Terrorism
and the International Legal Order

WITH SPECIAL REFERENCE TO THE UN, THE EU AND CROSS-BORDER ASPECTS

edited by

Peter J. van Krieken

T·M·C·Asser Press

The Hague

Published by T.M.C.ASSER PRESS
P.O.Box 16163, 2500 BD The Hague, The Netherlands

Sold and distributed in North, Central and South America
by Kluwer Law International,
101, Philip Drive, Norwell MA 02061

In all other countries, sold and distributed
by Kluwer Law International, Distribution Centre,
P.O.Box 322, 3300 AH Dordrecht, The Netherlands

to be cited as:
P.J. van Krieken, *Terrorism and the International Legal Order* (The Hague, 2002)

ISBN 90-6704-148-3

PREFACE

I am very pleased to welcome this book by Dr. Peter van Krieken, a widely known and recognized expert in the fields of migration and asylum law, who is now adding yet another important branch to his already impressive tree of publications in the domain of public international law: The international legal order on terrorism.

It indeed concerns a topic which, after the terrorist attacks in the United States of America on the 11th of September 2001, is certainly of the utmost importance, primarily because the lives of so many innocent people are at stake. It clearly demands a renewed call to free the world of this cruel flow of inhumanity.

In this context it is, on the one hand, quite disturbing that one needs to turn to legal experts for answers, suggestions and a framework, but, on the other hand, such an involvement could bring some order to an issue which is so overwhelming, so disturbing and so shocking at the same time. It also underlines the fact that international law can play a pivotal role in truly relevant issues.

In this respect the T.M.C. Asser Institute and its publishing house T.M.C. Asser Press try to be at the forefront by providing relevant information, analysis and guidance. The Asser Institute, an interuniversity organization, serves to promote free and independent scholarly research. The Institute operates as an academic community organizer through whose efforts research, education and documentation are collectively sustained and enhanced. It performs this task by conducting academic research, often in collaboration with its constituent Dutch universities and foreign universities, other academic institutions and international organizations, by organizing conferences, seminars and other educational programmes. It is also actively involved in the compilation and management of documentation which is disseminated through its own websites and in the publication of a great variety of books, journals and student readers.

This new book and the dedication to Bert V.A. Röling, one of the greatest international law professors from The Netherlands, fall perfectly into line with the above-mentioned activities.

Where the Security Council of the United Nations set the standard with one of the most important international instruments agreed upon thus far in the fight against terrorism, calling upon states to urgently cooperate to prevent and suppress terrorist acts, including for example 'to prevent and suppress the financing of terrorist acts', combined with international efforts to reach an agreed definition, 'Terrorism and the International Legal Order', which focuses on the UN, the EU, and cross-border aspects, provides an in-depth treatise on the emerging international legal order in this domain.

The author, Dr. Peter van Krieken, has a long-standing relationship with the Institute which is illustrated by the great number of titles he has published with T.M.C. Asser Press. In fact his very first publication (dating back to 1975) was published in our *Netherlands International Law Review* and dealt with hijacking and asylum, a topic that has once again come to the fore following the terrible September 2001 events. Therefore, it is only logical that T.M.C. Asser Press approached him to put today's terrorism in a broader legal context. The result is sound and comprehensive, containing a wealth of material, almost encyclopaedic in character, which I am sure will serve as an up to date source for anyone interested in this area. Thirty years after the terrorist attacks at the 1972 Olympic Games in Munich and now with the Twin Towers picture forever in our minds, the efforts to put the legal aspects into perspective are indeed laudable and deserve to be commended.

The Hague, July 2002   Prof. Dr. Frans A. Nelissen
                                                                                     Director, T.M.C. Asser Institute

ACKNOWLEDGEMENTS

This Volume is to some extent the logical follow-up to the 1999 *Refugee Law in Context: The Exclusion Clause*. In that publication due attention was paid to the issue of asylum seekers who are believed to have been involved in criminal acts. Although it referred to war crimes and common offences in the broadest of contexts, it also dealt with the issue of terrorism, and the need to formulate appropriate answers. The suggestion by my publisher following the September 2001 events to elaborate on the issue of terrorism hence sounded like music to my ears, also because in my various capacities I have encountered this issue in a variety of settings and with new challenges and viewpoints on each and every occasion.

The result does not claim to provide any definitive answers; it rather aims to place the many aspects in their proper context and to bring some order in the many instruments, resolutions, guidelines, papers, decisions and recommendations. To create some order in such chaos in no easy task, and the encouragements from colleagues and family were badly needed and highly appreciated. The moral obligation following my public role as 'Afghanistan expert' in the autumn of 2001 also added to the pressure to bring such an exercise to an end.

The traditional thanks, apart from family and colleagues, go to the Röling Foundation, Nico Schrijver for his introduction on Bert Röling to whom this publication has been dedicated, Frans Nelissen for his Preface, Johan Feitsma for his advice, and in particular to Otilia Urungeanu who in a diligent, industrious and patient manner has been instrumental in enabling this publication to see the day of light. Last but not least I owe the T.M.C. Asser Press team and Mr Peter Morris, the language editor, special thanks for their efficient and supportive roles.

RÖLING

This Volume has been dedicated to Professor Röling. Bert Röling (1906-1985) was a judge at the Tokyo War Crimes Tribunal and professor of international law and peace research at Groningen University, The Netherlands. He had a special interest in the emerging international criminal law in the context of war and peace.

Since September 11, 2001, international lawyers have been giving considerable thought on how to respond to acts of international terrorism. The debate has covered various strands of international law, including the law of self-defence, international criminal law, international anti-terrorism law, human rights and international law aimed at the promotion of justice.

The use of violence for politically motivated criminal acts is certainly not a new phenomenon. It was already practised in ancient times and the Middle Ages. Perhaps new are the widespread scale and the audacity of international terrorism as exemplified by the hijacking of aircraft, the use of extremely dangerous explosives and potential access to weapons of mass destruction.

At an early stage Röling had already identified these dangers and had sought to analyze their consequences to determine which direction international law should take to prevent such acts of violence and to promote peace and justice. Both Van Krieken and the author of this contribution, who, albeit at different times, took classes with Röling, cherished his views, teaching and his personal approach, and realized that he had been ahead of his time. Röling's work and opinions hence continue to have a profound impact on our thinking. Antonio Cassese rightly submits in his book on and with Röling on the 1946-1948 tribunal, *The Tokyo Trial and Beyond, reflections of a peacemonger* (Blackwell, 1993) that 'although Röling authored a great number of important writings, they do not fully convey the richness, complexity and liveliness of his verbal communication'.

Meanwhile, international law has developed progressively over the past decades, especially in the field of human rights, humanitarian law and international criminal law. One of the main issues now to be addressed is how the various chapters of international law can converge into one coherent and effective strategy in combating and, if possible, preventing international terrorism. This Volume brings together dozens of key documents on terrorism in the context of the international legal order. They are preceded by succinct introductions by Peter van Krieken who embodies rare combinations of extensive field experience (including close encounters with terrorists) in various hotbeds of this world (Beirut, Juba [Southern Sudan], Peshawar) and academic scholarship. As a matter of fact, Professor Röling 'instructed' Van Krieken, when he left for abroad to join the UN after completing his Ph.D., not to forego his academic interests.

To dedicate this Volume to Professor Röling is thus logical, commendable and indeed laudable. However, this Volume is more than just a (re-)collection: it is considered extremely useful for practitioners and academics alike who wish to acquaint themselves with the extensive emerging body of international anti-terrorism law and with the ways how international law can and ought to be employed in order to suppress and prevent international terrorism, to promote peace and justice, and to deny terrorists 'safe havens'.

Nico Schrijver,
Professor of International Law, *Vrije Universiteit*, Amsterdam
Chairman of the Academic Council on the UN System, NY

TABLE OF CONTENTS

CHAPTER 1
INTRODUCTION

The fight against terrorism requires a concerted and multifaceted strategy at both the domestic and international level and should involve military, economic, diplomatic and legal methods.[1] An international legal order is badly needed, but it should be stressed that in the context of terrorism, law and justice are more than ever a tool, and not a goal in themselves. Law and justice should above all provide the legal basis for the various military, economic and diplomatic activities and reactions. It is obvious, however, that the legal framework itself also needs to be updated and elaborated upon and should hence be turned into a practical tool.

This Volume aims to describe the various efforts made on the legal front towards an international legal order and will limit itself to that exercise only. It will for example not discuss the military activities in relation to Chapter VII of the Charter but will rather focus on building the international legal order, an aspect which is so urgently required in order to enable the politicians, the military and other actors to play their part in the most legal of manners.

The horror of the 11th of September 2001 had a number of effects on the legal front:
- it forced the debate on terrorism, protection and prosecution to be intensified (1.1 debate)
- it resulted in a reshuffle between freedom, security and justice (1.2 new balance)
- it influenced the migration & globalization discussions (1.3 cross-border aspects)
- it yielded a most important Security Resolution (1.4 SC Res. 1373), and
- it resulted in a reaffirmation of the relevance of international law and cooperation (1.5 reaffirmation)

1.1   DEBATE

Terrorism had already been high on the agenda for a couple of years. In fact, this may sound as an understatement as, for example in the year 1937, the League of Nations (LoN) organized a conference on this very issue. This LoN conference resulted in the 1937 Geneva Convention for the Prevention and Punishment of Terrorism.[2]

---

[1] See e.g. N.J. Schrijver, responding to international terrorism: moving the frontiers of international law for 'enduring freedom'?, in: XLVIII *Netherlands International Law Review* (2001) pp. 271-291 on p. 272.

[2] In 1937, after the attack against King Alexander of Yugoslavia and the French minister Louis Barthou in October 1934 in the city of Marseilles (France), the LoN (League Of Nations) drew up an

Apart from this Convention, a Convention for the Creation of an International Criminal Court was also adopted.[3] Both initiatives, however, were short-lived, which, of course, mainly had to do with the 1939 outbreak of WW II.

During the Cold War cooperation to fight terrorism fell prey to ideological and political differences. It was not until the aftermath of the decolonization process and its liberation war concept that the various actors started to review the use of violence for political aims. The 1989 events (the end of major antagonism between the West and the Soviet bloc) enabled major players to refocus on the purposes and principles of the United Nations, which, after all, laid down the principle of seeking peaceful settlements to the many conflicts which the world and society faces and will face.[4]

The new focus on efforts towards the peaceful settlement of conflict[5] also included a fresh approach towards violence of all sorts. Whatever remained of the romanticism and heroism of political of politically motivated offences became increasingly obscure and out of touch. The final blow, probably, to certain levels of understanding, appreciation or sympathy with violent acts was dealt by the revolutionary peaceful transition in South Africa under and with Nelson Mandela. He rightly won, together with F.W. de Klerk, the 1993 Nobel peace prize.[6] These two, together with yet another South African Nobel prize laureate (1984), Bishop Desmond Tutu, submitted the following statement in September 2001:

International Convention which was signed in Geneva on 16 November 1937 by twenty-five countries (but not by Italy and the United States). This Convention defined terrorist acts as 'criminal facts directed against a State and of which the goal or nature is to cause terror towards determined personalities, groups of people or the population'.

[3] The Convention for the Creation of an International Criminal Court was opened for signature in 1937 under the auspices of the League of Nations. The Court's proposed jurisdiction was confined to offences created by the Convention for the Prevention and Punishment of Terrorism, which was opened for signature at the same time. The entry into force of the Court Convention was made subject to the entry into force of the Terrorism Convention, which did not occur.

[4] The main purposes and principles (Arts. 1 and 2 of the UN Charter) have been defined as follows:
   – To maintain international peace and security, and to that end: to take effective collective measures for the prevention and removal of threats to the peace, and for the suppression of acts of aggression or other breaches of the peace, and to bring about by peaceful means, and in conformity with the principles of justice and international law, adjustment or settlement of international disputes or situations which might lead to a breach of the peace;
   – All Members shall settle their international disputes by peaceful means in such a manner that international peace and security, and justice, are not endangered.

[5] Art. 33 of the UN Charter enumerates the following means and methods for the peaceful settlement of conflicts: '... The parties to any dispute, the continuance of which is likely to endanger the maintenance of international peace and security, shall, first of all, seek a solution by negotiation, enquiry, mediation, conciliation, arbitration, judicial settlement, resort to regional agencies or arrangements, or other peaceful means of their own choice ...'

In fact, International Law could be defined as the set of rules and regulations a) to prevent conflict; b) to contain conflict; and c) to solve conflict.

[6] It was also quite logical that in the context of the terrorism debate 'freedom' movements like the Turkish/Kurdish PKK, the Tamil Tigers and various Kashmiri organizations were on the one hand labelled as 'terrorist' and on the other changed track as regards the pursuance of their (political) goals, i.e. political (negotiations) rather than with violent means.

The terrorist attacks in the United States of America last week shook all of humanity. It starkly reminded us again of the depth to which we can sink in our inhumanity towards one another.

It was a source of encouragement to note that almost the entire world responded with utter revulsion to such cowardly acts that cruelly and horrendously took the lives of so many innocent people merely going about their ordinary daily lives. Amidst the indescribable tragedy the overwhelming decency of human beings the world over found expression in the unreserved condemnation of those terrible deeds of cruelty. (...)

The events of last week are also a renewed call to rid the world of the scourge of terrorism. Those acts emphasised that we are all vulnerable to terrorism. We hope that the culprits will be identified, apprehended and severely punished.

This is a time that the world should stand together in pursuit of those objectives. Terrorism seeks to put itself above and outside of the law. Our steps against terrorism should studiously be within international law and the charter of our world body.

We need wise leadership and statesmanship in this period of looming crisis. The actions taken should not deepen tensions and further divide the world for it is in those circumstances of strife and division that terrorism finds fertile ground.

The recent history of our own country has taught that negotiation is the surest means of finding lasting solutions to even the most seemingly intractable political problems. (...)

If out of the tragic events of last week the world can find a renewed will to cooperate in finding just solutions to the problems that threaten the safety, security and well-being of us all, the highest tribute would have been paid to those who lost their lives.

As indicated above, terrorism did not come to the fore in 2001 only, but had been on the agendas throughout the 20th century, with a renewed urge since the 1970s (hijacking, the terrorist attacks at the Munich 1972 Olympics, the many abductions and subsequent killings, etc.), resulting in the various hijacking instruments. The debate truly got under way after 1989, resulting in instruments on hostage taking, terrorist bombings, attacks aimed at diplomatic staff, as well as the financing of terrorist acts.

Moreover, this development can not be separated from the efforts to secure that major criminals will be tried, either in local courts[7] or in international tribunals. That process, with the Yugoslavia and Rwanda tribunals as important landmarks of the early 1990s, culminated in the 1998 Statute of Rome which opened the door to the setting up of the International Criminal Court (ICC) in 2002. The Tribunals and the ICC focus on war crimes but in fact, many of the terrorist offences do amount to such crimes.[8]

It remains to be seen in how far the ICC will be competent to put terrorists (non-war criminals) on trial (see Chapter 3.6). The Security Council, however, in no uncertain terms, demanded that national legislation be adopted to enable terrorists to be prosecuted, and insisted that no protection, no safe haven whatsoever be provided

---

[7] SC Resolution 1373 (September 2001) stated quite clearly that all States shall ensure that any person who participates in the financing, planning, preparation or perpetration of terrorist acts or in supporting terrorist acts is brought to justice and shall ensure that, in addition to any other measures against them, such terrorist acts are established as serious criminal offences in domestic laws and regulations and that the punishment duly reflects the seriousness of such terrorist acts.

[8] On this issue see e.g. E. Chadwick, *Self-Determination, terrorism and the International Humanitarian Law of Armed Conflict,* The Hague 1996, and below, Chapter 4.4.

for (would be) terrorists. The maxim *aut dedere aut judicare* covers the need to solve the inherent challenges either at home, or in good cooperation with other States.

As we will see in this Volume, an international legal framework was already in the process of being developed in the 1990s, and the September 2001 events only stressed the need to continue building on that framework and accelerated the various efforts concerned.

1.2   NEW BALANCE

The major Western democracies, as a Twin Tower aftershock, embarked on a debate on how far the balance between freedom, security and justice should be reviewed and/or adjusted.

It is quite remarkable that in the European Union for example, the description of the Union as '… an area of freedom, security and justice …' is a fairly recent one, as it goes back to the Copenhagen summit of 1993. Indeed, these criteria are also known as the Copenhagen criteria, and it should be noted that the concept of security apparently precedes that of justice.

Law could be defined as an instrument to regulate (potential) conflict, to prevent it from emerging, to prevent it from escalating and/or to find solutions thereto. One should also recognize that 'justice' in this context stands for equity, fairness and reasonableness, rather than the administration of law (the English language lacks a clear-cut separation between the German terminology *Recht* and *Gerechtigkeit*.[9] It should also be acknowledged that the challenge of the legislature, the lawmaker, is to continuously strive for codifying 'justice' (in the meaning of *Gerechtigkeit*), and that 'law', by definition, is a number of steps behind developments in the concept of 'justice'. Moreover, 'justice' as a concept, is a product of continuously changing ideas, perceptions and developments as well.[10]

If we admit the interdependency of freedom, security and justice, in the meaning that more of the one, almost always means less of the other, it should come as no surprise that following September 2001, public opinion, the executive and the legislator alike were willing to exchange some elements of 'freedom' for increased levels of 'security'.[11] This, of course, on the one hand has an impact on the conceptualization of 'justice' and on the other on the guidelines for the administration of law.

Terrorism's impact on balancing freedom, security and justice will have long-term consequences.

---

[9] See e.g. Von Kleist and Dürrenmat.

[10] It is recalled that the idea of the 'progressive development of international law' is embedded in the UN Charter.

[11] It should be emphasized, though, that this debate is not at all new, but rather an ongoing one; see e.g. a 1999 US publication on this issue by Dempsey and Cole: *Terrorism & The Constitution, Sacrificing Civil Liberties in the Name of National Security.*

1.3   CROSS-BORDER ASPECTS

It remains to be seen in how far the September 2001 events will have an impact on the globalization process. This will depend on the definition of globalization, and in particular on the question whether flexible approaches towards wide-scale migration should be considered part and parcel of the globalization process.

The present author is of the opinion that globalization first and foremost focuses on economic liberalization and privatization and on the free movement of goods,[12] capital, services and technical innovation, rather than on the free movement of 'labour'. Yet, globalization should be considered as 'given' and will, of course, involve a fairly high level of free movement, the contours of which will only be slowly specified.

It comes as no surprise, however, that in the wake of the 2001 events, border control and the increased screening of migrants and would be migrants alike became in many countries an issue of the utmost relevance.[13] Moreover, the links between a country's residents and (potential) terrorist organizations also became the subject of further scrutiny.

In fact, the Security Council in a September 2001 Resolution (1373) decided that all States shall (inter alia):

–   Deny safe haven to those who finance, plan, support, or commit terrorist acts, or provide safe havens;
–   Prevent those who finance, plan, facilitate or commit terrorist acts from using their respective territories for those purposes against other States or their citizens; and
–   Prevent the movement of terrorists or terrorist groups by effective border controls and controls on issuance of identity papers and travel documents, and through measures for preventing counterfeiting, forgery or fraudulent use of identity papers and travel documents.

It goes virtually without saying that these obligations have major implications on the freedom of movement and hence the asylum and migration regime in general (see below 1.4.6).

1.4   SC RES. 1373

The most important instrument agreed upon thus far is probably Security Council Resolution 1373 (SC Res. 1373 (2001)). In view of its status and standing, this Volume should, to the greatest extent possible, follow the line of thought and conclusions as elaborated and agreed upon in this resolution.

---

[12] Which may indeed include (material to manufacture) biological, chemical or nuclear arms. See e.g. The Economist, April 6th 2002 on the container trade ('when commerce and security clash').

[13] Also efforts to strive for a so-called multicultural society were considered to be in need of a rethink; this was also true for cultural relativism and cultural identity as such.

This resolution reaffirmed Resolution 1269 (1999) of 19 October 1999 and should indeed be seen as a logical follow-up, repeating the 1269 text but adding some new, often essential elements.

1.4.1   Threats to the Peace: Chapter VII

The resolution reaffirmed that the September 2001 terrorist attacks, like any act of international terrorism, constitute a threat to international peace and security, which makes Chapter VII of the Charter applicable, and enables the SC to act under Chapter VII. The SC reaffirmed the need to combat by all means, in accordance with the Charter of the United Nations, threats to international peace and security caused by terrorist acts,

The need to link terrorism with other forms of crime was highlighted and a close connection was noted between international terrorism and transnational organized crime, illicit drugs, money-laundering, illegal arms trafficking, and the illegal movement of nuclear, chemical, biological and other potentially deadly materials, and in this regard the need to enhance the coordination of efforts on national, subregional, regional and international levels in order to strengthen a global response to this serious challenge and threat to international security was emphasized.

1.4.2   Contrary to Purposes and Principles: Chapter I

Moreover, it was also declared that acts, methods, and practices of terrorism are contrary to the purposes and principles of the United Nations and that knowingly financing, planning and inciting terrorist acts are also contrary to the purposes and principles of the United Nations.

1.4.3   International Treaties

Of particular relevance for this Volume, States were called upon to become parties as soon as possible to the relevant international conventions and protocols relating to terrorism, including the International Convention for the Suppression of the Financing of Terrorism of 9 December 1999; and to increase cooperation and fully implement the relevant international conventions and protocols relating to terrorism and Security Council Resolutions 1269 (1999) and 1368 (2001).

1.4.4   Cooperation

The SC called on States to work together urgently to prevent and suppress terrorist acts, including through increased cooperation and the full implementation of the relevant international conventions relating to terrorism – an important text as it refers to cooperation and implementation. The SC then focused on the financing aspects in recognizing the need for States to complement international cooperation by taking additional measures to prevent and suppress, in their territories through all lawful means, the financing and preparation of any acts of terrorism.

As for early warning, prevention and the exchange of information, all States (which includes the non-UN members) were called upon to (a) find ways of intensifying and accelerating the exchange of operational information, especially regarding actions or movements of terrorist persons or networks; forged or falsified travel documents; traffic in arms, explosives or sensitive materials; use of communications technologies by terrorist groups; and the threat posed by the possession of weapons of mass destruction by terrorist groups; (b) exchange information in accordance with international and domestic law and cooperate on administrative and judicial matters to prevent the commission of terrorist acts; (c) cooperate, particularly through bilateral and multilateral arrangements and agreements, to prevent and suppress terrorist attacks and take action against the perpetrators of such acts.

1.4.5 **Obligations**

Moreover, States were reminded that they have the duty to refrain from organizing, instigating, assisting or participating in terrorist acts in another State or acquiescing in organized activities within its territory directed towards the commission of such acts.

The SC also took the decision that all States shall (a) prevent and suppress the financing of terrorist acts; (b) criminalize the wilful provision or collection, by any means, directly or indirectly, of funds by their nationals or in their territories with the intention that the funds should be used, or in the knowledge that they are to be used, in order to carry out terrorist acts; (c) freeze without delay funds and other financial assets or economic resources of persons who commit, or attempt to commit, terrorist acts or participate in or facilitate the commission of terrorist acts; of entities owned or controlled directly or indirectly by such persons; and of persons and entities acting on behalf of, or at the direction of such persons and entities, including funds derived or generated from property owned or controlled directly or indirectly by such persons and associated persons and entities; (d) prohibit their nationals or any persons and entities within their territories from making any funds, financial assets or economic resources or financial or other related services available, directly or indirectly, for the benefit of persons who commit or attempt to commit or facilitate or participate in the commission of terrorist acts, of entities owned or controlled, directly or indirectly, by such persons and of persons and entities acting on behalf of or at the direction of such persons.

As to obligations 'at home' and abroad, it was moreover decided that States shall (e) refrain from providing any form of support, active or passive, to entities or persons involved in terrorist acts, including by suppressing recruitment of members of terrorist groups and eliminating the supply of weapons to terrorists; (f) take the necessary steps to prevent the commission of terrorist acts, including by the provision of early warning to other States by exchange of information; (g) ensure that any person who participates in the financing, planning, preparation or perpetration of terrorist acts or in supporting terrorist acts is brought to justice and ensure that, in addition to any other measures against them, such terrorist acts are established as serious criminal offences in domestic laws and regulations and that the punishment duly reflects the seriousness of such terrorist acts; and (h) afford one another the greatest measure of assistance in connection with criminal investigations or criminal proceedings relating to the financing or support of terrorist acts, including assistance in obtaining evidence in their possession necessary for the proceedings.

1.4.6   Cross-Border Movements

In addition, and of relevance to the cross-border movement of individuals and 'services', it was decided (a) to deny safe haven to those who finance, plan, support, or commit terrorist acts, or provide safe havens; (b) to prevent those who finance, plan, facilitate or commit terrorist acts from using their respective territories for those purposes against other States or their citizens; (c) to prevent the movement of terrorists or terrorist groups by effective border controls and controls on the issuance of identity papers and travel documents, and through measures for preventing counterfeiting, forgery or fraudulent use of identity papers and travel documents; and (d) to take appropriate measures in conformity with the relevant provisions of national and international law, including international standards of human rights, before granting refugee status, for the purpose of ensuring that the asylum seeker has not planned, facilitated or participated in the commission of terrorist acts; and (e) to ensure, in conformity with international law, that refugee status is not abused by the perpetrators, organizers or facilitators of terrorist acts, and that claims of political motivation are not recognized as grounds for refusing requests for the extradition of alleged terrorists. The various implications will be dealt with in depth in Chapter 7.

1.4.7   New Committee

It was decided to establish, in accordance with rule 28 of its provisional rules of procedure, a Committee of the Security Council, consisting of all the members of the Council, to monitor the implementation of this resolution, with the assistance of appropriate expertise, and to call upon all States to report to the Committee, no later than 90 days from the date of adopting this resolution and thereafter according to a timetable to be proposed by the Committee, on the steps they have taken to implement this resolution. The Committee was directed to delineate its tasks, to submit a work programme within 30 days of the adoption of this resolution, and to consider the support it requires, in consultation with the Secretary-General.

1.5   REAFFIRMATION OF THE RELEVANCE OF INTERNATIONAL LAW AND COOPERATION

Whatever the reactions to terrorism, the underlying legal principles are a quintessential condition for their success. Not only should military or armed action be embedded in a legal framework giving those (re)actions the status of legality, but efforts should also be taken to develop the general framework of conventions, treaties and Security Council resolutions to ensure agreement on definitions, jurisdiction, extradition and other forms of cooperation, in short in the context of an adequate legal response. Hereto the basis of international law deserves to be highlighted as no new starting points need to be invented: international law as it stands is completely capable of dealing with the various challenges arising out of the terrorism issue. That does not mean that the necessary work has been completed. More needs to be done in the field of the various aspects of the legal response. The purpose of this Volume is indeed to describe and to provide an inventory of what has been accomplished thus far and what still needs to be done: it concerns and tries to cover the International Legal Order.

As a starting point, however, it should be agreed that the existing framework of international law which indeed encompasses international humanitarian law and human rights law is completely sufficient as a badly needed starting point and term of reference. This was eloquently worded by ICRC President Kellenberger in his March 2002 statement upon the occasion of the Annual Session of the UN Commission on Human Rights:

(...) It has been said that the world will never be the same after the heinous crimes of September 11, 2001, which shocked the world's conscience. The September 11 attacks delivered a blow to the most fundamental values of human society, particularly those at the heart of international humanitarian and human rights law. One should however be careful not to allow these events to overshadow the seriousness of many – often forgotten or neglected – conflict zones around the world. Losing sight of them, neglecting the violations that occur in them, one runs the serious risk of weakening the body of international humanitarian law.

The crisis generated by the attacks has posed a host of questions, some of which I will outline and to which I will attempt to briefly respond.

One line of reasoning appears to suggest that certain individuals are undeserving of the protection of the law because of the heinous nature of their criminal acts. Such assumptions should be rejected. Human beings, by virtue of being human, are entitled to the protection of the law. Just as no state, group or individual can place themselves above the law, so also, no person can be placed outside the law.

It would be misleading to think that recent or present-day international crimes surpass the evils that humans have historically inflicted on humans. Does anyone really believe that the suffering caused by current conflicts around the globe surpasses the ravages of World War II and the atrocities that accompanied it? Can it really be said that the laws devised in response to that very dark time in human history, such as the Geneva Conventions of 1949, are outdated or quaint? I think not.

Another question that has been raised is whether international law in general, and international humanitarian law specifically, are adequate tools for dealing with the post-September 11th reality. My answer to this is that international law, if correctly applied, is one of the strongest tools that the community of nations has at its disposal in the effort to reestablish international order and stability. What we have to be clear about is which body of law is the right tool. It is the rules of the United Nations Charter, and not international humanitarian law, that regulate the use of force in international relations. The relevant provisions of the UN Charter provide guidance on questions such as legitimate resort to force, the right to self-defense and lawful responses to threats or breaches of international peace and security. It is the UN Charter that allows the international community to pass political and other judgment on the use of force in international relations.

International humanitarian law is, quite distinctly, the body of rules that regulates the protection of persons and conduct of hostilities once an armed conflict has occurred. Its aim is to alleviate the suffering of individuals affected by war regardless of the underlying causes – and therefore regardless of any justification – for the armed conflict. There are no 'just' or 'unjust' wars in terms of international humanitarian law because civilians, to name just one category of persons protected by its rules, have the right to be spared murder, torture or rape, no matter which side they happen to belong to.

A related doubt that has been raised in the aftermath of September 11 is whether international humanitarian law is applicable to the new security threats posed by acts of terrorism. Several bodies of law, including national and international rules of criminal law, are relevant in the struggle against terrorism. As for international humanitarian law, it is that body of rules that is applicable whenever the fight against terrorism amounts to or includes armed conflict. There is no question that its norms are adequate to deal with security risks in war because its provisions were designed specifically for the exceptional situation of armed conflict. The generations of experts and diplomats who crafted international humanitarian law over the last two centuries were fully aware of the need to balance state security and the preservation of human life, health and dignity. That balance has always been at the very core of the laws of war (…).

1.6   CONCLUSION

The challenge to interdependency through free movement, the search for new balances within society, the efforts to intensify the quest for agreed definitions, and, far more important, the fight against terrorism are all obvious results of the September 2001 events. Yet, these events represented just one element in an ongoing process. One might be tempted to state that there is in fact no news. That, however, would be incorrect: seldom has the world witnessed a more flagrant violation of norms and values which hold universal value. Yet, over the years many more people have become victims of terrorist acts, the 'Lockerbie' passengers, the traumatized victims of hostage-taking, the wheel-chair passenger on the Achillo Lauro who was thrown overboard, the Berlin, Buenos Aires or Jerusalem disco dancers, the many diplomats who have given their life in the course of duty and the thousands of innocent victims of indiscriminate killings and bombings. The war against terrorism is indeed a timely one and the need to define the rules and regulations underpinning such a war is an obvious one, as any legitimate fight needs to trace its legitimization to a well-defined legal basis. This Volume aims to provide the state of the art in the present, highly relevant, legal debate on the issue of terrorism. It takes the UN as the main norm-setter, it being a forum, instrument and actor alike. Due attention will also be paid to the EU. This Volume will hence focus on Conventions, Treaties, Declarations and the like, in short, on the legal response in general, whilst acknowledging that any response, any framework should never be considered a goal but an utmost tool, and a modest one at that. Yet, it is believed that the legal response should be effective, pragmatic and solution-orientated, aiming at creating a working international, legal order. If that proves to be impossible, then the legal experts should sit back and watch TV as the happenings and developments unfold.

This Volume, dedicated to the living memory of Bert V.A. Röling as reflected in Schrijver's introductory piece, provides in Chapter 2 a survey of the various definitions used and proposed in order to create some order in the legal chaos – a chaos resulting from the different political interests.

In Chapter 3 the (need for) cooperation will be underlined in the legal field, international criminal law in particular, under the heading *aut dedere aut judicare,* the old maxim for the principle to either extradite the alleged offender or to put him/her on trial. It will be concluded that virtually all instruments contain a variety of clauses underlying the need for cooperation and that proper implementation will hence yield the necessary results.

Chapter 4 then continues with the activities undertaken within the realm of the United Nations. All organs will be duly dealt with, as all organs have indeed been confronted or identified with the various challenges involved.

Chapter 5 contains the texts of virtually all the relevant international instruments in this field, including the main regional ones and in Chapter 6 due attention will be paid to the reactions and proposals as initiated in the European Union.

The cross-border aspects will be dealt with in a separate chapter (Chapter 7) as both arms and offenders can, by moving freely, have an impact on the issue at stake: any international legal order should focus on cross-border aspects as goods, people and ideas may originate in one place, but become effective in another: the very subject which international law should be concerned with.

As usual, the final chapter will contain some conclusions and ideas for the (near) future.

CHAPTER 2
DEFINITIONS

2.1   GENERAL/SEMANTICS

Thousands of people and organizations have been involved in acts of terrorism.[1] It may concern individual hostage-takers, bombers, murderers, hijackers, the mentally challenged, (members of) the Baader Meinhoff gang, Brigada Rossa, the Red Army, the (Real) IRA, ETA, PLO, DFLP, Abu Sayyaf, al-Qaeda, Hezbollah, Revolutionary Guards, Bolsheviks, ANC, Frelimo, PKK, Tamil Tigers – a list far too long to be included in full.[2] The urge to create a law on terrorism is hence obvious.

Yet, an important differentiation needs to be highlighted. This concerns the need not to forget that there are already a great number of laws and treaties which deal with various (other) heinous crimes like genocide, crimes against humanity, war

---

[1] For a survey that provides information on terrorist groups, events, and prominent figures spanning the period from the Zealot insurrections against Roman rule in first century Judea to the present, reference should be made to Anderson & Sloan, *A Historical Dictionary of Terrorism,* NJ and London 2002. Entries on terrorist groups and movements provide information on their histories, programmes, and leadership, as well as some discussion of the numbers and kinds of action perpetrated by each group. The introduction discusses essential components of terrorism that distinguish it from other forms of political violence. The flyer adds that terrorism has consistently dogged this supposedly modern and enlightened age. It has merely adopted new shapes and forms in keeping with the times. The causes have also evolved over the years, as old problems are solved and new ones created. Moreover, it has gone high-tech, like everything else. The book's chronology inserts terrorism into its historical context. And it also contains a section, which deals with weapons of mass destruction, 'cyber-terrorism', as well as more conventional terrorist threats.

[2] Bruce Hoffman, in his *Inside Terrorism* (Columbia University Press NY 1999) indicates that the word 'terrorism' first became popular during the French Revolution, when the *régime de la terreur* was initially viewed as a *positive* political system that used fear to remind citizens of the necessity of virtue. The use of violence to 'educate' people about ideological issues has continued, but it has taken on decidedly negative connotations – and has become predominantly, though not exclusively, a tactic deployed by those who do not have the powers of state at their disposal. Bruce Hoffman, the Director of the Centre for the Study of Terrorism and Political Violence, has written a clear summary of some of the major historical trends in international terrorism. He makes careful distinctions between the motivations that drive political (or ethno-nationalist) terrorism and religious terrorism, and he also shows why the rise of religious terrorism, coupled with the increased availability of weapons of mass destruction, may foretell an era of even greater violence. In the past, Hoffman argues, the main goal of the terrorist was not to kill, but to attract media attention to his cause in the hope of initiating reform. 'For the religious terrorist', however, 'violence is first and foremost a sacramental act or divine duty executed in direct response to some theological demand or imperative ... religious terrorists see themselves not as components of a system worth preserving but as "outsiders", seeking fundamental changes in the existing order'. Hoffman does not 'choose sides' in this framework, pointing to the bombings of the World Trade Center and Oklahoma City and to the sarin nerve gas attacks in Tokyo in order to demonstrate that fundamentalists of *any* religious denomination are capable of extreme acts of terrorism.

crimes, narcotics, illegal arms trade, trafficking, slave-trading, counterfeiting, piracy and so on. Thus, many of the terrorist acts do not need to be newly codified as 'crimes', as most, if not all societies already have ample opportunities to put those offenders on trial. Yet, by using the term 'terrorist', not only emotional, but also legal doors will be opened which would otherwise have remained closed. This primarily deals with the issue of jurisdiction (personal, territorial, universal), international cooperation (deportation, surrender, extradition) and obligations as to the non-provision of any form of protection (safe haven, refugee law). By labelling a crime as a terrorist act enables and obliges the various actors to apply a different range of instruments and means. It also results in increasing both the minimum and maximum penalties. It is therefore in the interest of the individual offender, the victim and the international regime to know exactly when a certain act amounts to terrorism and when it does not.

In a 1983 study, Alex Schmid compiled no less than 109 definitions of terrorism.[3] Since then, the number has probably doubled. Schmid defined terrorism as follows:

Terrorism is a method of combat in which random or symbolic victims serve as instrumental targets of violence. These instrumental victims share group or class characteristics which form the basis for their selection for victimization. Through previous use of violence or the credible threat of violence other members of that group or class are put in a state of chronic fear (terror). This group or class, whose members' sense of security is purposively undermined, is the target of terror. The victimizati-on of the target of violence is considered extranormal by most observers from the witnessing audien-ce on the basis of its atrocity; the time (e.g., peacetime) or place (not a battlefield) of victimization or the disregard for rules of combat accepted in conventional warfare. The norm violation creates an attentive audience beyond the target of terror; sectors of this audience might in turn form the main object of manipulation. The purpose of this indirect method of combat is either to immobilise the target of terror in order to produce disorientation and/or compliance, or to mobilise secondary targets of demands (e.g., a govern-ment) or targets of attenti-on (e.g., public opinion) to changes of attitude or behaviour favouring the short or long-term interests of the users of this method of combat.[4]

---

[3] See Schmid, *Political Terrorism: A Research Guide to Concepts, Theories, Data Bases and Litera-ture* (1983), pp. 119-152. In an excellent and thorough work, Schmid examines the various definitions of terro-rism and the relationships between terrorism and such other phenomena as guerrilla warfare, political assassi-nation, anarchism and 'terror'. Id. at pp. 20-71.

[4] Schmid's 1988 definition is even more 'academic': Terrorism is an anxiety-inspiring method of repeated violent action, employed by (semi-)clandestine individual, group or state actors, for idiosyncratic, criminal or political reasons, whereby – in contrast to assassination – the direct targets of violence are not the main targets. The immediate human victims of violence are generally chosen randomly (targets of opportunity) or selectively (representative or symbolic targets) from a target population, and serve as message generators. Threat- and violence-based communication processes between terrorist (organization), (imperilled) victims, and main targets are used to manipulate the main target (audience(s)), turning it into a target of terror, a target of demands, or a target of attention, depending on whether intimidation, coercion, or propaganda is primarily sought (from the UNDCP website).

As Lambert[5] comments, this definition does not include as terrorism those acts where there is no 'target of terror', i.e., where the act of violence has a more immediate and direct purpose. Examples of acts excluded would be a hijacking where the perpetrator's only purpose is to get to a destination which is not the intended one of the aircraft (a situation which would be covered by the Hague Convention on hijacking) and the assassination of a political figure which is intended only to eliminate that one person. It also excludes violence against objects, as opposed to violence against people. Partly for these reasons, Schmid acknowledges that this definition is flawed. However, it is a good definition in that it includes acts of violence committed both by indivi-duals (or groups) and by State actors. The purpose can be either revolutionary or to enforce the authority of the State. In fact, the definition does not allow any consideration of the motive behind the act or of the identity of the perpetrator. As Schmid states, '[w]hether the perpetrator is a "lone wolf", a criminal, a vigilante, a psychopath, an insurgent or an agent of a regime should be irrelevant in assessing whether or not certain forms of violence should be defined as terroristic'.

A simpler definition of terrorism, proffered by the US Department of State, deserves due attention:

> 'premeditated, politically motivated violence perpetrated against non-combatant targets by subnational groups or clandestine state agents, usually intended to influence an audience'.[6]

This definition requires a political motivation, but does not favour one political viewpoint over another. Similar to Schmid's definition, it does not allow for a relativist concept of terrorism, i.e. that 'one man's terrorist is another man's freedom fighter'. The motives or causes driving the actors are irrelevant, at least in theory (application of the definition to a certain set of circumstances, however, still involves a degree of subjectivity). The definition includes terror by the State, but only in so far as it involves 'clandestine state agents'. Its advantage over Schmid's definition is that it does not absolutely require a 'target of terror' and could thus include, for example, hijackings and assassinations such as those excluded from Schmid's definition. It should be noted that neither of these definitions would seemingly be acceptable to some developing States which have argued, (...) that the legitimate causes of certain groups, specifically national liberation movements, should take their actions outside the concept of terrorism.[7] (...)

It is exactly the discussion on 'State Terrorism' which prevented and still prevents the international community from embarking on a common search for a definition

---

[5] Joseph J. Lambert, *Terrorism and Hostages in International Law*, Grotius (1992), parts of which are included in Van Krieken, *Refugee Law in Context, The Exclusion Clause*, Asser/Kluwer (1999), pp. 177-194.

[6] US Department of State, *Patterns of Global Terrorism 1988* (1989), p. v.

[7] It goes without saying that the reports by special rapporteur Koufa (see the annex to Chapter 4.3) contains a wealth of material on this very definition issue (e.g. the 2001 progress report, paragraphs 24-31).

which would be acceptable to all, the developed world, the developing world, the de-facto world powers and the self-conceived oppressed.[8] As Lambert submits:

> Approaching the concept of terrorism by reference to the actors in a situation, two basic types may be identified: 'Individual' (or group) terrorism and 'State' terrorism. Individual terrorism has many manifestations, and is used by groups large and small, nationalists, separatists, liberation fighters, etc. Because of its many manifestations, it is difficult to generalize on this aspect of terrorism without sacrificing accuracy, and it is enough to say for now that individual terrorism is terrorism 'from below' rather than terrorism committed by organs of the State. The vast bulk of the literature on the subject of terrorism deals with individual terrorism, and, in general, the use of the term 'terrorism' in this study refers to this aspect of the problem. In contrast to individual terrorism stands the concept of 'State' terrorism. Traditionally, State terrorism refers to acts of terror, such as torture, killings, mass arrests, etc., which are conducted by the organs of the State against its own population, whether the entire population, a certain segment thereof (such as a minority community or political opposition), or the population of an occupied country. While individual terrorism is usually anti-State, and, therefore, subversive, the purpose of State terrorism is to enforce the authority and power of the State.[9]

Another important feature would appear to be the international character and the international nature of terrorism. This represents a common misperception. Terrorism was and is more often than not domestic in nature. Domestic terrorism, as the name implies, involves the citizens and territory of one State and is directed against (or by) that State. For terrorism to be international, there must be an 'internationalizing' element, and many definitions and criteria have been advanced for deciding when that element exists. The US State Department, for example, defines terrorism as international when it involves 'citizens or territory of more than one country.' Laqueur observes that the term 'international terrorism' can refer to State-sponsored terrorism against foreign countries, to cooperation between terrorist groups and to attacks against foreign nationals or property in the terrorist's own country or elsewhere. Wilkinson suggests that terrorism is international when it is 'directed against foreigners or foreign targets', when it is 'concerted by the governments or factions of more than one state', or when it is 'aimed at influencing the policies of a foreign govern-ment'. Another commentator notes, somewhat vaguely, that terrorism is international when 'the interests of more than one state are involved'. It can readily be seen that there are no contradictions between these various formulations, and that whenever the citizens, territory or entity of a second State are involved in a terrorist act, that act can be considered as international terrorism. In any event, for the purposes of studying the Hostages Convention it may be noted that the instrument ap-

---

[8] See also below, Chapter 4.3 on ECOSOC, and in particular in the annex to that chapter, the 2001 Koufa progress report paragraphs 42-67; it is the opinion of the present author that the differences *between ius ad bellum, ius in bello* and terrorism should always be stressed in the strongest of terms.

[9] Lambert, op. cit., in Van Krieken (1999) pp. 178-179. It is the opinion of the present author that the issue of state terrorism too much part of the Israel/Middle east issue to ever put the discussion on state terrorism on a neutral and hence productive level. See also Chapter 4.3 (ECOSOC, the reports of the special rapporteur) and Chapter 4.1 (GA, the ad hoc committee and the efforts to reach agreement on a comprehensive convention.

plies only to international acts of hostage-taking and that the criteria for whether or not such an act is international in nature are contained in [that Convention].[10]

It has been indicated above that there was a general feeling that no agreement on an all-encompassing definition of terrorism would be reached in the short term. As Elagad argues, there are several reasons why it is so difficult to offer a precise and objective definition:

(a) terrorism takes different forms: although it is usually equated with political subversion, it is employed at times by governments, and is used as an instrument of syndicated crime;

(b) the criteria for defining the term 'terrorism' is generally subjective since it is mainly based on political considerations;

(c) above all, terrorism is prompted by a wide range of motives, depending on the point in time and the prevailing political ideology. In this respect, it would be recalled that during wartime, members of the French resistance to the German occupation were regarded as criminals and were pursued accordingly. Another example is the division in French public opinion created by the Algerian War, some regarded the movements involved in the uprising as plain terrorists, while others viewed them as genuine liberation movements. Finally, Yasir Arafat who was once branded in the United States as a terrorist, is now being received in the White House by the President of the United States.[11]

Elagab then offers his own definition:

> The term terrorism is used to define criminal acts based on the use of violence or threat thereof, and which are directed against a country or its inhabitants and calculated to create a state of terror in the minds of the government officials, an individual or a group of persons, or the general public at large. It could be the work of one individual, but more often than not is the effect of organised groups whose philosophy is based on the theory that 'the end justifies the means'.

For the purpose of this Volume, and as long as no overall all-encompassing definition has been agreed upon in the legal arena (read: General Assembly, Security Council, ICJ, Conventions and/or Treaties), it would have been tempting to stick to a definition provided by the International Law Commission. This important Commission (functioning within the realm of the United Nations) concluded in the 1980s that the following categories constitute terrorist acts:

i. Any act causing death or grievous bodily harm or loss of liberty to a Head of State, persons exercising the prerogatives of the Head of State, their hereditary or designated successors, the spouse of such persons, or persons charged with public functions or holding public positions when the act is directed against them in their public capacity;

---

[10] Lambert, op. cit., in Van Krieken (1999) pp. 181-182.

[11] Omer Y. Elagab, *International law Documents relating to Terrorism*, London/Sydney 1997, p. xix.

ii.   Acts calculated to destroy or damage public property or property devoted to a public
      purpose;
iii. Any act likely to imperil human lives through the creation of a public danger, in par-
      ticular the seizure of aircraft, the taking of hostages and any form of violence di-
      rected against persons who enjoy internatio-nal protection or diplomatic immunity;
iv.   The manufacture, obtaining, possession or supplying of arms, ammunition, explo-
      sives or harmful substances with a view to the commission of a terrorist act.

Yet, it is quite obvious that this definition lacks important elements (the intention to
influence an audience, the 'spread' of terror) and does not cover nuclear terrorism
and, for example, the financing of terrorist acts. It is hence submitted that reference
should rather be made to the following definitions which would appear to sublime
the relevant aspects:[12]

–   Terrorism is the use or threatened use of force designed to bring about political
    change (*Brian Jenkins*);
–   Terrorism is the premeditated, deliberate, systematic murder, mayhem, and
    threatening of the innocent to create fear and intimidation in order to gain a
    political or tactical advantage, usually to influence an audience (*James M.
    Poland*);
–   Terrorism is the unlawful use of force or violence against persons or property to
    intimidate or coerce a government, the civilian population, or any segment
    thereof, in furtherance of political or social objectives (*FBI Definition*);
–   Terrorism is the unlawful use or threat of violence against persons or property to
    further political or social objectives. It is usually intended to intimidate or co-
    erce a government, individuals or groups, or to modify their behaviour or poli-
    tics (*Vice-President Gore's Task Force, 1986*);
–   Terrorism constitutes the illegitimate use of force to achieve a political objective
    when innocent people are targeted (*Walter Laqueur*).

However, as this Volume first and foremost deals with and covers International
Law, the following definition, as agreed upon by the General Assembly in 1996 (GA
Res. 51/210 on measures to eliminate international terrorism) shall serve as the lead-
ing notion throughout:

> criminal acts intended or calculated to provoke a state of terror in the general public, a
> group of persons or particular persons for political purposes.

And it was added, in no uncertain terms, that these acts

> are in any circumstance unjustifiable, whatever the considerations of a political, philoso-
> phical, ideological, racial, ethnic, religious or other nature that may be invoked to justify
> them.

---

[12] From the Terrorism Research Center website.

This definition is to be preferred over and above the one presently being circulated for the sake of a Comprehensive Convention. A United Nations General Assembly Ad-Hoc Committee in conjunction with the GA's Sixth Committee would appear to be able to agree on a definition which, in spite of a great many efforts, lacks the badly needed clarity:

1.   Any person commits an offence within the meaning of this Convention if that person, by any means, unlawfully and intentionally, causes:
     (a) Death or serious bodily injury to any person; or
     (b) Serious damage to public or private property, including a place of public use, a State or government facility, a public transportation system, an infrastructure facility or the environment; or
     (c) Damage to property, places, facilities, or systems referred to in paragraph 1(b) of this article, resulting or likely to result in major economic loss, when the purpose of the conduct, by its nature or context, is to intimidate a population, or to compel a Government or an international organization to do or abstain from doing any act.

It should be emphasized that the last part of this draft Article 2.1 (… when the purpose …) is a condition for all three parts (a to c). However, although 'to intimidate' and 'to compel' are useful legal concepts, not including the terror aspect ('provoking terror') is to be regretted.

The European Commission, in September 2001, confirmed a line of thinking which would be more efficient. It talked about:

> a list of offences treated as acts of terrorism where they are committed intentionally by individuals or groups against one or more countries or their institutions or population in order to threaten them and seriously undermine or even destroy their political, economic or social structures.[13]

In conclusion, for the time being, the GA 1996 definition is hence the most useful and straightforward one.

2.2   DETAILED/SPECIFIC[14]

Hereinbelow the definitions as contained in the various international instruments have all been included. That survey is preceded by a list of the relevant international

---

[13] See for details below, Chapter 6.

[14] This Volume focuses on the UN and the EU, and hence on post WW II developments. But mention should also be made – as has been done in the Introduction – to League of Nations efforts. The 1937 Convention contains the following definition:
(Article 2). The signatories of the text thus drew up the detailed list of the various forms of terrorism:
1. Facts intentionally directed against the life, the physical integrity, health or freedom of:
a)   heads of States, people who exert the prerogatives of head of State, their hereditary or designated successors;

instruments, together with an indication as to entry into force, Member States and signatories as per 1 May 2002.

In this Volume the various international instruments have been divided for easy reference as follows:

TC1: instruments adopted within the UN system (often as an Annex to a GA Resolution and with the UN Secretariat as the 'depository');
TC2: international instruments adopted outside the UN system, with normally a Government or an international organization as the 'depository'; and
TC3: regional instruments.

In view of ever ongoing developments the decision has been taken to pay due attention to two main draft conventions as well, the comprehensive one (in the version of February 2002) and the one on nuclear terrorism, in its 1999 version.

The full texts of all these conventions have been included in Chapter 5 of this Volume.

2.2.1   List of relevant Conventions

TC1: UN CONVENTIONS[15]

–   ***TC1A***: Convention on the Prevention and Punishment of Crimes against Internationally Protected Persons, including Diplomatic Agents, adopted by the General Assembly of the United Nations on 14 December 1973; entry into force: 20 February 1977; 119 parties and 25 signatories, as per May 2002;[16]
–   ***TC1B:*** International Convention against the Taking of Hostages, adopted by the General Assembly of the United Nations on 17 December 1979; entry into force: 3 June 1983; 107 parties and 39 signatories, as per May 2002;[17]
–   ***TC1C***: International Convention for the Suppression of Terrorist Bombings, adopted by the General Assembly of the United Nations on 15 December 1997;

---

b) husband or wife of the above peoples;
c) invested people of functions or public offices when the above-mentioned fact was made because of the functions or the responsibilities which these people exert.
2. The fact of destroying or of intentionally damaging public goods or goods intended for a public use, which belong to another State signatory or which belong to the State.
3. The fact of intentionally endangering human lives in order to create a common danger.
4. The attempt to commit offences envisaged by the preceding provisions of this article
    The fact of manufacturing, of getting, of holding or of providing weapons, ammunition, explosive products or harmful substances for the execution, in any country, of an infringement envisaged by this article
   [15] Another convention which has been concluded by the UN is the Convention on the Safety of United Nations and Associated Personnel, adopted by the General Assembly on 9 December 1994 and not yet in force (its text has not been included in this volume).
   [16] UN Treaty Series, vol. 1035, p. 167.
   [17] UN Treaty Series, vol. 1316, p. 205.

entry into force: 23 May 2001; 61 parties and 58 signatories, as per May 2002;[18]

- **TC1D:** Draft International Convention for the Suppression of Acts of Nuclear Terrorism, 22 October 1998;
- **TC1E**: International Convention for the Suppression of the Financing of Terrorism, adopted by the General Assembly of the United Nations on 9 December 1999; entry into force: 10 April 2002; 33 parties and 132 signatories, as per May 2001;[19]
- **TC1F**: Draft Comprehensive Convention (Ad-Hoc Committee established by the General Assembly Resolution 51/210 of 17 December 1996), 11 February 2002.

TC2: NON-UN CONVENTIONS

- **TC2A**: Convention on Offences and Certain Other Acts Committed on Board Aircraft, signed at Tokyo on 14 September 1963; entry into force: 4 December 1969; 173 parties, as per 1 May 2002;
- **TC2B**: Convention for the Suppression of Unlawful Seizure of Aircraft, signed at the Hague on 16 December 1970; entry into force:14 October; 175 parties, as per 1 May 2002;
- **TC2C**: Convention for the Suppression of Unlawful Acts against the Safety of Civil Aviation, signed at Montreal on 23 September 1971; entry into force:26 January 1973; 173 parties, as per 1 May 2002;
- **TC2D**: Convention on the Physical Protection of Nuclear Material, signed at Vienna on 3 March 1980; entry into force: 8 February 1987; 75 parties; 45 signatories, as per 1 May 2002;
- **TC2E**: Protocol on the Suppression of Unlawful Acts of Violence at Airports Serving International Civil Aviation, supplementary to the Convention for the Suppression of Unlawful Acts against the Safety of Civil Aviation, signed at Montreal on 24 February 1988; entry into force: 6 August 1989; 114 parties, as per 1 May 2002;
- **TC2F**: Convention for the Suppression of Unlawful Acts against the Safety of Maritime Navigation, done at Rome on 10 March 1988; entry into force: 1 March 1992; 67 parties, as per 1 May 2002;
- **TC2G**: Protocol for the Suppression of Unlawful Acts against the Safety of Fixed Platforms Located on the Continental Shelf, done at Rome on 10 March 1988; entry into force: 1 March 1992; 60 parties, as per 1 May 2002;
- **TC2H:** Convention on the Marking of Plastic Explosives for the Purpose of Detection, signed at Montreal on 1 March 1991; entry into force: 21 June 1998; 77 parties, as per 1 May 2002.

---

[18] Doc. A/RES/52/164.
[19] Res. A/RES/54/109.

TC3: REGIONAL INSTRUMENTS

- **TC3A**: Arab Convention on the Suppression of Terrorism, signed at a meeting held at the General Secretariat of the League of Arab States in Cairo on 22 April 1998;
- **TC3B:** Convention of the Organization of the Islamic Conference on Combating International Terrorism, adopted at Ouagadougou on 1 July 1999;
- **TC3C**: European Convention on the Suppression of Terrorism,[20] concluded at Strasbourg on 27 January 1977; entry into force: 4 August 1978; 38 ratifications and signatories, as per 1 May 2002;
- **TC3D**: OAS Convention to Prevent and Punish Acts of Terrorism Taking the Form of Crimes against Persons and Related Extortion that are of International Significance, concluded at Washington, D.C. on 2 February 1971; 14 ratifications, as per 1 May 2002;
- **TC3E**: OAU Convention on the Prevention and Combating of Terrorism, adopted at Algiers on 14 July 1999;
- **TC3F**: SAARC Regional Convention on Suppression of Terrorism, signed at Kathmandu on 4 November 1987;
- **TC3G**: Treaty on Cooperation among States Members of the Commonwealth of Independent States in Combating Terrorism, done at Minsk on 4 June 1999.

2.2.2   Definitions used

The definitions provided for and/or included in these respective instruments read as follows:

TC1: UN CONVENTIONS

TC1A
Convention on the Prevention and Punishment of Crimes against Internationally Protected Persons, including Diplomatic Agents, adopted by the General Assembly of the United Nations on 14 December 1973

Article 2, para. 1
The intentional commission of:
   (a) a murder, kidnapping or other attack upon the person or liberty of an internationally protected person;
   (b) a violent attack upon the official premises, the private accommodation or the means of transport of an internationally protected person likely to endanger his person or liberty.

---

[20] In relation with this convention, the European Union Member States have concluded the Dublin Agreement Concerning the Application of the European Convention on the Suppression of Terrorism among Member States (European Union), signed at Dublin on 4 December 1979, which has not been included in this volume.

TC1B

International Convention against the Taking of Hostages, adopted by the General Assembly of the United Nations on 17 December 1979

Article 1

1. Any person who seizes or detains and threatens to kill, to injure or to continue to detain another person (hereinafter referred to as the 'hostage') in order to compel a third party, namely, a State, an international intergovernmental organization, a natural or juridical person, or a group of persons, to do or abstain from doing any act as an explicit or implicit condition for the release of the hostage commits the offence of taking of hostages ('hostage-taking') within the meaning of this Convention.

TC1C

International Convention for the Suppression of Terrorist Bombings, adopted by the General Assembly of the United Nations on 15 December 1997

Article 2

1. Any person commits an offence within the meaning of this Convention if that person unlawfully and intentionally delivers, places, discharges or detonates an explosive or other lethal device in, into or against a place of public use, a State or government facility, a public transportation system or an infrastructure facility:
    (a) with the intent to cause death or serious bodily injury; or
    (b) with the intent to cause extensive destruction of such a place, facility or system, where such destruction results in or is likely to result in major economic loss.

TC1D

Draft International Convention for the Suppression of Acts of Nuclear Terrorism, 22 October 1998

Article 2

1. Any person commits an offence within the meaning of this Convention if that person unlawfully and intentionally:
    (a) Possesses radioactive material or makes or possesses a device:
        (i) With the intent to cause death or serious bodily injury; or
        (ii) With the intent to cause substantial damage to property or the environment;
    (b) Uses in any way radioactive material or a device, or uses or damages a nuclear facility in a manner which releases or risks the release of radioactive material:
        (i) With the intent to cause death or serious bodily injury; or
        (ii) With the intent to cause substantial damage to property or the environment; or
        (iii) With the intent to compel a natural or legal person, an international organization or a State to do or refrain from doing an act.
2. Any person also commits an offence if that person:
    (a) Threatens, under circumstances which indicate the credibility of the threat, to commit an offence as set forth in subparagraph 1 (b) of the present article; or
    (b) Demands unlawfully and intentionally radioactive material, a device or a nuclear facility by threat, under circumstances which indicate the credibility of the threat, or by use of force.

TC1E
International Convention for the Suppression of the Financing of Terrorism, adopted by
the General Assembly of the United Nations on 9 December 1999

Article 2
1. Any person commits an offence within the meaning of this Convention if that person by
any means, directly or indirectly, unlawfully and wilfully, provides or collects funds with the
intention that they should be used or in the knowledge that they are to be used, in full or in
part, in order to carry out:
    (a) An act which constitutes an offence within the scope of and as defined in one of the
         treaties listed in the annex; or
    (b) Any other act intended to cause death or serious bodily injury to a civilian, or to
         any other person not taking an active part in the hostilities in a situation of armed
         conflict, when the purpose of such act, by its nature or context, is to intimidate a
         population, or to compel a Government or an international organization to do or to
         abstain from doing any act.
(...)
3. For an act to constitute an offence set forth in paragraph 1, it shall not be necessary that the
funds were actually used to carry out an offence referred to in paragraph 1, subparagraph *(*a)
or *(*b).

TC1F
Draft Comprehensive Convention (Report of the Ad-Hoc Committee established by the
General Assembly Resolution 51/210 of 17 December 1996), 11 February 2002

Article 2
1. Any person commits an offence within the meaning of this Convention if that person, by
any means, unlawfully and intentionally, causes:
    (a) Death or serious bodily injury to any person; or
    (b) Serious damage to public or private property, including a place of public use, a
         State or government facility, a public transportation system, an infrastructure facil-
         ity or the environment; or
    (c) Damage to property, places, facilities, or systems referred to in paragraph 1(b) of
         this article, resulting or likely to result in major economic loss, when the purpose of
         the conduct, by its nature or context, is to intimidate a population, or to compel a
         Government or an international organization to do or abstain from doing any act:
         (i)   Be made with the aim of furthering the criminal activity or criminal purpose
               of the group, where such activity or purpose involves the commission of an
               offence as set forth in paragraph 1 of this article; or
         (ii) Be made in the knowledge of the intention of the group to commit an offence
               as set forth in paragraph 1 of this article (...)

Article 2 bis
Where this Convention and a treaty dealing with a specific category of terrorist offence
would be applicable in relation to the same act as between States that are parties to both treaties, the provisions of the latter shall prevail.

TC2: NON-UN CONVENTIONS

TC2A
Convention on Offences and Certain Other Acts Committed on Board Aircraft, signed at Tokyo on 14 September 1963

Article 2
1. This Convention shall apply in respect of:
    (a) offences against penal law;
    (b) acts which, whether or not they are offences, may or do jeopardize the safety of the aircraft or of persons or property therein or which jeopardize good order and discipline on board.
2. Except as provided in Chapter III, this Convention shall apply in respect of offences committed or acts done by a person on board any aircraft registered in a Contracting State, while that aircraft is in flight or on the surface of the high seas or of any other area outside the territory of any State.
3. For the purposes of this Convention, an aircraft is considered to be in flight from the moment when power is applied for the purpose of take-off until the moment when the landing run ends.
4. This Convention shall not apply to aircraft used in military, customs or police services.

TC2B
Convention for the Suppression of Unlawful Seizure of Aircraft, signed at the Hague on 16 December 1970

Article 1
Any person who on board an aircraft in flight:
    (a) unlawfully, by force or threat thereof, or by any other form of intimidation, seizes, or exercises control of, that aircraft, or attempts to perform any such act.

TC2C
Convention for the Suppression of Unlawful Acts against the Safety of Civil Aviation, signed at Montreal on 23 September 1971

Article 1
1. Any person commits an offence if he unlawfully and intentionally:
    (a) performs an act of violence against a person on board an aircraft in flight if that act is likely to endanger the safety of that aircraft; or
    (b) destroys an aircraft in service or causes damage to such an aircraft which renders it incapable of flight or which is likely to endanger its safety in flight; or
    (c) places or causes to be placed on an aircraft in service, by any means whatsoever, a device or substance which is likely to destroy that aircraft, or to cause damage to it which renders it incapable of flight, or to cause damage to it which is likely to endanger its safety in flight; or
    (d) destroys or damages air navigation facilities or interferes with their operation, if any such act is likely to endanger the safety of aircraft in flight; or
    (e) communicates information which he knows to be false, thereby endangering the safety of an aircraft in flight.

TC2D
Convention on the Physical Protection of Nuclear Material, signed at Vienna on 3 March 1980

Article 7
1. The intentional commission of:
    (a) an act without lawful authority which constitutes the receipt, possession, use, transfer, alteration, disposal or dispersal of nuclear material and which causes or is likely to cause death or serious injury to any person or substantial damage to property;
    (b) a theft or robbery of nuclear material;
    (c) an embezzlement or fraudulent obtaining of nuclear material;
    (d) an act constituting a demand for nuclear material by threat or use of force or by any other form of intimidation;
    (e) a threat:
        (i) to use nuclear material to cause death or serious injury to any person or substantial property damage, or
        (ii) to commit an offence described in sub-paragraph (b) in order to compel a natural or legal person, international organization or State to do or to refrain from doing any act.

TC2E
Protocol on the Suppression of Unlawful Acts of Violence at Airports Serving International Civil Aviation, supplementary to the Convention for the Suppression of Unlawful Acts against the Safety of Civil Aviation, signed at Montreal on 24 February 1988

Article 2
1. In Article 1 of the Convention, the following shall be added as new paragraph 1 bis:
        '1 bis. Any person commits an offence if he unlawfully and intentionally, using any device, substance or weapon:
        performs an act of violence against a person at an airport serving international civil aviation which causes or is likely to cause serious injury or death; or
        destroys or seriously damages the facilities of an airport serving international civil aviation or aircraft not in service located thereon or disrupts the services of the airport, if such an act endangers or is likely to endanger safety at that airport.'

TC2F
Convention for the Suppression of Unlawful Acts against the Safety of Maritime Navigation, done at Rome on 10 March 1988 (Deposited with the Secretary-General of the International Maritime Organization)

Article 3
1. Any person commits an offence if that person unlawfully and intentionally:
    (a) seizes or exercises control over a ship by force or threat thereof or any other form of intimidation; or
    (b) performs an act of violence against a person on board a ship if that act is likely to endanger the safe navigation of that ship; or
    (c) destroys a ship or causes damage to a ship or to its cargo which is likely to endanger the safe navigation of that ship; or

    (d) places or causes to be placed on a ship, by any means whatsoever, a device or sub-stance which is likely to destroy that ship, or cause damage to that ship or its cargo which endangers or is likely to endanger the safe navigation of that ship; or

    (e) destroys or seriously damages maritime navigational facilities or seriously inter-feres with their operation, if any such act is likely to endanger the safe navigation of a ship; or

    (f) communicates information which he knows to be false, thereby endangering the safe navigation of a ship; or

    (g) injures or kills any person, in connection with the commission or the attempted commission of any of the offences set forth in subparagraphs (a) to (f).

TC2G
Protocol for the Suppression of Unlawful Acts against the Safety of Fixed Platforms Located on the Continental Shelf, done at Rome on 10 March 1988

Article 2
1. Any person commits an offence if that person unlawfully and intentionally:

    (a) seizes or exercises control over a fixed platform by force or threat thereof or any other form of intimidation; or

    (b) performs an act of violence against a person on board a fixed platform lf that act is likely to endanger its safety; or

    (c) destroys a fixed platform or causes damage to it which is likely to endanger its safety; or

    (d) places or causes to be placed on a fixed platform, by any means whatsoever, a de-vice or substance which is likely to destroy that fixed platform or likely to endanger its safety; or

    (e) injures or kills any person in connection with the commission or the attempted commission of any of the offences set forth in subparagraphs (a) to (d).

TC2H
Convention on the Marking of Plastic Explosives for the Purpose of Detection, signed at Montreal on 1 March 1991

[no definition included in that Convention]

TC3: REGIONAL INSTRUMENTS

TC3A
Arab Convention on the Suppression of Terrorism, signed at a meeting held at the General Secretariat of the League of Arab States in Cairo on 22 April 1998

Part One, Definitions and General Provisions
Article 1
Each of the following terms shall be understood in the light of the definition give;

(…)

b. Terrorism
Any act or threat of violence, whatever its motives or purposes, that occurs in the advancement of an individual or collective criminal agenda and seeking to sow panic among people, causing fear by harming them, or placing their lives, liberty or security in danger, or seeking to cause damage to the environment or to public or private installations or property or to occupying or seizing them, or seeking to jeopardize a national resources.

c. Terrorist offence
Any offence or attempted offence committed in furtherance of a terrorist objective in any of the Contracting States, or against their nationals, property or interests, that is punishable by their domestic law. The offences stipulated in the following conventions, except where conventions have not been ratified by Contracting States or where offences have been excluded by their legislation, shall also be regarded as terrorist offences:
  (a) The Tokyo Convention on offences and Certain Other Acts Committed on Board Aircraft, of 14 September 1963;
  (b) The Hague Convention for the Suppression of Unlawful Seizure of Aircraft, of 16 December 1970;
  (c) The Montreal Convention for the Suppression of Unlawful Acts against the Safety of Civil Aviation, of 23 September 1971, and the Protocol thereto of 10 May 1984;
  (d) The Convention on the Prevention and Punishment of Crimes against Internationally Protected Persons, including Diplomatic Agents, of 14 December 1973;
  (e) The International Convention against the Taking of Hostages, of 17 December 1979;
  (f) The provisions of the United Nations Convention on the Law of the Sea, of 1982, relating to piracy on the high seas.

TC3B
Convention of the Organization of the Islamic Conference on Combating International Terrorism, adopted at Ouagadougou on 1 July 1999

Article 1
For the purposes of this Convention:
'Terrorism' means any act of violence or threat thereof notwithstanding its motives or intentions perpetrated to carry out an individual or collective criminal plan with the aim of terrorizing people or threatening to harm them or imperiling their lives, honour, freedoms, security or rights or exposing the environment or any facility or public or private property to hazards or occupying or seizing them, or endangering a national resource, or international facilities, or threatening the stability, territorial integrity, political unity or sovereignty of independent States.

'Terrorist Crime' means any crime executed, started or participated in to realize a terrorist objective in any of the Contracting States or against its nationals, assets or interests or foreign facilities and nationals residing in its territory punishable by its internal law.
Crimes stipulated in the following conventions are also considered terrorist crimes with the exception of those excluded by the legislations of Contracting States or those who have not ratified them:
  (a) Convention on 'Offences and Other Acts Committed on Board of Aircrafts' (Tokyo, 14.9.1963);
  (b) Convention on 'Suppression of Unlawful Seizure of Aircraft' (The Hague, 16.12.1970);

(c) Convention on 'Suppression of Unlawful Acts Against the Safety of Civil Aviation' signed at Montreal on 23.9.1971 and its Protocol (Montreal, 10.12.1984);

(d) Convention on the 'Prevention and Punishment of Crimes Against Persons Enjoying International Immunity, Including Diplomatic Agents' (New York, 14.12.1973);

(e) International Convention Against the Taking of Hostages (New York, 1979);

(f) The United Nations Law of the Sea Convention of 1988 and its related provisions on piracy at sea;

(g) Convention on the 'Physical Protection of Nuclear Material' (Vienna, 1979);

(h) Protocol for the Suppression of Unlawful Acts of Violence at Airports Serving International Civil Aviation-Supplementary to the Convention for the Suppression of Unlawful Acts Against the Safety of Civil Aviation (Montreal, 1988);

(i) Protocol for the Suppression of Unlawful Acts Against the Safety of Fixed Platforms on the Continental Shelf (Rome, 1988);

(j) Convention for the Suppression of Unlawful Acts Against the Safety of Maritime Navigation (Rome, 1988);

(k) International Convention for the Suppression of Terrorist Bombings (New York, 1997);

(l) Convention on the Marking of Plastic Explosives for the purposes of Detection (Montreal, 1991).

TC3C
European Convention on the Suppression of Terrorism, concluded at Strasbourg on 27 January 1977[21]

Article 1
For the purposes of extradition between Contracting States, none of the following offences shall be regarded as a political offence or as an offence connected with a political offence or as an offence inspired by political motives:

- an offence within the scope of the Convention of the Suppression of Unlawful Seizure of Aircraft, signed at The Hague on 16 December 1970;
- an office within the scope of the Convention for the Suppression of Unlawful Acts against the Safety of Civil Aviation, signed at Montreal on 23 September 1971;
- a serious offence involving an attack against the life, physical integrity or liberty of internationallyprotected persons, including diplomatic agents;
- an offence involving kidnapping, the taking of a hostage or serious unlawful detention;
- an offence involving the use of a bomb, grenade, rocket, automatic firearm or letter or parcel bomb if this use endangers persons;
- an attempt to commit any of the foregoing offences or participation as an accomplice of a person who commits orattempts to commit such an offence.

---

[21] In September 2001 the European Commission provided the following indications:
There is a list of offences treated as acts of terrorism where they are committed intentionally by individuals or groups against one or more countries or their institutions or population in order to threaten them and seriously undermine or even destroy their political, economic or social structures.

TC3D
OAS Convention to Prevent and Punish Acts of Terrorism Taking the Form of Crimes against Persons and Related Extortion that are of International Significance, concluded at Washington, D.C. on 2 February 1971

Article 2
For the purposes of this convention, kidnapping, murder, and other assaults against the life or personal integrity of those persons to whom the state has the duty to give special protection according to international law, as well as extortion in connection with those crimes, shall be considered common crimes of international significance, regardless of motive.

TC3E
OAU Convention on the Prevention and Combating of Terrorism, adopted at Algiers on 14 July 1999

Article 1
For the purposes of this Convention:
3. 'Terrorist act' means:
any act which is a violation of the criminal law of a State Party and which may endanger the life, physical integrity or freedom of, or
cause serious injury or death to, any person, any number or group of persons or causes or may cause damage to public or private property, natural resources, environmental or cultural heritage and is calculated or intended to:
  i.   intimidate, put in fear, force, coerce or induce any government, body, institution, the general public or any segment thereof, to do or abstain from doing any act, or to adopt or abandon a particular standpoint, or to act I according to certain principles; or
  ii. disrupt any public service, the delivery of any essential service to the public or to create a public emergency; or
  iii. create general insurrection in a State.

TC3F
SAARC Regional Convention on Suppression of Terrorism, signed at Kathmandu on 4 November 1987

Article 1
Subject to the overall requirements of the law of extradition, conduct constituting any of the following offences, according to the law of the Contracting State, shall be regarded as terroristic and for the purpose of extradition shall not be regarded as a political offence or as an offence connected with a political offence or as an offence inspired by political motives:
  (a) An offence within the scope of the Convention for the Suppression of Unlawful Seizure of Aircraft, signed at the Hague on December 16, 1970;
  (b) An offence within the scope of the Convention for the Suppression of Unlawful Acts against the Safety of Civil Aviation, signed at Montreal on September 23, 1971;
  (c) An offence within the scope of the Convention on the Prevention and Punishment of Crimes against Internationally Protected Persons, including Diplomatic Agents, signed at New York on December 14, 1973;

(d) An offence within the scope of any Convention to which the SAARC Member States concerned are parties and which obliges the parties to prosecute or grant extradition.

(e) Murder, manslaughter, assault causing bodily harm, kidnapping, hostage-taking and offences relating to firearms, weapons, explosives and dangerous substances when used as a means to perpetrate indiscriminate violence involving death or serious bodily injury to persons or serious damage to property;

(f) An attempt or conspiracy to commit an offence described in sub-paragraphs (a) to (e), aiding, abetting or counselling the commission of such an offence or participating as an accomplice in the offences so described.

TC3G
Treaty on Cooperation among States Members of the Commonwealth of Independent States in Combating Terrorism, done at Minsk on 4 June 1999

Article 1
For purposes of this Treaty, the terms used in it mean:

'Terrorism' – an illegal act punishable under criminal law committed for the purpose of undermining public safety, influencing decision making by the authorities or terrorizing the population, and taking the form of:

– Violence or threat of violence against natural or juridical persons;

– Destroying (damaging) or threatening to destroy (damage) property and other material objects so as to endanger people's lives;

– Causing substantial harm to property or the occurrence of other consequences dangerous to society;

– Threatening the life of a statesman or public figure for the purpose of putting an end to his State or other public activity or in revenge for such activity;

– Attacking a representative of a foreign State or an internationally protected staff member of an international organization, as well as the business premises or vehicles of internationally protected persons;

– Other acts classified as terrorist under the national legislation of the Parties or under universally recognized international legal instruments aimed at combating terrorism;

'Technological terrorism' – the use or threat of the use of nuclear, radiological, chemical or bacteriological (biological) weapons or their components, pathogenic micro-organisms, radioactive substances or other substances harmful to human health, including the seizure, putting out of operation or destruction of nuclear, chemical or other facilities posing an increased technological and environmental danger and the utility systems of towns and other inhabited localities, if these acts are committed for the purpose of undermining public safety, terrorizing the population or influencing the decisions of the authorities in order to achieve political, mercenary or any other ends.

CHAPTER 3
AUT DEDERE AUT JUDICARE

Whatever the definition of the act, it is of paramount importance that the offender be apprehended and be brought to justice. An essential element of modern societies having adopted the *trias politica* principle is that the monopoly of power, arms and enforcement has been handed over to a specific organ of the executive and that, on the basis of laws adopted by the legislature, the judiciary will take decisions as to culpability and will decide on the length and type of the penalty, if any. In this respect it is also important to underline that crime and justice have been removed from the offender-victim context and taken to the offender-society level as a whole.

Similarly, certain crimes are considered to be so far reaching that not just the direct victims and the affected local or national society are at stake, but the world community as a whole. Hence, efforts have been undertaken to ensure that the damage done be repaired in the broadest terms. In the context of terrorism we thus need to find out in how far (a) states have been obliged to include certain acts as criminal acts in their legislation; (b) whether the national courts have been declared competent also if it concerns crimes committed by non-nationals outside the territory; (c) whether extradition will be made possible if proceedings in another country would be the better alternative; (d) whether regard has to be had to those cases in which immunity prevents action from being taken; and (e) in how far would an international court be needed to fill legal, political or practical gaps. This chapter on *aut dedere aut judicare* (the principle to either extradite or put the culprits on trial) will hence be divided into five parts: part 1 deals with jurisdiction, part 2 with the accomplices issue, part 3 with extradition, part 4 with the topic of immunity; and finally part 5 with the ICC.

This chapter is indeed about closing the gaps in law enforcement.

3.1   JURISDICTION
(or: the strengthening of the *aut dedere aut judicare* principle)

3.1.1   Introduction

One of the main obstacles regarding the need to optimalize international cooperation in applying criminal law is related to the issue of jurisdiction. It may be recalled that Grotius already described piracy as 'an offence against the law of nations', an international crime. In the absence of international criminal tribunals, the punishment of piracy was left to any state that seized the offender, irrespective of whether the crime had been committed by one of its nationals, or whether the ship attacked had been sailing under its own flag, or whether the piracy took place in its territorial waters or some other state's territorial waters or on the high seas. It is obvious, in view of the very fact that all maritime states have an interest in ensuring safe passage for passengers and goods alike, that all efforts to combat piracy were welcomed and that this involved striving to put pirates on trial. Whether or not piracy per se is an international crime or rather a matter of international concern on which international law or international cooperation accepts the jurisdiction of all states, is not of quintessential importance.[1] Shared interests dictated the level of cooperation. This was also true for murdering the sovereign (king and emperor alike), counterfeiting, slavery (of both black and white) and to some extent desertion.[2] Of utmost relevance in this respect was whether the courts involved are competent to take on such cases, whether they would have 'jurisdiction' to try and possibility to apply the law.

International law normally differentiates between:

- **territorial jurisdiction**: the power of the court to render a ruling in crimes committed within the state where it resides;
- **personal jurisdiction**: the power of a court to adjudicate the personal legal rights of parties properly brought before it. It requires that the court not only has jurisdiction over the subject matter of the action, but also that it has jurisdiction over each party to the action;
- **universal jurisdiction**: a state prosecutes a person regardless of where the crime was committed or against whom.[3]

Strictly speaking the above differentiation could still result in cases which would go unpunished and untried. A new or amended set of principles was needed to cover potential gaps, and in 1987 the US thus reformulated the principles involved as follows:

- **The territorial principle;** under this principle, a state has jurisdiction over crimes committed within its territory, regardless of the fact whether the offender is a national of that state or a foreign citizen.[4]

---

[1] This paragraph is based on the reporter's note on para. 404 of Restatement (Third), Foreign Relations Law of the US, as reprinted in Steiner and Alston, *International Human Rights in Context,* Oxford 1996, pp. 1024-1025.

[2] As for desertion it should be noted that from the 1500s up until the 1790s most European armies consisted of mercenaries (still reflected in the Vatican's Swiss Guard and the French Foreign Legion). In order to prevent massive desertion when the going got tough or when more attractive contracts were on offer, there was widespread cooperation to prevent desertion to the greatest extent possible, although it fell short of calling desertion an international crime (see Van Krieken, *Deserteurs, Dienstweigeraars en Asielrecht,* Assen 1976).

[3] 'The principle of universal jurisdiction is based on the notion that certain crimes are so harmful to international interests that states are entitled – and even obliged – to bring proceedings against the perpetrator, regardless of the location of the crime or the nationality of the perpetrator or the victim. Human rights abuses widely considered to be subject to universal jurisdiction include genocide, crimes against humanity, war crimes and torture. While the principle of universal jurisdiction has long existed for these crimes, however, it is rapidly evolving as a result of significant recent developments' (Mary Robinson's Foreword to The Princeton Principles on Universal Jurisdiction, 2001). See also the Annex to this chapter containing these 2001 Princeton Principles on Universal Jurisdiction.

[4] A state can prescribe law with respect to conduct that, wholly or in substantial part, takes place

- **The effects principle;** what counts is the impact which the crime has had. It is a somewhat controversial concept, as some authors treat it as a separate principle, while others consider it as part of the territorial principle. It is often referred to as the objective territorial principle. An example which illustrates this concept is the person firing a weapon across the frontier and killing somebody in another country. Both states have jurisdiction: the state where the gun was fired has jurisdiction according to the territorial principle (where the act was committed), while the state in which the actual injury took place has jurisdiction under the effects doctrine (objective territorial jurisdiction).[5]
- **The nationality principle** reflects a state's jurisdiction to try its nationals for crimes committed both outside and within its territory. Generally, international law leaves the conditions for granting nationality to the domestic jurisdiction of states.[6]
- **The protective principle** asserts that a state may claim jurisdiction over aliens who have committed offences abroad which endanger the security of that state.[7]
- **The passive personality principle** provides that a state may claim jurisdiction to prosecute individuals for offences committed abroad which have a direct impact on the nationals of that state.[8]

However, other gaps continued to come to the fore: what if an Englishman, presumably guilty of a crime against a Frenchman whilst travelling in Germany, would be living in the Netherlands. In those cases a 'handing-over' scenario could yield some results and the legal instruments of deportation, expulsion, surrender and extradition would become relevant (see below, part 3 of this Chapter).

One of the main purposes of declaring a crime a terrorist act is indeed to facilitate the *aut dedere aut judicare* challenge. This stands for the obligation to either put the

---

within its territory. This most common basis for the exercise of jurisdiction to prescribe has generally been free from controversy (US Restatement 402, The Foreign Relations Law of the United States, 1987).

[5] A state can prescribe law with respect to conduct outside its territory that has 'substantial effect within its territory'. This principle is an aspect of jurisdiction based on territoriality, although it is sometimes viewed as a distinct category. A classic illustration would involve shooting or sending libellous publications across a boundary (ibid.).

[6] A state can prescribe law with respect to activities, interests, status, or relations of its nationals outside as well as within its territory. Typical criminal laws of the United States based on the nationality principle include a treason statute, statutes requiring citizens to register for military service, and judicial subpoenas addressed to nationals abroad. Many states provide that nationals may be prosecuted for all crimes, serious crimes, regardless of where they are committed (ibid.).

[7] A state can prescribe law with respect to conduct outside its territory by persons, not its nationals, that is directed against the security of the state or against a limited class of other state interests. That limited class concerns primarily offences threatening the integrity of governmental functions that are generally recognized as crimes by developed legal systems, including espionage, counterfeiting currency, and perjury before consular officials (ibid.).

[8] This principle asserts a state's jurisdiction to prescribe with respect to an act committed outside the state by a person not its national, where the victim of the act was its national. The principle has not been generally accepted for ordinary torts or crimes, but it is increasingly accepted as applied to terrorist and other organized attacks on a state's nationals by reason of their nationality. (ibid.)

offender on trial in the country where the offender is caught or to hand the offender over to any of the states interested in prosecuting him/her. This scenario can best be illustrated with the Pinochet case.

Pinochet was the military general in charge of the coup in Santiago de Chili, in September 1973. Whilst in the United Kingdom for medical treatment in 2000, a Spanish judge, interested in putting him on trial for alleged crimes (albeit torture, rather than terrorism) committed by the Chilean junta against Spanish citizens, asked for extradition. The UK High Court has originally refused extradition on the grounds that Pinochet, as the then Head of State, was immune under the 1978 State Immunity Act.[9] On appeal to the House of lords, however, a majority of the Law Lords (3 against 2) confirmed after lengthy procedures that certain crimes did indeed involve universal jurisdiction and that extradition to Spain was possible and acceptable. At a later stage the UK Government turned the Spanish extradition request down for medical reasons and returned Pinochet to his country of origin.[10]

It should be stressed that the Pinochet case concerned a former Head of State, a former dictator. Efforts have also been undertaken to file charges against persons in power. Reference can be made to Belgian prosecutors who, under a specific Belgian law filed charges against e.g. an actual Head of State and who consequently sent through Interpol an arrest warrant. This practice, however, has been ruled unlawful by the International Court of Justice (see below, under 'immunities' Chapter 3.4). Yet, for the purpose of this chapter, it can be safely concluded that there is an unstoppable move towards ensuring that no major criminal falls between the various stools of mazes of jurisdiction. This is being done by extending or rephrasing the territorial and personal principles and by agreeing that in a great many cases universal jurisdiction could be a proper response. This means that both on the national and international level appropriate action needs to be taken.

3.1.2   References to jurisdiction in relevant international instruments

As can be seen below, in virtually all terrorism instruments due attention has been paid to the jurisdiction issue. In most cases States have committed themselves to ensuring that jurisdiction over the crimes concerned should firmly be established

---

[9] More on immunity, see Chapter 3.5.

[10] Only for Mr. Pinochet to miraculously step out of his wheelchair on the very moment upon his return to Chili, in March 2000. As the NGO Human Rights Watch stated: On the night of October 16, 1998, London police arrested Gen. Augusto Pinochet Ugarte. They were acting on a Spanish warrant charging the former dictator with human rights crimes committed in Chile during his seventeen-year rule. Although Pinochet was returned to Chile on medical grounds in March 2000, his arrest and detention in London significantly advanced human rights both internationally and in Chile. The UK had confirmed that people accused of crimes such as torture can be prosecuted anywhere in the world. They have also firmly established that former heads of state are not immune from prosecution for such crimes. Amnesty International said:

This achievement is not affected by the UK Home Secretary decision not to extradite Augusto Pinochet to Spain'.

through and in their own legislation. The most repeated formula is: *States shall take such measures as may be necessary to establish its jurisdiction over the offences set forth in ... etc.* However, this obligation is more often than not limited to the cases in which the offences are committed: (a) in its territory; (b) by its nationals, and in some cases stateless persons with their habitual residence in that country; (c) on board its vessels or aircraft. This obligation in no way amounts to universal jurisdiction and also, remarkably, appears to often exclude legally residing aliens, and ever-growing category.

A second paragraph is hence normally added, in which no obligation has been formulated but rather an invitation: *A State Party may also establish its jurisdiction over any such offence when ...* (a) the offence is committed against a national; (b) against the State or e.g. an Embassy; (c) aimed at influencing the State in its actions. As can be noted below, the various instruments differ in what has been included under the obligation ('shall') and that which has been included under the additional phrase ('may'). It thus falls short of any coherent system, which, it could be submitted, will in due time result in efforts to arrive at a more streamlined and unified system altogether.

Apart from the balancing act described in the above paragraphs, it should nevertheless be stressed that virtually all instruments carry the important clause on the *aut dedere aut judicare* principle: *Each State shall take such measures as may be necessary to establish its jurisdiction in cases where the alleged offender is present in its territory and it does not extradite him to [another] State.* This would indeed appear to amount to an obligation to introduce a form of 'universal jurisdiction' in the case of non-extradition, by which the possible 'gaps' could be considered closed and/or covered. Due attention will be paid to the extradition aspect in part 3 of this Chapter.

As to JURISDICTION, the various instruments display the following details:[11]

TC1: UN CONVENTIONS

TC1A
Convention on the Prevention and Punishment of Crimes against Internationally Protected Persons, including Diplomatic Agents, adopted by the General Assembly of the United Nations on 14 December 1973

Article 3
1. Each State Party shall take such measures as may be necessary to establish its jurisdiction over the crimes set forth in Article 2 in the following cases:
  - (a) when the crime is committed in the territory of that State or on board a ship or aircraft registered in that State;
  - (b) when the alleged offender is a national of that State;
  - (c) when the crime is committed against an internationally protected person as defined in Article 1 who enjoys his status as such by virtue of functions which he exercises on behalf of that State.

---

[11] More often than not, the word 'jurisdiction' has been underlined (*jurisdiction*); it, of course relates to '*emphasis added*'.

2. Each State Party shall likewise take such measures as may be necessary to establish its jurisdiction over these crimes in cases where the alleged offender is present in its territory and it does not extradite him pursuant to Article 8 to any of the States mentioned in paragraph 1 of this Article.

3. This Convention does not exclude any criminal jurisdiction exercised in accordance with internal law.

TC1B
International Convention against the Taking of Hostages, adopted by the General Assembly of the United Nations on 17 December 1979

Article 5

1. Each State Party shall take such measures as may be necessary to establish its jurisdiction over any of the offences set forth in Article 1 which are committed:

    (a) in its territory or on board a ship or aircraft registered in that State;

    (b) by any of its nationals or, if that State considers it appropriate, by those stateless persons who have their habitual residence in its territory;

    (c) in order to compel that State to do or abstain from doing any act; or

    (d) with respect to a hostage who is a national of that State, if that State considers it appropriate.

2. Each State Party shall likewise take such measures as may be necessary to establish its jurisdiction over the offences set forth in Article 1 in cases where the alleged offender is present in its territory and it does not extradite him to any of the States mentioned in paragraph 1 of this Article.

3. This Convention does not exclude any criminal jurisdiction exercised in accordance with internal law.

TC1C
International Convention for the Suppression of Terrorist Bombings, adopted by the General Assembly of the United Nations on 15 December 1997

Article 6

1. Each State Party shall take such measures as may be necessary to establish its jurisdiction over the offences set forth in Article 2 when:

    (a) The offence is committed in the territory of that State; or

    (b) The offence is committed on board a vessel flying the flag of that State or an aircraft which is registered under the laws of that State at the time the offence is committed; or

    (c) The offence is committed by a national of that State.

2. A State Party may also establish its jurisdiction over any such offence when:

    (a) The offence is committed against a national of that State; or

    (b) The offence is committed against a State or government facility of that State abroad, including an embassy or other diplomatic or consular premises of that State; or

    (c) The offence is committed by a stateless person who has his or her habitual residence in the territory of that State; or

    (d) The offence is committed in an attempt to compel that State to do or abstain from doing any act; or

    (e) The offence is committed on board an aircraft which is operated by the Government of that State.

3. Upon ratifying, accepting, approving or acceding to this Convention, each State Party shall notify the Secretary-General of the United Nations of the jurisdiction it has established under its domestic law in accordance with paragraph 2 of the present Article. Should any change take place, the State Party concerned shall immediately notify the Secretary-General.
4. Each State Party shall likewise take such measures as may be necessary to establish its jurisdiction over the offences set forth in Article 2 in cases where the alleged offender is present in its territory and it does not extradite that person to any of the States Parties which have established their jurisdiction in accordance with paragraph 1 or 2 of the present Article.
5. This Convention does not exclude the exercise of any criminal jurisdiction established by a State Party in accordance with its domestic law.

Article 18
Nothing in this Convention entitles a State Party to undertake in the territory of another State Party the exercise of jurisdiction and performance of functions which are exclusively reserved for the authorities of that other State Party by its domestic law.

TC1D
Draft International Convention for the Suppression of Acts of Nuclear Terrorism, 22 October 1998

Article 9
1. Each State Party shall take such measures as may be necessary to establish its jurisdiction over the offences set forth in Article 2 when:
    (a)   The offence is committed in the territory of that State; or
    (b)   The offence is committed on board a vessel flying the flag of that State or an aircraft which is registered under the laws of that State at the time the offence is committed; or
    (c)   The offence is committed by a national of that State.
2. A State Party may also establish its jurisdiction over any such offence when:
    (a)   The offence is committed against a national of that State; or
    (b)   The offence is committed against a State or government facility of that State abroad, including an embassy or other diplomatic or consular premises of that State; or
    (c)   The offence is committed by a stateless person who has his or her habitual residence in the territory of that State; or
    (d)   The offence is committed in an attempt to compel that State to do or abstain from doing any act; or
    (e)   The offence is committed on board an aircraft which is operated by the Government of that State.
3. Upon ratifying, accepting, approving or acceding to this Convention, each State Party shall notify the Secretary-General of the United Nations of the jurisdiction it has established under its national law in accordance with paragraph 2 of the present Article. Should any change take place, the State Party concerned shall immediately notify the Secretary-General.
4. Each State Party shall likewise take such measures as may be necessary to establish its jurisdiction over the offences set forth in Article 2 in cases where the alleged offender is present in its territory and it does not extradite that person to any of the States Parties which have established their jurisdiction in accordance with paragraph 1 or 2 of the present Article.
5. This Convention does not exclude the exercise of any criminal jurisdiction established by a State Party in accordance with its national law.

TC1E
International Convention for the Suppression of the Financing of Terrorism, adopted by the General Assembly of the United Nations on 9 December 1999

Article 7
1. Each State Party shall take such measures as may be necessary to establish its jurisdiction over the offences set forth in Article 2 when:
   - (a) The offence is committed in the territory of that State;
   - (b) The offence is committed on board a vessel flying the flag of that State or an aircraft registered under the laws of that State at the time the offence is committed;
   - (c) The offence is committed by a national of that State.
2. A State Party may also establish its jurisdiction over any such offence when:
   - (a) The offence was directed towards or resulted in the carrying out of an offence referred to in Article 2, paragraph 1, subparagraph *(a)* or *(b)*, in the territory of or against a national of that State;
   - (b) The offence was directed towards or resulted in the carrying out of an offence referred to in Article 2, paragraph 1, subparagraph *(a)* or *(b)*, against a State or government facility of that State abroad, including diplomatic or consular premises of that State;
   - (c) The offence was directed towards or resulted in an offence referred to in Article 2, paragraph 1, subparagraph *(a)* or *(b)*, committed in an attempt to compel that State to do or abstain from doing any act;
   - (d) The offence is committed by a stateless person who has his or her habitual residence in the territory of that State;
   - (e) The offence is committed on board an aircraft which is operated by the Government of that State.
3. Upon ratifying, accepting, approving or acceding to this Convention, each State Party shall notify the Secretary-General of the United Nations of the jurisdiction it has established in accordance with paragraph 2. Should any change take place, the State Party concerned shall immediately notify the Secretary-General.
4. Each State Party shall likewise take such measures as may be necessary to establish its jurisdiction over the offences set forth in Article 2 in cases where the alleged offender is present in its territory and it does not extradite that person to any of the States Parties that have established their jurisdiction in accordance with paragraphs 1 or 2.
5. When more than one State Party claims jurisdiction over the offences set forth in Article 2, the relevant States Parties shall strive to coordinate their actions appropriately, in particular concerning the conditions for prosecution and the modalities for mutual legal assistance.
6. Without prejudice to the norms of general international law, this Convention does not exclude the exercise of any criminal jurisdiction established by a State Party in accordance with its domestic law

TC1F
Draft Comprehensive Convention (Report of the Ad-Hoc Committee established by the General Assembly Resolution 51/210 of 17 December 1996), 11 February 2002

Article 6
1. Each State Party shall take such measures as may be necessary to establish its jurisdiction over the offences set forth in Article 2 when:
   - (a) The offence is committed in the territory of that State; or

(b) The offence is committed on board a vessel flying the flag of that State or an aircraft which is registered under the laws of that State at the time the offence is committed; or

(c) The offence is committed by a national of that State.

2. A State may also establish its jurisdiction over any such offence when:

(a) The offence is committed by a stateless person who has his or her habitual residence in the territory of that State; or

(b) The offence is committed wholly or partially outside its territory, if the effects of the conduct or its intended effects constitute or result in, within its territory, the commission of an offence set forth in Article 2;

(c) The offence is committed against a national of that State; or

(d) The offence is committed against a State or government facility of that State abroad, including an embassy or other diplomatic or consular premises of that State; or

(e) The offence is committed in an attempt to compel that State to do or to abstain from doing any act; or

(f) The offence is committed on board an aircraft which is operated by the Government of that State.

3. Upon ratifying, accepting, approving or acceding to this Convention, each State Party shall notify the Secretary-General of the United Nations of the jurisdiction it has established under its domestic law in accordance with paragraph 2 of the present Article. Should any change take place, the State Party concerned shall immediately notify the Secretary-General.

4. Each State Party shall likewise take such measures as may be necessary to establish its  jurisdiction over the offences referred to in Article 2 in cases where the alleged offender is present in its territory and where it does not extradite such a person to any of the States Parties that have established their jurisdiction in accordance with paragraphs 1 or 2.

5. When more than one State Party claims jurisdiction over the offences set forth in Article 2, the relevant States Parties shall strive to coordinate their actions appropriately, in particular concerning the conditions for prosecution and the modalities for mutual legal assistance.

6. Without prejudice to the norms of general international law, this Convention does not exclude any criminal jurisdiction established by a State Party in accordance with its domestic law.

TC2: NON-UN CONVENTIONS

TC2A
Convention on Offences and Certain Other Acts Committed on Board Aircraft, signed at Tokyo on 14 September 1963

CHAPTER II
JURISDICTION

Article 3
1. The State of registration of the aircraft is competent to exercise jurisdiction over offences and acts committed.

2. Each Contracting State shall take such measures as may be necessary to establish its jurisdiction as the State of registration over offences committed on board aircraft registered in such State.

3. This Convention does not exclude any criminal jurisdiction exercised in accordance with national law.

Article 4

A Contracting State which is not the State of registration may not interfere with an aircraft in flight in order to exercise its criminal <u>jurisdiction</u> over an offence committed on board except in the following cases:

 (a) the offence has effect on the territory of such State;

 (b) the offence has been committed by or against a national or permanent resident of such State;

 (c) the offence is against the security of such State;

 (d) the offence consists of a breach of any rules or regulations relating to the flight or manoeuvre of aircraft in force in such State;

 (e) the exercise of <u>jurisdiction</u> is necessary to ensure the observance of any obligation of such State under a multilateral international agreement.

TC2B
Convention for the Suppression of Unlawful Seizure of Aircraft, signed at the Hague on 16 December 1970

Article 4

1. Each Contracting State shall take such measures as may be necessary to establish its <u>jurisdiction</u> over the offence and any other act of violence against passengers or crew committed by the alleged offender in connection with the offence, in the following cases:

 (a) when the offence is committed on board an aircraft registered in that State;

 (b) when the aircraft on board which the offence is committed lands in its territory with the alleged offender still on board;

 (c) when the offence is committed on board an aircraft leased without crew to a lessee who has his principal place of business or, if the lessee has no such place of business, his permanent residence, in that State.

2. Each Contracting State shall likewise take such measures as may be necessary to establish its <u>jurisdiction</u> over the offence in the case where the alleged offender is present in its territory and it does not extradite him pursuant to Article 8 to any of the States mentioned in paragraph 1 of this Article.

3. This Convention does not exclude any criminal <u>jurisdiction</u> exercised in accordance with national law.

TC2C
Convention for the Suppression of Unlawful Acts against the Safety of Civil Aviation, signed at Montreal on 23 September 1971

Article 5

1. Each Contracting State shall take such measures as may be necessary to establish its <u>jurisdiction</u> over the offences in the following cases:

 (a) when the offence is committed in the territory of that State;

 (b) when the offence is committed against or on board an aircraft registered in that State;

 (c) when the aircraft on board which the offence is committed lands in its territory with the alleged offender still on board;

 (d) when the offence is committed against or on board an aircraft leased without crew to a lessee who has his principal place of business or, if the lessee has no such place of business, his permanent residence, in that State.

2. Each Contracting State shall likewise take such measures as may be necessary to establish its <u>jurisdiction</u> over the offences mentioned in Article 1, paragraph 1 (a), (b) and (c), and in Article 1, paragraph 2, in so far as that paragraph relates to those offences, in the case where the alleged offender is present in its territory and it does not extradite him pursuant to Article 8 to any of the States mentioned in paragraph 1 of this Article.

3. This Convention does not exclude any criminal <u>jurisdiction</u> exercised in accordance with national law.

TC2D
Convention on the Physical Protection of Nuclear Material, signed at Vienna on 3 March 1980

Article 8
1. Each State Party shall take such measures as may be necessary to establish its <u>jurisdiction</u> over the offences set forth in Article 7 in the following cases:
   (a)   when the offence is committed in the territory of that State or on board a ship or aircraft registered in that State;
   (b)   when the alleged offender is a national of that State.

2. Each State Party shall likewise take such measures as may be necessary to establish its <u>jurisdiction</u> over these offences in cases where the alleged offender is present in its territory and it does not extradite him pursuant to Article 11 to any of the States mentioned in paragraph 1.

3. This Convention does not exclude any criminal <u>jurisdiction</u> exercised in accordance with national law.

4. In addition to the States Parties mentioned in paragraphs I and 2, each State Party may, consistent with international law, establish its <u>jurisdiction</u> over the offences set forth in Article 7 when it is involved in international nuclear transport as the exporting or importing State.

TC2E
Protocol on the Suppression of Unlawful Acts of Violence at Airports Serving International Civil Aviation, supplementary to the Convention for the Suppression of Unlawful Acts against the Safety of Civil Aviation, signed at Montreal on 24 February 1988

Article 3
In Article 5 of the Convention, the following shall be added as paragraph 2 bis:
> '2 bis. Each Contracting State shall likewise take such measures as may be necessary to establish its <u>jurisdiction</u> over the offences mentioned in Article 1, paragraph 1 bis, and in Article 1, paragraph 2, in so far as that paragraph relates to those offences, in the case where the alleged offender is present in its territory and it does not extradite him pursuant to Article 8 to the State mentioned in paragraph 1(a) of this Article'.

TC2F
Convention for the Suppression of Unlawful Acts against the Safety of Maritime Navigation, done at Rome on 10 March 1988 (Deposited with the Secretary-General of the International Maritime Organization)

Article 6
1. Each State Party shall take such measures as may be necessary to establish its <u>jurisdiction</u> over the offences set forth in Article 3 when the offence is committed:

    (a) against or on board a ship flying the flag of the State at the time the offence is committed; or

    (b) in the territory of that State, including its territorial sea; or

    (c) by a national of that State.

2. A State Party may also establish its jurisdiction over any such offence when:

    (a) it is committed by a stateless person whose habitual residence is in that State; or

    (b) during its commission a national of that State is seized, threatened, injured or killed; or

    (c) it is committed in an attempt to compel that State to do or abstain from doing any act.

3. Any State Party which has established jurisdiction mentioned in paragraph 2 shall notify the Secretary-General of the International Maritime Organization (hereinafter referred to as 'the Secretary-General'). If such State Party subsequently rescinds that jurisdiction it shall notify the Secretary-General.

4. Each State Party shall take such measures as may be necessary to establish its jurisdiction over the offences set forth in Article 3 in cases where the alleged offender is present in its territory and it does not extradite him to any of the States Parties which have established their jurisdiction in accordance with paragraphs 1 and 2 of this Article.

5. This Convention does not exclude any criminal jurisdiction exercised in accordance with national law.

TC2G
Protocol for the Suppression of Unlawful Acts against the Safety of Fixed Platforms Located on the Continental Shelf, done at Rome on 10 March 1988

Article 3

1. Each State Party shall take such measures as may be necessary to establish its jurisdiction over the offences set forth in Article 2 when the offence is committed:

    (a) against or on board a fixed platform while it is located on the continental shelf of that State; or

    (b) by a national of that State.

2. A State Party may also establish its jurisdiction over any such offence when:

    (a) it is committed by a stateless person whose habitual residence is in that State;

    (b) during its commission a national of that State is seized, threatened, injured or killed; or

    (c) it is committed in an attempt to compel that State to do or abstain from doing any act.

3. Any State Party which has established jurisdiction mentioned in paragraph 2 shall notify the Secretary-General of the International Maritime Organisation (hereinafter referred to as 'the Secretary-General'). If such State Party subsequently rescinds that jurisdiction, it shall notify the Secretary-General.

4. Each State Party shall take such measures as may be necessary to establish its jurisdiction over the offences set forth in Article 2 in cases where the alleged offender is present in its territory and it does not extradite him to any of the States Parties which have established their jurisdiction in accordance with paragraphs 1 and 2 of this Article.

5. This Protocol does not exclude any criminal jurisdiction exercised in accordance with national law.

TC2H
Convention on the Marking of Plastic Explosives for the Purpose of Detection, signed at Montreal on 1 March 1991

No reference to jurisdiction.

TC3: REGIONAL INSTRUMENTS

TC3A
Arab Convention on the Suppression of Terrorism, signed at a meeting held at the General Secretariat of the League of Arab States in Cairo on 22 April 1998

Article 14
(a) Where one of the Contracting States has jurisdiction to prosecute a person suspected of a terrorist offence, it may request the State in which the suspect is present to take proceedings against him for that offence, subject to the agreement of that State and provided that the offence is punishable in the prosecuting State by deprivation of liberty for a period of at least one your or more. The requesting state shall, in this event, provide the requested state with all the investigation documents and evidence relating to the offence.
(b) The investigation or prosecution shall be conducted on the basis of the charge or charges made by the requesting state against the suspect, in accordance with the provisions and procedures of the law of the prosecuting state.

TC3B
Convention of the Organization of the Islamic Conference on Combating International Terrorism, adopted at Ouagadougou on 1 July 1999

Article 15
1. If judicial competence accrues to one of the Contracting States for the prosecution of a subject accused of a terrorist crime, this State may request the country which hosts the suspect to prosecute him for this crime subject to the host country's consent and providing the crime is punishable in that country by a freedom restraining sentence for at least one year or by a more severe sanction. In such a case the requesting State shall pass all investigation documents and evidence related to the crime to the requested State.
2. Investigation or trial shall be conducted on the grounds of the case or cases brought by the requesting State against the accused in accordance with the legal provisions and procedures of the country holding the trial.

TC3C
European Convention on the Suppression of Terrorism, concluded at Strasbourg on 27 January 1977

Article 6
1. Each Contracting State shall take such measures as may be necessary to establish its jurisdiction over an offence mentioned in Article 1 in the ease where the suspected offender is present in its territory and it does not extradite him after receiving a request for extradition from a Contracting State whose jurisdiction is based on a rule of jurisdiction existing equally in the law of the requested State.

2. This Convention does not exclude any criminal jurisdiction exercised in accordance with national law.

TC3D
OAS Convention to Prevent and Punish Acts of Terrorism Taking the Form of Crimes against Persons and Related Extortion that are of International Significance, concluded at Washington, D.C. on 2 February 1971

No reference to jurisdiction

TC3E
OAU Convention on the Prevention and Combating of Terrorism, adopted at Algiers on 14 July 1999

Article 6
1. Each State Party has jurisdiction over terrorist acts as defined in Article 1 when:
   (a) the act is committed in the territory of that State and the perpetrator of the act is arrested in its territory or outside it if this is punishable by its national law;
   (b) the act is committed on board a vessel or a ship flying the flag of that State or an aircraft which is registered under the laws of that State at the time the offence is committed; or
   (c) the act is committed by a national or a group of nationals of that State.
2. A State Party may also establish its jurisdiction over any such offence when:
   (a) the act is committed against a national of that State; or
   (b) the act is committed against a State or government facility of that State abroad, including an embassy or other diplomatic or consular premises, and any other property, of that State; or
   (c) the act is committed by a stateless person who has his or her habitual residence in the territory of that State; or
   (d) the act is committed on board an aircraft which is operated by any carrier of that State; and
   (e) the act is committed against the security of the State Party.
3. Upon ratifying or acceding to this Convention, each State Party shall notify the Secretary General of the Organization of African Unity of the jurisdiction it has established in accordance with paragraph 2 under its national law. Should any change take place, the State Party concerned shall immediately notify the Secretary General.
4. Each State Party shall likewise take such measures as may be necessary to establish its jurisdiction over the acts set forth in Article 1 in cases where the alleged offender is present in its territory and it does not extradite that person to any of the States Parties which have established their jurisdiction in accordance with paragraphs 1 or 2.

TC3F
SAARC Regional Convention on Suppression of Terrorism, signed at Kathmandu on 4 November 1987

Article 5
For the purpose of Article IV, each Contracting State may take such measures as it deems appropriate, consistent with its national laws, subject to reciprocity, to exercise its jurisdiction in the case of an offence under Article I or agreed to in terms of Article II.

TC3G
Treaty on Cooperation among the States Members of the Commonwealth of Independent States in Combating Terrorism, done at Minsk on 4 June 1999

No mention regarding jurisdiction.

3.1.3   The Princeton Principles on Universal Jurisdiction

As has been indicated above, universal jurisdiction tends to become more than just a trend: it represents mutual dependency, globalization, the desire to cooperate and, not least, an awareness of increasing responsibility.

In an effort to reach an agreement on this issue, and in order to streamline thinking, drafting, planning in cooperation, an initiative was taken to define a set of principles. Most major actors, academia and politicians alike (e.g. Cherif Bassiouni,[12] Mary Robinson, Cees Flinterman, Richard A. Falk) were present and many an interesting statement and idea was submitted. Yet, the outcome is something of a disappointment, particularly also with regard to the ICC-related developments. That Court is very much based on the principle of ensuring that somewhere, somehow jurisdiction will be vested, more often than not on the basis of the concept of universal jurisdiction. Of course, the conference took place in January 2000, well ahead of the September 2001 events. Having said this, terrorism had already positioned itself on the leading agendas. The Security Council had adopted in October 1999 the important SC Res. 1269 and it is, therefore, remarkable that terrorism has not been included. It should hence be concluded that the Princeton Principles look backward, rather than forward, also as too many safeguards appear to have been included, based on an overriding fear of abuse of power, thus making the universal character somewhat illusionary. A more forward-looking document over and above the 1998 ICC Rome Statute would have been welcomed. The text reads as follows:

During the last century millions of human beings perished as a result of genocide, crimes against humanity, war crimes, and other serious crimes under international law. Perpetrators deserving of prosecution have only rarely been held accountable. To stop this cycle of violence and to promote justice, impunity for the commission of serious crimes must yield to

---

[12] M. Cherif Bassiouni is probably one of the foremost experts in international criminal law; he published widely on e.g. the ICC and is the editor of *International Terrorism: multilateral conventions 1937-2001*, Transnational Publishers, 2001. In this regard mention should also be made of Rosalyn Higgins & Maurice Flory: *Terrorism and International Law*, Routledge 1997. T&IL claims to be the first to address in one volume the wide variety of responses to terrorism as they exist in both international and domestic contexts. It is also claims to represent the first ever comprehensive collection of documents referring to terrorism which are to be found in the laws of the UK and France as well as in international law. Terrorism and International Law comprises contributions by thirteen well-known authorities in the areas of international, French and UK law, and is divided into four main sections: international cooperation against terrorism, the French and British responses to terrorism, the limits of state action and a documentary supplement.

accountability. But how can this be done, and what will be the respective roles of national courts and international tribunals?

National courts administer systems of criminal law designed to provide justice for victims and due process for accused persons. A nation's courts exercise jurisdiction over crimes committed in its territory and proceed against those crimes committed abroad by its nationals, or against its nationals, or against its national interests. When these and other connections are absent, national courts may nevertheless exercise jurisdiction under international law over crimes of such exceptional gravity that they affect the fundamental interests of the international community as a whole. This is universal jurisdiction: it is jurisdiction based solely on the nature of the crime. National courts can exercise universal jurisdiction to prosecute and punish, and thereby deter, heinous acts recognized as serious crimes under international law. When national courts exercise universal jurisdiction appropriately, in accordance with internationally recognized standards of due process, they act to vindicate not merely their own interests and values but the basic interests and values common to the international community.

Universal jurisdiction holds out the promise of greater justice, but the jurisprudence of universal jurisdiction is disparate, disjointed, and poorly understood. So long as that is so, this weapon against impunity is potentially beset by incoherence, confusion, and, at times, uneven justice.

International criminal tribunals also have a vital role to play in combating impunity as a complement to national courts. In the wake of mass atrocities and of oppressive rule, national judicial systems have often been unable or unwilling to prosecute serious crimes under international law, so international criminal tribunals have been established. Treaties entered into in the aftermath of World War II have strengthened international institutions, and have given greater clarity and force to international criminal law. A signal achievement of this long historic process occurred at a United Nations Conference in July 1998 when the Rome Statute of the International Criminal Court was adopted. When this permanent court becomes effective, the international community will acquire an unprecedented opportunity to hold accountable some of those accused of serious crimes under international law. The jurisdiction of the International Criminal Court will, however, be available only if justice cannot be done at the national level. The primary burden of prosecuting the alleged perpetrators of these crimes will continue to reside with national legal systems. Enhancing the proper exercise of universal jurisdiction by national courts will help close the gap in law enforcement that has favoured perpetrators of serious crimes under international law. Fashioning clearer and sounder principles to guide the exercise of universal jurisdiction by national courts should help to punish, and thereby to deter and prevent, the commission of these heinous crimes. Nevertheless, the aim of sound principles cannot be simply to facilitate the speediest exercise of criminal jurisdiction, always and everywhere, and irrespective of circumstances. Improper exercises of criminal jurisdiction, including universal jurisdiction, may be used merely to harass political opponents, or for aims extraneous to criminal justice. Moreover, the imprudent or untimely exercise of universal jurisdiction could disrupt the quest for peace and national reconciliation in nations struggling to recover from violent conflict or political oppression. Prudence and good judgement are required here, as elsewhere in politics and law.

What is needed are principles to guide, as well as to give greater coherence and legitimacy to, the exercise of universal jurisdiction. These principles should promote greater accountability for perpetrators of serious crimes under international law, in ways consistent with a prudent concern for the abuse of power and a reasonable solicitude for the quest for peace.

The participants in the Princeton Project on Universal Jurisdiction propose the following principles for the purposes of advancing the continued evolution of international law and the application of international law in national legal systems:

Principle 1 – Fundamentals of Universal Jurisdiction

1. For purposes of these Principles, universal jurisdiction is criminal jurisdiction based solely on the nature of the crime, without regard to where the crime was committed, the nationality of the alleged or convicted perpetrator, the nationality of the victim, or any other connection to the state exercising such jurisdiction.

2. Universal jurisdiction may be exercised by a competent and ordinary judicial body of any state in order to try a person duly accused of committing serious crimes under international law as specified in Principle 2(1), provided the person is present before such judicial body.

3. A state may rely on universal jurisdiction as a basis for seeking the extradition of a person accused or convicted of committing a serious crime under international law as specified in Principle 2(1), provided that it has established a prima facie case of the person's guilt and that the person sought to be extradited will be tried or the punishment carried out in accordance with international norms and standards on the protection of human rights in the context of criminal proceedings.

4. In exercising universal jurisdiction or in relying upon universal jurisdiction as a basis for seeking extradition, a state and its judicial organs shall observe international due process norms including but not limited to those involving the rights of the accused and victims, the fairness of the proceedings, and the independence and impartiality of the judiciary (hereinafter referred to as 'international due process norms').

5. A state shall exercise universal jurisdiction in good faith and in accordance with its rights and obligations under international law.

Principle 2 – Serious Crimes Under International Law

1. For purposes of these Principles, serious crimes under international law include: (1) piracy; (2) slavery; (3) war crimes; (4) crimes against peace; (5) crimes against humanity; (6) genocide; and (7) torture.

2. The application of universal jurisdiction to the crimes listed in paragraph 1 is without prejudice to the application of universal jurisdiction to other crimes under international law.

Principle 3 – Reliance on Universal Jurisdiction in the Absence of National Legislation

With respect to serious crimes under international law as specified in Principle 2(1), national judicial organs may rely on universal jurisdiction even if their national legislation does not specifically provide for it.

Principle 4 – Obligation to Support Accountability

1. A state shall comply with all international obligations that are applicable to: prosecuting or extraditing persons accused or convicted of crimes under international law in accordance with a legal process that complies with international due process norms, providing other states investigating or prosecuting such crimes with all available means of administrative and judicial assistance, and undertaking such other necessary and appropriate measures as are consistent with international norms and standards.

2. A state, in the exercise of universal jurisdiction, may, for purposes of prosecution, seek judicial assistance to obtain evidence from another state, provided that the requesting state has a good faith basis and that
the evidence sought will be used in accordance with international due process norms

Principle 5 – Immunities

With respect to serious crimes under international law as specified in Principle 2(1), the official position of any accused person, whether as head of state or government or as a responsible government official, shall not relieve such person of criminal responsibility nor mitigate punishment.

Principle 6 – Statutes of Limitations

Statutes of limitations or other forms of prescription shall not apply to serious crimes under international law as specified in Principle 2(1).

Principle 7 – Amnesties

1. Amnesties are generally inconsistent with the obligation of states to provide accountability for serious
crimes under international law as specified in Principle in 2(1).
2. The exercise of universal jurisdiction with respect to serious crimes under international law as specified in Principle 2(1) shall not be precluded by amnesties which are incompatible with the international legal obligations of the granting state.

Principle 8 – Resolution of Competing National Jurisdictions

Where more than one state has or may assert jurisdiction over a person and where the state that has custody of the person has no basis for jurisdiction other than the principle of universality, that state or its judicial organs shall, in deciding whether to prosecute or extradite, base their decision on an aggregate balance of the following criteria:

     (a)   multilateral or bilateral treaty obligations;
     (b)   the place of commission of the crime;
     (c)   the nationality connection of the alleged perpetrator to the requesting state;
     (d)   the nationality connection of the victim to the requesting state;
     (e)   any other connection between the requesting state and the alleged perpetrator, the crime, or the victim;
     (f)   the likelihood, good faith, and effectiveness of the prosecution in the requesting state;
     (g)   the fairness and impartiality of the proceedings in the requesting state;
     (h)   convenience to the parties and witnesses, as well as the availability of evidence in the requesting state; and
     (i)   the interests of justice.

Principle 9 – Non Bis In Idem/ Double Jeopardy

1. In the exercise of universal jurisdiction, a state or its judicial organs shall ensure that a person who is subject to criminal proceedings shall not be exposed to multiple prosecutions or punishment for the same criminal conduct where the prior criminal proceedings or other accountability proceedings have been conducted in good faith and in accordance with international norms and standards. Sham prosecutions or derisory punishment resulting from a conviction or other accountability proceedings shall not be recognized as falling within the scope of this Principle.
2. A state shall recognize the validity of a proper exercise of universal jurisdiction by another state and shall recognize the final judgement of a competent and ordinary national judicial body or a competent international judicial body exercising such jurisdiction in accordance with international due process norms.
3. Any person tried or convicted by a state exercising universal jurisdiction for serious crimes under international law as specified in Principle 2(1) shall have the right and legal standing to raise before any national or international judicial body the claim of non bis in idem in opposition to any further criminal proceedings.

Principle 10 – Grounds for Refusal of Extradition

1. A state or its judicial organs shall refuse to entertain a request for extradition based on universal jurisdiction if the person sought is likely to face a death penalty sentence or to be subjected to torture or any other cruel, degrading, or inhuman punishment or treatment, or if it is likely that the person sought will be subjected to sham proceedings in which international due process norms will be violated and no satisfactory assurances to the contrary are provided.

2. A state which refuses to extradite on the basis of this Principle shall, when permitted by international law, prosecute the individual accused of a serious crime under international law as specified in Principle 2(1) or extradite such person to another state where this can be done without exposing him or her to the risks referred to in paragraph 1.

Principle 11 – Adoption of National Legislation

A state shall, where necessary, enact national legislation to enable the exercise of universal jurisdiction and the enforcement of these Principles.

Principle 12 – Inclusion of Universal Jurisdiction in Future Treaties

In all future treaties, and in protocols to existing treaties, concerned with serious crimes under international law as specified in Principle 2(1), states shall include provisions for universal jurisdiction.

Principle 13 – Strengthening Accountability and Universal Jurisdiction

1. National judicial organs shall construe national law in a manner that is consistent with these Principles.

2. Nothing in these Principles shall be construed to limit the rights and obligations of a state to prevent or punish, by lawful means recognized under international law, the commission of crimes under international law.

3. These Principles shall not be construed as limiting the continued development of universal jurisdiction in international law.

Principle 14 – Settlement of Disputes

1. Consistent with international law and the Charter of the United Nations states should settle their disputes arising out of the exercise of universal jurisdiction by all available means of peaceful settlement of disputes and in particular by submitting the dispute to the International Court of Justice.

2. Pending the determination of the issue in dispute, a state seeking to exercise universal jurisdiction shall not detain the accused person nor seek to have that person detained by another state unless there is a reasonable risk of flight and no other reasonable means can be found to ensure that person's eventual appearance before the judicial organs of the state seeking to exercise its jurisdiction.

3.2   ACCOMPLICES
the status of those 'who finance, plan, support or commit': the impact of the
notion of accomplices.

3.2.1 Introduction

Security Council Resolution 1373 (2001) pays due attention to those who plan, finance, facilitate, support or commit a terrorist act. It has been indicated that the
circle of terrorist offenders is not limited to the actual offenders alone. The group of
'accomplices' is fairly large, and the question of to whom the various legal instruments apply is not just relevant, but is in many aspects a central one. SC Res. 1373
refers to *persons who commit, or attempt to commit, terrorist acts or participate in
or facilitate the commission of terrorist acts.* Elsewhere in the same resolution it can
be read that also persons and entities fall under the concept of terrorism if they are
found to be *making any funds, financial assets or economic resources or financial
or other related services available, directly or indirectly, for the benefit of persons
who commit or attempt to commit.* In addition to these two categories, a third category has been highlighted, namely ... *any person who participates in the financing,
planning, preparation or perpetration of terrorist acts or in supporting terrorist acts*
... It is implied that this group of 'accomplices' also falls under the category of terrorist offenders. It is herewith underlined that neither of the instruments concerned,
nor any preceding GA or SC resolutions have gone this far, which indeed means that
the general concern is far-reaching and has a tremendous impact.

The relevant European 'inclusion' can be seen from the Council's December 2001
Common Position:[1]
–   persons who commit, or attempt to commit, terrorist acts or participate in or fa-
     cilitate the commission of terrorist acts;
–   entities owned or controlled, directly or indirectly, by such persons; and
–   persons and entities acting on behalf of or under the direction of such persons
     and entities
–   measures shall be taken to suppress any form of support, active or passive, to
     entities or persons involved in terrorist acts, including measures aimed at sup-
     pressing the recruitment of members of terrorist groups and eliminating the sup-
     ply of weapons to terrorists.

---

[1] Included in full in this Volume as Chapter 6.3.3.

- safe haven shall be denied to those who finance, plan, support, or commit terrorist acts, or provide safe havens.
- persons who finance, plan, facilitate or commit terrorist acts
- persons who participate in the financing, planning, preparation or perpetration of terrorist acts or in supporting terrorist acts.

This clearly shows that the 'accomplices' issue has gained momentum and that the 'circle' of terrorist offenders would appear to be far greater than hitherto thought. The above references to SC Res. 1373 and the EU Common Position, however, differ to some extent from the more modest 'inclusion' as agreed upon in the various international instruments. The draft comprehensive convention includes participation, organization and contribution, which, from a terminology point of view, would indeed ensure a certain flexibility, which is indispensable for creating an effective international legal order. Yet, the SC Res. 1373 deserves to be highlighted and elaborated upon. It is obvious that hitherto only very few prosecutors and judges, human rights experts or lobby have paid sufficient attention to this issue in this context. It is the opinion of the present author that existing international law, also those instruments with only limited or no reference to the topic of accomplices, should be interpreted with SC Res. 1373 in mind.

3.2.2   References to accomplices in international instruments

The definitions provided for and/or included in the respective international instruments read as follows:

TC1: UN CONVENTIONS

TC1A
Convention on the Prevention and Punishment of Crimes against Internationally Protected Persons, including Diplomatic Agents, adopted by the General Assembly of the United Nations on 14 December 1973

Article 2
1. The intentional commission of:
    (a) (...)
    (b) (...)
    (c) a threat to commit any such attack;
    (d) an attempt to commit any such attack; and
    (e) an act constituting participation as an accomplice in any such attack shall be made by each State Party a crime under its internal law.

TC1B
International Convention against the Taking of Hostages, adopted by the General Assembly of the United Nations on 17 December 1979

Article 1
2. Any person who:
    (a) attempts to commit an act of hostage-taking, or

(b) participates as an accomplice of anyone who commits or attempts to commit an act of hostage-taking likewise commits an offence for the purposes of this Convention.

TC1C
International Convention for the Suppression of Terrorist Bombings, adopted by the General Assembly of the United Nations on 15 December 1997

Article 2
2. Any person also commits an offence if that person attempts to commit an offence as set forth in paragraph 1 of the present Article.
3. Any person also commits an offence if that person:
   (a) participates as an accomplice in an offence as set forth in paragraph 1 or 2 of the present Article; or
   (b) organizes or directs others to commit an offence as set forth in paragraph 1 or 2 of the present Article; or
   (c) in any other way contributes to the commission of one or more offences as set forth in paragraph 1 or 2 of the present Article by a group of persons acting with a common purpose; such contribution shall be intentional and either be made with the aim of furthering the general criminal activity or purpose of the group or be made in the knowledge of the intention of the group to commit the offence or offences concerned.

TC1D
Draft International Convention for the Suppression of Acts of Nuclear Terrorism, 22 October 1998

Article 2
4. Any person also commits an offence if that person:
   (a) Participates as an accomplice in an offence as set forth in paragraph 1, 2 or 3 of the present Article; or
   (b) Organizes or directs others to commit an offence as set forth in paragraph 1, 2 or 3 of the present Article; or
   (c) In any other way contributes to the commission of one or more offences as set forth in paragraph 1, 2 or 3 of the present Article by a group of persons acting with a common purpose; such contribution shall be intentional and either be made with the aim of furthering the general criminal activity or purpose of the group or be made in the knowledge of the intention of the group to commit the offence or offences concerned.

TC1E
International Convention for the Suppression of the Financing of Terrorism, adopted by the General Assembly of the United Nations on 9 December 1999

Article 2
(…)
4. Any person also commits an offence if that person attempts to commit an offence as set forth in paragraph 1 of this Article.
5. Any person also commits an offence if that person:
   (a) Participates as an accomplice in an offence as set forth in paragraph 1 or 4 of this Article;

(b) Organizes or directs others to commit an offence as set forth in paragraph 1 or 4 of this Article;

(c) Contributes to the commission of one or more offences as set forth in paragraph 1 or 4 of this Article by a group of persons acting with a common purpose. Such contribution shall be intentional and shall either:

   (i) Be made with the aim of furthering the criminal activity or criminal purpose of the group, where such activity or purpose involves the commission of an offence as set forth in paragraph 1 of this Article; or

   (ii) Be made in the knowledge of the intention of the group to commit an offence as set forth in paragraph 1 of this Article. (Article 2, para 4, 5)

TC1F
Draft Comprehensive Convention (Report of the Ad-Hoc Committee established by the General Assembly Resolution 51/210 of 17 December 1996), 11 February 2002

Article 2
(...)

4. Any person also commits an offence if that person:

   (a) Participates as an accomplice in an offence as set forth in paragraph 1, 2 or 3 of this Article;

   (b) Organizes or directs others to commit an offence as set forth in paragraph 1, 2 or 3 of this Article; or

   (c) Contributes to the commission of one or more offences as set forth in paragraph 1, 2 or 3 of this Article by a group of persons acting with a common purpose. Such contribution shall be intentional and shall either:

   (i) Be made with the aim of furthering the criminal activity or criminal purpose of the group, where such activity or purpose involves the commission of an offence as set forth in paragraph 1 of this Article; or

   (ii) Be made in the knowledge of the intention of the group to commit an offence as set forth in paragraph 1 of this Article.

TC2: NON-UN CONVENTIONS

TC2A
Convention on Offences and Certain Other Acts Committed on Board Aircraft, signed at Tokyo on 14 September 1963

No references

TC2B
Convention for the Suppression of Unlawful Seizure of Aircraft, signed at the Hague on 16 December 1970

Article 1
Any person who on board an aircraft in flight:

   (...)

   (d) is an accomplice of a person who performs or attempts to perform any such act commits an offence

   (hereinafter referred to as 'the offence').

TC2C
Convention for the Suppression of Unlawful Acts against the Safety of Civil Aviation, signed at Montreal on 23 September 1971

Article 1
(...)
2. Any person also commits an offence if he:
> (a) attempts to commit any of the offences mentioned in paragraph 1 of this Article; or
> (b) is an accomplice of a person who commits or attempts to commit any such offence.

TC2D
Convention on the Physical Protection of Nuclear Material, signed at Vienna on 3 March 1980

Article 7
1. The intentional commission of:
(...)
> (f) a threat:
>> (i) (...)
>> (ii) to commit an offence described in sub-paragraph (b) in order to compel a natural or legal person, international organization or State to do or refrain from doing an act;

TC2E
Protocol on the Suppression of Unlawful Acts of Violence at Airports Serving International Civil Aviation, supplementary to the Convention for the Suppression of Unlawful Acts against the Safety of Civil Aviation, signed at Montreal on 24 February 1988

No references

TC2F
Convention for the Suppression of Unlawful Acts against the Safety of Maritime Navigation, done at Rome on 10 March 1988. (Deposited with the Secretary-General of the International Maritime Organization)

Article 3
(...)
2. Any person also commits an offence if that person:
> (a) attempts to commit any of the offences set forth in paragraph 1; or
> (b) abets the commission of any of the offences set forth in paragraph 1 perpetrated by any person or is otherwise an accomplice of a person who commits such an offence; or
> (c) threatens, with or without a condition, as is provided for under national law, aimed at compelling a physical or juridical person to do or refrain from doing any act, to commit any of the of fences set forth in paragraph 1, subparagraphs (b), (c) and (e), if that threat is likely to endanger the safe navigation of the ship in question.

TC2G
Protocol for the Suppression of Unlawful Acts against the Safety of Fixed Platforms Located on the Continental Shelf, done at Rome on 10 March 1988

Article 2
(…)
2. Any person also commits an offence if that person:
   (a) attempts to commit any of the offences set forth in paragraph 1; or
   (b) abets the commission of any such offences perpetrated by any person or is otherwise an accomplice of a person who commits such an offence; or
   (c) threatens, with or without a condition, as is provided for under national law, aimed at compelling a physical or juridical person to do or refrain from doing any act, to commit any of the offences set forth in paragraph 1, subparagraphs (b) and (c), if that threat is likely to endanger the safety of the fixed platform.

TC2H
Convention on the Marking of Plastic Explosives for the Purpose of Detection, signed at Montreal on 1 March 1991

No references

TC3: REGIONAL INSTRUMENTS

TC3A
Arab Convention on the Suppression of Terrorism, signed at a meeting held at the General Secretariat of the League of Arab States in Cairo on 22 April 1998

No references

TC3B
Convention of the Organization of the Islamic Conference on Combating International Terrorism, adopted at Ouagadougou on 1 July 1999

Article 1
   (c) 'Terrorist Crime' means any crime executed, started or participated in to realize a terrorist objective in any of the Contracting States or against its nationals, assets or interests or foreign facilities and nationals residing in its territory punishable by its internal law.

TC3C
European Convention on the Suppression of Terrorism, concluded at Strasbourg on 27 January 1977

Article 1
For the purposes of extradition between Contracting States, none of the following offences shall be regarded as a political offence or as an offence connected with a political offence or as an offence inspired by political motives:

- (...)
- an attempt to commit any of the foregoing offences or participation as an accomplice of a person who commits orattempts to commit such an offence.

TC3D
OAS Convention to Prevent and Punish Acts of Terrorism Taking the Form of Crimes against Persons and Related Extortion that are of International Significance, concluded at Washington, D.C. on 2 February 1971

No references

TC3E
OAU Convention on the Prevention and Combating of Terrorism, adopted at Algiers on 14 July 1999

Article 1
3. 'Terrorist act' means:
(...)
    (b) any promotion, sponsoring, contribution to, command, aid, incitement, encouragement, attempt, threat, conspiracy, organizing, or procurement of any person, with the intent to commit any act referred to in paragraph (a) (i) to (iii).

TC3F
SAARC Regional Convention on Suppression of Terrorism, signed at Kathmandu on 4 November 1987

Article 1
    (f) An attempt or conspiracy to commit an offence described in sub-paragraphs (a) to (e), aiding, abetting or counselling the commission of such an offence or participating as an accomplice in the offences so described.

TC3G
Treaty on Cooperation among States Members of the Commonwealth of Independent States in Combating Terrorism, done at Minsk on 4 June 1999

Article 1 (...)
'Technological terrorism' – the use or threat of the use of nuclear, radiological, chemical or bacteriological (biological) weapons or their components, pathogenic micro-organisms, radioactive substances or other substances harmful to human health, including the seizure, putting out of operation or destruction of nuclear, chemical or other facilities posing an increased technological and environmental danger and the utility systems of towns and other inhabited localities, if these acts are committed for the purpose of undermining public safety, terrorizing the population or influencing the decisions of the authorities in order to achieve political, mercenary or any other ends, as well as attempts to commit one of the crimes listed above for the same purposes and leading, financing or acting as the instigator, accessory or accomplice of a person who commits or attempts to commit such a crime;
'Facilities posing an increased technological and environmental danger' – enterprises, installations, plant and other facilities whose inoperability may lead to loss of human life, the impairment of human health, pollution of the environment or destabilization of the situation in a given region or a given State as a whole.

3.3   EXTRADITION

3.3.1   Introduction

There is no rule under international law indicating that international cooperation in criminal matters would prevent any state to expel, deport, surrender or extradite aliens, foreign residents or nationals. The two main exceptions can be found in the fields of refugee law and human rights in general.[1] Rules on extradition, however, give countries the possibility not to extradite one's own subjects, but it is then generally assumed that the accused should may face trial in the country which refuses to follow up on an extradition request. In the case of terrorism, extradition may be the best of options, depending on the question where the prosecution would be most successful, in other words, where issues like investigation, burden of proof and witnesses are best available to ensure a successful outcome of the trial. Generally, non-extradition should amount to prosecution fully in accordance with the *aut dedere aut judicare* principle. In other words, jurisdiction, immunity and extradition are part and parcel of the same challenge, whereby in certain cases extradition may be the most desirable outcome and in other cases the contrary, again as long as local prosecution is then assured.

---

[1] The main provision of the 1951 Refugee Convention can be found in Art. 33.1 where it can be read that:

'No Contracting State shall expel or return ("refouler") a refugee in any manner whatsoever to the frontiers of territories where his life or freedom would be threatened on account of his race, religion, nationality, membership of a particular social group or political opinion'.

However, this obligation is not absolute as paragraph 2 of this Article indicates in fairly general terms in which cases the non-refoulement principle of paragraph 1 would not apply (nb: the wording 'reasonable grounds'): 'The benefit of the present provision may not, however, be claimed by a refugee whom there are reasonable grounds for regarding as a danger to the security of the country in which he is, or who, having been convicted by a final judgement of a particularly serious crime, constitutes a danger to the community of that country'.

In Europe, Art. 3 of the European Convention on Human Rights is, however, absolute in character (although some observers voice second thoughts on this absolute character). This Article reads: 'prohibition of torture: No one shall be subjected to torture or to inhuman or degrading treatment or punishment'.

Thirdly, the Convention against Torture (CAT, 1984) also contains an absolute prohibition:

'No State Party shall expel, return ("refouler") or extradite a person to another State where there are substantial grounds for believing that he would be in danger of being subjected to torture. For the purpose of determining whether there are such grounds, the competent authorities shall take into account all relevant considerations including, where applicable, the existence in the State concerned of a consistent pattern of gross, flagrant or mass violations of human rights'.

The 1957 European Convention on Extradition contains the following relevant indications, whereby it shall be noted that this instrument covers all possible crimes and not just terrorism.

Article 1 – Obligation to extradite
The Contracting Parties undertake to surrender to each other, subject to the provisions and conditions laid down in this Convention, all persons against whom the competent authorities of the requesting Party are proceeding for an offence or who are wanted by the said authorities for the carrying out of a sentence or detention order.

Article 6 – Extradition of nationals
A Contracting Party shall have the right to refuse extradition of its nationals.
Each Contracting Party may, by a declaration made at the time of signature or of deposit of its instrument of ratification or accession, define as far as it is concerned the term 'nationals' within the meaning of this Convention.
Nationality shall be determined as at the time of the decision concerning extradition. If, however, the person claimed is first recognised as a national of the requested Party during the period between the time of the decision and the time contemplated for the surrender, the requested Party may avail itself of the provision contained in sub-paragraph a of this Article.
If the requested Party does not extradite its national, it shall at the request of the requesting Party submit the case to its competent authorities in order that proceedings may be taken if they are considered appropriate. For this purpose, the files, information and exhibits relating to the offence shall be transmitted without charge by the means provided for in Article 12, paragraph 1. The requesting Party shall be informed of the result of its request.

Article 7 – Place of commission
The requested Party may refuse to extradite a person claimed for an offence which is regarded by its law as having been committed in whole or in part in its territory or in a place treated as its territory.
When the offence for which extradition is requested has been committed outside the territory of the requesting Party, extradition may only be refused if the law of the requested Party does not allow prosecution for the same category of offence when committed outside the latter Party's territory or does not allow extradition for the offence concerned.

Exceptions
Part of the 1950s philosophy was to 'pay tribute' to political offenders, and it was believed logical to protect this category. Once upon a time political offenders were believed to be heroes, fighting for the good cause, and indeed many of the 'offenders' deserve sympathy, as they pursued their goals in a peaceful manner. Each century appeared to feature its own characteristic attitude towards this issue: non-protection (read: extradition) was followed by absolute protection, and that

rigid approach was quite recently replaced by a more subtle, pragmatic and realistic one.

Changes occurred on three levels:

- case law;
- new conventions, and
- new attitudes towards jurisdiction (expanding the offences to fall under universal jurisdiction).

It is recalled that history witnessed (a) agreements on extradition; (b) a high level of cooperation; (c) a general exclusion for political crimes (with some exceptions for e.g. assassinations on heads of state); and (d) that these principles had been reconfirmed in most extradition treaties (e.g. Europe: 1957).

However, (i) crimes became more heinous; (ii) cooperation changed in character; mutual assistance and shared interests were underlined; and (iii) new ways of looking at the concept of political crimes and the exception to the extradition principle emerged.

One of the ways to yield results in an ambiance of increased cooperation was to ex-pand and extend jurisdiction, mainly as an alternative to extradition, and as a main maxim, agreement was reached – as we saw above – on the ***aut dedere aut judicare*** principle.

Within the extradition world a different solution was found by aiming at re-interpreting extradition treaties, e.g. by agreeing that some (obviously political) crimes will *not* be considered as a political offence or an offence inspired by political motives whereby those crimes became extraditable after all. Hereby the extradition treaties could remain in force and the political crime exception could be disregarded. This approach was reflected in some instruments in which it was specifically laid down that certain offences would whatever the character not be considered political in character.[2] As a main example is the European Convention on the Suppression of Terrorism, 1977, Article 1 in particular in which it can be read: 'For the purposes of extradition between contracting states, *none* of the following offences shall be considered as a political offence or as an offence connected with a political offence or as an offence inspired by political motives' (emphasis added). As we will see below it concerns an effective, exhaustive, and clear-cut list, which includes certain terrorist acts.

These developments can be considered to have taken place well within the triangle of freedom, security and justice, as it was considered logical to review the rule not to extradite political offenders and to declare certain prima face political offences as non-political. This development occurred in the context of increased international cooperation and a change of mind on the character of certain crimes and of an reappraisal of the such offences in general.

---

[2] Maybe remarkable, maybe in line with a trend, the Arab Convention concerned still contains the exception that an offence of a political nature will not result in extradition being permissible (TC3A, Art. 6).

Again, in the European context, in 1975 an Additional Protocol to the above 1957 Extradition Convention was adopted indicating which crimes would not be considered political (thus preceding the 1977 Convention on Terrorism).[3]

Meanwhile, in view of the many developments that took place in the European Union, it is quite logical that efforts are underway to go beyond the mechanism of extradition where it concerns cooperation in criminal matters. In fact, in 2001 agreement was reached on a European warrant of arrest, which would facilitate such cooperation and would in fact abolish extradition and its fairly complicated and time-consuming procedures as a phenomenon between EU Member States.[4]

---

[3] Art. 3 of the 1957 Convention read: Extradition shall not be granted if the offence in respect of which it is requested is regarded by the requested Party as a political offence or as an offence connected with a political offence. The same rule shall apply if the requested Party has substantial grounds for believing that a request for extradition for an ordinary criminal offence has been made for the purpose of prosecuting or punishing a person on account of his race, religion, nationality or political opinion, or that that person's position may be prejudiced for any of these reasons. The taking or attempted taking of the life of a Head of State or a member of his family shall not be deemed to be a political offence for the purposes of this Convention. This Article shall not affect any obligations which the Contracting Parties may have undertaken or may undertake under any other international convention of a multilateral character.

The 1975 Protocol agreed that: For the application of Article 3 of the Convention, political offences shall not be considered to include the following: the crimes against humanity specified in the Convention on the Prevention and Punishment of the Crime of Genocide adopted on 9 December 1948 by the General Assembly of the United Nations; the violations specified in Article 50 of the 1949 Geneva Convention for the Amelioration of the Condition of the Wounded and Sick in Armed Forces in the Field, Article 51 of the 1949 Geneva Convention for the Amelioration of the Condition of Wounded, Sick and Shipwrecked members of Armed Forces at Sea, Article 130 of the 1949 Geneva Convention relative to the Treatment of Prisoners of War and Article 147 of the 1949 Geneva Convention relative to the Protection of Civilian Persons in Time of War; any comparable violations of the laws of war having effect at the time when this Protocol enters into force and of customs of war existing at that time, which are not already provided for in the above-mentioned provisions of the Geneva Conventions.

[4] At the December 2001 Laeken summit, an agreement on a European arrest warrant was reached and it was hailed that extradition will no longer be necessary between EU Member States. As was stated in the related press release:

'European Union (EU) Member States' judiciary will no longer have to go through the formal extradition procedure in order to forcibly transfer a person from one Member State to another for conducting a criminal prosecution or executing a custodial sentence or detention order. On 11 December 2001, the EU reached a political agreement on the European arrest warrant. Its purpose is to facilitate law enforcement right across the EU. On 6 and 7 December 2001, the ministers responsible for justice and home affairs in the Member States of the European Union (EU) studied a draft EU decision based on a European Commission proposal, at the initiative of Commissioner Antonio Vitorino (document reference COM (2001) 522 final/2). A political agreement was reached on 11 December 2001 at EU level on a European arrest warrant valid for the entire territory of the European Union, and on the surrender procedures between the Member States. The European arrest warrant will come into force on 1 January 2004. The agreement carries through the European Council conclusions of October 1999, in Tampere, which state that the formal extradition procedure should be abolished among the Member States as far as persons are concerned who are fleeing from justice after having been finally sentenced. Criminals like anybody else can take advantage of the free movement of persons. Up till now, extradition was the only instrument available to the judiciary of a Member State to catch criminals beyond its national borders. This entailed a cumbersome and complex process. A high level of mutual trust and coopera-

Extradition involving many an administrative and judicial step is considered by many to be unnecessarily complicated. They wonder whether a simple expulsion or deportation would yield a similar result.

It is thus emphasized that extradition is still in many cases the preferable means to reach the goal of making sure that terrorist acts do not go unpunished. Although the extension of jurisdiction – be it by re-interpreting the territorial or personal principles or by adopting the universal jurisdiction principle – is laudable and important, more effect can probably be had by turning extradition into an effective and pragmatic tool.[5] It should hence come as no surprise that most terrorist instruments refer to extradition in no uncertain terms. Moreover, as we saw above in Chapter 2 on definitions, the GA 1996 Resolution (51/210) on measures to eliminate international terrorism) indicated that an act of terrorism can never be 'covered' by the excuse that they are political in character: these acts '*are in any circumstance unjustifiable, whatever the considerations of a political, philosophical, ideological, racial, ethnic, religious or other nature that may be invoked to justify them.*' In such cases extradition should hence be considered a practical alternative, if not the preferred option.

3.3.2 References to extradition in relevant international instruments

The paragraphs on extradition in the main international instruments read as follows:[6]

---

tion between the Member States who share the same highly demanding conception of the rule of law, has made it possible to simplify and improve the surrendering procedure. In doing so, they are developing the European Union into a single European judicial area.'

The Framework Decision concerned refers to the fundamental rights, in particular those mentioned in the Chapter VI of the 2000 Charter of fundamental rights of the European Union (a non-binding instrument) which relates to justice. The European arrest warrant applies to all offences. In practice, the judiciary of each Member State will be able to issue a European arrest warrant when a person is being prosecuted for an offence punishable by a custodial sentence of over a year or when the person has been sentenced to custodial or detention order exceeding four months. When an arrest is carried out on the basis of a European arrest warrant in a Member State, the person will be handed over by the judiciary of the state where the arrest has taken place pending minimal control over a maximum period of three months. For a list of 32 serious offences – punishable by deprivation of liberty of at least 3 years – the surrender of the person does not require the verification of the double criminality of the act. Dual discrimination requires that the facts which motivated issuing an arrest warrant are also incriminated in the Member State where the surrender is to be carried out. The serious offences subject to European arrest warrant include: participation in a criminal organisation, terrorism, trafficking in human beings, sexual exploitation of children and child pornography, illicit trafficking in arms, ammunition and explosives, corruption, fraud including fraud pertaining to the financial interest of the European Union, recycling the benefits of crime and counterfeiting.

[5] Or by 'replacing' it with 'surrender' as indicated in the preceding footnote.

[6] Unlike the sub-chapter on jurisdiction, in this survey the word extradition has not been underlined in view of the frequency this word (and extraditable offences) appear.

TC1: UN CONVENTIONS

TC1A
Convention on the Prevention and Punishment of Crimes against Internationally Protected Persons, including Diplomatic Agents, adopted by the General Assembly of the United Nations on 14 December 1973

Article 8
To the extent that the crimes set forth in Article 2 are not listed as extraditable offences in any extradition treaty existing between States Parties, they shall be deemed to be included as such therein. States Parties undertake to include those crimes as extraditable offences in every future extradition treaty to be concluded between them.

If a State Party which makes extradition conditional on the existence of a treaty receives a request for extradition from another State Party with which it has no extradition treaty, it may, if it decides to extradite, consider this Convention as the legal basis for extradition in respect of those crimes. Extradition shall be subject to the procedural provisions and the other conditions of the law of the requested State.

States Parties which do not make extradition conditional on the existence of a treaty shall recognize those crimes as extraditable offences between themselves subject to the procedural provisions and the other conditions of the law of the requested State.

Each of the crimes shall be treated, for the purpose of extradition between States Parties, as if it had been committed not only in the place in which it occurred but also in the territories of the States required to establish their jurisdiction in accordance with paragraph 1 of Article 3.

Article 9
A request for the extradition of an alleged offender, pursuant to this Convention, shall not be granted if the requested State Party has substantial grounds for believing:

that the request for extradition for an offence set forth in Article 1 has been made for the purpose of prosecuting or punishing a person on account of his race, religion, nationality, ethnic origin or political opinion; or

that the person's position may be prejudiced:

for any of the reasons mentioned in subparagraph (a) of this paragraph, or

for the reason that communication with him by the appropriate authorities of the State entitled to exercise rights of protection cannot be effected.

With respect to the offences as defined in this Convention, the provisions of all extradition treaties and arrangements applicable between States Parties are modified as between States Parties to the extent that they are incompatible with this Convention.

Article 10
The offences set forth in Article 1 shall be deemed to be included as extraditable offences in any extradition treaty existing between States Parties. States Parties undertake to include such offences as extraditable offences in every extradition treaty to be concluded between them.

If a State Party which makes extradition conditional on the existence of a treaty receives a request for extradition from another State Party with which it has no extradition treaty, the requested State may at its option consider this Convention as the legal basis for extradition in respect of the offences set forth in Article 1. Extradition shall be subject to the other conditions provided by the law of the requested State.

States Parties which do not make extradition conditional on the existence of a treaty shall recognize the offences set forth in Article 1 as extraditable offences between themselves subject to the conditions provided by the law of the requested State.

The offences set forth in Article I shall be treated, for the purpose of extradition between States Parties, as if they had been committed not only in the place in which they occurred but also in the territories of the States required to establish their jurisdiction in accordance with paragraph 1 of Article 5.

TC1B
International Convention against the Taking of Hostages, adopted by the General Assembly of the United Nations on 17 December 1979

Article 10
The offences set forth in Article 1 shall be deemed to be included as extraditable offences in any extradition treaty existing between States Parties. States Parties undertake to include such offences as extraditable offences in every extradition treaty to be concluded between them.

If a State Party which makes extradition conditional on the existence of a treaty receives a request for extradition from another State Party with which it has no extradition treaty, the requested State may at its option consider this Convention as the legal basis for extradition in respect of the offences set forth in Article 1. Extradition shall be subject to the other conditions provided by the law of the requested State.

States Parties which do not make extradition conditional on the existence of a treaty shall recognize the offences set forth in Article 1 as extraditable offences between themselves subject to the conditions provided by the law of the requested State.

The offences set forth in Article I shall be treated, for the purpose of extradition between States Parties, as if they had been committed not only in the place in which they occurred but also in the territories of the States required to establish their jurisdiction in accordance with paragraph 1 of Article 5.

TC1C
International Convention for the Suppression of Terrorist Bombings, adopted by the General Assembly of the United Nations on 15 December 1997

Article 8
The State Party in the territory of which the alleged offender is present shall, in cases to which Article 6 applies, if it does not extradite that person, be obliged, without exception whatsoever and whether or not the offence was committed in its territory, to submit the case without undue delay to its competent authorities for the purpose of prosecution, through proceedings in accordance with the laws of that State. Those authorities shall take their decision in the same manner as in the case of any other offence of a grave nature under the law of that State.

Whenever a State Party is permitted under its domestic law to extradite or otherwise surrender one of its nationals only upon the condition that the person will be returned to that State to serve the sentence imposed as a result of the trial or proceeding for which the extradition or surrender of the person was sought, and this State and the State seeking the extradition of the person agree with this option and other terms they may deem appropriate, such a conditional extradition or surrender shall be sufficient to discharge the obligation set forth in paragraph 1 of the present Article.

Article 9

The offences set forth in Article 2 shall be deemed to be included as extraditable offences in any extradition treaty existing between any of the States Parties before the entry into force of this Convention. States Parties undertake to include such offences as extraditable offences in every extradition treaty to be subsequently concluded between them.

When a State Party which makes extradition conditional on the existence of a treaty receives a request for extradition from another State Party with which it has no extradition treaty, the requested State Party may, at its option, consider this Convention as a legal basis for extradition in respect of the offences set forth in Article 2. Extradition shall be subject to the other conditions provided by the law of the requested State.

States Parties which do not make extradition conditional on the existence of a treaty shall recognize the offences set forth in Article 2 as extraditable offences between themselves, subject to the conditions provided by the law of the requested State.

If necessary, the offences set forth in Article 2 shall be treated, for the purposes of extradition between States Parties, as if they had been committed not only in the place in which they occurred but also in the territory of the States that have established jurisdiction in accordance with Article 6, paragraphs 1 and 2.

The provisions of all extradition treaties and arrangements between States Parties with regard to offences set forth in Article 2 shall be deemed to be modified as between State Parties to the extent that they are incompatible with this Convention.

TC1D
Draft International Convention for the Suppression of Acts of Nuclear Terrorism, 22 October 1998

Article 11

1. The State Party in the territory of which the alleged offender is present shall, in cases to which Article 9 applies, if it does not extradite that person, be obliged, without exception whatsoever and whether or not the offence was committed in its territory, to submit the case without undue delay to its competent authorities for the purpose of prosecution, through proceedings in accordance with the laws of that State. Those authorities shall take their decision in the same manner as in the case of any other offence of a grave nature under the law of that State.

2. Whenever a State Party is permitted under its national law to extradite or otherwise surrender one of its nationals only upon the condition that the person will be returned to that State to serve the sentence imposed as a result of the trial or proceeding for which the extradition or surrender of the person was sought, and this State and the State seeking the extradition of the person agree with this option and other terms they may deem appropriate, such a conditional extradition or surrender shall be sufficient to discharge the obligation set forth in paragraph 1 of the present Article.

Article 13

1. The offences set forth in Article 2 shall be deemed to be included as extraditable offences in any extradition treaty existing between any of the States Parties before the entry into force of this Convention. States Parties undertake to include such offences as extraditable offences in every extradition treaty to be subsequently concluded between them.

2. When a State Party which makes extradition conditional on the existence of a treaty receives a request for extradition from another State Party with which it has no extradition treaty, the requested State Party may, at its option, consider this Convention as a legal basis for extradition in respect of the offences set forth in Article 2. Extradition shall be subject to the other conditions provided by the law of the requested State.

3. States Parties which do not make extradition conditional on the existence of a treaty shall recognize the offences set forth in Article 2 as extraditable offences between themselves, subject to the conditions provided by the law of the requested State.

4. If necessary, the offences set forth in Article 2 shall be treated, for the purposes of extradition between States Parties, as if they had been committed not only in the place in which they occurred but also in the territory of the States that have established jurisdiction in accordance with Article 9, paragraphs 1 and 2.

5. The provisions of all extradition treaties and arrangements between States Parties with regard to offences set forth in Article 2 shall be deemed to be modified as between States Parties to the extent that they are incompatible with this Convention.

TC1E
International Convention for the Suppression of the Financing of Terrorism, adopted by the General Assembly of the United Nations on 9 December 1999

Article 11
1. The offences set forth in Article 2 shall be deemed to be included as extraditable offences in any extradition treaty existing between any of the States Parties before the entry into force of this Convention. States Parties undertake to include such offences as extraditable offences in every extradition treaty to be subsequently concluded between them.

2. When a State Party which makes extradition conditional on the existence of a treaty receives a request for extradition from another State Party with which it has no extradition treaty, the requested State Party may, at its option, consider this Convention as a legal basis for extradition in respect of the offences set forth in Article 2. Extradition shall be subject to the other conditions provided by the law of the requested State.

3. States Parties which do not make extradition conditional on the existence of a treaty shall recognize the offences set forth in Article 2 as extraditable offences between themselves, subject to the conditions provided by the law of the requested State.

4. If necessary, the offences set forth in Article 2 shall be treated, for the purposes of extradition between States Parties, as if they had been committed not only in the place in which they occurred but also in the territory of the States that have established jurisdiction in accordance with Article 7, paragraphs 1 and 2.

5. The provisions of all extradition treaties and arrangements between States Parties with regard to offences set forth in Article 2 shall be deemed to be modified as between States Parties to the extent that they are incompatible with this Convention.

TC1F
Draft Comprehensive Convention (Report of the Ad-Hoc Committee established by the General Assembly Resolution 51/210 of 17 December 1996), 11 February 2002

Article 11
1. The State Party in whose territory the alleged offender is present shall, in cases to which Article 6 applies, if it does not extradite the person, be obliged, without exception whatsoever and whether or not the offence was committed in its territory, to submit the case, without undue delay, to its competent authorities for the purpose of prosecution through proceedings in

accordance with the laws of that State. Those authorities shall take their decision in the same manner as in the case of any other offence of a grave nature under the law of that State.

2. Whenever a State Party is permitted under its domestic law to extradite or otherwise surrender one of its nationals only upon the condition that the person will be returned to that State to serve the sentence imposed as a result of the trial or proceeding for which the extradition or surrender of the person was sought, and that State and the State seeking the extradition of the person agree with this option and other terms they may deem appropriate, such a conditional extradition or surrender shall be sufficient to discharge the obligation set forth in paragraph 1.

Article 17

1. The offences referred to in Article 2 shall be deemed to be included as extraditable offences in any extradition treaty existing between any of the States Parties before the entry into force of this Convention. States Parties undertake to include such offences as extraditable offences in every extradition treaty to be subsequently concluded between them.

2. When a State Party which makes extradition conditional on the existence of a treaty receives a request from another State Party with which it has no extradition treaty, the requested State may, at its option, consider this Convention as a legal basis for extradition in respect of the offences set forth in Article 2. Extradition shall be subject to the other conditions provided by the law of the requested State.

3. States Parties which do not make extradition conditional on the existence of a treaty shall recognize the offences referred to in Article 2 as extraditable offences between themselves, subject to the conditions provided for by the law of the requested State.

4. If necessary, the offences set forth in Article 2 shall be treated, for the purposes of extradition between States Parties, as if they had been committed not only in the place in which they occurred but also in the territory of the States that have established jurisdiction in accordance with Article 6, paragraphs 1 and 2.

5. The provisions of all extradition treaties and arrangements between States Parties with regard to offences set forth in Article 2 shall be deemed to be modified as between States Parties to the extent that they are incompatible with this Convention.

TC2: NON-UN CONVENTIONS

TC2A
Convention on Offences and Certain Other Acts Committed on Board Aircraft, signed at Tokyo on 14 September 1963

Article 15

Without prejudice to Article 14, any person who has been disembarked in accordance with Article 8, paragraph 1, or delivered in accordance with Article 9, paragraph 1, or has disembarked after committing an act contemplated in Article 11, paragraph 1, and who desires to continue his journey shall be at liberty as soon as practicable to proceed to any destination of his choice unless his presence is required by the law of the State of landing for the purpose of extradition or criminal proceedings.

Without prejudice to its law as to entry and admission to, and extradition and expulsion from its territory, a Contracting State in whose territory a person has been disembarked in accordance with Article 8, paragraph 1, or delivered in accordance with Article 9, paragraph 1 or has disembarked and is suspected of having committed an act contemplated in Article 11, paragraph 1, shall accord to such person treatment which is no less favourable for his protection and security than that accorded to nationals of such Contracting State in like circumstances

TC2B
Convention for the Suppression of Unlawful Seizure of Aircraft, signed at the Hague on 16 December 1970

Article 8
The offence shall be deemed to be included as an extraditable offence in any extradition treaty existing between Contracting States. Contracting States undertake to include the offence as an extraditable offence in every extradition treaty to be concluded between them.

If a Contracting State which makes extradition conditional on the existence of a treaty receives a request for extradition from another Contracting State with which it has no extradition treaty, it may at its option consider this Convention as the legal basis for extradition in respect of the offence. Extradition shall be subject to the other conditions provided by the law of the requested State.

Contracting States which do not make extradition conditional on the existence of a treaty shall recognize the offence as an extraditable offence between themselves subject to the conditions provided by the law of the requested State.

The offence shall be treated, for the purpose of extradition between Contracting States, as if it had been committed not only in the place in which it occurred but also in the territories of the States required to establish their jurisdiction in accordance with Article 4, paragraph 1.

TC2C
Convention for the Suppression of Unlawful Acts against the Safety of Civil Aviation, signed at Montreal on 23 September 1971

Article 8
The offences shall be deemed to be included as extraditable offences in any extradition treaty existing between Contracting States. Contracting States undertake to include the offences as extraditable offences in every etradition treaty to be concluded between them.

If a Contracting State which makes extradition conditional on the existence of a treaty receives a request for extradition from another Contracting State with which it has no extradition treaty, it may at its option consider this Convention as the legal basis for extradition in respect of the offences. Extradition shall be subject to the other conditions provided by the law of the requested State.

Contracting States which do not make extradition conditional on the existence of a treaty shall recognize the offences as extraditable offences between themselves subject to the conditions provided by the law of the requested State.

Each of the offences shall be treated, for the purpose of extradition between Contracting States, as if it had been committed not only in the place in which it occurred but also in the territories of the States required to establish their jurisdiction in accordance with Article 5, paragraph 1 (b), (c) and (d).

TC2D
Convention on the Physical Protection of Nuclear Material, signed at Vienna on 3 March 1980

Article 10
The State Party in whose territory the alleged offender is present shall, if it does not extradite him, submit, without exception whatsoever and without undue delay, the case to its competent authorities for the purpose of prosecution, through proceedings in accordance with the laws of that State.

Article 11
The offences in article 7 shall be deemed to be included as extraditable offences in any extradition treaty existing between States Parties. States Parties undertake to include those offences as extraditable offences in every future extradition treaty to be concluded between them.
If a State Party which makes extradition conditional on the existence of a treaty receives a request for extradition from another State Party with which it has no extradition treaty, it may at its option consider this Convention as the legal basis for extradition in respect of those offences. Extradition shall be subject to the other conditions provided by the law of the requested State.
States Parties which do not make extradition conditional on the existence of a treaty shall recognize those offences as extraditable offences between themselves subject to the conditions provided by the law of the requested State.
Each of the offences shall be treated, for the purpose of extradition between States Parties, as if it had been committed not only in the place in which it occurred but also in the territories of the States Parties required to establish their jurisdiction in accordance with paragraph I of Article 8.

TC2E
Protocol on the Suppression of Unlawful Acts of Violence at Airports Serving International Civil Aviation, supplementary to the Convention for the Suppression of Unlawful Acts against the Safety of Civil Aviation, signed at Montreal on 24 February 1988

No reference to extradition

TC2F
Convention for the Suppression of Unlawful Acts against the Safety of Maritime Navigation, done at Rome on 10 March 1988 (Deposited with the Secretary-General of the International Maritime Organization)

Article 11
The offences set forth in Article 3 shall be deemed to be included as extraditable offences in any extradition treaty existing between any of the States Parties. States Parties undertake to include such offences as extraditable offences in every extradition treaty to be concluded between them.
If a State Party which makes extradition conditional on the existence of a treaty receives a request for extradition from another State Party with which it has no extradition treaty, the requested State Party may, at its option, consider this Convention as a legal basis for extradition in respect of the offences set forth in Article 3. Extradition shall be subject to the other conditions provided by the law of the requested State Party.

States Parties which do not make extradition conditional on the existence of a treaty shall recognize the offences set forth in Article 3 as extraditable offences between themselves, subject to the conditions provided by the law of the requested State.

If necessary, the offences set forth in Article 3 shall be treated, for the purposes of extradition between States Parties, as if they had been committed not only in the place in which they occurred but also in a place within the jurisdiction of the State Party requesting extradition.

A State Party which receives more than one request for extradition from States which have established jurisdiction in accordance with Article 7 and which decides not to prosecute shall, in selecting the State to which the offender or alleged offender is to be extradited, pay due regard to the interests and responsibilities of the State Party whose flag the ship was flying at the time of the commission of the offence.

In considering a request for the extradition of an alleged offender pursuant to this Convention, the requested State shall pay due regard to whether his rights as set forth in Article 7, paragraph 3, can be effected in the requesting State.

With respect to the offences as defined in this Convention, the provisions of all extradition treaties and arrangements applicable between States Parties are modified as between States Parties to the extent that they are incompatible with this Convention.

TC2G
Protocol for the Suppression of Unlawful Acts against the Safety of Fixed Platforms Located on the Continental Shelf, done at Rome on 10 March 1988

No reference to extradition

TC3: REGIONAL INSTRUMENTS

TC3A
Arab Convention on the Suppression of Terrorism, signed at a meeting held at the General Secretariat of the League of Arab States in Cairo on 22 April 1998

CHAPTER II: THE JUDICIAL FIELD
SECTION I: EXTRADITION OF OFFENDERS

Article 5
Contracting States shall undertake to extradite those indicated for or convicted of terrorist offences whose extradition is requested by any of these states in accordance with the rules and conditions stipulated in this convention.

Article 6
Extradition shall not be permissible in any of the following circumstances:
  (a) If the offence for which extradition is requested is regarded under the laws in force in the requested State as an offence of a political nature;
  (b) If the offence for which extradition is requested relates solely to a dereliction of military duties;
  (c) If the offence for which extradition is requested was committed in the territory of the requested contracting State, except where the offence has harmed the interests of the requesting State and its laws provide for the prosecution and punishment for

such offences and where the requested State has not initiated any investigation or prosecution;

(d) If a final judgement having the force of res judicata has been rendered in respect of the offence in the requested Contracting State or in a third Contracting State;

(e) If, on delivery of the request for extradition, proceedings have been terminated or punishment has, under the law of the requesting State, lapsed because of the passage of time;

(f) If the offence was committed outside the territory of the requesting State by a person who is not a national of that State and the law of the requested State does not allow prosecution for the same category of offence when committed outside its territory by such a person;

(g) If the requesting State has granted amnesty to perpetrators of offences that include the offence in question;

(h) If the legal system of the requested State does not allow it to extradite its nationals. In this case, the requested State shall prosecute any such persons who commit in any of the other Contracting States a terrorist offence that is punishable in both States by deprivation of liberty for a period of at least one year or more. The nationality of the person whose extradition is sought shall be determined as at the date on which the offence in question was committed, and use shall be made in this regard of the investigation conducted by the requesting state.

Article 7

Should the person whose extradition is sought be under investigation, on trial or already convicted for another offence in the requested State, his concluded, the trial is completed or the sentence is imposed. The requested State may nevertheless extradite him on an interim basis for questioning or trial provided that he is returned to that State before serving the sentence imposed on him in the requesting State.

Article 8

For purposes of the extradition of offenders under this Convention, no account shall be taken of any difference there may be in the domestic legislation of Contracting States in the legal designation of the offence as a felony or a misdemeanour or in the penalty assigned to it, provided that it is punishable under the laws of both States by deprivation of liberty for a period of at least one year or more.

TC3B
Convention of the Organization of the Islamic Conference on Combating International Terrorism, adopted at Ouagadougou on 1 July 1999

CHAPTER II: IN THE JUDICIAL FIELD
SECTION I: EXTRADITING CRIMINALS

Article 5

Contracting States shall undertake to extradite those indicted or convicted of terrorist crimes, requested for extradition by any of these countries in compliance with the rules and conditions stipulated in this Convention.

Article 6

Extradition shall not be permissible in the following cases:

(a) If the Crime for which extradition is requested is deemed by the laws enforced in the requested Contracting State as one of a political nature and without prejudice to the provisions of Article 2, paragraphs 2 and 3 of this Convention for which extradition is requested;

(b) If the Crime for which extradition is sought relates solely to a dereliction of military obligations;

(c) If the Crime for which extradition is requested, was committed in the territory of the requested Contracting State, unless this crime has undermined the interests of the requesting Contracting State and its laws stipulate that the perpetrators of those crimes shall be prosecuted and punished providing that the requested country has not commenced investigation or trial;

(d) If the Crime has been the subject of a final sentence which has the force of law in the requested Contracting State;

(e) If the action at the time of the extradition request elapsed or the penalty prescribed in accordance with the law in the Contacting State requesting extradition;

(f) Crimes committed outside the territory of the requesting Contracting State by a person who was not its national and the law of the requested Contracting State does not prosecute such a crime if perpetrated outside its territory by such a person;

(g) If pardon was granted and included the perpetrators of these crimes in the requesting Contracting State;

(h) If the legal system of the requested State does not permit extradition of its national, then it shall be obliged to prosecute whosoever commits a terrorist crime if the act is punishable in both States by a freedom restraining sentence for a minimum period of one year or more. The nationality of the person requested for extradition shall be determined according to the date of the crime taking into account the investigation undertaken in this respect by the requesting State.

Article 7
If the person requested for extradition is under investigation or trial for another crime in the requested State, his extradition shall be postponed until the investigation is disposed of or the trial is over and the punishment implemented. In this case, the requested State shall extradite him provisionally for investigation or trial on condition that he shall be returned to it before execution of the sentence issued in the requested State.

Article 8
For the purpose of extraditing crime perpetrators according to this Convention, the domestic legislations of Contracting States shall not have any bearing as to their differences with respect to the crime being classified as a felony or misdemeanor, nor as to the penalty prescribed for it.

TC3C
European Convention on the Suppression of Terrorism, concluded at Strasbourg on 27 January 1977

Article 3
The provisions of all extradition treaties and arrangements applicable between Contracting States, including the European Convention on Extradition, are modified as between Contracting States to the extent that they are incompatible with this Convention.

Article 4
For the purpose of this Convention and to the extent that any offence mentioned in Article 1 or 2 is not listed as an extraditable offence in any extradition convention or treaty existing between Contracting States, it shall be deemed to be included as such therein.

Article 5
Nothing in this Convention shall be interpreted as imposing an obligation to extradite if the requested State has substantial grounds for believing that the request for extradition for an offence mentioned in Article 1 or 2 has been made for the purpose of prosecuting or punishing a person on account of his race, religion, nationality or political opinion, or that that person's position may be prejudiced for any of these reasons.

TC3D
OAS Convention to Prevent and Punish Acts of Terrorism Taking the Form of Crimes against Persons and Related Extortion that are of International Significance, concluded at Washington, D.C. on 2 February 1971

Article 3
Persons who have been charged or convicted for any of the crimes referred to in Article 2 of this convention shall be subject to extradition under the provisions of the extradition treaties in force between the parties or, in the case of states that do not make extradition dependent on the existence of a treaty, in accordance with their own laws.

TC3E
OAU Convention on the Prevention and Combating of Terrorism, adopted at Algiers on 14 July 1999

Article 8
1. Subject to the provisions of paragraphs 2 and 3 of this Article, the States Parties shall undertake to extradite any person charged with or convicted of any terrorist act carried out on the territory of another State Party and whose extradition is requested by one of the States Parties in conformity with the rules and conditions provided for in this Convention or under extradition agreements between the States Parties and within the limits of their national laws.
2. Any State Party may, at the time of the deposit of its instrument of ratification or accession, transmit to the Secretary General of the OAU the grounds on which extradition may not be granted and shall at the same time indicate the legal basis in its national legislation or international conventions to which it is a party which excludes such extradition. The Secretary General shall forward these grounds to the States Parties.
3. Extradition shall not be granted if final judgement has been passed by a competent authority of the requested State upon the person in respect of the terrorist act or acts for which extradition is requested. Extradition may also be refused if the competent authority of the

requested State has decided either not to institute or terminate proceedings in respect of the same act or acts.

4. A State Party in whose territory an alleged offender is present shall be obliged, whether or not the offence was committed in its territory, to submit the case without undue delay to its competent authorities for the purpose of prosecution if it does not extradite that person.

Article 9
Each State Party undertakes to include as an extraditable offence any terrorist act as defined in Article 1, in any extradition treaty existing between any of the States Parties before or after the entry into force of this Convention.

Article 10
Exchange of extradition requests between the States Parties to this Convention shall be effected directly either through diplomatic channels or other appropriate organs in the concerned States.

Article 11
Extradition requests shall be in writing, and shall be accompanied in particular by the following:

    (a) an original or authenticated copy of the sentence, warrant of arrest or any order or other judicial decision made, in accordance with the procedures laid down in the laws of the requesting State;

    (b) a statement describing the offences for which extradition is being requested, indicating the date and place of its commission, the offence committed, any convictions made and a copy of the provisions of the applicable law; and

    (c) as comprehensive a description as possible of the wanted person together with any other information which may assist in establishing the person's identity and nationality.

Article 12
In urgent cases, the competent authority of the State making the extradition may, in writing, request that the State seized of the extradition request arrest the person in question provisionally. Such provisional arrest shall be for a reasonable period in accordance with the national law of the requested State.

Article 13
1. Where a State Party receives several extradition requests from different States Parties in respect of the same suspect and for the same or different terrorist acts, it shall decide on these requests having regard to all the prevailing circumstances, particularly the possibility of subsequent extradition, the respective dates of receipt of the requests, and the degree of seriousness of the crime.

2. Upon agreeing to extradite, States Parties shall seize and transmit all funds and related materials purportedly used in the commission of the terrorist act to the requesting State as well as relevant incriminating evidence.

3. Such funds, incriminating evidence and related materials, upon confirmation of their use in the terrorist act by the requested State, shall be transmitted to the requesting State even if, for reasons of death or escape of the accused, the extradition in question cannot take place.

4. The provisions in paragraphs 1, 2 and 3 of this Article shall not affect the rights of any of the States Parties or bona fide third parties regarding the materials or revenues mentioned above.

TC3F
SAARC Regional Convention on Suppression of Terrorism, signed at Kathmandu on 4 November 1987.

Article 2
For the purpose of extradition between SAARC Member States, any two or more Contracting States may, by agreement, decide to include any other serious offence involving violence, which shall not be regarded as a political offence or an offence connected with a political offence or an offence inspired by political motives.

Article 3
1. The provisions of all extradition treaties and arrangements applicable between Contracting States are hereby amended as between Contracting States to the extent that they are incompatible with the Convention.
2. For the purpose of this Convention and to the extent that any offence referred to in Article I or agreed to in terms of Article II is not listed as an extraditable offence in any extradition treaty existing between Contracting States, it shall be deemed to be included as such therein.
3. Contracting States undertake to include these offences as extraditable offences in any future extradition treaty to be concluded between them.
4. If a Contracting State which makes extradition conditional on the existence of a treaty receives a request for extradition from another Contracting State with which it has no extradition treaty, the requested State may, at its option, consider this Convention as the basis for extradition in respect of the offences set forth in Article I or agreed to in terms of Article II. Extradition shall be subject to the law of the requested State.
5. Contracting States which do not make extradition conditional on the existence of a treaty, shall recognise the offences set forth in Article I or agreed to in terms of Article II as extraditable offences between themselves, subject to the law of the requested State.

Article 6
A Contracting State in whose territory an alleged offender is found, shall upon receiving a request for extradition from another Contracting State, take appropriate measures, subject to its national laws, so as to ensure his presence for purposes of extradition or prosecution. Such measures shall immediately be notified to the requesting State.

Article 7
Contracting States shall not be obliged to extradite, if it appears to the requested State that by reason of the trivial nature of the case or by reason of the request for the surrender or return of a fugitive offender not being made in good faith or in the interests of justice or for any other reason it is unjust or inexpedient to surrender or return the fugitive offender.

TC3G
Treaty on Cooperation among the States Members of the Commonwealth of Independent States in Combating Terrorism, done at Minsk on 4 June 1999

Article 5
2. The procedure for sending and executing requests for extradition, for the provision of legal aid in criminal cases and for the institution of criminal proceedings shall be determined by the international agreements to which the Parties concerned are parties.

3.4 OTHER FORMS OF COOPERATION

3.4.1 Types of Cooperation

Regarding the forms of cooperation between states, such as exchange of information, assistance in investigation, and exchange of statistics, the pertinent international instruments contain interesting provisions. These provisions should be seen in addition to, and not necessarily replacing the other main forms of cooperation and mutual responsibility, namely those in the fields of jurisdiction and extradition.

The relevance of other forms of cooperation is to be found in the very fact that even if jurisdiction has been agreed upon and even if the extradition of the alleged offender has taken place, no guarantee whatsoever can be given as to the success of the trial. The need for additional cooperation is obvious, and this may take various forms: investigation *in situ*, assistance towards investigation, interrogation of persons of relevance to the case, exchange of (classified) information, the sending of witnesses and many other obvious examples.

The need for cooperation has been laid down in SC Res. 1373 (2001), in which the UN Security Council decided in no uncertain terms that all States shall *afford one another the greatest measure of assistance in connection with criminal investigations or criminal proceedings relating to the financing or support of terrorist acts, including assistance in obtaining evidence in their possession necessary for the proceedings.* And similarly, the Security Council in that same resolution called upon all States to *exchange information in accordance with international and domestic law and cooperate on administrative and judicial matters to prevent the commission of terrorist acts [and to] cooperate, particularly through bilateral and multilateral arrangements and agreements, to prevent and suppress terrorist attacks and take action against perpetrators of such acts.*

In the earlier SC Resolution 1269(1999) similar language can be found and it can thus be assumed that various forms of cooperation are a *sine-qua-non* in the context of finding adequate legal responses to terrorism.

On the European level, the Council, in its 27 December 2001 Common Position also refers in clear language to the obligation and use of cooperation. Article 9, for instance, reads:

> Member States shall afford one another, as well as third States, the greatest measure of assistance in connection with criminal investigations or criminal proceedings relating to the financing or support of terrorist acts in accordance with international and domestic

law, including assistance in obtaining evidence in the possession of a Member State or a third State which is necessary for the proceedings.

And Articles 12 and 13 state the following:

> Information shall be exchanged among Member States or between Member States and third States in accordance with international and national law, and cooperation shall be enhanced among Member States or between Member States and third States on administrative and judicial matters to prevent the commission of terrorist acts.
> Cooperation among Member States or between Member States and third States, particularly through bilateral and multilateral arrangements and agreements, to prevent and suppress terrorist attacks and take action against perpetrators of terrorist acts shall be enhanced.

The various international instruments have included the following formulations in this respect. It is assumed, now that the Security Council has made this cooperation imperative, that the Articles below should be read in the spirit and context of the SC resolutions. This means that also if no cooperation has been specifically agreed upon, the SC text shall apply. Similarly, if what has been agreed upon in the specific convention differs from the SC text, the latter shall overrule the former.

3.4.2 References to cooperation in relevant international instruments

TC1: UN CONVENTIONS

TC1A
Convention on the Prevention and Punishment of Crimes against Internationally Protected Persons, including Diplomatic Agents, adopted by the General Assembly of the United Nations on 14 December 1973

Article 4
States Parties shall cooperate in the prevention of the crimes set forth in Article 2, particularly by:
    (a)   taking all practicable measures to prevent preparations in their respective territories for the commission of those crimes within or outside their territories;
    (b)   exchanging information and coordinating the taking of administrative and other measures as appropriate to prevent the commission of those crimes

Article 5
The State Party in which any of the crimes set forth in Article 2 has been committed shall, if it has reason to believe that an alleged offender has fled from its territory, communicate to all other States concerned, directly or through the Secretary-General of the United Nations, all the pertinent facts regarding the crime committed and all available information regarding the identity of the alleged offender.
Whenever any of the crimes set forth in Article 2 has been committed against an internationally protected person, any State Party which has information concerning the victim and the circumstances of the crime shall endeavour to transmit it, under the conditions provided

for in its internal law, fully and promptly to the State Party on whose behalf he was exercising his functions.

Article 7
The State Party in whose territory the alleged offender is present shall, if it does not extradite him, submit, without exception whatsoever and without undue delay, the case to its competent authorities for the purpose of prosecution, through proceedings in accordance with the laws of that State.

TC1B
International Convention against the Taking of Hostages, adopted by the General Assembly of the United Nations on 17 December 1979

Article 4
States Parties shall cooperate in the prevention of the offences set forth in Article 1, particularly by:
  (a) taking all practicable measures to prevent preparations in their respective territories for the commission of those offences within or outside their territories, including measures to prohibit in their territories illegal activities of persons, groups and organizations that encourage, instigate, organize or engage in the perpetration of acts of taking of hostages;
  (b) exchange information and coordination the taking of administrative and other measures as appropriate to prevent the commission of those offences

Article 11
States Parties shall afford one another the greatest measure of assistance in connexion with criminal proceedings brought in respect of the offences set forth in Article 1, including the supply of all evidence at their disposal necessary for the proceedings.
The provisions of paragraph 1 of this Article shall not affect obligations concerning mutual judicial assistance embodied in any other treaty.

TC1C
International Convention for the Suppression of Terrorist Bombings, adopted by the General Assembly of the United Nations on 15 December 1997

Article 10
States Parties shall afford one another the greatest measure of assistance in connection with investigations or criminal or extradition proceedings brought in respect of the offences set forth in Article 2, including assistance in obtaining evidence at their disposal necessary for the proceedings.
States Parties shall carry out their obligations under paragraph 1 of the present Article in conformity with any treaties or other arrangements on mutual legal assistance that may exist between them. In the absence of such treaties or arrangements, States Parties shall afford one another assistance in accordance with their domestic law.

TC1D
Draft International Convention for the Suppression of Acts of Nuclear Terrorism, 22 October 1998

Article 7
1. States Parties shall cooperate by:
    (a)   Taking all practicable measures, including, if necessary, adapting their national law, to prevent and counter preparations in their respective territories for the commission within or outside their territories of the offences set forth in Article 2, including measures to prohibit in their territories illegal activities of persons, groups and organizations that encourage, instigate, organize, knowingly finance or knowingly provide technical assistance or information or engage in the perpetration of those offences;
    (b)   Exchanging accurate and verified information in accordance with their national law and in the manner of and subject to the conditions specified herein, and coordinating administrative and other measures taken as appropriate to detect, prevent, suppress and investigate the offences set forth in Article 2 and also in order to institute criminal proceedings against persons alleged to have committed those crimes. In particular, a State Party shall take appropriate measures in order to inform without delay the other States referred to in Article 9 in respect of the commission of the offences set forth in Article 2 as well as preparations to commit such offences about which it has learned, and also to inform, where appropriate, international organizations.

2. States Parties shall take appropriate measures consistent with their national law to protect the confidentiality of any information which they receive in confidence by virtue of the provisions of this Convention from another State Party or through participation in an activity carried out for the implementation of this Convention. If States Parties provide information to international organizations in confidence, steps shall be taken to ensure that the confidentiality of such information is protected.

3. States Parties shall not be required by this Convention to provide any information which they are not permitted to communicate pursuant to national law or which would jeopardize the security of the State concerned or the physical protection of nuclear material.

4. States Parties shall inform the Secretary-General of the United Nations of their competent authorities and liaison points responsible for sending and receiving the information referred to in the present Article. The Secretary-General of the United Nations shall communicate such information regarding competent authorities and liaison points to all States Parties and the International Atomic Energy Agency. Such authorities and liaison points must be accessible on a continuous basis.

Article 14
1. States Parties shall afford one another the greatest measure of assistance in connection with investigations or criminal or extradition proceedings brought in respect of the offences set forth in Article 2, including assistance in obtaining evidence at their disposal necessary for the proceedings.

2. States Parties shall carry out their obligations under paragraph 1 of the present Article in conformity with any treaties or other arrangements on mutual legal assistance that may exist between them. In the absence of such treaties or arrangements, States Parties shall afford one another assistance in accordance with their national law.

TC1E
International Convention for the Suppression of the Financing of Terrorism, adopted by the General Assembly of the United Nations on 9 December 1999

Article 12
1. States Parties shall afford one another the greatest measure of assistance in connection with criminal investigations or criminal or extradition proceedings in respect of the offences set forth in Article 2, including assistance in obtaining evidence in their possession necessary for the proceedings.
2. States Parties may not refuse a request for mutual legal assistance on the ground of bank secrecy.
3. The requesting Party shall not transmit or use information or evidence furnished by the requested Party for investigations, prosecutions or proceedings other than those stated in the request without the prior consent of the requested Party.
4. Each State Party may give consideration to establishing mechanisms to share with other States Parties information or evidence needed to establish criminal, civil or administrative liability pursuant to Article 5.
5. States Parties shall carry out their obligations under paragraphs 1 and 2 in conformity with any treaties or other arrangements on mutual legal assistance or information exchange that may exist between them. In the absence of such treaties or arrangements, States Parties shall afford one another assistance in accordance with their domestic law.

TC1F
Draft Comprehensive Convention (Report of the Ad-Hoc Committee established by the General Assembly Resolution 51/210 of 17 December 1996), 11 February 2002

Article 8
1. States Parties shall cooperate in the prevention of the offences set forth in Article 2 by taking all practicable measures, including, if necessary and where appropriate, adapting their domestic legislation, to prevent and counter preparations in their respective territories for the commission, within or outside their territories, of those offences, including:
   (a) Measures to prohibit the illegal activities of persons, groups and organizations that encourage, instigate, organize, knowingly finance or engage in the commission of offences set forth in Article 2;
   (b) In particular, measures to prohibit the establishment and operation of installations and training camps for the commission of offences set forth in Article 2.
2. States Parties shall further cooperate in the prevention of the offences set forth in Article 2, in accordance with their national law, by exchanging accurate and verified information and coordinating administrative and other measures taken as appropriate to prevent the commission of offences set forth in Article 2, in particular by:
   (a) Establishing and maintaining channels of communication between their competent agencies and services to facilitate the secure and rapid exchange of information concerning all aspects of offences set forth in Article 2;
   (b) Cooperating with one another in conducting inquiries, with respect to the offences set forth in Article 2, concerning:
      (i) The identity, whereabouts and activities of persons in respect of whom reasonable suspicion exists that they are involved in such offences;
      (ii) The movement of funds, property, equipment or other instrumentalities relating to the commission of such offences.

3. States Parties may exchange information through the International Criminal Police Organization (Interpol) or other international and regional organizations.

Article 13

1. States Parties shall afford one another the greatest measure of assistance in connection with investigations or criminal or extradition proceedings brought in respect of the offences set forth in Article 2, including assistance in obtaining evidence at their disposal necessary for the proceedings.

2. States Parties shall carry out their obligations under paragraph 1 in conformity with any treaties or other arrangements on mutual legal assistance that may exist between them. In the absence of such treaties or arrangements, States Parties shall afford one another assistance in accordance with their domestic law.

3. Each State Party may give consideration to establishing mechanisms to share with other States Parties information or evidence needed to establish criminal, civil or administrative liability pursuant to Article 9.

TC2: NON-UN CONVENTIONS

TC2A
Convention on Offences and Certain Other Acts Committed on Board Aircraft, signed at Tokyo on 14 September 1963

Other forms of Cooperation

CHAPTER V
POWERS AND DUTIES OF STATES

Article 12
Any Contracting State shall allow the commander of an aircraft registered in another Contracting State to disembark any person pursuant to Article 8, paragraph 1.

Article 13
Any Contracting State shall take delivery of any person whom the aircraft commander delivers pursuant to Article 9, paragraph 1.

Upon being satisfied that the circumstances so warrant, any Contracting State shall take custody or other measures to ensure the presence of any person suspected of an act contemplated in Article 11, paragraph 1 and of any person of whom it has taken delivery. The custody and other measures shall be as provided in the law of that State but may only be continued for such time as is reasonably necessary to enable any criminal or extradition proceedings to be instituted.

Any person in custody pursuant to the previous paragraph shall be assisted in communicating immediately with the nearest appropriate representative of the State of which he is a national.

Any Contracting State, to which a person is delivered pursuant to Article 9, paragraph 1, or in whose territory an aircraft lands following the commission of an act contemplated in Article 11, paragraph 1, shall immediately make a preliminary enquiry into the facts.

When a State, pursuant to this Article, has taken a person into custody, it shall immediately notify the State of registration of the aircraft and the State of nationality of the detained person and, if it considers it advisable, any other interested State of the fact that such person is in custody and of the circumstances which warrant his detention. The State which makes the preliminary enquiry contemplated in paragraph 4 of this Article shall promptly report its findings to the said States and shall indicate whether it intends to exercise jurisdiction.

Article 14

When any person has been disembarked in accordance with Article 8, paragraph 1, or delivered in accordance with Article 9, paragraph 1, or has disembarked after committing an act contemplated in Article 11, paragraph 1, and when such person cannot or does not desire to continue his journey and the State of landing refuses to admit him, that State may, if the person in question is not a national or permanent resident of that State, return him to the territory of the State of which he is a national or permanent resident or to the territory of the State in which he began his journey by air.

Neither disembarkation, nor delivery, not the taking of custody or other measures contemplated in Article 13, paragraph 2, nor return of the person concerned, shall be considered as admission to the territory of the Contracting State concerned for the purpose of its law relating to entry or admission of persons and nothing in this Convention shall affect the law of a Contracting State relating to the expulsion of persons from its territory.

TC2B
Convention for the Suppression of Unlawful Seizure of Aircraft, signed at the Hague on 16 December 1970

Article 5

The Contracting States which establish joint air transport operating organizations or international operating agencies, which operate aircraft which are subject to joint or international registration shall, by appropriate means, designate for each aircraft the State among them which shall exercise the jurisdiction and have the attributes of the State of registration for the purpose of this Convention and shall give notice thereof to the International Civil Aviation Organization which shall communicate the notice to all States Parties to this Convention.

Article 10

Contracting States shall afford one another the greatest measure of assistance in connection with criminal proceedings brought in respect of the offence and other acts mentioned in Article 4. The law of the State requested shall apply in all cases.

The provisions of paragraph 1 of this Article shall not affect obligations under any other treaty, bilateral or multilateral, which governs or will govern, in whole or in part, mutual assistance in criminal matters.

TC2C
Convention for the Suppression of Unlawful Acts against the Safety of Civil Aviation, signed at Montreal on 23 September 1971

Article 11

Contracting States shall afford one another the greatest measure of assistance in connection with criminal proceedings brought in respect of the offences. The law of the State requested shall apply in all cases.

The provisions of paragraph 1 of this Article shall not affect obligations under any other treaty, bilateral or multilateral, which governs or will govern, in whole or in part, mutual assistance in criminal matters.

Article 12

Any Contracting State having reason to believe that one of the offences mentioned in Article 1 will be committed shall, in accordance with its national law, furnish any relevant information in its possession to those States which it believes would be the States mentioned in Article 5, paragraph 1.

TC2D
Convention on the Physical Protection of Nuclear Material, signed at Vienna on 3 March 1980

Article 5

States Parties shall identify and make known to each other directly or through the International Atomic Energy Agency their central authority and point of contact having responsibility for physical protection of nuclear material and for coordinating recovery and response operations in the event of any unauthorized removal, use or alteration of nuclear material or in the event of credible threat thereof.

In the case of theft, robbery or any other unlawful taking of nuclear material or of credible threat thereof, States Parties shall, in accordance with their national law, provide cooperation and assistance to the maximum feasible extent in the recovery and protection of such material to any State that so requests. In particular:

each State Party shall take appropriate steps to inform as soon as possible other States, which appear to it to be concerned, of any theft, robbery or other unlawful taking of nuclear material or credible threat thereof and to inform, where appropriate, international organizations:

as appropriate, the States Parties concerned shall exchange information with each other or international organizations with a view to protecting threatened nuclear material, verifying the integrity of the shipping container, or recovering unlawfully taken nuclear material and shall:

    (a)   coordinate their efforts through diplomatic and other agreed channels;

    (b)   render assistance, if requested;

    (c)   ensure the return of nuclear material stolen or missing as a consequence of the above-mentioned events.

The means of implementation of this cooperation shall be determined by the States Parties concerned.

States Parties shall cooperate and consult as appropriate, with each other directly or through international organizations, with a view to obtaining guidance on the design, maintenance and improvement of systems of physical protection of nuclear material in international transport.

Article 13

States Parties shall afford one another the greatest measure of assistance in connection with criminal proceedings brought in respect of the offences set forth in Article 7, including the supply of evidence at their disposal necessary for the proceedings. The law of the State requested shall apply in all cases.

The provisions of paragraph I shall not affect obligations under any other treaty, bilateral or multilateral, which governs or will govern, in whole or in part, mutual assistance in criminal matters.

TC2E
Protocol on the Suppression of Unlawful Acts of Violence at Airports Serving International Civil Aviation, supplementary to the Convention for the Suppression of Unlawful Acts against the Safety of Civil Aviation, signed at Montreal on 24 February 1988

No references to cooperation included

TC2F
Convention for the Suppression of Unlawful Acts against the Safety of Maritime Navigation, done at Rome on 10 March 1988 (Deposited with the Secretary-General of the International Maritime Organization)

Article 12
State Parties shall afford one another the greatest measure of assistance in connection with criminal proceedings brought in respect of the offences set forth in Article 3, including assistance in obtaining evidence at their disposal necessary for the proceedings.
States Parties shall carry out their obligations under paragraph 1 in conformity with any treaties on mutual assistance that may exist between them. In the absence of such treaties, States Parties shall afford each other assistance in accordance with their national law.

Article 13
States Parties shall cooperate in the prevention of the offences set forth in Article 3, particularly by:
taking all practicable measures to prevent preparations in their respective territories for the commission of those offences within or outside their territories;
exchanging information in accordance with their national law, and coordinating administrative and other measures taken as appropriate to prevent the commission of offences set forth in Article 3.
When, due to the commission of an offence set forth in Article 3, the passage of a ship has been delayed or interrupted, any State Party in whose territory the ship or passengers or crew are present shall be bound to exercise all possible efforts to avoid a ship, its passengers, crew or cargo being unduly detained or delayed.

Article 14
Any State Party having reason to believe that an offence set forth in Article 3 will be committed shall, in accordance with its national law, furnish as promptly as possible any relevant information in its possession to those States which it believes would be the States having established jurisdiction in accordance with Article 6.

Article 15
Each State Party shall, in accordance with its national law) provide to the Secretary-General, as promptly as possible, any relevant information in its possession concerning:
the circumstances of the offence;
the action taken pursuant to Article 13, paragraph 2;
the measures taken in relation to the offender or the alleged offender and, in particular, the results of any extradition proceedings or other legal proceedings.
The State Party where the alleged offender is prosecuted shall, in accordance with its national law, communicate the final outcome of the proceedings to the Secretary-General.
The information transmitted in accordance with paragraphs 1 and 2 shall be communicated by the Secretary-General to all States Parties, to Members of the International Maritime Or-

ganization (hereinafter referred to as 'the Organization'), to the other States concerned, and to the appropriate international intergovernmental organizations.

TC2G
Protocol for the Suppression of Unlawful Acts against the Safety of Fixed Platforms Located on the Continental Shelf, done at Rome on 10 March 1988

No reference to cooperation included.

TC2H
Convention on the Marking of Plastic Explosives for the Purpose of Detection, signed at Montreal on 1 March 1991

Article 8
States Parties shall, if possible, transmit to the Council information that would assist the Commission in the discharge of its functions under paragraph 1 of Article VI.
States Parties shall keep the Council informed of measures they have taken to implement the provisions of this Convention. The Council shall communicate such information to all States Parties and international organizations concerned.

TC3: REGIONAL INSTRUMENTS

TC3A
Arab Convention on the Suppression of Terrorism, signed at a meeting held at the General Secretariat of the League of Arab States in Cairo on 22 April 1998

Article 4
Contracting States shall cooperate for the prevention and suppression of terrorist offences, in accordance with the domestic laws and regulations of each State, as set forth hereunder:
Exchanging of information
Contracting States shall undertake to promote the exchange of information between and among them concerning:
The activities and crimes of terrorist groups and of their leaders and members; their headquarters and training; the means and sources by which they are funded and armed; the types of weapons, munitions and explosives used by them; and other means of aggression, murder and destruction;
The means of communication and propaganda used by terrorist groups, their modus operandi; the movements of their leaders and members; and the travel documents that they use.
Each contracting State shall undertake to notify any other Contracting State in an expeditious manner of the information it has concerning any terrorist offence that takes place in its territory and is intended to harm the interests of that State or of its nationals and to include in such notification statements concerning the circumstances surrounding the offence, those who committed it, its victims, the losses occasioned by it and the devices and methods used in its perpetration, to the extent compatible with the requirements of the investigation and inquiry.
Contracting States shall undertake to cooperate with each other in the exchange of information for the suppression of terrorist offences and promptly to notify other Contracting States of all the information or data in their possession that may prevent the occurrence of terrorist offences in their territory, against their nationals or residents or against their interests.

Each Contracting State shall undertake to furnish any other Contracting State with any information or data in its possession that may:

Assist in the arrest of a person or persons accused of committing a terrorist offence against the interests of that State or of being implicated in such an offence whether by aiding and abetting, collusion or incitement;

Lead to the seizure of any weapons, munitions or explosives or any devices or funds used or intended for use to commit a terrorist offence.

Contracting States shall undertake to maintain the confidentiality of the information that they exchange among themselves and not to furnish it to any State that is not a Contracting State or any other party without the prior consent of the State that was the source of the information.

Investigations:

Contracting States shall undertake to promote cooperation among themselves and to provide assistance with respect to measures for the investigation and arrest of fugitives suspected or convicted of terrorist offences in accordance with the laws and regulations of each state.

Exchange of expertise:

Contracting States shall cooperate in the conduct and exchange of research studies for the suppression of terrorist offences and shall exchange expertise in the counter-terrorism field.

Contracting States shall cooperate, within the limits of their resources, in providing all possible technical assistance for the formulation of programmes or the holding of joint training courses or training courses intended for one state or for a group of Contracting Sttes, as required for the benefit of those working in counter-terrorism with the aim of developing their scientific and practical abilities and enhancing their performance.

Judicial Delegation

Article 9

Each Contracting State may request any other Contracting State to undertake in its territory and on its behalf any judicial procedure relating to an action arising out of a terrorist offence and, in particular:

 (a)   To hear the testimony of witnesses and take depositions as evidence;
 (b)   To effect service of judicial documents;
 (c)   To execute searches and seizures;
 (d)   To examine and inspect evidence;
 (e)   To obtain relevant documents and records or certified copies thereof.

Article 10

Each of the Contracting States shall undertake to implement judicial delegations relating to terrorist offences, but such assistance may be refused in either of the two following cases:

Where the request relates to an offence that is subject to investigation or prosecution in the requested State;

Where granting the request might be prejudicial to the sovereignty, security or public order of the requested State.

Article 11

The request for judicial delegation shall be granted promptly in accordance with the provisions of the domestic law of the requested State. The latter may postpone the execution of the request until such time as any ongoing investigation or prosecution involving the same matter are completed or any compelling reasons for postponement cease to exist, provided that the requesting State is notified of such postponement.

Article 12

A measure that is undertaken by means of a judicial delegation, in accordance with the provisions of this Conventions, shall have the same legal effect as if it had been taken by the competent authority of the requesting State

The result of implementing the judicial delegation may be used only for the purpose for which the delegation is issued.

Judicial cooperation

Article 13

Each Contracting State shall provide the other States with all possible and necessary assistance for investigations or prosecutions relating to terrorist offences.

Article 14

Where one of the Contracting States has jurisdiction to prosecute a person suspected of a terrorist offence, it may request the State in which the suspect is present to take proceedings against him for that offence, subject to the agreement of that State and provided that the offence is punishable in the prosecuting State by deprivation of liberty for a period of at least one your or more. The requesting state shall, in this event, provide the requested state with all the investigation documents and evidence relating to the offence.

The investigation or prosecution shall be conducted on the basis of the charge or charges made by the requesting state against the suspect, in accordance with the provisions and procedures of the law of the prosecuting state.

Article 15

The submission by the requesting state of a request for prosecution in accordance with paragraph (a) of the preceding Article shall entail the suspension of the measures taken by it to pursue, investigate and prosecute the suspect whose prosecution is being requested, with the exception of those required for the purposes of the judicial cooperation and assistance, or the judicial delegation, sought by the State requested to conduct the prosecution.

Article 16

The measures taken in either the requesting State or that in which the prosecution takes place shall be subject to the law of the State in which they are taken and they shall have the force accorded to them by that law.

The requesting State may try or retry a person whose prosecution it has requested only if the requested State declines to prosecute him.

The State requested to take proceedings shall in all cases undertake to notify the requesting State of what action it has taken with regard to the request and of the outcome of the investigation or prosecution.

Article 17

The State requested to take proceedings may take all the measures and steps established by its law with respect to the accused both before the request to take proceedings reaches it and subsequently.

Article 18

The transfer of competence for prosecution shall not prejudice the rights of the victim of the offence, who reserves the right to approach the courts of the requesting State or the prosecuting State with a view to claiming his civil-law rights as a result of the offence.

Exchange of evidence

Article 21

Contracting States shall undertake to have the evidence of any terrorist offence committed in their territory against another Contracting State examined by their competent agencies, and they may seek the assistance of any other Contracting State in doing so. They shall take the necessary measures to preserve such evidence and ensure its legal validity. They alone shall examination to the State against whose interests the offence was committed, and the Contracting State or States whose assistance is sought shall not pass this information to any third party.

TC3B
Convention of the Organization of the Islamic Conference on Combating International Terrorism, adopted at Ouagadougou on 1 July 1999

Areas of Islamic cooperation for preventing and combating terrorist crimes.

Article 4
Contracting States shall cooperate among themselves to prevent and combat terrorist crimes in accordance with the respective laws and regulations of each State in the following areas:
First: Exchange of Information
Contracting States shall undertake to promote exchange of information among them as such regarding:
Activities and crimes committed by terrorist groups, their leaders, their elements, their headquarters, training, means and sources that provide finance and weapons, types of arms, ammunition and explosives utilized as well as other ways and means to attack, kill and destroy.
Means of communications and propaganda utilized by terrorist groups, how they act, movement of their leaders, their elements and their travel documents.
Contracting States shall expeditiously inform any other Contracting State regarding available information about any terrorist crime perpetrated in its territory aimed at undermining the interests of that State or its nationals and to state the facts surrounding the crime in terms of its circumstances, criminals involved, victims, losses, devices and methods utilized to carry out the crime, without prejudicing investigation and inquiry requisites.
Contracting States shall exchange information with the other Parties to combat terrorist crimes and to inform the Contracting State or other States of all available information or data that could prevent terrorist crimes within its territory or against its nationals or residents or interests.
The Contracting States shall provide any other Contracting State with available information or data that will
Assist in arresting those accused of committing a terrorist crime against the interests of that country or being implicated in such acts either by assistance, collusion, instigation, or financing.
Contribute to confiscating any arms, weapons, explosives, devices or funds spent or meant to be spent to commit a terrorist crime.
The Contracting States undertake to respect the confidentiality of information exchanged between them and shall refrain from passing it to any non-Contracting States or other parties without prior consent of the source country.
Second: Investigation
Each Contracting State pledges to promote cooperation with other contracting states and to extend assistance in the field of investigation procedures in terms of arresting escaped sus-

pects or those convicted for terrorist crimes in accordance with the laws and regulations of each country.

Third: Exchange of Expertise

Contracting States shall cooperate with each other to undertake and exchange studies and researches on combating terrorist crimes as well as exchange of expertise in this field.

Contracting States shall cooperate within the scope of their capabilities to provide available technical assistance for preparing programmes or holding joint training sessions with one or more Contracting State if the need arises for personnel required in the field of combating terrorism in order to improve their scientific and practical potential and upgrade their performance standards.

Fourth: Education and Information Field

The Contracting States shall cooperate in:

Promoting information activities and supporting the mass media in order to confront the vicious campaign against Islam, by projecting the true image of tolerance of Islam, and exposing the designs and danger of terrorist groups against the stability and security of Islamic States.

Including the noble human values, which proscribe the practice of terrorism in the educational curricula of Contracting States.

Supporting efforts aimed at keeping abreast of the age by introducing an advanced Islamic thought based on ijtihad by which Islam is distinguished.

TC3C
European Convention on the Suppression of Terrorism, concluded at Strasbourg on 27 January 1977

Article 8

Contracting States shall afford one another the widest measure of mutual assistance in criminal matters in connection with proceedings brought in respect of the offences mentioned in Article 1 or 2. The law of the requested State concerning mutual assistance in criminal matters shall apply in all cases. Nevertheless this assistance may not be refused on the sole ground that it concerns a political offence or an offence connected with a political offence or an offence inspired by political motives.

Nothing in this Convention shall be interpreted as imposing an obligation to afford mutual assistance if the requested State has substantial grounds for believing that the request for mutual assistance in respect of an offence mentioned in Article 1 or 2 has been made for the purpose of prosecuting or punishing a person on account of his race, religion, nationality or political opinion or that person's position may be prejudiced for any of these reasons.

The provisions of all treaties and arrangements concerning mutual assistance in criminal matters applicable between Contracting States, including the European Convention on Mutual Assistance in Criminal Matters, are modified as between Contracting States to the extent that they are incompatible with this Convention.

TC3D
OAS Convention to Prevent and Punish Acts of Terrorism Taking the Form of Crimes against Persons and Related Extortion that are of International Significance, concluded at Washington, D.C. on 2 February 1971

Article 1

The Contracting States undertake to cooperate among themselves by taking all the measures that they may consider effective, under their own laws, and especially those established in this convention, to prevent and punish acts of terrorism, especially kidnapping, murder, and other assaults against the life or physical integrity of those persons to whom the state has the duty according to international law to give special protection, as well as extortion in connection with those crimes.

Article 8

To cooperate in preventing and punishing the crimes contemplated in Article 2 of this convention, the contracting states accept the following obligations:

(a)   To take all measures within their power, and in conformity with their own laws, to prevent and impede the preparation in their respective territories of the crimes mentioned in Article 2 that are to be carried out in the territory of another contracting state;

(b)   To exchange information and consider effective administrative measures for the purpose of protecting the persons to whom Article 2 of this convention refers;

(c)   To guarantee to every person deprived of his freedom through the application of this convention every right to defend himself;

(d)   To endeavour to have the criminal acts contemplated in this convention included in their penal laws, if not already so included;

(e)   To comply most expeditiously with the requests for extradition concerning the criminal acts contemplated in this convention.

TC3E
OAU Convention on the Prevention and Combating of Terrorism, adopted at Algiers on 14 July 1999

Article 5

States Parties shall cooperate among themselves in preventing and combating terrorist acts in conformity with national legislation and procedures of each State in the following areas:

1. States Parties undertake to strengthen the exchange of information among them regarding:

(a)   acts and crimes committed by terrorist groups, their leaders and elements, their headquarters and training camps, their means and sources of funding and acquisition of arms, the types of arms, ammunition and explosives used, and other means in their possession;

(b)   the communication and propaganda methods and techniques used by the terrorists groups, the behaviour of these groups, the movement of their leaders and elements, as well as their travel documents.

2. States Parties undertake to exchange any information that leads to:

(a)   the arrest of any person charged with a terrorist act against the interests of a State Party or against its nationals, or attempted to commit such an act or participated in it as an accomplice or an instigator;

(b)   the seizure and confiscation of any type of arms, ammunition, explosives, devices or funds or other instrumentalities of crime used to commit a terrorist act or intended for that purpose.

3. States Parties undertake to respect the confidentiality of the information exchanged among them and not to provide such information to another State that is not party to this Convention, or to a third State Party, without the prior consent of the State from where such information originated.

4. States Parties undertake to promote cooperation among themselves and to help each other with regard to procedures relating to the investigation and arrest of persons suspected of, charged with or convicted of terrorist acts, in conformity with the national law of each State.

5. States Parties shall cooperate among themselves in conducting and exchanging studies and researches on how to combat terrorist acts and to exchange expertise relating to control of terrorist acts.

6. States Parties shall cooperate among themselves, where possible, in providing any available technical assistance in drawing up programmes or organizing, where necessary and for the benefit of their personnel, joint training courses involving one or several States Parties in the area of control of terrorist acts, in order to improve their scientific, technical and operational capacities to prevent and combat such acts.

TC3F
SAARC Regional Convention on Suppression of Terrorism, signed at Kathmandu on 4 November 1987

Article 8
1. Contracting States shall, subject to their national laws, afford one another the greatest measure of mutual assistance in connection with proceedings brought in respect of the offences referred to in Article I or agreed to in terms of Article II, including the supply of all evidence at their disposal necessary for the proceedings.

2. Contracting States shall cooperate among themselves, to the extent permitted by their national laws, through consultations between appropriate agencies, exchange of information, intelligence and expertise and such other cooperative measures as may be appropriate, with a view to preventing terrorist activities through precautionary measures.

TC3G
Treaty on Cooperation among the States Members of the Commonwealth of Independent States in Combating Terrorism, done at Minsk on 4 June 1999

Article 5
1. The competent authorities of the Party shall, in accordance with this Treaty, other international agreements and national legislation, cooperate and assist one another by:

(a)   Exchanging information;

(b)   Responding to enquiries regarding the conduct of investigations;

(c)   Developing and adopting agreed measures for preventing, uncovering, halting or investigating acts of terrorism, and informing one another about such measures;

(d)   Adopting measures to prevent and halt preparations in their territory for the commission of acts of terrorism in the territory of another Party;

(e)   Assisting in assessing the condition of the system for physical protection of facilities posing an increased technological and environmental danger, and developing and implementing measures to improve that system;

(f)   Exchanging legislative texts and materials on the practice with respect to their application;

(g)   Sending, by agreement between interested Parties, special anti-terrorist units to render practical assistance in halting acts of terrorism and combating their consequences;

(h)   Exchanging experience on the prevention and combating of terrorist acts, including the holding of training courses, seminars, consultations and workshops;

(i)   Training and further specialized training of personnel;

(j)   Joint financing, by agreement between Parties, and conduct of research and development work on systems for and means of physically protecting facilities posing an increased technological and environmental danger;

    (k)   Implementation on a contractual basis of deliveries of special items, technology and equipment for anti-terrorist activity.

2. The procedure for sending and executing requests for extradition, for the provision of legal aid in criminal cases and for the institution of criminal proceedings shall be determined by the international agreements to which the Parties concerned are parties.

Article 6

The Parties shall, through consultations, jointly draw up recommendations for achieving concerted approaches to the legal regulation of issues relating to the prevention and combating of terrorist acts.

Article 9

1. The rendering of assistance under this Treaty shall be denied in whole part or in part if the requested Party believes that fulfillment of the request may impair its sovereignty, security, social order or other vital interests or it is in contravention of its legislation or international obligations.

2. The rendering of assistance may be defined if the act in relation to which the request was made is not a crime under the legislation of the requested Party.

3. The requesting Party shall be notified in writing of a refusal to fulfil a request in whole or in part, with an indication of the reasons for refusal listed in paragraph 1 of this Article.

Article 11

The competent authorities of the Parties shall exchange information on issues of mutual interest, including:

    (a)   Materials distributed in the territory of their States containing information on terrorist threats, terrorist acts in the course of preparation or committed and the identified intentions of given persons, groups of persons or organizations to commit acts of terrorism;

    (b)   Acts of terrorism in the course of preparation that are directed against the heads of State, internationally protected persons, staff of diplomatic missions, consular institutions and international organizations of the Parties and participants in State visits and international and national political, sporting and other activities;

    (c)   Instances of illegal circulation of nuclear materials, chemical, bacteriological (biological) weapons or their components, highly toxic chemicals and pathogenic micro-organisms;

    (d)   Terrorist organizations, groups and individuals that present a threat to the State security of the Parties and the establishment of contacts between terrorist organizations, groups or individuals;

    (e)   Illegal armed formations employing methods of terrorist activity, their structure, members, aims and objectives;

    (f)   Ways, means and methods of terrorist action they have identified;

    (g)   Supplies and equipment that may be provided by the Parties to one another to the extent of their ability;

    (h)   Practice with respect to the legal and other regulatory settlement of issues related to the extent of their ability;

    (i)   Identified and presumed channels for the financing and illegal delivery to the territory of their States of weapons and other means of committing terrorist acts;

    (j)   Terrorist encroachments aimed at violating the sovereignty and territorial integrity of Parties;

3.5   IMMUNITY

3.5.1   **Introduction**

International law is a complex system of rules and regulations, some of which diverge. This is also true for the subject of jurisdiction. Above an effort has been made to indicate in which circumstances a state may or shall exercise its jurisdiction in criminal matters. Yet, reference should also be made to cases in which broad jurisdiction would be counterproductive. This notion is normally referred to as immunity but can also be seen as part of the domestic jurisdiction concept, meaning that 'the actions of the organs of government and administration are supreme, free from international legal principles and interference'.[1]

At the same time, however, it should be acknowledged that one of the main developments over the last fifty years or so, has been exactly a reappraisal of the domestic jurisdiction concept (Charter, Art. 2.7). Not only has this concept become obsolete in the case of a threat to the peace (Chapter VII of the Charter), but in many more cases, through acceding to international instruments with specific provisions on supervision, monitoring and/or reporting on the implementation of that instrument (e.g. the human rights treaties and their treaty-based bodies) level of sovereignty has de-facto been handed over. This is in particular the case in the field of human rights and humanitarian law (including weaponry and nuclear devices), but increasingly so in e.g. environmental law and trade law.

Traditionally, immunity was an issue for the sovereigns, the government and the envoys. It also covered the property of any state which is designated for public use. Over the years, shifts can be noticed from an absolute immunity approach, through a restrictive approach to today's efforts to limit immunity to an absolute minimum. Reflective of this development are the efforts to codify state responsibility.[2] In Europe, the European Convention on State Immunity dates from 1972 and it already prohibited sovereign immunity in certain specific cases mainly to ensure trade and other forms of economic interaction.

---

[1] Shaw, *International Law* (4th, CUP 1997) p.491.

[2] See Kamminga's *Inter-State Accountability for Violations of Human Rights*, Philadelphia 1992, as well as ILA and ILC proceedings and proposals on this subject: the fifty-third session of the International Law Commission (2001) resulted in the adoption of the draft Articles on the responsibility of states for internationally wrongful acts. In 2001 the GA adopted a resolution on this subject (56/83): *Responsibility of States for internationally wrongful acts.*

Of relevance to the subject of this volume, the treatment of persons who might have been involved in terrorist acts or other serious crimes, is the apparent 'clash' between human rights law and international criminal law on the one hand, and other aspects of international law on the other, namely the need to ensure that the basic function of international law, the prevention or solution of conflict, will not be hampered.

This issue came to the fore in an interesting way: in April 2000, a Belgian investigating judge issued and internationally circulated an arrest warrant against the then Minister for Foreign Affairs of the Democratic Republic of the Congo. This, obviously, hindered this Minister in carrying out his tasks and it was submitted that the warrant of arrest should be regarded as a violation of the rule of customary international law concerning the absolute inviolability and immunity from criminal process of incumbent foreign ministers.

Early in 2002, the ICJ ruled accordingly and found that Belgium must cancel the arrest warrant and in this respect inform the authorities to whom that warrant had been circulated (see 3.5.2). This, indeed, is an important indication of the limits to 'universal' jurisdiction, and should be seen in the context of international law as a whole, of which human rights and international criminal law are mere parts, and which should not be viewed as *primus inter pares*.

It is thus noted that even in the case of 'terrorism' a balance needs to be found as to when and where appropriate action can be taken.

3.5.2   The ICJ and Immunity

On 14 February 2002 the ICJ issued a press release on the case concerned (Arrest Warrant of 11 April 2000 – *Democratic Republic of the Congo* v. *Belgium*) on which the following is based (emphasis added).

In its Application, the Congo contended that in respect of a dispute concerning an international arrest warrant issued on 11 April 2000 by a Belgian investigating judge against the Minister for Foreign Affairs in office of the Democratic Republic of the Congo, Mr. Abdulaye Yerodia Ndombasi, Belgium had violated the principle that a State may not exercise its authority on the territory of another State, the principle of sovereign equality among all Members of the United Nations, as laid down in Article 2, paragraph 1, of the Charter of the United Nations, as well as the diplomatic immunity of the Minister for Foreign Affairs of a sovereign State, as recognized by the jurisprudence of the Court and following from Article 41, paragraph 2, of the Vienna Convention of 18 April 1961 on Diplomatic Relations.

The Congo also filed a request for the indication of a provisional measure and by an Order of 8 December 2000 the Court, on the one hand, rejected Belgium's request that the case be removed from the List and, on the other, held that the circumstances, as they then presented themselves to the Court, were not such as to require the exercise of its power under Article 41 of the Statute to indicate provisional measures. In the same Order, the Court also held that it was desirable that the issues before the Court should be determined as soon as possible and that it was therefore appropriate to ensure that a decision on the Congo's Application be reached with all expedition.

In light of the facts and arguments set out during the written and oral proceedings, the Government of the Democratic Republic of the Congo requested the Court to adjudge and declare that:

1. by issuing and internationally circulating the arrest warrant of 11 April 2000 against Mr. Abdulaye Yerodia Ndombasi, Belgium committed a violation in regard to the Democratic Republic of the Congo of the rule of customary international law concerning the absolute inviolability and immunity from criminal process of incumbent foreign ministers; in so doing, it violated the principle of sovereign equality among States;

2. a formal finding by the Court of the unlawfulness of that act constitutes an appropriate form of satisfaction, providing reparation for the consequent moral injury to the Democratic Republic of the Congo;

3. the violations of international law underlying the issue and international circulation of the arrest warrant of 11 April 2000 preclude any State, including Belgium, from executing it;

4. Belgium shall be required to recall and cancel the arrest warrant of 11 April 2000 and to inform the foreign authorities to whom the warrant was circulated that Belgium renounces its request for their cooperation in executing the unlawful warrant.

Belgium requested the Court, as a preliminary matter, to adjudge and declare that the Court lacks jurisdiction in this case and/or that the Application by the Democratic Republic of the Congo against Belgium is inadmissible.

If, contrary to the submissions of Belgium with regard to the Court's jurisdiction and the admissibility of the Application, the Court concludes that it does have jurisdiction in this case and that the Application by the Democratic Republic of the Congo is admissible, Belgium requested the Court to reject the submissions of the Democratic Republic of the Congo on the merits of the case and to dismiss the Application.

On 11 April 2000 an investigating judge of the Brussels *tribunal de première instance* issued 'an international arrest warrant *in absentia* against Mr. Abdulaye Yerodia Ndombasi, charging him, as perpetrator or co-perpetrator, with offences constituting grave breaches of the Geneva Conventions of 1949 and of the Additional Protocols thereto, and with crimes against humanity. The arrest warrant was circulated internationally through Interpol. At the time when the arrest warrant was issued Mr. Yerodia was the Minister for Foreign Affairs of the Congo. The crimes with which Mr. Yerodia was charged were punishable in Belgium under the Law of 16 June 1993 'concerning the Punishment of Grave Breaches of the International Geneva Conventions of 12 August 1949 and of Protocols I and II of 8 June 1977 Additional Thereto', as amended by the Law of 19 February 1999 'concerning the Punishment of Serious Violations of International Humanitarian Law' (hereinafter referred to as the 'Belgian Law'). On 17 October 2000, the Congo instituted proceedings before the International Court of Justice, requesting the Court 'to declare that the Kingdom of Belgium shall annul the international arrest warrant issued on 11 April 2000'. After the proceedings were instituted, Mr. Yerodia ceased to hold office as Minister for Foreign Affairs, and subsequently ceased to hold any ministerial office. Belgium, of course submitted an objection that the case was now without object and that the

Court should accordingly decline to proceed to judgment on the merits of the case, but to no avail.

In its Application instituting proceedings, the Congo relied on two separate legal grounds. First, it claimed that the *universal jurisdiction* that the Belgian State attributes to itself under Article 7 of the Law in question constituted a violation of the principle that a State may not exercise its authority on the territory of another State and of the principle of sovereign equality among all Members of the United Nations. Secondly, it claimed that the non-recognition, on the basis of Article 5 of the Belgian Law, of the immunity of a Minister for Foreign Affairs in office constitutes a violation of the diplomatic immunity of the Minister for Foreign Affairs of a sovereign State. However, the Congo's Memorial and its final submissions refer only to a violation in regard to the Congo of the rule of customary international law concerning the absolute inviolability and immunity from criminal process of incumbent foreign ministers.

Belgium had pointed out that the Congo initially advanced a twofold argument, based, on the one hand, on the Belgian judge's lack of jurisdiction and, on the other, on the immunity from jurisdiction enjoyed by its Minister for Foreign Affairs. According to Belgium, the Congo now confines itself to arguing the latter point, and the Court consequently cannot rule on the issue of *universal jurisdiction* in any decision it renders on the merits of the case.

The Court recalled the well-established principle that 'it is the duty of the Court not only to reply to the questions as stated in the final submissions of the parties, but also to abstain from deciding points not included in those submissions' The Court observed that, while it is thus not entitled to decide upon questions not asked of it, the *non ultra petita* rule nonetheless cannot preclude the Court from addressing certain legal points in its reasoning. Thus in the present case the Court may not rule, in the operative part of its Judgment, on the question whether the disputed arrest warrant, issued by the Belgian investigating judge in exercise of his purported *universal jurisdiction*, complied in that regard with the rules and principles of international law governing the jurisdiction of national courts. This does not mean, however, that the Court may not deal with certain aspects of that question in the reasoning of its Judgment, should it deem this necessary or desirable.

As to immunity and inviolability of an incumbent Foreign Minister in general the Court observed at the outset that in international law it is firmly established that, as also diplomatic and consular agents, certain holders of high-ranking office in a State, such as the Head of State, Head of Government and Minister for Foreign Affairs, enjoy immunities from jurisdiction in other States, both civil and criminal. For the purposes of the present case, it is only the immunity from criminal jurisdiction and the inviolability of an incumbent Minister for Foreign Affairs that fall for the Court to consider.

The Court noted that a certain number of treaty instruments were cited by the Parties in this regard, including the Vienna Convention on Diplomatic Relations of 18 April 1961 and the New York Convention on Special Missions of 8 December 1969. The Court found that these conventions provide useful guidance on certain aspects of the question of immunities, but that they do not contain any provision specifically defining the immunities enjoyed by Ministers for Foreign Affairs. It is consequently on the basis of customary international law that the Court must decide the questions relating to the immunities of such Ministers raised in the present case.

In customary international law, the immunities accorded to Ministers for Foreign Affairs are not granted for their personal benefit, but to ensure the effective performance of their functions on behalf of their respective States. In order to determine the extent of these immunities, the Court must therefore first consider the nature of the functions exercised by a Minister for Foreign Affairs. After an examination of those functions, the Court concludes that they are such that, throughout the duration of his or her office, a Minister for Foreign Affairs when abroad enjoys full immunity from criminal jurisdiction and inviolability. That immunity and that inviolability protect the individual concerned against any act of authority of another State which would hinder him or her in the performance of his or her duties.

The Court found that in this respect no distinction can be drawn between acts performed by a Minister for Foreign Affairs in an 'official' capacity and those claimed to have been performed in a 'private capacity', or, for that matter, between acts performed before the person concerned assumed office as Minister for Foreign Affairs and acts committed during the period of office. Thus, if a Minister for Foreign Affairs is arrested in another State on a criminal charge, he or she is clearly thereby prevented from exercising the functions of his or her office. Furthermore, even the mere risk that, by travelling to or transiting another State, a Minister for Foreign Affairs might be exposing himself or herself to legal proceedings could deter the Minister from travelling internationally when required to do so for the purposes of the performance of his or her official functions.

The Court then addressed Belgium's argument that immunities accorded to incumbent Ministers for Foreign Affairs can in no case protect them where they are suspected of having committed war crimes or crimes against humanity.

The Court stated that it has carefully examined State practice, including national legislation and those few decisions of national higher courts, such as the House of Lords in the United Kingdom or the French Court of Cassation, and that it has been unable to deduce from this practice that there exists under customary international law any form of exception to the rule according immunity from criminal jurisdiction and inviolability to incumbent Ministers for Foreign Affairs, where they are suspected of having committed war crimes or crimes against humanity. The Court added that it has also examined the rules concerning the immunity or criminal responsibility of persons having an official capacity contained in the legal instruments creating international criminal tribunals, and which are specifically applicable to the latter (see Charter of the International Military Tribunal of Nuremberg, Art. 7; Charter of the International Military Tribunal of Tokyo, Art. 6; Statute of the International Criminal Tribunal for the former Yugoslavia, Art. 7, para. 2; Statute of the International Criminal Tribunal for Rwanda, Art. 6, para. 2; Statute of the International Criminal Court, Art. 27), and that it finds that these rules likewise do not enable it to conclude that any such exception exists in customary international law in regard to national courts. Finally, the Court observes that none of the decisions of the Nuremberg and Tokyo international military tribunals, or of the International Criminal Tribunal for the former Yugoslavia, cited by Belgium deal with the question of the immunities of incumbent Ministers for Foreign Affairs before national courts where they are accused of having committed war crimes or crimes against humanity. The Court accordingly noted that those decisions are in no way at variance with the findings it has reached above. The Court accordingly did not accept Belgium's argument in this regard.

It further noted that the rules governing the jurisdiction of national courts must be carefully distinguished from those governing jurisdictional immunities: jurisdiction does not imply absence of immunity, while absence of immunity does not imply jurisdiction. Thus, although various international conventions on the prevention and punishment of certain serious crimes impose on States obligations of prosecution or extradition, thereby requiring them to extend their criminal jurisdiction, such extension of jurisdiction in no way affects immunities under customary international law, including those of Ministers for Foreign Affairs. The Court emphasized, however, that the *immunity* from jurisdiction enjoyed by incumbent Ministers for Foreign Affairs does not mean that they enjoy *impunity* in respect of any crimes they might have committed, irrespective of their gravity. Jurisdictional immunity may well bar prosecution for a certain period or for certain offences; it cannot exonerate the person to whom it applies from all criminal responsibility. Accordingly, the immunities enjoyed under international law by an incumbent or former Minister for Foreign Affairs do not represent a bar to criminal prosecution in certain circumstances. The Court refers to circumstances where such persons are tried in their own countries, where the State which they represent or have represented decides to waive that immunity, where such persons no longer enjoy all of the immunities accorded by international law in other States after ceasing to hold the office of Minister for Foreign Affairs, and where such persons are subject to criminal proceedings before certain international criminal courts, where they have jurisdiction.

After examining the terms of the arrest warrant, the Court noted that its *issuance*, as such, represents an act by the Belgian judicial authorities intended to enable the arrest on Belgian territory of an incumbent Minister for Foreign Affairs on charges of war crimes and crimes against humanity. The fact that the warrant is enforceable is clearly apparent from the order given in it to 'all bailiffs and agents of public authority ... to execute this arrest warrant' and from the assertion in the warrant that 'the position of Minister for Foreign Affairs currently held by the accused does not entail immunity from jurisdiction and enforcement.' The Court notes that the warrant did admittedly make an exception for the case of an official visit by Mr. Yerodia to Belgium, and that Mr. Yerodia never suffered arrest in Belgium. The Court considered itself bound, however, to find that, given the nature and purpose of the warrant, its mere issue violated the immunity which Mr. Yerodia enjoyed as the Congo's incumbent Minister for Foreign Affairs. The Court accordingly concluded that the issue of the warrant constituted a violation of an obligation of Belgium towards the Congo, in that it failed to respect the immunity of that Minister and, more particularly, infringed the immunity from criminal jurisdiction and the inviolability then enjoyed by him under international law.

The Court also noted that Belgium admits that the purpose of the international *circulation* of the disputed arrest warrant was to establish a legal basis for the arrest of Mr. Yerodia abroad and his subsequent extradition to Belgium. The Court finds that, as in the case of the warrant's issue, its international circulation from June 2000 by the Belgian authorities, given its nature and purpose, effectively infringed Mr. Yerodia's immunity as the Congo's incumbent Minister for Foreign Affairs and was furthermore liable to affect the Congo's conduct of its international relations. The Court concluded that the circulation of the warrant, whether or not it significantly interfered with Mr. Yerodia's diplomatic activity, constituted a violation of an obligation of Belgium towards the Congo, in that it failed to respect the immunity of the incumbent Minister for Foreign Affairs of the Congo and, more particularly, infringed the immunity from criminal jurisdiction and inviolability then enjoyed by him under international law.

> 'For these reasons, The Court,
> (1. A) By fifteen votes to one, *Rejects* the objections of the Kingdom of Belgium relating to jurisdiction, mootness and admissibility;
> (1. B) By fifteen votes to one, *Finds* that it has jurisdiction to entertain the Application filed by the Democratic Republic of the Congo on 17 October 2000;
> (1. C) By fifteen votes to one, *Finds* that the Application of the Democratic Republic of the Congo is not without object and that accordingly the case is not moot;
> (1. D) By fifteen votes to one, *Finds* that the Application of the Democratic Republic of the Congo is admissible;
> (2) By thirteen votes to three, *Finds* that the issue against Mr. Abdulaye Yerodia Ndombasi of the arrest warrant of 11 April 2000, and its international circulation, constituted violations of a legal obligation of the Kingdom of Belgium towards the Democratic Republic of the Congo, in that they failed to respect the immunity from criminal jurisdiction and the inviolability which the incumbent Minister for Foreign Affairs of the Democratic Republic of the Congo enjoyed under international law;
> (3) By ten votes to six, *Finds* that the Kingdom of Belgium must, by means of its own choosing, cancel the arrest warrant of 11 April 2000 and so inform the authorities to whom that warrant was circulated'.

3.6   ICC AND TERRORISM

On the 1st of July 2002, the July 1998 Rome Statute entered into force. The creation of an International Criminal Court thereby became a reality. For many observers this was somewhat surprising, not that they did not believe that the Rome Statute would enter into force sooner or later, but rather the timing: most were thinking in terms of 2008 or even 2010. Although many are tempted to argue that the September 2001 events had their impact, it is hereby submitted that given the status of signatures and ratifications by late summer 2001, those events only had a marginal influence.[1]

Yet, the coming into being of the ICC is of the uttermost importance. The question, however, remains whether the ICC will also be competent to deal with terrorist acts. Initial reactions appeared to indicate that such an inclusion was only logical. Others were of the opinion that such an inclusion would be detrimental and would in the end undermine the status of the Court. It will be argued in this sub-chapter that inclusion in the long run is logical and should be supported, as it might also enable the USA to join the Court, at last.

The ICC has not come out of the blue. As indicated in Chapter 1, already in 1937 a convention had been agreed upon for the creation of an international court, as an 'annex' to the 1937 (LoN) Geneva Convention for the Prevention and Punishment of Terrorism.[2] WW II discontinued a sincere interest in this issue also because the issue of genocide and war crimes – rightly – dominated the (legal) discussion and debate, resulting in the Military Tribunals of Nuremberg and Tokyo (1945-1948). These Tribunals took place in a spirit of pragmatic cooperation, part of the initial positive WW II aftermath. If the discussion had started after 1948, then agreement between the USA and the USSR would most probably not have been reached: efforts could have fallen prey to vetoes in the Security Council.

---

[1] By late August 2001, almost 140 States had signed the Statute, and some 40 had already deposited their instrument of ratification; with this 'trend', the required total of 60 would be reached by early summer 2002 also without the September 2001 events.

[2] The Convention for the Creation of an International Criminal Court was opened for signature in 1937 under the auspices of the League of Nations. The Court's proposed jurisdiction was confined to offences created by the Convention for the Prevention and Punishment of Terrorism, which was opened for signature at the same time. The entry into force of the Court Convention was made subject to the entry into force of the Terrorism Convention, which did not occur. See LN Doc. C.546(I).M.383(I).1937.V; and LN Doc. C.547(I).M.384(I).1937.V. respectively.

It therefore took until 1989 before renewed efforts in this field had a chance of success.[3] And indeed, in an environment of common concern, new avenues of cooperation and common goals, the Security Council was able to agree on a statute for an International Criminal Tribunal on Yugoslavia (ICTY) in 1993.[4] The ICTY started functioning shortly afterwards and is believed to have enough cases and material to continue its operations until at least 2010.

A similar Tribunal was set up for the events which took place in Rwanda 1994,[5] and here too, the Tribunal might still be operational in the year 2010.

It was in the context of these two tribunals that the international community realized that the time was ripe for a more general tribunal, also because there was talk of similar exercises for Cambodia, Sierra Leone and even East Timor. And indeed, after due considerations and lengthy conferences, a statute for a permanent International Criminal Court was adopted on 17 July 1998 by 160 states, meeting at a Diplomatic Conference in Rome, hence the name 'the 1998 Rome Statute'. It is underlined that this Statute has no direct link with the UN, although the General Assembly has subsequently endorsed the results and has on numerous occasions called upon the UN members to sign and/or ratify this Statute.[6] Yet, the Court will be brought into a certain relationship with the UN through an agreement to be approved by the ICC Assembly of States Parties and thereafter concluded by the President of the Court on its behalf.[7]

The 60th instrument of ratification was deposited in New York on April 11th, 2002, and the Statute thus entered into force on July 1st, 2002, as per its Art. 126.

The Rome Statute first and foremost establishes a Court which shall be a permanent institution and which shall have the power to exercise its jurisdiction over persons

---

[3] It was Trinidad and Tobago that, in 1989, put the question of the creation of an ICC back on the agenda of the UN General Assembly.

[4] SC Resolution 827, 25 May 1993.

[5] SC Resolution 955, 8 November 1994.

[6] In 1992, the United Nations General Assembly asked the International Law Commission (ILC) to draft a statute for an international criminal court as a matter of priority. In 1996, the UN General Assembly approved a series of Preparatory Committee meetings for 1997 and 1998 and set the summer of 1998 as the date for a Diplomatic Conference to discuss a draft Statute for an International Criminal Court. With the July 1998 agreement, the GA adopted yearly Resolutions, like the December 2001 one in which it requested the Secretary-General to reconvene the Preparatory Commission, in accordance with resolution F [of the 1998 Rome Diplomatic Conference], to continue to carry out the mandate of that resolution and, in that connection, to discuss ways to enhance the effectiveness and acceptance of the Court. The GA also requested the Secretary-General to undertake the preparations necessary to convene, in accordance with Article 112, paragraph 1, of the Rome Statute, the meeting of the Assembly of States Parties to be held at United Nations Headquarters upon the entry into force of the Statute in accordance with Article 126, paragraph 1, of the Statute (GA Res. 56/85 of 12 December 2001).

[7] Rome Statute, Art. 2 (relationship with the UN) in conjunction with Art. 112 (Assembly) and Art. 38 (Presidency). The GA noted in Resolution 56/85 '... with regard to the work of the Preparatory Commission and related working groups, the adoption by the Commission on 5 October 2001 of the report on its sixth to eighth sessions, containing the draft texts of the Relationship Agreement between the Court and the United Nations, the Financial Regulations, the Agreement on the Privileges and Immunities of the Court and the Rules of Procedure of the Assembly of States Parties'.

for the most serious crimes of international concern, as referred to in the Statute (Art. 1). Of relevance is, of course, that terrorism as such has not been included among those most serious crimes as referred to in the Statute. Moreover, of the utmost importance for the jurisdiction, immunity and extradition debate, the Court's jurisdiction shall be complementary to national criminal jurisdictions. This would appear to underline the trend to place the responsibility for jurisdiction primarily with the Nation State. The Court acts as an additional, complementary safeguard.

As to the crimes which fall under the Court's jurisdiction, these have been limited to (a) the crime of genocide; (b) crimes against humanity; (c) war crimes; and (d), upon the adoption of an additional provision, the crime of aggression.[8] Terrorism does not fall under these criteria, and it would be counterproductive to define terrorism in such a way that it should equal or should be considered to amount to, for example, a crime against humanity. The definition as contained in the Statute's Art. 7 is well-balanced, and should primarily focus on what has been *prima facie* included in this definition, in accordance with the *Textes Préparatoires*, and not on extending the scope and purposes. However, it is herewith submitted that many would label acts which fall under the scope of Art. 7 as terrorist acts. In other words, by labelling them as 'crimes against humanity' those acts would then fall under the Statute and the ICC would then be competent and would have jurisdiction. An example will probably suffice: the suicide bombing in Israel spreading terror in early 2002 by aiming at bus stations, discothèques and markets could well be defined as an act (murder), committed as part of a widespread or systematic attack against a civilian population, with knowledge of the attack, as per the 'chapeau' of the Statute's Art. 7.[9] In fact, it could also be submitted that the condition as contained in Art. 7.2 could also be considered to have been met:

---

[8] Statute, Art. 5.

[9] This Art. 7 reads in full: Crimes against humanity

1. For the purpose of this Statute, 'crime against humanity' means any of the following acts when committed as part of a widespread or systematic attack directed against any civilian population, with knowledge of the attack:

(a)   Murder;

(b)   Extermination;

(c)   Enslavement;

(d)   Deportation or forcible transfer of population;

(e)   Imprisonment or other severe deprivation of physical liberty in violation of fundamental rules of international law;

(f)   Torture;

(g)   Rape, sexual slavery, enforced prostitution, forced pregnancy, enforced sterilization, or any other form of sexual violence of comparable gravity;

(h)   Persecution against any identifiable group or collectivity on political, racial, national, ethnic, cultural, religious, gender as defined in paragraph 3, or other grounds that are universally recognized as impermissible under international law, in connection with any act referred to in this paragraph or any crime within the jurisdiction of the Court;

(i)   Enforced disappearance of persons;

(j)   The crime of apartheid;

(k)   Other inhumane acts of a similar character intentionally causing great suffering, or serious injury to body or to mental or physical health.

'Attack directed against any civilian population' means a course of conduct involving the multiple commission of acts referred to in paragraph 1 against any civilian population, pursuant to or in furtherance of a State or organizational policy to commit such attack.

Yet, although in certain instances 'terrorism' equals an act which falls under the terms of the Rome Statute, and would hence result in the ICC being competent, it should be emphasized that most terrorist acts do not fall within the ambit of the Rome Statute, and that the ICC is not competent to 'deal' with such acts.

Of course, some observers fall prey to wishful thinking and argue that the ICC may play an important role in the war against terrorism.[10] And indeed, they have the

---

2. For the purpose of paragraph 1:

(a)   'Attack directed against any civilian population' means a course of conduct involving the multiple commission of acts referred to in paragraph 1 against any civilian population, pursuant to or in furtherance of a State or organizational policy to commit such attack;

(b)   'Extermination' includes the intentional infliction of conditions of life, inter alia, the deprivation of access to food and medicine, calculated to bring about the destruction of part of a population;

(c)   'Enslavement' means the exercise of any or all of the powers attaching to the right of ownership over a person and includes the exercise of such power in the course of trafficking in persons, in particular women and children;

(d)   'Deportation or forcible transfer of population' means forced displacement of the persons concerned by expulsion or other coercive acts from the area in which they are lawfully present, without grounds permitted under international law;

(e)   'Torture' means the intentional infliction of severe pain or suffering, whether physical or mental, upon a person in the custody or under the control of the accused; except that torture shall not include pain or suffering arising only from, inherent in or incidental to, lawful sanctions;

(f)   'Forced pregnancy' means the unlawful confinement of a woman forcibly made pregnant, with the intent of affecting the ethnic composition of any population or carrying out other grave violations of international law. This definition shall not in any way be interpreted as affecting national laws relating to pregnancy;

(g)   'Persecution' means the intentional and severe deprivation of fundamental rights contrary to international law by reason of the identity of the group or collectivity;

(h)   'The crime of apartheid' means inhumane acts of a character similar to those referred to in paragraph 1, committed in the context of an institutionalized regime of systematic oppression and domination by one racial group over any other racial group or groups and committed with the intention of maintaining that regime;

(i)   'Enforced disappearance of persons' means the arrest, detention or abduction of persons by, or with the authorization, support or acquiescence of, a State or a political organization, followed by a refusal to acknowledge that deprivation of freedom or to give information on the fate or whereabouts of those persons, with the intention of removing them from the protection of the law for a prolonged period of time.

3. For the purpose of this Statute, it is understood that the term 'gender' refers to the two sexes, male and female, within the context of society. The term 'gender' does not indicate any meaning different from the above.

[10] See for instance some remarks made in early October 2001 upon the UK ratifying the Rome Statute: 'This week, the American Servicemembers' Protection Act (ASPA), a piece of extreme anti-ICC legislation, was re-introduced in Congress by Senator Jesse Helms (R-NC). It threatens to cut off military aid to countries that ratify the ICC treaty and would prohibit US cooperation even in a case of international terrorism'. When asked about the UK government's response to ASPA, the UK's Ambassador to the UN Greenstock remarked, 'The US is one of the UK's strongest allies, and the UK hopes the US will continue working with us in creating a permanent ICC. It is important to have the US in the ICC

Statute to support such thinking: Seven years after the entry into force of the Statute, i.e. 1 July 2009, a Review Conference shall be convened *to consider any amendments* to the Statute: *such review may include the list of crimes contained in Article 5*.[11]

Although one may be tempted, given the present developments, to convene such a review Conference at an earlier stage, this would appear to be impossible. That, however, does not mean that one should not prepare for adding terrorism to the list of crimes for which the ICC would have jurisdiction (of course, also in a complementary way). Yet, first of all, efforts to agree on a general definition of terrorism should yield results, and secondly, the ICC should prove its worth over the above period of seven years. But efforts could already be undertaken now to prepare for widening the list of crimes so as to include terrorism. This should be done in the context of a wider agreement with the USA: the inclusion of terrorism and US support (read: ratification[12]) for the ICC. The present author, though fully aware of many US peculiarities, insists that the Nuremberg-ICC process has lasted more than 50 years and that being patient for another 25 years or so should be considered part and parcel of the 'progressive development of international law' as per the UN Charter.[13]

process and I hope the US will ratify the ICC Statute as soon as possible'. Mr. Pace commented, 'The UK ratification could not be a more timely or clear refutation of USA Congressional extremists' efforts to pass ASPA, at the same time the USA is trying to build a global coalition against terrorism'.

A European delegate at the United Nations remarked that U.S. opposition to the ICC can 'potentially alienate allies, thereby eroding support for the global coalition against terrorism'. Another delegate said that legislation 'imposing military and legal reprisals is unprecedented and unacceptable'. Heather Hamilton, of the American Coalition for the ICC (AMICC) added, 'The administration should realize that supporting legislation penalizing countries that join an international law enforcement mechanism is not the way to strengthen international efforts to bring terrorists to justice'. (Source: Nuclear Age Peace Foundation; website: wagingpeace.org). It is obvious that the US Administration's action in this regard in May 2002 did not raise the stakes on an early accession of the US to the ICC. See also the conclusions in Chapter 8.

[11] Rome Statute, Article 123.

[12] It is recalled that President Clinton signed the Rome Statute on 31 December 2000, just before handing over to his successor.

[13] UN Charter, Art. 13.a.

CHAPTER 4
THE UNITED NATIONS AND TERRORISM

As per Article 7 of the UN Charter, the United Nations consists of six organs: the General Assembly, the Security Council, ECOSOC (the Economic and Social Council), the Trusteeship Council (now more or less defunct), the International Court of Justice (ICJ) and the Secretariat (read: the Secretary-General). All six bodies have in one way or another dealt with the terrorism issue.

- The General Assembly (GA), through resolutions, lengthy debates, the adoption of draft Conventions and since 1996 a special committee;
- The Security Council (SC), through some fairly effective and clearly worded resolutions and the establishment of the CTC, the Counter-Terrorism Committee;
- The ECOSOC (the Economic and Social Council), by linking the topic of human rights with terrorism, inter alia, through a Special Rapporteur;
- The Trusteeship Council, through the non-debate on liberation fighters v. terrorists and the link to self-determination;
- The International Court of Justice (ICJ), in e.g. the Lockerbie and the Iranian Hostage Taking cases; and
- The Secretariat (the Secretary-General/SG), through numerous initiatives and statements.

Attention shall be paid to all the relevant moves, motions and results. From the outset, however, it must be stressed that the United Nations as a structure can in no way be compared with the traditional Trias Politica system as adhered to in most democratic societies. The General Assembly does not serve as a legislative or controlling body, its resolutions being 'soft' in character, the ICJ is not entitled to screen the Resolutions of the Security Council[1] and the only conclusion worth draw-

---

[1] Although that is exactly what Libya wants the ICJ to do in the case of Libya v. the US and the UK (Lockerbie). However, the present author sides with Judge Schwebel who submitted in that case that the terms and drafting history of the Charter demonstrate that the Security Council is subject to the rule of law, and at the same time is empowered to derogate from international law if the maintenance of international peace requires this. It does not follow from the fact that the Council is so subject, and that the Court is the United Nation's principal judicial organ, that the Court is authorized to ensure that the Council's decisions are in accordance with the law. In many legal systems, subjecting the acts of an organ to the law by no means entails the legality of its actions to judicial review. The tenor of the discussions at San Francisco indicate the intention of the Charter's drafters not to accord the Court the power of judicial review. To engraft the power of judicial review upon the Charter regime would not be a development but a departure which is neither justified by the Charter's terms nor by customary international law or by the general principles of law.

ing from an analysis of the Charter and almost 60 years of 'action' is that the SC is the first and foremost organ, setting the tone, giving directions and adopting binding resolutions.

When Mr. Milosovic complained at the beginning of his trial at the ICTY, the Yugoslavia Tribunal, that the Statute of the Tribunal had not been approved or adopted by the General Assembly, he should have been informed of the difference in standing and authority between the GA and the SC.[2] The Security Council enjoys the 'ultimate' power within the UN system and thus under international law, because the UN Members conferred on the SC *'primary responsibility for the maintenance of international peace and security'*, and agreed *'that in carrying out its duties, the SC acts on their behalf'*.[3]

This having been said, this Volume will nevertheless follow the structure of the Charter and starts with an analysis of the involvement of the General Assembly in tackling the issue of terrorism, also because the GA did set the tone in this matter. The SC more often than not simply followed suit, albeit in a straightforward, pragmatic and realistic manner, and hence with significant added value. The order in this chapter is thus: (4.1) GA; (4.2) SC; (4.3) ECOSOC; (4.4) Trusteeship Council; (4.5) ICJ; and (4.6) SG.

As will be shown, the main activities take place in the following three (sub-)bodies:

– the Counter-Terrorism Committee, which falls under the SC;
– the Ad Hoc Committee, a GA Committee working closely with – and to some extent within or under the aegis of – the GA's Sixth Committee, and
– the (Sub-)Commission on Human Rights, with a Special Rapporteur on human rights and terrorism.

The focus of these three bodies differs to a great extent: the CTC deals first and foremost with the threat to peace as posed by terrorism; the Ad Hoc Committee elaborates and discusses draft conventions; and the Special Rapporteur focuses on the possible impact of the war against terrorism on freedoms and human rights in general, whilst describing all the conceivable aspects of terrorism in fairly great detail.

A different focus yields a different result, and it is hereby submitted that further efforts need to be undertaken in order to bring these three actors into line, whilst fully appreciating the hierarchy or chain of command: the Security Council is and remains the uttermost body: The members of the UN have after all agreed to accept and carry out the decisions of the SC in accordance with the Charter.[4]

---

[2] The ICTY has been set up under SC Resolutions 820 and 827 (1993).
[3] UN Charter, art. 24.1; this in spite of GA Res. 377(V), 1950, the so-called Uniting for Peace Resolution.
[4] As per the Charter's Art. 25.

4.1 GENERAL ASSEMBLY

4.1.1 From 'understanding' to straightforwardness and back (1989-2001)

4.1.1.1 *'Understanding'*

As will be appreciated from the point of view that many UN members have an obsession with Middle East developments, it should come as no surprise that even in the late 1980s efforts were undertaken to look upon terrorism with some understanding. References were made to the underlying causes and a fairly ambiguous terminology was quite common. This ambiguity was even reflected in the official title of the item as it appeared on the agenda of the General Assembly's (GA) Sixth Committee, the reports and the (draft) resolutions:

> 'Measures to prevent international terrorism which endangers or takes innocent human lives or jeopardizes fundamental freedoms and study of the underlying causes of those forms of terrorism and acts of violence which lie in misery, frustration, grievance and despair and which cause some people to sacrifice human lives, including their own, in an attempt to effect radical changes.'

Two comments need to be made here: (1) the GA apparently limited its attention to those forms of terrorism which endanger or take innocent lives or jeopardize fundamental freedoms, implying that there are other forms of terrorism which do not fall under this definition and which do not deserve to be taken up as an issue; and (2) by immediately adding the need to study the underlying causes, the GA appears to have an understanding, if not an appreciation, of the offenders, who are sometimes so desperate that they even ('including') take their own lives ... This can only be understood with the Israel challenge in mind, and one of the main goals of both the GA's Sixth Committee and the GA itself was to convene an international conference, under the auspices of the UN,

> 'to define terrorism and to differentiate it from the struggle of peoples for national liberation.'

This very sentence indeed reflects the 'frustration' that some countries either deny certain peoples the right to struggle (read: use violence) for national liberation and/ or equate such struggle with terrorism. By separating these issues it was hoped that the struggle for national liberation could be made legitimate and that certain organizations (read: PLO) could be dissociated from its many terrorist acts.[1]

Keeping this in mind, it should come as no surprise that, e.g., the Western European countries again and again submitted draft resolutions which were far more straightforward in character. Some illustrations of the 'war of words' in the late 1980s (in this case 1989, at the time of major changes on the East-West level) might be useful. The West gives priority to e.g. the following:

'... Once again unequivocally condemns, as criminal and unjustifiable under any circumstances, all acts, methods and practices of terrorism wherever and by whomever committed ...'

Such drafts contained no reference whatsoever to frustration or despair.

Most Eastern Europeans tried to find a middle course: they wanted to set up 'a fact-finding body to deal with acts of international terrorism at the request of the States directly affected' and to consider the establishment within the Secretariat of 'a centre on international terrorism with a view, inter alia, to collecting and analysing information on serious aspects of the problem', which indeed ever so slightly goes in the direction of aiming for the root causes and the implied 'understanding'.

The non-aligned (through Yugoslavia) submitted drafts which touched upon State terrorism (read: Israel) and *the inalienable right to self-determination and independence of all peoples under colonial and racist régimes and other forms of alien domination and foreign occupation and upholding the legitimacy of their struggle, in particular the struggle of national liberation movements.*[2]

In view of the composition of the General Assembly, it was quite logical that the resolution which was finally adopted was a fair blend, leaning towards the non-aligned point of view (not repeating the frustration and despair parts from the title, stressing the national liberation struggle, albeit in line with GA Res. 2625 (XXV).[3]

---

[1] Yet, even in 2002 there were serious efforts to deny that the Palestinian suicide bombings are terrorist acts: Muslim nations avoided a definition of terrorism at an April 2002 Kuala Lumpur OIC conference as any attempt 'to link terrorism to the struggle of the Palestinian people [including suicide bombers]' was rejected by the OIC foreign ministers (IHT, 3 April 2002). See on this issue, below, Chapter 4.4 on self-determination and the Trusteeship Council.

[2] It took until 1991 when the equation of Zionism with racism was finally revoked. In 1975, the General Assembly, by a vote of 89 to 67, passed Resolution 3379 (XXX) determining 'that Zionism is a form of racism and racial discrimination'. That resolution remained on the books until 1991 when it was revoked by a vote of 87 to 25. In 2001, at the Durban anti-racism conference this issue once again emerged, to be suppressed only at a very late stage.

[3] This Res. 2625 (XXV) also stipulates in principle 1 that every State has the duty to refrain from organizing, instigating, assisting or participating in acts of civil strife *or terrorist acts* in another State or acquiescing in organized activities within its territory directed towards the commission of such acts, when the acts referred to involve a threat or use of force. And in principle 3 it can be read that no State shall organize, assist, foment, finance, incite or tolerate subversive, *terrorist or armed activities* directed towards the violent overthrow of the regime in another State. Yet, references to terrorism in this important 'Declaration on Principles' were embedded in the general context of (armed) intervention and are hence indirect at most.

Finally, yet another interesting development was a proposal made during the spring 2002 session of the GA Ad Hoc Committee under 51/210 to include in the preamble of the (draft) comprehensive convention a paragraph which would once again refer to underlying causes and pay 'special attention to all situations [including ...] involving alien occupation that may give rise to international terrorism and may endanger international peace and security'. Some delegations appear to be unable to focus on the scourge of terrorism and still appear to introduce elements of understanding, if not appreciation. The fight for an appropriate legal response has not yet been won.

4.1.1.2 'Straightforward', practical

A turning point came in the mid-1990s. The 1991 Resolution (46/51) had already replaced the title which referred to the causes and the offender with a simple, straightforward *'Measures to eliminate international terrorism'*. Yet, self-determination and the struggle of national liberation movements was still included. In 1994 (**GA Res. 49/60**, adopted without a vote) the Resolution itself was a mere introduction to a *novum:* the adoption of a ***Declaration on Measures to Eliminate International Terrorism*** (included in full in this Volume, 4.1.5.2.A).

In this Declaration references to liberation movements were omitted, the issue of state terrorism was avoided and any understanding for the offender was firmly dropped. The language finally became palpable, pragmatic and reflected the serious reality. States solemnly reaffirmed *their unequivocal condemnation of all acts, methods and practices of terrorism as criminal and unjustifiable, wherever and by whomever committed.* It was declared that *Acts, methods and practices of terrorism constitute a grave violation of the purposes and principles of the United Nations, which may pose a threat to international peace and security* thereby linking terrorism firmly to both Chapter I and Chapter VII of the Charter.[4] Moreover, the unjustifiable character of terrorism was stressed: *criminal acts, intended or calculated to provoke a state of terror in the general public, a group of persons or particular persons for political purposes are in any circumstance unjustifiable, whatever the considerations of a political, philosophical, racial, ethnic, religious or any other nature that may be invoked to justify them.*

As indicated above, Resolution 49/60, with the Declaration as an Annex, was adopted without a vote. It may be recalled, however, that GA Declarations and Resolutions have a limited impact due to the soft law character of such instruments.

Two years later, in 1996, yet another Declaration was adopted (this time as an annex to **GA Res. 51/210**). This Declaration was meant to Supplement the earlier 1994 declaration, by focusing on efforts to limit the freedom of movement of assumed perpetrators, on the exclusion clause of the 1951 Refugee Convention, and on the need to further facilitate cooperation in ensuring that the accused be brought to justice.

---

[4] The UN Charter Chapter I deals with purposes and principles; and Chapter VII with 'action with respect to threats to the peace, breaches of the peace, and acts of aggression'.

Moreover, under this Declaration an Ad-Hoc Committee was set up in order to streamline work on (draft) Conventions and remaining gaps.[5] The Committee's formal title is the Ad Hoc Committee Established by General Assembly Resolution 51/210 of 17 December 1996; it was initially given a mandate to harmonize legal structures for combating international terrorism, a mandate which was slightly updated in 2001 (see also 4.1.3).[6]

---

[5] Such an Ad-Hoc Committee reports primarily to the GA's Sixth Committee. Illustrative in this context may be a report on the Sixth Committee's meeting of 19 November 2001: The Sixth Committee had before it two reports on 'Measures to eliminate international terrorism': the first, from the Ad Hoc Committee on Terrorism, which held five meetings as a working group of the Sixth Committee from 15 to 26 October 2001 (document A/C.6/56/L.9); and the second is a report from the Secretary-General (document A/56/160) on the status of previously adopted anti-terrorism conventions. The Ad Hoc Committee on Terrorism, which was established by the General Assembly in 1996 to elaborate a comprehensive legal framework of conventions dealing with international terrorism, was mandated to examine the possibility of developing a comprehensive instrument on the subject as well as to continue negotiations on a convention on nuclear terrorism. It also keeps on its agenda the question of convening a high-level United Nations conference to formulate an international response to all forms of terrorism. The working group focused on a paper first submitted by India at the General Assembly's fifty-first session [1996], which was intended to serve as the basis for negotiations on a comprehensive convention. The objective of a comprehensive convention is to close the gaps on offences that are currently outside the scope of the existing specialized anti-terrorism conventions, and to provide further legal support to them. Delegates began negotiations on the 27-article draft comprehensive convention at the Ad Hoc Committee's fifth session from 12 to 23 February [2001]. Negotiations continued in the form of a Sixth Committee (Legal) Working Group in mid-October where delegates reached agreement on most of the articles. In the hope of being able to present an agreed draft convention to the Assembly in December, the Sixth Committee has appointed a coordinator to continue negotiations on the few remaining articles of the text. The text of the draft Comprehensive Convention has been included in this Volume, Chapter 5.

[6] Under the terms of General Assembly Resolution 56/88 adopted on 12 December 2001 (operative paragraph 16), the Ad Hoc Committee shall continue to elaborate a comprehensive convention on international terrorism as a matter of urgency, and shall continue its efforts to resolve the outstanding issues relating to the elaboration of a draft international convention for the suppression of acts of nuclear terrorism, as a means of further developing a comprehensive legal framework of conventions dealing with international terrorism, and it shall keep on its agenda the question of convening a high-level conference under the auspices of the United Nations to formulate a joint organized response of the international community to terrorism in all its forms and manifestations.

Since its establishment, the Ad Hoc Committee has negotiated several texts resulting in the adoption of two treaties (1) the **International Convention for the Suppression of Terrorist Bombings** adopted by the General Assembly in Resolution 52/164 of 15 December 1997; and (2) the **International Convention for the Suppression of the Financing of Terrorism** adopted by the General Assembly in Resolution 54/109 of 9 December 1999 (somewhat later slightly amended);

Moreover, a draft international convention for the suppression of nuclear terrorism (A/C.6/53/L.4, Annex I) has been agreed upon, and by the end of 2000, work had begun on a draft comprehensive convention on international terrorism.

The Ad Hoc Committee has adopted the pattern of holding one session per year over a one or two week period, usually early in the year. The work is then continued in the framework of a Working Group of the Sixth Committee held later in the year.

The Committee is open to all States which are members of the United Nations or members of specialized agencies or of the International Atomic Energy Agency.

Below (Chapter 7.2) more attention will be paid to the transborder aspects as reflected in asylum and refugee law. **GA Res. 51/120 and the Declaration to supplement the 1994 Declaration** have been included in full in this sub-chapter (4.1.5.3).

Subsequent resolutions (e.g., 52/165, 53/108, 54/110 and 55/158) did not contain significant new aspects and were more often than not adopted without a vote. Of relevance was the commitment to work towards a convention on the suppression of acts of nuclear terrorism.

GA Res. 54/109 (1999), however, proved to be a major step forward as it represented agreement on the International Convention for the Suppression of the Financing of Terrorism.

4.1.1.3 'And back': the human rights angle

Whereas the elimination of international terrorism could count on broad support, a new element was introduced into the discussion: the link between human rights and terrorism. Terrorism as a subject had reached the (Sub-)Commission on Human Rights (a charter-based organ) and the results were presented to the GA through ECOSOC. This subject, although resulting in a number of GA Resolutions, will hence be dealt with under the heading of ECOSOC. It suffices to state here that a) the 'human rights and terrorism' resolutions seemed to divert from the gist of the 'measures against terrorism' resolutions, but b) that the 2001 resolution concerned would appear to follow the mainstream of thinking. And then again, as we will see, the 2002 Commission on Human Rights' discussions focused on the human rights of the assumed offenders and the fear of oppressive measures in the wake of the September 2001 events rather than on the issue of terror and the victims of terror.

4.1.2   The General Assembly after September 2001

The condemnation of the terrorist attacks in the USA, the subject of the General Assembly's first resolution of 2001 (**GA Res. 56/1**), was somewhat non-descriptive in that it neither opened new venues nor embarked on new visions.[7]

However, a special session on this issue was organized from 1-5 October 2001. In his concluding remarks, the Chairman submitted that Member States concurred with the view that a primary task facing the international community was to ensure that an effective legal framework for the prevention and elimination of international terrorism is in place. To this end, he called upon all Member States that had not yet

---

[7] (The GA) Strongly condemns the heinous acts of terrorism, which have caused enormous loss of human life, destruction and damage in the cities of New York, host city of the United Nations, and Washington, D.C., and in Pennsylvania; Expresses its condolences and solidarity with the people and Government of the United States of America in these sad and tragic circumstances; Urgently calls for international cooperation to bring to justice the perpetrators, organizers and sponsors of the outrages of 11 September 2001; Also urgently calls for international cooperation to prevent and eradicate acts of terrorism, and stresses that those responsible for aiding, supporting or harbouring the perpetrators, organizers and sponsors of such acts will be held accountable.

done so to become, as a matter of priority, parties to the existing international conventions relating to terrorism.[8]

---

[8] Statement by General Assembly President H.E. Dr. Han Seung-soo at the Conclusion of the Plenary Meetings on 'Measures to Eliminate International Terrorism', 5 October 2001:

(...) We have had an unusually long but very important and constructive debate during the last five days. It is unprecedented in the history of the UN for 168 Member States to participate in the debate on a single agenda item. This fact alone eloquently demonstrates how seriously all Member States and the whole international community regard the acts of terrorism that took place on 11 September. It was because we all believed that they were not only attacks on the United States but assaults on the whole civilized world.

As we all know, this agenda item 'Measures to Eliminate International Terrorism' (item 166) has long been on the agenda of the Sixth Committee. However, in light of the importance and urgency of the issue in the aftermath of the tragedy of 11 September, we decided that the debate on this item be held in plenary meetings while consideration of the technical aspects of the item remain within the purview of the Sixth Committee. (...)

During our deliberations, all participants joined wholeheartedly in condemning the terrorist attacks of 11 September, reaffirming General Assembly Resolution 56/1 of 12 September 2001 in which the General Assembly condemned these attacks in the strongest terms and called for international cooperation to bring to justice the perpetrators, organizers, and sponsors of the outrages.

Member States voiced the view that international terrorism constitutes a threat to international peace and security as well as a crime against humanity. Undoubtedly, international terrorism is one of the most formidable challenges to the world community in the 21st century, and the United Nations should to play the key role in intensifying international efforts to eliminate such terrorism.

In this regard, I wish to recall that the General Assembly has taken important steps by adopting the Declaration on Measures to Eliminate International Terrorism in 1994 and its supplementary Declaration in 1996. The Security Council has also taken initiatives such as the adoption of Resolutions 1269 of 19 October 1999, 1368 of 12 September 2001 and 1373 of 28 September 2001, which not only condemned all forms of terrorism but also specified measures to be taken by Member States to prevent and suppress terrorist acts.

Member States recognized the urgency of dealing with all forms and manifestations of international terrorism and those who harbour and support the perpetrators, organizers, and sponsors of international terrorism. They stressed the need to enhance international cooperation and to promptly take all necessary measures to prevent and suppress terrorist activities.

Member States concurred in the view that a primary task facing the international community at present is to ensure that an effective legal framework for the prevention and elimination of international terrorism is in place. To this end, I call upon all Member States that have not yet done so to become, as a matter of priority, parties to the existing international conventions relating to terrorism. In this context, it is noteworthy that the Commission on Crime Prevention and Criminal Justice has recently adopted the revised Draft Action Plan for the Implementation of the Vienna Declaration on Crime and Justice. Many Member States also expressed their intention to take necessary measures to implement international conventions within their domestic jurisdiction.

I would like to take this opportunity to urge Member States to accelerate the work of the General Assembly with a view to early conclusion of the pending conventions on international terrorism in order to enhance the capacity of the international community to combat terrorism. As President of the General Assembly, I also wish to kindly request the Sixth Committee to expedite its work and submit its report to the General Assembly as early possible, preferably by 15 November 2001.

Finally, I recall that during our debate Member States shared the view that the international community should resolve to fight terrorism as a phenomenon separate from any religion or ethnic group. In this regard, the necessity of dialogue among civilizations was stressed. Also some delegates suggested a high level conference on international terrorism, while some others called upon the international community to address the root causes of terrorism. At the same time, the need for a clearer definition of terrorism was raised for our further consideration.

It is quite remarkable that the unique 5-day session did not result in a more tangible outcome. And indeed the subsequent 'normal' December 2001 GA Resolution (**GA Res. 56/88**, included in full, 4.1.5.5) reaffirms 56/1, and continues by saying, inter alia:

Stressing the need to strengthen further international cooperation among States and among international organizations and agencies, regional organizations and arrangements and the United Nations in order to prevent, combat and eliminate terrorism in all its forms and manifestations, wherever and by whomsoever committed, in accordance with the principles of the Charter, international law and relevant international conventions, (…)

1. Strongly condemns all acts, methods and practices of terrorism as criminal and unjustifiable, wherever and by whomsoever committed;

2. Reiterates that criminal acts intended or calculated to provoke a state of terror in the general public, a group of persons or particular persons for political purposes are in any circumstances unjustifiable, whatever the considerations of a political, philosophical, ideological, racial, ethnic, religious or other nature that may be invoked to justify them;

3. Reiterates its call upon all States to adopt further measures in accordance with the Charter of the United Nations and the relevant provisions of international law, including international standards of human rights, to prevent terrorism and to strengthen international cooperation in combating terrorism (…)

4. Also reiterates its call upon all States, with the aim of enhancing the efficient implementation of relevant legal instruments, to intensify, as and where appropriate, the exchange of information on facts related to terrorism and, in so doing, to avoid the dissemination of inaccurate or unverified information;

5. Further reiterates its call upon States to refrain from financing, encouraging, providing training for or otherwise supporting terrorist activities;

6. Reaffirms that international cooperation as well as actions by States to combat terrorism should be conducted in conformity with the principles of the Charter, international law and relevant international conventions;

7. Urges all States that have not yet done so to consider, as a matter of priority, and in accordance with Security Council Resolution 1373 (2001), becoming parties to relevant conventions (…) and calls upon all States to enact, as appropriate, domestic legislation necessary to implement the provisions of those conventions and protocols, to ensure that the jurisdiction of their courts enables them to bring to trial the perpetrators of terrorist acts, and to cooperate with and provide support and assistance to other States and relevant international and regional organizations to that end;

(…)

16. Decides that the Ad Hoc Committee shall continue to elaborate a comprehensive convention on international terrorism as a matter of urgency(…) and that it shall keep on its agenda the question of convening a high-level conference under the auspices of the United Nations to formulate a joint organized response of the international community to terrorism in all its forms and manifestations.

Our week-long deliberation was instrumental in reaffirming the central role of the United Nations in dealing with global and high profile issues such as international terrorism. It is my sincere hope that the United Nations and the international community will take further necessary measures to combat international terrorism, building on the deliberations we have had for the last five days.

4.1.3   The Ad Hoc Committee

We have seen that the issue of terrorism is being dealt with mainly in the GA's Sixth Committee (dealing with legal matters) but that also the Third Committee (on social affairs) is involved through the human rights angle.

More or less under the aegis of the Sixth Committee a Special Committee operates to deal with the problems and challenges involved with the task of finding solutions, on the legal level in particular. It concerns 'the Ad Hoc Committee'. In 1996 the General Assembly, in Resolution 51/210 of 17 December, decided to establish such an Ad Hoc Committee to elaborate an international convention for the suppression of terrorist bombings and, subsequently, an international convention for the suppression of acts of nuclear terrorism, to supplement related existing international instruments, and thereafter to address means of further developing a comprehensive legal framework of conventions dealing with international terrorism.[9] This mandate continued to be renewed and revised on an annual basis by the General Assembly in its resolutions on the topic of measures to eliminate international terrorism. The Committee's formal title is the Ad Hoc Committee Established by General Assembly Resolution 51/210 of 17 December 1996. It functions within the framework of a working group of the Sixth Committee.

The present mandate of the Ad Hoc Committee can best be described as follows. Under the terms of General Assembly Resolution 56/88 adopted on 12 December 2001 (operative paragraph 16), the Ad Hoc Committee shall continue to elaborate a comprehensive convention on international terrorism as a matter of urgency, and shall continue its efforts to resolve the outstanding issues relating to the elaboration of a draft international convention for the suppression of acts of nuclear terrorism, as a means of further developing a comprehensive legal framework of conventions dealing with international terrorism, and it shall keep on its agenda the question of convening a high-level conference under the auspices of the United Nations to formulate a joint organized response of the international community to terrorism in all its forms and manifestations.

Since its establishment in 1996, the Ad Hoc Committee has negotiated several texts resulting in the adoption of two treaties:

- the **International Convention for the Suppression of Terrorist Bombings** adopted by the General Assembly in Resolution 52/164 of 15 December 1997; and
- the **International Convention for the Suppression of the Financing of Terrorism** adopted by the General Assembly in Resolution 54/109 of 9 December 1999 (and slightly amended shortly afterwards);

---

[9] This Ad Hoc Committee had already been preceded in the 1970s by another one: as a result of the work of the Sixth Committee, the General Assembly adopted Resolution 3034 (XXVII) of 18 December 1972, providing for the setting up of an ad hoc committee, consisting of 35 members, to study the issues relating to international terrorism and to report to it. The Ad Hoc Committee on International Terrorism, which met in 1973, 1977 and 1979, examined the problem of international terrorism under three main parts – the definition, the underlying causes and the measures to be taken to combat international terrorism.

as well as

- a **draft international convention for the suppression of nuclear terrorism** (A/C.6/53/L.4, Annex I, included in Chapter 5.1); moreover, by the end of 2000, work had begun on
- a **draft comprehensive convention on international terrorism**, the 2002 text of which is included in full in this Volume (see Chapter 5.1).

The Ad Hoc Committee has adopted the pattern of holding one session per year over a one or two week period, usually early in the year. The work is then continued in the framework of a Working Group of the Sixth Committee held later in the year. The Committee is open to all States members of the United Nations or members of specialized agencies or of the International Atomic Energy Agency.

The 2002 session (the report on which is included in part in this sub-chapter, 4.1.5.6) not only dealt in extenso with the comprehensive convention, but also touched upon the issue of nuclear terrorism. It is foreseen that in the future also the biological and chemical aspects will be dealt with in a more elaborated manner. As indicated, the (draft) comprehensive convention has been included in full in the chapter containing the text of all the major conventions. Moreover, reference has been made to it in the sub-chapters on jurisdiction, accomplices, extradition and other forms of cooperation.

4.1.4   Some Concluding Remarks

The General Assembly has come a long way. Or rather, it should be submitted that the Members of the GA have gained a new insight. The reality is different: the GA is first and foremost a political body that reflects the political opinion of a majority of the UN Member States, influenced up to 1989 by the ideological divide between East and West and since 1948 by a clash of history in the Middle East. The latter issue in particular has poisoned the legal debate on terrorism as cultural identity, frustration and politically-motivated arguments have not only crept into the equation but have long dominated the debate. It is to be hoped that the 'unjustifiability' formula of the recent GA resolutions continue to be included, upheld and respected. Long-term concern as regards terrorism should enable the world community as represented in the GA to overcome short-term differences.

4.1.5   The General Assembly annexes

4.1.5.1   Res. 44/29
4.1.5.2.A   Res. 49/60
4.1.5.2.B   Declaration
4.1.5.3.A   Res. 51/210
4.1.5.3.B   Declaration
4.1.5.4   Res. 56/1
4.1.5.5   Res. 56/88
4.1.5.6   February 2002 Report Ad-Hoc Committee

4.1.5.1   *GA Res. 44/29*

Measures to prevent international terrorism which endangers or takes innocent human lives or jeopardizes fundamental freedoms and study of the underlying causes
of those forms of terrorism and acts of violence which lie in misery, frustration,
grievance and despair and which cause some people to sacrifice human lives, including their own, in an attempt to effect radical changes: (a) Report of the Secretary-General; (b) Convening, under the auspices of the United Nations, of an
international conference to define terrorism and differentiate it from the struggle of
peoples for national liberation:[10]

The General Assembly,
Recalling its Resolutions 3034 (XXVII) of 18 December 1972, 31/102 of 15 Decem-
ber 1976, 32/147 of 16 December 1977, 34/145 of 17 December 1979, 36/109 of 10
December 1981, 38/130 of 19 December 1983, 40/61 of 9 December 1985 and 42/
159 of 7 December 1987,
Recalling also the recommendations of the Ad Hoc Committee on International Terrorism contained in its report to the General Assembly at its thirty-fourth session,
Recalling further the Declaration on Principles of International Law concerning
Friendly Relations and Cooperation among States in accordance with the Charter of
the United Nations, the Declaration on the Strengthening of International Security,
the Definition of Aggression and relevant instruments on international humanitarian
law applicable in armed conflict,
Recalling moreover the existing international conventions relating to various aspects
of the problem of international terrorism, inter alia, the Convention on Offences and
Certain Other Acts Committed on Board Aircraft, signed at Tokyo on 14 September
1963, the Convention for the Suppression of Unlawful Seizure of Aircraft, signed at
The Hague on 16 December 1970, the Convention for the Suppression of Unlawful
Acts against the Safety of Civil Aviation, concluded at Montreal on 23 September
1971, the Convention on the Prevention and Punishment of Crimes against Internationally Protected Persons, including Diplomatic Agents, adopted in New York on
14 December 1973, the International Convention against the Taking of Hostages,

---

[10] General Assembly A/RES/44/29, 72nd plenary meeting, 4 December 1989.

adopted in New York on 17 December 1979, the Convention on the Physical Protection of Nuclear Material, adopted at Vienna on 3 March 1980, the Protocol for the Suppression of Unlawful Acts of Violence at Airports Serving International Civil Aviation, supplementary to the Convention for the Suppression of Unlawful Acts against the Safety of Civil Aviation, signed at Montreal on 24 February 1988, the Convention for the Suppression of Unlawful Acts against the Safety of Maritime Navigation, done at Rome on 10 March 1988, and the Protocol for the Suppression of Unlawful Acts against the Safety of Fixed Platforms located on the Continental Shelf, done at Rome on 10 March 1988,

Convinced that a policy of firmness and effective measures should be taken in accordance with international law in order that all acts, methods and practices of international terrorism may be brought to an end,

Noting the ongoing work within the International Civil Aviation Organization regarding research as to the detection of plastic or sheet explosives and the devising of an international regime for the marking of such explosives for the purposes of detection, and taking note of Security Council Resolution 635 (1989) of 14 June 1989 relating thereto,

Taking note of Security Council Resolution 638 (1989) of 31 July 1989 on the taking of hostages,

Deeply disturbed by the world-wide persistence of acts of international terrorism in all its forms, including those in which States are directly or indirectly involved, which endanger or take innocent lives, have a deleterious effect on international relations and may jeopardize the territorial integrity and security of States,

Calling attention to the growing connection between terrorist groups and drug traffickers,

Convinced of the importance of the observance by States of their obligations under the relevant international conventions to ensure that appropriate law-enforcement measures are taken in connection with the offences
addressed in those conventions,

Convinced also of the importance of expanding and improving international cooperation among States, on a bilateral, regional and multilateral basis, which will contribute to the elimination of acts of international terrorism and their underlying causes and to the prevention and elimination of this criminal scourge,

Convinced further that international cooperation in combating and preventing terrorism will contribute to the strengthening of confidence among States, reduce tensions and create a better climate among them,

Mindful of the need to enhance the role of the United Nations and the relevant specialized agencies in combating international terrorism,

Mindful also of the necessity of maintaining and protecting the basic rights of, and guarantees for, the individual in accordance with the relevant international human rights instruments and generally accepted international standards,

Reaffirming the principle of self-determination of peoples as enshrined in the Charter of the United Nations,

Reaffirming also the inalienable right to self-determination and independence of all peoples under colonial and racist regimes and other forms of alien domination and foreign occupation, and upholding the legitimacy of their struggle, in particular the struggle of national liberation movements, in accordance with the purposes and principles of the Charter and the Declaration on Principles of International Law concerning Friendly Relations and Cooperation among States in accordance with the Charter of the United Nations,

Noting the efforts and important achievements of the International Civil Aviation Organization and the International Maritime Organization in promoting the security of international air and sea transport against acts of terrorism,

Recognizing that the effectiveness of the struggle against terrorism could be enhanced by the establishment of a generally agreed definition of international terrorism,

Taking into account the proposal made at its forty-second session to hold an international conference on international terrorism, as referred to in agenda item 139(b),

Taking note of the report of the Secretary-General,

1. Once again unequivocally *condemns*, as criminal and unjustifiable, all acts, methods and practices of terrorism wherever and by whomever committed, including those which jeopardize the friendly relations among States and their security;

2. *Deeply deplores* the loss of human lives which results from such acts of terrorism, as well as the pernicious impact of these acts on relations of cooperation among States;

3. *Calls upon* all States to fulfil their obligations under international law to refrain from organizing, instigating, assisting or participating in terrorist acts in other States, or acquiescing in or encouraging activities

within their territory directed towards the commission of such acts;

4. *Urges* all States to fulfil their obligations under international law and take effective and resolute measures for the speedy and final elimination of international terrorism and to that end, in particular:

   (a) *To prevent* the preparation and organization in their respective territories, for commission within or outside their territories, of terrorist and subversive acts directed against other States and their citizens;

   (b) *To ensure* the apprehension and prosecution or extradition of perpetrators of terrorist acts;

   (c) *To endeavour* to conclude special agreements to that effect on a bilateral, regional and multilateral basis;

   (d) *To cooperate* with one another in exchanging relevant information concerning the prevention and combating of terrorism;

   (e) *To take* promptly all steps necessary to implement the existing international conventions on this subject to which they are parties, including the harmonization of their domestic legislation with those conventions;

5. *Appeals to* all States that have not yet done so to consider becoming party to the international conventions relating to various aspects of international terrorism referred to in the preamble to the present resolution;

6. *Urges* all States, unilaterally and in cooperation with other States, as well as relevant United Nations organs, to contribute to the progressive elimination of the causes underlying international terrorism and to pay special attention to all situations, including colonialism, racism and situations involving mass and flagrant vio-

lations of human rights and fundamental freedoms and those involving alien domination and foreign occupation, that may give rise to international terrorism and may endanger international peace and security;

7. *Firmly calls for the immediate and* safe release of all hostages and abducted persons, wherever and by whomever they are being held;

8. *Calls upon* all States to use their political influence in accordance with the Charter of the United Nations and the principles of international law to secure the safe release of all hostages and abducted persons and to prevent the commission of acts of hostage-taking and abduction;

9. *Expresses* concern at the growing and dangerous links between terrorist groups, drug traffickers and their paramilitary gangs, which have resorted to all types of violence, thus endangering the constitutional order of States and violating basic human rights;

10. *Welcomes* the efforts undertaken by the International Civil Aviation Organization aimed at promoting universal acceptance of, and strict compliance with, international air-security conventions, and welcomes its recent adoption of the Protocol for the Suppression of Unlawful Acts of Violence at Airports Serving International Civil Aviation;

11. *Also welcomes* the adoption by the International Maritime Organization of the Convention for the Suppression of Unlawful Acts against the Safety of Maritime Navigation and the Protocol for the Suppression of Unlawful Acts against the Safety of Fixed Platforms located on the Continental Shelf;

12. *Urges* the International Civil Aviation Organization to intensify its work on devising an international regime for the marking of plastic or sheet explosives for the purposes of detection;

13. *Requests* the other relevant specialized agencies and intergovernmental organizations, in particular the Universal Postal Union, the World Tourism Organization and the International Atomic Energy Agency, within their respective spheres of competence, to consider what further measures can usefully be taken to combat and eliminate terrorism;

14. *Requests* the Secretary-General to continue seeking the views of Member States on international terrorism in all its aspects and on ways and means of combating it, including the convening, under the auspices of the United Nations, of an international conference to deal with international terrorism in the light of the proposal referred to in the penultimate preambular paragraph of the present resolution;

15. *Also requests* the Secretary-General to seek the views of Member States on the ways and means of enhancing the role of the United Nations and the relevant specialized agencies in combating international terrorism, as well as on proposals made during the debate on this item in the Sixth Committee at the forty-fourth session of the General Assembly;

16. *Further requests* the Secretary-General to follow up, as appropriate, the implementation of the present resolution and to submit a report in this respect to the General Assembly at its forty-sixth session;

17. *Considers* that nothing in the present resolution could in any way prejudice the right to self-determination, freedom and independence, as derived from the Charter of the United Nations, of peoples forcibly deprived of that right referred to in the

Declaration on Principles of International Law concerning Friendly Relations and Cooperation among States in accordance with the Charter of the United Nations, particularly peoples under colonial and racist regimes or other forms of alien domination, or the right of these peoples to struggle legitimately to this end and to seek and receive support in accordance with the principles of the Charter, the above-mentioned Declaration and the relevant General Assembly resolutions, including the present resolution;

18. *Decides* to include the item in the provisional agenda of its forty-sixth session.

 4.1.5.2.A *GA Res. 49/60. Measures to eliminate international terrorism*[11]

The General Assembly,
Recalling its Resolution 46/51 of 9 December 1991 and its decision 48/411 of 9 December 1993,
Taking note of the report of the Secretary-General,
Having considered in depth the question of measures to eliminate international terrorism,
Convinced that the adoption of the declaration on measures to eliminate international terrorism should contribute to the enhancement of the struggle against international terrorism,

1. *Approves* the Declaration on Measures to Eliminate International Terrorism, the text of which is annexed to the present resolution;
2. *Invites* the Secretary-General to inform all States, the Security Council, the International Court of Justice and the relevant specialized agencies, organizations and organisms of the adoption of the Declaration;
3. *Urges* that every effort be made in order that the Declaration becomes generally known and is observed and implemented in full;
4. *Urges* States, in accordance with the provisions of the Declaration, to take all appropriate measures at the national and international levels to eliminate terrorism;
5. *Invites* the Secretary-General to follow up closely the implementation of the present resolution and the Declaration, and to submit to the General Assembly at its fiftieth session a report thereon, relating, in particular, to the modalities of implementation of paragraph 10 of the Declaration;
6. *Decides* to include in the provisional agenda of its fiftieth session the item entitled 'Measures to eliminate international terrorism', in order to examine the report of the Secretary-General requested in paragraph 5 above, without prejudice to the annual or biennial consideration of the item.

4.1.5.2.B *Declaration on Measures to Eliminate International Terrorism, 1994*

The General Assembly,
Guided by the purposes and principles of the Charter of the United Nations,

---

[11] General Assembly, A/RES/49/60, 84th plenary meeting, 9 December 1994.

Recalling the Declaration on Principles of International Law concerning Friendly Relations and Cooperation among States in accordance with the Charter of the United Nations, the Declaration on the Strengthening of International Security, the Definition of Aggression, the Declaration on the Enhancement of the Effectiveness of the Principle of Refraining from the Threat or Use of Force in International Relations, the Vienna Declaration and Programme of Action, adopted by the World Conference on Human Rights, the International Covenant on Economic, Social and Cultural Rights and the International Covenant on Civil and Political Rights,

Deeply disturbed by the world-wide persistence of acts of international terrorism in all its forms and manifestations, including those in which States are directly or indirectly involved, which endanger or take innocent lives, have a deleterious effect on international relations and may jeopardize the security of States,

Deeply concerned by the increase, in many regions of the world, of acts of terrorism based on intolerance or extremism,

Concerned at the growing and dangerous links between terrorist groups and drug traffickers and their paramilitary gangs, which have resorted to all types of violence, thus endangering the constitutional order of States and violating basic human rights,

Convinced of the desirability for closer coordination and cooperation among States in combating crimes closely connected with terrorism, including drug trafficking, unlawful arms trade, money laundering and smuggling of nuclear and other potentially deadly materials, and bearing in mind the role that could be played by both the United Nations and regional organizations in this respect,

Firmly determined to eliminate international terrorism in all its forms and manifestations,

Convinced also that the suppression of acts of international terrorism, including those in which States are directly or indirectly involved, is an essential element for the maintenance of international peace and security,

Convinced further that those responsible for acts of international terrorism must be brought to justice,

Stressing the imperative need to further strengthen international cooperation between States in order to take and adopt practical and effective measures to prevent, combat and eliminate all forms of terrorism that affect the international community as a whole,

Conscious of the important role that might be played by the United Nations, the relevant specialized agencies and States in fostering widespread cooperation in preventing and combating international terrorism, inter alia, by increasing public awareness of the problem,

Recalling the existing international treaties relating to various aspects of the problem of international terrorism, inter alia, the Convention on Offences and Certain Other Acts Committed on Board Aircraft, signed atTokyo on 14 September 1963, the Convention for the Suppression of Unlawful Seizure of Aircraft, signed at The Hague on 16 December 1970, the Convention for the Suppression of Unlawful Acts against the Safety of Civil Aviation, concluded at Montreal on 23 September 1971, the Convention on the Prevention and Punishment of Crimes against Internationally Protected Persons, including Diplomatic Agents, adopted in New York on 14 December 1973, the International Convention against the Taking of Hostages, adopted

in New York on 17 December 1979, the Convention on the Physical Protection of
Nuclear Material, adopted at Vienna on 3 March 1980, the Protocol for the Suppression of Unlawful Acts of Violence at Airports Serving International Civil Aviation,
supplementary to the Convention for the Suppression of Unlawful Acts against the
Safety of Civil Aviation, signed at Montreal on 24 February 1988, the Convention
for the Suppression of Unlawful Acts against the Safety of Maritime Navigation,
done at Rome on 10 March 1988, the Protocol for the Suppression of Unlawful Acts
against the Safety of Fixed Platforms located on the Continental Shelf, done at
Rome on 10 March 1988, and the Convention on the Marking of Plastic Explosives
for the Purpose of Detection, done at Montreal on 1 March 1991,

Welcoming the conclusion of regional agreements and mutually agreed declarations
to combat and eliminate terrorism in all its forms and manifestations,

Convinced of the desirability of keeping under review the scope of existing international legal provisions to combat terrorism in all its forms and manifestations, with
the aim of ensuring a comprehensive legal framework for the prevention and elimination of terrorism,

Solemnly declares the following:

1. The States Members of the United Nations solemnly *reaffirm* their unequivocal
condemnation of all acts, methods and practices of terrorism, as criminal and unjustifiable, wherever and by whomever committed, including those which jeopardize
the friendly relations among States and peoples and threaten the territorial integrity
and security of States;

2. Acts, methods and practices of terrorism constitute a grave violation of the purposes and principles of the United Nations, which may pose a threat to international
peace and security, jeopardize friendly relations among States, hinder international
cooperation and aim at the destruction of human rights, fundamental freedoms and
the democratic bases of society;

3. Criminal acts intended or calculated to provoke a state of terror in the general
public, a group of persons or particular persons for political purposes are in any circumstance unjustifiable, whatever the considerations of a political, philosophical,
ideological, racial, ethnic, religious or any other nature that may be invoked to justify them;

4. States, guided by the purposes and principles of the Charter of the United Nations
and other relevant rules of international law, must refrain from organizing, instigating, assisting or participating in terrorist acts in territories of other States, or from
acquiescing in or encouraging activities within their territories directed towards the
commission of such acts;

5. States must also fulfil their obligations under the Charter of the United Nations
and other provisions of international law with respect to combating international terrorism and are urged to take effective and resolute measures in accordance with the
relevant provisions of international law and international standards of human rights
for the speedy and final elimination of international terrorism, in particular:

   (a) *To refrain* from organizing, instigating, facilitating, financing, encouraging
       or tolerating terrorist activities and to take appropriate practical measures to
       ensure that their respective territories are not used for terrorist installations

or training camps, or for the preparation or organization of terrorist acts intended to be committed against other States or their citizens;

(b) *To ensure* the apprehension and prosecution or extradition of perpetrators of
terrorist acts, in accordance with the relevant provisions of their national
law;

(c) *To endeavour* to conclude special agreements to that effect on a bilateral, regional and multilateral basis, and to prepare, to that effect, model agreements on cooperation;

(d) *To cooperate* with one another in exchanging relevant information concerning the prevention and combating of terrorism;

(e) *To take promptly all steps* necessary to implement the existing international
conventions on this subject to which they are parties, including the harmonization of their domestic legislation with those conventions;

(f) *To take appropriate measures*, before granting asylum, for the purpose of
ensuring that the asylum seeker has not engaged in terrorist activities and,
after granting asylum, for the purpose of ensuring that the refugee status is
not used in a manner contrary to the provisions set out in subparagraph (a)
above;

6. In order to combat effectively the increase in, and the growing international character and effects of, acts of terrorism, States should enhance their cooperation in this
area through, in particular, systematizing the exchange of information concerning
the prevention and combating of terrorism, as well as by effective implementation of
the relevant international conventions and conclusion of mutual judicial assistance
and extradition agreements on a bilateral, regional and multilateral basis;

7. In this context, States are encouraged to review urgently the scope of the existing
international legal provisions on the prevention, repression and elimination of terrorism in all its forms and manifestations, with the aim of ensuring that there is a comprehensive legal framework covering all aspects of the matter;

8. Furthermore States that have not yet done so are urged to consider, as a matter of
priority, becoming parties to the international conventions and protocols relating to
various aspects of international terrorism referred to in the preamble to the present
Declaration;

9. The United Nations, the relevant specialized agencies and intergovernmental
organizations and other relevant bodies must make every effort with a view to promoting measures to combat and eliminate acts of terrorism and to strengthening
their role in this field;

10. The Secretary-General should assist in the implementation of the present Declaration by taking, within existing resources, the following practical measures to enhance international cooperation:

(a) A collection of data on the status and implementation of existing multilateral, regional and bilateral agreements relating to international terrorism, including information on incidents caused by international terrorism and
criminal prosecutions and sentencing, based on information received from
the depositaries of those agreements and from Member States;

(b) A compendium of national laws and regulations regarding the prevention and suppression of international terrorism in all its forms and manifestations, based on information received from Member States;

(c) An analytical review of existing international legal instruments relating to international terrorism, in order to assist States in identifying aspects of this matter that have not been covered by such instruments and could be addressed to develop further a comprehensive legal framework of conventions dealing with international terrorism;

(d) A review of existing possibilities within the United Nations system for assisting States in organizing workshops and training courses on combating crimes connected with international terrorism;

11. All States are urged to promote and implement in good faith and effectively the provisions of the present Declaration in all its aspects;

12. Emphasis is placed on the need to pursue efforts aiming at liminating definitively all acts of terrorism by the strengthening of international cooperation and progressive development of international law and its codification, as well as by enhancement of coordination between, and increase of the efficiency of, the United Nations and the relevant specialized agencies, organizations and bodies.

4.1.5.3.A   *GA Res. 51/210. Measures to eliminate international terrorism 1996*[12]

The General Assembly,

Recalling its Resolution 49/60 of 9 December 1994, by which it adopted the Declaration on Measures to eliminate International Terrorism, and its Resolution 50/53 of 11 December 1995,

Recalling also the Declaration on the Occasion of the Fiftieth Anniversary of the United Nations,

Guided by the purposes and principles of the Charter of the United Nations,

Deeply disturbed by the persistence of terrorist acts, which have taken place worldwide,

Stressing the need further to strengthen international cooperation between States and between international organizations and agencies, regional organizations and arrangements and the United Nations in order to prevent, combat and eliminate terrorism in all its forms and manifestations, wherever and by whomsoever committed,

Mindful of the need to enhance the role of the United Nations and the relevant specialized agencies in combating international terrorism,

Noting, in this context, all regional and international efforts to combat international terrorism, including those of the Organization of African Unity, the Organization of American States, the Organization of the Islamic Conference, the South Asian Association for Regional Cooperation, the European Union, the Council of Europe, the Movement of Non-Aligned Countries and the countries of the group of seven major industrialized countries and the Russian Federation,

---

[12] General Assembly, A/RES/51/210, 88th plenary meeting, 17 December 1996.

Taking note of the report of the Director-General of the United Nations Educational, Scientific and Cultural Organization on educational activities under the project entitled 'Towards a culture of peace',

Recalling that in the Declaration on Measures to Eliminate International Terrorism the General Assembly encouraged States to review urgently the scope of the existing international legal provisions on the prevention, repression and elimination of terrorism in all its forms and manifestations, with the aim of ensuring that there was a comprehensive legal framework covering all aspects of the matter,

Bearing in mind the possibility of considering in the future the elaboration of a comprehensive convention on international terrorism,

Noting that terrorist attacks by means of bombs, explosives or other incendiary or lethal devices have become increasingly widespread, and stressing the need to supplement the existing legal instruments in order to address specifically the problem of terrorist attacks carried out by such means,

Recognizing the need to enhance international cooperation to prevent the use of nuclear materials for terrorist purposes and to develop an appropriate legal instrument,

Recognizing also the need to strengthen international cooperation to prevent the use of chemical and biological materials for terrorist purposes,

Convinced of the need to implement effectively and supplement the provisions of the Declaration on Measures to Eliminate International Terrorism,

Having examined the report of the Secretary-General,

1. *Strongly condemns* all acts, methods and practices of terrorism as criminal and unjustifiable, wherever and by whomsoever committed;

2. *Reiterates* that criminal acts intended or calculated to provoke a state of terror in the general public, a group of persons or particular persons for political purposes are in any circumstance unjustifiable, whatever the considerations of a political, philosophical, ideological, racial, ethnic, religious or other nature that may be invoked to justify them;

3. *Calls upon* all States to adopt further measures in accordance with the relevant provisions of international law, including international standards of human rights, to prevent terrorism and to strengthen international cooperation in combating terrorism and, to that end, to consider the adoption of measures such as those contained in the official document adopted by the group of seven major industrialized countries and the Russian Federation at the Ministerial Conference on Terrorism, held in Paris on 30 July 1996, and the plan of action adopted by the Inter-American Specialized Conference on Terrorism, held at Lima from 23 to 26 April 1996 under the auspices of the Organization of American States, and in particular calls upon all States:

(a) *To recommend* that relevant security officials undertake consultations to improve the capability of Governments to prevent, investigate and respond to terrorist attacks on public facilities, in particular means of public transport, and to cooperate with other Governments in this respect;

(b) *To accelerate* research and development regarding methods of detection of explosives and other harmful substances that can cause death or injury, undertake consultations on the development of standards for marking explosives in order to identify their origin in post-blast investigations, and promote cooperation and transfer of technology, equipment and related materials, where appropriate;

(c) *To note* the risk of terrorists using electronic or wire communications systems and networks to carry out criminal acts and the need to find means, consistent with national law, to prevent such criminality and to promote cooperation where appropriate;

(d) *To investigate*, when sufficient justification exists according to national laws, and acting within their jurisdiction and through appropriate channels of international cooperation, the abuse of organizations, groups or associations, including those with charitable, social or cultural goals, by terrorists who use them as a cover for their own activities;

(e) *To develop*, if necessary, especially by entering into bilateral and multilateral agreements and arrangements, mutual legal assistance procedures aimed at facilitating and speeding investigations and collecting evidence, as well as cooperation between law enforcement agencies in order to detect and prevent terrorist acts;

(f) *To take steps* to prevent and counteract, through appropriate domestic measures, the financing of terrorists and terrorist organizations, whether such financing is direct or indirect through organizations which also have or claim to have charitable, social or cultural goals or which are also engaged in unlawful activities such as illicit arms trafficking, drug dealing and racketeering, including the exploitation of persons for purposes of funding terrorist activities, and in particular to consider, where appropriate, adopting regulatory measures to prevent and counteract movements of funds suspected to be intended for terrorist purposes without impeding in any way the freedom of legitimate capital movements and to intensify the exchange of information concerning international movements of such funds;

4. Also *calls upon* all States, with the aim of enhancing the efficient implementation of relevant legal instruments, to intensify, as and where appropriate, the exchange of information on facts related to terrorism and, in so doing, to avoid the dissemination of inaccurate or unverified information;

5. *Reiterates* its call upon States to refrain from financing, encouraging, providing training for or otherwise supporting terrorist activities;

6. *Urges* all States that have not yet done so to consider, as a matter of priority, becoming parties to the Convention on Offences and Certain Other Acts Committed on Board Aircraft, signed at Tokyo on 14 September 1963, the Convention for the Suppression of Unlawful Seizure of Aircraft, signed at The Hague on 16 December 1970, the Convention for the Suppression of Unlawful Acts against the Safety of Civil Aviation, concluded at Montreal on 23 September 1971, the Convention on the Prevention and Punishment of Crimes against Internationally Protected Persons, including Diplomatic Agents, adopted in New York on 14 December 1973, the International Convention against the Taking of Hostages, adopted in New York on 17 December 1979, the Convention on the Physical Protection of Nuclear Material, signed at Vienna on 3 March 1980, the Protocol for the Suppression of Unlawful Acts of Violence at Airports Serving International Civil Aviation, supplementary to the Convention for the Suppression of Unlawful Acts against the Safety of Civil

Aviation, signed at Montreal on 24 February 1988, the Convention for the Suppression of Unlawful Acts against the Safety of Maritime Navigation, done at Rome on 10 March 1988, the Protocol for the Suppression of Unlawful Acts against the Safety of Fixed Platforms located on the Continental Shelf, done at Rome on 10 March 1988, and the Convention on the Marking of Plastic Explosives for the Purpose of Detection, done at Montreal on 1 March 1991, and calls upon all States to enact, as appropriate, domestic legislation necessary to implement the provisions of those Conventions and Protocols, to ensure that the jurisdiction of their courts enables them to bring to trial the perpetrators of terrorist acts and to provide support and assistance to other Governments for those purposes;

7. *Reaffirms* the Declaration on Measures to Eliminate International Terrorism contained in the annex to Resolution 49/60;

8. *Approves* the Declaration to Supplement the 1994 Declaration on Measures to Eliminate International Terrorism, the text of which is annexed to the present resolution;

9. *Decides* to establish an Ad Hoc Committee, open to all States Members of the United Nations or members of specialized agencies or of the International Atomic Energy Agency, to elaborate an international convention for the suppression of terrorist bombings and, subsequently, an international convention for the suppression of acts of nuclear terrorism, to supplement related existing international instruments, and thereafter to address means of further developing a comprehensive legal framework of conventions dealing with international terrorism;

10. *Decides* also that the Ad Hoc Committee will meet from 24 February to 7 March 1997 to prepare the text of a draft international convention for the suppression of terrorist bombings, and recommends that work continue during the fifty-second session of the General Assembly from 22 September to 3 October 1997 in the framework of a working group of the Sixth Committee;

11. *Requests* the Secretary-General to provide the Ad Hoc Committee with the necessary facilities for the performance of its work;

12. *Requests* the Ad Hoc Committee to report to the General Assembly at its fifty-second session on progress made towards the elaboration of the draft convention;

13. *Recommends* that the Ad Hoc Committee be convened in 1998 to continue its work as referred to in paragraph 9 above;

14. *Decides* to include in the provisional agenda of its fifty-second session the item entitled 'Measures to eliminate international terrorism'.

4.1.5.3.B   *Declaration to Supplement the 1994 Declaration on Measures to*
            Eliminate International Terrorism 1996

The General Assembly,
Guided by the purposes and principles of the Charter of the United Nations,
Recalling the Declaration on Measures to Eliminate International Terrorism adopted by the General Assembly by its Resolution 49/60 of 9 December 1994,
Recalling also the Declaration on the Occasion of the Fiftieth Anniversary of the United Nations,

Deeply disturbed by the worldwide persistence of acts of international terrorism in all its forms and manifestations, including those in which States are directly or indirectly involved, which endanger or take innocent lives, have a deleterious effect on international relations and may jeopardize the security of States,

Underlining the importance of States developing extradition agreements or arrangements as necessary in order to ensure that those responsible for terrorist acts are brought to justice,

Noting that the Convention relating to the Status of Refugees, done at Geneva on 28 July 1951, does not provide a basis for the protection of perpetrators of terrorist acts, noting also in this context articles 1, 2, 32 and 33 of the Convention, and emphasizing in this regard the need for States parties to ensure the proper application of the Convention,

Stressing the importance of full compliance by States with their obligations under the provisions of the 1951 Convention and the 1967 Protocol relating to the Status of Refugees, including the principle of non-refoulement of refugees to places where their life or freedom would be threatened on account of their race, religion, nationality, membership in a particular social group or political opinion, and affirming that the present Declaration does not affect the protection afforded under the terms of the Convention and Protocol and other provisions of international law,

Recalling article 4 of the Declaration on Territorial Asylum adopted by the General Assembly by its Resolution 2312 (XXII) of 14 December 1967,

Stressing the need further to strengthen international cooperation between States in order to prevent, combat and eliminate terrorism in all its forms and manifestations, Solemnly declares the following:

1. The States Members of the United Nations solemnly *reaffirm* their unequivocal condemnation of all acts, methods and practices of terrorism as criminal and unjustifiable, wherever and by whomsoever committed, including those which jeopardize friendly relations among States and peoples and threaten the territorial integrity and security of States;

2. The States Members of the United Nations *reaffirm* that acts, methods and practices of terrorism are contrary to the purposes and principles of the United Nations; they declare that knowingly financing, planning and inciting terrorist acts are also contrary to the purposes and principles of the United Nations;

3. The States Members of the United Nations *reaffirm* that States should take appropriate measures in conformity with the relevant provisions of national and international law, including international standards of human rights, before granting refugee status, for the purpose of ensuring that the asylum-seeker has not participated in terrorist acts, considering in this regard relevant information as to whether the asylum-seeker is subject to investigation for or is charged with or has been convicted of offences connected with terrorism and, after granting refugee status, for the purpose of ensuring that that status is not used for the purpose of preparing or organizing terrorist acts intended to be committed against other States or their citizens;

4. The States Members of the United Nations *emphasize* that asylum-seekers who are awaiting the processing of their asylum applications may not thereby avoid prosecution for terrorist acts;

5. The States Members of the United Nations *reaffirm* the importance of ensuring effective cooperation between Member States so that those who have participated in terrorist acts, including their financing, planning or incitement, are brought to justice; they stress their commitment, in conformity with the relevant provisions of international law, including international standards of human rights, to work together to prevent, combat and eliminate terrorism and to take all appropriate steps under their domestic laws either to extradite terrorists or to submit the cases to their competent authorities for the purpose of prosecution;

6. In this context, and while *recognizing* the sovereign rights of States in extradition matters, States *are encouraged*, when concluding or applying extradition agreements, not to regard as political offences excluded from the scope of those agreements offences connected with terrorism which endanger or represent a physical threat to the safety and security of persons, whatever the motives which may be invoked to justify them;

7. States *are also encouraged*, even in the absence of a treaty, to consider facilitating the extradition of persons suspected of having committed terrorist acts, insofar as their national laws permit;

8. The States Members of the United Nations *emphasize* the importance of taking steps to share expertise and information about terrorists, their movements, their support and their weapons and to share information regarding the investigation and prosecution of terrorist acts.

4.1.5.4 *GA Res. 56/1. Condemnation of terrorist attacks in the United States of America, 2001*[13]

The General Assembly,
Guided by the purposes and principles of the Charter of the United Nations,

1. *Strongly condemns* the heinous acts of terrorism, which have caused enormous loss of human life, destruction and damage in the cities of New York, host city of the United Nations, and Washington, D.C., and in Pennsylvania;

2. *Expresses its condolences and solidarity* with the people and Government of the United States of America in these sad and tragic circumstances;

3. *Urgently calls* for international cooperation to bring to justice the perpetrators, organizers and sponsors of the outrages of 11 September 2001;

4. *Also urgently calls* for international cooperation to prevent and eradicate acts of terrorism, and stresses that those responsible for aiding, supporting or harbouring the perpetrators, organizers and sponsors of such acts will be held accountable.

---

[13] United Nations General Assembly Fifty-sixth session, *1st plenary meeting, 12 September 2001.*

4.1.5.5 *GA Res. 56/88. Measures to eliminate international terrorism, 2001*[14]

The General Assembly,
Guided by the purposes and principles of the Charter of the United Nations,
Recalling the Declaration on the Occasion of the Fiftieth Anniversary of the United Nations,[15]
Recalling also the United Nations Millennium Declaration,[16]
Recalling further all General Assembly and Security Council resolutions on measures to eliminate international terrorism,
Convinced of the importance of the consideration of measures to eliminate international terrorism by the General Assembly as the universal organ having competence to do so,
Deeply disturbed by the persistence of terrorist acts, which have been carried out worldwide,
Reaffirming its strong condemnation of the heinous acts of terrorism that caused enormous loss of human life, destruction and damage in the cities of New York, host city of the United Nations, and Washington, D.C., and in Pennsylvania, which prompted the adoption of General Assembly Resolution 56/1 of 12 September 2001, as well as Security Council Resolutions 1368 (2001) of 12 September 2001, 1373 (2001) of 28 September 2001 and 1377 (2001) of 12 November 2001,
Recalling its debate on the item entitled 'Measures to eliminate international terrorism', held in plenary meeting from 1 to 5 October 2001,
Stressing the need to strengthen further international cooperation among States and among international organizations and agencies, regional organizations and arrangements and the United Nations in order to prevent, combat and eliminate terrorism in all its forms and manifestations, wherever and by whomsoever committed, in accordance with the principles of the Charter, international law and relevant international conventions,
Mindful of the need to enhance the role of the United Nations and the relevant specialized agencies in combating international terrorism, and of the proposals of the Secretary-General to enhance the role of the Organization in this respect,
Recalling the Declaration on Measures to Eliminate International Terrorism, contained in the annex to Resolution 49/60 of 9 December 1994, wherein the General Assembly encouraged States to review urgently the scope of the existing international legal provisions on the prevention, repression and elimination of terrorism in all its forms and manifestations, with the aim of ensuring that there was a comprehensive legal framework covering all aspects of the matter,
Taking note of the final document of the Thirteenth Ministerial Conference of the Movement of Non-Aligned Countries, held at Cartagena, Colombia, on 8 and 9 April 2000,[17] which reiterated the collective position of the Movement of Non-

---

[14] General Assembly 56/88, Fifty-sixth session, Resolution adopted by the General Assembly, 12 December 2001, *[on the report of the Sixth Committee (A/56/593)]*.
[15] See Resolution 50/6.
[16] See Resolution 55/2.
[17] A/54/917-S/2000/580, annex.

Aligned Countries on terrorism and reaffirmed the previous initiative of the Twelfth Conference of Heads of State or Government of Non-Aligned Countries, held at Durban, South Africa, from 29 August to 3 September 1998,[18] calling for an international summit conference under the auspices of the United Nations to formulate a joint organized response of the international community to terrorism in all its forms and manifestations, and other relevant initiatives,

Recalling its decision in Resolutions 54/110 of 9 December 1999 and 55/158 of 12 December 2000 that the Ad Hoc Committee established by General Assembly Resolution 51/210 of 17 December 1996 should address, and keep on its agenda, the question of convening a high-level conference under the auspices of the United Nations to formulate a joint organized response of the international community to terrorism in all its forms and manifestations,

Noting regional efforts to prevent, combat and eliminate terrorism in all its forms and manifestations, wherever and by whomsoever committed, including through the elaboration of and adherence to regional conventions,

Having examined the report of the Secretary-General,[19] the report of the Ad Hoc Committee[20] and the report of the Working Group of the Sixth Committee established pursuant to Resolution 55/158,[21]

1. *Strongly condemns* all acts, methods and practices of terrorism as criminal and unjustifiable, wherever and by whomsoever committed;

2. *Reiterates* that criminal acts intended or calculated to provoke a state of terror in the general public, a group of persons or particular persons for political purposes are in any circumstances unjustifiable, whatever the considerations of a political, philosophical, ideological, racial, ethnic, religious or other nature that may be invoked to justify them;

3. *Reiterates its call* upon all States to adopt further measures in accordance with the Charter of the United Nations and the relevant provisions of international law, including international standards of human rights, to prevent terrorism and to strengthen international cooperation in combating terrorism and, to that end, to consider in particular the implementation of the measures set out in paragraphs 3(a) to (f) of Resolution 51/210; consider in particular the implementation of the measures set out in paragraphs 3(a) to (f) of Resolution 51/210;

4. *Also reiterates its call* upon all States, with the aim of enhancing the efficient implementation of relevant legal instruments, to intensify, as and where appropriate, the exchange of information on facts related to terrorism and, in so doing, to avoid the dissemination of inaccurate or unverified information;

5. *Further reiterates its call* upon States to refrain from financing, encouraging, providing training for or otherwise supporting terrorist activities;

---

[18] See A/53/667-S/1998/1071, annex I, paras. 149-162.
[19] A/56/160 and Corr.1 and Add.1.
[20] Official Records of the General Assembly, 56th session, Supplement No. 37 (A/56/37).
[21] A/C.6/56/L.9.

6. *Reaffirms* that international cooperation as well as actions by States to combat terrorism should be conducted in conformity with the principles of the Charter, international law and relevant international conventions;

7. *Urges* all States that have not yet done so to consider, as a matter of priority, and in accordance with Security Council Resolution 1373 (2001), becoming parties to relevant conventions and protocols as referred to in paragraph 6 of General Assembly Resolution 51/210, as well as the International Convention for the Suppression of Terrorist Bombings[22] and the International Convention for the Suppression of the Financing of Terrorism,[23] and calls upon all States to enact, as appropriate, domestic legislation necessary to implement the provisions of those conventions and protocols, to ensure that the jurisdiction of their courts enables them to bring to trial the perpetrators of terrorist acts, and to cooperate with and provide support and assistance to other States and relevant international and regional organizations to that end;

8. *Urges* States to cooperate with the Secretary-General and with one another, as well as with interested intergovernmental organizations, with a view to ensuring, where appropriate within existing mandates, that technical and other expert advice is provided to those States requiring and requesting assistance in becoming parties to the conventions and protocols referred to in paragraph 7 above;

9. *Notes with appreciation and satisfaction* that, consistent with the call contained in paragraph 7 of General Assembly Resolution 55/158, a number of States became parties to the relevant conventions and protocols referred to therein, thereby realizing the objective of wider acceptance and implementation of those conventions;

10. *Reaffirms* the Declaration on Measures to Eliminate International Terrorism, contained in the annex to Resolution 49/60, and the Declaration to Supplement the 1994 Declaration on Measures to Eliminate International Terrorism, contained in the annex to Resolution 51/210, and calls upon all States to implement them;

11. *Urges* all States and the Secretary-General, in their efforts to prevent international terrorism, to make best use of the existing institutions of the United Nations;

12. *Welcomes* the efforts of the Terrorism Prevention Branch of the Centre for International Crime Prevention in Vienna, after reviewing existing possibilities within the United Nations system, to enhance, through its mandate, the capabilities of the United Nations in the prevention of terrorism;

13. *Invites* States that have not yet done so to submit to the Secretary-General information on their national laws and regulations regarding the prevention and suppression of acts of international terrorism;

14. *Invites* regional intergovernmental organizations to submit to the Secretary-General information on the measures they have adopted at the regional level to eliminate international terrorism;

15. *Welcomes* the important progress attained in the elaboration of the draft comprehensive convention on international terrorism during the meetings of the Ad Hoc Committee established by General Assembly Resolution 51/210 of 17 December

---

[22] Resolution 52/164, annex.
[23] Resolution 54/109, annex.

1996 and the Working Group of the Sixth Committee established pursuant to General Assembly Resolution 55/158;

16. *Decides* that the Ad Hoc Committee shall continue to elaborate a comprehensive convention on international terrorism as a matter of urgency, and shall continue its efforts to resolve the outstanding issues relating to the elaboration of a draft international convention for the suppression of acts of nuclear terrorism as a means of further developing a comprehensive legal framework of conventions dealing with international terrorism, and that it shall keep on its agenda the question of convening a high-level conference under the auspices of the United Nations to formulate a joint organized response of the international community to terrorism in all its forms and manifestations;

17. *Also decides* that the Ad Hoc Committee shall meet from 28 January to 1 February 2002 to continue the elaboration of a draft comprehensive convention on international terrorism, with appropriate time allocated to the continued consideration of outstanding issues relating to the elaboration of a draft international convention for the suppression of acts of nuclear terrorism, that it shall keep on its agenda the question of convening a high-level conference under the auspices of the United Nations to formulate a joint organized response of the international community to terrorism in all its forms and manifestations, and that the work shall continue, if necessary, during the fifty-seventh session of the General Assembly, within the framework of a working group of the Sixth Committee;

18. *Requests* the Secretary-General to continue to provide the Ad Hoc Committee with the necessary facilities for the performance of its work;

19. *Requests* the Ad Hoc Committee to report to the General Assembly at its fifty-sixth session in the event of the completion of the draft comprehensive convention on international terrorism or the draft international convention for the suppression of acts of nuclear terrorism;

20. *Also requests* the Ad Hoc Committee to report to the General Assembly at its fifty-seventh session on progress made in the implementation of its mandate;

21. *Decides* to include in the provisional agenda of its fifty-seventh session the item entitled 'Measures to eliminate international terrorism'.

4.1.5.6 *2002 Report Ad Hoc Committee*[24]

Report of the Ad Hoc Committee established by General Assembly Resolution 51/210 of 17 December 1996

1. The sixth session of the Ad Hoc Committee established by General Assembly Resolution 51/210 of 17 December 1996 was convened in accordance with paragraphs 16 and 17 of Assembly Resolution 56/88 of 12 December 2001. The Committee met at Headquarters from 28 January to 1 February 2002.

---

[24] Sixth session (28 January-1 February 2002) GAOR, 57th session, Supplement No. 37 (A/57/37).

2. In accordance with paragraph 9 of General Assembly Resolution 51/210, the Ad Hoc Committee was open to all States Members of the United Nations or members of specialized agencies or of the International Atomic Energy Agency (IAEA).
(…)
8. The Ad Hoc Committee held five meetings: the 22nd and the 23rd, on 28 January; the 24th, on 30 January; the 25th, on 31 January; and the 26th, on 1 February 2002.
9. At the 23rd meeting, the Ad Hoc Committee adopted its work programme and decided to proceed with discussions in informal consultations. The informal consultations were coordinated by the Vice-Chairman, Mr. Richard Rowe.
10. The informal consultations were held in two stages. The first commenced with discussion on article 18 of the draft comprehensive convention and was followed by consideration of the preamble and article 1 of the draft convention.
11. The second stage, the informal consultations, focused on the outstanding issues pertaining to the draft international convention for the suppression of acts of nuclear terrorism. The representative of IAEA briefed delegations on the measures under consideration by the Agency aimed at combating acts of terrorism involving nuclear materials and other radioactive materials.
(…)
20. At the 26th meeting, the Ad Hoc Committee, bearing in mind General Assembly Resolution 56/88, decided to recommend that the Sixth Committee, at the fifty-seventh session of the General Assembly, consider establishing a working group, preferably to be convened from 14 to 18 October 2002, to continue, as a matter of urgency, the elaboration of a draft comprehensive convention on international terrorism,[25] with appropriate time allocated to the continued consideration of outstanding issues relating to the elaboration of a draft international convention for the suppression of acts of nuclear terrorism, and keeping on its agenda the question of convening a high-level conference under the auspices of the United Nations to formulate a joint organized response of the international community to terrorism in all its forms and manifestations.

---

[25] (Ed.) The draft comprehensive convention has been included in this Volume in Chapter 5.1.

4.2   THE SECURITY COUNCIL

4.2.1   **Survey**

Totally different from the General Assembly and its dual approach (on the one hand the resolutions fielded by the Sixth Committee, on the other the ones emanating from the Third Committee), the Security Council has persistently delivered resolutions which leave no doubt as to their language, meaning or direction.

Of course, the Security Council (SC), being exposed to the mechanism of veto voting (the five SC permanent members enjoy a veto), was up until 1989 basically a victim of ideological warfare. The SC was basically not able to agree on terrorism-related issues until 1989.
Resolutions have since then been adopted on the following issues:

- marking of plastic or sheet explosives for the purpose of detection; SC Res. 635 (1989);
- on the destruction of Pan American flight 103 and Union des transports aériens flight 772; SC Res. 731 (1992);
- on sanctions against the Libyan Arab Jamahiriya; SC Res. 748 (1992);
- calling upon Sudan to extradite to Ethiopia the three suspects wanted in connection with the assassination attempt against President Mubarak of Egypt; SC Res. 1044 (1996);
- on sanctions against Sudan in connection with non-compliance with SC Res. 1044 (1996) demanding extradition to Ethiopia of the three suspects wanted in connection with the assassination attempt on President Mubarak of Egypt; SC Res. 1054 (1996);
- concerning the terrorist bomb attacks of 7 August 1998 in Kenya and Tanzania SC Res. 1189 (1998);
- on the situation in Afghanistan; SC Res. 1214 (1998);
- on measures against the Taliban; SC Res. 1267 (1999) and 1333 (2000);
- on international cooperation in the fight against terrorism; **SC Res. 1269 (1999);**
- on the establishment of a mechanism to monitor the implementation of measures imposed by Resolutions 1267 (1999) and 1333 (2000) [i.e. on the Taliban]; SC Res. 1363 (2001);
- condemning the terrorist attacks of 11 September 2001 in New York, Washington, D.C. and Pennsylvania, United States of America; **SC Res. 1368 (2001);**
- on international cooperation to combat threats to international peace and security caused by terrorist acts; **SC Res. 1373 (2001)** [under this resolution, the SC

established a Committee to monitor implementation of that resolution, the counter-terrorism committee CTC];
- reaffirmation on the ministerial level of SC Res. 1373; **SC Res. 1377 (2001,** November 12th);
- confirming and elaborating on the fight against the Taliban; SC Res. 1378 (2001, November 14th).[1]

From the above it should be concluded that Resolutions 1269, 1368, 1373 and 1377 are the main instruments to have regard to. The most striking element contained in these resolutions is the very fact that the subject is being dealt with within the realm of Chapter VII, on threats against the peace. Terrorism is no longer a nuisance, an aberration, but is now considered worthy of being labelled a threat to the peace or even an act of aggression. The Security Council unanimously agreed that terrorism constitutes not just a threat but one of the most serious threats to peace. In the context of 1377 the following should hence be noted:

Declaring that acts of international terrorism constitute one of the most serious threats to international peace and security in the twenty-first century, and that such acts further constitute a challenge to all countries and all humanity, the Security Council on 12 November called on all States to intensify their efforts to eliminate international terrorism.

It took that action at the end of a ministerial meeting when it unanimously adopted Resolution 1377 (2001). By other terms it affirmed that a sustained, comprehensive approach, involving the active participation and collaboration of Member States was essential to combat international terrorism.

The Council stressed that continuing international efforts to broaden the understanding among civilizations and to address regional conflicts and the full range of global issues, including those related to development, would contribute to international cooperation and collaboration, which themselves were necessary to sustain the broadest possible fight against international terrorism. States were also called on to become parties as soon as possible to the international conventions and protocols relating to terrorism.

The text further called on States to take urgent steps to fully implement Resolution 1373 (2001), and to assist each other in doing so. It also underlined the obligation of States to deny financial and all other forms of support and safe haven to terrorists and the supporters of terrorism.

On 28 September, the Council adopted Resolution 1373 (2001) – a wide-ranging comprehensive resolution with steps and strategies to combat international terrorism. By that text, the Council established a Committee to monitor the implementation of the resolution and called on all States to report on action they had taken to that end no later than 90 days from 28 September. Among the steps and strategies were calls for suppressing the financing of terrorism and improving international cooperation in the area of counter-terrorism activities.

By other terms of this latest resolution, the Council expressed its determination to proceed with the implementation of Resolution 1373 (2001) in full cooperation with the whole United Nations membership, and welcomed the progress made so far by the Counter-Terrorism Committee to monitor implementation of the resolution.

Furthermore the Council recognized that many States would require assistance in imple-

---

[1] The Resolutions indicated in bold have been included in full in sub-chapter 4.2.3.

menting all the requirements of 1373 (2001), and invited such States to inform the Counter-Terrorism Committee of areas in which they required support.

Secretary-General Kofi Annan said the United Nations was uniquely placed to facilitate cooperation between governments in the fight against terrorism. That fight must begin with ensuring that the existing instruments on international terrorism under United Nations auspices were signed, ratified and implemented without delay by all States. It was also important to obtain agreement on a comprehensive convention on international terrorism. He emphasized the need for moral clarity and said there could be no acceptance of those who sought to justify the deliberate taking of innocent civilian life regardless of cause or grievance.

'Action is needed and action is needed now', United States Secretary of State Colin Powell said. His country was taking the fight directly to the terrorists and their supporters. The swift action of the Council had made clear that the perpetrators and their supporters would be held accountable. Resolution 1373 (2001) was a mandate to fundamentally change how the international community responded to terrorism – but to be effective, it required a new resolve. States must now work together bilaterally and multilaterally.

For many, he said, implementation of the resolution would involve complicated and difficult challenges to their legal systems and require changes on many levels. The United States was ready to provide technical assistance in areas ranging from aviation security to the tracking measures used by law enforcement (…).[2]

4.2.2   Analysis

Already before 1989 the Security Council proved that the dual system, resulting in GA Resolutions which are rightly called soft law, can in no way be compared with the SC's hard law resolutions. The gap in conception, perception and outcome is sometimes staggering and demonstrates that the drafters of the Charter had some foresight which has prevented the UN from falling apart.

Yet, the difference in tone, subject and outcome is every now and then remarkable and would appear to indicate that more efforts need to be undertaken to bridge the gaps. It is also important that understanding and appreciation for the role of the Security Council be enhanced in no uncertain terms. Then again, it should be stressed that the important 1999 resolution, which indeed set the SC tone, is very much based on the GA texts of 1994 and 1996. As we saw above, those GA texts can be commended for their pragmatism and realism[3] and it thus should thus come as no surprise that when the GA displays a constructive approach, the SC is ready to elaborate on a job well done.

As can be seen from the resolutions which have been included in this Volume, and which in tone and substance do not differ significantly from the other resolutions related to terrorism which had been adopted before 1999, the SC has embarked on a process which at the end of the day should include a comprehensive approach. The main pitfalls will relate to the issue of state terrorism, but as the present draft of a comprehensive convention shows, progress has been made and results can be expected in the not too distant future.

---

[2] UN Association U.K: press release.
[3] Which, as we saw above in Chapter 4.1, can not be said of all GA resolutions.

The hierarchy in international law making should be stressed again and again. As we will see below, a UNHCR document 'concluding' that SC Resolution 1373 (2001) is in accordance with international human rights law would appear to indicate that the drafter of that document does not fully appreciate that the SC indicates the direction in which human rights law will go, rather than the other way around. In this respect it was not surprising that the tenure of the 1997-2002 High Commissioner for Human Rights was not extended.

The four most relevant Resolutions are 1269, 1368, 1373 and 1377. Of these 1269 and 1373 are quintessential. 1368 was a unique reaction to the 11th of September events, as it was already adopted one day afterwards. And 1377, apart from welcoming the 1-5 October 2001 GA session on terrorism, merely reconfirms 1373.

The 2001 resolutions are also very important as they convincingly place terrorism within the realm of Charter Chapter VII on threats to the peace. This is a most significant development which has a major impact on the issue and the various legal responses. These resolutions have thereby become the cornerstone of the international legal order concerned.

The most important conclusion that can be drawn from a comparison between SC Res. 1269 and SC Res. 1373 is that the points of view, the line of thinking and the goal to be attained do not differ significantly. In other words, the September 2001 events have not forced the Security Council to change track. 1373 should hence be seen as an elaboration of 1269. It mainly reinforced the need to strive for tangible results. Of course, a few new points of attention were added, like the additional focus on those who *support* terrorists or terrorist acts. Also a Special Committee to monitor the implementation of this Resolution was set up under the aegis of the Security Council, in accordance with rule 28 of the provisional rules of procedure, which indeed may make some difference.

For this survey it suffices to refer to the texts of the SC Resolutions 1269, 1368, 1373 and 1377, resolutions which have all been included in full in this Volume. Moreover, the UN press release of 28th of September 2001 would appear to correctly summarize the various motions and environment. Due note should be taken of the fact that that day's meeting started at 10:50 pm and concluded at 10:53 pm, a sign of proper preparation and total agreement.

> Security Council unanimously adopts wide-ranging anti-terrorism resolution; calls for suppressing financing, improving international cooperation.
> Resolution 1373 (2001) also creates committee to monitor implementation.
> Reaffirming its unequivocal condemnation of the terrorist acts that took place in New York, Washington, D.C., and Pennsylvania on 11 September, the Security Council this evening unanimously adopted a wide-ranging, comprehensive resolution with steps and strategies to combat international terrorism.
> By Resolution 1373 (2001) the Council also established a Committee of the Council to monitor the resolution's implementation and called on all States to report on actions they had taken to that end no later than 90 days from today.
> Under terms of the text, the Council decided that all States should prevent and suppress the financing of terrorism, as well as criminalize the wilful provision or collection of funds for such acts. The funds, financial assets and economic resources of those who

commit or attempt to commit terrorist acts or participate in or facilitate the commission of terrorist acts and of persons and entities acting on behalf of terrorists should also be frozen without delay.

The Council also decided that States should prohibit their nationals or persons or entities in their territories from making funds, financial assets, economic resources, financial or other related services available to persons who commit or attempt to commit, facilitate or participate in the commission of terrorist acts. States should also refrain from providing any form of support to entities or persons involved in terrorist acts; take the necessary steps to prevent the commission of terrorist acts; deny safe haven to those who finance, plan, support, commit terrorist acts and provide safe havens as well.

By other terms, the Council decided that all States should prevent those who finance, plan, facilitate or commit terrorist acts from using their respective territories for those purposes against other countries and their citizens. States should also ensure that anyone who has participated in the financing, planning, preparation or perpetration of terrorist acts or in supporting terrorist acts is brought to justice. They should also ensure that terrorist acts are established as serious criminal offences in domestic laws and regulations and that the seriousness of such acts is duly reflected in sentences served.

By further terms, the Council decided that States should afford one another the greatest measure of assistance for criminal investigations or criminal proceedings relating to the financing or support of terrorist acts. States should also prevent the movement of terrorists or their groups by effective border controls as well.

Also by the text, the Council called on all States to intensify and accelerate the exchange of information regarding terrorist actions or movements; forged or falsified documents; traffic in arms and sensitive material; use of communications and technologies by terrorist groups; and the threat posed by the possession of weapons of mass destruction.

States were also called on to exchange information and cooperate to prevent and suppress terrorist acts and to take action against the perpetrators of such acts. States should become parties to, and fully implement as soon as possible, the relevant international conventions and protocols to combat terrorism.

By the text, before granting refugee status, all States should take appropriate measures to ensure that the asylum seekers had not planned, facilitated or participated in terrorist acts. Further, States should ensure that refugee status was not abused by the perpetrators, organizers or facilitators of terrorist acts, and that claims of political motivation were not recognized as grounds for refusing requests for the extradition of alleged terrorists.

The Council noted with concern the close connection between international terrorism and transnational organized crime, illicit drugs, money laundering and illegal movement of nuclear, chemical, biological and other deadly materials. In that regard, it emphasized the need to enhance the coordination of national, subregional, regional and international efforts to strengthen a global response to that threat to international security.

Reaffirming the need to combat by all means, in accordance with the Charter, threats to international peace and security caused by terrorist acts, the Council expressed its determination to take all necessary steps to fully implement the current resolution.

4.2.3 The Counter-Terrorism Committee (CTC)

This Committee which was, as we saw, established pursuant to SC Res. 1373(2001) has the following mandate:
'to monitor implementation of this resolution, with the assistance of appropriate expertise'. It consists of all the 15 members of the Council. It is assisted by appropri-

ate experts. Accordingly, the Committee invited all States in a position to do so, to contribute to the compilation of a directory of sources of advice and expertise in the areas of legislative and administrative practice (SC A/20/01(8)). The directory is divided into eight sections broadly corresponding to the areas of activity covered by Resolution 1373 and reflected in the Committee's first Work Programme (S/2001/986):

- drafting of counter-terrorism legislation;
- financial law and practice;
- customs law and practice;
- immigration law and practice;
- extradition law and practice;
- police and enforcement work;
- illegal arms trafficking;
- other.

As in most bureaucracies a letter was sent out to the UN Member States with a questionnaire on the steps taken (pursuant to para. 6 of 1373). Responses were received, but it remains to be seen whether this Committee will be as effective as needed. A March 2002 press release is perhaps illustrative and might give reason for some doubt:

> Ambassador Greenstock, Chairman of the Counter-Terrorism Committee, briefed interested Member States on 11 March on work of the CTC. He said the Sub-Committees had considered over 50 reports to date, and would continue to keep up the pace.
> The CTC had been briefed on 28 February by the Secretary-General of the Organisation of American States (OAS) on the work it was doing to improve cooperation in the area of counter-terrorism. The OAS had formed an international committee to take this forward and to act as a forum for Member States to share best practice.
> Ambassador Greenstock said the CTC would continue to develop links with other international and regional organisations.
> The Directory of Assistance had been established and was available to Member States on the CTC website. It would be updated as new information was made available.
> Ambassador Greenstock said the CTC had agreed to the appointment of an additional expert to take forward work in the area of assistance to Member States and hoped to appoint the expert by the end of April. The expert would liaise with States, international and regional organisations on assistance matters.

Yet, it is hereby submitted that as long as the permanent SC members agree on the rationale behind the fight or war against terrorism, the CTC may be able to avoid the fate of a great many committees and commissions, and may after all be able to 'deliver'.

4.2.4   SC Resolutions relevant to terrorism

This sub-chapter contains the four most relevant SC Resolutions: 1269 (1999) and the September-November 2001 ones: 1368, 1373 and 1377, respectively to be found herein as 4.2.4.1-4.2.4.4. It is once again underlined that the issue of terrorism has been firmly placed within the realm of UN Charter Chapter VII and that the 'ministerial' Resolution 1377 subscribes to the utmost importance of SC Res. 1373 (2001).

4.2.4.1 *SC Resolution 1269 (1999)*[4]

The Security Council,

Deeply concerned by the increase in acts of international terrorism which endangers the lives and well-being of individuals worldwide as well as the peace and security of all States,

Condemning all acts of terrorism, irrespective of motive, wherever and by whomever committed,

Mindful of all relevant resolutions of the General Assembly, including Resolution 49/60 of 9 December 1994, by which it adopted the Declaration on Measures to Eliminate International Terrorism,

Emphasizing the necessity to intensify the fight against terrorism at the national level and to strengthen, under the auspices of the United Nations, effective international cooperation in this field on the basis of the principles of the Charter of the United Nations and norms of international law, including respect for international humanitarian law and human rights,

Supporting the efforts to promote universal participation in and implementation of the existing international anti-terrorist conventions, as well as to develop new international instruments to counter the terrorist threat,

Commending the work done by the General Assembly, relevant United Nations organs and specialized agencies and regional and other organizations to combat international terrorism,

Determined to contribute, in accordance with the Charter of the United Nations, to the efforts to combat terrorism in all its forms,

Reaffirming that the suppression of acts of international terrorism, including those in which States are involved, is an essential contribution to the maintenance of international peace and security,

1. *Unequivocally condemns* all acts, methods and practices of terrorism as criminal and unjustifiable, regardless of their motivation, in all their forms and manifestations, wherever and by whomever committed, in particular those which could threaten international peace and security;

2. *Calls upon* all States to implement fully the international anti-terrorist conventions to which they are parties, *encourages* all States to consider as a matter of priority adhering to those to which they are not parties, and *encourages also* the speedy adoption of the pending conventions;

3. *Stresses* the vital role of the United Nations in strengthening international cooperation in combating terrorism and, *emphasizes* the importance of enhanced coordination among States, international and regional organizations;

4. *Calls upon* all States to take, inter alia, in the context of such cooperation and coordination, appropriate steps to:

---

[4] Adopted by the Security Council at its 4053rd meeting on 19 October 1999.

- cooperate with each other, particularly through bilateral and multilateral agreements and arrangements, to prevent and suppress terrorist acts, protect their nationals and other persons against terrorist attacks and bring to justice the perpetrators of such acts;
- prevent and suppress in their territories through all lawful means the preparation and financing of any acts of terrorism;
- deny those who plan, finance or commit terrorist acts safe havens by ensuring their apprehension and prosecution or extradition;
- take appropriate measures in conformity with the relevant provisions of national and international law, including international standards of human rights, before granting refugee status, for the purpose of ensuring that the asylum-seeker has not participated in terrorist acts;
- exchange information in accordance with international and domestic law, and cooperate on administrative and judicial matters in order to prevent the commission of terrorist acts;

5. *Requests* the Secretary-General, in his reports to the General Assembly, in particular submitted in accordance with its Resolution 50/53 on measures to eliminate international terrorism, to pay special attention to the need to prevent and fight the threat to international peace and security as a result of terrorist activities;

6. *Expresses* its readiness to consider relevant provisions of the reports mentioned in paragraph 5 above and to take necessary steps in accordance with its responsibilities under the Charter of the United Nations in order to counter terrorist threats to international peace and security;

7. *Decides* to remain seized of this matter.

4.2.4.2 *SC Resolution 1368 (2001)*[5]

The Security Council,
Reaffirming the principles and purposes of the Charter of the United Nations,
Determined to combat by all means threats to international peace and security caused by terrorist acts,
Recognizing the inherent right of individual or collective self-defence in accordance with the Charter,

1. *Unequivocally condemns* in the strongest terms the horrifying terrorist attacks which took place on 11 September 2001 in New York, Washington, D.C. and Pennsylvania and *regards* such acts, like any act of international terrorism, as a threat to international peace and security;

2. *Expresses* its deepest sympathy and condolences to the victims and their families and to the people and Government of the United States of America;

3. *Calls* on all States to work together urgently to bring to justice the perpetrators, organizers and sponsors of these terrorist attacks and *stresses* that those responsible for aiding, supporting or harbouring the perpetrators, organizers and sponsors of these acts will be held accountable;

---

[5] Adopted by the Security Council at its 4370th meeting on 12 September 2001.

4. *Calls also* on the international community to redouble their efforts to prevent and suppress terrorist acts including by increased cooperation and full implementation of the relevant international anti-terrorist conventions and Security Council Resolutions, in particular Resolution 1269 (1999) of 19 October 1999;

5. *Expresses* its readiness to take all necessary steps to respond to the terrorist attacks of 11 September 2001, and to combat all forms of terrorism, in accordance with its responsibilities under the Charter of the United Nations;

6. *Decides* to remain seized of the matter.

4.2.4.3 *SC Resolution 1373 (2001)*[6]

The Security Council,

Reaffirming its Resolutions 1269 (1999) of 19 October 1999 and 1368 (2001) of 12 September 2001,

Reaffirming also its unequivocal condemnation of the terrorist attacks which took place in New York, Washington, D.C., and Pennsylvania on 11 September 2001, and expressing its determination to prevent all such acts,

Reaffirming further that such acts, like any act of international terrorism, constitute a threat to international peace and security,

Reaffirming the inherent right of individual or collective self-defence as recognized by the Charter of the United Nations as reiterated in Resolution 1368 (2001),

Reaffirming the need to combat by all means, in accordance with the Charter of the United Nations, threats to international peace and security caused by terrorist acts,

Deeply concerned by the increase, in various regions of the world, of acts of terrorism motivated by intolerance or extremism,

Calling on States to work together urgently to prevent and suppress terrorist acts, including through increased cooperation and full implementation of the relevant international conventions relating to terrorism,

Recognizing the need for States to complement international cooperation by taking additional measures to prevent and suppress, in their territories through all lawful means, the financing and preparation of any acts of terrorism,

Reaffirming the principle established by the General Assembly in its declaration of October 1970 (Resolution 2625 (XXV)) and reiterated by the Security Council in its Resolution 1189 (1998) of 13 August 1998, namely that every State has the duty to refrain from organizing, instigating, assisting or participating in terrorist acts in another State or acquiescing in organized activities within its territory directed towards the commission of such acts,

Acting under Chapter VII of the Charter of the United Nations,

1. *Decides* that all States shall:
   (a) Prevent and suppress the financing of terrorist acts;
   (b) Criminalize the wilful provision or collection, by any means, directly or indirectly, of funds by their nationals or in their territories with the intention

---

[6] Security Council SC/7158, 4385th Meeting (Night), 28 September 2001.

that the funds should be used, or in the knowledge that they are to be used, in order to carry out terrorist acts;

(c) Freeze without delay funds and other financial assets or economic resources of persons who commit, or attempt to commit, terrorist acts or participate in or facilitate the commission of terrorist acts; of entities owned or controlled directly or indirectly by such persons; and of persons and entities acting on behalf of, or at the direction of such persons and entities, including funds derived or generated from property owned or controlled directly or indirectly by such persons and associated persons and entities;

(d) Prohibit their nationals or any persons and entities within their territories from making any funds, financial assets or economic resources or financial or other related services available, directly or indirectly, for the benefit of persons who commit or attempt to commit or facilitate or participate in the commission of terrorist acts, of entities owned or controlled, directly or indirectly, by such persons and of persons and entities acting on behalf of or at the direction of such persons;

2. *Decides* also that all States shall:

(a) Refrain from providing any form of support, active or passive, to entities or persons involved in terrorist acts, including by suppressing recruitment of members of terrorist groups and eliminating the supply of weapons to terrorists;

(b) Take the necessary steps to prevent the commission of terrorist acts, including by provision of early warning to other States by exchange of information;

(c) Deny safe haven to those who finance, plan, support, or commit terrorist acts, or provide safe havens;

(d) Prevent those who finance, plan, facilitate or commit terrorist acts from using their respective territories for those purposes against other States or their citizens;

(e) Ensure that any person who participates in the financing, planning, preparation or perpetration of terrorist acts or in supporting terrorist acts is brought to justice and ensure that, in addition to any other measures against them, such terrorist acts are established as serious criminal offences in domestic laws and regulations and that the punishment duly reflects the seriousness of such terrorist acts;

(f) Afford one another the greatest measure of assistance in connection with criminal investigations or criminal proceedings relating to the financing or support of terrorist acts, including assistance in obtaining evidence in their possession necessary for the proceedings;

(g) Prevent the movement of terrorists or terrorist groups by effective border controls and controls on issuance of identity papers and travel documents, and through measures for preventing counterfeiting, forgery or fraudulent use of identity papers and travel documents;

3. *Calls upon* all States to:

(a) Find ways of intensifying and accelerating the exchange of operational information, especially regarding actions or movements of terrorist persons or networks; forged or falsified travel documents; traffic in arms, explosives or sensitive materials; use of communications technologies by terrorist groups; and the threat posed by the possession of weapons of mass destruction by terrorist groups;

(b) Exchange information in accordance with international and domestic law and cooperate on administrative and judicial matters to prevent the commission of terrorist acts;

(c) Cooperate, particularly through bilateral and multilateral arrangements and agreements, to prevent and suppress terrorist attacks and take action against perpetrators of such acts;

(d) Become parties as soon as possible to the relevant international conventions and protocols relating to terrorism, including the International Convention for the Suppression of the Financing of Terrorism of 9 December 1999;

(e) Increase cooperation and fully implement the relevant international conventions and protocols relating to terrorism and Security Council Resolutions 1269 (1999) and 1368 (2001);

(f) Take appropriate measures in conformity with the relevant provisions of national and international law, including international standards of human rights, before granting refugee status, for the purpose of ensuring that the asylum seeker has not planned, facilitated or participated in the commission of terrorist acts;

(g) Ensure, in conformity with international law, that refugee status is not abused by the perpetrators, organizers or facilitators of terrorist acts, and that claims of political motivation are not recognized as grounds for refusing requests for the extradition of alleged terrorists;

4. *Notes* with concern the close connection between international terrorism and transnational organized crime, illicit drugs, money-laundering, illegal arms-trafficking, and illegal movement of nuclear, chemical, biological and other potentially deadly materials, and in this regard emphasizes the need to enhance coordination of efforts on national, subregional, regional and international levels in order to strengthen a global response to this serious challenge and threat to international security;

5. *Declares* that acts, methods, and practices of terrorism are contrary to the purposes and principles of the United Nations and that knowingly financing, planning and inciting terrorist acts are also contrary to the purposes and principles of the United Nations;

6. *Decides* to establish, in accordance with rule 28 of its provisional rules of procedure, a Committee of the Security Council, consisting of all the members of the Council, to monitor implementation of this resolution, with the assistance of appropriate expertise, and calls upon all States to report to the Committee, no later than 90 days from the date of adoption of this resolution and thereafter according to a timetable to be proposed by the Committee, on the steps they have taken to implement this resolution;

7. *Directs* the Committee to delineate its tasks, submit a work programme within 30 days of the adoption of this resolution, and to consider the support it requires, in consultation with the Secretary-General;

8. *Expresses* its determination to take all necessary steps in order to ensure the full implementation of this resolution, in accordance with its responsibilities under the Charter;

9. *Decides* to remain seized of this matter.

4.2.4.4 *SC Resolution 1377 (2001)*[7]

The Security Council,

Meeting at the Ministerial level,

Recalling its Resolutions 1269 (1999) of 19 October 1999, 1368 (2001) of 12 September 2001 and 1373 (2001) of 28 September 2001,

Declares that acts of international terrorism constitute one of the most serious threats to international peace and security in the twenty-first century,

Further declares that acts of international terrorism constitute a challenge to all States and to all of humanity,

Reaffirms its unequivocal condemnation of all acts, methods and practices of terrorism as criminal and unjustifiable, regardless of their motivation, in all their forms and manifestations, wherever and by whomever committed,

Stresses that acts of international terrorism are contrary to the purposes and principles of the Charter of the United Nations, and that the financing, planning and preparation of as well as any other form of support for acts of international terrorism are similarly contrary to the purposes and principles of the Charter of the United Nations,

Underlines that acts of terrorism endanger innocent lives and the dignity and security of human beings everywhere, threaten the social and economic development of all States and undermine global stability and prosperity,

Affirms that a sustained, comprehensive approach involving the active participation and collaboration of all Member States of the United Nations, and in accordance with the Charter of the United Nations and international law, is essential to combat the scourge of international terrorism,

Stresses that continuing international efforts to broaden the understanding among civilizations and to address regional conflicts and the full range of global issues, including development issues, will contribute to international cooperation and collaboration, which themselves are necessary to sustain the broadest possible fight against international terrorism,

Welcomes the commitment expressed by States to fight the scourge of international terrorism, including during the General Assembly plenary debate from 1-5 October 2001, calls on all States to become parties as soon as possible to the relevant international conventions and protocols relating to terrorism, and encourages Member States to take forward work in this area,

Calls on all States to take urgent steps to implement fully Resolution 1373 (2001), and to assist each other in doing so, and underlines the obligation on States to deny financial and all other forms of support and safe haven to terrorists and those supporting terrorism,

---

[7] Adopted 12 November 2001.

Expresses its determination to proceed with the implementation of that resolution in full cooperation with the whole membership of the United Nations, and welcomes the progress made so far by the Counter-Terrorism Committee established by paragraph 6 of Resolution 1373 (2001) to monitor implementation of that resolution,

Recognizes that many States will require assistance in implementing all the requirements of Resolution 1373 (2001), and invites States to inform the Counter-Terrorism Committee of areas in which they require such support,

In that context, invites the Counter-Terrorism Committee to explore ways in which States can be assisted, and in particular to explore with international, regional and subregional organizations:

- the promotion of best-practice in the areas covered by Resolution 1373 (2001), including the preparation of model laws as appropriate,
- the availability of existing technical, financial, regulatory, legislative or other assistance programmes which might facilitate the implementation of Resolution 1373 (2001),
- the promotion of possible synergies between these assistance programmes,

Calls on all States to intensify their efforts to eliminate the scourge of international terrorism.

4.3   ECOSOC

4.3.1   **Human Rights and Terrorism**

ECOSOC stands for the Economic and Social Council as set up under Chapter X of the Charter and is meant to deal with various aspects enumerated in Chapter IX which include stability and well-being, peaceful relations and human rights. Although the issue of human rights is also dealt with by the General Assembly, the Third Committee in particular, the human rights hierarchy now dictates that primary discussions and resolutions are adopted in the (Sub-)Commission on Human Rights, the results of which more often than not find their way to the General Assembly through ECOSOC.[1]

---

[1] The main relevant reports are:

Resolutions of the Commission on Human Rights (all on: Human rights and terrorism):
E/CN.4/RES/2001/37; E/CN.4/RES/2000/30; E/CN.4/RES/1999/27; E/CN.4/RES/1998/47; E/CN.4/RES/1997/42; E/CN.4/RES/1996/47; E/CN.4/RES/1995/43.

Resolutions of the Subcommission on the Promotion and Protection of Human Rights on 'terrorism and human rights': E/CN.4/Sub.2/RES/2001/18; E/CN.4/Sub.2/RES/1999/26.

Resolutions of the Subcommission on the Promotion and Protection of Human Rights on 'human rights and terrorism':
E/CN.4/Sub.2/RES/1998/29; E/CN.4/Sub.2/RES/1997/39; E/CN.4/Sub.2/RES/1996/20; E/CN.4/Sub.2/RES/1994/18.

Reports by the Special Rapporteur Ms. Kalliopi K. Koufa:
E/CN.4/Sub.2/2001/31: Terrorism and human rights (progress report); E/CN.4/Sub.2/1999/27 Terrorism and human rights (preliminary report).

Resolution of the Commission on the Status of Women: E/CN.6/RES/36/7 Advancement of women and acts of terrorism against women.

One of the subsidiary bodies reporting to ECOSOC is indeed the Commission on Women, which in 1992 adopted a resolution on the issue of women and terrorism, which on the one hand indicates that terrorism is indeed a subject which in way or another touches upon each and every subject, while on the other, it provides an insight into a different angle in dealing with the challenge (Resolution 36/7. Advancement of women and acts of terrorism against women):

The Commission on the Status of Women,

Taking into account the fact that the Nairobi Forward-looking Strategies for the Advancement of Women have identified violence against women as one of the major obstacles to the achievement of the objectives of the United Nations Decade for Women: Equality, Development and Peace,

Recalling Commission on Human Rights resolution 1992/82 of 5 March 1992, concerning the promotion and furtherance of human rights and fundamental freedoms,

Profoundly concerned about the persistent acts of violence perpetrated in various countries by armed groups and by drug traffickers who terrorize the population and threaten in particular the safety and lives of women and children,

Reaffirming that such acts prevent the full exercise of civil and political rights, such as participation in

As indicated above in Chapter 1, one of the main challenges facing modern society is to find the right balance between freedom, security and justice. The main question is whether the sum of the three would amount to a fixed total, meaning that if more attention were to be paid to security, some of the freedoms would have to suffer. Alternatively, if the total is not fixed, more security might be combined with more freedom. The present author is of the opinion that this is not the case: justice is and should be maximalized, whereas freedom and security do have an impact on each other. That indeed means that more security might come at the cost of some freedom.

It, therefore, comes as no surprise that the human rights world is concerned about the aftermath of the September 2001 events in that it is afraid that some basic human rights might be infringed by the zeal to hunt terrorists or the obligation to prevent terrorist acts. As we will see, however, the human rights lobby, sometimes appears to be overconcerned, as the challenge to optimize security against terrorism seems to be met without sacrificing human rights. Yet, at the same time, it should be emphasized that the Security Council, rather than the Commission on Human Rights – which falls under ECOSOC – is instrumental in indicating the direction in which any new balance should go.[2]

In 1993, the General Assembly adopted a first Resolution on Human Rights and Terrorism (GA Res. 48/122) which in the preamble included a text which could be misinterpreted as a reference to the causes and roots of terrorism (the earlier frustration and despair aspects). It was reiterated that *all Member States have an obligation to promote and protect human rights and fundamental freedoms, and also that every individual should strive to secure their universal and effective recognition and observance* (sic), a blurred and ambiguous text at best. The Resolution itself condemns terrorism, calls upon States to take all necessary and effective measures to prevent, combat and eliminate terrorism, and urges the international community to enhance cooperation. It could be concluded that this human rights v. terrorism text somewhat differs from the main elimination resolutions of the 1990s, which is to be regretted.

---

free elections, the right to peaceful assembly, freedom of association and trade union rights, as well as the exercise of economic, social and cultural rights, thus undermining the welfare of the people and seriously harming the economic infrastructure and production,

1. *Strongly condemns* the acts of violence perpetrated by armed groups and by drug traffickers who terrorize and threaten the safety and lives of the population, especially women, and, in particular, women who have been democratically elected to public office, or who are leaders of community organizations or welfare associations, or who have been appointed by the Government to positions of responsibility;

2. *Expresses* its profound concern about the adverse effect on the enjoyment of human rights caused by armed groups and by drug traffickers who terrorize the population and threaten the safety and lives of women;

3. *Requests* governmental and non-governmental organizations to pay particular attention to these violations of human rights;

4. *Decides* to consider this question under the priority theme 'Peace' at its thirty-seventh session.

    [2] On 12 April 2002, the UN SG Kofi Annan addressed the Commission and said, inter alia, that security against terrorism could not be achieved by sacrificing human rights, – that '*to try and do so would hand the terrorists a victory beyond their dreams*'.

The human rights effort was repeated in 1994 (49/185), 1995 (50/186), 1997 (52/133) and 1999 (54/164) and gained major support. For instance, the 1995 resolution was adopted without a vote (included in the annex to this sub-chapter).

Moreover, in its Resolution 1996/20 of 29 August 1996, entitled 'Human Rights and Terrorism', the Sub-Commission on Prevention of Discrimination and Protection of Minorities decided to entrust Ms. Kalliopi K. Koufa with the task of preparing a working paper on the question of terrorism and human rights. **The 1999 preliminary report on the question of terrorism and human rights**[3] was prepared pursuant to paragraph 1 of Sub-Commission Resolution 1998/29. Its purpose was to outline the main questions to be analysed in the study and thus provide a basis for discussion.

Ms. Koufa, the Special Rapporteur concerned, came to the conclusion that there was a need to illuminate and elaborate the reality of the link between terrorism and human rights, which, as she claims, for a long time the United Nations has not been so ready to recognize as a result of deep ideological divisions in the attitudes of Member States concerning the issue of terrorism and its implications for the full enjoyment of human rights and fundamental freedoms. The Rapporteur then states that 'this approach involves consideration of three major, relatively distinct areas, in which terrorism puts under threat those social and political values that relate, either directly or indirectly, to the full enjoyment of human rights and fundamental freedoms, namely the areas of: (a) the life, liberty and dignity of the individual; (b) democratic society; and (c) social peace and public order'.

Although attention is paid to the concern that States abuse the issue of terrorism or terrorist threats to reach agreement on oppressive measures, the main conclusions of the report appear to focus on the need for the UN system to deal effectively with the challenge posed by non-State terrorist groups, and for better cooperation among the various Agencies, including the Vienna-based Drugs and Crime Prevention Agency.

A major part of the Report, which was preceded by a Working Paper in 1997,[4] has been included in full in this Volume (below, 4.3.3.1).

In June 2001, the Special Rapporteur submitted a progress report.[5] That report was divided into five chapters: chapter one provides information on the development of international action on terrorism since the preliminary report was issued; chapter two addresses problems regarding the definition of terrorism and focuses in particu-

---

[3] E/CN.4/Sub.2/1999/27, 7 June 1999, REVIEW OF FURTHER DEVELOPMENTS IN FIELDS WITH WHICH THE SUB-COMMISSION HAS BEEN OR MAY BE CONCERNED; REVIEW OF ISSUES NOT PREVIOUSLY THE SUBJECT OF STUDIES BUT WHICH THE SUB-COMMISSION HAS DECIDED TO EXAMINE: Terrorism and human rights, Preliminary report prepared by Ms. Kalliopi K. Koufa, Special Rapporteur.

[4] In 1997 Ms. Koufa submitted a working paper (E/CN.4/Sub.2/1997/28) to the Sub-Commission identifying the diverse issues and problems involved in the discussion of this question and containing a number of proposals for a study on terrorism and human rights.

[5] E/CN.4/Sub.2/2001/31, 27 June 2001. COMMISSION ON HUMAN RIGHTS, Sub-Commission on the Promotion and Protection of Human Rights; Fifty-third session: OTHER ISSUES, Terrorism and Human Rights, Progress report prepared by Ms. Kalliopi K. Koufa, Special Rapporteur. The main excerpts are included in this Volume, below, 4.3.3.2.

lar on the actors or potential perpetrators of terrorism, as well as on the necessity to distinguish terrorism from armed conflict; chapter three explores the threat of mass destruction terrorism and the wide-ranging debate that is currently taking place concerning contemporary forms of terrorism; chapter four is devoted to the impact of terrorism on human rights and to the Commission's requests that the Special Rapporteur should devote attention to the questions presented in some of its resolutions; chapter five sums up the conclusion.

It is worth quoting the main concluding observations (paragraphs 129-131) as they appear to once again raise the issue of the causes and other roots in a (in the opinion of the present author) non-productive manner, also because the Rapporteur would appear to indicate that 'an international order that generates terrorism hardly qualifies as a social and international order in which the rights and freedoms set forth in the Universal Declaration on Human Rights can be fully realized.' A turnaround in the process of coming to terms with terrorism and terrorists is thereby almost complete, a regrettable development indeed.

> In reviewing contemporary terrorism, one might roughly observe that those States with the best human rights records are the States with the least likelihood of problems with domestic terrorism. Similarly, those States with international relationships that most conform to the goals and principles of the Charter are likely to be the States least affected by international terrorism. It follows that an obvious step to reduce terrorism is the full realization of human rights and the practice of genuine democratic processes throughout the world, among States and in every State. All efforts must be made to address better the realization of human rights, in particular in relation to self-determination, racism, internal ethnic and political representation, and class-based economic or cultural divisions in society.
>
> Violations of human rights, humanitarian law and basic principles of the Charter, then, are among the major causal factors of terrorism. As noted earlier in this progress report, careful attention to causal factors of terrorism is one of the duties of all States regarding terrorism and human rights. The overall result of addressing causal factors could be a reduction in terrorist acts. Thus, rather than being viewed as 'legitimizing' terrorist groups, as some States have suggested, careful study of causal factors should be an essential logical component of any plan to reduce terrorism, especially with regard to problem areas or situations in which terrorist acts occur with frequency.
>
> The full realization of human rights also involves achievement of economic balance among States, including the right to development. In similar fashion, better efforts should be made to achieve improved relations between States, not only because this is mandated in the Charter, but also because it is viewed as essential to the global realization of human rights as indicated in Article 28 of the Universal Declaration: quite clearly an international order that is generating terrorist acts hardly qualifies as a social and international order in which the rights and freedoms set forth in the Declaration can be fully realized.

The Sub-Commission adopted **Resolution 2001/18** on this issue, in which it expressed its deep appreciation and thanks to the Special Rapporteur for her excellent [sic] progress report and her introductory statement. The 2002 Session focused on the possible abuse of activities aimed at terrorists rather than on violations of human rights by terrorists.[6]

---

[6] As the International Herald Tribune stated in its 18 March, 2002 issue: The United Nations' chief

The above development is even more remarkable now that the actors focusing on human rights would appear to neglect not only the tone and contents of the Security Council resolutions but also the December 2001 GA resolution on this theme as even the latter resolution has in a way 'hardened' the approach concerned. This **GA Res. 56/160** has been included in full below (4.3.2.2).

4.3.2   The General Assembly

The General Assembly, as indicated in the introduction to this Chapter 4, has dealt with the issue of terrorism in an ambiguous manner. On the one hand, since 1989, a rather pragmatic approach, but on the other a reference to human rights which could easily be misunderstood. Of course, the Third Committee should act as a 'screen' for everything coming on its table from the (Sub-)Commission on Human Rights through ECOSOC. Indeed, the GA resolutions differ from the Commission resolutions, but the dual approach should nevertheless be subject to scrupulous investigation, as the GA, as a consequence of this dual approach (Third Committee v. Sixth Committee) tends to be unable to speak with a single voice. The resolutions contained in this Chapter 4.3.2 should be compared with one another, but in particular with the resolutions adopted by the Commission on Human Rights, as included in Chapter 4.3.4. Moreover, due attention should be paid to the very fact that the special rapporteur, by dealing with terrorism from the broadest point of view possible, is perhaps intervening with the work of the Ad Hoc Committee (Sixth Committee) (Chapter 4.1.5.6) and probably with the CTC set up under the Security Council (Chapter 4.2.3).

4.3.2.1 *GA Res. 50/186 on Human Rights and Terrorism*[7]

The General Assembly,
Guided by the Charter of the United Nations, the Universal Declaration of Human Rights, the Declaration on Principles of International Law concerning Friendly Relations and Cooperation among States in accordance with the Charter of the United Nations and the International Covenants on Human Rights,

---

human rights body, composed of 53 countries, will begin its annual review of abuses worldwide while facing concerns that the international commitment to human rights is being eroded by the war against terrorism. Human rights campaigners have accused the United States, Russia, China and other countries of adopting security measures that jeopardize basic rights. The United States, which is reproved annually for its use of the death penalty, is also likely to be criticized this year for its treatment of captured Al Qaeda and Taliban fighters at the Guantanamo Bay naval base in Cuba, and its proposal that suspected foreign terrorists be tried by military tribunals. 'The United States government has cynically used the banner of terrorism to support rewriting of international humanitarian law to suit its own purposes', said a representative for Human Rights Watch. Amnesty International is also urging countries to take up the matter of the hundreds of people held in the United States after a sweep for possible suspects after the September 11 terrorist attacks. Rights campaigners say they are worried that Russia is hiding behind the terrorism issue as an excuse to cover up rights violations in Chechnya. They criticize Russia for failing to act on two previous commission recommendations to investigate abuses in the province and to punish those responsible.

[7] Adopted without a vote on 22 December 1995.

Bearing in mind the Declaration on the Occasion of the Fiftieth Anniversary of the United Nations,

Taking into account the fact that acts of terrorism in all its forms and manifestations aimed at the destruction of human rights have continued despite national and international efforts,

Bearing in mind that the most essential and basic human right is the right to life,

Bearing in mind also that terrorism creates an environment that destroys the freedom from fear of the people,

Recalling the Vienna Declaration and Programme of Action, adopted by the World Conference on Human Rights on 25 June 1993,

Recalling also its Resolutions 48/122 of 20 December 1993 and 49/185 of 23 December 1994,

Taking note of Commission on Human Rights Resolution 1995/43 of 3 March 1995,

Reiterating that all States have an obligation to promote and protect human rights and fundamental freedoms, and also that every individual should strive to secure their universal and effective recognition and observance,

Seriously concerned at the gross violations of human rights perpetrated by terrorist groups,

Profoundly deploring the increasing number of innocent persons, including women, children and the elderly, killed, massacred and maimed by terrorists in indiscriminate and random acts of violence and terror, which cannot be justified under any circumstances,

Noting with great concern the growing connection between the terrorist groups and other criminal organizations engaged in the illegal traffic in arms and drugs at the national and international levels, as well as the consequent commission of serious crimes such as murder, extortion, kidnapping, assault, taking of hostages and robbery,

Mindful of the need to protect human rights of and guarantees for the individual in accordance with the relevant international human rights principles and instruments, particularly the right to life,

Reaffirming that all measures to counter terrorism must be in strict conformity with international human rights standards,

1. *Expresses* its solidarity with the victims of terrorism;

2. *Reiterates* its unequivocal condemnation of the acts, methods and practices of terrorism as activities aimed at the destruction of human rights, fundamental freedoms and democracy, threatening the territorial integrity and security of States, destabilizing legitimately constituted Governments, undermining pluralistic civil society and having adverse consequences on the economic and social development of States;

3. *Calls upon* States to take all necessary and effective measures in accordance with international standards of human rights to prevent, combat and eliminate all acts of terrorism wherever and by whomever committed;

4. *Urges* the international community to enhance cooperation at regional and international levels in the fight against terrorism in accordance with relevant interna-

tional instruments, including those relating to human rights, with the aim of its eradication;

5. *Condemns* incitement of ethnic hatred, violence and terrorism;

6. *Requests* the Secretary-General to continue to seek the views of Member States on the possible establishment of a United Nations voluntary fund for victims of terrorism, as well as ways and means to rehabilitate the victims of terrorism and to reintegrate them into society, and to submit to the General Assembly at its fifty-second session, for its consideration, a report containing comments made by Member States on the subject;

7. *Also requests* the Secretary-General to transmit the text of the present resolution to all Member States and to competent specialized agencies and intergovernmental organizations for their consideration;

8. *Encourages* special rapporteurs, special representatives and working groups of the Commission on Human Rights, as well as treaty bodies, to pay appropriate attention, within their mandates, to the consequences of the acts, methods and practices of terrorist groups;

9. *Decides* to consider this question at its fifty-second session under the item entitled 'Human rights questions'.

4.3.2.2 *GA Res. 56/160 on Human Rights and Terrorism*[8]

The General Assembly,

Guided by the Charter of the United Nations, the Universal Declaration of Human Rights, the Declaration on Principles of International Law concerning Friendly Relations and Cooperation among States in accordance with the Charter of the United Nations and the International Covenants on Human Rights,

Recalling the Declaration on the Occasion of the Fiftieth Anniversary of the United Nations, as well as the Declaration on Measures to Eliminate International Terrorism,

Recalling also the Vienna Declaration and Programme of Action adopted by the World Conference on Human Rights on 25 June 1993, in which the Conference reaffirmed that the acts, methods and practices of terrorism in all its forms and manifestations, as well as its linkage in some countries to drug trafficking, are activities aimed at the destruction of human rights, fundamental freedoms and democracy, threatening territorial integrity and the security of States and destabilizing legitimately constituted Governments, and that the international community should take the necessary steps to enhance cooperation to prevent and combat terrorism,

Recalling further the United Nations Millennium Declaration adopted by the General Assembly,

Recalling its Resolutions 48/122 of 20 December 1993, 49/185 of 23 December 1994, 50/186 of 22 December 1995, 52/133 of 12 December 1997 and 54/164 of 17 December 1999,

---

[8] Adopted on 19 December 2002.

Recalling in particular that, in its Resolution 52/133, it requested the Secretary-General to seek the views of Member States on the implications of terrorism in all its forms and manifestations for the full enjoyment of human rights and fundamental freedoms,

Recalling previous resolutions of the Commission on Human Rights, and taking note in particular of Commission Resolution 2001/37 of 23 April 2001, as well as the relevant resolutions of the Subcommission on the Promotion and Protection of Human Rights, in particular its Resolution 2001/18, adopted unanimously on 16 August 2001,

Bearing in mind all other relevant General Assembly Resolutions,

Bearing in mind also relevant Security Council Resolutions,

Aware that, at the dawn of the twenty-first century, the world is witness to historic and far-reaching transformations, in the course of which forces of aggressive nationalism and religious and ethnic extremism continue to produce fresh challenges,

Alarmed that acts of terrorism in all its forms and manifestations aimed at the destruction of human rights have continued despite national and international efforts,

Bearing in mind that the right to life is the basic human right, without which a human being can exercise no other right,

Bearing in mind also that terrorism creates an environment that destroys the right of people to live in freedom from fear,

Reiterating that all States have an obligation to promote and protect all human rights and fundamental freedoms and that every individual should strive to secure their universal and effective recognition and observance,

Seriously concerned about the gross violations of human rights perpetrated by terrorist groups,

Profoundly deploring the increasing number of innocent persons, including women, children and the elderly, killed, massacred and maimed by terrorists in indiscriminate and random acts of violence and terror, which cannot be justified under any circumstances,

Expressing its deepest sympathy and condolences to all the victims of terrorism and their families,

Noting with great concern the growing connection between terrorist groups and other criminal organizations engaged in the illegal traffic in arms and drugs at the national and international levels, as well as the consequent commission of serious crimes such as murder, extortion, kidnapping, assault, the taking of hostages and robbery,

Alarmed in particular at the possibility that terrorist groups may exploit new technologies to facilitate acts of terrorism, which may cause massive damage, including huge loss of human life,

Emphasizing the need to intensify the fight against terrorism at the national level, to enhance effective international cooperation in combating terrorism in conformity with international law and to strengthen the role of the United Nations in this respect,

Emphasizing also the importance of Member States taking appropriate steps to deny safe haven to those who plan, finance or commit terrorist acts by ensuring their apprehension and prosecution or extradition,

Reaffirming that all measures to counter terrorism must be in strict conformity with the relevant provisions of international law, including international human rights standards,

Mindful of the need to protect the human rights of and guarantees for the individual in accordance with the relevant human rights principles and instruments, in particular the right to life,

Noting the growing consciousness within the international community of the negative effects of terrorism in all its forms and manifestations on the full enjoyment of human rights and fundamental freedoms and on the establishment of the rule of law and democratic freedoms as enshrined in the Charter of the United Nations and the International Covenants on Human Rights,

1. *Expresses its solidarity* with the victims of terrorism;

2. *Strongly condemns* the violations of the right to live free from fear and of the right to life, liberty and security;

3. *Reiterates its unequivocal condemnation* of the acts, methods and practices of terrorism in all its forms and manifestations as activities aimed at the destruction of human rights, fundamental freedoms and democracy, threatening the territorial integrity and security of States, destabilizing legitimately constituted Governments, undermining pluralistic civil society and having adverse consequences for the economic and social development of States;

4. *Reaffirms* the decision of the heads of State and Government, as contained in the United Nations Millennium Declaration, to take concerted action against international terrorism and to accede as soon as possible to all the relevant regional and international conventions;

5. *Urges* the international community to enhance cooperation at the regional and international levels in the fight against terrorism, in accordance with relevant international instruments, including those relating to human rights, with the aim of its eradication;

6. *Calls upon* States to take all necessary and effective measures, in accordance with relevant provisions of international law, including international human rights standards, to prevent, combat and eliminate terrorism in all its forms and manifestations, wherever and by whomever it is committed, and also calls upon States to strengthen, where appropriate, their legislation to combat terrorism in all its forms and manifestations;

7. *Urges* all States to deny safe haven to terrorists;

8. *Calls upon* States to take appropriate measures, in conformity with relevant provisions of national and international law, including international human rights standards, before granting refugee status, for the purpose of ensuring that an asylum-seeker has not planned, facilitated or participated in the commission of terrorist acts, including assassinations, and in this context urges those States that have granted refugee status or asylum to persons involved in or claiming to have committed acts of terrorism to review these situations;

9. *Condemns* the incitement to ethnic hatred, violence and terrorism;

10. *Commends* those Governments that have communicated their views on the implications of terrorism in response to the notes verbales by the Secretary-General dated 16 August 1999 and 4 September 2000;

11. *Welcomes* the report of the Secretary-General, and requests him to continue to seek the views of Member States on the implications of terrorism in all its forms and manifestations for the full enjoyment of all human rights and fundamental freedoms and on the possible establishment of a voluntary fund for the victims of terrorism, as well as on ways and means to rehabilitate the victims of terrorism and to reintegrate them into society, with a view to incorporating his findings in his report to the General Assembly;

12. *Decides* to consider this question at its fifty-eighth session under the item entitled 'Human rights questions'.

4.3.3   The Special Rapporteur

1. In its Resolution 1996/20 of 29 August 1996, entitled 'Human rights and terrorism', the Sub-Commission on Prevention of Discrimination and Protection of Minorities decided to entrust Ms. Kalliopi K. Koufa with the task of preparing a working paper on the question of terrorism and human rights, to be considered at its forty-ninth session. In response to this request Ms. Koufa submitted a working paper (E/CN.4/Sub.2/1997/28) to the Sub-Commission identifying the diverse issues and problems involved in the discussion of this question and containing a number of proposals for a study on terrorism and human rights.

2. At its forty-ninth session, the Sub-Commission examined this working paper and in its Resolution 1997/39 of 28 August 1997 expressed its deep appreciation to Ms. Koufa for her analytical, very comprehensive and well-documented paper, recommending that the Commission on Human Rights authorize her appointment as Special Rapporteur to conduct a comprehensive study on terrorism and human rights on the basis of her working paper and it requested her to submit a preliminary report at its fiftieth session, a progress report at its fifty-first session and a final report at its fifty-second session.

3. At its fifty-fourth session, the Commission on Human Rights, in its decision 1998/107 of 17 April 1998, approved the appointment of Ms. Koufa as Special Rapporteur and requested the Secretary-General to provide the Special Rapporteur with all the assistance necessary to enable her to accomplish her task. The Economic and Social Council, in its decision 1998/278 of 30 July 1998, endorsed decision 1998/107 of the Commission on Human Rights.

4. Owing to the insufficient time between the confirmation of her appointment by the Commission and the deadline for submitting Sub-Commission documents, the Special Rapporteur was unable to prepare a preliminary report for the fiftieth session of the Sub-Commission. However, she made an oral presentation at that session, in which she highlighted the essential elements of her study, discussed her ideas on the purpose, scope, sources and structure of her future report, and expressed her wish to elaborate on them further in the framework of a substantial preliminary report, to be submitted to the Sub-Commission at its fifty-first session. After expressing its interest in the study on human rights and terrorism and in the oral statement by the

Special Rapporteur concerning the basis and the orientation of the study, the Sub-Commission adopted Resolution 1998/29 on 26 August 1998, in which it requested the Special Rapporteur to submit her preliminary report at its fifty-first session.[9]

In this sub-chapter 4.3.3 major parts of both the preliminary 1999 report as well as the 2001 progress report (which, it should be duly noted, was dated 27 June 2001) have been included. No new report was prepared for the (Sub-)Commission's spring 2002 session.

4.3.3.1 *Terrorism and human rights*

The 1999 Preliminary report prepared by Ms. Kalliopi K. Koufa, Special Rapporteur[10]

I.   INTRODUCTION

A.   Mandate and purpose (…)

5. The present preliminary report on the question of terrorism and human rights is prepared pursuant to paragraph 1 of Sub-Commission Resolution 1998/29. Its purpose is to outline the main questions to be analysed in the study and thus provide a basis for discussion by the Sub-Commission at its fifty-first session. It is expected that this discussion will assist the Special Rapporteur in finalizing the framework of the study and delimiting the problem areas to be dealt with in the study. Consequently, this preliminary report is to be understood as a sequel to the working paper (E/CN.4/Sub.2/1997/28) and as a set of hypotheses requiring further thought, elaboration and refinement.

B.   Historical background

6. Before embarking upon the essential task of this preliminary report, reference should be made to the historical background of the present study. It may be well to recall also that attempts to study the problem of terrorism as a common danger to be confronted by international law were already made before the Second World War. For an account of these attempts, see the study prepared by the United Nations Secretariat for the Sixth Committee, under the title 'Measures to prevent international terrorism which endangers or takes innocent human lives or jeopardizes fundamental freedoms, and study of the underlying causes of those forms of terrorism and acts of violence which lie in misery, frustration, grievance and despair and which cause some people to sacrifice human lives, including their own, in an attempt to effect radical changes' (A/C.6/418 of 2 November 1972 (…)). However, since it would not

---

[9] From Ms Koufa's 1999 preliminary report, paragraphs 1-4.
[10] COMMISSION ON HUMAN RIGHTS, Sub-Commission on Prevention of Discrimination and Protection of Minorities Human rights report 1999; E/CN.4/Sub.2/1999/27, 7 June 1999. The text has been slightly edited and most of the footnotes have been deleted.

be appropriate to try to review here the history of these attempts in order to draw from it valid conclusions for solving the problems with which the international community is confronted today with regard to human rights and terrorism, suffice it to note at this point that the pre-Second World War attempts culminated in the abortive Convention for the Prevention and Punishment of Terrorism, adopted under the auspices of the League of Nations on 16 November 1937.

7. Following the Second World War, the United Nations made no attempt to revive this Convention. Nonetheless, the problem of terrorism has been the subject of a number of actions in the course of the work carried out by the United Nations on the codification and progressive development of international law, since the early 1950s (…).

8. It was not until 1972, soon after the spectacular kidnapping and killing of 11 Israeli athletes during the Olympic Games at Munich, that the issue of terrorism became the epicentre of attention and contention in the General Assembly when, by a note dated 8 September 1972, the then Secretary-General Kurt Waldheim requested that the General Assembly include in the agenda of its twenty-seventh session an additional item of an important and urgent character, entitled 'Measures to prevent terrorism and other forms of violence which endanger or take innocent human lives or jeopardize fundamental freedoms'.

9. On 20 September 1972, the Secretary-General stated in support of his request that, while fully aware of the immense complexity of the problem of terrorism and violence and of the difficulties that a number of Governments would have in formulating their approach to the problem, he had nevertheless proposed the item because there was a deep and general concern with the phenomenon of international terrorism, because the scope of terrorist activity as well as its underlying causes had become increasingly international and because modern technology had added a formidable new dimension to this ancient problem. The Secretary-General felt strongly that the United Nations should face up to the international aspects of terrorism, for there was also the risk of a steady erosion, through indiscriminate violence, of the already tenuous structure of international law, order and behaviour, in which innocent people, often completely unconnected with the issues involved, would increasingly fall victims. In his opinion, it was no good to consider the very complex phenomenon of terrorism without at the same time considering the underlying situations which gave rise to it. The roots of terrorism in many cases lay in misery, frustration, grievance and despair so deep that men were prepared to sacrifice human lives, including their own, in the attempt to effect radical changes. The Secretary-General made it clear that it was not his intention, in proposing the item, to affect principles enunciated by the General Assembly regarding colonial and dependent peoples seeking independence and liberation.

10. On 23 September 1972, the General Assembly decided to include the item on its agenda, under the amended title 'Measures to prevent international terrorism which endangers or takes innocent human lives or jeopardizes fundamental freedoms, and

study of the underlying causes of those forms of terrorism and acts of violence which lie in misery, frustration, grievance and despair and which cause some people to sacrifice human lives, including their own, in an attempt to effect radical changes' and allocated it to the Sixth (Legal) Committee for consideration. Pursuant to a decision by the Sixth Committee requesting that the Secretariat submit to it 'a thorough study on the problem of terrorism, including its origins'.

11. As a result of the work of the Sixth Committee, the General Assembly adopted Resolution 3034 (XXVII) of 18 December 1972, providing for the setting up of an ad hoc committee, consisting of 35 members, to study the issues relating to international terrorism and to report to it. The Ad Hoc Committee on International Terrorism, which met in 1973, 1977 and 1979, examined the problem of international terrorism under three main parts – the definition, the underlying causes and the measures to be taken to combat international terrorism. The reports of the Ad Hoc Committee clearly demonstrate how far apart the Member States were on practically all aspects of the issues examined. After the failure of the Ad Hoc Committee of Thirty-Five on International Terrorism, established by General Assembly Resolution 3034 (XXVII) of 18 December 1972, other ad hoc committees established by the General Assembly with a view to studying or dealing with specific questions and aspects of the fight against international terrorism have been the Ad Hoc Committee for the drafting of the International Convention against the Taking of Hostages (General Assembly Resolution 31/103 of 15 December 1976) and the Ad Hoc Committee for the elaboration of the International Convention for the Suppression of Terrorist Bombings and, subsequently, other conventions dealing with international terrorism (General Assembly Resolution 51/210 of 17 December 1996).

12. Nonetheless, in the period between 1972 and 1998, despite debates at cross purposes and persisting differences of opinion, the General Assembly managed to develop a pioneering role in the global struggle against terrorism, by adopting 4 (of the existing 12) international conventions that address crimes associated with terrorism.

13. The resolutions of the General Assembly addressing terrorism clearly reflect, on the one hand, an increasing resolve within the international community to condemn all acts, methods and practices of terrorism wherever and by whomever committed and, on the other hand, a growing international awareness of the existing relationship between human rights and terrorism. In this context, it is important to recall that the Vienna Declaration and Programme of Action, adopted by the 1993 World Conference on Human Rights, has substantiated the danger posed by terrorism not only to the life and dignity of the individual but also to the very concepts of human rights, fundamental freedoms and democracy that underlie the creation of the United Nations, by affirming that 'the acts, methods and practices of terrorism in all its forms and manifestations as well as linkage in some countries to drug trafficking are activities aimed at the destruction of human rights, fundamental freedoms and democracy, threatening territorial integrity, security of States and destabilizing legitimately constituted Governments' and by prompting the international community to take the necessary steps to prevent and combat terrorism.

14. As a result of this evolution in approach and of the broadening of interest on the part of the General Assembly in the human rights dimension of terrorism, it was hardly surprising that the Commission on Human Rights and the Sub-Commission on Prevention of Discrimination and Protection of Minorities should follow suit by adopting a series of resolutions on 'Human rights and terrorism'.[11] As reflected in these resolutions, the Commission has, since 1994, entertained the idea of entrusting the Sub-Commission with the task of preparing a study on the question of terrorism and human rights, evidence proving beyond any doubt the concern of these two human rights bodies to clarify conceptually, morally and legally the neglected human rights aspects and effects of terrorism.

15. The resolutions mentioned in the preceding paragraphs refer to a number of problems relating to the human rights aspects of terrorism. The working paper on terrorism and human rights, submitted by the Special Rapporteur (E/CN.4/Sub.2/1997/28), as well as the ensuing discussions by the Sub-Commission at its forty-ninth and fiftieth sessions, highlight the central issues relevant to the understanding of the human rights dimension of terrorism and contain a number of ideas as to the scope and content of the present study. Since the purpose of this preliminary report is to present a tentative framework for the study, to identify possible priorities and to indicate the methods to be used, it is now necessary to proceed by considering briefly certain conceptual and other relevant questions that are basic to the subject-matter of terrorism and human rights.

II.   SOME CONCEPTUAL AND OTHER FUNDAMENTAL QUESTIONS
        THAT ARE RELEVANT TO THE STUDY

A.   The link between terrorism and human rights in fact and law

16. Little, if any, attention has been given to the link between terrorism and human rights. Although some of the more obvious effects of terrorism on human rights have been documented in numerous resolutions of the General Assembly, the inextricable link between terrorism and human rights and its broader international implications were largely ignored before the 1993 Vienna World Conference on Human Rights.

17. This delay is interesting and merits further discussion inasmuch as it is due to the traditional view that human rights concern only a Government and its subjects, for human rights are both the responsibility and the privilege of the Government. This traditional view has a profound conceptual basis and an important bearing on the nature and content of the link between terrorism and human rights and will, therefore, have to be looked into in the course of the study. As will be seen later, it

---

[11] See Commission Resolutions 1994/46 of 4 March 1994; 1995/43 of 3 March 1995; 1996/47 of 19 April 1996; 1997/42 of 11 April 1997; 1998/47 of 17 April 1998; 1999/27 of 26 April 1999. And see Sub-Commission Resolutions 1994/18 of 25 August 1994; 1996/20 of 29 August 1996; 1997/39 of 28 August 1997; 1998/29 of 26 August 1998.

also involves the question of the scope of application of human rights law (see below, paras. 44-46) and, in particular, the question already raised in the working paper of whether human rights law is actually moving beyond the traditional
dichotomy of individual versus State and towards the creation of obligations applicable also to non-State entities.

18. The question here is rather to illuminate and elaborate on the reality of the link
between terrorism and human rights, which for a long time the United Nations has
not been so ready to recognize, as a result of deep ideological divisions in the attitudes of Member States concerning the issue of terrorism and its implications for the
full enjoyment of human rights and fundamental freedoms. This approach involves
consideration of three major, relatively distinct areas, in which terrorism puts under
threat those social and political values that relate, either directly or indirectly, to the
full enjoyment of human rights and fundamental freedoms, namely the areas of (1)
the life, liberty and dignity of the individual; (2) democratic society; and (3) social
peace and public order.

19. These three areas are very important and relevant to the present study. It is,
therefore, proposed that at subsequent stages of preparation of the study the analysis
to be made include all three of them, in their theoretical as well as practical dimensions. In the present preliminary report, however, only a few remarks will need to be
made with regard to their immediate relevance in this context.

1. The life, liberty and dignity of the individual

20. Articles 3 and 5 of the Universal Declaration of Human respectively state that
'everyone has the right to life, liberty and security of person' and that 'no one shall
be subjected to torture or to cruel, inhuman or degrading treatment or punishment'.
The International Covenant on Civil and Political Rights, aiming at the protection of
the supreme right to life as well as the dignity and the physical and mental integrity
of the individual, from which no derogation is allowed even in situations of public
emergency. Article 6, paragraph 1, and Article 7 respectively provide that 'every human being has the inherent right to life. This right shall be protected by law. No one
shall be arbitrarily deprived of his life' and that 'no one shall be subjected to torture
or to cruel, inhuman or degrading treatment or punishment'.

21. While there is no doubt that both the Universal Declaration of Human Rights
and the International Covenant on Civil and Political Rights envisage positive or
negative obligations of States, and that the procedures for the implementation of the
International Covenant on Civil and Political Rights envisage actions only against
States, it is obvious that groups or persons can also act in violation of human rights
and freedoms enumerated therein of other persons, especially the human rights and
freedoms that concern the life, liberty and dignity of the individual. This is particularly true in the case of terrorism, for terrorism not only disregards human life and
human dignity but actually leads to the death and injury of innocent people.

22. In this connection, it is appropriate to recall yet another provision of both International Covenants on Human Rights, namely common Article 5, paragraph 1, which – using almost identical language to that of Article 30 of the Universal Declaration – stipulates that 'nothing in the present Covenant may be interpreted as implying for any State, group or person any right to engage in any activity or perform any act aimed at the destruction of any of the rights and freedoms recognized herein or at their limitation to a greater extent than is provided for in the present Covenant'.

23. Now this provision, which clearly applies not only to States but also to groups and individuals, forbids the abuse of human rights. It forbids the misuse and exploitation of the International Covenants as a pretext for violating human rights and is, therefore, very pertinent to the discussion of the issue of terrorism and human rights. For it is a well-known fact that the destruction or limitation of human rights and freedoms recognized in the International Covenants – and in the Universal Declaration – through unacceptable acts and abuses justified in terms of human rights, is a practice which is very often resorted to by terrorists, be they individuals, groups or Governments.

24. Indeed, terrorist acts and methods not only violate the rights of their victims but, at the same time, provoke or give an excuse for serious breaches of human rights and freedoms by overreacting State authorities that feel threatened by terrorism. Furthermore, it should be borne in mind that terrorists anticipate, and often aim to provoke the State authorities into, the kind of suppressive reaction and response that will eventually involve them in a spiral of terrorist abuse and violations of human rights, in order to create fear and dissatisfaction among the general public. Hence, the intractable problems and legal dilemmas posed by the human rights notions and pretexts invoked by the opposing sides engaged in this vicious circle of controversial aims and doubtful means.

25. Thus, it is clear that there is a close link between terrorism and the enjoyment of human rights and freedoms. This link is seen directly when groups or individuals resort to acts of terrorism and, in so doing, kill or injure individuals, deprive them of their freedom, destroy their property, or use threats and intimidation to sow fear. The link can be seen indirectly when a State's response to terrorism leads to the adoption of policies and practices that exceed the bounds of what is permissible under international law and result in human rights violations, such as extrajudicial executions, torture, unfair trials and other acts of unlawful repression, that violate the human rights not only of the terrorists but of innocent civilians. There seems to be widespread agreement on both the direct and indirect link between terrorism and respect for human rights. Moreover, the devastating effects of terrorism on the life, liberty and dignity of the individual have been clearly expressed and documented in the debates and the related pronouncements on terrorism of the competent organs and bodies of the United Nations.

2.   Democratic society

26. The preceding observations point already to the second area, that of democratic society, which is threatened by terrorism. The words 'democratic society' are among the most used and abused of the political vocabulary. While they may mean different things to different people, is a vital concept for human rights based on common values shared by human beings throughout the world community.

27. Indeed, Article 29, paragraph 2, of the Universal Declaration, Articles 4 and 8, paragraph 1(a), of the International Covenant on Economic, Social and Cultural Rights, and Articles 14, paragraph 1, 21 and 22, paragraph 2, of the International Covenant on Civil and Political Rights refer to the concept of democratic society in order to authorize restrictions on the rights and freedoms of the individual. [It] relates this concept to the freedoms of the individual and their necessary limitation within the framework of organized society in order to achieve the essential balance and harmony between the individual and the community. The fundamental reasoning here, of course, is that rights and freedoms have first to exist in order to permit of their restriction or limitation; furthermore, that the reasons which may justify their restriction or limitation must be basic values 'in a democratic society', the degree of democracy in society being tested by the extent of participation in the decision-making processes, the extent of popular control of governmental decisions and the extent of the experience by ordinary citizens of ruling and being ruled.

28. In the words of the Vienna Declaration and Programme of Action, adopted by the 1993 World Conference on Human Rights, which undoubtedly have marked the evolution and current status as well as the new trends and visions of the international community, as represented in the United Nations, in the field of human rights: 'Democracy is based on the freely expressed will of the people to determine their own political, economic, social and cultural systems and their full participation in all aspects of their lives'. The then Secretary-General, Boutros Boutros-Ghali, in his opening statement, in which, inter alia, he linked democracy with the guarantee of human rights and with the 'reconciliation of individual rights and collective rights, the rights of peoples and the rights of persons', spelled out 'forcefully, that democracy is the private domain of no one. It can and ought to be assimilated by all cultures. It can take many forms in order to accommodate local realities more effectively. Democracy is not a model to copy from certain States, but a goal to be achieved by all peoples! It is the political expression of our common heritage ... like human rights, democracy has a universal dimension'.

29. Proceeding from these ideas, it is assumed that a democratic society requires the existence and free exercise of certain basic individual and group rights and freedoms, which the Universal Declaration and the International Covenants – not to mention at this juncture other international, regional and national human rights instruments, norms and standards – define and thereby indicate their limits. These basic rights and freedoms are, inter alia: liberty and security of person, equality and

non-discrimination, due process of law, freedom of opinion and expression, freedom of assembly and association, judicial access and review.

30. A democratic society, moreover, whatever may be the cultural, political, social and economic framework in which it is achieved, is identified by certain principles and institutions, such as pluralism, the rule of law, legitimacy, political equality, popular control and public accountability of government, which, again, have their starting point in human rights and freedoms. It follows that the concept of democratic society is inseparable from fundamental human rights and freedoms, and from respect for the rights and freedoms of others. In any event, there seems to be ample consensus that a democratic society is characterized by differences of opinion, considerable freedom, and tolerance of diversity of cultures and identities subject to the law and the principle of equality and non-discrimination.

31. It will be apparent from the foregoing that terrorism is totally at odds with the concept of democratic society. Terrorist acts and methods utilized to coerce others from a free choice and full participation in the political process offend democratic society. As aptly stated by United Nations Secretary-General Boutros Boutros-Ghali in his message to the 1996 preparatory meeting for the Cairo International Symposium on Terrorism: 'Terrorists threaten the very foundation of civilized life. By seeking to achieve their aims through violence, they reveal their unwillingness to subject their views to the test of a fair political process'.

32. In fact, terrorism can threaten democratic society in various ways. By using violence and fear as a political tool, terrorism can undermine the legitimate authority of Governments; influence ideological and political factors in order to impose its own model of society; impede citizens in their use of their rights to have a say in the decisions that affect their lives; subvert pluralism and democratic institutions through the creation of negative conditions for the functioning of the constitution; halt the democratic process and democratization; undermine free political, economic, social and cultural development; impair the quality of democratic society for all, even when it does not actually threaten its survival; lead to more terrorism and militancy; and so on. In this context, it should be recalled that the threats posed by terrorism to democratic society have already found their expression in a number of authoritative pronouncements by the organs and competent human rights bodies of the United Nations.

3.   Social peace and public order

33. Lastly, there is the area of social peace and public order, where the effects of terrorism can also be devastating. Terrorist acts and methods involving impermissible violence and fear, whether engaged in by private individuals or in the name of the official State, will inevitably create social and political disorder and affect stability and peace. In this connection, it is appropriate to consider the actual and potential threat to stability, peace and order posed by terrorism in both its national and international dimensions.

34. To begin with the national dimension, the actual and potential threat to stability, peace and order posed by terrorism will be easily deduced from what has already been developed in the preceding sections. Terrorist outrages aiming at the destruction of human rights in order to create fear and provoke conditions that are propitious to the destruction of the prevailing social order may destabilize Governments.

35. Indeed, killing innocent people, destroying property and fostering an atmosphere of alarm and terror amount not merely to a violation of the rights of the direct victims but to a solicitation of further serious breaches of human rights. In response to the terrorists' despicable conduct and the threats posed to society, the authorities of the State which is responsible for bringing the terrorist violence to an end are entitled to adopt counter-terrorist measures and may not be constrained by the normal limits of official measures for the prevention of ordinary crime. As a consequence, there is a real danger that the State will overreact to the threat of terrorism and slide towards repression and violation of the human rights not only of the terrorists but of the rest of society whose rights and liberties might be diminished in the course of discovering, apprehending and convicting the terrorists. The damaging impact and effects of terrorism on social peace and public order may, in the long run, threaten the very existence of the State.

36. This is particularly true in cases where terrorist activity becomes strongly linked to illicit trafficking in narcotic drugs, arms traffic, political assassinations and other international organized criminal activity, or in cases where terrorism takes the form of violent insurgent activity – devoted to the violent overthrow of authority – that succeeds in creating a crisis which overshadows public order and destabilizes the Government. In such cases, which are likely to have international repercussions, the potential danger posed by terrorism to regional and international stability, peace and order also becomes very clear.

37. In fact, as the Special Rapporteur pointed out in her working paper, terrorism is an international as well as a domestic phenomenon. In this age of increasing internationalization and interdependence, the national and international dimensions of terrorism are but two facets of the same dangerous social phenomenon which infringes upon the interests of all States, not only as an assault against their public order and the institutions that protect the life, liberty, dignity and security of their citizens but, at the same time, as a serious danger to peaceful international relations and cooperation, which in our day is clearly understood as encompassing human rights and values, as well as the principle of equal rights and self-determination of peoples.

38. It is no wonder, then, that the General Assembly, in the Declaration on Principles of International Law concerning Friendly Relations and Cooperation among States in accordance with the Charter of the United Nations, approved in its Resolution 2625 (XXV) of 24 October 1970, expressed its opposition to terrorism in the following terms:

> Every State has the duty to refrain from organizing, instigating, assisting or participating
> in acts of civil strife or terrorist acts in another State or acquiescing in organized activities

within its territory directed towards the commission of such acts ... no State shall organize, assist, foment, finance, incite or tolerate subversive, terrorist or armed activities directed towards the violent overthrow of the regime of another State, or interfere in civil strife in another State.

39. These widely recognized prescriptions are characteristic of the general awareness within the international community of the increased role of terrorism as a catalyst for wider conflict. The involvement of States in mounting long-range terrorist activity may not only put at risk the constitutional order, the territorial integrity and the security of targeted States but may also have profound effects on regional and international balances, and jeopardize friendly relations and international peace and order. International terrorism, then, evinces similar characteristics to those of terrorist acts and methods in the domestic context: arbitrariness, indiscriminateness in effects, non-recognition of any rules or conventions of war, inhumanity and barbaric cruelty.

B.   The question of defining terrorism

40. Once the connection between human rights and terrorism is established, the Special Rapporteur would proceed further to identify other controversial questions that are deserving of study and analysis. Further, given that the Special Rapporteur has been asked to examine the human rights aspects of terrorism, it will be important for the purposes of the study to focus also on issues which are relevant to the study and which have not been fully dealt with elsewhere in the United Nations system.

41. At the outset, there are issues of definition and terminology that need to be clarified. For example, what is an act of terrorism? Who can be identified and labelled as engaging in the exercise of terrorism? Governments? State and sub-State actors? Non-State groups and individuals? In modern international relations, there is a growing concern that States are using terrorism in inter-State conflicts. On the other hand, particular crimes, including crimes that are the subject of international treaties for their suppression and punishment, such as hijacking and kidnapping, are commonly referred to as 'acts of terrorism', as are bombings aimed at civilians. International humanitarian law includes specific prohibitions against the use of terror or terrorism, but does not provide a clear definition of all such acts. Furthermore, the terms 'terror' and 'terrorism' are not referred to at all in human rights treaties.

42. As indicated in the working paper, the international community has not yet arrived at a comprehensive, universally accepted, definition of 'terrorism'. In the course of the study, the Special Rapporteur may have to explore some working definitions, in order to delimit the subject matter with greater precision and, in particular, with a view to identifying its major aspects and its possible relationship to the question of accountability. In this context, it is valuable to recall that the Rome Statute of the International Criminal Court, adopted on 17 July 1998, contains a number of provisions on genocide, war crimes and crimes against humanity that prohibit the commission of certain acts that in essence form part of a terrorist campaign. There

are also provisions in global and regional instruments in international human rights law, international humanitarian law and international criminal law which, to varying degrees, relate to terrorist acts. These sources, as well as jurisprudence arising from the pronouncements of the International Court of Justice and other international and regional courts and tribunals, may also provide some guidance on the definitional components of terrorism at the international level, and will, therefore, be examined in a next phase of this study.

43. As a consequence, although finding an all-encompassing and generally acceptable definition of 'terrorism' is too ambitious an aim, the Special Rapporteur considers that it may be valuable in future reports to try to elaborate with some precision on the specific acts that can be considered as 'acts of terrorism' for the purposes of the study. In doing so, attention must also be given to the actors or perpetrators of terrorism, whether they are States or non-State entities.

C.   The interrelated questions of the scope of application of international human
        rights law and of the accountability of the non-State actor

44. It must be acknowledged that the Special Rapporteur has been entrusted with a controversial mandate, and that some States which are members of the Commission on Human Rights did not vote in favour of this study. Looking to the reasons why a number of States seem to be uncomfortable with the study helps, however, to identify more accurately the controversial issues that are in need of objective analysis. Pivotal among them are the issues of the scope of application of international human rights law and of the accountability of the non-State actor. These issues are also relevant to the question of defining terrorism and of assessing who may be a perpetrator of terrorist acts. In fact, a consideration of the debates on human rights and terrorism shows, more specifically, that there is a basic disagreement on the following two key and interrelated questions.

45. First, there is the question of whether certain acts committed by terrorists, or members of armed groups acting outside the State's control, are properly characterized as human rights violations. No State seems to be in doubt that terrorist acts are deserving of condemnation and that the perpetrators of terrorism need to be punished. However, a number of States do question whether this can or should be accomplished through the application of international human rights law. (See, for instance, the different statements and explanations of vote recorded in the General Assembly and in the Commission on Human Rights during the adoption of their resolutions on human rights and terrorism.) This question is a complex one. It raises issues concerning the scope of application not only of the main United Nations human rights treaties, but also of international humanitarian law. It also involves questions concerning individual criminal responsibility under international law for crimes such as genocide, war crimes and crimes against humanity. The Special Rapporteur intends to take account of the new developments in all these different areas of law, including those brought about by the adoption of the Rome Statute of the International Criminal Court, in a subsequent stage of the study.

46. Related to this question of accountability under human rights law is a second controversial question, namely, whether acts of terrorism perpetrated by non-State groups are properly the subject of scrutiny and condemnation by United Nations human rights bodies. There is no doubt that a main impetus for the creation of the Special Rapporteur's mandate has been the perception by some States that the United Nations human rights programme lacks balance as it fails to address consistently abuses perpetrated by terrorist groups. In particular, some States which face terrorist activity, and whose own counter-terrorism activities might be criticized by United Nations human rights bodies, may take the view that this perceived lack of balance paints a false picture of the human rights situation in the country. Of course, dealing with this question will require a consideration of the extent to which this perception is accurate. This in turn might require some survey of the degree to which existing United Nations human rights mechanisms do deal with terrorist acts and whether it is appropriate to ensure that these mechanisms follow this issue more closely in the future.

D.   Recent trends in international terrorism

47. It is essential that the more ominous characteristics of contemporary terrorism should also solicit the attention of the Special Rapporteur. At the dawn of the new millennium, new forms of terrorist threat and assault that are harder to distinguish from other criminal activity seem to point to a new era of indiscriminate violence, more dangerous and deadly than in the past. In order for the study to proceed on some empirical basis, it will also be helpful, as indicated in the working paper, to highlight some recent trends in international terrorism and provide some survey of the scope and nature of contemporary terrorism. For example, what are the new types, if any, of terrorist acts which are said to violate human rights, and how and where do they occur? What, if any, are the new kinds or breeds of terrorists? Of course, it will be difficult to provide an accurate and comprehensive survey, but we do need some sense of the scope of the problem. This survey might be based on material submitted by States and intergovernmental and non-governmental organizations, as well as further research in the framework of the competent organs and bodies of the United Nations system.

48. Admittedly, terrorism in our day is undergoing all kinds of mutations. New adversaries, new motivations and new rationales which have emerged in recent years can couple with today's increased opportunities and capabilities to launch terrorism on a trajectory towards higher levels of lethality, mass destruction and mass killing, and to challenge the conventional knowledge about it. Certain recent trends in terrorist activities highlight not only the increased potential deadliness of terrorism, but also the increased role non-State actors may play in future as perpetrators. These developments concern primarily the spread of nuclear, biological and chemical weapons, as well as the proliferation of small calibre weapons. They further concern the growth of a variety of terrorist groups and organizations with diversified motivations, funding mechanisms and strategies, and the great dispersion of power existing now at the transnational level.

49. Indeed, nobody can remain unaware of the proliferation and availability of increasingly sophisticated weaponry and weapons of mass destruction, and of the disquieting possibilities and consequences their possession by terrorists can have. In the first place, with regard to nuclear weapons, the danger of fissile material falling into the hands of terrorist elements has risen dramatically with the fall of the former Soviet Union and the putative illicit market in nuclear materials that is reportedly surfacing in Eastern and Central Europe. According to a recent report of the Director General of the International Atomic Energy Agency, the number of incidents of theft and illicit trafficking involving the unauthorized movement of both nuclear material and other radioactive sources, i.e. material which could contribute to the production of a nuclear weapon as well as material that can pose health hazards but cannot be used in the development of a nuclear weapon, has been rising.

50. In the second place, terrorist access to biological and chemical weapons, such as anthrax, ricin or sarin is easier than access to nuclear materials. Biological agents and man-made chemical compounds which attack the nervous system, skin or blood and which can kill or harm humans, animals or plants over a large area and result in a simultaneous and widespread outbreak of disease, depending on the kind of pathogen or toxic spread, can now be produced by graduate students or laboratory technicians, and general recipes are available on the Internet. The relative ease and low cost with which these weapons can be produced or acquired has therefore raised the risk of increasing recourse to them by sophisticated terrorists. In fact, the spread of sarin nerve gas on the Tokyo subway on 20 March 1995, killing 12 and injuring some 5,700 people, dramatically demonstrated the potential magnitude of the threat posed by terrorists armed with weapons of mass destruction.

51. Also relevant to the discussion of recent trends in terrorism affecting the enjoyment of human rights and freedoms is, in the third place, the rapid proliferation of small calibre weapons and the illicit trade in small arms. While the rapid and widespread proliferation and increasing deadliness of small calibre weapons strengthen the position of criminal organizations which resort to terrorist acts and methods, the close relationship between the illicit trade in small arms and terrorism, drug trafficking, money laundering and other transnational crime has been recently underlined also in a number of General Assembly resolutions which do not focus specifically on terrorism. For example, in its resolutions on 'International action to combat drug abuse and illicit production and trafficking', the General Assembly has repeatedly expressed its deep alarm for 'the growing violence and economic power of criminal organizations and terrorist groups engaged in drug-trafficking activities and other criminal activities, such as money laundering, and illicit traffic of arms and precursors and essential chemicals, and by the increasing transnational links between them' and reaffirmed 'the danger and threat posed to civil society by drug trafficking and its links to terrorism, transnational crime, money laundering and the arms trade'.

52. Indeed, with the increasing globalization of the world economy, terrorists have managed to expand their activities, to establish networks of alliances with

transnational criminal organizations and to hinder law and order, particularly in a number of developing countries where criminal law enforcement may be susceptible to pressure and bribery from powerful drug barons. According to [Clutterbuck] an expert on terrorism: 'The cultivation, processing, transport and distribution of narcotics is probably the greatest single generator of political violence and crime in the world. Its profits are used to finance and arm rural guerrillas, urban terrorists and criminal gangs; also to facilitate the trade by intimidation and corruption and by keeping the army and police away'.

53. Thus, another trend of serious concern is the combination of terrorism and drug trafficking and its corrosive effect on the integrity of State institutions, especially in those countries in which coca and heroin growing has fallen into the hands of powerful cartels. In fact, in those cases where police officers, judges, politicians, customs officials and others responsible for law and order find the combination of threats and bribes irresistible, or where standing up for the rule of law may risk exposing oneself or family members to kidnapping, assault and murder by organized terrorist gangs, the combination of terrorism and large-scale trafficking in illicit drugs forms yet another lethal assault weapon against human rights and the rule of law.

54. Finally, academics and experts are currently emphasizing the recent rise and proliferation of religious- or quasi-religious-inspired terrorist organizational entities.

III.   CONCLUDING OBSERVATIONS

55. The issues and trends in terrorism discussed above demonstrate the actual and potential threat that the various agents of terrorism pose to human rights and freedoms, to democratic society and public order. They further magnify the rise of non-State terrorist entities with transnational reach, their potential role in challenging the ability of States to protect the rule of law and the rights of their citizens, and in threatening international peace and security.

56. While the direct relevance of international and human rights law to human rights violations resulting from State or State-sponsored terrorist activity cannot be doubted, the relevance and adequacy of international and human rights law with regard to terrorist activities of non-State actors is questionable. For non-State actors are not, strictly speaking, legally bound by the supervisory mechanisms of international and human rights law. As a consequence, in these days when transnational terrorism is making full use of the gaps in legal systems, international concern about the grave human rights abuses being committed by non-State terrorist actors is, indeed, growing.

57. As already indicated by the Special Rapporteur in her working paper and in the present preliminary report, the question of the legal accountability of non-State actors involved in the violation of human rights through acts of terrorism is a vital one. It should, therefore, be discussed further at an appropriate stage of the study, with a

view also to contributing towards a more balanced approach to the major diver-
gences of opinion regarding the proper standard of accountability, taking into account new developments in international and human rights law.

58. In the present preliminary report, other pertinent trends and issues mentioned in
the working paper, such as, for example, the increasing incidence in the post-cold
war era of terrorist campaigns perpetrated by or against particular minority groups
or elements of the population in the framework of ethnic or nationalist/separatist
conflict, or the continuing controversy about wars of national liberation and the motives advanced to justify violence in the context of the efforts of peoples to realize
the right to self-determination, have not been discussed. It is clear, however, that
these questions should be addressed at subsequent stages of the study, in connection
with the analysis and further elaboration of other interrelated issues referred to in the
present preliminary report.

59. The next phase of preparation of the study on terrorism and human rights will be
devoted to analytical work on the main problems referred to in this preliminary report. The primary sources of information will be: relevant international conventions,
resolutions, studies, reports and other documents prepared within the United Nations
system as well as by the regional intergovernmental organizations; relevant specialized literature; and relevant information provided by governmental and non-governmental organizations. A further source of information will be the replies by States
on the implications of terrorism, as well as on the effects of the fight against terrorism, on the full enjoyment of human rights, collected by the Secretary-General from
all relevant sources, including Governments, specialized agencies, intergovernmental and non-governmental organizations and academic institutions, in accordance
with Commission Resolution 1999/27 of 26 April 1999, and made available to the
Special Rapporteur also for consideration. The members of the Sub-Commission are
invited to make their suggestions to the Special Rapporteur regarding the sources of
information.

60. An additional method that might be used at subsequent stages could be to attempt to collect information on and to study particular examples of the impact of terrorism on the full enjoyment of human rights in different States, particularly those
States that are experiencing problems in the fight against terrorism. The Special
Rapporteur is ready to consult with Governments that so wish in order to present
their experience in subsequent reports on terrorism and human rights.

61. The Special Rapporteur considers that, in the light of the multidimensional character of the issues concerning the relationship between human rights and terrorism,
and given that terrorism is a particular form of criminality, it would be valuable to
coordinate with the United Nations Commission on Crime Prevention and Criminal
Justice and the Centre for International Crime Prevention of the Office for Drug
Control and Crime Prevention, based in Vienna, which is the focal point for the integrated efforts of the United Nations in drug control, crime prevention and combating

international terrorism, in order to reduce possible overlap and better harmonize the Special Rapporteur's work with efforts and developments on related issues.

62. Moreover, the Special Rapporteur believes it is important to liaise and coordinate with special rapporteurs, representatives, experts and chairpersons of working groups of the special procedures of the Commission on Human Rights and of the advisory services programme, whose mandates touch on the topic of human rights and terrorism. To this end, the Special Rapporteur would appreciate being given the opportunity to participate in their annual gathering in Geneva, in order also to receive and benefit from their insights.

63. Finally, the Special Rapporteur is conscious of the importance of and the need for gathering further information and carrying out further research in order to be able to elaborate further the subjects covered in this preliminary report. To this effect, it would be particularly useful if the Sub-Commission would consider authorizing the Special Rapporteur to visit Geneva, New York and Vienna, with a view to holding consultations with the competent services and bodies of the United Nations system, complementing her research and collecting all the essential and up-to-date information and data required for the preparation of the final report. In all these efforts, the Special Rapporteur would, of course, rely on the Office of the High Commissioner for Human Rights to support her work with all the assistance required.

64. With the present study, the Sub-Commission has the opportunity to contribute to filling yet another void in existing international human rights law in an area of burning, contemporary significance and practical under-response. It is the hope of the Special Rapporteur that she will be enabled to proceed with vigour, taking into account the new trends and developments that pertain to the substance of the questions and issues contained in the present report.

4.3.3.2 *Terrorism and Human Rights*

2001 Progress report prepared by Ms. Kalliopi K. Koufa, Special Rapporteur[12]

Introduction (…)

8. At its fifty-fourth session, the Commission on Human Rights, in its Resolution 2000/30 of 20 April 2000, taking note of Sub-Commission Resolution 1999/26, requested the Secretary-General to continue to collect information, including a compilation of studies and publications, on the implications of terrorism, as well as the effects of the fight against terrorism, on the full enjoyment of human rights from all relevant sources, and to make it available to the concerned special rapporteurs, including the Special Rapporteur on human rights and terrorism of the Sub-Commis-

---

[12] COMMISSION ON HUMAN RIGHTS, Sub-Commission on the Promotion and Protection of Human Rights E/CN.4/Sub.2/2001/31, 27 June 2001. The text has been slightly edited and most of the footnotes have been deleted.

sion. The Commission endorsed the Sub-Commission's request to the Secretary-General to give the Special Rapporteur all the assistance necessary, in order to hold consultations with the competent services and bodies of the United Nations system to complement her essential research and to collect all the needed and up-to-date information and data for the preparation of her progress report. The Economic and Social Council, in its decision 2000/260 of 28 July 2000, approved this request to the Secretary-General.

9. The Secretariat, in a note to the Sub-Commission at its fifty-second session (E/CN.4/Sub.2/2000/31), set out the technical reasons for the inability of the Special Rapporteur to finalize her progress report within the time available for the preparation of documents for that session. In an oral statement explaining the substantive and procedural reasons and delays that had made the submission of her progress report at the fifty-second session impossible, the Special Rapporteur requested that the Sub-Commission allow her to submit her progress report at its fifty-third session. The Sub-Commission, in its decision 2000/115 of 18 August 2000, requested the Special Rapporteur to submit the progress report on her study at its fifty-third session.

10. The Special Rapporteur has proceeded with the preparation of this progress report on terrorism and human rights from the bases laid down in the working paper (E/CN.4/Sub.2/1997/28) and the preliminary report (E/CN.4/Sub.2/1999/27). Therefore, the present report should be studied with the aforementioned documents in mind. The report will not revert to the analysis of the relationship of terrorism to human rights and its broader international implications as discussed in the preliminary report. Its main purpose is to move ahead and explore other priority areas touched upon in the earlier documents prepared by the Special Rapporteur, namely the problem of definition and of the actors involved in the exercise or use of 'terrorist' activity, the development of new forms of terrorism and the probability of mass destruction terrorism and, finally, a number of issues associated with the consequences of terrorism for human rights. It also attempts to provide an update on recent international action on terrorism and to give attention to issues raised by the Commission on Human Rights in its Resolutions 1999/27 of 26 April 1999, 2000/30 of 20 April 2000 and 2001/37 of 23 April 2001.

11. Accordingly, the present progress report is divided into five chapters. Chapter one provides information on the development of international action on terrorism since the preliminary report was issued. Chapter two addresses problems regarding the definition of terrorism and focuses in particular on the actors or potential perpetrators of terrorism, as well as on the necessity to distinguish terrorism from armed conflict. Chapter three explores the threat of mass destruction terrorism and the wide-ranging debate that is currently carried on concerning contemporary forms of terrorism. Chapter four is devoted to the impact of terrorism on human rights and to the Commission's requests that the Special Rapporteur give attention to the questions presented in its Resolutions 1999/27, 2000/30 and 2000/31. Concluding observations can be found in chapter five.

12. The mode of analysis of the subject matter at hand follows the perspective of international law, including the law of human rights, international humanitarian and criminal law, but not only that. Terrorism is a distinctive form of criminal activity in that it encompasses elements of politics and conflict. The Special Rapporteur initiated the necessary direct contacts with the Office of Legal Affairs of the United Nations in New York and the Terrorism Prevention Branch of the United Nations Office for Drug Control and Crime Prevention, based in Vienna. The documents which have so far been made available to the Special Rapporteur suggest that further analysis and consultation with these focal points that address the international phenomenon of terrorism from different perspectives would be extremely useful. Given the complexity and diversity of questions to be considered in the framework of the study on terrorism and human rights, it also seems necessary that a second progress report be prepared for consideration by the Sub-Commission. A recommendation to this effect is included at the end of the report.

I.   AN UPDATE ON INTERNATIONAL ACTION

13. Since the submission of the working paper and the preliminary report there has been recent additional international action on terrorism that should be taken into account.

14. On 19 October 1999, the Security Council voted unanimously to wage a common fight against terrorists anywhere. In its historic Resolution 1269 (1999) – its first resolution ever to address the matter of terrorism in general – the Security Council, emphasizing the necessity to intensify the fight against terrorism at the national level and to strengthen, under the auspices of the United Nations, effective international cooperation in this field on the basis of the principles of the Charter and norms of international law, including respect for international humanitarian law and human rights, stressed the vital role of the United Nations in strengthening international cooperation in combating terrorism and emphasized the importance of enhanced coordination among States, international and regional organizations. It also called upon States to take appropriate steps to deny those who plan, finance or commit terrorist acts safe havens by ensuring their apprehension and prosecution or extradition, and to take appropriate measures in conformity with the relevant provisions of national and international law, including international standards of human rights, before granting refugee status, for the purpose of ensuring that the asylum-seeker has not participated in terrorist acts.

15. The General Assembly, in its Resolution 54/109 of 9 December 1999, adopted the International Convention for the Suppression of the Financing of Terrorism, the full text of which is set out in the annex to that resolution. In its Resolution 54/110 of 9 December 1999 entitled 'Measures to eliminate international terrorism', the General Assembly decided that the Ad Hoc Committee established by its Resolution 51/210 of 17 December 1996 should continue to elaborate a draft international convention for the suppression of acts of nuclear terrorism, should address means of further developing a comprehensive legal framework of conventions dealing with

international terrorism, including considering the elaboration of a comprehensive convention on international terrorism, and should address the question of convening a high-level conference under the auspices of the United Nations to formulate a joint organized response of the international community to terrorism in all its forms and manifestations. The Ad Hoc Committee met from 14 to 18 February 2000 and discussed all three items. Its report reflects a serious divergence of views regarding both the nuclear terrorism draft and the high-level conference. There was recognition that the question of the elaboration of a comprehensive convention on international terrorism was not then before the Ad Hoc Committee but that completion of work on the other two items would facilitate work on such a convention.

16. In his report on human rights and terrorism to the General Assembly at its fifty-fourth session (A/54/439 of 6 October 1999), the Secretary-General set out, in summary fashion, the content of the replies received from a number of Governments on the implications of terrorism, in all its forms and manifestations, for the full enjoyment of all human rights and fundamental freedoms, pursuant to General Assembly Resolution 52/133 of 12 December 1997.

17. In its Resolution 54/164 of 17 December 1999 entitled 'Human rights and terrorism', the General Assembly condemned the violations of the right to live free from fear and of the right to life, liberty and security, as well as the incitement of ethnic hatred, violence and terrorism. It reiterated its unequivocal condemnation of the acts, methods and practices of terrorism as activities aimed at the destruction of human rights, fundamental freedoms and democracy, threatening the territorial integrity and security of States, destabilizing legitimately constituted Governments, undermining pluralistic civil society and having adverse consequences for economic and social development. It also urged the international community to enhance cooperation at the regional and international levels in the fight against terrorism, in accordance with relevant international instruments, including those relating to human rights.

18. The Secretary-General, in his most recent report, entitled 'Measures to eliminate international terrorism' (A/55/179 of 26 July 2000 and A/55/179/Add.1 of 9 October 2000), sets out additional information received from Governments and international organizations in the light of General Assembly Resolution 49/60 of 9 December 1994, a list of the existing 19 international conventions (global and regional) pertaining to international terrorism, and progress in the preparation of a compendium on national laws and regulations relating to the prevention and suppression of international terrorism. The report also has a chart indicating accession to or ratification by States of the 19 conventions.

19. On 8 September 2000, in its Resolution 55/2, the General Assembly adopted the United Nations Millennium Declaration, which, in paragraph 9, includes the pledge to take 'concerted action against international terrorism, and to accede ... to all the relevant international conventions'. On 12 December 2000, the General Assembly adopted Resolution 55/158, entitled 'Measures to eliminate international terrorism',

in which it decided that its Ad Hoc Committee on international terrorism should continue to elaborate a comprehensive convention on international terrorism and should continue its efforts to resolve the outstanding issues relating to the elaboration of a draft international convention for the suppression of acts of nuclear terrorism, and that it should keep on its agenda the question of convening a high-level conference on terrorism. The Ad Hoc Committee met from 12 to 23 February 2001 and continued its work on the above-mentioned items, building upon the work accomplished during the fifty-fifth session of the General Assembly within the framework of a working group of the Sixth Committee.

20. On 16 March 2000, the European Parliament made mention of terrorism in its resolution on respect for human rights in the European Union. This resolution 'reiterates that terrorism is a violation of human rights' and underlines the importance of cooperation between States in combating it and the need for appropriate indemnity for victims of terrorism 'in conformity with the guidelines of the Commission communication on crime victims in the European Union'.

21. In April 2000, the Thirteenth Ministerial Conference of the Movement of Non-Aligned Countries reiterated its position on terrorism and reaffirmed its 1998 initiative calling for an international summit conference under the auspices of the United Nations.

22. The Organization of the Islamic Conference (OIC) has also addressed terrorism. At its twenty-sixth session, held at Ouagadougou, Burkina Faso, from 28 June to 1 July 1999, the Islamic Conference of Foreign Ministers adopted the Convention of the Organization of the Islamic Conference on Combating International Terrorism. At its Ninth Summit Conference (Qatar, 2000) the OIC reiterated its support for a high-level international conference on terrorism and again stressed the OIC concerns about the need to distinguish clearly terrorism from people's struggle for 'national liberation ... and the elimination of foreign occupation and colonial hegemony as well as for regaining the right to self determination'. In its Resolution No. 65/9 – P(IS), the Ninth Summit endorsed the OIC Convention for Combating International Terrorism and in its Resolution No. 64/9 – P(IS) reiterated its support for convening an international conference under the auspices of the United Nations to define terrorism.

23. Finally, the Organization of African Unity (OAU) adopted the OAU Convention on the Prevention and Combating of Terrorism during the 35th Ordinary Session of the Assembly of Heads of State and Government, in July 1999, in Algiers, whereas a Treaty on Cooperation among States Members of the Commonwealth of Independent States in Combating Terrorism was signed at Minsk on 4 June 1999.

II.   THE PROBLEM OF DEFINITION

A.   The controversy before the Sub-Commission

24. As indicated in her working paper and in her preliminary report, the Special Rapporteur considers the issue of terrorism to be one of the most controversial issues in the contemporary international legal and political arena. This has been apparent since 1937, when concerted international effort to promulgate the International Convention for the Prevention and Punishment of Terrorism, adopted under the auspices of the League of Nations, failed. Since the failed 1937 effort, the international community has addressed terrorism only in a piecemeal fashion (i.e. crime by crime/issue by issue) rather than comprehensively. The controversial issue of terrorism has thus been approached from such different perspectives and in such different contexts that it has been impossible for the international community to arrive at a generally acceptable definition to this very day. Instead, there exists a plethora of definitions and working definitions advanced by scholars and practitioners, which tend to be either too expansive and broad, so as not to omit any possible interpretation of the phenomenon, or more restricted and narrow, focusing eventually on particular terrorist acts and excluding wide-ranging interpretations.

25. Indeed, it may be that the definitional problem is the major factor in the controversy regarding terrorism. This is all the more true when considering the high political stakes attendant upon the task of definition. For the term terrorism is emotive and highly loaded politically. It is habitually accompanied by an implicit negative judgement and is used selectively. In this connection, some writers have aptly underlined a tendency amongst commentators in the field to mix definitions with value judgements and either qualify as terrorism violent activity or behaviour which they are opposed to or, conversely, reject the use of the term when it relates to activities and situations which they approve of. Hence the famous phrase 'one man's terrorist is another man's freedom fighter'.

26. Because of these problems, the Special Rapporteur has pointed out that in view of the complexity and amplitude of the human rights dimensions of terrorism it would be premature and counterproductive to proceed with a definition before the Sub-Commission determines which issues it considers worth developing, and that finding an all-encompassing and generally acceptable definition of terrorism is too ambitious an aim. However, she had also indicated her leaning towards the view that, in future reports, she may have to explore some working definitions, in order to delimit the subject matter with greater precision and, in particular, with a view to identifying its major aspects and possible relationship to the question of accountability. (…)

30. It has been and remains the position of the Special Rapporteur that the study does not need to make use of a precise and/or generally accepted definition of terrorism and that, in any case, a definition should not yet be used. However, the study does not need to shy away from the conceptual analysis of terrorism or from scruti-

nizing its essential elements and manifestations, with a view to obtaining and drawing together basic definitional components and criteria that could eventually guide
the Sub-Commission towards the advancement or articulation of a definition of terrorism, for the purposes of the study, before the study is completed.

31. Since this is a progress report, it is at this time more important to continue discussing questions in order to induce more comments from Sub-Commission members, observers and non-governmental organizations, rather than pursue final
answers. In this respect, the Special Rapporteur also accepts the suggestion, already
made some time ago, by another Sub-Commission expert who, noting the differing
interpretations within the Sub-Commission, said that the Sub-Commission's task
would be 'to prune away and to discuss, so that opinions could coalesce'.

B.   The question of the actors involved in the exercise of terror or terrorism

1.   Introduction

32. One of the major reasons for the failure to come to a generally acceptable definition of terrorism is that different users of definition concentrate almost entirely on
behavioural description (i.e. on certain conduct or behaviour and its effects) and do
not spell out clearly who can use terrorism. Yet, the term 'terrorism' carries almost
always the flavour of some (subjective) moral judgement: some classes of political
violence are justified whereas others are not. The same type of conduct or behaviour
will or will not be viewed as terrorism by a particular observer according to the
moral meaning or justification ascribed to it. Thus, the labelling of a particular act as
'terrorist' may be more a formulation of a social judgement than a description of a
set of phenomena. As a consequence, a descriptive (objective) definition of terrorism which focuses on certain behaviour and its effects, and does not allow consideration of the identity of the author or perpetrator, may be useful but not absolutely
precise or satisfactory in containing and explaining a relativist concept, tempered by
considerations of motive and politics, such as terrorism.

33. The above observations are illustrated well by the very practice within the
United Nations, where among the main stumbling blocks in the effort to define terrorism has been the question of who can be identified and labelled as 'terrorist'. In
fact, review of action undertaken by the General Assembly and the Commission, as
well as records of the discussions held in the framework of these organs, and of the
various ad hoc committees on terrorism established by the General Assembly, as this
issue has progressed, reveal that a certain degree of consensus has been obtained on
some of the elements of conduct that comprise terrorism, but not on who can use
terrorism, or – to put it otherwise – on who can be a potential author of terrorism.

34. Thus, in considering alternative approaches to definition, it may be valuable not
to start by seeking to determine at present what conduct or acts should be included
under the concept of terrorism but by attempting to approach the concept of terrorism by reference to the authors or instigators in situations that are commonly per-

ceived and interpreted (or characterized) in both academic discussion and ordinary parlance as 'terrorism'. This approach has the advantage of seeking to lessen the controversy or, at least, make it more manageable by spelling it out clearly and trying to explain it.

35. This approach involves examination of the basic distinction made between State terrorism and sub-State or individual terrorism and understanding of the multifold manifestations of both State and sub-State or individual terrorism. The distinction and categorization of the above types of terrorism are, in the opinion of the Special Rapporteur, not only important and relevant to the present study but also the proper basis to ask for guidance on whether, eventually, it will be desirable, for the purposes of the study, to exclude any category or form of terrorism. Such guidance will, in turn, help the Special Rapporteur in delimiting more precisely the scope of the study as to the acts and the targets of terrorism.

2.   State and sub-State (or individual) terrorism

36. In considering the concept of terrorism by reference to potential actors or instigators in a situation recognized in both academic discussion and common parlance as terror or terrorism, there is a foremost distinction to be made between State terrorism (i.e. terrorism used by the State) and sub-State (or individual) terrorism (i.e. terrorism exercised 'from below', or against the State). This foremost distinction between State and sub-State (or individual) terrorism is now a generally acceptable component of the debate on terrorism, despite the fact that some commentators prefer to focus attention on State terrorism and others on sub-State (or individual) terrorism. This distinction is, moreover, useful in that it covers not only the historical genesis of modern terrorism and the evolutionary alteration that its ordinary meaning has undergone since it first came into use, but also current concepts of international terrorism, as will be seen in greater detail below.

37. Indeed, the concept of State terrorism or terror of State originated from the 'régime de la terreur' which evolved between 1792 and 1794, during the French Revolution, wherein terror-violence was used intentionally and systematically by the revolutionary government as an instrument of political repression and social control. Confronted with external and internal crises (i.e. the threat of foreign invasion, civil war, economic hardship, counterrevolution and the possibility of a complete breakdown of State authority) the French Government under Robespierre responded by creating machinery and legislation that made the (Jacobin) 'terror' possible, i.e. a ruthless policy directed against suspected enemies that consisted of arrests, imprisonments, confiscations of property, torture and executions, and the spreading of intimidation and fear in order to consolidate State authority.

38. The concept of sub-State (or individual) terrorism emerged almost a century later, between 1878 and 1881, and evolved with the passage of time as part of the terrorist process, first in tsarist Russia, and then across Europe and in the United States. The concept embraced the anti-State terror tactics of individuals and groups

inspired and affected by the anarchist ideology and philosophy that rejected the State, all government-made laws and private property. Acts of violence and intimidation (such as assassinations – targeting in particular heads of State, ministers or other government officials and prominent political or business personalities – bombings, sabotage and robberies) by individuals and groups who tried to enforce their political ideas by terrorizing the State and the public, in order to revolutionize the masses and bring about social and political change, generated considerable attention and eventually became a prominent feature of life in many countries.

39. Both the concept of State terrorism and the concept of sub-State (or individual) terrorism significantly expanded and evolved in the course of the twentieth century, as social and technological changes manifestly affected terrorist operations and tactics, and their effectiveness, as well as terrorist philosophy.

40. In particular, the spread of ideological violence and the fragmentation or dismantling of existing socio-political structures, on the one hand, and the advances in the fields of transport, communications and weaponry, on the other hand, facilitated the emergence of transnational and international terrorism. Increased mobility, cooperation and links not only between non-State terrorist actors from divergent political, ethnic and geographical backgrounds but also between State and non-State terrorist actors appeared, and the manifestations of both State and sub-State (or individual) terrorism multiplied and changed. Furthermore, the dividing line between terrorism and criminality gradually became less and less distinct and the targets of terrorism less and less concrete.

41. However, despite the ever expanding and evolving behavioural and stylistic variables which have come to characterize terrorism in our days, the dual conceptual distinction between State and sub-State (or individual) terrorism retains all its validity and utility for purposes of analysis, and to help illuminate and understand the two different – i.e. State and anti-State – basic dimensions of the phenomenon of terrorism. After all, it is obvious that almost all modern variants of terrorism trace their immediate antecedents to these two different expressions or dimensions of the phenomenon.

3.   Manifestations of State terrorism

(a)   Regime or government terror

42. There are different manifestations of terrorism used by the State. In the first place, there is the so-called 'regime' or 'government' terror, i.e. the traditional type or form of State terrorism, which is conducted by the organs of the State against its own population or the population of an occupied territory, in order to preserve a given regime or suppress challenges to its authority. The most widely known historical examples of this type of State terrorism include the 'reign of terror' in France under Robespierre, mentioned already, the atrocities of the Stalinist regime in the Soviet Union between 1929 and 1946, and the State terror of Hitler's Nazi Germany

culminating in the genocide of the Jews and Gypsies and the mass slaughter of Slavic people between 1933 and 1945. More recent examples include the reign of terror, from 1971 to 1979 of Idi Amin Dada, Ugandan President for Life Pol Pot's reign of terror in Cambodia from 1975 to 1979, and the notorious 'dirty war' against 'subversive elements' and the treatment of the 'disappeared' by Argentina's military junta between 1976 and 1983.

43. State terrorism in the form of 'regime' or 'government terror' is characterized by such actions as the kidnapping and assassination of political opponents of the government by the police or the secret service or security forces or the army; systems of imprisonment without trial; persecution and torture; massacres of racial or religious minorities or of certain social classes; incarceration of citizens in concentration camps; and, generally speaking, government by fear. It is quite obvious that almost all dictators and dictatorial or totalitarian and militarist regimes, as well as old-fashioned autocracies, have resorted to this form of State terrorism, which is, in essence, a misuse and an abuse of the powers of government, whether in the domestic or the occupied territory setting.

44. It is equally obvious that this form of State terrorism can also be deployed by a democratic government in a situation of 'emergency', internal strife or civil war, in which overreactions to the dangers of terrorism and a cult of counter-terrorism tactics could result in the deprivation of individual freedom, the increase of potential government violations of human rights and, generally speaking, 'terror from above', with no one left to protect the public from intimidation and repression.

45. State terrorism in the context of 'regime' or 'government terror' is, then, a global phenomenon confined to no particular ideology or location. Even when trying to operate secretly, this type of bureaucratized terror intimidates, injures and abuses whole groups, sometimes whole nations, and it is the type of terrorism that historically and today produces the most harm.

46. A further point that deserves particular mention is the role of the law in the reification and legitimacy of 'regime' or 'government terror'. In fact, 'regime' or 'government terror' is exercised according to the law that the public authorities have themselves created. To put it differently, the organization and administration of terror-violence and coercion by the State against its population, a segment thereof or the population of an occupied territory usually involves its national or domestic law. It follows that official regimes which practise terrorism assert the legality of their activities drawing on well-recognized claims of legitimacy based upon national or domestic law. However, it is with regard to the very same law that the difficult question of the legitimacy of power and of resistance to oppression inevitably arises. Hence the familiar terrorist cycle of action and reaction that permits each side to regard itself as the wronged party; in other words, the cycle of State and anti-State terrorism.

47. It will also be noted that the use of terror by a State against its own population does not generally fit within the scope of 'international' terrorism. As a consequence, it does not prima facie come into the ambit of international law. Nonetheless, it is all too well known that, with the involvement of the United Nations in human rights matters constantly expanding and deepening, the treatment by a State of its own nationals is now viewed in the context of international human rights regulations. The principle of domestic jurisdiction as mirrored in Article 2, paragraph 7, of the UN Charter having increasingly eroded, as humanitarian concerns prevail over respect for a State's right to manage or mismanage its affairs, human rights issues are no longer recognized as being solely within the domestic jurisdiction of States. Accordingly, the basic duty of non-intervention in the domestic affairs of States has been subject to a process of reinterpretation in the human rights field since 1945, so that States can no longer plead it successfully as a bar to international concern and consideration of internal human rights situations.

48. This evolutionary development has been further accelerated by the multiplication of the State's human rights obligations through the expansion not only of international human rights law but also of international humanitarian and criminal law. Thus, for instance, in the area of human rights, a wide-ranging series of international and regional instruments dealing with the establishment of standards and norms have limited the State's freedom of action and given birth to an ever expanding institutional framework of mechanisms for dealing with human rights violations. Treaty provisions such as the prohibition of torture, genocide, slavery and the principle of non-discrimination may now be regarded as having entered into the category of customary international law in the light of international practice, while other human rights provisions established under treaty may constitute obligations erga omnes for States parties.

49. In situations of armed conflict, international law, by virtue of customary and humanitarian law, condemns State terror perpetrated in violation of the applicable provisions of the Geneva Conventions of 12 August 1949, relating to the protection of victims of armed conflicts, and of their two Additional Protocols of 8 June 1977. This is notably the case in the event of disregard for the rules of international humanitarian law protecting civilians, as well as the wounded and prisoners of war.

50. From this perspective, it has been pertinently argued that State or government terror that is carried out in peacetime essentially raises human rights problems, whereas during wartime it involves problems relating to humanitarian law. Nonetheless, it has also been convincingly maintained that the fundamental principles of international law recognized in the Charter of the Nürnberg Tribunal (the 'Nürnberg Principles') should also be taken into consideration, since they too deal with terrorist acts in times of peace and of war. In this respect, it is instructive to consider also the

jurisprudence of the more recent international criminal tribunals for the former Yugoslavia and for Rwanda.

(b)   State sponsored terrorism

51. Central to the deliberation of the important international dimensions of terrorism is the marked increase in the involvement of States in terrorism in pursuance of their immediate foreign policy goals. Thus, in recent years, a wider view of the concept of State terrorism has been taken in both the policy and the scholarly communities, a view that expands the scope of State terrorism to include any form of overt or covert support or assistance given by a State to terrorist agents for the purpose of subverting or destabilizing another State or its government.

52. State-sponsored terrorism occurs when a government plans, aids, directs and controls terrorist operations in another country. The activities may be carried out by individuals or by government officials. As suggested by its very name, 'State-sponsored terrorism' generally involves terrorist activities against one State which are 'sponsored' by another State. The sponsoring State benefits by distancing itself from the terrorist activity, since it can easily deny any involvement. The support of guerrilla insurgents in Mozambique and Angola by the Government of South Africa in the 1980s is a classic example. Weaker States, however, have also employed the technique of sponsorship as a useful method of striking out at opponents who outgun them in terms of military strength.

53. State-sponsorship of terrorism may take many forms ranging from moral and diplomatic encouragement to the supply of material assistance, such as arms and other equipment, training, funds and sanctuary to terrorists directly or indirectly controlled by the sponsoring State. For States targeted by State-sponsored terrorism, it can often be difficult to find the link that ties terrorists to their sponsors, and thus to bring the sponsoring State to be held responsible. As noted by Laqueur, this type of terrorism is characterized by 'an almost impenetrable maze of linkages, intrigues, common and conflicting interests, including open and covert collaboration with foreign governments who preferred to stay in the shadows'.

54. The fact that State-sponsored terrorism encompasses such a variety of behaviours has led some commentators to further distinguish between 'State sponsorship' and 'State support' of terrorism, the latter implying a lesser degree of State involvement and control of the terrorists. Thus, according to this distinction, 'State sponsorship' would refer to those situations where the State actively contributes to the planning, direction and control of terrorist operations, whereas 'State support' would include situations such as tacit support, provision of transportation, permission for use of territory and financial support for terrorists. As can be readily appreciated, however, the line between 'State sponsorship' and 'State support' of terrorism can be blurred in the practice of States. Moreover, because of the lack of precise legal content of these terms, there is major disagreement over what constitutes State sponsorship, support of, or involvement in international terrorism, what strategic, domes-

tic or foreign policy goals are intended to be pursued by it, which States are involved in sponsoring or influencing terrorist groups, and how to evaluate the alleged
evidence of State involvement.

55. It should further be noted that State-sponsored terrorism is not a novel phenomenon nor a unique feature of the contemporary international landscape. It was an established practice in ancient times in the Oriental empires, in Rome and Byzantium,
in Asia and Europe, and there are countless examples of it in modern history. For
instance, in the late nineteenth century, Russia provided support to revolutionary
groups in the Balkans trying to set up Slavic States. During the First World War,
Germany supplied arms to the Irish nationalists fighting British rule. In the twentieth
century, numerous States have backed terrorist groups. Nonetheless, it is only since
the mid-1970s that this form of State terrorism has received increased international
attention, when United States analysts first classed it as 'surrogate warfare' and suggested that such sponsorship was a coherent programme undertaken by various
Communist bloc and Arab States.

56. Admittedly, there has been growing recognition among experts in the field that
in an age of nuclear strategy and sophisticated technological means, State-sponsored
terrorism, along with other forms of unconventional and 'indirect warfare', constitutes a particularly attractive mode of low-intensity warfare, allowing a State to
strike at its enemies in a way that is easily deniable, clandestine, relatively cheap,
high yielding and less risky militarily than conventional armed conflict.

57. In the words of Murphy, 'State involvement that takes the form of sponsorship
of terrorism may constitute the waging of secret or undeclared warfare against an
adversary State ... [B]ecause of the dangers of military escalation in today's world of
high technology, this form of so-called low-intensity conflict is becoming increasingly prevalent'. Other specialists, however, have warned against the labelling of
terrorism as warfare and, in particular, against the categorization of State-sponsored
terrorism as low-intensity warfare, or as 'surrogate warfare' in the eventual interests
of States at yet a further remove, arguing that such categorization confuses the essential nature of State-sponsored terrorism, which does not constitute a unitary phenomenon and a single type of conflict. In the same line of argument, it has been
convincingly maintained that equating State-sponsored terrorism with low-intensity
warfare leads to military analyses and military solutions and, thence, to accompanying excessive use of force and interventionism, which may contribute to further destabilization and terrorism.

58. It is undeniable that, as with domestic terrorism, the labelling of an act as one of
State-sponsored terrorism depends largely on the political perspective of the
labeller. Indeed, the boundaries of the term 'State-sponsored terrorism' are often expanded to encompass almost any act of violence or threat of violence which suits the
purpose of the labeller or, alternatively, are limited and skewed to take in only those
acts with whose perpetrators or aims the labeller is at odds. Such propagandistic and
explicitly politicized use of the concept of State-sponsored terrorism has not only

contributed to the already existing general confusion (both accidental and deliberate) over the precise legal content of terms and labels relating to terrorism, but has also resulted in a wide range of nations being identified as terrorist sponsors, even where the evidence for it is not solid or lacks the necessary clarity. Conversely, political and economic considerations and pressures, and the realities of international relations, have often been the reasons behind the extreme reluctance of States to name others as terrorist sponsors, even in those cases where clear and solid evidence has existed.

59. This double-standard morality and the ensuing basic dishonesty that allows States to look for a State sponsor behind almost all acts of terrorism that are against their interests while themselves denying that there is any remote similarity in their own aiding of repressive regimes or revolutionary movements in other parts of the world, have stood in the way of objective analysis and understanding of the relation of State-sponsored terrorism to other forms of conflict between States. They have also led to misleading estimates of the threat that State-sponsored terrorism poses to both the domestic and the international society, and have often engendered unwarranted overreaction and counter-terror, thereby increasing the terrorism-generating qualities of certain foreign policies and undermining the already vulnerable international democratic institutions or the balance of international relations.

60. It hardly needs to be said in this context that State-sponsored terrorism raises many serious and difficult problems under different aspects or areas of international law, namely the law of armed conflict and humanitarian law, the law of responsibility and that of sanctions, including legitimate self-defence. Obviously, this is not the place to discuss these in any detail. Nor is it the place to consider tactics and measures adopted in response to State-sponsored terrorism. For present purposes, it suffices to focus attention on the repudiation of State-sponsored terrorism of all varieties contained in the Declaration on Principles of International Law concerning Friendly Relations and Cooperation among States in accordance with the Charter of the United Nations, adopted by the General Assembly in its Resolution 2625 (XXV) of 24 October 1970 – an instrument that is regarded as an authoritative interpretation of broad principles of international law expressed in the Charter and which marks an important development in the area of international law pertaining to international terrorism.

61. This significant international instrument establishes in principle 1 (containing the basic prohibition of the use of force in international relations) the duty of every State to refrain from 'organizing or encouraging the organization of irregular forces or armed bands, including mercenaries, for incursion into the territory of another State' and, further, the duty of every State to refrain from 'organizing, instigating, assisting or participating in acts of civil strife or terrorist acts in another State or acquiescing in organized activities within its territory directed towards the commission of such acts'. Moreover, it asserts in principle 3 (containing the basic prohibition of foreign intervention), that 'no State shall organize, assist, foment, finance, incite or

tolerate subversive, terrorist or armed activities directed towards the violent over-throw of the regime of another State, or interfere in civil strife in another State'.

(c)   International State terrorism

62. While the concept of State terrorism usually refers to regime or government ter-ror in the domestic or occupied territory setting (as already described under (a) above), or to current international political terrorism that is State-sponsored or State-directed (as explained under (b) above), it is necessary to note, for reasons of com-pleteness, an even wider view of this concept which is sometimes taken in the international relations scholarly community and in debates within the framework of the United Nations. This view does not simply expand the scope of the concept of State terrorism from the domestic to the international plane but enlarges it still fur-ther to a degree that would include – and literally amount to – the resort to force in international relations.

63. Thus, starting from such premises as that the State is as much a user of terror in its international affairs as in its domestic activities, some international relations scholars have argued that coercive diplomacy and other overt State behaviour such as resort to the application of terror tactics in international relations (i.e. reprisals and bombing raids designed to produce damage and instil fear or, alternatively, the show of force or use of force as employed in the cold war period by the two super-Powers within their respective spheres of influence, nuclear deterrence and the 'bal-ance of terror') are cases of (international) State terrorism, whether in war or non-war situations.

64. The same enlarged concept of State terrorism has been taken by some State rep-resentatives when discussing issues of terrorism in the relevant organs and bodies of the United Nations and is, therefore, reflected in official documents along with the record of debates. Thus, for instance, the 1973 report of the Ad Hoc Committee on International Terrorism refers to this concept of State terrorism endorsed by a num-ber of States, in the following terms:

> Terror inflicted on a large scale and with the most modern means on whole populations for purposes of domination or interference in their internal affairs, armed attacks perpe-trated under the pretext of reprisals or of preventive action by States against the sover-eignty and integrity of third States, and the infiltration of terrorist groups or agents into the territory of other States.

65. There is, however, strong disagreement in both the policy and the scholarly com-munities over such an expansion of the concept of State terrorism, an expansion which, in turn, has an impact on the already overloaded term 'terrorism' to the point where it becomes unmanageable.

66. Without regard to one's view of the extent to which State activities such as those mentioned above do or do not qualify as State terrorism, the Special Rapporteur would like to recall at this point that recourse to war and the prohibition of force are

governed by international law. As is well known, the basic notion embodied in the Chapter of the United Nations is that the threat or use of force is prohibited in international relations (art. 2, para. 4), unless undertaken in self-defence (art. 51) or in terms of the exception provided for in the final sentence of the domestic jurisdiction clause (art. 2, para. 7). It is, moreover, well-understood that the 'illegal' use of force in international relations will be considered under customary international law, international human rights and humanitarian law, the law of armed conflict and international criminal law. It could result in individual criminal liability for the leading policy makers and engage as well the responsibility of the State.

67. Of course, this is not the place to go into this matter in any detail. It is sufficient for our purposes to specify at this juncture the following considerations. (a) While war is not necessarily, or even normally, a species of terrorism, belligerent practices and threats may be. (b) Terrorist acts can be committed by States against States, in both war and non-war situations. (c) State-sponsored terrorism in the modern world can, indeed, take many forms, and does not only consist of the assisting or directing of terrorist groups abroad but of other types of terrorist attacks also. This factual situation, coupled with the current inconsistencies and imprecisions in the terminology used by both commentators and policy makers, often results in confounding the boundaries between (international) State terrorism and State-sponsored terrorism. (d) From the legal point of view, the distinction between (international) State terrorism and State-sponsored terrorism is immaterial, since the invocation of either one of them would have exactly the same results (i.e. identification of the violated international law norms, articulation of charges reflected in the relevant international law norms, renunciation of alleged behaviour, etc., and the attendant question of responsibility).

4.   Manifestation of sub-State (or individual) terrorism

68. In contrast to the phenomenon of State terrorism stands the phenomenon of sub-State (or individual) terrorism, which is much more diverse in the forms it takes. As is well known, scholarly concern and the vast bulk of the literature on the subject of terrorism has until now concentrated primarily on this type of terrorism, which embraces the anti-State terror tactics of individuals and groups large and small, nationalists, separatists, liberation fighters, and so on.

69. On the diversity of sub-State (or individual) terrorism, one of the leading scholars on terrorism, Laqueur, has written pertinently:

'Terrorism, interpreted here as the use of covert violence by a group for political ends, is usually directed against a government but is also used against other ethnic groups, classes or parties. The aims may vary from the redress of specific grievances to the overthrow of a government and the seizure of power, or to the liberation of a country from foreign rule. Terrorists seek to cause political, social and economic disruption, and for this purpose frequently engage in planned or indiscriminate murder. Terrorism may appear in conjunction with a political campaign or with guerrilla war, but it also has a 'pure' form. It has been waged by national and religious groups, by the left and the right, by nationalist as well as internationalist movements, and it has been State-sponsored ... Terrorist movements have frequently consisted of members of the educated middle classes, but there has also been agrarian terrorism, terror by the uprooted and the rejected, and trade union and working-class terror ... Terror has been directed against autocratic regimes as well as democracies; sometimes there has been an obvious link with social dislocation and economic crisis, at other times there has been no such connection'.

70. As the above citation clearly shows, this dimension of terrorism is so disparate and vast that it is difficult to reduce and comment on it here in a manageable way. In addition, some of its aspects are extremely controversial, with many diverse and contending points of view. In her previous work, the Special Rapporteur has already drawn the attention of the Sub-Commission to a number of problems of sub-State terrorism in relation to international and human rights law which need to be carefully examined, stressing especially the question of the accountability of non-State actors. She has also received a number of submissions from Governments and non-governmental organizations, some important ones arriving too late to receive the attention they are due and at a time when the size limitation placed on progress reports has already been surpassed. At this point, the Special Rapporteur is convinced that further review of and reflection on this topic would better serve its examination. Accordingly, she will postpone the discussion on the manifestations of sub-State terrorism to a later stage, in order to present it in a more integrated form.

C.   Lessening the controversy: the necessity to distinguish terrorism from armed conflict

71. In seeking a definition of terrorism it is essential to set out the difference between armed conflict and terrorism. The Special Rapporteur recognized from the beginning of her work that this issue has been quite contentious in the international community, as illustrated by the oft repeated phrase 'one person's terrorist is another person's freedom fighter'. Concerns have been raised by many States about wars of national liberation in the context of the right to self-determination. These States are determined not to allow the terrorism debate to encroach unduly on this fundamental principle. Others have focused on what is increasingly called 'ethnic conflict' or even 'nationalist/separatist conflict', even at times giving the impression that any conflict described with those labels is necessarily related to terrorism. The debates in the framework of all United Nations organs and bodies reflect these concerns. However, the Special Rapporteur notes the almost total absence of any legal analysis of these critical areas in the international dialogue. As a consequence, she thinks that it is time to address this issue, because without the clear separation of war and terrorism, there will be no meaningful progress towards a definition of terrorism and, more importantly, no chance to implement meaningful measures to combat terrorism.

72. An obvious reason to distinguish clearly armed conflict from terrorism is because the law of armed conflict (and humanitarian law) automatically comes into effect when there is an armed conflict. This body of law has long-settled definitions, as well as clear obligations, regarding all aspects of military conduct involving both

military operations and weaponry (The Hague law) and the protection of victims of armed conflict (Geneva law). Under the law of armed conflict, acts of war are not chargeable as either criminal or terrorist acts. Most importantly, there are clear obligations regarding their enforcement, not the least of which is to respect humanitarian law in all circumstances. Thus it is necessary to distinguish war from terrorism and acts of war from acts of terrorism.

1.   Armed conflict and terrorism

73. Armed conflict is a situation where two or more parties armed with military materiel engage in military operations (acts of war) sufficient to meet the customary definitions of armed conflict. What is sufficient in terms of military operations varies depending on whether the conflict is an international armed conflict or not.

74. There is scant guidance in customary humanitarian law regarding the degree of military activity required to constitute an international armed conflict and, hence, to entail the automatic application of international armed conflict law to the situation. However, practice seems to indicate that even very little military aggression on the part of one State against another State is viewed as being sufficient. Most military aggression, however, is quite overt and, although a declaration of war may not be made, the international community is aware that there is an armed conflict.

75. In the case of armed conflict 'not of an international character occurring within the territory' of a State (in the terms of common Article 3 of the 1949 Geneva Conventions), Article 1.1 of the 1977 Protocol Additional to the 1949 Geneva Conventions, and Relating to the Protection of Victims of Non-International Armed Conflicts (Protocol II) rounds off the vagueness of common Article 3 of the Geneva Conventions and supplies the criteria of military action sufficient to define non-international armed conflicts (otherwise, 'internal' or 'civil' wars). Article 1.1 provides that Protocol II applies to all armed conflicts which take place in the territory of a State between its armed forces and dissident armed forces or other organized armed groups in sufficient control over a part of its territory as to enable such groups to carry out sustained and concerted military operations and to implement Protocol II. Like common Article 3 of the 1949 Geneva Conventions, Protocol II does not apply to situations of internal disturbance and tension, such as riots, isolated and sporadic acts of violence and other acts of a similar nature (which are not deemed to be 'armed conflicts'). At lower levels of violence, the distinction between 'armed conflicts' and internal disturbances is not free from difficulty, and yet it is also open to abuse.

76. A particular war may arise in an ethnic context – hence the currently popular term 'ethnic conflict'. Nevertheless, the situation is still a war governed by humanitarian norms and is either a civil war or an international war – which in the case of the 'ethnic conflict' label is more than likely a war of national liberation. Similarly, a particular war may arise in a 'national/separatist' context; like an 'ethnic conflict', it is nonetheless governed by humanitarian law. The popular use of these terms can-

not legally annul the obvious application of humanitarian law to the combatants in these armed conflicts.

77. For purposes of determining if a situation is an armed conflict or terrorism, it is rarely necessary to decide whether an armed conflict is a civil war or one in which a group with a claim to self-determination is fighting for national liberation. Many groups engaged in armed conflict claim the right to self-determination. Legal and factual analysis may or may not support such claims. However, if there is armed conflict sufficient to invoke humanitarian law, then humanitarian law has to be applied. Where the international community will have political difficulty is not as to whether there is a war or terrorism, but in determining what type of armed conflict it is. This legal/political controversy, however, belongs not in the debate on terrorism but in debates on which provisions of humanitarian law apply – those governing civil wars or those governing wars identified in Article 1.4 of Additional Protocol I. That debate would have to take into account, of course, the principle of self-determination, as set out in the Charter of the United Nations, human rights instruments and resolutions, with regard to the armed conflict in question. Legitimate concerns, raised by the OIC and others in many forums, that the attempt to define terrorism could result in an erosion of the principle of self-determination, could be favourably addressed in the framework of humanitarian law.

78. This is not to say that a situation which is clearly an armed conflict between either two governments, or a government and a group engaged in armed conflict in the defence of its right to self-determination, or a group meeting the test for civil war may not also generate groups unaffiliated with the combatant forces that engage relatively exclusively in terrorist acts. Thus, there may be groups that could be called terrorist groups whose acts may arise from a political position regarding the armed conflict, but who are, for want of a better term, acting outside the armed conflict.

79. Requiring rigour in these determinations does not mean that all acts undertaken in the course of armed conflict are legal acts of war. Humanitarian law identifies acts that are prohibited under the laws and customs of war and, hence, are chargeable as illegal acts. Customary international law, as well as the Geneva Conventions and their Additional Protocols identify those illegal acts that are considered especially serious international crimes when taking place in armed conflicts. While there is no mention of terrorist acts in the 1907 Hague Convention and Regulations or the 1949 Geneva Conventions, specific mention of a prohibition of terrorism as a method of warfare is made in Additional Protocol II, Article 4.2 (d). Additional Protocol I, Article 51.2 prohibits war-time 'acts or threats of violence the primary purpose of which is to spread terror among the civilian population'. It makes no legal sense to focus solely on terrorist acts carried out by combatants in the context of armed conflict and to disregard other acts that also violate the rules of war at the same level of gravity. Allegations of any and all violations of the rules of war should be made in the context of applicable armed conflict law, its enforcement provisions and all the protection and guarantees they provide.

80. There is sometimes an obvious reluctance among States to take seriously and impartially their obligations under the enforcement provisions of humanitarian law instruments. This might be one of the reasons why debate regarding certain armed conflicts is sometimes shifted to debate on terrorism. In any case, the Special Rapporteur notes that in the cases of the former Yugoslavia and Rwanda there has been concerted international effort to address violations of the parties in an impartial way. It remains to be seen how the International Criminal Court, once it is established, will improve the overall situation. Regardless of the status of the Rome Statute, existing international humanitarian law rules provide that any State may seek out and try alleged violators of the laws and customs of war in its national courts or turn such persons over for trial in another State, provided that they do so with impartiality and in proceedings that meet minimum standards. Whatever the perceived gain that may be behind States' unwillingness to do this and address wars as wars, the removal of some of the current armed conflicts from the terrorism debate would be a major gain in the potential for progress in defining and acting on reducing terrorism.

81. There remain, however, cases where there may be political or other difficulties in determining whether a situation is an armed conflict or terrorism. Thus, for example, in the context of Article 2 common to the Geneva Conventions, which provides that humanitarian law applies in all cases of partial or total occupation of territory 'even if the said occupation meets with no armed resistance', the following situations may be envisaged. (a) A situation where there has been long-time acquiescence to an occupation but where the occupied people subsequently try to restore or gain their claim to self-determination to the point of taking up arms. Their military actions may be few in number, or relatively ineffective – in other words, not meeting a minimum definition of armed conflict. The occupying power may, then, invoke its long occupancy as proof that its occupation is legitimate and characterize any and all use of force against it as terrorism. (b) There is a situation of nascent civil war – i.e. a situation where there are armed groups who either do not control sufficient territory, or who engage in military activities that are more than sporadic but less than sustained, or whose actions do not qualify as military actions under the laws and customs of war. The group may or may not claim the right to self-determination, but if so, the claim may be, at best, dubious. (c) In yet another situation, a group with a strong self-determination claim may use force, but almost exclusively in ways that clearly violate the laws and customs of war. With regard to the above situations, it can be argued that, in the first, characterization as terrorism could be incorrect, while in the second it could be correct. In the third situation, the perpetrators of acts that violate the laws and customs of war could be charged under applicable humanitarian law provisions or even anti-terrorism laws applicable in the given situation. It goes without saying that, in any event, the peoples' underlying self-determination claim remains intact.

III.   CONTEMPORARY FORMS OF TERRORISM

82. Resolutions adopted by the Commission and Sub-Commission have indicated their concern over the possible exploitation of new technologies by terrorist groups. The Special Rapporteur recognizes the importance of the wide-ranging debate being carried on among academics, policy makers and non-governmental organizations on contemporary forms of terrorism. While such ill-defined labels as 'superterrorism', 'catastrophic terrorism', or 'megaterrorism' are used with increasing frequency to describe manifestations of political violence that have arisen in the past 10 to 20 years, it is essential to disaggregate the elements grouped under these rubrics in order to achieve analytical clarity with regard to the actors and forms of violence. At first reading, the Special Rapporteur leans towards the view that (i) the plausibility of the threat must be grounded in the practicalities of the act, not in worst-case speculation; and (ii) that much of what is being described as terrorism could in fact also be categorized as non-terrorist activity. These conclusions should be taken into consideration if a realistic account is to be made of possible solutions to the problems of human rights and contemporary forms of terrorism.

83. In studying this topic, the Special Rapporteur notes that most of the literature relating to it is by political scientists or sociologists and other scientists, not lawyers or human rights specialists, and is presented in a factual or speculatively factual way rather than as legal analysis. For this reason, the Special Rapporteur's discussion has to depart from her usual form of legal analysis. Thus, she begins by examining possible terrorist use of weapons of mass destruction (WMD) as this is the form of new technology that generates the most commentary. She then comments on the role of new information technologies in contemporary terrorism, giving special attention to the concept of 'cyberterrorism'. Other issues relating to new technologies may be presented at a later stage in her work.

A.   Weapons of mass destruction and terrorism

84. The spectre of the terrorist use of WMD is unquestionably frightening. Apocalyptic depictions of hundreds of thousands of gruesome deaths caused by the detonation of a nuclear weapon or the release of anthrax in an urban area abound in the literature and are frequently invoked by States to justify counter-terrorist policies. Precisely because of the potentially grave implications that both the terrorist use of WMD and counter-terrorism policy hold for the enjoyment of human rights, it is essential to consider carefully the reality of the threat and the efficacy of the counterstrategy.

1.   Chemical weapons

85. Chemical weapons have existed for most of the twentieth Century. They can take liquid or gaseous forms and are generally separated into four categories: blister agents such as mustard gas; blood agents such as hydrogen cyanide; choking agents such as phosgene and chlorine; and nerve agents such as sarin, VX, tabun and

soman. Nerve agents are the most deadly as they block the enzyme cholinesterase, effectively short-circuiting the neuromuscular system and killing the victim almost immediately, and are also of most interest to a group or individual intending to kill large numbers of people.

86. The technical feasibility of the terrorist use of chemical weapons can be broken down into two areas: production and delivery. While all the ingredients and equipment needed to produce chemical weapons are dual-use and most are readily available through commercial dealers, the actual production of such weapons presents difficulties. Although estimates of the amount of experience needed to produce chemical weapons range from a high-school knowledge of chemistry to extensive post-graduate work, most experts agree that some graduate education is necessary to produce nerve agents, for example, safely in large quantities. Estimates of the cost of setting up a functioning nerve agent production plant similarly range widely, from US$ 20,000 to US$ 20 million. The only effort to regulate the export of dual-use equipment and chemical precursors has been that of the 30 countries comprising the Australia Group, whose effort must be expanded and intensified if it is to function effectively.

87. Nerve agents can be delivered by many devices, from bombs to sprayers to punctured plastic bags. Most experts agree that the only effective way of distributing nerve agents over large areas outdoors is via aerosolization, a means that requires high levels of technical skill and is easily disturbed by environmental conditions. Moreover, even under optimal conditions, 'hundreds to thousands of kilograms' of agent are necessary per square kilometre. An outdoor attack would likely kill no more than several hundred people. At best, dispersing the agent inside a building might kill a few thousand. Thus, for terrorist use a chemical weapon would do nothing that a conventional bomb could not do more easily and with more certainty. The amounts necessary would take months or years to produce in any but the largest production facilities.

88. The experience of the Aum Shinrikyo cult in Japan provides insight into the problems for potential terrorists of using chemical weapons. Aum executed two effective nerve agent attacks: the 27 June 1994 sarin attack in Matsumoto, Japan, that led to seven deaths and 144 persons being injured and the 20 March 1995 sarin attack on the Tokyo subway that left 12 dead and over a thousand injured. At its peak in 1995, Aum had 40,000 members worldwide, with total assets reported as ranging from tens of millions to 1.4 billion United States dollars. Their membership included a number of young scientists and technicians, and Aum had established an international network to obtain chemicals and equipment. Despite their massive funds, infrastructure, skills and apparent determination to produce mass casualties, their nine attempts at using biological weapons were unmitigated failures. They then switched to chemical agents and conducted their two deadly attacks. However, neither produced deaths on the scale that is usually cited in the WMD terrorism literature or, indeed, that Aum had hoped for. The delivery methods were crude: in the first attack, a large fan and a heating element, and in the second, punctured plastic bags.

Even Aum, the paradigmatic example of a terrorist group using chemical weapons to cause mass casualties, could not surmount the technical obstacles to do it.

2.   Biological weapons

89. Biological weapons are exponentially more deadly than chemical weapons but, fortunately, also more difficult to produce and deliver. Biological weapons are generally separated into four categories: bacteria, including anthrax and plague; viruses, including yellow fever, Ebola, and Venezuelan equine encephalitis; rickettsiae, including Q fever; and toxins, including ricin and botulinum toxin. Some are communicable, and many have an incubation period, making them hard to diagnose and counteract.

90. In terms of production, the acquisition of seed cultures is the most difficult obstacle. While some cultures could in the past be ordered legally from international collections, export controls are now being more strictly enforced. Growth media and equipment are relatively easy to obtain. As with chemical weapons, estimates of the technical knowledge needed to produce biological weapons range from a basic knowledge of biology to years of post-doctoral work, though again it is generally agreed that some graduate-level experience is required. The total cost of building a small biological weapons production facility might range from US$ 200,000 to 2 million. There are several trade-offs involved in production: while wet agents are easier to produce, they are much less effective than dry agents, and the more pure an agent is, the less stable it is. Doctors and medical researchers generally cite anthrax, plague, smallpox, and botulinum toxin as the most probable candidates for use by terrorist organizations.

91. Because of the extreme sensitivity of biological agents to environmental factors like sunlight, humidity and temperature, they are very difficult to deliver effectively in large quantities. The creation of a respirable aerosol represents the most difficult technical challenge, as was evident in Aum's series of failures at spreading anthrax through aerosolizers. In fact, there has never been a biological weapons attack by a terrorist that resulted in more than one death, testament to the inherent difficulty of producing and delivering a biological agent over a large area.

3.   Nuclear terrorism

92. Experts generally agree that the acquisition and use of nuclear weapons by terrorists is less likely than the possible use of chemical or biological weapons. Although stories abound of the smuggling of stolen nuclear weapons, including the notorious 'suitcase bombs', there has been no confirmed sale of a nuclear weapon and no non-State actor has ever been confirmed as possessing a nuclear weapon, let alone detonating one. Still, the problem of 'loose nukes', as it has been termed, requires a concerted multilateral effort to account for nuclear weapons and to put them under safeguards.

93. Those, groups or individuals, who cannot obtain a ready-made nuclear weapon could try to construct one themselves, although this would require a high level of technical knowledge and the acquisition of a suitable amount of weapons-grade, or at least weapons-usable, fissile material, either highly enriched uranium (HEU) or plutonium. Although rumours likewise abound around the putative market for nuclear materials, there has not been a single case involving enough material to actually make a bomb. Some experts even question the existence of a demand for fissile material or nuclear weapons. The most difficult manner of obtaining a nuclear weapon is to produce one's own HEU in a reactor. The prime example of a clandestine project of this sort is South Africa, where the total cost was nearly US$ 200 million. The cost of a project that had obtained fissile materials would be much lower.

94. Other possible forms of nuclear terrorism may include the use of radiation-dispersion devices, radiological weapons that utilize more easily obtained non-fissile radioactive isotopes to disperse a powder of radioactive materials. Although generally considered impractical for standard military use, they could be useful for instilling terror in a population even if the casualty count would probably be quite low. Another potential form of nuclear terrorism is the sabotage of nuclear reactors. Chechen rebels, for example, have repeatedly threatened to do this in Russia, and some experts consider this to be the most plausible form of nuclear terrorism.

4.   Potential use of weapons of mass destruction

95. Most chemical biological and nuclear weapons have existed for decades. Terrorism is a phenomenon with a centuries-longer history. It has been suggested that in the recent explosion in writing and policy-making concerning the possibility of their combination, the Aum Shinrikyo subway attack was the most important catalyst, as it represented the first significant instance of the terrorist use of WMD in a modern urban environment. Suddenly, the debate was transformed from 'will it happen?', to 'when will it happen again?', as experts assumed that terrorists' normal fondness for mimicry would lead others to attempt similar attacks. In addition, new interest in alleged biochemical weapons programmes and concern over vulnerable nuclear, chemical and biological weapons stockpiles in the hands of certain Governments gave rise to the fear that WMD were more easily available, either from 'State sponsors' or on the black market.

96. But the question of why terrorists would use WMD remains. In the oft-quoted phrase of a well-known expert on terrorism: 'terrorists want a lot of people watching, not a lot of people dead'. That is to say, terrorists are cognizant that an extremely lethal WMD attack could alienate their supporters or cause a fatal counter-attack by the Government. Moreover, terrorists might be fearful of handling and using such dangerous substances themselves, and might consider conventional weapons as satisfactory for their needs. In the face of this orthodoxy, two arguments are generally made by experts and policy makers to support the possibility of the terrorist use of WMD. First, many point to the 'increasing lethality' of terrorist attacks and, extrapolating from the trend, argue that terrorists will turn to WMD as they be-

come more familiar with their deadly capacities. Second, many have sketched out the portrait of a 'new breed' of terrorists who, breaking from the traditional terrorist mould, are willing to use WMD. This new breed is variously characterized as 'nihilistic', 'religiously-oriented', 'fanatical', 'fundamentalist', 'apocalyptic', 'ethnic' and always 'extremist'. These new actors' other-worldly orientation and lack of concrete political objectives release them from the restraints of orthodox terrorists and they are willing to use WMD to carry out their agenda of mass destruction.

97. The Special Rapporteur believes that it is essential to avoid falling prey to alarmist analyses of the potential for WMD terrorism and, hence, becoming complacent towards the possible violations of human rights that can easily accompany a counter-terrorist strategy premised on these dire warnings. Some of the technical obstacles to obtaining and utilizing WMD were outlined earlier. Even if these obstacles are overcome, the evidence still speaks against the possibility of an imminent WMD attack by terrorists. Worldwide in the last 25 years, there have only been five WMD attacks by terrorists that caused 10 or more deaths (the most being only 19) and all used chemical weapons with 'low-tech' delivery methods. In total, according to one source, from 1975 to July 2000, there were two fatalities and 752 injuries due to the terrorist use of biological weapons, and 150 fatalities and 2,492 injuries due to chemical weapons. These data are clearly dwarfed by the hundreds of deaths caused by many conventional terrorist attacks.

98. All this does not mean, of course, that these numbers are trivial, or even that the probability of a future slide to mass destruction terrorism is unlikely and, therefore, should not capture our attention. It only means that the link between the recent increased lethality of terrorist attacks and the use of WMD appears questionable. Indeed, this increased lethality has not been a result of the use of WMD but rather of a string of deadly conventional terrorist attacks, such as the 13 simultaneous bombings in Bombay in 1993, the 1995 bombing of the Federal Building in Oklahoma City and the 1998 bombing of the United States Embassies in Nairobi and Dar-es-Saalam. Further, experts in the field have convincingly argued that an analytic distinction should be drawn between the small-scale use of WMD in tactical attacks and the use of WMD for the purpose of mass destruction. Be that as it may, this is not the place to speculate in more detail on the potential use by terrorists of WMD. The Special Rapporteur thinks that given the serious doubts about the likelihood of imminent use of WMD by terrorists we should be wary of overinflating the dangers of 'catastrophic', 'postmodern' terrorism or 'superterrorism', which carry with them potential justification of counter-terrorist machinery with the associated potential infringements upon civil liberties and human rights. For example, the threat of WMD could lead to the invoking of stringent restrictions and an increase in police powers. These and other adverse effects of a climate of fear (engendered by the fear of terrorism) can prompt a reduction of human rights as readily as an actual terrorist presence.

B.   Terrorism and new information technologies

99. There are a number of delineations that must be made concerning the rhetoric surrounding contemporary forms of terrorism and the new information technologies (NIT). First, NIT can be used by terrorists or other groups for organizational purposes and as a means of disseminating their own information. This use of NIT can give rise to new network forms of organization that are especially useful for terrorists, criminals and other organizations working in opposition to States. The all-channel network is especially effective, as it allows for an organization that is cemented ideologically and linked by constant information flows from every node to every other node, while not presenting any single privileged point at which the enemy can attack. E-mail, Web pages, bulletin boards, fax machines and cellular telephones provide the technical infrastructure for these new forms of organization and also provide ways for small groups with few resources to disseminate their information throughout the world instantly. It must be made clear that the use of NIT by terrorist groups for propagandistic or organizational purposes may not necessarily qualify as terrorism itself, unless it meets legal standards for incitement.

100. The use of NIT as a destructive tool has become popularized under the name 'cyberterrorism'. But, just as the use of NIT for propagandistic purposes may not be terrorism, so many uses of NIT for disruptive or destructive purposes may not be terrorism either. Thanks to the rapid spread of the Internet, would-be hackers around the world have a wealth of tools at their disposal, ranging from notorious viruses to such lesser-known weapons as 'logic bombs', 'worms', and 'Trojan horses'.

101. Moreover, as personal computing capacities have increased dramatically over the last decade, hackers can launch multinational coordinated attacks upon computer systems, breaking in and crashing networks, destroying data, and shutting down systems dependent upon computer networks. While a number of different categories of actions fit within this framework, they do not all fit under the rubric of 'cyberterrorist'. The Special Rapporteur would reserve the label of cyberterrorism for those acts whose intention is to cause disruption or destruction sufficient enough to terrorize the population. Oft-cited examples of this are attacks upon air traffic control systems, the commandeering of weapons systems and the disruption of emergency medical communications. Actions of this sort seem indeed to qualify as the use of NIT for terrorism, but the label should not be allowed to spill over onto other classes of actions. Further, it should be noted that, despite the alarmist rhetoric, amongst the reportedly thousands of attacks by hackers which major computer systems face daily, to date there has been no confirmed report of a cyberterrorist attack. In fact, many experts deem such an attack as extremely unlikely, because of its difficulty and potential inefficacy.

IV.   THE IMPACT OF TERRORISM ON HUMAN RIGHTS

102. Terrorist acts, whether committed by States or non-State actors, may affect the right to life, the right to freedom from torture and arbitrary detention, women's

rights, children's rights, health, subsistence (food), democratic order, peace and security, the right to non-discrimination, and any number of other protected human
rights norms. Actually, there is probably not a single human right exempt from the
impact of terrorism.

103. In its Resolutions 1999/27 of 26 April 1999 and 2000/30 of 20 April 2000, the
Commission requested the Special Rapporteur to give attention to the questions presented in these resolutions: certain human rights, concern for the victims, concern
that counter-terrorist action may not fully comply with international human rights
standards, and special concern about hostage-taking, kidnapping and extortion. The
Commission's Resolution 2001/37 of 23 April 2001, is essentially identical on these
points to the two aforementioned resolutions. It is also worth noting in this context
that during the preceding debates many statements by Governments as well as non-
governmental organizations drew particular attention to the curtailment of procedural rights provided in international human rights instruments in cases of persons
charged under national anti-terrorism laws. As usual, there was a large divergence of
views expressed regarding the issue of non-State actors. Accordingly, the Special
Rapporteur will now attempt to address some of these questions, although, regrettably, briefly owing to the size constraints on reports.

A.   Direct impact

1.   General concerns

104. In her review of terrorist hostage-taking, kidnapping and extortion carried out
by terrorist groups, the Special Rapporteur has found that these acts are mostly carried out by known groups who predominate in only a few areas. The political issues
involved in these areas are also well known. In the context of a study on terrorism
and human rights, it is difficult to know what the Commission wishes of the Special
Rapporteur regarding these acts except to note again that there have been few new
instances of new groups engaging in them. This does not mean that such acts may
not be committed in the future in other areas by new groups, but it is difficult if not
impossible to predict where they might occur. Criminal liability for these acts remains a concern of national and existing international law, including the requirement of international cooperation in apprehending persons alleged to have engaged
in such acts.

105. The Commission has also expressed its concern about rape by terrorist groups.
In this connection, the Special Rapporteur draws attention not only to the work of
the Commission regarding violence against women and the work of the
Commission's Special Rapporteur on violence against women, its causes and consequences, but also to the relevant work of the Sub-Commission and of its Special
Rapporteur on systematic rape, sexual slavery and slavery-like practices during
armed conflict. The Commission has already resolved that rape by non-State actors
constitutes a violation of the rights of women.

106. States have an affirmative duty to promote and protect the human rights of all persons under their jurisdictions. While this is a basic tenet of human rights law, it is important to recall it here as both the Commission and the Sub-Commission have stressed this point in the context also of terrorism. States that resort to State terrorism, whether international or internal, grossly violate the basic concepts of human rights. Such States should be subjected to both international condemnation and international action in the light of instruments and mechanisms of human rights and, where applicable, humanitarian law. Such action, if effective, would greatly diminish incidence of terrorism today.

107. When terrorist acts or threats of terrorist acts by non-State actors threaten the lives and safety of persons under a State's jurisdiction, it is the responsibility and the duty of the State to protect those persons. A State's minimum response should not be limited to proscribing terrorist acts in its criminal law system or in the training of local and national law enforcement or military personnel. Such a response would be, in the Special Rapporteur's view, too narrow and limited, and would not result in meaningful protection from terrorist acts. A State must also undertake a thorough study of all aspects of terrorism, including causal factors and the implications of its foreign and domestic policies in the light of international law (especially in terms of human rights) that have generated a risk of terrorist acts being committed against its citizens or persons under its jurisdiction. Were all States to do this in an unbiased way, and then adopt meaningful responses – which may or may not require changes in policies – the incidence of terrorist acts by non-State actors would also dramatically decline.

108. Unfortunately, some States consider that to focus any attention on the causes of terrorism has the undesired effect of generating sympathy for, if not the terrorist acts, at least, the context in which they arise. Public opinion may then be rallied to pressure a State to change a policy that it does not want to change, even at the cost of increased fear of terrorism. Additionally, some are of the opinion that focus on the causes that might result in changes of policy could be viewed as giving in to terrorist demands. Even so, States are sometimes obliged to change policies that contravene international law. Yet this is not viewed as giving in to terrorist demands, in spite of the fact that a terrorist group may seek those very changes.

109. Sometimes, a State may utterly fail to protect its people in an effective way from acts of terrorism. In these situations, one could say that the State is either unable (incapable) or unwilling – or both – to control those acts. The State, then, has effectively reneged on its affirmative duty to protect its own people. Such a State, in these situations, can itself be liable for acts carried out by non-State actors. On the other hand, a State's over-response to terrorism can also effect human rights. Thus, the Commission has repeatedly expressed concern over counter-terrorist measures, as evinced in its latest resolutions on human rights and terrorism that state yet again that measures to counter terrorism must be in strict conformity with international human rights law.

110. In this context, the rights to freedom of speech, association, belief, religion and movement, and the rights of refugees are particularly vulnerable to undue suspension in the guise of anti-terrorist measures. This may sometimes occur when individuals or groups in a State express support for a political position that is in opposition to the government's position but conforms with that espoused by a group labelled as terrorist.

111. It should, finally, be noted that a number of States either have or are in the process of enacting anti-terrorism legislation which is frequently criticized by legal scholars and human rights defenders. Some of this legislation contains no definition of terrorism, while some contains lists of certain acts. Some of it includes provisions in which groups are put on an official terrorist list, frequently with no analysis of the particulars of the situation or the nature of the group. Those groups and others espousing similar views but uninvolved with the groups concerned may face severe consequences. As will be set out below, judicial proceedings to challenge this false labelling or to defend a person charged with an offence under such anti-terrorism legislation may leave room for serious negation of a wide range of procedural rights.

2.   Special note on judicial process rights

112. The Special Rapporteur has reviewed a number of national laws regarding terrorism and the comments of States that have responded either to the initiative of the General Assembly or to this study. While some national laws take full account of international human rights norms, others do not in very significant ways. Accordingly, she thinks it should be of high interest to set out some of the situations that could give rise to a serious possibility of misuse and abuse of defendants' rights.

113. In some States, detained persons considered as terrorists may be denied visitation rights. This can include the denial of access to a defendant's own attorney, or such severe restriction of access to counsel, including the constant presence of State officials in attorney-client sessions, as to reduce the right to counsel to a nullity. The defendant is held, essentially, incommunicado.

114. States may have special procedures that allow identity checks, house-to-house searches and other acts that have implications for both privacy rights and fair trial provisions. The State may lower the standard for a warrant, for example, or eliminate the need for a warrant at all. Not only a defendant but also large numbers of uninvolved persons may be subjected to serious encroachment on their rights, especially with house-to-house searches and other intrusions into privacy.

115. Some States have provisions that affect the actual judicial proceedings. For example, persons accused of terrorist acts may be limited in the number of witnesses that may be called, or may even be denied any witnesses at all. This can seriously impair any attempt by a defendant to prove he or she has no association with a particular group considered to be terrorist, or had nothing to do with a particular act.

This could be of great importance if the person is charged not with a terrorist act directly but under group liability statutes.

116. A defendant may also seek to prove that a group to which he or she is ascribed is not by law a terrorist group. Curtailment of witnesses such as experts in international or national law relating to the analysis of terrorism could seriously hinder the defence. The Special Rapporteur is keenly aware that there are complex legal questions at stake – questions that an ordinary defence counsel is ill-prepared to address even in the most highly educated of legal communities. Further, in many States the judiciary might be reluctant to countermand the State in these matters. Even in States with a relatively impartial, independent judiciary, there are few lawyers and judges with sufficient education in international human rights and humanitarian law standards to rule fairly, especially if a defendant is not allowed experts or other witnesses.

117. Judicial process rights may be especially at risk when a State uses group liability or conspiracy laws against alleged members of groups labelled as terrorist. For example, a person who may have once distributed literature relating to the same goal as an alleged terrorist group could be charged with aiding and abetting terrorism and could be charged with any acts proved to have been carried out by the group – acts of which a defendant has no involvement or even awareness. Conspiracy laws can be especially harmful to procedural rights in situations of internal or international armed conflict that a State has labelled as 'terrorist'. Such situations can dramatically impair rights under humanitarian law in cases where there is no group liability and where both legitimate military acts and acts in support of humanitarian relief cannot be criminalized.

B.   Indirect impact

118. Either State or non-State actors may intentionally fan the fear of terrorist acts against a population. Fear out of proportion to actual risk can generate, for example, attitudes of generalized fear of a particular race or religion. Clearly, in a number of countries orchestrated denouncing of certain groups has already resulted in generalized racism and religious intolerance. Undue fear leads to weakened resistance to overly harsh anti-terrorism measures. The desire of a State to have such measures may lie behind fear campaigns. Some States may consider that the resulting racism and religious intolerance is useful to its political agenda and therefore worth the price. However, from a human rights perspective such cynicism is offensive and has had a serious negative effect on human rights wherever these policies occur. In any case, there may be a serious risk of curtailment of basic civil liberties.

119. There are two related sub-issues to the undue fear situation, which – although highly political – have a direct relationship to human rights. A State's people may be motivated into an irrational fear of other States and of their leaders and people far out of proportion to any risk actually posed. This, of course, has a negative impact on the idea of international solidarity. The imposition of unilateral sanctions or other

penalties by States sometimes, in an attempt to extend these sanctions and penalties to third party States, is a policy that the General Assembly has repeatedly and forcefully rejected as being in violation of the Charter. While having an impact on civil and political rights, this also has and can continue to have a serious impact on economic, social and cultural rights, both in obvious and not so obvious ways. In any case, the practice of unilateral action can be viewed as violating the spirit of the international organization's appeals for international cooperation in addressing terrorism and terrorist acts.

120. The second of the sub-issues relating to undue fear of terrorism arises in the context of the 'my freedom fighter is your terrorist' debate that the Special Rapporteur has already referred to above and in her previous work. Indeed, there may be a number of reasons why some States would purposefully mislabel armed conflict situations as terrorism, but the Special Rapporteur does not need to dwell on this here.

C.   The question of impunity

121. The Commission and the Sub-Commission have both raised the issue of impunity in relation to terrorism. Clearly, an important method of reducing terrorist acts is to deter future acts by resolute prosecution of those involved. Rather than deterring terrorism, State practices of impunity can only be viewed as encouraging terrorism.

122. The Sub-Commission has already addressed impunity involving civil and political rights, as well as economic, social and cultural rights, in two excellent studies. While neither study directly addresses terrorist acts, terrorist acts viewed as impairing civil and political rights have been those drawing the most attention in the Commission and the Sub-Commission and on the part of the Special Rapporteur in her previous work and in the present report as well. Yet a review of the types of acts mentioned by Mr. Guissé in his report addressing economic, social and cultural rights leads the Special Rapporteur to consider that the following current practices could potentially be considered in the context of terrorism and human rights: structural adjustment programmes that severely impair subsistence-level economic rights, embargoes, corruption of government officials, monetary fraud, human caused ecological disasters, the manipulation of health systems and pharmaceuticals and the manipulation of foodstuffs. Mr. Guissé provides a two-part scheme for judicial measures addressing impunity: compensation for victims and prosecution of violators. He recommends that violations of economic, social and cultural rights should be declared international crimes with universal jurisdiction.

123. The Special Rapporteur rejects any impunity for terrorist acts, whether perpetrated by State or non-State actors, and involving civil, political, economic, social or cultural acts. Regrettably, impunity occurs, and in many guises. In the case of non-State actors, impunity can occur under the guise of selective prosecution or prosecutorial discretion. While this is occasionally valid, due to a realistic appraisal

that existing evidence against persons accused of terrorist acts is unconvincing, in some situations there is sufficient evidence to prosecute but the State chooses to ignore it. In some States, victims of the alleged terrorist acts, or their survivors, may not have legal standing to compel a State to prosecute the perpetrators. These victims or their survivors may also be unable to bring a civil action for damages because of a wide array of judicial barriers.

124. A key question that arises in the context of impunity is the degree to which a head of State or other State official can avoid judicial consequences for State terrorism under the theory of sovereign immunity. However, as has been made clear in post-Second World War tribunals, as well as in the tribunals recently established to address issues arising in the former Yugoslavia and Rwanda, there can be no sovereign immunity for war crimes, genocide or crimes against humanity. To this list, the Special Rapporteur thinks that State terrorism could be added, although, as already made clear above, in many instances of State terrorism, the State has engaged in either war crimes, crimes against humanity or genocide against its own people or nationals of another State. Nevertheless, the Rome Statute of the International Criminal Court has not included acts of State terrorism occurring outside the context of armed conflict or genocide.

D.   Extradition

125. Extradition of a person alleged to have committed a terrorist act from one State to another, legally-interested State is one way the international community can address impunity. International anti-terrorism instruments and most of the existing regional comprehensive conventions on terrorism have a heavy focus on the issue of extradition, in large part because extradition is almost universally viewed as a powerful tool in preventing impunity and, as a consequence, reducing terrorism. The fear of extradition to a State targeted by their acts or to a State that will prosecute is considered a major deterrent for potential terrorists. Thus, it is important that persons who might be persuaded to commit terrorist acts know that, if captured, they would surely be prosecuted. Such persons must also understand the relationship between the law of political asylum and the evolving law of terrorism, under which persons who have committed terrorist acts may not be granted asylum. Thus, an international regime with operative extradition laws, in which there is no safe haven for persons who have committed terrorist acts, could be viewed as an effective deterrent to terrorist acts.

126. Of course, there should be careful scrutiny of calls by one State to another State to hand over persons accused by that State of having committed terrorist acts. Likewise, when calls for extradition are subject to judicial proceedings, courts should carefully review such appeals to ensure correct application of, inter alia, humanitarian law.

127. Extradition requests can also generate conflicts in the area of requisite evidence for a prima facie case, burdens of proof and other procedural issues that are not fully

addressed in the regional conventions. Such conflicts could lead to a denial of an extradition request. Requested States or alleged perpetrators may also invoke a variety of forum non conveniens defences. For example, a requested State may refuse to turn over an alleged perpetrator to a State that might directly, or through its judicial system, violate a defendant's rights. In this regard, action has been taken to prevent return of requested persons to States having the death penalty. There are other factors relating to human rights compliance that a requested State may take into consideration prior to ordering extradition. In this regard, it is especially important that States have practices and judicial systems that fully comply with international human rights and humanitarian law norms, so as not to impair the use of extradition as a preventive force and a remedy against terrorism.

V.   CONCLUDING OBSERVATIONS

128. Both the Commission and the Sub-Commission have requested the Special Rapporteur to address other issues related to terrorism that are best discussed here because they are actually means of reducing terrorism. Most of these issues relate directly to human rights and humanitarian law norms.

129. In reviewing contemporary terrorism, one might roughly observe that those States with the best human rights records are the States with the least likelihood of problems with domestic terrorism. Similarly, those States with international relationships that most conform to the goals and principles of the Charter are likely to be the States least affected by international terrorism. It follows that an obvious step to reduce terrorism is the full realization of human rights and the practice of genuine democratic processes throughout the world, among States and in every State. All efforts must be made to address better the realization of human rights, in particular in relation to self-determination, racism, internal ethnic and political representation, and class-based economic or cultural divisions in society.

130. Violations of human rights, humanitarian law and basic principles of the Charter, then, are among the major causal factors of terrorism. As noted earlier in this progress report, careful attention to causal factors of terrorism is one of the duties of all States regarding terrorism and human rights. The overall result of addressing causal factors could be a reduction in terrorist acts. Thus, rather than being viewed as 'legitimizing' terrorist groups, as some States have suggested, careful study of causal factors should be an essential logical component of any plan to reduce terrorism, especially with regard to problem areas or situations in which terrorist acts occur with frequency.

131. The full realization of human rights also involves achievement of economic balance among States, including the right to development. In similar fashion, better efforts should be made to achieve improved relations between States, not only because this is mandated in the Charter, but also because it is viewed as essential to the global realization of human rights as indicated in Article 28 of the Universal Declaration: quite clearly an international order that is generating terrorist acts hardly

qualifies as a 'social and international order in which the rights and freedoms set forth in the Declaration can be fully realized'.

132. In the course of her work, the Special Rapporteur became aware that the scale and scope of this topic is perhaps larger than other topics undertaken by the Sub-Commission. In this progress report, she has sought to provide more theoretical insight into some of the many complex issues relevant to the study on terrorism and human rights, giving attention to the issues raised by the Commission and Sub-Commission. However, limitations concerning the size of Sub-Commission reports have not made it possible to fully address all the issues that the Special Rapporteur believes should be included in this progress report.

133. There is much more that needs to be assessed concerning extradition in the context of terrorism. As already mentioned, the new regional conventions place great emphasis on extradition. The issue of a sovereign immunity defence when a State actor is charged with acts of State terrorism also deserves more attention, as it stands prominently before the international community in several cases recently or not yet resolved. The Special Rapporteur would also like to review some ongoing or recently concluded cases relating to international terrorism and she considers that review of all the existing comprehensive regional instruments on terrorism would be very useful in the context of definition as well. Last but not least, she would like to complete her consideration of sub-State (or individual) terrorism and of the related question of the accountability of non-State actors before the final report.

134. In the light of her concerns about this array of topics that need more attention, the Special Rapporteur recommends that the Sub-Commission consider authorizing her to prepare a second progress report.

4.3.4   The (Sub-)Commission on Human Rights

In view of the September 2001 events, it is of relevance to compare the 2001 resolution with the 2002 one. As one can notice, the 'fear' that the war against terrorism might violate human rights has been slightly reinforced, but the overall impression would appear to be that the Commission acts as a 'mini-GA' and tries to cover also the aspects which belong firmly to the Sixth Committee.

4.3.4.1 *Sub-Commission Resolution 2001/18: Terrorism and human rights*

The Sub-Commission on the Promotion and Protection of Human Rights,
Guided by the principles embodied in the Charter of the United Nations, the Universal Declaration of Human Rights, the Declaration on Principles of International Law concerning Friendly Relations and Cooperation among States in accordance with the Charter of the United Nations, the International Covenants on Human Rights and other international and regional instruments, relating to human rights and international humanitarian law,

Recalling the Vienna Declaration and Programme of Action adopted on 25 June 1993 by the World Conference on Human Rights, in which the Conference reaffirmed that terrorism is indeed aimed at the destruction of human rights, fundamental freedoms and democracy,

Recalling also the Declaration on the Occasion of the Fiftieth Anniversary of the United Nations and the United Nations Millennium Declaration adopted by the General Assembly at its fiftieth and fifty-fifth sessions, respectively,

Recalling further General Assembly Resolution 54/164 of 17 December 1999, as well as Commission on Human Rights Resolution 2001/37 of 23 April 2001 and its own Resolution 1999/26 of 26 August 1999,

Regretting that the negative impact of terrorism, in all its dimensions, on human rights continues to remain alarming, despite national and international efforts to combat it,

Convinced that terrorism, in all its forms and manifestations, wherever and by whomever committed, can never be justified in any instance, including as a means to promote and protect human rights,

Bearing in mind that the most essential and basic human right is the right to life,

Bearing in mind also that terrorism creates an environment that destroys the freedom from fear of the people,

Convinced that terrorism in many cases poses a severe challenge to democracy, civil society and the rule of law,

Deploring the large number of innocent persons killed, massacred and maimed by terrorism in indiscriminate and random acts of violence and terror, which cannot be justified under any circumstances,

Emphasizing the need to intensify the fight against terrorism at the national level, to enhance effective international cooperation in combating terrorism in conformity with international law and to strengthen the role of the United Nations system in this respect,

Reiterating that all States have an obligation to promote and protect all human rights and fundamental freedoms, and that every individual should strive to secure their universal and effective recognition and observance,

Reaffirming that all measures to counter terrorism must be in strict conformity with international law, including international human rights and humanitarian law standards,

Reiterating the great importance of the study on terrorism and human rights,

Having considered the analytical and well-documented progress report (E/CN.4/Sub.2/2001/31) prepared by the Special Rapporteur, Ms. Kalliopi Koufa, and having heard her comprehensive introductory statement,

1. *Expresses* its deep appreciation and thanks to the Special Rapporteur, Ms. Kalliopi Koufa for her excellent progress report (E/CN.4/Sub.2/2001/31) and her introductory statement;

2. *Requests* the Special Rapporteur to continue her work, taking into consideration the views and comments made during the discussion of the topic at the Sub-Commission, as well as the replies submitted by Governments, competent organs and

bodies of the United Nations system and intergovernmental and non-governmental organizations;

3. *Requests* the Special Rapporteur, keeping in mind the importance and the complexity of the study, to continue her direct contacts with the competent services and bodies of the United Nations, in particular those in New York and Vienna, and also requests the Special Rapporteur to visit those Offices, as soon as possible, in order to expand her research, to update data and information for the study and to expedite her work;

4. *Requests* the Secretary-General to transmit the progress report of the Special Rapporteur to Governments, specialized agencies and concerned intergovernmental and non-governmental organizations with the request that they submit to the Special Rapporteur, as soon as possible, comments, information and data relating to the study on terrorism and human rights;

5. *Requests* the Secretary-General to continue to collect information, including a compilation of studies and publications, on the implications of terrorism for, as well as the effects of the fight against terrorism on, the enjoyment of human rights from all relevant sources, including Governments, specialized agencies, intergovernmental and non-governmental organizations and academic institutions, and to make them available to the Special Rapporteur;

6. *Requests* the Special Rapporteur to submit a second progress report to the Sub-Commission at its fifty-fourth session;

7. *Requests* the Secretary-General to give the Special Rapporteur all the necessary assistance in order to hold consultations with the above-mentioned competent services and bodies of the United Nations system, in particular those located in New York and Vienna, to complement and expand her essential research and to collect all the up-to-date information and data needed for the preparation of her second progress report;

8. *Recommends* the following draft decision to the Commission on Human Rights for adoption:

'The Commission on Human Rights, taking note of Resolution 2001/18 of 16 August 2001 of the Sub-Commission on the Promotion and Protection of Human Rights, approves the Sub-Commission's request to the Secretary-General to give the Special Rapporteur all the assistance necessary for the preparation of her second progress report, in particular by providing for visits to Vienna and New York in order to hold consultations with the competent services and bodies of the United Nations located there, to complement and expand her essential research and to collect all the needed and up-to-date information and data.'

4.3.4.2 *Commission Resolution 2002/... Human rights and terrorism*[13]

The Commission on Human Rights,
Guided by the Charter of the United Nations, the Universal Declaration of Human Rights, the Declaration on Principles of International Law concerning Friendly Rela-

---

[13] E/CN.4/2002/L.50/Rev.1, 16 April 2002, COMMISSION ON HUMAN RIGHTS Fifty-eighth session; resolution number not yet known; this resolution had been adopted on 22 April 2002, with 32

tions and Cooperation among States in Accordance with the Charter of the United Nations and the International Covenants on Human Rights,

Recalling the Declaration on the Occasion of the Fiftieth Anniversary of the United Nations, as well as the Declaration on Measures to Eliminate International Terrorism, adopted by the General Assembly at its fiftieth and forty-ninth sessions, respectively,

Recalling also the United Nations Millennium Declaration adopted by the General Assembly on 8 September 2000 at its fifty-fifth session,

Recalling further the Vienna Declaration and Programme of Action adopted in June 1993 by the World Conference on Human Rights (A/CONF.157/23),

Noting all previous General Assembly resolutions on the issue of terrorism, including Resolutions 46/51 of 9 December 1991, 48/122 of 20 December 1993, 49/185 of 23 December 1994, 50/186 of 22 December 1995, 52/133 of 12 December 1997 and 56/160 of 19 December 2001, as well as its own Resolutions 2000/30 of 20 April 2000 and 2001/37 of 23 April 2001,

Recalling General Assembly Resolutions 54/164 of 17 December 1999 and 54/110 of 9 December 1999, in which it decided that the Ad Hoc Committee established by Assembly Resolution 51/210 of 17 December 1996 should continue to elaborate a draft international convention for the suppression of acts of nuclear terrorism with a view to completing the instrument, should address means of further developing a comprehensive legal framework of conventions dealing with international terrorism, including considering the elaboration of a comprehensive convention on international terrorism, and should address the question of convening a high-level conference under the auspices of the United Nations to formulate a joint organized response of the international community to terrorism in all its forms and manifestations,

Reaffirming the need for the implementation of General Assembly Resolution 54/109 of 9 December 1999, in which the Assembly adopted the International Convention for the Suppression of the Financing of Terrorism,

Taking note of the importance of General Assembly Resolution 55/158 of 12 December 2000, in which the Assembly stressed the need to strengthen further international cooperation between States and between international organizations and agencies, regional organizations and arrangements and the United Nations in order to prevent, combat and eliminate terrorism in all its forms and manifestations, wherever and by whomever committed, in accordance with the principles of the Charter, international law and relevant international conventions,

Noting with great concern the growing connection between terrorist groups and other criminal organizations engaged in the illegal traffic in arms and drugs at the national and international levels, as well as the consequent commission of serious

---

votes in favour, 0 against and 21 abstentions. The resolution was based on an Algerian proposal and supported by China, Russia and most Third World countries. An alternative proposal, submitted by Mexico and supported by the West, was far more modest and straightforward. It became clear, however, that once the Algerian delegation started to propose amendments to the Mexican text the West would lack support for that alternative proposal (see E/CN.4/2002/L.110, also dated 22 April 2002).

crimes, such as murder, extortion, kidnapping, assault, the taking of hostages and robbery,

Alarmed in particular at the possibility that the terrorist groups may exploit new technologies to facilitate acts of terrorism which may cause massive damage, including huge loss of human life,

Mindful that the Security Council adopted Resolution 1373 (2001) of 28 September 2001, requiring States to adopt counter-terrorism measures, and Resolution 1377 (2001) of 12 November 2001, by which it adopted a declaration on the global effort to combat terrorism,

Convinced that terrorism, in all its forms and manifestations, wherever and by whomever committed, can never be justified in any instance, including as a means to promote and protect human rights,

Bearing in mind that the most essential and basic human right is the right to life,

Bearing in mind also that terrorism in all its forms and manifestations creates an environment that destroys the ideal of free human beings enjoying freedom from fear and want, and makes it difficult for States to promote and protect human rights and fundamental freedoms,

Bearing in mind further that terrorism in many cases poses a severe challenge to democracy, civil society and the rule of law,

Recalling in this regard the horrific events of 11 September 2001 in the United States of America which led to the loss of the lives of several thousand civilians,

Reiterating that all States have an obligation to promote and protect all human rights and fundamental freedoms and to ensure effective implementation of their obligations under international humanitarian law,

Profoundly deploring the large number of civilians killed, massacred and maimed by terrorists in indiscriminate and random acts of violence and terror, which cannot be justified under any circumstances,

Emphasizing the need to intensify the fight against terrorism in all its forms and manifestations at the national level and to enhance effective international cooperation in combating terrorism in conformity with international law, including relevant State obligations under international human rights and international humanitarian law, and to strengthen the role of the United Nations in this respect,

Recognizing the need to improve international cooperation on criminal matters and national measures so as to address impunity, which can contribute to the continued occurrence of terrorism,

Emphasizing that States shall deny safe haven to those who finance, plan, support or commit terrorist acts, or provide safe havens,

Reaffirming that all measures to counter terrorism must be in strict conformity with international law, including international human rights standards and obligations,

Seriously concerned at the gross violations of human rights perpetrated by terrorist groups,

Deciding further to promote the growing consciousness of the international community of the negative effects of terrorism in all its forms and manifestations on the full enjoyment of human rights and fundamental freedoms and on the establishment of the rule of law and democratic freedoms as enshrined in the Charter and the International Covenants on Human Rights,

1. *Reiterates its unequivocal condemnation* of all acts, methods and practices of terrorism, regardless of their motivation, in all their forms and manifestations, wherever, whenever and by whomever committed, as acts aimed at the destruction of human rights, fundamental freedoms and democracy, threatening the territorial integrity and security of States, destabilizing legitimately constituted Governments, undermining pluralistic civil society and the rule of law and having adverse consequences for the economic and social development of the State;

2. *Strongly condemns* the violations of the right to life, liberty and security;

3. *Expresses its solidarity* with the victims of terrorism;

4. *Condemns* incitement of ethnic hatred, violence and terrorism;

5. *Urges* States to fulfil their obligations under the Charter in strict conformity with international law, including human rights standards and obligations and international humanitarian law, to prevent, combat and eliminate terrorism in all its forms and manifestations, wherever, whenever and by whomever committed, and calls upon States to strengthen, where appropriate, their legislation to combat terrorism in all its forms and manifestations;

6. *Urges* States to enhance cooperation at the regional and international levels in the fight against terrorism in all its forms and manifestations, in accordance with relevant international obligations under human rights instruments and international humanitarian law, with the aim of eliminating terrorism in all its forms and manifestations, and to further strengthen cooperation with a view to bringing terrorists to justice;

7. *Calls upon* States to take appropriate measures in conformity with the relevant provisions of national and international law, including international human rights standards, before granting refugee status, with the purpose of ensuring that the asylum-seeker has not planned, facilitated or participated in the commission of terrorist acts, and to ensure, in conformity with international law, that refugee status is not abused by the perpetrators, organizers or facilitators of terrorist acts and that claims of political motivation are not recognized as grounds for refusing requests for the extradition of alleged terrorists;

8. *Urges* all relevant human rights mechanisms and procedures, as appropriate, to address the consequences of the acts, methods and practices of terrorist groups in their forthcoming reports to the Commission;

9. *Invites* the Office of the High Commissioner to respond to requests from interested Governments for assistance and advice on ensuring full compliance with international human rights standards and obligations when undertaking measures to combat terrorism;

10. *Welcomes* the report of the Secretary-General (A/56/190), and invites him to continue to seek the views of Member States on the implications of terrorism in all its forms and manifestations for the full enjoyment of all human rights and fundamental freedoms and on how the needs and concerns of victims of terrorism might be addressed, including through the possible establishment of a voluntary fund for the victims of terrorism, as well as on ways and means to rehabilitate the victims of terrorism and to reintegrate them into society, with a view to incorporating his findings in his reports to the Commission and the General Assembly;

11. *Endorses* the decision of the Sub-Commission on the Promotion and Protection of Human Rights requesting the Secretary-General to give the Special Rapporteur of the Sub-Commission all the assistance necessary, in order to hold consultations with the competent services and bodies of the United Nations system to complement her essential research and to collect all the needed and up-to-date information and data for the preparation of her second progress report;

12. *Requests* the Special Rapporteur to give attention in her next report on human rights and terrorism to the questions raised in the present resolution;

13. *Decides* to remain seized of the matter at its fifty-ninth session.

4.4   TRUSTEESHIP COUNCIL

4.4.1   **Self-determination and terrorism**

In early April 2002, the foreign ministers of Islamic countries meeting in Kuala Lumpur in Malaysia condemned international terrorism. *But they rejected 'any attempt to link terrorism' with the struggles of Palestinians and others fighting against foreign occupation.*[1]

One of the most complicated issues which the UN has been dealing with is the right to self-determination. This right has, indeed, been embedded in the Charter itself, to start with in Art. 1.2 in which it has been stated that one of the purposes of the UN is *'to develop friendly relations among nations based on respect for the principle of equal rights and self-determination of peoples ...'* The right to self-determination has, among others, also been included in the two human rights Covenants of 1966 and continues to dominate debates within the human rights world, the field of humanitarian law, and within those circles focusing on international law at large. The main questions are whether every 'people' is entitled to self-determination, what the concept exactly entails, and last but not least, whether violence or armed struggle may be used to attain that goal. We will see that also in this context the applicable principle is that solutions to disputes should be brought about by peaceful means. Moreover, if armed conflict arises, whether this in itself is justified or not, humanitarian law shall apply. That means that in certain cases the law of warfare may be violated, and in certain others the law on terrorism.[2] In no situation can an act of terrorism be justified. Similarly, one can not deny a certain act being labelled as an act of terrorism. Although the heading is somewhat artificial, it is believed that this issue can be best dealt with in the context of the UN with the Trusteeship Council as a starting point.

---

[1] The Economist April 6th 2002.

[2] In her *Self-Determination, Terrorism and the International Humanitarian Law of Armed Conflict* (The Hague, 1996), Chadwick concludes that a separability of 'liberationalist' terrorism from individual, sporadic acts, e.g. for personal gain be acknowledged. She submits that international law has developed to such an extent that (p. 206) 'it is thus now possible to prosecute acts of terrorism perpetrated during an armed conflict for self-determination as "grave breaches", or terrorist war crimes. All parties to a liberation armed conflict are restrained legally in their use of force, where previously there had been little or no reason for such restraint. Acts of terrorism which in the past have characterized 'civil' liberation wars can now be prosecuted under international law, in trials which should reflect standardized, civilized notions of justice ...'

This Trusteeship Council was set up under Chapter XIII of the UN Charter. It was above all meant to deal with the territories which had been handed over to certain UN Member States in the wake of the Second World War. The idea was that the Member States concerned would look after the well-being ('advancement') of those territories, and the concept of 'well-being' in due time amounted to self-determination and independence.[3]

The Trusteeship Council suspended its operation on 1 November 1994, with the independence of Palau, the last remaining trust territory one month earlier. By a resolution adopted on 25 May 1994, the Council had already amended its rules of procedure to drop the obligation to meet annually and had agreed to meet as and when required (by its own decision or the decision of its President, or at the request of a majority of its members or the General Assembly or the Security Council).

It is hereby again submitted that it is, legally speaking, completely erroneous to deal with 'national liberation' under the heading of trusteeship, as it concerns a different matter altogether. Yet, the UN as a whole had been struggling over the years with the concept of self-determination in so many different, often confusing ways, that it was considered somewhat logical to place terrorism and national liberation within the realm of Chapter XIII whilst admitting that the concept of self-determination has also been touched upon in, e.g., Art. 1.2 and Art. 55. Remarkably, Art. 73 on non-self-governing territories does not contain the concept of self-determination, but the aim of that article is obviously to strive for exactly that goal. The same would appear to be true for Art. 76.b.

Self-determination became en vogue in the late 1950s. This resulted in two interesting 1960 UN GA Resolutions (1514(XV) and 1540(XV)) slightly different from each other although adopted in the very same week (December 1960).

On a number of occasions the General Assembly allowed so-called liberation forces to pursue their struggle 'by all (available) means' which is believed to allow these movements to embark on armed struggle.[4]

---

[3] Under the Charter, the Trusteeship Council is authorized to examine and discuss reports from the Administering Authority on the political, economic, social and educational advancement of the peoples of Trust Territories and, in consultation with the Administering Authority, to examine petitions from and undertake periodic and other special missions to Trust Territories. In setting up an International Trusteeship System, the Charter established the Trusteeship Council as one of the main organs of the United Nations and assigned to it the task of supervising the administration of Trust Territories placed under the Trusteeship System. Major goals of the System were to promote the advancement of the inhabitants of Trust Territories and their progressive development towards self-government or independence. The aims of the Trusteeship System have been fulfilled to such an extent that all Trust Territories have attained self-government or independence, either as separate States or by joining neighbouring independent countries

[4] For instance in GA Resolution 47/82 the GA (...)
1. *Calls upon* all States to implement fully and faithfully all the relevant resolutions of the United Nations regarding the exercise of the right to self-determination and independence by peoples under colonial and foreign domination;
2. *Reaffirms* the legitimacy of the struggle of peoples for independence, territorial integrity, national unity and liberation from colonial domination, apartheid and foreign occupation, in all its forms and by all available means; (...)

Some observers are of the opinion that wars of national liberation are almost by definition legal and do not need a 'green light' from the GA and/or the SC. Others claim that all individuals are bound by, e.g., the Universal Declaration of Human Rights, particularly if they wage their war claiming the fulfilment of human rights. The latter group refers to, e.g., UDHR's Art. 29.3 in which it can be read that human rights and freedoms may in no case be exercised contrary to the purposes and principles of the United Nations', which should then be read in conjunction with Chapter I of the UN Charter in which the goals and purposes have been defined. This can indeed be summarized by the obligation to strive for the peaceful ('pacific') settlement of conflict.[5]

As to terrorism in this context, it can be noted that up until the early 1990s there was some understanding for the acts of those who were involved in national liberation struggles. To many, the 'freedom fighter' had become a hero, also if he/she was involved in acts of terrorism (hijacking, hostage taking, terrorist bombing). Thereafter something of a shift occurred: on the one hand the development towards agreeing that even in liberation struggles terrorism should be considered unacceptable, while on the other hand towards implying that national liberation struggles never amount to terrorism but fall in a different category altogether. If the latter approach would have been accepted, a very dangerous dilemma would have been created whereby liberation struggles would be placed above the law.

It should thus be underlined that

Yet, as with so many other resolutions, it is of the utmost importance to analyze the voting pattern. This was adopted with 107 in favour, 22 against and 33 abstentions. 2525(XXV) and 50/6, for instance, were adopted 'without a vote', i.e. unanimously, and thus carry far greater weight. Moreover, even in the case of 'all available means' this does not mean that humanitarian law may be violated or that use could be made of terrorism in order to attain the desired goal.

It is also quite remarkable that later resolutions appear to have dropped the 'all means' formula in the annual resolutions (47/82 being the last one, in as far as the present author could trace);

E.g. 54/155 from 1999, the GA (…)

1. *Reaffirms* that the universal realization of the right of all peoples, including those under colonial, foreign and alien domination, to self-determination is a fundamental condition for the effective guarantee and observance of human rights and for the preservation and promotion of such rights;

2. *Declares* its firm opposition to acts of foreign military intervention, aggression and occupation, since these have resulted in the suppression of the right of peoples to self-determination and other human rights in certain parts of the world; (…)

This major change coincided with a change of heading: since 1993 'Universal realization of the right of peoples to self-determination' and until 1992: 'Importance of the universal realization of the right of peoples to self-determination and of the speedy granting of independence to colonial countries and peoples for the effective guarantee and observance of human rights'.

[5] Indeed, the present author is of the opinion that Art. 33.1 of the UN Charter is probably the most important article of the Charter and present international law: 'The parties to any dispute, the continuance of which is likely to endanger the maintenance of international peace and security, shall, first of all seek a solution by negotiation, enquiry, mediation, conciliation, arbitration, judicial settlement, resort to regional agencies or arrangements, or other peaceful means of their own choice'.

- national liberation struggles by all accounts fall within the realm of UN law;
- the struggle by violent means should be allowed in no uncertain terms (by the Security Council, in some specific cases by General Assembly and even then one should have regard to the voting pattern);
- and even then the law of warfare would apply, which equally forbids terrorist acts.

Moreover, by equating terrorist acts with acts contrary to the goals and purposes of the United Nations as, e.g., has been done in SC Res. 1373, no room whatsoever is left to whatever excuse or understanding and the efforts to imply that national liberation struggles belong to a different category should be properly dealt with, i.e., totally rejected.

4.4.2 The TC Annexes

The two documents contained in this Annex are so-called 'anniversary declarations', adopted at the occasion of the UN's 50th and 25th anniversary respectively (October 1995 and October 1970). The Declarations are considered to have a major impact as a) they have been adopted unanimously; b) they reflect the 25/50 years development in dealing with UN law and the Charter; and c) they can be seen as an updated interpretation of the principles laid down in the Charter, the main ones being (i) conflicts should be solved in a peaceful/pacific manner; (ii) this includes the enjoyment of the right to self-determination; (iii) a status of self-determination can be considered to have been reached when the 'people' concerned enjoy political, cultural and economic rights; (iv) any 'armed struggle' should in principle receive the green light from the Security Council.

This indeed means that the 'unjustifiability' in all circumstances also holds true for the struggle for self-determination and the fight against foreign occupation: suicide bombers commit an act of terrorism, irrespective of their motivation, the circumstances or the lack of freedom or even repression under which they have to live.

4.4.2.1 *GA Res. 50/6, Declaration on the Occasion of the Fiftieth Anniversary of the United Nations*[6]

(...) The United Nations has been tested by conflict, humanitarian crisis and turbulent change, yet it has survived and played an important role in preventing another global conflict and has achieved much for people all over the world. The United Nations has helped to shape the very structure of relations between nations in the modern age. Through the process of decolonization and the elimination of apartheid, hundreds of millions of human beings have been and are assured the exercise of the fundamental right of self-determination. (...)

1. To meet these challenges, and while recognizing that action to secure global peace, security and stability will be futile unless the economic and social needs of people are addressed, we will: (...)

---

[6] General Assembly, A/RES/50/6, 24 October 1995.

Continue to reaffirm the right of self-determination of all peoples, taking into account the particular situation of peoples under colonial or other forms of alien domination or foreign occupation, and recognize the right of peoples to take legitimate action in accordance with the Charter of the United Nations to realize their inalienable right of self-determination. This shall not be construed as authorizing or encouraging any action that would dismember or impair, totally or in part, the territorial integrity or political unity of sovereign and independent states conducting themselves in compliance with the principle of equal rights and self-determination of peoples and thus possessed of a Government representing the whole people belonging to the territory without distinction of any kind (…).

4.4.2.2 *GA Res. 2625(XXV), Declaration on Principles of International Law Concerning Friendly Relations and Cooperation among States in accordance with the Charter of the United Nations*[7]

(…) The principle of equal rights and self-determination of peoples
By virtue of the principle of equal rights and self-determination of peoples enshrined in the Charter of the United Nations, all peoples have the right freely to determine, without external interference, their political status and to pursue their economic, social, and cultural development, and every State has the duty to respect this right in accordance with the provisions of the Charter.

Every State has the duty to promote, through joint and separate action, realization of the principle of equal rights and self-determination of peoples in accordance with the provisions of the Charter, and to render assistance to the United Nations in carrying out the responsibilities entrusted to it by the Charter regarding the implementation of the Principle, in order:
To promote friendly relations and cooperation among States; and
To bring a speedy end to colonization, having due regard to the freely expressed will of the peoples concerned;
And bearing in mind that subjection of peoples to alien subjugation, domination and exploitation constitutes a violation of the principle, as well as a denial of fundamental human rights, and is contrary to the Charter.
The establishment of a sovereign and independent State, the free association or integration with an independent State, or the emergence into any other political status freely determined by a people constitutes modes of implementing the right to self-determination by that people.
Every State has the duty to refrain from any forcible action which deprives people referred to above in the elaboration of the present principle of their right to self-determination and freedom and independence. In their actions against, and resistance to, such forcible action in pursuit of the existence of their right to self-determination, such peoples are entitled to seek and to receive support in accordance with the purposes and principles of the Charter.

---

[7] General Assembly, Resolution 2625(XXV), 24 October 1970.

The territory of a colony or other Non-Self-Governing Territory has, under the Charter, a status separate and distinct from the territory of the State administering it; and such separate and distinct status under the Charter shall exist until the people of the colony or Non-Self-Governing Territory have exercised their right to self-determination in accordance with the Charter, and particular its purposes and principles.

Nothing in the foregoing paragraphs shall be construed as authorizing or encouraging any action which would dismember or impair, totally or in part, the territorial integrity or political unity of sovereign and independent State conducting themselves in compliance with the principle of equal rights and self-determination of peoples as described above and thus possessed of a government representing the whole people belonging to the territory without distinction as to race, creed or colour.

Every State shall refrain from any action aimed at the partial or total disruption of the national unity and territorial integrity of any other State or country.

4.5   THE INTERNATIONAL COURT OF JUSTICE

Chapter XIV of the UN Charter deals with the International Court of Justice, the ICJ. Moreover, an Annex has been attached to the Charter in which the Statute of the Court has been laid down.

The ICJ too has dealt with the issue of terrorism. But it has also ruled on another very important aspect of the fight against terrorism, namely the question of jurisdiction and prosecution.[1]

A first case goes back to 1980, the case of the USA v. Iran on the issue of the hostages in the US Embassy, Tehran. The case was brought before the Court by Appli-

---

[1] Moreover, the ICJ also found itself in a 'constitutional' fight, as it was asked to rule on the question whether the SC had acted out of turn. Libya had, inter alia, submitted that the United Kingdom is under a legal obligation to respect Libya's right not to have the Convention set aside by means which would in any case be at variance with the principles of the United Nations Charter and with the mandatory rules of general international law prohibiting the use of force and the violation of the sovereignty, territorial integrity, sovereign equality and political independence of States. In the present case, the United Kingdom contended, however, that even if the Montreal Convention did confer on Libya the rights it claims, they could not be exercised in this case because they were superseded by Security Council Resolutions 748 (1992) and 883 (1993) which, by virtue of Articles 25 and 103 of the United Nations Charter, have priority over all rights and obligations arising out of the Montreal Convention. The Respondent also argued that, because of the adoption of those resolutions, the only dispute which existed from that point on was between Libya and the Security Council; this, clearly, would not be a dispute falling within the terms of Article 14, paragraph 1, of the Montreal Convention and thus not one which the Court could entertain. The Court found that it could not uphold this line of argument. Security Council Resolutions 748 (1992) and 883 (1993) were in fact adopted after the filing of the Application on 3 March 1992. In accordance with its established jurisprudence, if the Court had jurisdiction on that date, it continued to do so; the subsequent adoption of the above-mentioned resolutions cannot affect its jurisdiction once established.
However, the present author, as indicated above in the introduction to Chapter 4, in principle sides with Judge Schwebel who submitted: that the terms and drafting history of the Charter demonstrate that the Security Council is subject to the rule of law, and at the same time is empowered to derogate from international law if the maintenance of international peace so requires. It does not follow from the fact that the Council is so subject, and that the Court is the United Nation's principal judicial organ, that the Court is authorized to ensure that the Council's decisions do accord with the law. In many legal systems, subjecting the acts of an organ to the law by no means entails the legality of its actions to judicial review. The tenor of the discussions at San Francisco indicate the intention of the Charter's drafters not to accord the Court the power of judicial review. To engraft the power of judicial review upon the Charter régime would not be a development but a departure which is neither justified by the Charter's terms nor by customary international law or by the general principles of law.

cation by the US following the occupation of its Embassy in Tehran by Iranian militants on 4 November 1979, and the capture and holding as hostages of its diplomatic and consular staff. On a request by the United States for the indication of provisional measures, the Court held that there was no more fundamental prerequisite for relations between States than the inviolability of diplomatic envoys and embassies, and it indicated provisional measures for ensuring the immediate restoration of the Embassy premises to the United States and the release of the hostages. In its decision on the merits of the case, at a time when the situation complained of still persisted, the Court, in its ruling of 24 May 1980, found

- that Iran had violated and was still violating obligations owed by it to the United States under conventions in force between the two countries and rules of general international law;
- that the violation of these obligations engaged its responsibility, and
- that the Iranian Government was bound to secure the immediate release of the hostages, to restore the Embassy premises, and to make reparation for the injury caused to the United States Government.

The Court reaffirmed the cardinal importance of the principles of international law governing diplomatic and consular relations. It pointed out that while, during the events of 4 November 1979, the conduct of militants could not be directly attributed to the Iranian State – for lack of sufficient information – that State had however done nothing to prevent the attack, to stop it before it reached its completion or to oblige the militants to withdraw from the premises and release the hostages. The Court noted that, after 4 November 1979, certain organs of the Iranian State had endorsed the acts complained of and decided to perpetuate them, so that those acts were transformed into acts of the Iranian State.

The Court pronounced its judgment, notwithstanding the absence of the Iranian Government and after rejecting the reasons put forward by Iran in two communications addressed to the Court in support of its assertion that the Court could not and should not entertain the case. The Court was not called upon to deliver a further judgement on the reparation for the injury caused to the United States Government since, by Order of 12 May 1981, the case was removed from the List following discontinuance.[2]

Another famous ICJ case (still ongoing) concerns Lockerbie, not the case against the culprits (a Scottish trial in Zeist on 'neutral' Netherlands territory, with a final judgment in spring 2002), but regarding the question whether the US and UK first had to apply the conflict resolution devices as laid down in treaties and only thereafter – i.e. in the case of failure – were entitled to request the Security Council to intervene.

On 3 March 1992 the Libya filed two separate Applications with the Court instituting proceedings against the USA and the UK in respect of a dispute over the interpretation and application of the Convention for the Suppression of Unlawful Acts

---

[2] This summary is based on relevant ICJ information contained in its so-called 'blue book'.

against the Safety of Civil Aviation signed in Montreal on 23 September 1971. This dispute arose from acts resulting in the aerial incident that occurred over Lockerbie, Scotland, on 21 December 1988. In its Applications, Libya referred to the charging and indictment of two Libyan nationals by a Grand Jury of the United States and by the Lord Advocate of Scotland, respectively, for having caused a bomb to be placed aboard Pan Am flight 103. The bomb subsequently exploded, causing the plane to crash, all persons aboard being killed as well as additional victims on the ground. Libya pointed out that the acts alleged constituted an offence within the meaning of Article 1 of the Montreal Convention, which it claimed to be the only appropriate Convention in force between the Parties, and asserted that it had fully complied with its own obligations under that instrument, Article 5 of which required a State to establish its own jurisdiction over alleged offenders present in its territory in the event of their non-extradition; and that there was no extradition treaty between Libya and the respective other Parties, so that Libya was obliged under Article 7 of the Convention to submit the case to its competent authorities for the purpose of prosecution. Libya contended that the USA and the UK were in breach of the Montreal Convention in that they had rejected its efforts to resolve the matter within the framework of international law, including the Convention itself, and that they were placing pressure upon Libya to surrender the two Libyan nationals for trial. On 3 March 1992, Libya made two separate requests to the Court to indicate certain provisional measures forthwith, namely: *(a)* to enjoin the US and the UK respectively from taking any action against Libya calculated to coerce or compel it to surrender the accused individuals to any jurisdiction outside Libya; and *(b)* to ensure that no steps were taken that would in any way prejudice the rights of Libya with respect to the legal proceedings that were the subject of Libya's Applications. On 14 April 1992, the Court read two Orders on those requests for the indication of provisional measures, in which it found that the circumstances of the cases were not such as to require the exercise of its powers to indicate such measures. Within the time-limit fixed for the filing of its Counter-Memorial, each of the respondent States filed preliminary objections: the USA filed certain preliminary objections requesting the Court to adjudge and declare that it lacked jurisdiction and could not entertain the case; the UK filed certain preliminary objections to the jurisdiction of the Court and to the admissibility of the Libyan claims. In accordance with the provisions of Article 79 of the Rules of Court, the proceedings on the merits were suspended in those two cases. Libya, for its part, filed a written statement of its observations and submissions on the Preliminary Objections within the time-limit fixed by the Court. Hearings were held between 13 and 22 October 1997.

As to the Jurisdiction of the Court, the Court first considered the objection to its jurisdiction raised by the United Kingdom. Libya submitted that the Court has jurisdiction on the basis of Article 14, paragraph 1, of the Montreal Convention.[3] Having

---

[3] This article reads: 'Any dispute between two or more Contracting States concerning the interpretation or application of this Convention which cannot be settled through negotiation, shall, at the request of one of them, be submitted to arbitration. If within six months from the date of the request for arbitration the Parties are unable to agree on the organization of the arbitration, any one of those Parties may refer the dispute to the International Court of Justice by request in conformity with the Statute of the Court.

examined the various arguments the Court concluded that the alleged dispute between the Parties could not be settled by negotiation or submitted to arbitration under the Montreal Convention, and the refusal of the Respondent to enter into arbitration to resolve that dispute absolved Libya from any obligation under Article 14, paragraph 1, of the Convention to observe a six-month period starting from the request for arbitration, before seizing the Court.

As to the question of the existence of a legal dispute of a general nature concerning the Convention, Libya maintained that the Montreal Convention was the only instrument applicable to the destruction of the Pan Am aircraft over Lockerbie. The UK did not deny that, as such, the facts of the case could fall within the terms of the Montreal Convention. However, it emphasized that, in the present case, from the time Libya invoked the Montreal Convention, the UK had claimed that it was not relevant as the question to be resolved concerned the reaction of the international community to the situation arising from Libya's failure to respond effectively to the most serious accusations of State involvement in acts of terrorism. The Court found that consequently the Parties did differ on the question whether the destruction of the Pan Am aircraft over Lockerbie can be governed by the Montreal Convention. A dispute thus existed between the Parties as to the legal regime applicable to this event. Such a dispute, in the view of the Court, concerns the interpretation and application of the Montreal Convention, and, in accordance with Article 14, paragraph 1, of the Convention, falls to be decided by the Court.

As to the existence of a specific dispute concerning Article 7 of the Montreal Convention, it should be noted that this article is of relevance to the issue of jurisdiction, as it clearly states that the Contracting State in the territory of which the alleged offender is found shall, if it does not extradite him, be obliged, without exception whatsoever and whether or not the offence was committed in its territory, to submit the case to its competent authorities for the purpose of prosecution. Those authorities shall take their decision in the same manner as in the case of any ordinary offence of a serious nature under the law of that State.

Furthermore, the Court concluded that a dispute equally existed between the Parties concerning the interpretation and application of Article 11 on levels of assistance and other obligations under international law:

1. Contracting States shall afford one another the greatest measure of assistance in connection with criminal proceedings brought in respect of the offences. The law of the State requested shall apply in all cases.
2. The provisions of paragraph 1 of this Article shall not affect obligations under any other treaty, bilateral or multilateral, which governs or will govern, in whole or in part, mutual assistance in criminal matters.

Finally, as to the admissibility of the Application, Libya contended that the Court can usefully determine on the interpretation and application of the Montreal Convention, independently of the legal effects of Resolutions 748 (1992) and 883 (1993). Libya furthermore drew the Court's attention to the principle that the critical date for determining the admissibility of an application is the date on which it is filed. The Court agreed. The case is still pending.[4]

In conclusion it can be submitted that the ICJ is bound to play a crucial role every now and then. Some submit that the Court may compete with the newly established ICC, or could act as a potential 'spoiler' by denying countries the opportunity of bringing cases to justice, by interfering in procedures, and last but not least, by potentially dealing the SC a fatal blow. Yet, the present author is of the opinion that the ICJ will play its legal part, whilst optimalizing its role, by sticking to the pattern and hierarchy as laid down in the Charter with due regard to the (political) global reality: law, after all, is a means rather than a goal. This is true not only for constitutional relationships but also in the efforts to create an international legal order which is able to cope with the terrorism phenomenon.

---

[4] Summing up, the February 1998 ruling was as follows:
For these reasons: THE COURT,
1a: by thirteen votes to three, *rejects* the objection to jurisdiction raised by the United Kingdom on the basis of the alleged absence of a dispute between the Parties concerning the interpretation or application of the Montreal Convention of 23 September 1971;
1b: by thirteen votes to three, *finds* that it has jurisdiction, on the basis of Article 14, paragraph 1, of the Montreal Convention of 23 September 1971, to hear the disputes between Libya and the United Kingdom as to the interpretation or application of the provisions of that Convention;
2a: by twelve votes to four, *rejects* the objection to admissibility derived by the United Kingdom from Security Council Resolutions 748 (1992) and 883 (1993);
2b: by twelve votes to four, *finds* that the Application filed by Libya on 3 March 1992 is admissible.
3: by ten votes to six, declares that the objection raised by the United Kingdom according to which Security Council Resolutions 748 (1992) and 883 (1993) have rendered the claims of Libya without object does not, in the circumstances of the case, have an exclusively preliminary character.
By Orders dated 30 March 1998, the Court fixed 30 December 1998 as the time-limit for the filing of the Counter-Memorials of the United Kingdom and of the United States. The time-limit was subsequently extended to 31 March 1999 at the request of the United Kingdom and of the United States. The Counter-Memorials were filed within the time-limit thus extended.
By Orders of 29 June 1999, the Court authorized the submission of Replies by Libya and Rejoinders by the United Kingdom and the United States, fixing 29 June 2000 as the time-limit for the filing of Libya's Replies. Libya's Replies were filed within the prescribed time-limit.

CHAPTER 4
THE UNITED NATIONS AND TERRORISM

4.6   THE SECRETARY-GENERAL

The Secretary-General (SG) forms part of the Secretariat and hence falls under Chapter XV of the Charter (Arts. 97-101). As the highest and most prominent employee of the UN he attends and participates in the meetings of the various organs. He also submits reports to various organs, normally at the request of those organs, the General Assembly in particular. His main challenge, however, can be found in art. 99:

> The Secretary-General may bring to the attention of the Security Council any matter which in his opinion may threaten the maintenance of international peace and security.

It is in this position that the SG can play an active role, and, in certain situations, can make a great deal of difference.

As to terrorism, the SG has been quite outspoken. In his address to the Security Council in November 2001 (a session during which the SC adopted Resolution 1377), he was quoted as follows:

> The fight against terrorism must begin with ensuring that the dozen legal instruments on international terrorism adopted under United Nations auspices were signed, ratified and implemented 'without delay', Secretary-General Kofi Annan told the Security Council today as it began a ministerial-level meeting on the threats to peace caused by terrorists acts.
> In his opening address, the Secretary-General said that while he understood and accepted the need for legal precision in defining terrorism, there was also a need for moral clarity. 'There can be no acceptance of those who seek to justify the deliberate taking of innocent civilian life, regardless of cause or grievance', he said.
> Mr. Annan also called for the strengthening of global norms against the use or proliferation of weapons of mass destruction as well as any types of weapons – such as small arms and landmines – that 'pose grave dangers through terrorist use'.
> In welcoming the international community's resolve to fight terrorism, the Secretary-General pointed out 'the reality is that like war, terrorism is an immensely complicated phenomenon with multiple objectives and causes, a multitude of weapons and agents, and virtually limitless manifestations'.
> 'The only common denominator among different variants of terrorism is the calculated use of deadly violence against civilians for political purposes', he said. 'It is, however, this common denominator that provides the UN a common cause and a common agenda'.
> Ultimately, the world community's success would be measured in terrorist acts thwarted

and lives saved, Mr. Annan said, 'but I am confident that the unity born of 11 September can be sustained in the months and years ahead'.

Over the last five years or so, the SG has regularly submitted reports to the General Assembly on both the 'measures to eliminate terrorism' and 'human rights and terrorism'.[1]

The July 2001 report on 'measures' (A/56/160) starts by saying:

1. The present report has been prepared pursuant to General Assembly Resolution 50/53 of 11 December 1995, entitled 'Measures to eliminate international terrorism', in which the Assembly requested the Secretary-General to follow up closely the implementation of the Declaration on Measures to Eliminate International Terrorism (Resolution 49/60, annex) and to submit an annual report on the implementation of paragraph 10 of the Declaration, taking into account the modalities set out in his report to the Assembly at its fiftieth session (A/50/372 and Add.1) and the views expressed by States in the debate of the Sixth Committee during that session.

2. In paragraph 10 of the Declaration, the General Assembly requested the Secretary-General to assist in the implementation of the Declaration by taking, within existing resources, the following practical measures to enhance international cooperation:

(a)   A collection of data on the status and implementation of existing multilateral, regional and bilateral agreements relating to international terrorism, including information on incidents caused by international terrorism and criminal prosecutions and sentencing, based on information received from the depositaries of those agreements and from Member States;

(b)   A compendium of national laws and regulations regarding the prevention and suppression of international terrorism in all its forms and manifestations, based on information received from Member States;

(c)   An analytical review of existing international legal instruments relating to international terrorism, in order to assist States in identifying aspects of this matter that have not been covered by such instruments and could be addressed to develop further a comprehensive legal framework of conventions dealing with international terrorism;

(d)   A review of existing possibilities within the United Nations system for assisting States in organizing workshops and training courses on combating crimes connected with international terrorism.

3. By a note dated 16 January 2001, the Secretary-General drew the attention of all States to Resolution 49/60 of 9 December 1994 and the Declaration annexed thereto and requested them to submit information on the implementation of the Declaration under paragraphs 10(a) and (b) thereof by 31 May 2001. In the note, the Secretary-General also noted that in the information to be submitted by States they might wish to give particular attention to paragraph 5 of Security Council Resolution 1269 (1999). By a letter dated 16

---

[1] The SG reports on this theme go back to 1981 and their frequency had intensified by the mid-1990s:

A/56/190 Human rights and terrorism A/56/160 Measures to eliminate international terrorism; A/54/439 Human rights and terrorism; A/55/179 + Add.1 Measures to eliminate international terrorism; A/54/301 +Add. 1. Measures to eliminate international terrorism; A/53/314 + Add.1 Measures to eliminate international terrorism; A/52/304 + Add.1 Measures to eliminate international terrorism; A/51/336 + Add.1 Measures to eliminate international terrorism; A/50/685 Human rights and terrorism, etc.

January 2001, the Secretary-General invited relevant specialized agencies and other organizations to submit information or other relevant material on the implementation of the
Declaration, pursuant to its paragraphs 10(a) and (d), by 31 May 2001 (…)

The July 2001 report on human rights and terrorism[2] which up until May 2002 had
no sequence or follow-up[3] forms part of the communication between the Secretariat
and the UN human rights' niche:[4]

> The present report, submitted pursuant to that request, summarizes the replies received
> from the Governments that responded to the note verbale by the Secretary-General dated
> 4 September 2000, namely, Azerbaijan, Egypt, Kuwait, Qatar and Turkey. Also covered
> are replies to the note verbale dated 16 August 1999 that were not included in the previ-
> ous report (A/54/439), namely, those received from Cuba, India and the United Arab
> Emirates. (…) The full texts of the replies received are available for consultation in the
> files of the Secretariat.

The reports, both the one on 'measures' and the one on 'human rights' can not be
labelled as eye-openers, as the Secretariat functions as a Secretariat, an exchange for
information. However, they are informative in that they contain a wealth of material
and provide an interesting survey on how concerns developed and how the challenges are believed to be met.

In his communication with the Security Council, the SG has consistently ham-
mered home the need to yield results and it can be safely submitted that the SC and
SG work closely together with the same concerns, the same goals and the same approaches. Mr. Annan's 2002 re-election as SG was proof of this submission.

---

[2] United Nations, A/56/190, General Assembly, 17 July 2001, Fifty-sixth session, Human rights
questions: human rights questions, including alternative approaches for improving the effective enjoyment of human rights and fundamental freedoms; Human rights and terrorism, Report of the Secretary-
General.

[3] The Commission on Human Rights specifically refers to this 56/190 report (see above Chapter
4.3.4) in its April 2002 resolution.

[4] As 56/190 indicates:

1. In its Resolution 54/164 of 17 December 1999, recalling its previous resolutions on human rights and
   terrorism and those of the Commission on Human Rights and the Subcommission on the Promotion
   and Protection of Human Rights on the same subject, the General Assembly reiterated its unequivocal condemnation of the acts, methods and practices of terrorism; and called upon States to take all
   necessary and effective measures in accordance with relevant provisions of international law, including international human rights standards, to prevent, combat and eliminate terrorism in all its forms
   and manifestations, wherever and by whomever committed.

2. In the same resolution, the General Assembly requested the Secretary-General to continue to seek the
   views of Member States on the implications of terrorism, in all its forms and manifestations, for the
   full enjoyment of all human rights and fundamental freedoms, with a view to incorporating them into
   his report to the Assembly at its fifty-sixth session.

CHAPTER 5
INTERNATIONAL INSTRUMENTS: TEXTS

INTRODUCTION

Chapter 5 includes in full the texts of the main international (sub-chapters 5.1 and 5.2) and regional instruments (sub-chapter 5.3) on terrorism.[1] In classifying the international conventions, a distinction has been made between the UN conventions, often adopted by the General Assembly and deposited with the UN Secretary General, and the non-UN conventions, other international instruments, deposited with various international organizations (such as the International Civil Aviation, the International Maritime Organization etc.) or with governments (UK, former USSR, USA). Sub-chapter 5.3 contains the regional instruments. The main draft conventions (comprehensive and nuclear) have been included as TC1F and TC1D respectively. An overview of the various signatures and ratifications can be found in Chapter 2, 'Definitions'.

TC1: UN CONVENTIONS[2]

–   ***TC1A***: Convention on the Prevention and Punishment of Crimes against Internationally Protected Persons, including Diplomatic Agents, adopted by the General Assembly of the United Nations on 14 December 1973; entry into force: 20 February 1977; 119 parties and 25 signatories, as per May 2002;[3]
–   ***TC1B:*** International Convention against the Taking of Hostages, adopted by the General Assembly of the United Nations on 17 December 1979; entry into force: 3 June 1983; 107 parties and 39 signatories, as per May 2002;[4]
–   ***TC1C***: International Convention for the Suppression of Terrorist Bombings, adopted by the General Assembly of the United Nations on 15 December 1997; entry into force: 23 May 2001; 61 parties and 58 signatories, as per May 2002;[5]
–   ***TC1D:*** Draft International Convention for the Suppression of Acts of Nuclear Terrorism, 22 October 1998;
–   ***TC1E***: International Convention for the Suppression of the Financing of Terrorism, adopted by the General Assembly of the United Nations on 9 December

---

[1] For a complete list of international and regional conventions, see Chapter 2, 'Definitions'.

[2] Another convention which has been concluded by the UN is the Convention on the Safety of United Nations and Associated Personnel, adopted by the General Assembly on 9 December 1994 and not yet in force (its text has not been included in this volume).

[3] UN Treaty Series, vol. 1035, p. 167.

[4] UN Treaty Series, vol. 1316, p. 205.

[5] Doc. A/RES/52/164.

1999; entry into force: 10 April 2002; 33 parties and 132 signatories, as per May 2001;[6]

– **TC1F**: Draft Comprehensive Convention (Ad-Hoc Committee established by the General Assembly Resolution 51/210 of 17 December 1996), 11 February 2002.

TC2: NON-UN CONVENTIONS

– **TC2A**: Convention on Offences and Certain Other Acts Committed on Board Aircraft, signed at Tokyo on 14 September 1963; entry into force: 4 December 1969; 173 parties, as per 1 May 2002;

– **TC2B**: Convention for the Suppression of Unlawful Seizure of Aircraft, signed at the Hague on 16 December 1970; entry into force: 14 October; 175 parties, as per 1 May 2002;

– **TC2C**: Convention for the Suppression of Unlawful Acts against the Safety of Civil Aviation, signed at Montreal on 23 September 1971; entry into force: 26 January 1973; 173 parties, as per 1 May 2002;

– **TC2D**: Convention on the Physical Protection of Nuclear Material, signed at Vienna on 3 March 1980; entry into force: 8 February 1987; 75 parties; 45 signatories, as per 1 May 2002;

– **TC2E**: Protocol on the Suppression of Unlawful Acts of Violence at Airports Serving International Civil Aviation, supplementary to the Convention for the Suppression of Unlawful Acts against the Safety of Civil Aviation, signed at Montreal on 24 February 1988; entry into force: 6 August 1989; 114 parties, as per 1 May 2002;

– **TC2F**: Convention for the Suppression of Unlawful Acts against the Safety of Maritime Navigation, done at Rome on 10 March 1988; entry into force: 1 March 1992; 67 parties, as per 1 May 2002;

– **TC2G**: Protocol for the Suppression of Unlawful Acts against the Safety of Fixed Platforms Located on the Continental Shelf, done at Rome on 10 March 1988; entry into force: 1 March 1992; 60 parties, as per 1 May 2002;

– **TC2H:** Convention on the Marking of Plastic Explosives for the Purpose of Detection, signed at Montreal on 1 March 1991; entry into force: 21 June 1998; 77 parties, as per 1 May 2002;

TC3: REGIONAL INSTRUMENTS

– **TC3A**: Arab Convention on the Suppression of Terrorism, signed at a meeting held at the General Secretariat of the League of Arab States in Cairo on 22 April 1998;

– **TC3B:** Convention of the Organization of the Islamic Conference on Combating International Terrorism, adopted at Ouagadougou on 1 July 1999;

---

[6] Res. A/RES/54/109

- **TC3C**: European Convention on the Suppression of Terrorism,[7] concluded at Strasbourg on 27 January 1977; entry into force: 4 August 1978; 38 ratifications and signatories, as per 1 May 2002;
- **TC3D**: OAS Convention to Prevent and Punish Acts of Terrorism Taking the Form of Crimes against Persons and Related Extortion that are of International Significance, concluded at Washington, D.C. on 2 February 1971; 14 ratifications, as per 1 May 2002;
- **TC3E**: OAU Convention on the Prevention and Combating of Terrorism, adopted at Algiers on 14 July 1999;
- **TC3F**: SAARC Regional Convention on Suppression of Terrorism, signed at Kathmandu on 4 November 1987;
- **TC3G**: Treaty on Cooperation among States Members of the Commonwealth of Independent States in Combating Terrorism, done at Minsk on 4 June 1999.

Subject List

For the sake of easy reference a survey follows on the basis of subjects dealt with by the various instruments; an alphabetical order has been chosen, hence financing, hijacking ... terrorist bombing.

1. Financing

TC1E   International Convention for The Suppression of the Financing of Terrorism (1999)

2. Hijacking and related attacks on Civil Aviation

The relevant Conventions which tackle this subject are:

TC2A   Convention on Offences and Certain Other Acts Committed on Board Aircraft (1963)
TC2B   Convention for the Suppression of Unlawful Seizure of Aircraft (Hague, 1970)
TC2C   Convention for the Suppression of Unlawful Acts against the Safety of Civil Aviation (Montreal, 1971)
TC2E   Protocol of the Montreal Convention for the Suppression of Unlawful Acts of violence at Airports Serving International Civil Aviation, supplementary to the Convention for the Suppression of Unlawful Acts against the Saftey of Civil Aviation, 1988
TC2G   Convention on the Marking of Plastic Explosives for the purpose of Detection (Montreal, 1991)

---

[7] In relation with this convention, the European Union Member States have concluded the Dublin Agreement Concerning the Application of the European Convention on the Suppression of Terrorism among Member States (European Union), signed at Dublin on 4 December 1979, which has not been included in this volume.

3. Hostage taking

TC1B   International Convention Against the Taking of Hostages Signed at New York on 18 December 1979

4. Maritime Terrorism

TC2F   Convention for the Suppression of Unlawful Acts against the Safety of Maritime Navigation (Rome, 1988)
TC2G   Protocol for the Suppression of Unlawful Acts against the Safety of Fixed Platforms Located on the Continental Shelf (Rome, 1988)

5. Nuclear Terrorism

TC1D   Draft International Convention for the Suppression of Acts of Nuclear Terrorism, 22 October 1998

6. Terrorist Acts against internationally Protected Persons, including Diplomatic Agents

This topic has been captured in the following conventions:

TC1A   Convention on the Prevention and Punishment of Crimes against Internationally Protected Persons, including Diplomatic Agents, 1973
TC3D   OAS Convention to Prevent and Punish Acts of Terrorism Taking the form of Crimes against Persons and Related Extortion that are of International Significance (Washington, 1971).

7. Suppressing, Combating and Preventing Terrorism and Financing terrorism

TC1C   International Convention for the Suppression of Terrorist Bombing (New York, 12 January 1998)
TC1D   Draft International Convention for the Suppression of Acts of Nuclear Terrorism, 22 October 1998
TC1E   International Convention for the Suppression of the Financing of Terrorism (1999)
TC1F   Draft Comprehensive Convention (2002)
TC3A   The Arab Convention for the Suppression of Terrorism (1998)
TC3B   Convention of the Organization of The Islamic Conference on Combating International Terrorism (Ouagadougou, 1999)
TC3C   European Convention on the Suppression of Terrorism (Strasbourg, 1977)
TC3E   OAU Convention on the Prevention and Combating of Terrorism (Algiers, 1999)
TC3F   SAARC Regional Convention on Suppression of Terrorism (Kathmandu, 1987)
TC3G   Treaty on Cooperation among States Member to the Commonwealth of Independent states in Combating Terrorism (Minsk, 1999)

8. Terrorist Bombing

TC1C International Convention for the Suppression of Terrorist Bombing (New York, 12 January 1998)

Chronological List
In order to fully appeciate the various developments, a chronological overview may be useful:

1963: *TC2A*. Convention on Offences and Certain Other Acts Committed on Board Aircraft, signed at Tokyo on 14 September 1963

1970: *TC2B*. Convention for the Suppression of Unlawful Seizure of Aircraft, signed at the Hague on 16 December 1970

1971: *TC2C*. Convention for the Suppression of Unlawful Acts against the Safety of Civil Aviation, signed at Montreal on 23 September 1971
TC3D. OAS Convention to Prevent and Punish Acts of Terrorism Taking the Form of Crimes against Persons and Related Extortion that are of International Significance, concluded at Washington, D.C. on 2 February 1971

1973: *TC1A*. Convention on the Prevention and Punishment of Crimes against Internationally Protected Persons, including Diplomatic Agents, adopted by the General Assembly of the United Nations on 14 December 1973

1977: *TC3C*. European Convention on the Suppression of Terrorism, concluded at Strasbourg on 27 January 1977

1979: *TC1B*. International Convention against the Taking of Hostages, adopted by the General Assembly of the United Nations on 17 December 1979

1980: *TC2D*. Convention on the Physical Protection of Nuclear Material, signed at Vienna on 3 March 1980

1987: *TC3F*. SAARC Regional Convention on Suppression of Terrorism, signed at Kathmandu on 4 November 1987

1988: *TC2E*. Protocol on the Suppression of Unlawful Acts of Violence at Airports Serving International Civil Aviation, supplementary to the Convention for the Suppression of Unlawful Acts against the Safety of Civil Aviation, signed at Montreal on 24 February 1988
TC2F. Convention for the Suppression of Unlawful Acts against the Safety of Maritime Navigation, done at Rome on 10 March 1988. (Deposited with the Secretary-General of the International Maritime Organization)
TC2G. Protocol for the Suppression of Unlawful Acts against the Safety of Fixed Platforms Located on the Continental Shelf, done at Rome on 10 March 1988

1991: *TC2H.* Convention on the Marking of Plastic Explosives for the purpose of Detection (Montreal, 1991)

1998: *TC1C.* International Convention for the Suppression of Terrorist Bombing (New York, 12 January 1998)

TC3A. Arab Convention on the Suppression of Terrorism, signed at a meeting held at the General Secretariat of the League of Arab States in Cairo on 22 April 1998

TC1D. Draft International Convention for the Suppression of Acts of Nuclear Terrorism, 22 October 1998

1999:   *TC3G*. Treaty on Cooperation among States Member to the Commonwealth of Independent states in Combating terrorism (Minsk, 1999)

TC3B. Convention of the Organization of the Islamic Conference on Combating International Terrorism, adopted at Ouagadougou on 1 July 1999

TC3E. OAU Convention on the Prevention and Combating of terrorism (Algiers, 1999)

TC1E. International Convention for the Suppression of the Financing of Terrorism, adopted by the General Assembly of the United Nations on 9 December 1999

2002:   *TC1F.* Draft Comprehensive Convention (February, 2002)

TC1: The UN Conventions
– ratifications/ successions /accessions (•) and signatures (s) –

Participant	Convention on the Prevention and Punishment of Crimes against Internationally Protected Persons, including Diplomatic Agents (TC1A)	International Convention against the taking of hostages (TC1B)	International Convention for the Suppression of Terrorist Bombings(TC1C)	International Convention for the Suppression of the Financing of Terrorism (TC1E)
Albania	•	•	•	•
Algeria	•	•	•	•
Antigua and Barbuda	•	•		•
Andorra				(s)
Argentina	•	•	(s)	(s)
Armenia	•			(s)
Australia	•	•		(s)
Austria	•	•	•	•
Azerbaidjan	•	•	•	•
Bahamas	•	•		(s)
Bahrain				(s)
Barbados	•	•		(s)
Belarus	•	•	•	(s)
Belgium		•	(s)	(s)
Belize	•	•	•	(s)
Benin				(s)
Bhutan	•	•		(s)
Bolivia	•	•	•	•
Bosnia and Herzegovina	•	•		(s)
Botswana	•	•	•	•
Brazil	•	•	(s)	(s)
Brunei Darussalam		•	•	
Bulgaria	•	•	•	•
Burundi	•		(s)	(s)
Cambodia				(s)
Cameroon	•	•		
Canada	•	•	•	•
Cape Verde			•	•
Central African Republic				(s)
Chile	•	•	•	•
China	•	•	•	(s)
Colombia	•			(s)
Comoros			(s)	(s)
Congo				(s)
Cook Islands				(s)
Costa Rica	•		•	(s)
Côte d'Ivoire	•	•	•	•
Croatia	•			(s)
Cuba	•	•	•	•
Cyprus	•	•	•	•
Czech Republic	•	•	•	(s)

Participant	Convention on the Prevention and Punishment of Crimes against Internationally Protected Persons, including Diplomatic Agents (TC1A)	International Convention against the taking of hostages (TC1B)	International Convention for the Suppression of Terrorist Bombings(TC1C)	International Convention for the Suppression of the Financing of Terrorism (TC1E)
Democratic People's Republic of Korea	•	•		(s)
Democratic Republic of the Congo	•	(s)		(s)
Denmark	•	•	•	(s)
Djibouti				(s)
Dominica		•		
Dominican Republic	•	(s)		(s)
Ecuador	•	•		(s)
Egypt	•	•	(s)	(s)
El Salvador	•	•		
Estonia	•	•	•	•
Finland	•	•	•	(s)
France		•	•	•
Gabon	•	(s)		(s)
Georgia				(s)
Germany	•	•	(s)	(s)
Ghana	•	•		(s)
Greece	•	•	(s)	(s)
Grenada	•	•	•	•
Guatemala	•	•	•	•
Guinea			•	(s)
Guinea-Bissau				(s)
Haiti	•	•		
Honduras		•		(s)
Hungary	•	•	•	(s)
Iceland	•	•	•	•
India	•	•	•	(s)
Indonesia				(s)
Iran (Islamic Republic of)	•			
Iraq	•	(s)		
Ireland			(s)	(s)
Israel	•	(s)	(s)	(s)
Italy	•	•	(s)	(s)
Jamaica	•	(s)		(s)
Japan	•	•	•	(s)
Jordan	•	•		(s)
Kazakhstan	•	•		
Kenya	•	•	•	(s)
Kuwait	•	•		
Kyrgyzstan			•	
Latvia	•			(s)
Lebanon	•	•		
Lesotho		•	•	•
Liberia	•	(s)		
Libyan Arab Jamahiriya	•	•	•	(s)
Liechtenstein	•	•		(s)

Participant	Convention on the Prevention and Punishment of Crimes against Internationally Protected Persons, including Diplomatic Agents (TC1A)	International Convention against the taking of hostages (TC1B)	International Convention for the Suppression of Terrorist Bombings(TC1C)	International Convention for the Suppression of the Financing of Terrorism (TC1E)
Lithuania		•	(s)	
Luxembourg		•	(s)	(s)
Madagascar			(s)	(s)
Malawi	•	•		
Maldives	•		•	
Mali	•	•	•	•
Malta	•	•	•	•
Mauritania	•	•		
Mauritius		•		(s)
Mexico	•	•		(s)
Micronesia (Federated States of)				(s)
Monaco		•	•	•
Mongolia	•	•	•	(s)
Morocco	•			(s)
Mozambique				(s)
Myanmar			•	(s)
Namibia				(s)
Nauru				(s)
Nepal	•	•	(s)	
Netherlands	•	•	•	•
New Zealand	•	•		(s)
Nicaragua	•			(s)
Niger	•			
Nigeria				(s)
Norway	•	•	•	(s)
Oman	•	•		
Pakistan	•	•		
Palau	•	•	•	•
Panama	•	•	•	(s)
Paraguay	•			(s)
Peru	•	•	•	•
Philippines	•	•	(s)	(s)
Poland	•	•	(s)	(s)
Portugal	•	•	•	(s)
Qatar	•			
Republic of Korea	•	•	(s)	(s)
Republic of Moldova	•			(s)
Romania	•	•	(s)	(s)
Russian Federation	•	•	•	(s)
Rwanda	•	•	•	•
Saint Kitts and Nevis		•	•	•
Saint Vincent and the Grenadines	•	•		•
Samoa				(s)
San Marino			•	•
Saudi Arabia		•		(s)
Senegal		•		

Participant	Convention on the Prevention and Punishment of Crimes against Internationally Protected Persons, including Diplomatic Agents (TC1A)	International Convention against the taking of hostages (TC1B)	International Convention for the Suppression of Terrorist Bombings(TC1C)	International Convention for the Suppression of the Financing of Terrorism (TC1E)
Seychelles	•			(s)
Sierra Leone				(s)
Singapore				(s)
Slovakia	•	•	•	(s)
Slovenia	•	•	(s)	(s)
Somalia				(s)
South Africa			(s)	(s)
Spain	•	•	•	•
Sri Lanka	•	•	•	•
Sudan	•	•	•	(s)
Suriname		•		
Sweden	•	•	•	(s)
Switzerland	•	•		(s)
Syrian Arab Republic	•			
Tajikistan	•			(s)
Thailand				(s)
The Former Yugoslav Republic of Macedonia	•	•	(s)	(s)
Togo	•	•	(s)	(s)
Trinidad and Tobago	•	•	•	
Tunisia	•	•		(s)
Turkey	•	•	(s)	(s)
Turkmenistan	•	•	•	
Uganda		(s)	(s)	(s)
Ukraine	•	•	•	(s)
United Kingdom of Great Britain and Northern Ireland	•	•	•	•
United States of America	•	•	(s)	(s)
Uruguay	•		•	(s)
Uzbekistan	•	•	•	•
Venezuela		•	(s)	(s)
Viet Nam	•			
Yemen	•	•	•	
Yugoslavia	•	•		(s)

NB TC1D on nuclear terrorism and **TC1E**, the comprehensive convention, are drafts only and have not yet been finalized.

TC2: Non-UN Conventions
– ratifications/ successions /accessions (•) and signatures (s) –

Participant	Convention on Offences and Certain Other Acts Committed on Board Aircraft (TC2A)	Convention for the Suppression of Unlawful Seizure of Aircraft (TC2B)	Convention for the Suppression of Unlawful Acts against the Safety of Civil Aviation(TC2C)	Convention on the Physical Protection of Nuclear Material (TC2D)	Protocol on the Suppression of Unlawful Acts of Violence at Airports Serving International Civil Aviation (TC2E)	Convention for the Suppression of Unlawful Acts against the Safety of Maritime Navigation(TC2F)	Protocol for the Suppression of Unlawful Acts against the Safety of Fixed Platforms Located on the Continental Shelf(TC2G)	Convention on the Marking of Plastic Explosives for the Purpose of Detection (TC2H)
Afghanistan	•	•	•					(s)
Albania	•	•	•	•	•			
Algeria	•	•	•		•	•		•
Angola	•	•	•					
Antigua and Barbuda	•	•	•	•				
Argentina	•	•	•	•	•	•	(s)	•
Armenia				•				
Australia	•	•	•	•	•	•	•	
Austria	•	•	•		•	•	•	•
Azerbaijan	•	•	•		•			
Bahamas	•	•	•			(s)	(s)	
Bahrain	•	•	•		•			•
Bangladesh	•	•	•					
Barbados	•	•	•			•	•	
Belarus	•	•	•	•	•			•
Belgium	•	•	•		•	(s)	(s)	(s)
Belize	•	•	•					(s)
Benin		•						
Bhutan	•	•	•					
Bolivia	•	•	•	•	•			•
Bosnia and Herzegovina	•	•	•	•	•			
Botswana	•	•	•	•	•	•	•	•
Brazil	•	•	•	•	•	(s)	(s)	•
Brunei Darussalam	•	•	•		•	(s)	(s)	
Bulgaria	•	•	•		•	•	•	•
Burkina Faso	•	•	•		•			
Burundi	•	(s)	•					
Byelorussian SSR						(s)	(s)	
Cambodia	•	•	•		•			
Cameroon	•	•	•		(s)			•
Canada	•	•	•	•	•	•	•	
Cape Verde	•	•	•					
Cape Verde	•	•	•					
Central African Republic	•	•	•		•			
Chad	•	•	•					
Chile	•	•	•	•	•	•	•	•
China	•	•	•	•	•	•	•	(s)
Colombia	•	•	•					(s)
Comoros	•	•	•					
Congo	•	•	•		(s)			
Costa Rica	•	•	•		(s)	(s)	(s)	(s)
Côte d'Ivoire	•	•	•		(s)			(s)

Participant	Convention on Offences and Certain Other Acts Committed on Board Aircraft (TC2A)	Convention for the Suppression of Unlawful Seizure of Aircraft (TC2B)	Convention for the Suppression of Unlawful Acts against the Safety of Civil Aviation (TC2C)	Convention on the Physical Protection of Nuclear Material (TC2D)	Protocol on the Suppression of Unlawful Acts of Violence at Airports Serving International Civil Aviation (TC2E)	Convention for the Suppression of Unlawful Acts against the Safety of Maritime Navigation (TC2F)	Protocol for the Suppression of Unlawful Acts against the Safety of Fixed Platforms Located on the Continental Shelf (TC2G)	Convention on the Marking of Plastic Explosives for the Purpose of Detection (TC2H)
Croatia	•	•	•	•	•			
Cuba	•	•	•	•	•			•
Cyprus	•	•	•	•	•	•	•	
Czech Republic	•	•	•	•	•			•
Czechoslovakia						(s)	(s)	
Democratic People's Republic of Korea	•	•	•		•			
Democratic Republic of the Congo	•	•	•		(s)			
Denmark	•	•	•	•	•	•	•	•
Djibouti	•	•	•					
Dominican Republic	•	•	•	(s)				
Ecuador	•	•	•	•		(s)	(s)	•
Egypt	•	•	•		•	•	•	•
El Salvador	•	•	•		•	•	•	•
Equatorial Guinea	•	•	•					
Eritrea								•
Estonia	•	•	•	•	•			•
Ethiopia	•	•	•		•			
Fiji	•	•	•					
Finland	•	•	•	•	•	•		
France	•	•	•	•	•			
Gabon	•	•	•		(s)			(s)
Gambia	•	•	•		•	•		•
Georgia	•	•	•		•			•
Germany	•	•	•	•	•	•	•	•
Ghana	•	•	•		•			•
Greece	•	•	•	•	•	•	•	•
Grenada	•	•	•	•	•			•
Guatemala	•	•	•		•			•
Guinea	•	•	•		•			(s)
Guinea-Bissau		•	•					(s)
Guyana	•	•	•					
Haiti	•	•	•	(s)				
Holy See	(s)							
Honduras	•	•	•					(s)
Hungary	•	•	•	•	•	•	•	
Iceland	•	•	•		•			•
India	•	•	•	•	•	•		•
Indonesia	•	•	•	•	(s)			
Iran, Islamic Republic of	•	•	•		•			
Iraq	•	•	•		•	(s)	(s)	
Ireland	•	•	•	•	•			
Israel	•	•	•	•	•	(s)	(s)	(s)
Italy	•	•	•	•	•	•	•	

Participant	Convention on Offences and Certain Other Acts Committed on Board Aircraft (TC2A)	Convention for the Suppression of Unlawful Seizure of Aircraft (TC2B)	Convention for the Suppression of Unlawful Acts against the Safety of Civil Aviation (TC2C)	Convention on the Physical Protection of Nuclear Material (TC2D)	Protocol on the Suppression of Unlawful Acts of Violence at Airports Serving International Civil Aviation (TC2E)	Convention for the Suppression of Unlawful Acts against the Safety of Maritime Navigation (TC2F)	Protocol for the Suppression of Unlawful Acts against the Safety of Fixed Platforms Located on the Continental Shelf(TC2G)	Convention on the Marking of Plastic Explosives for the Purpose of Detection (TC2H)
Jamaica	•	•	•		(s)			
Japan	•	•	•	•	•	•	•	•
Jordan	•	•	•		•	(s)	(s)	•
Kazakhstan	•	•	•		•			•
Kenya	•	•	•	•	•			
Kuwait	•	•	•		•			•
Kyrgyzstan	•	•	•		•			•
Lao People's Democratic Republic	•	•	•					
Latvia	•	•	•		•			•
Lebanon	•	•	•	•	•	•	•	•
Lesotho	•	•	•					
Liberia	(s)	•	•		(s)	•	•	
Libyan Arab Jamahiriya	•	•	•	•	•			
Liechtenstein	•	•	•	•	•			
Lithuania	•	•	•	•	•			•
Luxembourg	•	•	•	•	(s)			
Madagascar	•	•	•		•			(s)
Malawi	•	•	•		(s)			
Malaysia	•	•	•		(s)			
Maldives	•	•	•		•			•
Mali	•	•	•	•	•			•
Malta	•	•	•		•			•
Marshall Islands	•	•	•		•	•	•	
Mauritania	•	•	•					
Mauritius	•	•	•		•			(s)
Mexico	•	•	•	•	•	•	•	•
Monaco	•	•	•	•	•			•
Mongolia	•	•	•	•	•			•
Morocco	•	•	•	(s)	•	(s)	(s)	•
Myanmar	•	•	•		•			
Nauru	•	•	•					
Nepal	•	•	•					
Netherlands	•	•	•	•	•	•	•	•
New Zealand	•	•	•		•	•	•	
Nicaragua	•	•	•		•			(s)
Niger	•	•	•	(s)	(s)			
Nigeria	•	•	•			(s)	(s)	•
Norway	•	•	•	•	•	•	•	•
Oman	•	•	•		•	•	•	•
Pakistan		•	•	•	•	•	•	(s)
Palau	•	•	•		•			•
Panama	•	•	•	•	•			•
Papua New Guinea	•	•	•					
Paraguay	•	•	•	•				
Peru	•	•	•	•	•			•
Philippines	•	•	•	•	(s)	(s)	(s)	

Participant	Convention on Offences and Certain Other Acts Committed on Board Aircraft (TC2A)	Convention for the Suppression of Unlawful Seizure of Aircraft (TC2B)	Convention for the Suppression of Unlawful Acts against the Safety of Civil Aviation (TC2C)	Convention on the Physical Protection of Nuclear Material (TC2D)	Protocol on the Suppression of Unlawful Acts of Violence at Airports Serving International Civil Aviation (TC2E)	Convention for the Suppression of Unlawful Acts against the Safety of Maritime Navigation (TC2F)	Protocol for the Suppression of Unlawful Acts against the Safety of Fixed Platforms Located on the Continental Shelf (TC2G)	Convention on the Marking of Plastic Explosives for the Purpose of Detection (TC2H)
Poland	•	•	•	•	(s)	•	•	
Portugal	•	•	•	•	•	•		
Qatar	•	•	•					•
Republic of Korea	•	•	•	•	•			•
Republic of Moldova	•	•	•	•	•			•
Romania	•	•	•	•	•	•	•	•
Russian Federation	•	•	•	•	•			(s)
Rwanda	•	•	•		•			
Saint Lucia	•	•	•		•			
Saint Kitts and Nevis								•
Saint Vincent and the Grenadines	•	•	•		•			
Samoa	•	•	•		•			
Saudi Arabia	•	•	•		•	(s)	(s)	•
Senegal	•	•	•		(s)			(s)
Seychelles	•	•	•			•	•	
Sierra Leone	•	•	•					
Singapore	•	•	•		•			
Slovakia	•	•	•	•	•	•	•	•
Slovenia	•	•	•	•	%			•
Solomon Islands	•		•					
South Africa	•	•	•	(s)	•			•
Spain	•	•	•	•	•	•	•	•
Sri Lanka	•	•	•		•	•		
Sudan	•	•	•	%	•	•	•	•
Suriname	•	•	•					
Swaziland	•	•	•					
Sweden	•	•	•	•	•	•	•	(s)
Switzerland	•	•	•	•	•	•	•	•
Syrian Arab Republic	•	•	•					
Tajikistan	•	•	•	•	•			
Thailand	•	•	•		•			
The former Yugoslav Republic of Macedonia	•	•	•	•	•			•
Togo	•	•	•		•			(s)
Tonga	•	•	•					
Trinidad and Tobago	•	•	•	•	•	•	•	•
Tunisia	•	•	•	•	•	•	•	•
Turkey	•	•	•	•	•	•	•	•
Turkmenistan	•	•	•		•	•	•	
Uganda	•	•	•					
Ukraine	•	•	•	•	•	•	•	
Ukrainean SSR						(s)	(s)	
United Arab Emir.	•	•	•		•			•

Participant	Convention on Offences and Certain Other Acts Committed on Board Aircraft (TC2A)	Convention for the Suppression of Unlawful Seizure of Aircraft (TC2B)	Convention for the Suppression of Unlawful Acts against the Safety of Civil Aviation (TC2C)	Convention on the Physical Protection of Nuclear Material (TC2D)	Protocol on the Suppression of Unlawful Acts of Violence at Airports Serving International Civil Aviation (TC2E)	Convention for the Suppression of Unlawful Acts against the Safety of Maritime Navigation (TC2F)	Protocol for the Suppression of Unlawful Acts against the Safety of Fixed Platforms Located on the Continental Shelf(TC2G)	Convention on the Marking of Plastic Explosives for the Purpose of Detection (TC2H)
United Kingdom	•	•	•	•	•	•	•	•
United Republic of Tanzania	•	•	•					
United States	•	•	•	•	•	•		•
Uruguay	•	•	•		•			•
USSR						(s)	(s)	
Uzbekistan	•	•	•	•	•	•	•	•
Vanuatu	•	•	•			•	•	
Venezuela	•	•	•		(s)			
Viet Nam	•	•	•		•			
Yemen	•	•	•			•	•	
Yugoslavia, (F.R. of)	•	•	•	•	•			
Zambia	•	•	•					•
Zimbabwe	•	•	•					

5.1   TC1: UN CONVENTIONS

TC1A
Convention on the Prevention and Punishment of Crimes against Internationally Protected Persons, including Diplomatic Agents, adopted by the General Assembly of the United Nations on 14 December 1973

The States Parties to this Convention,
Having in mind the purposes and principles of the Charter of the United Nations concerning the maintenance of international peace and the promotion of friendly relations and cooperation among States,
Considering that crimes against diplomatic agents and other internationally protected persons jeopardizing the safety of these persons create a serious threat to the maintenance of normal international relations which are necessary for cooperation among States,
Believing that the commission of such crimes is a matter of grave concern to the international community,
Convinced that there is an urgent need to adopt appropriate and effective measures for the prevention and punishment of such crimes,
Have agreed as follows:

Article 1
For the purposes of this Convention:
1. *'internationally protected person'* means:
    (a) a Head of State, including any member of a collegial body performing the functions of a Head of State under the constitution of the State concerned, a Head of Government or a Minister for Foreign Affairs, whenever any such person is in a foreign State, as well as members of his family who accompany him;
    (b) any representative or official of a State or any official or other agent of an international organization of an intergovernmental character who, at the time when and in the place where a crime against him, his official premises, his private accommodation or his means of transport is committed, is entitled pursuant to international law to special protection from any attack on his person, freedom or dignity, as well as members of his family forming part of his household.
2. *'alleged offender'* means a person as to whom there is sufficient evidence to determine prima facie that he has committed or participated in one or more of the crimes set forth in Article 2.

Article 2
1. The intentional commission of:
    (a) a murder, kidnapping or other attack upon the person or liberty of an internationally protected person;

(b) a violent attack upon the official premises, the private accommodation or the means of transport of an internationally protected person likely to endanger his person or liberty;

(c) a threat to commit any such attack;

(d) an attempt to commit any such attack; and

(e) an act constituting participation as an accomplice in any such attack shall be made by each State Party a crime under its internal law.

2. Each State Party shall make these crimes punishable by appropriate penalties which take into account their grave nature.

3. Paragraphs 1 and 2 of this Article in no way derogate from the obligations of States Parties under international law to take all appropriate measures to prevent other attacks on the person, freedom or dignity of an internationally protected person.

Article 3

1. Each State Party shall take such measures as may be necessary to establish its jurisdiction over the crimes set forth in Article 2 in the following cases:

(a) when the crime is committed in the territory of that State or on board a ship or aircraft registered in that State;

(b) when the alleged offender is a national of that State;

(c) when the crime is committed against an internationally protected person as defined in Article 1 who enjoys his status as such by virtue of functions which he exercises on behalf of that State.

2. Each State Party shall likewise take such measures as may be necessary to establish its jurisdiction over these crimes in cases where the alleged offender is present in its territory and it does not extradite him pursuant to Article 8 to any of the States mentioned in paragraph 1 of this Article.

3. This Convention does not exclude any criminal jurisdiction exercised in accordance with internal law.

Article 4

States Parties shall cooperate in the prevention of the crimes set forth in Article 2, particularly by:

(a) taking all practicable measures to prevent preparations in their respective territories for the commission of those crimes within or outside their territories;

(b) exchanging information and coordinating the taking of administrative and other measures as appropriate to prevent the commission of those crimes.

Article 5

1. The State Party in which any of the crimes set forth in Article 2 has been committed shall, if it has reason to believe that an alleged offender has fled from its territory, communicate to all other States concerned, directly or through the Secretary-General of the United Nations, all the pertinent facts regarding the crime committed and all available information regarding the identity of the alleged offender.

2. Whenever any of the crimes set forth in Article 2 has been committed against an internationally protected person, any State Party which has information concerning the victim and the circumstances of the crime shall endeavour to transmit it, under the conditions provided for in its internal law, fully and promptly to the State Party on whose behalf he was exercising his functions.

Article 6

1. Upon being satisfied that the circumstances so warrant, the State Party in whose territory the alleged offender is present shall take the appropriate measures under its internal law so as to ensure his presence for the purpose of prosecution or extradition. Such measures shall be notified without delay directly or through the Secretary-General of the United Nations to:

    (a) the State where the crime was committed;

    (b) the State or States of which the alleged offender is a national or, if he is a state-less person, in whose territory he permanently resides;

    (c) the State or States of which the internationally protected person concerned is a national or on whose behalf he was exercising his functions;

    (d) all other States concerned; and

    (e) the international organization of which the internationally protected person concerned is an official or an agent.

2. Any person regarding whom the measures referred to in paragraph 1 of this Article are being taken shall be entitled:

    (a) to communicate without delay with the nearest appropriate representative of the State of which he is a national or which is otherwise entitled to protect his rights or, if he is a stateless person, which he requests and which is willing to protect his rights, and

    (b) to be visited by a representative of that State.

Article 7

The State Party in whose territory the alleged offender is present shall, if it does not extradite him, submit, without exception whatsoever and without undue delay, the case to its competent authorities for the purpose of prosecution, through proceedings in accordance with the laws of that State.

Article 8

1. To the extent that the crimes set forth in Article 2 are not listed as extraditable offences in any extradition treaty existing between States Parties, they shall be deemed to be included as such therein. States Parties undertake to include those crimes as extraditable offences in every future extradition treaty to be concluded between them.

2. If a State Party which makes extradition conditional on the existence of a treaty receives a request for extradition from another State Party with which it has no extradition treaty, it may, if it decides to extradite, consider this Convention as the legal basis for extradition in respect of those crimes. Extradition shall be subject to the procedural provisions and the other conditions of the law of the requested State.

3. States Parties which do not make extradition conditional on the existence of a treaty shall recognize those crimes as extraditable offences between themselves subject to the procedural provisions and the other conditions of the law of the requested State.

4. Each of the crimes shall be treated, for the purpose of extradition between States Parties, as if it had been committed not only in the place in which it occurred but also in the territories of the States required to establish their jurisdiction in accordance with paragraph 1 of Article 3.

Article 9

Any person regarding whom proceedings are being carried out in connexion with any of the crimes set forth in Article 2 shall be guaranteed fair treatment at all stages of the proceedings.

Article 10

1. States Parties shall afford one another the greatest measure of assistance in connexion with criminal proceedings brought in respect of the crimes set forth in Article 2, including the supply of all evidence at their disposal necessary for the proceedings.

2. The provisions of paragraph 1 of this Article shall not affect obligations concerning mutual judicial assistance embodied in any other treaty.

Article 11

The State Party where an alleged offender is prosecuted shall communicate the final outcome of the proceedings to the Secretary-General of the United Nations, who shall transmit the information to the other States Parties.

Article 12

The provisions of this Convention shall not affect the application of the Treaties on Asylum, in force at the date of the adoption of this Convention, as between the States which are parties to those Treaties; but a State Party to this Convention may not invoke those Treaties with respect to another State Party to this Convention which is not a party to those Treaties.

Article 13

1. Any dispute between two or more States Parties concerning the interpretation or application of this Convention which is not settled by negotiation shall, at the request of one of them, be submitted to arbitration. If within six months from the date of the request for arbitration the parties are unable to agree on the organization of the arbitration, any one of those parties may refer the dispute to the International Court of Justice by request in conformity with the Statute of the Court.

2. Each State Party may at the time of signature or ratification of this Convention or accession thereto declare that it does not consider itself bound by paragraph 1 of this Article. The other States Parties shall not be bound by paragraph 1 of this Article with respect to any State Party which has made such a reservation.

3. Any State Party which has made a reservation in accordance with paragraph 2 of this Article may at any time withdraw that reservation by notification to the Secretary-General of the United Nations.

Article 14

This Convention shall be open for signature by all States, until 31 December 1974 at United Nations Headquarters in New York.

Article 15

This Convention is subject to ratification. The instruments of ratification shall be deposited with the Secretary-General of the United Nations.

Article 16

This Convention shall remain open for accession by any State. The instruments of accession shall be deposited with the Secretary- General of the United Nations.

Article 17

1. This Convention shall enter into force on the thirtieth day following the date of deposit of the twenty-second instrument of ratification or accession with the Secretary-General of the United Nations.

2. For each State ratifying or acceding to the Convention after the deposit of the twenty-second instrument of ratification or accession, the Convention shall enter into force on the thirtieth day after deposit by such State of its instrument of ratification or accession.

Article 18
1. Any State Party may denounce this Convention by written notification to the Secretary-General of the United Nations.
2. Denunciation shall take effect six months following the date on which notification is received by the Secretary-General of the United Nations.

Article 19
The Secretary-General of the United Nations shall inform all States, inter alia:
- (a) of signatures to this Convention, of the deposit of instruments of ratification or accession in accordance with Articles 14, 15 and 16 and of notifications made under Article 18.
- (b) of the date on which this Convention will enter into force in accordance with Article 17.

Article 20
The original of this Convention, of which the Chinese, English, French, Russian and Spanish texts are equally authentic, shall be deposited with the Secretary-General of the United Nations, who shall send certified copies thereof to all States.

IN WITNESS WHEREOF the undersigned, being duly authorized thereto by their respective Governments, have signed this Convention, opened for signature at New York on 14 December 1973.

TC1B
International Convention against the Taking of Hostages, signed at New York on 18 December 1979

The States Parties to this Convention,
Having in mind the purposes and principles of the Charter of the United Nations concerning the maintenance of international peace and security and the promotion of friendly relations and cooperation among States,
Recognizing in particular that everyone has the right to life, liberty and security of person, as set out in the Universal Declaration of Human Rights and the International Covenant on Civil and Political Rights,
Reaffirming the principle of equal rights and self-determination of peoples as enshrined in the Charter of the United Nations and the Declaration on Principles of International Law concerning Friendly Relations and Cooperation among States in accordance with the Charter of the United Nations, as well as in other relevant resolutions of the General Assembly,
Considering that the taking of hostages is an offence of grave concern to the international community and that, in accordance with the provisions of this Convention, any person committing an act of hostage taking shall either be prosecuted or extradited,
Being convinced that it is urgently necessary to develop international cooperation between States in devising and adopting effective measures for the prevention, prosecution and punishment of all acts of taking of hostages as manifestations of international terrorism,
Have agreed as follows:

Article 1

1. Any person who seizes or detains and threatens to kill, to injure or to continue to detain another person (hereinafter referred to as the 'hostage') in order to compel a third party, namely, a State, an international intergovernmental organization, a natural or juridical person, or a group of persons, to do or abstain from doing any act as an explicit or implicit condition for the release of the hostage commits the offence of taking of hostages ('hostage-taking') within the meaning of this Convention.

2. Any person who:

    (a) attempts to commit an act of hostage-taking, or

    (b) participates as an accomplice of anyone who commits or attempts to commit an act of hostage-taking likewise commits an offence for the purposes of this Convention.

Article 2

Each State Party shall make the offences set forth in Article 1 punishable by appropriate penalties which take into account the grave nature of those offences.

Article 3

1. The State Party in the territory of which the hostage is held by the offender shall take all measures it considers appropriate to ease the situation of the hostage, in particular, to secure his release and, after his release, to facilitate, when relevant, his departure.

2. If any object which the offender has obtained as a result of the taking of hostages comes into the custody of a State Party, that State Party shall return it as soon as possible to the hostage or the third party referred to in Article 1, as the case may be, or to the appropriate authorities thereof.

Article 4

States Parties shall cooperate in the prevention of the offences set forth in Article 1, particularly by:

    (a) taking all practicable measures to prevent preparations in their respective territories for the commission of those offences within or outside their territories, including measures to prohibit in their territories illegal activities of persons, groups and organizations that encourage, instigate, organize or engage in the perpetration of acts of taking of hostages;

    (b) exchanging information and coordinating the taking of administrative and other measures as appropriate to prevent the commission of those offences.

Article 5

1. Each State Party shall take such measures as may be necessary to establish its jurisdiction over any of the offences set forth in Article 1 which are committed:

    (a) in its territory or on board a ship or aircraft registered in that State;

    (b) by any of its nationals or, if that State considers it appropriate, by those stateless persons who have their habitual residence in its territory;

    (c) in order to compel that State to do or abstain from doing any act; or

    (d) with respect to a hostage who is a national of that State, if that State considers it appropriate.

2. Each State Party shall likewise take such measures as may be necessary to establish its jurisdiction over the offences set forth in Article 1 in cases where the alleged offender is present in its territory and it does not extradite him to any of the States mentioned in paragraph 1 of this Article.

3. This Convention does not exclude any criminal jurisdiction exercised in accordance with internal law.

Article 6

1. Upon being satisfied that the circumstances so warrant, any State Party in the territory of which the alleged offender is present shall, in accordance with its laws, take him into custody or take other measures to ensure his presence for such time as is necessary to enable any criminal or extradition proceedings to be instituted. That State Party shall immediately make a preliminary inquiry into the facts.

2. The custody or other measures referred to in paragraph 1 of this Article shall be notified without delay directly or through the Secretary-General of the United Nations to:

   (a) the State where the offence was committed;
   (b) the State against which compulsion has been directed or attempted;
   (c) the State of which the natural or juridical person against whom compulsion has been directed or attempted is a national;
   (d) the State of which the hostage is a national or in the territory of which he has his habitual residence;
   (e) the State of which the alleged offender is a national or, if he is a stateless person, in the territory of which he has his habitual residence;
   (f) the international intergovernmental organization against which compulsion has been directed or attempted;
   (g) all other States concerned.

3. Any person regarding whom the measures referred to in paragraph 1 of this Article are being taken shall be entitled:

   (a) to communicate without delay with the nearest appropriate representative of the State of which he is a national or which is otherwise entitled to establish such communication or, if he is a stateless person, the State in the territory of which he has his habitual residence;
   (b) to be visited by a representative of that State.

4. The rights referred to in paragraph 3 of this Article shall be exercised in conformity with the laws and regulations of the State in the territory of which the alleged offender is present subject to the proviso, however, that the said laws and regulations must enable full effect to be given to the purposes for which the rights accorded under paragraph 3 of this Article are intended.

5. The provisions of paragraphs 3 and 4 of this Article shall be without prejudice to the right of any State Party having a claim to jurisdiction in accordance with paragraph 1(b) of Article 5 to invite the International Committee of the Red Cross to communicate with and visit the alleged offender.

6. The State which makes the preliminary inquiry contemplated in paragraph 1 of this Article shall promptly report its findings to the States or organization referred to in paragraph 2 of this Article and indicate whether it intends to exercise jurisdiction.

Article 7

The State Party where the alleged offender is prosecuted shall in accordance with its laws communicate the final outcome of the proceedings to the Secretary-General of the United Nations, who shall transmit the information to the other States concerned and the international intergovernmental organizations concerned.

Article 8

1. The State Party in the territory of which the alleged offender is found shall, if it does not extradite him, be obliged, without exception whatsoever and whether or not the offence was committed in its territory, to submit the case to its competent authorities for the purpose of prosecution, through proceedings in accordance with the laws of that State. Those authorities shall take their decision in the same manner as in the case of any ordinary offence of a grave nature under the law of that State.

2. Any person regarding whom proceedings are being carried out in connexion with any of the offences set forth in Article 1 shall be guaranteed fair treatment at all stages of the proceedings, including enjoyment of all the rights and guarantees provided by the law of the State in the territory of which he is present.

Article 9

1. A request for the extradition of an alleged offender, pursuant to this Convention, shall not be granted if the requested State Party has substantial grounds for believing:

    (a) that the request for extradition for an offence set forth in Article 1 has been made for the purpose of prosecuting or punishing a person on account of his race, religion, nationality, ethnic origin or political opinion; or

    (b) that the person's position may be prejudiced:

        (i) for any of the reasons mentioned in subparagraph (a) of this paragraph, or

        (ii) for the reason that communication with him by the appropriate authorities of the State entitled to exercise rights of protection cannot be effected.

2. With respect to the offences as defined in this Convention, the provisions of all extradition treaties and arrangements applicable between States Parties are modified as between States Parties to the extent that they are incompatible with this Convention.

Article 10

1. The offences set forth in Article 1 shall be deemed to be included as extraditable offences in any extradition treaty existing between States Parties. States Parties undertake to include such offences as extraditable offences in every extradition treaty to be concluded between them.

2. If a State Party which makes extradition conditional on the existence of a treaty receives a request for extradition from another State Party with which it has no extradition treaty, the requested State may at its option consider this Convention as the legal basis for extradition in respect of the offences set forth in Article 1. Extradition shall be subject to the other conditions provided by the law of the requested State.

3. States Parties which do not make extradition conditional on the existence of a treaty shall recognize the offences set forth in Article 1 as extraditable offences between themselves subject to the conditions provided by the law of the requested State.

4. The offences set forth in Article 1 shall be treated, for the purpose of extradition between States Parties, as if they had been committed not only in the place in which they occurred but also in the territories of the States required to establish their jurisdiction in accordance with paragraph 1 of Article 5.

Article 11

1. States Parties shall afford one another the greatest measure of assistance in connexion with criminal proceedings brought in respect of the offences set forth in Article 1, including the supply of all evidence at their disposal necessary for the proceedings.

2. The provisions of paragraph 1 of this Article shall not affect obligations concerning mutual judicial assistance embodied in any other treaty.

Article 12

In so far as the Geneva Conventions of 1949 for the protection of war victims or the Additional Protocols to those Conventions are applicable to a particular act of hostage-taking, and in so far as States Parties to this Convention are bound under those conventions to prosecute or hand over the hostage-taker, the present Convention shall not apply to an act of hostage-taking committed in the course of armed conflicts as defined in the Geneva Conventions of 1949 and the Protocols thereto, including armed conflicts mentioned in Article 1, paragraph 4, of Additional Protocol I of 1977, in which peoples are fighting against colonial domination and alien occupation and against racist regimes in the exercise of their right of self- determination, as enshrined in the Charter of the United Nations and the Declaration on Principles of International Law concerning Friendly Relations and Cooperation among States in accordance with the Charter of the United Nations.

Article 13

This Convention shall not apply where the offence is committed within a single State, the hostage and the alleged offender are nationals of that State and the alleged offender is found in the territory of that State.

Article 14

Nothing in this Convention shall be construed as justifying the violation of the territorial integrity or political independence of a State in contravention of the Charter of the United Nations.

Article 15

The provisions of this Convention shall not affect the application of the Treaties on Asylum, in force at the date of the adoption of this Convention, as between the States which are parties to those Treaties; but a State Party to this convention may not invoke those Treaties with respect to another State Party to this Convention which is not a party to those treaties.

Article 16

1. Any dispute between two or more States Parties concerning the interpretation or application of this Convention which is not settled by negotiation shall, at the request of one of them, be submitted to arbitration. If within six months from the date of the request for arbitration the parties are unable to agree on the organization of the arbitration, any one of those parties may refer the dispute to the International Court of Justice by request in conformity with the Statute of the Court.

2. Each State may at the time of signature or ratification of this Convention or accession thereto declare that it does not consider itself bound by paragraph 1 of this Article. The other States Parties shall not be bound by paragraph 1 of this Article with respect to any State Party which has made such a reservation.

3. Any State Party which has made a reservation in accordance with paragraph 2 of this Article may at any time withdraw that reservation by notification to the Secretary-General in the United Nations.

Article 17

1. This Convention is open for signature by all States until 31 December 1980 at United Nations Headquarters in New York.

2. This Convention is subject to ratification. The instruments of ratification shall be deposited with the Secretary-General of the United Nations.

3. This Convention is open for accession by any State. The instruments of accession shall be deposited with the Secretary- General of the United Nations.

Article 18

1. This Convention shall enter into force on the thirtieth day following the date of deposit of the twenty-second instrument of ratification or accession with the Secretary-General of the United Nations.

2. For each State ratifying or acceding to the Convention after the deposit of the twenty-second instrument of ratification or accession, the Convention shall enter into force on the thirtieth day after deposit by such State of its instrument of ratification or accession.

Article 19

1. Any State Party may denounce this Convention by written notification to the Secretary-General of the United Nations.

2. Denunciation shall take effect one year following the date on which notification is received by the Secretary-General of the United Nations.

Article 20

The original of this Convention, of which the Arabic, Chinese, English, French, Russian and Spanish texts are equally authentic, shall be deposited with the Secretary General of the United Nations, who shall send certified copies thereof to all States.

IN WITNESS WHEREOF, the undersigned, being duly authorized thereto by their respective Governments, have signed this Convention, opened for signature at New York on 18 December 1979.

TC1C
International Convention for the Suppression of Terrorist Bombing (New York, 12 January 1998)

The States Parties to this Convention,

Having in mind the purposes and principles of the Charter of the United Nations concerning the maintenance of international peace and security and the promotion of good-neighbourliness and friendly relations and cooperation among States,

Deeply concerned about the worldwide escalation of acts of terrorism in all its forms and manifestations,

Recalling the Declaration on the Occasion of the Fiftieth Anniversary of the United Nations of 24 October 1995,

Recalling also the Declaration on Measures to Eliminate International Terrorism, annexed to General Assembly Resolution 49/60 of 9 December 1994, in which, inter alia, 'the States Members of the United Nations solemnly reaffirm their unequivocal condemnation of all acts, methods and practices of terrorism as criminal and unjustifiable, wherever and by whomever committed, including those which jeopardize the friendly relations among States and peoples and threaten the territorial integrity and security of States',

Noting that the Declaration also encouraged States 'to review urgently the scope of the existing international legal provisions on the prevention, repression and elimination of terrorism in all its forms and manifestations, with the aim of ensuring that there is a comprehensive legal framework covering all aspects of the matter',

Recalling General Assembly Resolution 51/210 of 17 December 1996 and the Declaration to Supplement the 1994 Declaration on Measures to Eliminate International Terrorism annexed thereto,

Noting that terrorist attacks by means of explosives or other lethal devices have become increasingly widespread,

Noting also that existing multilateral legal provisions do not adequately address these attacks,

Being convinced of the urgent need to enhance international cooperation between States in devising and adopting effective and practical measures for the prevention of such acts of terrorism and for the prosecution and punishment of their perpetrators,

Considering that the occurrence of such acts is a matter of grave concern to the international community as a whole,

Noting that the activities of military forces of States are governed by rules of international law outside the framework of this Convention and that the exclusion of certain actions from the coverage of this Convention does not condone or make lawful otherwise unlawful acts, or preclude prosecution under other laws,

Have agreed as follows:

Article 1

For the purposes of this Convention

1. 'State or government facility' includes any permanent or temporary facility or conveyance that is used or occupied by representatives of a State, members of Government, the legislature or the judiciary or by officials or employees of a State or any other public authority or entity or by employees or officials of an intergovernmental organization in connection with their official duties.

2. 'Infrastructure facility' means any publicly or privately owned facility providing or distributing services for the benefit of the public, such as water, sewage, energy, fuel or communications.

3. 'Explosive or other lethal device' means:
    (a) An explosive or incendiary weapon or device that is designed, or has the capability, to cause death, serious bodily injury or substantial material damage; or
    (b) A weapon or device that is designed, or has the capability, to cause death, serious bodily injury or substantial material damage through the release, dissemination or impact of toxic chemicals, biological agents or toxins or similar substances or radiation or radioactive material.

4. 'Military forces of a State' means the armed forces of a State which are organized, trained and equipped under its internal law for the primary purpose of national defence or security and persons acting in support of those armed forces who are under their formal command, control and responsibility.

5. 'Place of public use' means those parts of any building, land, street, waterway or other location that are accessible or open to members of the public, whether continuously, periodically or occasionally, and encompasses any commercial, business, cultural, historical, educational, religious, governmental, entertainment, recreational or similar place that is so accessible or open to the public.

6. 'Public transportation system' means all facilities, conveyances and instrumentalities, whether publicly or privately owned, that are used in or for publicly available services for the transportation of persons or cargo.

Article 2

1. Any person commits an offence within the meaning of this Convention if that person unlawfully and intentionally delivers, places, discharges or detonates an explosive or other le-

thal device in, into or against a place of public use, a State or government facility, a public transportation system or an infrastructure facility:

(a) With the intent to cause death or serious bodily injury; or

(b) With the intent to cause extensive destruction of such a place, facility or system, where such destruction results in or is likely to result in major economic loss.

2. Any person also commits an offence if that person attempts to commit an offence as set forth in paragraph 1 of the present Article.

3. Any person also commits an offence if that person:

(a) Participates as an accomplice in an offence as set forth in paragraph 1 or 2 of the present Article; or

(b) Organizes or directs others to commit an offence as set forth in paragraph 1 or 2 of the present Article; or

(c) In any other way contributes to the commission of one or more offences as set forth in paragraph 1 or 2 of the present Article by a group of persons acting with a common purpose; such contribution shall be intentional and either be made with the aim of furthering the general criminal activity or purpose of the group or be made in the knowledge of the intention of the group to commit the offence or offences concerned.

Article 3

This Convention shall not apply where the offence is committed within a single State, the alleged offender and the victims are nationals of that State, the alleged offender is found in the territory of that State and no other State has a basis under Article 6, paragraph 1 or paragraph 2, of this Convention to exercise jurisdiction, except that the provisions of Articles 10 to 15 shall, as appropriate, apply in those cases.

Article 4

Each State Party shall adopt such measures as may be necessary:

(a) To establish as criminal offences under its domestic law the offences set forth in Article 2 of this Convention;

(b) To make those offences punishable by appropriate penalties which take into account the grave nature of those offences.

Article 5

Each State Party shall adopt such measures as may be necessary, including, where appropriate, domestic legislation, to ensure that criminal acts within the scope of this Convention, in particular where they are intended or calculated to provoke a state of terror in the general public or in a group of persons or particular persons, are under no circumstances justifiable by considerations of a political, philosophical, ideological, racial, ethnic, religious or other similar nature and are punished by penalties consistent with their grave nature.

Article 6

1. Each State Party shall take such measures as may be necessary to establish its jurisdiction over the offences set forth in Article 2 when:

(a) The offence is committed in the territory of that State; or

(b) The offence is committed on board a vessel flying the flag of that State or an aircraft which is registered under the laws of that State at the time the offence is committed; or

(c) The offence is committed by a national of that State.

2. A State Party may also establish its jurisdiction over any such offence when:

(a) The offence is committed against a national of that State; or

(b) The offence is committed against a State or government facility of that State abroad, including an embassy or other diplomatic or consular premises of that State; or

(c) The offence is committed by a stateless person who has his or her habitual residence in the territory of that State; or

(d) The offence is committed in an attempt to compel that State to do or abstain from doing any act; or

(e) The offence is committed on board an aircraft which is operated by the Government of that State.

3. Upon ratifying, accepting, approving or acceding to this Convention, each State Party shall notify the Secretary-General of the United Nations of the jurisdiction it has established under its domestic law in accordance with paragraph 2 of the present Article. Should any change take place, the State Party concerned shall immediately notify the Secretary-General.

4. Each State Party shall likewise take such measures as may be necessary to establish its jurisdiction over the offences set forth in Article 2 in cases where the alleged offender is present in its territory and it does not extradite that person to any of the States Parties which have established their jurisdiction in accordance with paragraph 1 or 2 of the present Article.

5. This Convention does not exclude the exercise of any criminal jurisdiction established by a State Party in accordance with its domestic law.

Article 7

1. Upon receiving information that a person who has committed or who is alleged to have committed an offence as set forth in Article 2 may be present in its territory, the State Party concerned shall take such measures as may be necessary under its domestic law to investigate the facts contained in the information.

2. Upon being satisfied that the circumstances so warrant, the State Party in whose territory the offender or alleged offender is present shall take the appropriate measures under its domestic law so as to ensure that person's presence for the purpose of prosecution or extradition.

3. Any person regarding whom the measures referred to in paragraph 2 of the present Article are being taken shall be entitled to:

(a) Communicate without delay with the nearest appropriate representative of the State of which that person is a national or which is otherwise entitled to protect that person's rights or, if that person is a stateless person, the State in the territory of which that person habitually resides;

(b) Be visited by a representative of that State;

(c) Be informed of that person's rights under subparagraphs (a) and (b).

4. The rights referred to in paragraph 3 of the present Article shall be exercised in conformity with the laws and regulations of the State in the territory of which the offender or alleged offender is present, subject to the provision that the said laws and regulations must enable full effect to be given to the purposes for which the rights accorded under paragraph 3 are intended.

5. The provisions of paragraphs 3 and 4 of the present Article shall be without prejudice to the right of any State Party having a claim to jurisdiction in accordance with Article 6, subparagraph 1 (c) or 2 (c), to invite the International Committee of the Red Cross to communicate with and visit the alleged offender.

6. When a State Party, pursuant to the present Article, has taken a person into custody, it shall immediately notify, directly or through the Secretary-General of the United Nations, the States Parties which have established jurisdiction in accordance with Article 6, paragraphs 1

and 2, and, if it considers it advisable, any other interested States Parties, of the fact that that person is in custody and of the circumstances which warrant that person's detention. The State which makes the investigation contemplated in paragraph 1 of the present Article shall promptly inform the said States Parties of its findings and shall indicate whether it intends to exercise jurisdiction.

Article 8

1. The State Party in the territory of which the alleged offender is present shall, in cases to which Article 6 applies, if it does not extradite that person, be obliged, without exception whatsoever and whether or not the offence was committed in its territory, to submit the case without undue delay to its competent authorities for the purpose of prosecution, through proceedings in accordance with the laws of that State. Those authorities shall take their decision in the same manner as in the case of any other offence of a grave nature under the law of that State.
2. Whenever a State Party is permitted under its domestic law to extradite or otherwise surrender one of its nationals only upon the condition that the person will be returned to that State to serve the sentence imposed as a result of the trial or proceeding for which the extradition or surrender of the person was sought, and this State and the State seeking the extradition of the person agree with this option and other terms they may deem appropriate, such a conditional extradition or surrender shall be sufficient to discharge the obligation set forth in paragraph 1 of the present Article.

Article 9

1. The offences set forth in Article 2 shall be deemed to be included as extraditable offences in any extradition treaty existing between any of the States Parties before the entry into force of this Convention. States Parties undertake to include such offences as extraditable offences in every extradition treaty to be subsequently concluded between them.
2. When a State Party which makes extradition conditional on the existence of a treaty receives a request for extradition from another State Party with which it has no extradition treaty, the requested State Party may, at its option, consider this Convention as a legal basis for extradition in respect of the offences set forth in Article 2. Extradition shall be subject to the other conditions provided by the law of the requested State.
3. States Parties which do not make extradition conditional on the existence of a treaty shall recognize the offences set forth in Article 2 as extraditable offences between themselves, subject to the conditions provided by the law of the requested State.
4. If necessary, the offences set forth in Article 2 shall be treated, for the purposes of extradition between States Parties, as if they had been committed not only in the place in which they occurred but also in the territory of the States that have established jurisdiction in accordance with Article 6, paragraphs 1 and 2.
5. The provisions of all extradition treaties and arrangements between States Parties with regard to offences set forth in Article 2 shall be deemed to be modified as between State Parties to the extent that they are incompatible with this Convention.

Article 10

1. States Parties shall afford one another the greatest measure of assistance in connection with investigations or criminal or extradition proceedings brought in respect of the offences set forth in Article 2, including assistance in obtaining evidence at their disposal necessary for the proceedings.
2. States Parties shall carry out their obligations under paragraph 1 of the present Article in conformity with any treaties or other arrangements on mutual legal assistance that may exist

between them. In the absence of such treaties or arrangements, States Parties shall afford one another assistance in accordance with their domestic law.

Article 11
None of the offences set forth in Article 2 shall be regarded, for the purposes of extradition or mutual legal assistance, as a political offence or as an offence connected with a political offence or as an offence inspired by political motives. Accordingly, a request for extradition or for mutual legal assistance based on such an offence may not be refused on the sole ground that it concerns a political offence or an offence connected with a political offence or an offence inspired by political motives.

Article 12
Nothing in this Convention shall be interpreted as imposing an obligation to extradite or to afford mutual legal assistance, if the requested State Party has substantial grounds for believing that the request for extradition for offences set forth in Article 2 or for mutual legal assistance with respect to such offences has been made for the purpose of prosecuting or punishing a person on account of that person's race, religion, nationality, ethnic origin or political opinion or that compliance with the request would cause prejudice to that person's position for any of these reasons.

Article 13
1. A person who is being detained or is serving a sentence in the territory of one State Party whose presence in another State Party is requested for purposes of testimony, identification or otherwise providing assistance in obtaining evidence for the investigation or prosecution of offences under this Convention may be transferred if the following conditions are met:
　　(a) The person freely gives his or her informed consent; and
　　(b) The competent authorities of both States agree, subject to such conditions as those States may deem appropriate.
2. For the purposes of the present Article:
　　(a) The State to which the person is transferred shall have the authority and obligation to keep the person transferred in custody, unless otherwise requested or authorized by the State from which the person was transferred;
　　(b) The State to which the person is transferred shall without delay implement its obligation to return the person to the custody of the State from which the person was transferred as agreed beforehand, or as otherwise agreed, by the competent authorities of both States;
　　(c) The State to which the person is transferred shall not require the State from which the person was transferred to initiate extradition proceedings for the return of the person;
　　(d) The person transferred shall receive credit for service of the sentence being served in the State from which he was transferred for time spent in the custody of the State to which he was transferred.
3. Unless the State Party from which a person is to be transferred in accordance with the present Article so agrees, that person, whatever his or her nationality, shall not be prosecuted or detained or subjected to any other restriction of his or her personal liberty in the territory of the State to which that person is transferred in respect of acts or convictions anterior to his or her departure from the territory of the State from which such person was transferred.

Article 14

Any person who is taken into custody or regarding whom any other measures are taken or proceedings are carried out pursuant to this Convention shall be guaranteed fair treatment, including enjoyment of all rights and guarantees in conformity with the law of the State in the territory of which that person is present and applicable provisions of international law, including international law of human rights.

Article 15

States Parties shall cooperate in the prevention of the offences set forth in Article 2, particularly:

  (a) By taking all practicable measures, including, if necessary, adapting their domestic legislation, to prevent and counter preparations in their respective territories for the commission of those offences within or outside their territories, including measures to prohibit in their territories illegal activities of persons, groups and organizations that encourage, instigate, organize, knowingly finance or engage in the perpetration of offences as set forth in Article 2;

  (b) By exchanging accurate and verified information in accordance with their national law, and coordinating administrative and other measures taken as appropriate to prevent the commission of offences as set forth in Article 2;

  (c) Where appropriate, through research and development regarding methods of detection of explosives and other harmful substances that can cause death or bodily injury, consultations on the development of standards for marking explosives in order to identify their origin in post-blast investigations, exchange of information on preventive measures, cooperation and transfer of technology, equipment and related materials.

Article 16

The State Party where the alleged offender is prosecuted shall, in accordance with its domestic law or applicable procedures, communicate the final outcome of the proceedings to the Secretary-General of the United Nations, who shall transmit the information to the other States Parties.

Article 17

The States Parties shall carry out their obligations under this Convention in a manner consistent with the principles of sovereign equality and territorial integrity of States and that of non-intervention in the domestic affairs of other States.

Article 18

Nothing in this Convention entitles a State Party to undertake in the territory of another State Party the exercise of jurisdiction and performance of functions which are exclusively reserved for the authorities of that other State Party by its domestic law.

Article 19

1. Nothing in this Convention shall affect other rights, obligations and responsibilities of States and individuals under international law, in particular the purposes and principles of the Charter of the United Nations and international humanitarian law.

2. The activities of armed forces during an armed conflict, as those terms are understood under international humanitarian law, which are governed by that law, are not governed by this Convention, and the activities undertaken by military forces of a State in the exercise of

their official duties, inasmuch as they are governed by other rules of international law, are not governed by this Convention.

Article 20

1. Any dispute between two or more States Parties concerning the interpretation or application of this Convention which cannot be settled through negotiation within a reasonable time shall, at the request of one of them, be submitted to arbitration. If, within six months from the date of the request for arbitration, the parties are unable to agree on the organization of the arbitration, any one of those parties may refer the dispute to the International Court of Justice, by application, in conformity with the Statute of the Court.

2. Each State may at the time of signature, ratification, acceptance or approval of this Convention or accession thereto declare that it does not consider itself bound by paragraph 1 of the present Article. The other States Parties shall not be bound by paragraph 1 with respect to any State Party which has made such a reservation.

3. Any State which has made a reservation in accordance with paragraph 2 of the present Article may at any time withdraw that reservation by notification to the Secretary-General of the United Nations.

Article 21

1. This Convention shall be open for signature by all States from 12 January 1998 until 31 December 1999 at United Nations Headquarters in New York.

2. This Convention is subject to ratification, acceptance or approval. The instruments of ratification, acceptance or approval shall be deposited with the Secretary-General of the United Nations.

3. This Convention shall be open to accession by any State. The instruments of accession shall be deposited with the Secretary-General of the United Nations.

Article 22

1. This Convention shall enter into force on the thirtieth day following the date of the deposit of the twenty-second instrument of ratification, acceptance, approval or accession with the Secretary-General of the United Nations.

2. For each State ratifying, accepting, approving or acceding to the Convention after the deposit of the twenty-second instrument of ratification, acceptance, approval or accession, the Convention shall enter into force on the thirtieth day after deposit by such State of its instrument of ratification, acceptance, approval or accession.

Article 23

1. Any State Party may denounce this Convention by written notification to the Secretary-General of the United Nations.

2. Denunciation shall take effect one year following the date on which notification is received by the Secretary-General of the United Nations.

Article 24

The original of this Convention, of which the Arabic, Chinese, English, French, Russian and Spanish texts are equally authentic, shall be deposited with the Secretary-General of the United Nations, who shall send certified copies thereof to all States.

TC1D
*Draft International Convention for the Suppression of Acts of Nuclear Terrorism, 22
October 1998*[1]

The States Parties to this Convention,
Having in mind the purposes and principles of the Charter of the United Nations concerning
the maintenance of international peace and security and the promotion of good-
neighbourliness and friendly relations and cooperation among States,
Recalling the Declaration on the Occasion of the Fiftieth Anniversary of the United Nations
of 24 October 1995,
Recognizing the right of all States to develop and apply nuclear energy for peaceful purposes
and their legitimate interests in the potential benefits to be derived from the peaceful
application of nuclear energy,
Bearing in mind the Convention on the Physical Protection of Nuclear Material of 1980,
Deeply concerned about the worldwide escalation of acts of terrorism in all its forms and
manifestations,
Recalling also the Declaration on Measures to Eliminate International Terrorism, annexed to
General Assembly Resolution 49/60 of 9 December 1994, in which, inter alia, the States
Members of the United Nations solemnly reaffirm their unequivocal condemnation of all
acts, methods and practices of terrorism as criminal and unjustifiable, wherever and by

---

[1] Draft International Convention for the Suppression of Acts of Nuclear Terrorism; Revised text proposed by the Friends of the Chairman; (A/C.6/53/L.4, annex I), 22 October 1998. At the February 2002
meeting of the (GA) Ad Hoc Committee (set up under GA Res 51/210, see Chapter 4.1.3 for details) its
Chairman, Philippe Kirsch (Canada), said the Committee was still considering whether to elaborate a
new convention or a protocol to either the 1980 Convention on the Physical Protection of Nuclear Material or the 1997 Convention on the Suppression of Terrorist Bombings. Important elements of the proposed draft convention on nuclear terrorism were drawn from the 1980 Convention, which largely dealt
with the use of nuclear material for peaceful purposes. Continuing, he said if the Ad Hoc Committee or
the working group of the Sixth Committee (Legal) decided on a separate convention, rather than a protocol, then it would still have to be determined to what extent the new instrument took into account the
1997 Convention. There were still uncertainties on how to deal with several complex issues, including
the exact nature of the offence, the materials or facilities to be included and the scope of the convention.
Future work should focus on the content of the exchanges in the working group and how to build on the
progress made so far, and reflect general discussions rather then just individual suggestions.
    During the general debate, several speakers said universal adherence to a nuclear terrorism conven-
tion would address the emerging threats from groups operating across borders. The convention would
also help reduce the probability of nuclear and radioactive terrorism, and safeguard sites that produced
nuclear energy for peaceful purposes. Many speakers called for a close examination of the draft convention's relationship with existing legal instruments. Delegations cited three treaties that covered similar
issues: the 1980 Convention on the Physical Protection of Nuclear Material; the 1997 International Convention for the Suppression of Terrorist Bombings; and the Comprehensive Nuclear-Test-Ban Treaty
(CTBT) of 1996. Several speakers said the Committee should consider whether the most effective method of dealing with the nuclear threat would be to elaborate the draft convention or amend or add a protocol to the 1980 Convention. The Committee should clarify the draft convention's definition of nuclear
terrorism and the scope of its applications, some speakers said. The provisions concerning jurisdiction,
extradition and the rendering of mutual assistance should also be studied. In addition, the text should not
modify provisions of current international humanitarian law. Concerned that the draft only addressed terrorism by individuals, other speakers said that terrorism could also involve acts by States, especially in
the case of nuclear terrorism (from: Supplement no. 37 (A/57/37) UN NY, 2002).

whomever committed, including those which jeopardize the friendly relations among States and peoples and threaten the territorial integrity and security of States,

Noting that the Declaration also encouraged States to review urgently the scope of the existing international legal provisions on the prevention, repression and elimination of terrorism in all its forms and manifestations, with the aim of ensuring that there is a comprehensive legal framework covering all aspects of the matter,

Recalling General Assembly Resolution 51/210 of 17 December 1996 and the Declaration to Supplement the 1994 Declaration on Measures to Eliminate International Terrorism annexed thereto,

Recalling also that, pursuant to General Assembly Resolution 51/210, an ad hoc committee was established to elaborate, inter alia, an international convention for the suppression of acts of nuclear terrorism to supplement related existing international instruments,

Noting that acts of nuclear terrorism may result in the gravest consequences and may pose a threat to international peace and security,

Noting also that existing multilateral legal provisions do not adequately address those attacks,

Being convinced of the urgent need to enhance international cooperation between States in devising and adopting effective and practical measures for the prevention of such acts of terrorism and for the prosecution and punishment of their perpetrators,

Noting that the activities of military forces of States are governed by rules of international law outside of the framework of this Convention and that the exclusion of certain actions from the coverage of this Convention does not condone or make lawful otherwise unlawful acts, or preclude prosecution under other laws,

Have agreed as follows:

Article 1
For the purposes of this Convention:

1. 'Radioactive material' means nuclear material and other radioactive substances which contain nuclides which undergo spontaneous disintegration (a process accompanied by emission of one or more types of ionizing radiation, such as alpha-, beta-, neutron pArticles and gamma rays) and which may, owing to their radiological or fissile properties, cause death, serious bodily injury or substantial damage to property or to the environment.

2. 'Nuclear material' means plutonium, except that with isotopic concentration exceeding 80 per cent in plutonium-238; uranium-233; uranium enriched in the isotopes 235 or 233; uranium containing the mixture of isotopes as occurring in nature other than in the form of ore or ore residue; or any material containing one or more of the foregoing;

Whereby 'uraniumenriched in the isotope 235 or 233' means uranium containing the isotope 235 or 233 or both in an amount such that the abundance ratio of the sum of these isotopes to the isotope 238 is greater than the ratio of the isotope 235 to the isotope 238 occurring in nature.

3. 'Nuclear facility' means:
    (a) Any nuclear reactor, including reactors installed on vessels, vehicles, aircraft or space objects for use as an energy source in order to propel such vessels, vehicles, aircraft or space objects or for any other purpose;
    (b) Any plant or conveyance being used for the production, storage, processing or transport of radioactive material.

4. 'Device' means:
    (a) Any nuclear explosive device; or
    (b) Any radioactive material dispersal or radiation-emitting device which may, owing to its radiological properties, cause death, serious bodily injury or substantial damage to property or the environment.

5. 'State or government facility' includes any permanent or temporary facility or conveyance that is used or occupied by representatives of a State, members of Government, the legislature or the judiciary or by officials or employees of a State or any other public authority or entity or by employees or officials of an intergovernmental organization in connection with their official duties.

6. 'Military forces of a State' means the armed forces of a State which are organized, trained and equipped under its internal law for the primary purpose of national defence or security and persons acting in support of those armed forces who are under their formal command, control and responsibility.

Article 2

1. Any person commits an offence within the meaning of this Convention if that person unlawfully and intentionally:
   (a) Possesses radioactive material or makes or possesses a device:
       (i) With the intent to cause death or serious bodily injury; or
       (ii) With the intent to cause substantial damage to property or the environment;
   (b) Uses in any way radioactive material or a device, or uses or damages a nuclear facility in a manner which releases or risks the release of radioactive material:
       (i)   With the intent to cause death or serious bodily injury; or
       (ii) With the intent to cause substantial damage to property or the environment; or
       (iii) With the intent to compel a natural or legal person, an international organization or a State to do or refrain from doing an act.

2. Any person also commits an offence if that person:
   (a) Threatens, under circumstances which indicate the credibility of the threat, to commit an offence as set forth in subparagraph 1(b) of the present Article; or
   (b) Demands unlawfully and intentionally radioactive material, a device or a nuclear facility by threat, under circumstances which indicate the credibility of the threat, or by use of force.

3. Any person also commits an offence if that person attempts to commit an offence as set forth in paragraph 1 of the present Article.

4. Any person also commits an offence if that person:
   (a) Participates as an accomplice in an offence as set forth in paragraph 1, 2 or 3 of the present Article; or
   (b) Organizes or directs others to commit an offence as set forth in paragraph 1, 2 or 3 of the present Article; or
   (c) In any other way contributes to the commission of one or more offences as set forth in paragraph 1, 2 or 3 of the present Article by a group of persons acting with a common purpose; such contribution shall be intentional and either be made with the aim of furthering the general criminal activity or purpose of the group or be made in the knowledge of the intention of the group to commit the offence or offences concerned.

Article 3

This Convention shall not apply where the offence is committed within a single State, the alleged offender and the victims are nationals of that State, the alleged offender is found in the territory of that State and no other State has a basis under Article 9, paragraph 1 or paragraph 2, to exercise jurisdiction, except that the provisions of Articles 7, 12, 14, 15, 16 and 17 shall, as appropriate, apply in those cases.

Article 4

1. Nothing in this Convention shall affect other rights, obligations and responsibilities of States and individuals under international law, in particular the purposes and principles of the Charter of the United Nations and international humanitarian law.

2. The activities of armed forces during an armed conflict, as those terms are understood under international humanitarian law, which are governed by that law are not governed by this Convention, and the activities undertaken by military forces of a State in the exercise of their official duties, inasmuch as they are governed by other rules of international law, are not governed by this Convention.

3. The provisions of paragraph 2 of the present Article shall not be interpreted as condoning or making lawful otherwise unlawful acts, or precluding prosecution under other laws.

Article 5

Each State Party shall adopt such measures as may be necessary:

    (a) To establish as criminal offences under its national law the offences set forth in Article 2;

    (b) To make those offences punishable by appropriate penalties which take into account the grave nature of these offences.

Article 6

Each State Party shall adopt such measures as may be necessary, including, where appropriate, domestic legislation, to ensure that criminal acts within the scope of this Convention, in particular where they are intended or calculated to provoke a state of terror in the general public or in a group of persons or particular persons, are under no circumstances justifiable by considerations of a political, philosophical, ideological, racial, ethnic, religious or other similar nature and are punished by penalties consistent with their grave nature.

Article 7

1. States Parties shall cooperate by:

    (a) Taking all practicable measures, including, if necessary, adapting their national law, to prevent and counter preparations in their respective territories for the commission within or outside their territories of the offences set forth in Article 2, including measures to prohibit in their territories illegal activities of persons, groups and organizations that encourage, instigate, organize, knowingly finance or knowingly provide technical assistance or information or engage in the perpetration of those offences;

    (b) Exchanging accurate and verified information in accordance with their national law and in the manner of and subject to the conditions specified herein, and coordinating administrative and other measures taken as appropriate to detect, prevent, suppress and investigate the offences set forth in Article 2 and also in order to institute criminal proceedings against persons alleged to have committed those crimes. In particular, a State Party shall take appropriate measures in order to inform without delay the other States referred to in Article 9 in respect of the commission of the offences set forth in Article 2 as well as preparations to commit such offences about which it has learned, and also to inform, where appropriate, international organizations.

2. States Parties shall take appropriate measures consistent with their national law to protect the confidentiality of any information which they receive in confidence by virtue of the provisions of this Convention from another State Party or through participation in an activity carried out for the implementation of this Convention. If States Parties provide information to

international organizations in confidence, steps shall be taken to ensure that the confidentiality of such information is protected.

3. States Parties shall not be required by this Convention to provide any information which they are not permitted to communicate pursuant to national law or which would jeopardize the security of the State concerned or the physical protection of nuclear material.

4. States Parties shall inform the Secretary-General of the United Nations of their competent authorities and liaison points responsible for sending and receiving the information referred to in the present Article. The Secretary-General of the United Nations shall communicate such information regarding competent authorities and liaison points to all States Parties and the International Atomic Energy Agency. Such authorities and liaison points must be accessible on a continuous basis.

Article 8

For purposes of preventing offences under this Convention, States Parties shall make every effort to adopt appropriate measures to ensure the protection of radioactive material, taking into account relevant recommendations and functions of the International Atomic Energy Agency.

Article 9

1. Each State Party shall take such measures as may be necessary to establish its jurisdiction over the offences set forth in Article 2 when:
    (a) The offence is committed in the territory of that State; or
    (b) The offence is committed on board a vessel flying the flag of that State or an aircraft which is registered under the laws of that State at the time the offence is committed; or
    (c) The offence is committed by a national of that State.
2. A State Party may also establish its jurisdiction over any such offence when:
    (a) The offence is committed against a national of that State; or
    (b) The offence is committed against a State or government facility of that State abroad, including an embassy or other diplomatic or consular premises of that State; or
    (c) The offence is committed by a stateless person who has his or her habitual residence in the territory of that State; or
    (d) The offence is committed in an attempt to compel that State to do or abstain from doing any act; or
    (e) The offence is committed on board an aircraft which is operated by the Government of that State.
3. Upon ratifying, accepting, approving or acceding to this Convention, each State Party shall notify the Secretary-General of the United Nations of the jurisdiction it has established under its national law in accordance with paragraph 2 of the present Article. Should any change take place, the State Party concerned shall immediately notify the Secretary-General.

4. Each State Party shall likewise take such measures as may be necessary to establish its jurisdiction over the offences set forth in Article 2 in cases where the alleged offender is present in its territory and it does not extradite that person to any of the States Parties which have established their jurisdiction in accordance with paragraph 1 or 2 of the present Article.

5. This Convention does not exclude the exercise of any criminal jurisdiction established by a State Party in accordance with its national law.

Article 10

1. Upon receiving information that an offence set forth in Article 2 has been committed or is being committed in the territory of a State Party or that a person who has committed or who is alleged to have committed such an offence may be present in its territory, the State Party concerned shall take such measures as may be necessary under its national law to investigate the facts contained in the information.

2. Upon being satisfied that the circumstances so warrant, the State Party in whose territory the offender or alleged offender is present shall take the appropriate measures under its national law so as to ensure that person's presence for the purpose of prosecution or extradition.

3. Any person regarding whom the measures referred to in paragraph 2 of the present Article are being taken shall be entitled to:

    (a) Communicate without delay with the nearest appropriate representative of the State of which that person is a national or which is otherwise entitled to protect that person's rights or, if that person is a stateless person, the State in the territory of which that person habitually resides;

    (b) Be visited by a representative of that State;

    (c) Be informed of that person's rights under subparagraphs (a) and (b).

4. The rights referred to in paragraph 3 of the present Article shall be exercised in conformity with the laws and regulations of the State in the territory of which the offender or alleged offender is present, subject to the provision that the said laws and regulations must enable full effect to be given to the purposes for which the rights accorded under paragraph 3 are intended.

5. The provisions of paragraphs 3 and 4 of the present Article shall be without prejudice to the right of any State Party having a claim to jurisdiction in accordance with Article 9, subparagraph 1c or 2c, to invite the International Committee of the Red Cross to communicate with and visit the alleged offender.

6. When a State Party, pursuant to the present Article, has taken a person into custody, it shall immediately notify, directly or through the Secretary-General of the United Nations, the States Parties which have established jurisdiction in accordance with Article 9, paragraphs 1 and 2 and, if it considers it advisable, any other interested States Parties, of the fact that that person is in custody and of the circumstances which warrant that person's detention. The State which makes the investigation contemplated in paragraph 1 of the present Article shall promptly inform the said States Parties of its findings and shall indicate whether it intends to exercise jurisdiction.

Article 11

1. The State Party in the territory of which the alleged offender is present shall, in cases to which Article 9 applies, if it does not extradite that person, be obliged, without exception whatsoever and whether or not the offence was committed in its territory, to submit the case without undue delay to its competent authorities for the purpose of prosecution, through proceedings in accordance with the laws of that State. Those authorities shall take their decision in the same manner as in the case of any other offence of a grave nature under the law of that State.

2. Whenever a State Party is permitted under its national law to extradite or otherwise surrender one of its nationals only upon the condition that the person will be returned to that State to serve the sentence imposed as a result of the trial or proceeding for which the extradition or surrender of the person was sought, and this State and the State seeking the extradition of the person agree with this option and other terms they may deem appropriate,

such a conditional extradition or surrender shall be sufficient to discharge the obligation set forth in paragraph 1 of the present Article.

Article 12

Any person who is taken into custody or regarding whom any other measures are taken or proceedings are carried out pursuant to this Convention shall be guaranteed fair treatment, including enjoyment of all rights and guarantees in conformity with the law of the State in the territory of which that person is present and applicable provisions of international law, including international law of human rights.

Article 13

1. The offences set forth in Article 2 shall be deemed to be included as extraditable offences in any extradition treaty existing between any of the States Parties before the entry into force of this Convention. States Parties undertake to include such offences as extraditable offences in every extradition treaty to be subsequently concluded between them.
2. When a State Party which makes extradition conditional on the existence of a treaty receives a request for extradition from another State Party with which it has no extradition treaty, the requested State Party may, at its option, consider this Convention as a legal basis for extradition in respect of the offences set forth in Article 2. Extradition shall be subject to the other conditions provided by the law of the requested State.
3. States Parties which do not make extradition conditional on the existence of a treaty shall recognize the offences set forth in Article 2 as extraditable offences between themselves, subject to the conditions provided by the law of the requested State.
4. If necessary, the offences set forth in Article 2 shall be treated, for the purposes of extradition between States Parties, as if they had been committed not only in the place in which they occurred but also in the territory of the States that have established jurisdiction in accordance with Article 9, paragraphs 1 and 2.
5. The provisions of all extradition treaties and arrangements between States Parties with regard to offences set forth in Article 2 shall be deemed to be modified as between States Parties to the extent that they are incompatible with this Convention.

Article 14

1. States Parties shall afford one another the greatest measure of assistance in connection with investigations or criminal or extradition proceedings brought in respect of the offences set forth in Article 2, including assistance in obtaining evidence at their disposal necessary for the proceedings.
2. States Parties shall carry out their obligations under paragraph 1 of the present Article in conformity with any treaties or other arrangements on mutual legal assistance that may exist between them. In the absence of such treaties or arrangements, States Parties shall afford one another assistance in accordance with their national law.

Article 15

None of the offences set forth in Article 2 shall be regarded, for the purposes of extradition or mutual legal assistance, as a political offence or as an offence connected with a political offence or as an offence inspired by political motives. Accordingly, a request for extradition or for mutual legal assistance based on such an offence may not be refused on the sole ground that it concerns a political offence or an offence connected with a political offence or an offence inspired by political motives.

Article 16

Nothing in this Convention shall be interpreted as imposing an obligation to extradite or to afford mutual legal assistance if the requested State Party has substantial grounds for believing that the request for extradition for offences set forth in Article 2 or for mutual legal assistance with respect to such offences has been made for the purpose of prosecuting or punishing a person on account of that person's race, religion, nationality, ethnic origin or political opinion or that compliance with the request would cause prejudice to that person's position for any of these reasons.

Article 17

1. A person who is being detained or is serving a sentence in the territory of one State Party whose presence in another State Party is requested for purposes of testimony, identification or otherwise providing assistance in obtaining evidence for the investigation or prosecution of offences under this Convention may be transferred if the following conditions are met:
    (a) The person freely gives his or her informed consent; and
    (b) The competent authorities of both States agree, subject to such conditions as those States may deem appropriate.
2. For the purposes of the present Article:
    (a) The State to which the person is transferred shall have the authority and obligation to keep the person transferred in custody, unless otherwise requested or authorized by the State from which the person was transferred;
    (b) The State to which the person is transferred shall without delay implement its obligation to return the person to the custody of the State from which the person was transferred as agreed beforehand, or as otherwise agreed, by the competent authorities of both States;
    (c) The State to which the person is transferred shall not require the State from which the person was transferred to initiate extradition proceedings for the return of the person;
    (d) The person transferred shall receive credit for service of the sentence being served in the State fromwhich he was transferred for time spent in the custody of the State to which he was transferred.
3. Unless the State Party from which a person is to be transferred in accordance with the present Article so agrees, that person, whatever his or her nationality, shall not be prosecuted or detained or subjected to any other restriction of his or her personal liberty in the territory of the State to which that person is transferred in respect of acts or convictions anterior to his or her departure from the territory of the State from which such person was transferred.

Article 18

1. Upon seizing or otherwise taking control of radioactive material, devices or nuclear facilities, following the commission of an offence set forth in Article 2, the State Party in possession of it shall:
    (a) Take steps to render harmless the radioactive material, device or nuclear facility;
    (b) Ensure that any nuclear material is held in accordance with applicable International Atomic Energy Agency safeguards; and
    (c) Have regard to physical protection recommendations and health and safety standards published by the International Atomic Energy Agency.
2. Upon the completion of any proceedings connected with an offence set forth in Article 2, or sooner if required by international law, any radioactive material, device or nuclear facility shall be returned, after consultations (in particular, regarding modalities of return and storage) with the States Parties concerned to the State Party to which it belongs, to the State Party

of which the natural or legal person owning such radioactive material, device or facility is a national or resident, or to the State Party from whose territory it was stolen or otherwise unlawfully obtained.

3(1). Where a State Party is prohibited by national or international law from returning or accepting such radioactive material, device or nuclear facility or where the States Parties concerned so agree, subject to paragraph 3(2) of the present Article, the State Party in possession of the radioactive material, devices or nuclear facilities shall continue to take the steps described in paragraph 1 of the present Article; such radioactive material, devices or nuclear facilities shall be used only for peaceful purposes.

3(2). Where it is not lawful for the State Party in possession of the radioactive material, devices or nuclear facilities to possess them, that State shall ensure that they are as soon as possible placed in the possession of a State for which such possession is lawful and which, where appropriate, has provided assurances consistent with the requirements of paragraph 1 of the present Article in consultation with that State, for the purpose of rendering it harmless; such radioactive material, devices or nuclear facilities shall be used only for peaceful purposes.

4. If the radioactive material, devices or nuclear facilities referred to in paragraphs 1 and 2 of the present Article do not belong to any of the States Parties or to a national or resident of a State Party or was not stolen or otherwise unlawfully obtained from the territory of a State Party, or if no State is willing to receive such item pursuant to paragraph 3 of the present Article, a separate decision concerning its disposition shall, subject to paragraph 3(2) of the present Article, be taken after consultations between the States concerned and any relevant international organizations.

5. For the purposes of paragraphs 1, 2, 3 and 4 of the present Article, the State Party in possession of the radioactive material, device or nuclear facility may request the assistance and cooperation of other States Parties, in particular the States Parties concerned, and any relevant international organizations, in particular the International Atomic Energy Agency. States Parties and the relevant international organizations are encouraged to provide assistance pursuant to this paragraph to the maximum extent possible.

6. The States Parties involved in the disposition or retention of the radioactive material, device or nuclear facility pursuant to the present Article shall inform the Director General of the International Atomic Energy Agency of the manner in which such an item was disposed of or retained. The Director General of the International Atomic Energy Agency shall transmit the information to the other States Parties.

7. In the event of any dissemination in connection with an offence set forth in Article 2, nothing in the present Article shall affect in any way the rules of international law governing liability for nuclear damage, or other rules of international law.

Article 19

The State Party where the alleged offender is prosecuted shall, in accordance with its national law or applicable procedures, communicate the final outcome of the proceedings to the Secretary-General of the United Nations, who shall transmit the information to the other States Parties.

Article 20

States Parties shall conduct consultations with one another directly or through the Secretary-General of the United Nations, with the assistance of international organizations as necessary, to ensure effective implementation of this Convention.

Article 21

The States Parties shall carry out their obligations under this Convention in a manner consistent with the principles of sovereign equality and territorial integrity of States and that of non-intervention in the domestic affairs of other States.

Article 22

Nothing in this Convention entitles a State Party to undertake in the territory of another State Party the exercise of jurisdiction and performance of functions which are exclusively reserved for the authorities of that other State Party by its national law.

Article 23

1. Any dispute between two or more States Parties concerning the interpretation or application of this Convention which cannot be settled through negotiation within a reasonable time shall, at the request of one of them, be submitted to arbitration. If, within six months from the date of the request for arbitration, the parties are unable to agree on the organization of the arbitration, any one of those parties may refer the dispute to the International Court of Justice, by application, in conformity with the Statute of the Court.

2. Each State may, at the time of signature, ratification, acceptance or approval of this Convention or accession thereto, declare that it does not consider itself bound by paragraph 1 of the present Article. The other States Parties shall not be bound by paragraph 1 with respect to any State Party which has made such a reservation.

3. Any State which has made a reservation in accordance with paragraph 2 of the present Article may at any time withdraw that reservation by notification to the Secretary-General of the United Nations.

Article 24

1. This Convention shall be open for signature by all States from ... until ... at United Nations Headquarters in New York.

2. This Convention is subject to ratification, acceptance or approval. The instruments of ratification, acceptance or approval shall be deposited with the Secretary-General of the United Nations.

3. This Convention shall be open to accession by any State. The instruments of accession shall be deposited with the Secretary-General of the United Nations.

Article 25

1. This Convention shall enter into force on the thirtieth day following the date of the deposit of the twenty-second instrument of ratification, acceptance, approval or accession with the Secretary-General of the United Nations.

2. For each State ratifying, accepting, approving or acceding to the Convention after the deposit of the twenty-second instrument of ratification, acceptance, approval or accession, the Convention shall enter into force on the thirtieth day after deposit by such State of its instrument of ratification, acceptance, approval or accession.

Article 26

1. A State Party may propose an amendment to this Convention. The proposed amendment shall be submitted to the Depositary, who circulates it immediately to all States Parties.

2. If the majority of the States Parties request the Depositary to convene a Conference to consider the proposed amendments, the Depositary shall invite all States Parties to attend such a Conference to begin not sooner than three months after the invitations are issued.

3. The Conference shall make every effort to ensure amendments are adopted by consensus. Should this not be possible, amendments shall be adopted by a two-thirds majority of all States Parties. Any amendment adopted at the Conference shall be promptly circulated by the Depositary to all States Parties.

4. The amendment adopted pursuant to paragraph 3 of the present Article shall enter into force for each State Party that deposits its instrument of ratification, acceptance, accession or approval of the amendment on the thirtieth day after the date on which two thirds of the States Parties have deposited their relevant instrument. Thereafter, the amendment shall enter into force for any State Party on the thirtieth day after the date on which that State deposits its relevant instrument.

Article 27

1. Any State Party may denounce this Convention by written notification to the Secretary-General of the United Nations.

2. Denunciation shall take effect one year following the date on which notification is received by the Secretary-General of the United Nations.

Article 28

The original of this Convention, of which the Arabic, Chinese, English, French, Russian and Spanish texts are equally authentic, shall be deposited with the Secretary-General of the United Nations, who shall send certified copies thereof to all States.

IN WITNESS WHEREOF, the undersigned, being duly authorized thereto by their respective Governments, have signed this Convention, opened for signature at United Nations Headquarters in New York on ...

TC1E
International Convention for the Suppression of the Financing of Terrorism

United Nations General Assembly
Austral-asian Legal Information Institute
December 9, 1999

The convention, adopted unanimously by the UN General Assembly on December 9, 1999, will expand the legal framework for international cooperation in the investigation , arrest, prosecution, and extradition of persons who engage in terrorist financing.
International Convention for the Suppression of the Financing of Terrorism
(New York, 9 December 1999)
Preamble

The States Parties to this Convention,
Bearing in mind the purposes and principles of the Charter of the United Nations concerning the maintenance of international peace and security and the promotion of good-neighbourliness and friendly relations and cooperation among States,
Deeply concerned about the worldwide escalation of acts of terrorism in all its forms and manifestations,
Recalling the Declaration on the Occasion of the Fiftieth Anniversary of the United Nations, contained in General Assembly Resolution 50/6 of 24 October 1995,
Recalling also all the relevant General Assembly resolutions on the matter, including Resolution 49/60 of 9 December 1994 and its annex on the Declaration on Measures to Eliminate

International Terrorism, in which the States Members of the United Nations solemnly reaffirmed their unequivocal condemnation of all acts, methods and practices of terrorism as criminal and unjustifiable, wherever and by whomever committed, including those which jeopardize the friendly relations among States and peoples and threaten the territorial integrity and security of States,

Noting that the Declaration on Measures to Eliminate International Terrorism also encouraged States to review urgently the scope of the existing international legal provisions on the prevention, repression and elimination of terrorism in all its forms and manifestations, with the aim of ensuring that there is a comprehensive legal framework covering all aspects of the matter,

Recalling General Assembly Resolution 51/210 of 17 December 1996, paragraph 3, subparagraph (f), in which the Assembly called upon all States to take steps to prevent and counteract, through appropriate domestic measures, the financing of terrorists and terrorist organizations, whether such financing is direct or indirect through organizations which also have or claim to have charitable, social or cultural goals or which are also engaged in unlawful activities such as illicit arms trafficking, drug dealing and racketeering, including the exploitation of persons for purposes of funding terrorist activities, and in particular to consider, where appropriate, adopting regulatory measures to prevent and counteract movements of funds suspected to be intended for terrorist purposes without impeding in any way the freedom of legitimate capital movements and to intensify the exchange of information concerning international movements of such funds,

Recalling also General Assembly Resolution 52/165 of 15 December 1997, in which the Assembly called upon States to consider, in particular, the implementation of the measures set out in paragraphs 3(a) to (f) of its Resolution 51/210 of 17 December 1996,

Recalling further General Assembly Resolution 53/108 of 8 December 1998, in which the Assembly decided that the Ad Hoc Committee established by General Assembly Resolution 51/210 of 17 December 1996 should elaborate a draft international convention for the suppression of terrorist financing to supplement related existing international instruments,

Considering that the financing of terrorism is a matter of grave concern to international community as a whole,

Noting that the number and seriousness of acts of international terrorism depend on the financing that terrorists may obtain,

Noting also that existing multilateral legal instruments do not expressly address such financing,

Being convinced of the urgent need to enhance international cooperation among States in devising and adopting effective measures for the prevention of the financing of terrorism, as well as for its suppression through the prosecution and punishment of its perpetrators,

Have agreed as follows:

Article 1

For the purposes of this Convention:

1. 'Funds' means assets of every kind, whether tangible or intangible, movable or immovable, however acquired, and legal documents or instruments in any form, including electronic or digital, evidencing title to, or interest in, such assets, including, but not limited to, bank credits, travellers cheques, bank cheques, money orders, shares, securities, bonds, drafts, letters of credit.

2. 'A State or governmental facility' means any permanent or temporary facility or conveyance that is used or occupied by representatives of a State, members of Government, the legislature or the judiciary or by officials or employees of a State or any other public authority or entity or by employees or officials of an intergovernmental organization in connection with their official duties.

3. 'Proceeds' means any funds derived from or obtained, directly or indirectly, through the commission of an offence set forth in Article 2.

Article 2

1. Any person commits an offence within the meaning of this Convention if that person by any means, directly or indirectly, unlawfully and wilfully, provides or collects funds with the intention that they should be used or in the knowledge that they are to be used, in full or in part, in order to carry out:

   (a) An act which constitutes an offence within the scope of and as defined in one of the treaties listed in the Annex; or

   (b) Any other act intended to cause death or serious bodily injury to a civilian, or to any other person not taking an active part in the hostilities in a situation of armed conflict, when the purpose of such act, by its nature or context, is to intimidate a population, or to compel a government or an international organization to do or to abstain from doing any act.

2. (a) On depositing its instrument of ratification, acceptance, approval or accession, a State Party which is not a party to a treaty listed in the Annex may declare that, in the application of this Convention to the State Party, the treaty shall be deemed not to be included in the Annex referred to in paragraph 1, subparagraph(a) The declaration shall cease to have effect as soon as the treaty enters into force for the State Party, which shall notify the depositary of this fact;

   (b) When a State Party ceases to be a party to a treaty listed in the Annex, it may make a declaration as provided for in this Article, with respect to that treaty.

3. For an act to constitute an offence set forth in paragraph 1, it shall not be necessary that the funds were actually used to carry out an offence referred to in paragraph 1, subparagraphs (a) or (b).

4. Any person also commits an offence if that person attempts to commit an offence as set forth in paragraph 1 of this Article.

5. Any person also commits an offence if that person:

   (a) Participates as an accomplice in an offence as set forth in paragraph 1 or 4 of this Article;

   (b) Organizes or directs others to commit an offence as set forth in paragraph 1 or 4 of this Article;

   (c) Contributes to the commission of one or more offences as set forth in paragraphs 1 or 4 of this Article by a group of persons acting with a common purpose. Such contribution shall be intentional and shall either:

      (i) Be made with the aim of furthering the criminal activity or criminal purpose of the group, where such activity or purpose involves the commission of an offence as set forth in paragraph 1 of this Article; or

      (ii) Be made in the knowledge of the intention of the group to commit an offence as set forth in paragraph 1 of this Article.

Article 3

This Convention shall not apply where the offence is committed within a single State, the alleged offender is a national of that State and is present in the territory of that State and no other State has a basis under Article 7, paragraph 1, or Article 7, paragraph 2, to exercise jurisdiction, except that the provisions of Articles 12 to 18 shall, as appropriate, apply in those cases.

Article 4

Each State Party shall adopt such measures as may be necessary:

    (a) To establish as criminal offences under its domestic law the offences set forth in Article 2;

    (b) To make those offences punishable by appropriate penalties which take into account the grave nature of the offences.

Article 5

1. Each State Party, in accordance with its domestic legal principles, shall take the necessary measures to enable a legal entity located in its territory or organized under its laws to be held liable when a person responsible for the management or control of that legal entity has, in that capacity, committed an offence set forth in Article 2. Such liability may be criminal, civil or administrative.

2. Such liability is incurred without prejudice to the criminal liability of individuals having committed the offences.

3. Each State Party shall ensure, in particular, that legal entities liable in accordance with paragraph 1 above are subject to effective, proportionate and dissuasive criminal, civil or administrative sanctions. Such sanctions may include monetary sanctions.

Article 6

Each State Party shall adopt such measures as may be necessary, including, where appropriate, domestic legislation, to ensure that criminal acts within the scope of this Convention are under no circumstances justifiable by considerations of a political, philosophical, ideological, racial, ethnic, religious or other similar nature.

Article 7

1. Each State Party shall take such measures as may be necessary to establish its jurisdiction over the offences set forth in Article 2 when:

    (a) The offence is committed in the territory of that State;

    (b) The offence is committed on board a vessel flying the flag of that State or an aircraft registered under the laws of that State at the time the offence is committed;

    (c) The offence is committed by a national of that State.

2. A State Party may also establish its jurisdiction over any such offence when:

    (a) The offence was directed towards or resulted in the carrying out of an offence referred to in Article 2, paragraph 1, subparagraph (a) or (b), in the territory of or against a national of that State;

    (b) The offence was directed towards or resulted in the carrying out of an offence referred to in Article 2, paragraph 1, subparagraph (a) or (b), against a State or government facility of that State abroad, including diplomatic or consular premises of that State;

    (c) The offence was directed towards or resulted in an offence referred to in Article 2, paragraph 1, subparagraph (a) or (b), committed in an attempt to compel that State to do or abstain from doing any act;

    (d) The offence is committed by a stateless person who has his or her habitual residence in the territory of that State;

    (e) The offence is committed on board an aircraft which is operated by the Government of that State.

3. Upon ratifying, accepting, approving or acceding to this Convention, each State Party shall notify the Secretary-General of the United Nations of the jurisdiction it has established in accordance with paragraph 2. Should any change take place, the State Party concerned shall immediately notify the Secretary-General.

4. Each State Party shall likewise take such measures as may be necessary to establish its jurisdiction over the offences set forth in Article 2 in cases where the alleged offender is present in its territory and it does not extradite that person to any of the States Parties that have established their jurisdiction in accordance with paragraphs 1 or 2.

5. When more than one State Party claims jurisdiction over the offences set forth in Article 2, the relevant States Parties shall strive to coordinate their actions appropriately, in particular concerning the conditions for prosecution and the modalities for mutual legal assistance.

6. Without prejudice to the norms of general international law, this Convention does not exclude the exercise of any criminal jurisdiction established by a State Party in accordance with its domestic law.

Article 8
1. Each State Party shall take appropriate measures, in accordance with its domestic legal principles, for the identification, detection and freezing or seizure of any funds used or allocated for the purpose of committing the offences set forth in Article 2 as well as the proceeds derived from such offences, for purposes of possible forfeiture.

2. Each State Party shall take appropriate measures, in accordance with its domestic legal principles, for the forfeiture of funds used or allocated for the purpose of committing the offences set forth in Article 2 and the proceeds derived from such offences.

3. Each State Party concerned may give consideration to concluding agreements on the sharing with other States Parties, on a regular or case-by-case basis, of the funds derived from the forfeitures referred to in this Article.

4. Each State Party shall consider establishing mechanisms whereby the funds derived from the forfeitures referred to in this Article are utilized to compensate the victims of offences referred to in Article 2, paragraph 1, subparagraph (a) or (b), or their families.

5. The provisions of this Article shall be implemented without prejudice to the rights of third parties acting in good faith.

Article 9
1. Upon receiving information that a person who has committed or who is alleged to have committed an offence set forth in Article 2 may be present in its territory, the State Party concerned shall take such measures as may be necessary under its domestic law to investigate the facts contained in the information.

2. Upon being satisfied that the circumstances so warrant, the State Party in whose territory the offender or alleged offender is present shall take the appropriate measures under its domestic law so as to ensure that person's presence for the purpose of prosecution or extradition.

3. Any person regarding whom the measures referred to in paragraph 2 are being taken shall be entitled to:

   (a) Communicate without delay with the nearest appropriate representative of the State of which that person is a national or which is otherwise entitled to protect that person's rights or, if that person is a stateless person, the State in the territory of which that person habitually resides;

   (b) Be visited by a representative of that State;

   (c) Be informed of that person's rights under subparagraphs (a) and (b).

4. The rights referred to in paragraph 3 shall be exercised in conformity with the laws and regulations of the State in the territory of which the offender or alleged offender is present, subject to the provision that the said laws and regulations must enable full effect to be given to the purposes for which the rights accorded under paragraph 3 are intended.

5. The provisions of paragraphs 3 and 4 shall be without prejudice to the right of any State Party having a claim to jurisdiction in accordance with Article 7, paragraph 1, subparagraph

(b), or paragraph 2, subparagraph (b), to invite the International Committee of the Red Cross to communicate with and visit the alleged offender.

6. When a State Party, pursuant to the present Article, has taken a person into custody, it shall immediately notify, directly or through the Secretary-General of the United Nations, the States Parties which have established jurisdiction in accordance with Article 7, paragraph 1 or 2, and, if it considers it advisable, any other interested States Parties, of the fact that such person is in custody and of the circumstances which warrant that person's detention. The State which makes the investigation contemplated in paragraph 1 shall promptly inform the said States Parties of its findings and shall indicate whether it intends to exercise jurisdiction.

Article 10

1. The State Party in the territory of which the alleged offender is present shall, in cases to which Article 7 applies, if it does not extradite that person, be obliged, without exception whatsoever and whether or not the offence was committed in its territory, to submit the case without undue delay to its competent authorities for the purpose of prosecution, through proceedings in accordance with the laws of that State. Those authorities shall take their decision in the same manner as in the case of any other offence of a grave nature under the law of that State.

2. Whenever a State Party is permitted under its domestic law to extradite or otherwise surrender one of its nationals only upon the condition that the person will be returned to that State to serve the sentence imposed as a result of the trial or proceeding for which the extradition or surrender of the person was sought, and this State and the State seeking the extradition of the person agree with this option and other terms they may deem appropriate, such a conditional extradition or surrender shall be sufficient to discharge the obligation set forth in paragraph 1.

Article 11

1. The offences set forth in Article 2 shall be deemed to be included as extraditable offences in any extradition treaty existing between any of the States Parties before the entry into force of this Convention. States Parties undertake to include such offences as extraditable offences in every extradition treaty to be subsequently concluded between them.

2. When a State Party which makes extradition conditional on the existence of a treaty receives a request for extradition from another State Party with which it has no extradition treaty, the requested State Party may, at its option, consider this Convention as a legal basis for extradition in respect of the offences set forth in Article 2. Extradition shall be subject to the other conditions provided by the law of the requested State.

3. States Parties which do not make extradition conditional on the existence of a treaty shall recognize the offences set forth in Article 2 as extraditable offences between themselves, subject to the conditions provided by the law of the requested State.

4. If necessary, the offences set forth in Article 2 shall be treated, for the purposes of extradition between States Parties, as if they had been committed not only in the place in which they occurred but also in the territory of the States that have established jurisdiction in accordance with Article 7, paragraphs 1 and 2.

5. The provisions of all extradition treaties and arrangements between States Parties with regard to offences set forth in Article 2 shall be deemed to be modified as between States Parties to the extent that they are incompatible with this Convention.

Article 12

1. States Parties shall afford one another the greatest measure of assistance in connection with criminal investigations or criminal or extradition proceedings in respect of the offences

set forth in Article 2, including assistance in obtaining evidence in their possession necessary for the proceedings.

2. States Parties may not refuse a request for mutual legal assistance on the ground of bank secrecy.

3. The requesting Party shall not transmit nor use information or evidence furnished by the requested Party for investigations, prosecutions or proceedings other than those stated in the request without the prior consent of the requested Party.

4. Each State Party may give consideration to establishing mechanisms to share with other States Parties information or evidence needed to establish criminal, civil or administrative liability pursuant to Article 5.

5. States Parties shall carry out their obligations under paragraphs 1 and 2 in conformity with any treaties or other arrangements on mutual legal assistance or information exchange that may exist between them. In the absence of such treaties or arrangements, States Parties shall afford one another assistance in accordance with their domestic law.

Article 13
None of the offences set forth in Article 2 shall be regarded, for the purposes of extradition or mutual legal assistance, as a fiscal offence. Accordingly, States Parties may not refuse a request for extradition or for mutual legal assistance on the sole ground that it concerns a fiscal offence.

Article 14
None of the offences set forth in Article 2 shall be regarded for the purposes of extradition or mutual legal assistance as a political offence or as an offence connected with a political offence or as an offence inspired by political motives. Accordingly, a request for extradition or for mutual legal assistance based on such an offence may not be refused on the sole ground that it concerns a political offence or an offence connected with a political offence or an offence inspired by political motives.

Article 15
Nothing in this Convention shall be interpreted as imposing an obligation to extradite or to afford mutual legal assistance, if the requested State Party has substantial grounds for believing that the request for extradition for offences set forth in Article 2 or for mutual legal assistance with respect to such offences has been made for the purpose of prosecuting or punishing a person on account of that person's race, religion, nationality, ethnic origin or political opinion or that compliance with the request would cause prejudice to that person's position for any of these reasons.

Article 16
1. A person who is being detained or is serving a sentence in the territory of one State Party whose presence in another State Party is requested for purposes of identification, testimony or otherwise providing assistance in obtaining evidence for the investigation or prosecution of offences set forth in Article 2 may be transferred if the following conditions are met:
    (a) The person freely gives his or her informed consent;
    (b) The competent authorities of both States agree, subject to such conditions as those States may deem appropriate.

2. For the purposes of the present Article:
    (a) The State to which the person is transferred shall have the authority and obligation to keep the person transferred in custody, unless otherwise requested or authorized by the State from which the person was transferred;

(b) The State to which the person is transferred shall without delay implement its obligation to return the person to the custody of the State from which the person was transferred as agreed beforehand, or as otherwise agreed, by the competent authorities of both States;

(c) The State to which the person is transferred shall not require the State from which the person was transferred to initiate extradition proceedings for the return of the person;

(d) The person transferred shall receive credit for service of the sentence being served in the State from which he or she was transferred for time spent in the custody of the State to which he or she was transferred.

3. Unless the State Party from which a person is to be transferred in accordance with the present Article so agrees, that person, whatever his or her nationality, shall not be prosecuted or detained or subjected to any other restriction of his or her personal liberty in the territory of the State to which that person is transferred in respect of acts or convictions anterior to his or her departure from the territory of the State from which such person was transferred.

Article 17

Any person who is taken into custody or regarding whom any other measures are taken or proceedings are carried out pursuant to this Convention shall be guaranteed fair treatment, including enjoyment of all rights and guarantees in conformity with the law of the State in the territory of which that person is present and applicable provisions of international law, including international human rights law.

Article 18

1. States Parties shall cooperate in the prevention of the offences set forth in Article 2 by taking all practicable measures, inter alia, by adapting their domestic legislation, if necessary, to prevent and counter preparations in their respective territories for the commission of those offences within or outside their territories, including:

(a) Measures to prohibit in their territories illegal activities of persons and organizations that knowingly encourage, instigate, organize or engage in the commission of offences set forth in Article 2;

(b) Measures requiring financial institutions and other professions involved in financial transactions to utilize the most efficient measures available for the identification of their usual or occasional customers, as well as customers in whose interest accounts are opened, and to pay special attention to unusual or suspicious transactions and report transactions suspected of stemming from a criminal activity. For this purpose, States Parties shall consider:

(i) Adopting regulations prohibiting the opening of accounts the holders or beneficiaries of which are unidentified or unidentifiable, and measures to ensure that such institutions verify the identity of the real owners of such transactions;

(ii) With respect to the identification of legal entities, requiring financial institutions, when necessary, to take measures to verify the legal existence and the structure of the customer by obtaining, either from a public register or from the customer or both, proof of incorporation, including information concerning the customer's name, legal form, address, directors and provisions regulating the power to bind the entity;

(iii) Adopting regulations imposing on financial institutions the obligation to report promptly to the competent authorities all complex, unusual large transactions and unusual patterns of transactions, which have no apparent economic or obviously lawful purpose, without fear of assuming criminal or civil liability for breach of any restriction on disclosure of information if they report their suspicions in good faith;

(iv) Requiring financial institutions to maintain, for at least five years, all necessary records on transactions, both domestic or international.

2. States Parties shall further cooperate in the prevention of offences set forth in Article 2 by considering:

(a) Measures for the supervision, including, for example, the licensing, of all money-transmission agencies;

(b) Feasible measures to detect or monitor the physical cross-border transportation of cash and bearer negotiable instruments, subject to strict safeguards to ensure proper use of information and without impeding in any way the freedom of capital movements.

3. States Parties shall further cooperate in the prevention of the offences set forth in Article 2 by exchanging accurate and verified information in accordance with their domestic law and coordinating administrative and other measures taken, as appropriate, to prevent the commission of offences set forth in Article 2, in particular by:

(a) Establishing and maintaining channels of communication between their competent agencies and services to facilitate the secure and rapid exchange of information concerning all aspects of offences set forth in Article 2;

(b) Cooperating with one another in conducting inquiries, with respect to the offences set forth in Article 2, concerning:

(i) The identity, whereabouts and activities of persons in respect of whom reasonable suspicion exists that they are involved in such offences;

(ii) The movement of funds relating to the commission of such offences.

4. States Parties may exchange information through the International Criminal Police Organization (Interpol).

Article 19

The State Party where the alleged offender is prosecuted shall, in accordance with its domestic law or applicable procedures, communicate the final outcome of the proceedings to the Secretary-General of the United Nations, who shall transmit the information to the other States Parties.

Article 20

The States Parties shall carry out their obligations under this Convention in a manner consistent with the principles of sovereign equality and territorial integrity of States and that of non-intervention in the domestic affairs of other States.

Article 21

Nothing in this Convention shall affect other rights, obligations and responsibilities of States and individuals under international law, in particular the purposes of the Charter of the United Nations, international humanitarian law and other relevant conventions.

Article 22

Nothing in this Convention entitles a State Party to undertake in the territory of another State Party the exercise of jurisdiction or performance of functions which are exclusively reserved for the authorities of that other State Party by its domestic law.

Article 23

1. The Annex may be amended by the addition of relevant treaties that:
    (a) Are open to the participation of all States;
    (b) Have entered into force;
    (c) Have been ratified, accepted, approved or acceded to by at least twenty-two States Parties to the present Convention.
2. After the entry into force of this Convention, any State Party may propose such an amendment. Any proposal for an amendment shall be communicated to the depositary in written form. The depositary shall notify proposals that meet the requirements of paragraph 1 to all States Parties and seek their views on whether the proposed amendment should be adopted.
3. The proposed amendment shall be deemed adopted unless one third of the States Parties object to it by a written notification not later than 180 days after its circulation.
4. The adopted amendment to the Annex shall enter into force 30 days after the deposit of the twenty-second instrument of ratification, acceptance or approval of such amendment for all those States Parties having deposited such an instrument. For each State Party ratifying, accepting or approving the amendment after the deposit of the twenty-second instrument, the amendment shall enter into force on the thirtieth day after deposit by such State Party of its instrument of ratification, acceptance or approval.

Article 24

1. Any dispute between two or more States Parties concerning the interpretation or application of this Convention which cannot be settled through negotiation within a reasonable time shall, at the request of one of them, be submitted to arbitration. If, within six months from the date of the request for arbitration, the parties are unable to agree on the organization of the arbitration, any one of those parties may refer the dispute to the International Court of Justice, by application, in conformity with the Statute of the Court.
2. Each State may at the time of signature, ratification, acceptance or approval of this Convention or accession thereto declare that it does not consider itself bound by paragraph 1. The other States Parties shall not be bound by paragraph 1 with respect to any State Party which has made such a reservation.
3. Any State which has made a reservation in accordance with paragraph 2 may at any time withdraw that reservation by notification to the Secretary-General of the United Nations.

Article 25

1. This Convention shall be open for signature by all States from 10 January 2000 to 31 December 2001 at United Nations Headquarters in New York.
2. This Convention is subject to ratification, acceptance or approval. The instruments of ratification, acceptance or approval shall be deposited with the Secretary-General of the United Nations.
3. This Convention shall be open to accession by any State. The instruments of accession shall be deposited with the Secretary-General of the United Nations.

Article 26

1. This Convention shall enter into force on the thirtieth day following the date of the deposit of the twenty-second instrument of ratification, acceptance, approval or accession with the Secretary-General of the United Nations.
2. For each State ratifying, accepting, approving or acceding to the Convention after the deposit of the twenty-second instrument of ratification, acceptance, approval or accession, the Convention shall enter into force on the thirtieth day after deposit by such State of its instrument of ratification, acceptance, approval or accession.

Article 27
1. Any State Party may denounce this Convention by written notification to the Secretary-General of the United Nations.
2. Denunciation shall take effect one year following the date on which notification is received by the Secretary-General of the United Nations.

Article 28
The original of this Convention, of which the Arabic, Chinese, English, French, Russian and Spanish texts are equally authentic, shall be deposited with the Secretary-General of the United Nations who shall send certified copies thereof to all States.

IN WITNESS WHEREOF, the undersigned, being duly authorized thereto by their respective Governments, have signed this Convention, opened for signature at United Nations Headquarters in New York on 10 January 2000.
[Signatures not reproduced here.]

ANNEX
1. Convention for the Suppression of Unlawful Seizure of Aircraft, done at The Hague on 16 December 1970.
2. Convention for the Suppression of Unlawful Acts against the Safety of Civil Aviation, done at Montreal on 23 September 1971.
3. Convention on the Prevention and Punishment of Crimes against Internationally Protected Persons, including Diplomatic Agents, adopted by the General Assembly of the United Nations on 14 December 1973.
4. International Convention against the Taking of Hostages, adopted by the General Assembly of the United Nations on 17 December 1979.
5. Convention on the Physical Protection of Nuclear Material, adopted at Vienna on 3 March 1980.
6. Protocol for the Suppression of Unlawful Acts of Violence at Airports Serving International Civil Aviation, supplementary to the Convention for the Suppression of Unlawful Acts against the Safety of Civil Aviation, done at Montreal on 24 February 1988.
7. Convention for the Suppression of Unlawful Acts against the Safety of Maritime Navigation, done at Rome on 10 March 1988.
8. Protocol for the Suppression of Unlawful Acts against the Safety of Fixed Platforms located on the Continental Shelf, done at Rome on 10 March 1988.
9. International Convention for the Suppression of Terrorist Bombings, adopted by the General Assembly of the United Nations on 15 December 1997.

TC1F
Draft Comprehensive Convention

Preamble[2]

The States Parties to this Convention,
Recalling the existing international treaties relating to various aspects of the problem of international terrorism, in particular the Convention on Offences and Certain Acts Committed

---

[2] Preamble and Article 1 are based on the *Discussion paper on the preamble and Article 1 of the draft comprehensive convention, prepared by the Bureau as a basis for discussion in the Sixth Commit-*

on Board Aircraft, signed at Tokyo on 14 September 1963; the Convention for the Suppression of Unlawful Seizure of Aircraft, signed at The Hague on 16 December 1970; the Convention for the Suppression of Unlawful Acts against the Safety of Civil Aviation, signed at Montreal on 23 September 1971; the Convention on the Prevention and Punishment of Crimes against Internationally Protected Persons, including Diplomatic Agents, adopted by the General Assembly of the United Nations on 14 December 1973; the International Convention against the Taking of Hostages, adopted by the General Assembly of the United Nations on 17 December 1979; the Convention on the Physical Protection of Nuclear Material, signed at Vienna on 3 March 1980; the Protocol for the Suppression of Unlawful Acts of Violence at Airports Serving International Civil Aviation, supplementary to the Convention for the Suppression of Unlawful Acts against the Safety of Civil Aviation, signed at Montreal on 24 February 1988; the Convention for the Suppression of Unlawful Acts against the Safety of Maritime Navigation, done at Rome on 10 March 1988; the Protocol for the Suppression of Unlawful Acts against the Safety of Fixed Platforms Located on the Continental Shelf, done at Rome on 10 March 1988; the Convention on the Marking of Plastic Explosives for the Purpose of Detection, signed at Montreal on 1 March 1991; the International Convention for the Suppression of Terrorist Bombings, adopted by the General Assembly of the United Nations on 15 December 1997; the International Convention for the Suppression of the Financing of Terrorism, adopted by the General Assembly of the United Nations on 9 December 1999,

Recalling also General Assembly Resolution 49/60 of 9 December 1994 and the Declaration on Measures to Eliminate International Terrorism annexed thereto,

Recalling further General Assembly Resolution 51/210 of 17 December 1996 and the Declaration to supplement the 1994 Declaration on Measures to Eliminate International Terrorism annexed thereto,

Deeply concerned about the worldwide escalation of acts of terrorism in all its forms and manifestations, which endanger or take innocent lives, jeopardize fundamental freedoms and seriously impair the dignity of human beings,

Reaffirming their unequivocal condemnation of all acts, methods and practices of terrorism as criminal and unjustifiable, wherever and by whomever committed, including those which jeopardize friendly relations among States and peoples and threaten the territorial integrity and security of States,

---

tee at the fifty-seventh session of the General Assembly, as included in A/57/37. These texts represent the stage of consideration reached at the current session of the Ad Hoc Committee. It is understood that further consideration will be given to these texts, together with all written and oral proposals, in future discussions, including on outstanding issues.

– Article 2 is based on *The Informal texts of Articles 2 and 2 bis of the draft comprehensive convention, prepared by the Coordinator* (which are reproduced from document A/C.6/56/L.9, annex I.B.) These texts represent the stage of consideration reached at the 2001 session of the Working Group of the Sixth Committee. It is understood that further consideration will be given to these texts in future discussions, including on outstanding issues.

– Articles 3 – 17 bis. As well as Articles 20 – 29 are based on the *Texts of Articles 3 to 17 bis and 20 to 27 of the draft comprehensive convention, prepared by the Friends of the Chairman* (which are reproduced from document A/C.6/56/L.9, annex I.A.). This text represents the stage of consideration reached at the 2001 session of the Working Group of the Sixth Committee. It is understood that further consideration will be given to this text in future discussions, including on outstanding issues.

– Article 18 is based on the *Texts relating to Article 18 of the draft comprehensive conventions (Text circulated by the Coordinator for discussion* and *Text proposed by the Member States of the Organization of the Islamic Conference.*

Recognizing that acts, methods and practices of terrorism constitute a grave violation of the purposes and principles of the United Nations, which may pose a threat to international peace and security, jeopardize friendly relations among States, hinder international cooperation and aim at the undermining of human rights, fundamental freedoms and the democratic basis of society,

Recognizing also that the financing, planning and inciting of terrorist acts are also contrary to the purposes and principles of the United Nations, and that it is the duty of the States Parties to bring to justice those who have participated in such terrorist acts,

Convinced that the suppression of acts of international terrorism, including those which are committed or supported by States, directly or indirectly, is an essential element in the maintenance of international peace and security and the sovereignty and territorial integrity of States,

Noting that the Convention relating to the Status of Refugees signed at Geneva on 28 July 1951 and the Protocol relating to the Status of Refugees done at New York on 31 January 1967 do not provide a basis for the protection of perpetrators of terrorist acts, and stressing the importance of the full compliance by the parties to those instruments with the obligations embodied therein, including, in particular, the principle of non-refoulement,

Bearing in mind the necessity of respecting human rights and international humanitarian law in the fight against terrorism,

Realizing the need for a comprehensive convention on international terrorism,

Have resolved to take effective measures to prevent acts of terrorism and to ensure that perpetrators of terrorist acts do not escape prosecution and punishment by providing for their extradition or prosecution, and to that end

have agreed as follows:

Article 1[3]

For the purposes of this Convention:

1. 'State or government facility' includes any permanent or temporary facility or conveyance that is used or occupied by representatives of a State, members of government, the legislature or the judiciary or by officials or employees of a State or any other public authority or entity or by employees or officials of an intergovernmental organization in connection with their official duties.

2. 'Military forces of a State' means the armed forces of a State which are organized, trained and equipped under its internal law for the primary purpose of national defence or security, and persons acting in support of those armed forces who are under their formal command, control and responsibility.

3. 'Infrastructure facility' means any publicly or privately owned facility providing or distributing services for the benefit of the public, such as water, sewerage, energy, fuel, banking, communications, telecommunications and information networks.

4. 'Place of public use' means those parts of any building, land, street, waterway or other location that are accessible or open to members of the public, whether continuously, periodically or occasionally, and encompasses any commercial, business, cultural, historical, educational, religious, governmental, entertainment,

recreational or similar place that is so accessible or open to the public.

---

[3] Identical to the revised text of Article 1 prepared by India and contained in document A/C.6/55/L.2, annex I.

5. 'Public transportation system' means all facilities, conveyances and instrumentalities, whether publicly or privately owned, that are used in or for publicly available services for the transportation of persons or cargo.

Article 2
1. Any person commits an offence within the meaning of this Convention if that person, by any means, unlawfully and intentionally, causes:
    (a) Death or serious bodily injury to any person; or
    (b) Serious damage to public or private property, including a place of public use, a State or government facility, a public transportation system, an infrastructure facility or the environment; or
    (c) Damage to property, places, facilities, or systems referred to in paragraph 1 (b) of this Article, resulting or likely to result in major economic loss, when the purpose of the conduct, by its nature or context, is to intimidate a population, or to compel a Government or an international organization to do or abstain from doing any act.
2. Any person also commits an offence if that person makes a credible and serious threat to commit an offence as set forth in paragraph 1 of this Article.
3. Any person also commits an offence if that person attempts to commit an offence as set forth in paragraph 1 of this Article.
4. Any person also commits an offence if that person:
    (a) Participates as an accomplice in an offence as set forth in paragraph 1, 2 or 3 of this Article;
    (b) Organizes or directs others to commit an offence as set forth in paragraph 1, 2 or 3 of this Article; or
    (c) Contributes to the commission of one or more offences as set forth in paragraph 1, 2 or 3 of this Article by a group of persons acting with a common purpose. Such contribution shall be intentional and shall either:
        (i) Be made with the aim of furthering the criminal activity or criminal purpose of the group, where such activity or purpose involves the commission of an offence as set forth in paragraph 1 of this Article; or
        (ii) Be made in the knowledge of the intention of the group to commit an offence as set forth in paragraph 1 of this Article.

Article 2 bis
Where this Convention and a treaty dealing with a specific category of terrorist offence would be applicable in relation to the same act as between States that are parties to both treaties, the provisions of the latter shall prevail.

Article 3
This Convention shall not apply where the offence is committed within a single State, the alleged offender and the victims are nationals of that State, the alleged offender is found in the territory of that State and no other State has a basis under Article 6, paragraph 1, or Article 6, paragraph 2, of this Convention to exercise jurisdiction, except that the provisions of Articles 8 and 12 to 16 shall, as appropriate, apply in those cases.

Article 4
Each State Party shall adopt such measures as may be necessary:
    (a) To establish as criminal offences under its domestic law the offences set forth in Article 2;

(b)   To make those offences punishable by appropriate penalties which take into account
      the grave nature of those offences.

Article 5

Each State Party shall adopt such measures as may be necessary, including, where appropriate,
domestic legislation, to ensure that criminal acts within the scope of this Convention are
under no circumstances justifiable by considerations of a political, philosophical, ideological,
racial, ethnic, religious or other similar nature.

Article 6

1. Each State Party shall take such measures as may be necessary to establish its jurisdiction
over the offences set forth in Article 2 when:
    (a)   The offence is committed in the territory of that State; or
    (b)   The offence is committed on board a vessel flying the flag of that State or an aircraft
          which is registered under the laws of that State at the time the offence is committed;
          or
    (c)   The offence is committed by a national of that State.
2. A State may also establish its jurisdiction over any such offence when:
    (a)   The offence is committed by a stateless person who has his or her habitual residence
          in the territory of that State; or
    (b)   The offence is committed wholly or partially outside its territory, if the effects of
          the conduct or its intended effects constitute or result in, within its territory, the
          commission of an offence set forth in Article 2;
    (c)   The offence is committed against a national of that State; or
    (d)   The offence is committed against a State or government facility of that State abroad,
          including an embassy or other diplomatic or consular premises of that State; or
    (e)   The offence is committed in an attempt to compel that State to do or to abstain
          from doing any act; or
    (f)   The offence is committed on board an aircraft which is operated by the Government
          of that State.
3. Upon ratifying, accepting, approving or acceding to this Convention, each State Party
shall notify the Secretary-General of the United Nations of the jurisdiction it has established
under its domestic law in accordance with paragraph 2 of the present Article. Should any
change take place, the State Party concerned shall immediately notify the Secretary-General.
4. Each State Party shall likewise take such measures as may be necessary to establish its
jurisdiction over the offences referred to in Article 2 in cases where the alleged offender is
present in its territory and where it does not extradite such a person to any of the States
Parties that have established their jurisdiction in accordance with paragraphs 1 or 2.
5. When more than one State Party claims jurisdiction over the offences set forth in Article
2, the relevant States Parties shall strive to coordinate their actions appropriately, in particular
concerning the conditions for prosecution and the modalities for mutual legal assistance.
6. Without prejudice to the norms of general international law, this Convention does not
exclude any criminal jurisdiction established by a State Party in accordance with its domestic
law.

Article 7

States Parties shall take appropriate measures, in conformity with the relevant provisions of
national and international law, including international human rights law, for the purpose of
ensuring that refugee status is not granted to any person in respect of whom there are serious
reasons for considering that he or she has committed an offence referred to in Article 2.

Article 8

1. States Parties shall cooperate in the prevention of the offences set forth in Article 2 by taking all practicable measures, including, if necessary and where appropriate, adapting their domestic legislation, to prevent and counter preparations in their respective territories for the commission, within or outside their territories, of those offences, including:

    (a) Measures to prohibit the illegal activities of persons, groups and organizations that encourage, instigate, organize, knowingly finance or engage in the commission of offences set forth in Article 2;

    (b) In particular, measures to prohibit the establishment and operation of installations and training camps for the commission of offences set forth in Article 2.

2. States Parties shall further cooperate in the prevention of the offences set forth in Article 2, in accordance with their national law, by exchanging accurate and verified information and coordinating administrative and other measures taken as appropriate to prevent the commission of offences set forth in Article 2, in particular by:

    (a) Establishing and maintaining channels of communication between their competent agencies and services to facilitate the secure and rapid exchange of information concerning all aspects of offences set forth in Article 2;

    (b) Cooperating with one another in conducting inquiries, with respect to the offences set forth in Article 2, concerning:

        (i)   The identity, whereabouts and activities of persons in respect of whom reasonable suspicion exists that they are involved in such offences;

        (ii) The movement of funds, property, equipment or other instrumentalities relating to the commission of such offences.

3. States Parties may exchange information through the International Criminal Police Organization (Interpol) or other international and regional organizations.

Article 9

1. Each State Party, in accordance with its domestic legal principles, shall take the necessary measures to enable a legal entity located in its territory or organized under its laws to be held liable when a person responsible for the management or control of that legal entity has, in that capacity, committed an offence referred to in Article 2. Such liability may be criminal, civil or administrative.

2. Such liability is incurred without prejudice to the criminal liability of individuals having committed the   offences.

3. Each State Party shall ensure, in particular, that legal entities liable in accordance with paragraph 1 above are subject to effective, proportionate and dissuasive criminal, civil or administrative sanctions. Such sanctions may include monetary sanctions.

Article 10

1. Upon receiving information that a person who has committed or who is alleged to have committed an offence referred to in Article 2 may be present in its territory, the State Party concerned shall take such measures as may be necessary under its domestic law to investigate the facts contained in the information.

2. Upon being satisfied that the circumstances so warrant, the State Party in whose territory the offender or alleged offender is present shall take the appropriate measures under its domestic law so as to ensure that person's presence for the purpose of prosecution or extradition.

3. Any person regarding whom the measures referred to in paragraph 2 are being taken shall be entitled to:

    (a) Communicate without delay with the nearest appropriate representative of the State of which that person is a national or which is otherwise entitled to protect that

person's rights or, if that person is a stateless person, the State in the territory of
which that person habitually resides;

(b) Be visited by a representative of that State;

(c) Be informed of that person's rights under subparagraphs (a) and (b).

4. The rights referred to in paragraph 3 shall be exercised in conformity with the laws and
regulations of the State in the territory of which the offender or alleged offender is present,
subject to the provision that the said laws and regulations must enable full effect to be given
to the purposes for which the rights accorded under paragraph 3 are intended.

5. The provisions of paragraphs 3 and 4 shall be without prejudice to the right of any State
Party having a claim to jurisdiction in accordance with Article 6, paragraph 1, subparagraph
(c), or paragraph 2, subparagraph (a), to invite the International Committee of the Red Cross
to communicate with and visit the alleged offender.

6. When a State Party, pursuant to the present Article, has taken a person into custody, it
shall immediately notify, directly or through the Secretary-General of the United Nations,
the States Parties which have established jurisdiction in accordance with Article 6, paragraph
1 or 2, and if it considers it advisable, any other interested States Parties, of the fact that
such person is in custody and of the circumstances which warrant that person's detention.
The State which makes the investigation contemplated in paragraph 1 shall promptly inform
the said States Parties of its findings and shall indicate whether it intends to exercise jurisdiction.

Article 11

1. The State Party in whose territory the alleged offender is present shall, in cases to which
Article 6 applies, if it does not extradite the person, be obliged, without exception whatsoever
and whether or not the offence was committed in its territory, to submit the case, without
undue delay, to its competent authorities for the purpose of prosecution through proceedings
in accordance with the laws of that State. Those authorities shall take their decision in the
same manner as in the case of any other offence of a grave nature under the law of that
State.

2. Whenever a State Party is permitted under its domestic law to extradite or otherwise surrender
one of its nationals only upon the condition that the person will be returned to that State to
serve the sentence imposed as a result of the trial or proceeding for which the extradition
or surrender of the person was sought, and that State and the State seeking the extradition
of the person agree with this option and other terms they may deem appropriate, such a
conditional extradition or surrender shall be sufficient to discharge the obligation set forth
in paragraph 1.

Article 12

Any person who is taken into custody or regarding whom any other measures are taken or
proceedings are carried out pursuant to this Convention shall be guaranteed fair treatment,
including enjoyment of all rights and guarantees in conformity with the law of the State in
the territory of which that person is present and applicable provisions of international law,
including international human rights law and, in particular, the Standard minimum Rules
for the Treatment of Prisoners.

Article 13

1. States Parties shall afford one another the greatest measure of assistance in connection
with investigations or criminal or extradition proceedings brought in respect of the offences
set forth in Article 2, including assistance in obtaining evidence at their disposal necessary
for the proceedings.

2. States Parties shall carry out their obligations under paragraph 1 in conformity with any treaties or other arrangements on mutual legal assistance that may exist between them. In the absence of such treaties or arrangements, States Parties shall afford one another assistance in accordance with their domestic law.

3. Each State Party may give consideration to establishing mechanisms to share with other States Parties information or evidence needed to establish criminal, civil or administrative liability pursuant to Article 9.

Article 14

None of the offences referred to in Article 2 shall be regarded, for the purposes of extradition or mutual legal assistance, as a political offence or as an offence connected with a political offence or as an offence inspired by political motives. Accordingly, a request for extradition or for mutual legal assistance based on such an offence may not be refused on the sole ground that it concerns a political offence or an offence connected with a political offence or an offence inspired by political motives.

Article 15

Nothing in this Convention shall be interpreted as imposing an obligation to extradite or to afford mutual legal assistance, if the requested State Party has substantial grounds for believing that the request for extradition for offences set forth in Article 2 or for mutual legal assistance with respect to such offences has been made for the purpose of prosecuting or punishing a person on account of that person's race, religion, nationality, ethnic origin or political opinion or that compliance with the request would cause prejudice to that person's position for any of these reasons.

Article 16

1. A person who is being detained or is serving a sentence in the territory of one State Party whose presence in another State Party is requested for purposes of identification, testimony or otherwise providing assistance in obtaining evidence for the investigation or prosecution of offences under this Convention may be transferred if the following conditions are met:

    (a) The person freely gives his or her informed consent; and

    (b) The competent authorities of both States Parties agree, subject to such conditions as those States Parties may deem appropriate.

2. For the purposes of this Article:

    (a) The State to which the person is transferred shall have the authority and obligation to keep the person transferred in custody, unless otherwise requested or authorized by the State from which the person was transferred;

    (b) The State to which the person is transferred shall without delay implement its obligation to return the person to the custody of the State from which the person was transferred as agreed beforehand, or as otherwise agreed, by the competent authorities of both States;

    (c) The State to which the person is transferred shall not require the State from which the person was transferred to initiate extradition proceedings for the return of the person;

    (d) The person transferred shall receive credit for service of the sentence being served in the State from which he or she was transferred for the time spent in the custody of the State to which he or she was transferred.

3. Unless the State Party from which a person is to be transferred in accordance with this Article so agrees, that person, whatever his or her nationality, shall not be prosecuted or detained or subjected to any other restriction of his or her personal liberty in the territory

of the State to which that person is transferred in respect of acts or convictions anterior to his or her departure from the territory of the State from which such person was transferred.

Article 17

1. The offences referred to in Article 2 shall be deemed to be included as extraditable offences in any extradition treaty existing between any of the States Parties before the entry into force of this Convention. States Parties undertake to include such offences as extraditable offences in every extradition treaty to be subsequently concluded between them.

2. When a State Party which makes extradition conditional on the existence of a treaty receives a request from another State Party with which it has no extradition treaty, the requested State may, at its option, consider this Convention as a legal basis for extradition in respect of the offences set forth in Article 2. Extradition shall be subject to the other conditions provided by the law of the requested State.

3. States Parties which do not make extradition conditional on the existence of a treaty shall recognize the offences referred to in Article 2 as extraditable offences between themselves, subject to the conditions provided for by the law of the requested State.

4. If necessary, the offences set forth in Article 2 shall be treated, for the purposes of extradition between States Parties, as if they had been committed not only in the place in which they occurred but also in the territory of the States that have established jurisdiction in accordance with Article 6, paragraphs 1 and 2.

5. The provisions of all extradition treaties and arrangements between States Parties with regard to offences set forth in Article 2 shall be deemed to be modified as between States Parties to the extent that they are incompatible with this Convention.

Article 17 bis

The State Party where the alleged offender is prosecuted shall, in accordance with its domestic law or its applicable procedures, communicate the final outcome of the proceedings to the Secretary-General of the United Nations, who shall transmit the information to the other States Parties.

Article 18[4]

Text circulated by the Coordinator for discussion

1. Nothing in this Convention shall affect other rights, obligations and responsibilities of States, peoples and individuals under international law, in particular the purposes and principles of the Charter of the United Nations, and international humanitarian law.

2. The activities of armed forces during an armed conflict, as those terms are understood under international humanitarian law, which are governed by that law, are not governed by this Convention.

---

[4] There is also a proposal from the Organization of the Islamic Conference:

'1. Nothing in this Convention shall affect other rights, obligations and responsibilities of States, peoples and individuals under international law, in particular the purposes and principles of the Charter of the United Nations, and international humanitarian law.

2. The activities of the parties during an armed conflict, including in situations of foreign occupation, as those terms are understood under international humanitarian law, which are governed by that law, are not governed by this Convention.

3. The activities undertaken by the military forces of a State in the exercise of their official duties, inasmuch as they are in conformity with international law, are not governed by this Convention.

4. Nothing in this Article condones or makes lawful otherwise unlawful acts, nor precludes prosecution under other laws'.

3. The activities undertaken by the military forces of a State in the exercise of their official duties, inasmuch as they are governed by other rules of international law, are not governed by this Convention.

4. Nothing in this Article condones or makes lawful otherwise unlawful acts, nor precludes prosecution under other laws.

Article 19
[......]

Article 20
The States Parties shall carry out their obligations under this Convention in a manner consistent with the principles of sovereign equality and territorial integrity of States and that of non-intervention in the domestic affairs of other States.

Article 21
[Deleted]

Article 22
Nothing in this Convention entitles a State Party to undertake in the territory of another State Party the exercise of jurisdiction or performance of functions which are exclusively reserved for the authorities of that other State Party by the law in force in that State Party.

Article 23
1. Any dispute between two or more States Parties concerning the interpretation or application of this Convention which cannot be settled through negotiation within a reasonable time shall, at the request of one of them, be submitted to arbitration. If, within six months from the date of the request for arbitration, the parties are unable to agree on the organization of the arbitration, any one of those parties may refer the dispute to the International Court of Justice, by application, in conformity with the Statute of the Court.

2. Each State may at the time of signature, ratification, acceptance or approval of this Convention or accession thereto declare that it does not consider itself bound by paragraph 1. The other States Parties shall not be bound by paragraph 1 with respect to any State Party which has made such a reservation.

3. Any State which has made a reservation in accordance with paragraph 2 may at any time withdraw that reservation by notification to the Secretary-General of the United Nations.

Article 24
1. This Convention shall be open for signature by all States from ... to ... at United Nations Headquarters in New York.

2. This Convention is subject to ratification, acceptance or approval. The instruments of ratification, acceptance or approval shall be deposited with the Secretary-General of the United Nations.

3. This Convention shall be open to accession by any State. The instruments of accession shall be deposited with the Secretary-General of the United Nations.

These texts represent the stage of consideration reached at the current session of the Ad Hoc Committee. It is understood that further consideration will be given to these texts, together with all written and oral proposals, in future discussions, including on outstanding issues.

Article 25

1. This Convention shall enter into force thirty days after twenty-two instruments of ratification, acceptance, approval or accession have been deposited with the Secretary-General of the United Nations.

2. For each State ratifying, accepting, approving or acceding to the Convention after the deposit of the twenty-second instrument of ratification, acceptance, approval or accession, the Convention shall enter into force on the thirtieth day after the deposit by such State of its instrument of ratification, acceptance, approval or accession.

Article 26

1. A State may denounce this Convention by written notification to the Secretary-General of the United Nations.

2. Denunciation shall take effect one year following the date on which such notification is received by the Secretary-General of the United Nations.

Article 27

The original of this Convention, of which the Arabic, Chinese, English, French, Russian and Spanish texts are equally authentic, shall be deposited with the Secretary-General of the United Nations, who shall send certified copies thereof to all States.

IN WITNESS WHEREOF, the undersigned, being duly authorized thereto by their respective Governments, have signed this Convention, opened for signature at United Nations Headquarters in New York on ... 2002.

(...)
Annex II

A. List of written amendments and proposals submitted by delegations to the Working Group of the Sixth Committee at the fifty-sixth session of the General Assembly in connection with the elaboration of a draft comprehensive convention on international terrorism[5]

(...)

B. Written amendments and proposals submitted by delegations to the Working Group of the Sixth Committee at the fifty-sixth session of the General Assembly in connection with the elaboration of a draft international convention for the suppression of acts of nuclear terrorism[6]

(...)

Article 4, new paragraph
This Convention does not address, nor can it be interpreted as addressing, in any way the issue of the legality of the use or threat of use of nuclear weapons by States.

---

[5] It is understood that further consideration will be given to these written amendments and proposals, together with all other written and oral proposals, in future discussions, including on outstanding issues

[6] It is understood that further consideration will be given to these written amendments and proposals, together with all other written and oral proposals, in future discussions, including on outstanding issues

Annex III

Report of the Coordinator on the results of the informal consultations

1. I wish to report to the Committee, in my capacity as Coordinator, on the informal consultations which I chaired, on 28, 29 and 30 January 2002, concerning Article 18, the preamble and Article 1 of the draft comprehensive convention on international terrorism, and concerning the draft international convention for the suppression of acts of nuclear terrorism.

A. *Draft comprehensive convention on international terrorism*

Article 18
2. In relation to this key Article, which deals with the savings clause and exclusions from the scope of the convention, delegations had before them two texts of a draft Article for consideration, one which I had prepared as Coordinator at the end of the October 2001 session of the Working Group of the Sixth Committee and another proposed by the Member States of the Organization of the Islamic Conference. The key issues on which discussion focused are reflected in paragraphs 2 and 3 of the drafts, namely: (a) in paragraph 2, whether to refer to the activities of 'armed forces' or of 'the Parties' during an armed conflict, and whether to insert the words 'including in situations of foreign occupation' in that paragraph; and (b) in paragraph 3, whether to refer to excluding the activities undertaken by the military forces of a State in the exercise of their official duties by using the words 'inasmuch as they are governed by other rules of international law' or the words 'in conformity with international law'.
3. Views were expressed by many delegations in support of the various formulations, but there was no consensus on what the texts should be. Accordingly, it will be necessary to continue consultations on those two paragraphs. I suggest that we use as the basis the two texts that we had before us during the informal consultations at the current session (see annex IV to the present report).

Preamble
4. We had a very comprehensive and constructive consideration of the draft preamble based on the text contained in document A/C.6/55/L.2. We advanced our work on the preamble, building on the discussions we had had in October 2001. In relation to the 10 draft paragraphs of the preamble contained in document A/C.6/55/L.2, proposals were made in relation to the first to fourth and sixth to eighth preambular paragraphs. In addition, new ninth and tenth preambular paragraphs were inserted and a proposal was made in relation to the new tenth preambular paragraph. There was also a proposal to add a preambular paragraph taken from the Convention for the Suppression of Unlawful Acts against the Safety of Maritime Navigation.
5. It was agreed to replace the word 'conventions' with the word 'treaties' in the first preambular paragraph, to correct the reference to General Assembly Resolution 51/210 in the third preambular paragraph, and to insert the words 'and manifestations' after the words 'in all its forms' in the fourth preambular paragraph. Switzerland also informed the Committee of a revised formulation for its proposal contained in document A/C.6/55/WG.1/CRP.27, to read *'Bearing in mind* the necessity of respecting human rights and international humanitarian law in the fight against terrorism'.

Article 1

6. Discussion of the definitions contained in draft Article 1 was based on the text contained in document A/C.6/55/L.2, annex I. Comments were made on the five paragraphs. Specific proposals were made in relation to paragraphs 1 (relating to 'State or government facility') and 4 (relating to 'Place of public use'). No proposals were made in relation to paragraphs 2, 3 and 5. Some delegations noted that their position in relation to the amendments which had been proposed and their position in relation to the proposal contained in document A/C.6/55/WG.1/CRP.30, which remains on the table, would depend on the outcome of the text agreed upon for Article 18.

7. The proposals which were presented in relation to the preamble and Article 1 during the informal consultations are listed in the appendix to my report, for reference in relation to future discussion of those parts of the Convention; the text of the draft preamble and Article 1 are contained in annex I to the present report of the Ad Hoc Committee.

B.   *Draft international convention for the suppression of acts of nuclear terrorism*

8. Informal consultations were also held on the draft international convention for the suppression of acts of nuclear terrorism. The Director of the New York office of IAEA briefed delegations on the measures under consideration by the Agency aimed at combating acts of terrorism involving nuclear materials and other radioactive materials. His remarks were drawn from the report of the IAEA Director General to the IAEA Board of Governors on protection against nuclear terrorism.[7]

9. The reference document for the informal consultations on the draft convention was the revised text proposed by the Friends of the Chairman in October 1998,[8] which was based on a Russian draft text. The Coordinator noted that at the October 2001 meeting of the Working Group of the Sixth Committee, there had been a comprehensive exchange of views on the principal outstanding issues relating to the scope of application of the convention, and that the positions of delegations on those issues were well known. However, since there had been insufficient time in October to consider fully the proposal that had been put forward by Mexico relating to the scope Article, to the effect that 'This convention does not address, nor can it be interpreted as addressing, in any way, the issue of the legality of the use or threat of use of nuclear weapons by States', the Coordinator proposed that the consultations should focus on that proposal.

10. Some delegations, while reiterating their support for the current text of Article 4 in the draft convention, stated that they supported the proposal and thought that it could represent a possible compromise in addressing concerns about 'the armed forces of States' exclusion issue in relation to the Article. Other delegations stated that they could not support the proposal and did not regard it as a compromise solution to the issues raised by the current provisions of Article 4.

11. Some delegations reiterated their support for the conclusion of a convention for the suppression of acts of nuclear terrorism. Others suggested that it might be useful to reflect upon alternative approaches. Lebanon reiterated its proposal in relation to the dumping of radioactive waste material.[9]

---

[7] See S/2001/1164.
[8] See A/C.6/53/L.4.
[9] A/C.6/53/WG.1/CRP.33.

C. Conclusion

12. I wish to thank all delegations for their cooperation and application in engaging so readily in discussion of the issues addressed in informal consultations. Our understanding of the position of delegations on particular points has been enhanced and the issues for which we need to find broadly acceptable solutions have been more sharply clarified.

13. The key issue in relation to the comprehensive convention is clearly to resolve the text of Article 18. That has to be our priority. If we can do that, I believe, as many delegations have indicated, that the other outstanding matters will also be capable of resolution and we will be able to conclude the Convention on which so much progress has been made over the past four months.

Appendix

List of proposals made during informal consultations on the preamble and Article 1 of the draft comprehensive convention on international terrorism[10]

For reference only

Preamble

New preambular paragraph
• Insert the following text taken from document A/C.6/55/WG.1/CRP.37:
'*Guided* by the purposes and principles of the Charter of the United Nations'
• Insert the following text taken from document A/C.6/56/WG.1/CRP.4:
'*Having in mind* the purposes and principles of the Charter of the United Nations concerning the maintenance of international peace and security and the promotion of good-neighbourliness and friendly relations and cooperation among States'

New preambular paragraph
• Insert the following text taken from document A/C.6/55/WG.1/CRP.37:
'*Recalling* all relevant General Assembly resolutions, including Resolution 46/51 of 9 December 1991'

New preambular paragraph
• Add the following text taken from document A/C.6/55/WG.1/CRP.37:
'*Recalling* also the Declaration on the Occasion of the Fiftieth Anniversary of the United Nations contained in General Assembly Resolution 50/6 of 24 October 1995'

Sixth preambular paragraph
• Replace the words 'aim at the undermining of human rights' with the words 'undermine the protection of human rights' or 'undermine the enjoyment of human rights'.

---

[10] For the text of the draft preamble and Article 1, see annex I to the present report of the Ad Hoc Committee. It is understood that further consideration will be given to these proposals, together with all other written and oral proposals, in future discussions, including on outstanding issues

Seventh preambular paragraph
• Delete the word 'inciting' or replace it with the word 'encouraging'.
• Replace the words 'those who have participated in such terrorist acts' with the words 'those who have participated in terrorist acts'.

Eighth preambular paragraph
• Replace the words 'including those which are committed or supported by States, directly or indirectly' with the words 'including those in which States are directly or indirectly involved'.
• Replace the words 'committed or supported by States' with the words 'supported by States'.
• Delete the words 'including those which are committed or supported by States, directly or indirectly'.
• Delete the entire preambular paragraph.

Tenth preambular paragraph
• Insert the word 'law' after the words 'human rights'.

New preambular paragraph
• Add the following new preambular paragraph taken from the Convention for the Suppression of Unlawful Acts against the Safety of Maritime Navigation:

'*Recalling* General Assembly Resolution 40/61 of 9 December 1985, which, inter alia, "urges all States, unilaterally and in cooperation with other States, as well as relevant United Nations organs, to contribute to the progressive elimination of causes underlying international terrorism and to pay special attention to all situations, including colonialism, racism and situations involving mass and flagrant violations of human rights and fundamental freedoms and those involving alien occupation, that may give rise to international terrorism and may endanger international peace and security".'

Article 1
Paragraph 4
• Add a reference to the environment and the endangering of natural resources.

5.2   NON-UN CONVENTIONS

TC2A
Convention on Offences and Certain Other Acts Committed on Board Aircraft
signed at Tokyo, on 14 September 1963

The States Parties to this Convention,
Have agreed as follows:

CHAPTER I
SCOPE OF THE CONVENTION

Article 1
1. This Convention shall apply in respect of:
    (a) offences against penal law;
    (b) acts which, whether or not they are offences, may or do jeopardize the safety of the
         aircraft or of persons or property therein or which jeopardize good order and disci-
         pline on board.
2. Except as provided in Chapter III, this Convention shall apply in respect of offences committed or acts done by a person on board any aircraft registered in a Contracting State, while
that aircraft is in flight or on the surface of the high seas or of any other area outside the
territory of any State.
3. For the purposes of this Convention, an aircraft is considered to be in flight from the moment when power is applied for the purpose of take- off until the moment when the landing
run ends.
4. This Convention shall not apply to aircraft used in military, customs or police services.

Article 2
Without prejudice to the provisions of Article 4 and except when the safety of the aircraft or
of persons or property on board so requires, no provision of this Convention shall be interpreted as authorizing or requiring any action in respect of offences against penal laws of a
political nature or those based on racial or religious discrimination.

CHAPTER II
JURISDICTION

Article 3
1. The State of registration of the aircraft is competent to exercise jurisdiction over offences
and acts committed on board.
2. Each Contracting State shall take such measures as may be necessary to establish its jurisdiction as the State of registration over offences committed on board aircraft registered in
such State.

3. This Convention does not exclude any criminal jurisdiction exercised in accordance with national law.

Article 4

A Contracting State which is not the State of registration may not interfere with an aircraft in flight in order to exercise its criminal jurisdiction over an offence committed on board except in the following cases:

    (a) the offence has effect on the territory of such State;

    (b) the offence has been committed by or against a national or permanent resident of such State;

    (c) the offence is against the security of such State;

    (d) the offence consists of a breach of any rules or regulations relating to the flight or manoeuvre of aircraft in force in such State;

    (e) the exercise of jurisdiction is necessary to ensure the observance of any obligation of such State under a multilateral international agreement.

CHAPTER III
POWERS OF THE AIRCRAFT COMMANDER

Article 5

1. The provisions of this Chapter shall not apply to offences and acts committed or about to be committed by a person on board an aircraft in flight in the airspace of the State of registration or over the high seas or any other area outside the territory of any State unless the last point of take- off or the next point of intended landing is situated in a State other than that of registration, or the aircraft subsequently flies in the airspace of a State other than that of registration with such person still on board.

2. Notwithstanding the provisions of Article 1, paragraph 3, an aircraft shall for the purposes of this Chapter, be considered to be in flight at any time from the moment when all its external doors are closed following embarkation until the moment when any such door is opened for disembarkation. In the case of a forced landing, the provisions of this Chapter shall continue to apply with respect to offences and acts committed on board until competent authorities of a State take over the responsibility for the aircraft and for the persons and property on board.

Article 6

1. The aircraft commander may, when he has reasonable grounds to believe that a person has committed, or is about to commit, on board the aircraft, an offence or act contemplated in Article 1, paragraph 1, impose upon such person reasonable measures including restraint which are necessary:

    (a) to protect the safety of the aircraft, or of persons or property therein; or

    (b) to maintain good order and discipline on board; or

    (c) to enable him to deliver such person to competent authorities or to disembark him in accordance with the provisions of this Chapter.

2. The aircraft commander may require or authorize the assistance of other crew members and may request or authorize, but not require, the assistance of passengers to restrain any person whom he is entitled to restrain. Any crew member or passenger may also take reasonable preventive measures without such authorization when he has reasonable grounds to believe that such action is immediately necessary to protect the safety of the aircraft, or of persons or property therein.

Article 7

1. Measures of restraint imposed upon a person in accordance with Article 6 shall not be continued beyond any point at which the aircraft lands unless:

(a) such point is in the territory of a non-Contracting State and its authorities refuse to permit disembarkation of that person or those measures have been imposed in accordance with Article 6, paragraph 1(c) in order to enable his delivery to competent authorities;

(b) the aircraft makes a forced landing and the aircraft commander is unable to deliver that person to competent authorities; or

(c) that person agrees to onward carriage under restraint.

2. The aircraft commander shall as soon as practicable, and if possible before landing in the territory of a State with a person on board who has been placed under restraint in accordance with the provisions of Article 6, notify the authorities of such State of the fact that a person on board is under restraint and of the reasons for such restraint.

Article 8

1. The aircraft commander may, in so far as it is necessary for the purpose of subparagraph (a) or (b) or paragraph 1 of Article 6, disembark in the territory of any State in which the aircraft lands any person who he has reasonable grounds to believe has committed, or is about to commit, on board the aircraft an act contemplated in Article 1, paragraph 1(b).

2. The aircraft commander shall report to the authorities of the State in which he disembarks any person pursuant to this Article, the fact of, and the reasons for, such disembarkation.

Article 9

1. The aircraft commander may deliver to the competent authorities of any Contracting State in the territory of which the aircraft lands any person who he has reasonable grounds to believe has committed on board the aircraft an act which, in his opinion, is a serious offence according to the penal law of the State of registration of the aircraft.

2. The aircraft commander shall as soon as practicable and if possible before landing in the territory of a Contracting State with a person on board whom the aircraft commander intends to deliver in accordance with the preceding paragraph, notify the authorities of such State of his intention to deliver such person and the reasons therefor.

3. The aircraft commander shall furnish the authorities to whom any suspected offender is delivered in accordance with the provisions of this Article with evidence and information which, under the law of the State of registration of the aircraft, are lawfully in his possession.

Article 10

For actions taken in accordance with this Convention, neither the aircraft commander, any other member of the crew, any passenger, the owner or operator of the aircraft, nor the person on whose behalf the flight was performed shall be held responsible in any proceeding on account of the treatment undergone by the person against whom the actions were taken.

CHAPTER IV
UNLAWFUL SEIZURE OF AIRCRAFT

Article 11

1. When a person on board has unlawfully committed by force or threat thereof an act of interference, seizure, or other wrongful exercise of control of an aircraft in flight or when such an act is about to be committed, Contracting States shall take all appropriate measures to restore control of the aircraft to its lawful commander or to preserve his control of the aircraft.

2. In the cases contemplated in the preceding paragraph, the Contracting State in which the aircraft lands shall permit its passengers and crew to continue their journey as soon as practicable, and shall return the aircraft and its cargo to the persons lawfully entitled to possession.

CHAPTER V
POWERS AND DUTIES OF STATES

Article 12
Any Contracting State shall allow the commander of an aircraft registered in another Contracting State to disembark any person pursuant to Article 8, paragraph 1.

Article 13
1. Any Contracting State shall take delivery of any person whom the aircraft commander delivers pursuant to Article 9, paragraph 1.
2. Upon being satisfied that the circumstances so warrant, any Contracting State shall take custody or other measures to ensure the presence of any person suspected of an act contemplated in Article 11, paragraph 1 and of any person of whom it has taken delivery. The custody and other measures shall be as provided in the law of that State but may only be continued for such time as is reasonably necessary to enable any criminal or extradition proceedings to be instituted.
3. Any person in custody pursuant to the previous paragraph shall be assisted in communicating immediately with the nearest appropriate representative of the State of which he is a national.
4. Any Contracting State, to which a person is delivered pursuant to Article 9, paragraph 1, or in whose territory an aircraft lands following the commission of an act contemplated in Article 11, paragraph 1, shall immediately make a preliminary enquiry into the facts.
5. When a State, pursuant to this Article, has taken a person into custody, it shall immediately notify the State of registration of the aircraft and the State of nationality of the detained person and, if it considers it advisable, any other interested State of the fact that such person is in custody and of the circumstances which warrant his detention. The State which makes the preliminary enquiry contemplated in paragraph 4 of this Article shall promptly report its findings to the said States and shall indicate whether it intends to exercise jurisdiction.

Article 14
1. When any person has been disembarked in accordance with Article 8, paragraph 1, or delivered in accordance with Article 9, paragraph 1, or has disembarked after committing an act contemplated in Article 11, paragraph 1, and when such person cannot or does not desire to continue his journey and the State of landing refuses to admit him, that State may, if the person in question is not a national or permanent resident of that State, return him to the territory of the State of which he is a national or permanent resident or to the territory of the State in which he began his journey by air.
2. Neither disembarkation, nor delivery, not the taking of custody or other measures contemplated in Article 13, paragraph 2, nor return of the person concerned, shall be considered as admission to the territory of the Contracting State concerned for the purpose of its law relating to entry or admission of persons and nothing in this Convention shall affect the law of a Contracting State relating to the expulsion of persons from its territory.

Article 15
1. Without prejudice to Article 14, any person who has been disembarked in accordance with Article 8, paragraph 1, or delivered in accordance with Article 9, paragraph 1, or has disem-

barked after committing an act contemplated in Article 11, paragraph 1, and who desires to continue his journey shall be at liberty as soon as practicable to proceed to any destination of his choice unless his presence is required by the law of the State of landing for the purpose of extradition or criminal proceedings.

2. Without prejudice to its law as to entry and admission to, and extradition and expulsion from its territory, a Contracting State in whose territory a person has been disembarked in accordance with Article 8, paragraph 1, or delivered in accordance with Article 9, paragraph 1 or has disembarked and is suspected of having committed an act contemplated in Article 11, paragraph 1, shall accord to such person treatment which is no less favourable for his protection and security than that accorded to nationals of such Contracting State in like circumstances.

CHAPTER VI
OTHER PROVISIONS

Article 16

1. Offences committed on aircraft registered in a Contracting State shall be treated, for the purpose of extradition, as if they had been committed not only in the place in which they have occurred but also in the territory of the State of registration of the aircraft.

2. Without prejudice to the provisions of the preceding paragraph, nothing in this Convention shall be deemed to create an obligation to grant extradition.

Article 17

In taking any measures for investigation or arrest or otherwise exercising jurisdiction in connection with any offence committed on board an aircraft the Contracting States shall pay due regard to the safety and other interests of air navigation and shall so act as to avoid unnecessary delay of the aircraft, passengers, crew or cargo.

Article 18

If Contracting States establish joint air transport operating organizations or international operating agencies, which operate aircraft not registered in any one State those States shall, according to the circumstances of the case, designate the State among them which, for the purposes of this Convention, shall be considered as the State of registration and shall give notice thereof to the International Civil Aviation Organization which shall communicate the notice to all States Parties to this Convention.

CHAPTER VII
FINAL CLAUSES

Article 19

Until the date on which this Convention comes into force in accordance with the provisions of Article 21, it shall remain open for signature on behalf of any State which at that date is a Member of the United Nations or of any of the Specialized Agencies.

Article 20

1. This Convention shall be subject to ratification by the signatory States in accordance with their constitutional procedures.

2. The instruments of ratification shall be deposited with the International Civil Aviation Organization.

Article 21

1. As soon as twelve of the signatory States have deposited their instruments of ratification of this Convention, it shall come into force between them on the ninetieth day after the date of the deposit of the twelfth instrument of ratification. It shall come into force for each State ratifying thereafter on the ninetieth day after the deposit of its instrument of ratification.

2. As soon as this Convention comes into force, it shall be registered with the Secretary-General of the United Nations by the International Civil Aviation Organization.

Article 22

1. This Convention shall, after it has come into force, be open for accession by any State Member of the United Nations or of any of the Specialized Agencies.

2. The accession of a State shall be effected by the deposit of an instrument of accession with the International Civil Aviation Organization and shall take effect on the ninetieth day after the date of such deposit.

Article 23

1. Any Contracting State may denounce this Convention by notification addressed to the International Civil Aviation Organization.

2. Denunciation shall take effect six months after the date of receipt by the International Civil Aviation Organization of the notification of denunciation.

Article 24

1. Any dispute between two or more Contracting States concerning the interpretation or application of this Convention, which cannot be settled through negotiation, shall, at the request of one of them, be submitted to arbitration. If within six months from the date of the request for arbitration the Parties are unable to agree on the organization of the arbitration, any one of those Parties may refer the dispute to the International Court of Justice by request in conformity with the Statute of the Court.

2. Each State may at the time of signature or ratification of this Convention or accession thereto, declare that it does not consider itself bound by the preceding paragraph. The other Contracting States shall not be bound by the preceding paragraph with respect to any Contracting State having made such a reservation.

3. Any Contracting State having made a reservation in accordance with the preceding paragraph may at any time withdraw this reservation by notification to the International Civil Aviation Organization.

Article 25

Except as provided in Article 24 no reservation may be made to this Convention.

Article 26

The International Civil Aviation Organization shall give notice to all States Members of the United Nations or of any of the Specialized Agencies:

    (a) of any signature of this Convention and the date thereof;

    (b) of the deposit of any instrument of ratification or accession and the date thereof;

    (c) of the date on which this Convention comes into force in accordance with Article 21, paragraph 1;

    (d) of the receipt of any notification of denunciation and the date thereof; and

    (e) of the receipt of any declaration or notification made under Article 24 and the date thereof.

IN WITNESS WHEREOF the undersigned Plenipotentiaries, having been duly authorized, have signed this Convention.

DONE at Tokyo on the fourteenth day of September One Thousand Nine Hundred and Sixty-three in three authentic texts drawn up in the English, French and Spanish languages.
This Convention shall be deposited with the International Civil Aviation Organization with which, in accordance with Article 19, it shall remain open for signature and the said Organization shall send certified copies thereof to all States Members of the United Nations or of any Specialized Agency.

TC2B
Convention for the Suppression of Unlawful Seizure of Aircraft, signed at The Hague, on 16 December 1970 (The Hague Convention 1970)

The States Parties to this Convention,
Considering that unlawful acts of seizure or exercise of control of aircraft in flight jeopardize the safety of persons and property, seriously affect the operation of air services, and undermine the confidence of the peoples of the world in the safety of civil aviation;
Considering that the occurrence of such acts is a matter of grave concern;
Considering that, for the purpose of deterring such acts, there is an urgent need to provide appropriate measures for punishment of offenders;
Have agreed as follows:

Article 1
Any person who on board an aircraft in flight:
    (a) unlawfully, by force or threat thereof, or by any other form of intimidation, seizes, or exercises control of, that aircraft, or attempts to perform any such act, or
    (b) is an accomplice of a person who performs or attempts to perform any such act commits an offence (hereinafter referred to as 'the offence').

Article 2
Each Contracting State undertakes to make the offence punishable by severe penalties.

Article 3
1. For the purposes of this Convention, an aircraft is considered to be in flight at any time from the moment when all its external doors are closed following embarkation until the moment when any such door is opened for disembarkation. In the case of a forced landing, the flight shall be deemed to continue until the competent authorities take over the responsibility for the aircraft and for persons and property on board.
2. This Convention shall not apply to aircraft used in military, customs or police services.
3. This Convention shall apply only if the place of take-off or the place of actual landing of the aircraft on board which the offence is committed is situated outside the territory of the State of registration of that aircraft; it shall be immaterial whether the aircraft is engaged in an international or domestic flight.
4. In the cases mentioned in Article 5, this Convention shall not apply if the place of take-off and the place of actual landing of the aircraft on board which the offence is committed are situated within the territory of the same State where that State is one of those referred to in that Article.

5. Notwithstanding paragraphs 3 and 4 of this Article, Articles 6, 7, 8, and 10 shall apply whatever the place of take-off or the place of actual landing of the aircraft, if the offender or the alleged offender is found in the territory of a State other than the State of registration of that aircraft.

Article 4

1. Each Contracting State shall take such measures as may be necessary to establish its jurisdiction over the offence and any other act of violence against passengers or crew committed by the alleged offender in connection with the offence, in the following cases:
    (a) when the offence is committed on board an aircraft registered in that State;
    (b) when the aircraft on board which the offence is committed lands in its territory with the alleged offender still on board;
    (c) when the offence is committed on board an aircraft leased without crew to a lessee who has his principal place of business or, if the lessee has no such place of business, his permanent residence, in that State.
2. Each Contracting State shall likewise take such measures as may be necessary to establish its jurisdiction over the offence in the case where the alleged offender is present in its territory and it does not extradite him pursuant to Article 8 to any of the States mentioned in paragraph 1 of this Article.
3. This Convention does not exclude any criminal jurisdiction exercised in accordance with national law.

Article 5

The Contracting States which establish joint air transport operating organizations or international operating agencies, which operate aircraft which are subject to joint or international registration shall, by appropriate means, designate for each aircraft the State among them which shall exercise the jurisdiction and have the attributes of the State of registration for the purpose of this Convention and shall give notice thereof to the International Civil Aviation Organization which shall communicate the notice to all States Parties to this Convention.

Article 6

1. Upon being satisfied that the circumstances so warrant, any Contracting State in the territory of which the offender or the alleged offender is present, shall take him into custody or take other measures to ensure his presence. The custody and other measures shall be as provided in the law of that State but may only be continued for such time as is necessary to enable any criminal or extradition proceedings to be instituted.
2. Such State shall immediately make a preliminary enquiry into the facts.
3. Any person in custody pursuant to paragraph 1 of this Article shall be assisted in communicating immediately with the nearest appropriate representative of the State of which he is a national.
4. When a State, pursuant to this Article, has taken a person into custody, it shall immediately notify the State of registration of the aircraft, the State mentioned in Article 4, paragraph 1(c), the State of nationality of the detained person and, if it considers it advisable, any other interested States of the fact that such person is in custody and of the circumstances which warrant his detention. The State which makes the preliminary enquiry contemplated in paragraph 2 of this Article shall promptly report its findings to the said States and shall indicate whether it intends to exercise jurisdiction.

Article 7

The Contracting State in the territory of which the alleged offender is found shall, if it does not extradite him, be obliged, without exception whatsoever and whether or not the offence was committed in its territory, to submit the case to its competent authorities for the purpose of prosecution. Those authorities shall take their decision in the same manner as in the case of any ordinary offence of a serious nature under the law of that State.

Article 8

1. The offence shall be deemed to be included as an extraditable offence in any extradition treaty existing between Contracting States. Contracting States undertake to include the offence as an extraditable offence in every extradition treaty to be concluded between them.

2. If a Contracting State which makes extradition conditional on the existence of a treaty receives a request for extradition from another Contracting State with which it has no extradition treaty, it may at its option consider this Convention as the legal basis for extradition in respect of the offence. Extradition shall be subject to the other conditions provided by the law of the requested State.

3. Contracting States which do not make extradition conditional on the existence of a treaty shall recognize the offence as an extraditable offence between themselves subject to the conditions provided by the law of the requested State.

4. The offence shall be treated, for the purpose of extradition between Contracting States, as if it had been committed not only in the place in which it occurred but also in the territories of the States required to establish their jurisdiction in accordance with Article 4, paragraph 1.

Article 9

1. When any of the acts mentioned in Article 1(a) has occurred or is about to occur, Contracting States shall take all appropriate measures to restore control of the aircraft to its lawful commander or to preserve his control of the aircraft.

2. In the cases contemplated by the preceding paragraph, any Contracting State in which the aircraft or its passengers or crew are present shall facilitate the continuation of the journey of the passengers and crew as soon as practicable, and shall without delay return the aircraft and its cargo to the persons lawfully entitled to possession.

Article 10

1. Contracting States shall afford one another the greatest measure of assistance in connection with criminal proceedings brought in respect of the offence and other acts mentioned in Article 4. The law of the State requested shall apply in all cases.

2. The provisions of paragraph 1 of this Article shall not affect obligations under any other treaty, bilateral or multilateral, which governs or will govern, in whole or in part, mutual assistance in criminal matters.

Article 11

Each Contracting State shall in accordance with its national law report to the Council of the International Civil Aviation Organization as promptly as possible any relevant information in its possession concerning:

    (a)   the circumstances of the offence;

    (b)   the action taken pursuant to Article 9;

    (c)   the measures taken in relation to the offender or the alleged offender, and, in particular, the results of any extradition proceedings or other legal proceedings.

Article 12

1. Any dispute between two or more Contracting States concerning the interpretation or application of this Convention which cannot be settled through negotiation, shall, at the request of one of them, be submitted to arbitration. If within six months from the date of the request for arbitration the Parties are unable to agree on the organization of the arbitration, any one of those Parties may refer the dispute to the International Court of Justice by request in conformity with the Statute of the Court.

2. Each State may at the time of signature or ratification of this Convention or accession thereto, declare that it does not consider itself bound by the preceding paragraph. The other Contracting States shall not be bound by the preceding paragraph with respect to any Contracting State having made such a reservation.

3. Any Contracting State having made a reservation in accordance with the preceding paragraph may at any time withdraw this reservation by notification to the Depositary Governments.

Article 13

1. This Convention shall be open for signature at The Hague on 16 December 1970, by States participating in the International Conference on Air Law held at The Hague from 1 to 16 December 1970 (hereinafter referred to as The Hague Conference). After 31 December 1970, the Convention shall be open to all States for signature in Moscow, London and Washington. Any State which does not sign this Convention before its entry into force in accordance with paragraph 3 of this Article may accede to it at any time.

2. This Convention shall be subject to ratification by the signatory States. Instruments of ratification and instruments of accession shall be deposited with the Governments of the Union of Soviet Socialist Republics, the United Kingdom of Great Britain and Northern Ireland, and the United States of America, which are hereby designated the Depositary Governments.

3. This Convention shall enter into force thirty days following the date of the deposit of instruments of ratification by ten States signatory to this Convention which participated in The Hague Conference.

4. For other States, this Convention shall enter into force on the date of entry into force of this Convention in accordance with paragraph 3 of this Article, or thirty days following the date of deposit of their instruments of ratification or accession, whichever is later.

5. The Depositary Governments shall promptly inform all signatory and acceding States of the date of each signature, the date of deposit of each instrument of ratification or accession, the date of entry into force of this Convention, and other notices.

6. As soon as this Convention comes into force, it shall be registered by the Depositary Governments pursuant to Article 102 of the Charter of the United Nations and pursuant to Article 83 of the Convention on International Civil Aviation (Chicago, 1944).

Article 14

1. Any Contracting State may denounce this Convention by written notification to the Depositary Governments.

2. Denunciation shall take effect six months following the date on which notification is received by the Depositary Governments.

IN WITNESS WHEREOF the undersigned Plenipotentiaries, being duly authorised thereto by their Governments, have signed this Convention.

DONE at The Hague, this sixteenth day of December, one thousand nine hundred and seventy, in three originals, each being drawn up in four authentic texts in the English, French, Russian and Spanish languages.

TC2C
Convention for the Suppression of Unlawful Acts Against the Safety of Civil Aviation (Montreal 1971), entry into force: 26 January 1973

The States Parties to the Convention
Considering that unlawful acts against the safety of civil aviation jeopardize the safety of persons and property, seriously affect the operation of air services, and undermine the confidence of the peoples of the world in the safety of civil aviation;
Considering that the occurrence of such acts is a matter of grave concern;
Considering that, for the purpose of deterring such acts, there is an urgent need to provide appropriate measures for punishment of offenders;
Have agreed as follows:

Article 1
1. Any person commits an offence if he unlawfully and intentionally:
    (a) performs an act of violence against a person on board an aircraft in flight if that act is likely to endanger the safety of that aircraft; or
    (b) destroys an aircraft in service or causes damage to such an aircraft which renders it incapable of flight or which is likely to endanger its safety in flight; or
    (c) places or causes to be placed on an aircraft in service, by any means whatsoever, a device or substance which is likely to destroy that aircraft, or to cause damage to it which renders it incapable of flight, or to cause damage to it which is likely to endanger its safety in flight; or
    (d) destroys or damages air navigation facilities or interferes with their operation, if any such act is likely to endanger the safety of aircraft in flight; or
    (e) communicates information which he knows to be false, thereby endangering the safety of an aircraft in flight.
2. Any person also commits an offence if he:
    (a) attempts to commit any of the offences mentioned in paragraph 1 of this Article; or
    (b) is an accomplice of a person who commits or attempts to commit any such offence.

Article 2
For the purposes of this Convention:
    (a) an aircraft is considered to be in flight at any time from the moment when all its external doors are closed following embarkation until the moment when any such door is opened for disembarkation; in the case of a forced landing, the flight shall be deemed to continue until the competent authorities take over the responsibility for the aircraft and for persons and property on board;
    (b) an aircraft is considered to be in service from the beginning of the preflight preparation of the aircraft by ground personnel or by the crew for a specific flight until twenty-four hours after any landing; the period of service shall, in any event, extend for the entire period during which the aircraft is in flight as defined in paragraph (a) of this Article.

Article 3
Each Contracting State undertakes to make the offences mentioned in Article 1 punishable by severe penalties.

Article 4

1. This Convention shall not apply to aircraft used in military, customs or police services.

2. In the cases contemplated in subparagraphs (a), (b), (c) and (e) of paragraph 1 of Article 1, this Convention shall apply, irrespective of whether the aircraft is engaged in an international or domestic flight, only if:

    (a)   the place of take-off or landing, actual or intended, of the aircraft is situated outside the territory of the State of registration of that aircraft; or

    (b)   the offence is committed in the territory of a State other than the State of registration of the aircraft.

3. Notwithstanding paragraph 2 of this Article, in the cases contemplated in subparagraphs (a), (b), (c) and (e) of paragraph 1 of Article 1, this Convention shall also apply if the offender or the alleged offender is found in the territory of a State other than the State of registration of the aircraft.

4. With respect to the States mentioned in Article 9 and in the cases mentioned insubparagraphs (a), (b), (c) and (e) of paragraph 1 of Article 1, this Convention shall not apply if the places referred to in subparagraph (a) of paragraph 2 of this Article are situated within the territory of the same State where that State is one of those referred to in Article 9, unless the offence is committed or the offender or alleged offender is found in the territory of a State other than that State.

5. In the cases contemplated in subparagraph (d) of paragraph 1 of Article 1, this Convention shall apply only if the air navigation facilities are used in international air navigation.

6. The provisions of paragraphs 2, 3, 4 and 5 of this Article shall also apply in the cases contemplated in paragraph 2 of Article 1.

Article 5

1. Each Contracting State shall take such measures as may be necessary to establish its jurisdiction over the offences in the following cases:

    (a)   when the offence is committed in the territory of that State;

    (b)   when the offence is committed against or on board an aircraft registered in that State;

    (c)   when the aircraft on board which the offence is committed lands in its territory with the alleged offender still on board;

    (d)   when the offence is committed against or on board an aircraft leased without crew to a lessee who has his principal place of business or, if the lessee has no such place of business, his permanent residence, in that State.

2. Each Contracting State shall likewise take such measures as may be necessary to establish its jurisdiction over the offences mentioned in Article 1, paragraph 1 (a), (b) and (c), and in Article 1, paragraph 2, in so far as that paragraph relates to those offences, in the case where the alleged offender is present in its territory and it does not extradite him pursuant to Article 8 to any of the States mentioned in paragraph 1 of this Article.

3. This Convention does not exclude any criminal jurisdiction exercised in accordance with national law.

Article 6

1. Upon being satisfied that the circumstances so warrant, any Contracting State in the territory of which the offender or the alleged offender is present, shall take him into custody or take other measures to ensure his presence. The custody and other measures shall be as provided in the law of that State but may only be continued for such time as is necessary to enable any criminal or extradition proceedings to be instituted.

2. Such State shall immediately make a preliminary enquiry into the facts.

3. Any person in custody pursuant to paragraph 1 of this Article shall be assisted in communicating immediately with the nearest appropriate representative of the State of which he is a national.

4. When a State, pursuant to this Article, has taken a person into custody, it shall immediately notify the States mentioned in Article 5, paragraph 1, the State of nationality of the detained person and, if it considers it advisable, any other interested State of the fact that such person is in custody and of the circumstances which warrant his detention. The State which makes the preliminary enquiry contemplated in paragraph 2 of this Article shall promptly report its findings to the said States and shall indicate whether it intends to exercise jurisdiction.

Article 7

The Contracting State in the territory of which the alleged offender is found shall, if it does not extradite him, be obliged, without exception whatsoever and whether or not the offence was committed in its territory, to submit the case to its competent authorities for the purpose of prosecution. Those authorities shall take their decision in the same manner as in the case of any ordinary offence of a serious nature under the law of that State.

Article 8

1. The offences shall be deemed to be included as extraditable offences in any extradition treaty existing between Contracting States. Contracting States undertake to include the offences as extraditable offences in every etradition treaty to be concluded between them.

2. If a Contracting State which makes extradition conditional on the existence of a treaty receives a request for extradition from another Contracting State with which it has no extradition treaty, it may at its option consider this Convention as the legal basis for extradition in respect of the offences. Extradition shall be subject to the other conditions provided by the law of the requested State.

3. Contracting States which do not make extradition conditional on the existence of a treaty shall recognize the offences as extraditable offences between themselves subject to the conditions provided by the law of the requested State.

4. Each of the offences shall be treated, for the purpose of extradition between Contracting States, as if it had been committed not only in the place in which it occurred but also in the territories of the States required to establish their jurisdiction in accordance with Article 5, paragraph 1 (b), (c) and (d).

Article 9

The Contracting States which establish joint air transport operating organizations or international operating agencies, which operate aircraft which are subject to joint or international registration shall, by appropriate means, designate for each aircraft the State among them which shall exercise the jurisdiction and have the attributes of the State of registration for the purpose of this Convention and shall give notice thereof to the International Civil Aviation Organization which shall communicate the notice to all States Parties to this Convention.

Article 10

1. Contracting States shall, in accordance with international and national law, endeavour to take all practicable measure for the purpose of preventing the offences mentioned in Article 1.

2. When, due to the commission of one of the offences mentioned in Article 1, a flight has been delayed or interrupted, any Contracting State in whose territory the aircraft or passengers or crew are presentshall facilitate the continuation of the journey of the passengers and

crew as soon as practicable, and shall without delay return the aircraft and its cargo to the persons lawfully entitled to possession.

Article 11

1. Contracting States shall afford one another the greatest measure of assistance in connection with criminal proceedings brought in respect of the offences. The law of the State requested shall apply in all cases.

2. The provisions of paragraph 1 of this Article shall not affect obligations under any other treaty, bilateral or multilateral, which governs or will govern, in whole or in part, mutual assistance in criminal matters.

Article 12

Any Contracting State having reason to believe that one of the offences mentioned in Article 1 will be committed shall, in accordance with its national law, furnish any relevant information in its possession to those States which it believes would be the States mentioned in Article 5, paragraph 1.

Article 13

Each Contracting State shall in accordance with its national law report to the Council of the International Civil Aviation Organization as promptly as possible any relevant information in its possession concerning:
   (a)   the circumstances of the offence;
   (b)   the action taken pursuant to Article 10, paragraph 2;
   (c)   the measures taken in relation to the offender or the alleged offender and, in particular, the results of any extradition proceedings or other legal proceedings.

Article 14

1. Any dispute between two or more Contracting States concerning the interpretation or application of this Convention which cannot be settled through negotiation, shall, at the request of one of them, be submitted to arbitration. If within six months from the date of the request for arbitration the Parties are unable to agree on the organization of the arbitration, any one of those Parties may refer the dispute to the International Court of Justice by request in conformity with the Statute of the Court.

2. Each State may at the time of signature or ratification of this Convention or accession thereto, declare that it does not consider itself bound by the preceding paragraph. The other Contracting States shall not be bound by the preceding paragraph with respect to any Contracting State having made such a reservation.

3. Any Contracting State having made a reservation in accordance with the preceding paragraph may at any time withdraw this reservation by notification to the Depositary Governments.

Article 15

1. This Convention shall be open for signature at Montreal on 23 September 1971, by States participating in the International Conference on Air Law held at Montreal from 8 to 23 September 1971 (hereinafter referred to as the Montreal Conference). After 10 October 1971, the Convention shall be open to all States for signature in Moscow, London and Washington. Any State which does not sign this Convention before its entry into force in accordance with paragraph 3 of this Article may accede to it at any time.

2. This Convention shall be subject to ratification by the signatory States. Instruments of ratification and instruments of accession shall be deposited with the Governments of the Union of Soviet Socialist Republics, the United Kingdom of Great Britain and Northern Ireland, and the United States of America, which are hereby designated the Depositary Governments.

3. This Convention shall enter into force thirty days following the date of the deposit of instruments of ratification by ten States signatory to this Convention which participated in the Montreal Conference.

4. For other States, this Convention shall enter into force on the date of entry into force of this Convention in accordance with paragraph 3 of this Article, or thirty days following the date of deposit of their instruments of ratification or accession, whichever is later.

5. The Depositary Governments shall promptly inform all signatory andacceding States of the date of each signature, the date of deposit of each instrument of ratification or accession, the date of entry into force of this Convention, and other notices.

6. As soon as this Convention comes into force, it shall be registered by the Depositary Governments pursuant to Article 102 of the Convention on International Civil Aviation (Chicago, 1944).

Article 16

1. Any Contracting State may denounce this Convention by written notification to the Depositary Governments.

2. Denunciation shall take effect six months following the date on which notification is received by the Depositary Governments.

IN WITNESS WHEREOF the undersigned Plenipotentiaries, being duly authorized thereto by their Governments, have signed this Convention.

DONE at Montreal, this twenty-third day of September, one thousand nine hundred and seventy-one, in three originals, each being drawn up in four authentic texts in the English, French, Russian and Spanish languages.

TC2D
Convention on the Physical Protection of Nuclear Material, signed at Vienna, 3 March 1980

The States Parties to this Convention,

Recognizing the right of all States to develop and apply nuclear energy for peaceful purposes and their legitimate interests in the potential benefits to be derived from the peaceful application of nuclear energy,

Convinced of the need for facilitating international cooperation in the peaceful application of nuclear energy,

Desiring to avert the potential dangers posed by the unlawful taking and use of nuclear material,

Convinced that offences relating to nuclear material are a matter of grave concern and that there is an urgent need to adopt appropriate and effective measures to ensure the prevention, detection and punishment of such offences,

Aware of the need for international cooperation to establish, in conformity with the national law of each State Party and with this Convention, effective measures for the physical protection of nuclear material,

Convinced that this Convention should facilitate the safe transfer of nuclear material,
Stressing also the importance of the physical protection of nuclear material in domestic use.
storage and transport,
Recognizing the importance of effective physical protection of nuclear material used for military purposes, and understanding that such material is and will continue to be accorded stringent physical protection.
Have agreed as follows:

Article 1

For the purposes of this Convention:

(a) 'nuclear material' means plutonium except that with isotopic concentration exceeding 80% in plutonium-238; uranium-233; uranium enriched in the isotopes 235 or
233; uranium containing the mixture of isotopes as occurring in nature other than in
the form of ore or ore-residue; any material containing one or more of the foregoing;

(b) 'uranium enriched in the isotope 235 or 233' means uranium containing the isotopes 235 or 233 or both in an amount such that the abundance ratio of the sum of
these isotopes to the isotope 238 is greater than the ratio of the isotope 235 to the
isotope 238 occurring in nature;

(c) 'international nuclear transport' means the carriage of a consignment of nuclear
material by any means of transportation intended to go beyond the territory of the
State where the shipment originates beginning with the departure from a facility of
the shipper in that State and ending with the arrival at a facility of the receiver
within the State of ultimate destination.

Article 2

1. This Convention shall apply to nuclear material used for peaceful purposes while in international nuclear transport.

2. With the exception of Articles 3 and 4 and paragraph 3 of Article 5, this Convention shall
also apply to nuclear material used for peaceful purposes while in domestic use, storage and
transport.

3. Apart from the commitments expressly undertaken by States Parties in the articles covered
by paragraph 2 with respect to nuclear material used for peaceful purposes while in domestic
use, storage and transport, nothing in this Convention shall be interpreted as affecting the
sovereign rights of a State regarding the domestic use, storage and transport of such nuclear
material.

Article 3

Each State Party shall take appropriate steps within the framework of its national law and
consistent with international law to ensure as far as practicable that, during international
nuclear transport, nuclear material within its territory, or on board a ship or aircraft under its
jurisdiction insofar as such ship or aircraft is engaged in the transport to or from that State, is
protected at the levels described in Annex 1.

Article 4

1. Each State Party shall not export or authorize the export of nuclear material unless the
State Party has received assurances that such material will be protected during the international nuclear transport at the levels described in Annex 1.

2. Each State Party shall not import or authorize the import of nuclear material from a State not party to this Convention unless the State Party has received assurances that such material will during the international nuclear transport be protected at the levels described in Annex 1.

3. A State Party shall not allow the transit of its territory by land or internal waterways or through its airports or seaports of nuclear material between States that are not parties to this Convention unless the State Party has received assurances as far as practicable that this nuclear material will be protected during international nuclear transport at the levels described in Annex 1.

4. Each State Party shall apply within the framework of its national law the levels of physical protection described in Annex I to nuclear material being transported from a part of that State to another part of the same State through international waters or airspace.

5. The State Party responsible for receiving assurances that the nuclear material will be protected at the levels described in Annex I according to paragraphs I to 3 shall identify and inform in advance States which the nuclear material is expected to transit by land or internal waterways, or whose airports or seaports it is expected to enter.

6. The responsibility for obtaining assurances referred to in paragraph 1may be transferred, by mutual agreement, to the State Party involved in the transport as the importing State.

7. Nothing in this article shall be interpreted as in any way affecting the territorial sovereignty and jurisdiction of a State, including that over its airspace and territorial sea.

Article 5

1. States Parties shall identify and make known to each other directly or through the International Atomic Energy Agency their central authority and point of contact having responsibility for physical protection of nuclear material and for coordinating recovery and response operations in the event of any unauthorized removal, use or alteration of nuclear material or in the event of credible threat thereof.

2. In the case of theft, robbery or any other unlawful taking of nuclear material or of credible threat thereof, States Parties shall, in accordance with their national law, provide cooperation and assistance to the maximum feasible extent in the recovery and protection of such material to any State that so requests. In particular:

    (a)   each State Party shall take appropriate steps to inform as soon as possible other States, which appear to it to be concerned, of any theft, robbery or other unlawful taking of nuclear material or credible threat thereof and to inform, where appropriate, international organizations;

    (b)   as appropriate, the States Parties concerned shall exchange information with each other or international organizations with a view to protecting threatened nuclear material, verifying the integrity of the shipping container, or recovering unlawfully taken nuclear material and shall:

        (i)   coordinate their efforts through diplomatic and other agreed channels:

        (ii)   render assistance, if requested;

        (iii) ensure the return of nuclear material stolen or missing as a consequence of the above-mentioned events.

    The means of implementation of this cooperation shall be determined by the States Parties concerned.

3. States Parties shall cooperate and consult as appropriate, with each other directly or through international organizations, with a view to obtaining guidance on the design, maintenance and improvement of systems of physical protection of nuclear material in international transport.

Article 6

1. States Parties shall take appropriate measures consistent with their national law to protect the confidentiality of any information which they receive in confidence by virtue of the provisions of this Convention from another State Party or through participation in an activity carried out for the implementation of this Convention. If States Parties provide information to international organizations in confidence, steps shall be taken to ensure that the confidentiality of such information is protected.

2. States Parties shall not be required by this Convention to provide any information which they are not permitted to communicate pursuant to national law or which would jeopardize the security of the State concerned or the physical protection of nuclear material.

Article 7

1. The intentional commission of:
  (a) an act without lawful authority which constitutes the receipt, possession, use, transfer, alteration, disposal or dispersal of nuclear material and which causes or is likely to cause death or serious injury to any person or substantial damage to property;
  (b) a theft or robbery of nuclear material;
  (c) an embezzlement or fraudulent obtaining of nuclear material;
  (d) an act constituting a demand for nuclear material by threat or use of force or by any other form of intimidation;
  (e) a threat:
    (i)   to use nuclear material to cause death or serious injury to any person or substantial property damage, or
    (ii) to commit an offence described in sub-paragraph (b) in order to compel a natural or legal person, international organization or State to do or to refrain from doing any act;
  (f) an attempt to commit any offence described in paragraphs (a), (b) or (c); and
  (g) an act which constitutes participation in any offence described in paragraphs (a) to (f) shall be made a punishable offence by each State Party under its national law.

2. Each State Party shall make the offences described in this article punishable by appropriate penalties which take into account their grave nature.

Article 8

1. Each State Party shall take such measures as may be necessary to establish its jurisdiction over the offences set forth in Article 7 in the following cases:
  (a) when the offence is committed in the territory of that State or on board a ship or aircraft registered in that State;
  (b) when the alleged offender is a national of that State.

2. Each State Party shall likewise take such measures as may be necessary to establish its jurisdiction over these offences in cases where the alleged offender is present in its territory and it does not extradite him pursuant to Article 11 to any of the States mentioned in paragraph 1.

3. This Convention does not exclude any criminal jurisdiction exercised in accordance with national law.

4. In addition to the States Parties mentioned in paragraphs 1 and 2, each State Party may, consistent with international law, establish its jurisdiction over the offences set forth in Article 7 when it is involved in international nuclear transport as the exporting or importing State.

Article 9

Upon being satisfied that the circumstances so warrant, the State Party in whose territory the alleged offender is present shall take appropriate measures, including detention, under its national law to ensure his presence for the purpose of prosecution or extradition. Measures taken according to this article shall be notified without delay to the States required to establish jurisdiction pursuant to Article 8 and, where appropriate, all other States concerned.

Article 10

The State Party in whose territory the alleged offender is present shall, if it does not extradite him, submit, without exception whatsoever and without undue delay, the case to its competent authorities for the purpose of prosecution, through proceedings in accordance with the laws of that State.

Article 11

1. The offences in Article 7 shall be deemed to be included as extraditable offences in any extradition treaty existing between States Parties. States Parties undertake to include those offences as extraditable offences in every future extradition treaty to be concluded between them.

2. If a State Party which makes extradition conditional on the existence of a treaty receives a request for extradition from another State Party with which it has no extradition treaty, it may at its option consider this Convention as the legal basis for extradition in respect of those offences. Extradition shall be subject to the other conditions provided by the law of the requested State.

3. States Parties which do not make extradition conditional on the existence of a treaty shall recognize those offences as extraditable offences between themselves subject to the conditions provided by the law of the requested State.

4. Each of the offences shall be treated, for the purpose of extradition between States Parties, as if it had been committed not only in the place in which it occurred but also in the territories of the States Parties required to establish their jurisdiction in accordance with paragraph 1 of Article 8.

Article 12

Any person regarding whom proceedings are being carried out in connection with any of the offences set forth in Article 7 shall be guaranteed fair treatment at all stages of the proceedings.

Article 13

1. States Parties shall afford one another the greatest measure of assistance in connection with criminal proceedings brought in respect of the offences set forth in Article 7, including the supply of evidence at their disposal necessary for the proceedings. The law of the State requested shall apply in all cases.

2. The provisions of paragraph 1 shall not affect obligations under any other treaty, bilateral or multilateral, which governs or will govern, in whole or in part, mutual assistance in criminal matters.

Article 14

1. Each State Party shall inform the depositary of its laws and regulations which give effect to this Convention. The depositary shall communicate such information periodically to all States Parties.

2. The State Party where an alleged offender is prosecuted shall, wherever practicable, first communicate the final outcome of the proceedings to the States directly concerned. The State Party shall also communicate the final outcome to the depositary who shall inform all States.

3.Where an offence involves nuclear material used for peaceful purposes in domestic use, storage or transport, and both the alleged offender and the nuclear material remain in the territory of the State Party in which the offence was committed, nothing in this Convention shall be interpreted as requiring that State Party to provide information concerning criminal proceeding arising out of such an offence.

Article 15
The Annexes constitute an integral part of this Convention

Article 16
1. A conference of States Parties shall be convened by the depositary five years after the entry into force of this Convention to review the implementation of the Convention and its adequacy as concerns the preamble, the whole of the operative part and the annexes in the light of the then prevailing situation.

2. At intervals of not less than five years thereafter, the majority of States Parties may obtain, by submitting a proposal to this effect to the depositary, the convening of further conferences with the same objective.

Article 17
1. In the event of a dispute between two or more States Parties concerning the interpretation or application of this Convention, such States Parties shall consult with a view to the settlement of the dispute by negotiation, or by any other peaceful means of settling disputes acceptable to all parties to the dispute.

2. Any dispute of this character which cannot be settled in the manner prescribed in paragraph 1 shall, at the request of any party to such dispute, be submitted to arbitration or referred to the International Court of Justice for decision. Where a dispute is submitted to arbitration, if, within six months from the date of the request, the parties to the dispute are unable to agree on the organization of the arbitration, a party may request the President of the International Court of Justice or the Secretary-General of the United Nations to appoint one or more arbitrators. In case of conflicting requests by the parties to the dispute, the request to the Secretary-General of the United Nations shall have priority.

3. Each State Party may at the time of signature, ratification, acceptance or approval of this Convention or accession thereto declare that it does not consider itself bound by either or both of the dispute settlement procedures provided for in paragraph 2. The other States Parties shall not be bound by a dispute settlement procedure provided for in paragraph 2, with respect to a State Party which has made a reservation to that procedure.

4. Any State Party which has made a reservation in accordance with paragraph 3 may at any time withdraw that reservation by notification to the depositary.

Article 18
1. This Convention shall be open for signature by all States at the Headquarters of the International Atomic Energy Agency in Vienna and at the Headquarters of the United Nations in New York from 3 March 1980 until its entry into force.

2. This Convention is subject to ratification, acceptance or approval by the signatory States.

3. After its entry into force, this Convention will be open for accession by all States.

4. (a) This Convention shall be open for signature or accession by international organizations and regional organizations of an integration or other nature, provided that any such organization is constituted by sovereign States and has competence in respect of

the negotiation, conclusion and application of international agreements in matters covered by this Convention;

(b) In matters within their competence, such organizations shall, on their own behalf, exercise the rights and fulfill the responsibilities which this Convention attributes to States Parties;

(c) When becoming party to this Convention such an organization shall communicate to the depositary a declaration indicating which States are members thereof and which articles of this Convention do not apply to it;

(d) Such an organization shall not hold any vote additional to those of its Member States.

5. Instruments of ratification, acceptance, approval or accession shall be deposited with the depositary.

Article 19

1. This Convention shall enter into force on the thirtieth day following the date of deposit of the twenty first instrument of ratification, acceptance or approval with the depositary.

2. For each State ratifying, accepting, approving or acceding to the Convention after the date of deposit of the twenty first instrument of ratification, acceptance or approval, the Convention shall enter into force on the thirtieth day after the deposit by such State of its instrument of ratification, acceptance, approval or accession.

Article 20

1. Without prejudice to Article 16 a State Party may propose amendments to this Convention. The proposed amendment shall be submitted to the depositary who shall circulate it immediately to all States Parties. If a majority of States Parties request the depositary to convene a conference to consider the proposed amendments, the depositary shall invite all States Parties to attend such a conference to begin not sooner than thirty days after the invitations are issued. Any amendment adopted at the conference by a two-thirds majority of all States Parties shall be promptly circulated by the depositary to all States Parties.

2. The amendment shall enter into force for each State Party that deposits its instrument of ratification, acceptance or approval of the amendment on the thirtieth day after the date on which two thirds of the States Parties have deposited their instruments of ratification, acceptance or approval with the depositary. Thereafter, the amendment shall enter into force for any other State Party on the day on which that State Party deposits its instrument of ratification, acceptance or approval of the amendment.

Article 21

1. Any State Party may denounce this Convention by written notification to the depositary.

2. Denunciation shall take effect one hundred and eighty days following the date on which notification is received by the depositary.

Article 22

The depositary shall promptly notify all States of:

(a) each signature of this Convention;

(b) each deposit of an instrument of ratification, acceptance, approval or accession;

(c) any reservation or withdrawal in accordance with Article 17;

(d) any communication made by an organization in accordance with paragraph 4(c) of Article 18;

(e) the entry into force of this Convention;

(f) the entry into force of any amendment to this Convention; and

(g) any denunciation made under Article 21.

Article 23

The original of this Convention, of which the Arabic, Chinese, English, French, Russian and Spanish texts are equally authentic, shall be deposited with the Director General of the International Atomic Energy Agency who shall send certified copies thereof to all States.

IN WITNESS WHEREOF, the undersigned, being duly authorized, have signed this Convention,
opened for signature at Vienna and at New York on 3 March 1980.

Annex I

Levels of Physical Protection to be Applied in International Transport of Nuclear Material as Categorized in Annex II

1. Levels of physical protection for nuclear material during storage incidental to international nuclear transport include:
   (a) For Category 111 materials, storage within an area to which access is controlled;
   (b) For Category 11 materials, storage within an area under constant surveillance by guards or electronic devices, surrounded by a physical barrier with a limited number of points of entry under appropriate control or any area with an equivalent level of physical protection;
2. For Category I material, storage within a protected area as defined for Category 11 above, to which, in addition, access is restricted to persons whose trustworthiness has been determined, and which is under surveillance by guards who are in close communication with appropriate response forces. Specific measures taken in this context should have as their object the detection and prevention of any assault, unauthorized access or unauthorized removal of material.
3. Levels of physical protection for nuclear material during international transport include:
   (a) For Category 11 and 111 materials, transportation shall take place under special precautions including prior arrangements among sender, receiver, and carrier, and prior agreement between natural or legal persons subject to the jurisdiction and regulation of exporting and importing States, specifying time, place and procedures for transferring transport responsibility;
   (b) For Category I materials, transportation shall take place under special precautions identified above for transportation of Category 11 and 111 materials, and in addition, under constant surveillance by escorts and under conditions which assure close communication with appropriate response forces;
   (c) For natural uranium other than in the form of ore or ore-residue transportation protection for quantities exceeding 500 kilograms U shall include advance notification of shipment specifying mode of transport, expected time of arrival and confirmation of receipt of shipment.

Annex II

   (a) All plutonium except that with isotopic concentration exceeding 80% in plutonium-238.
   (b) Material not irradiated in a reactor or material irradiated in a reactor but with a radiation level equal to or less than 100 reds/hour at one metre unshielded.
   (c) Quantities not falling in Category III and natural uranium should be protected in accordance with prudent management practice,

(d) Although this level of protection is recommended, it would be open to States, upon evaluation of the specific circumstances, to assign a different category of physical protection.

(e) Other fuel which by virtue of its original fissile material content is classified as Category I and II before irradiation may be reduced one category level while the radiation level from the fuel exceeds 100 reds/hour at one metre unshielded.

TC2E
Protocol on the Suppression of Unlawful Acts of Violence at Airports Serving International Civil Aviation (1971), supplementary to the Convention for the Suppression of Unlawful Acts against the Safety of Civil Aviation, signed at Montreal on 24 February 1988

The States Parties to this Convention,

Considering that unlawful acts of violence which endanger or are likely to endanger the safety of persons at airports serving international civil aviation or which jeopardize the safe operation of such airports undermine the confidence of the peoples of the world in safety at such airports and disturb the safe and orderly conduct of civil aviation for all States;

Considering that the occurrence of such acts is a matter of grave concern to the international community and that, for the purpose of deterring such acts, there is an urgent need to provide appropriate measures for punishment of offenders;

Considering that it is necessary to adopt provisions supplementary to those of the Convention for the Suppression of Unlawful Acts against the Safety of Civil Aviation, done at Montreal on 23 September 1971, to deal with such unlawful acts of violence at airports serving international civil aviation;

Have agreed as follows:

Article I
This Protocol supplements the Convention for the Suppression of Unlawful Acts against the Safety of Civil Aviation, done at Montreal on 23 September 1971 (hereinafter referred to as 'the Convention'), and, as between the Parties to this Protocol, the Convention and the Protocol shall be read and interpreted together as one single instrument.

Article II
1. In Article 1 of the Convention, the following shall be added as new paragraph 1 bis:
'1 bis. Any person commits an offence if he unlawfully and intentionally, using any device, substance or weapon:
    (a) performs an act of violence against a person at an airport serving international civil aviation which causes or is likely to cause serious injury or death; or
    (b) destroys or seriously damages the facilities of an airport serving international civil aviation or aircraft not in service located thereon or disrupts the services of the airport, if such an act endangers or is likely to endanger safety at that airport'.
2. In paragraph 2(a) of Article 1 of the Convention, the following words shall be inserted after the words 'paragraph 1': 'or paragraph 1 bis'.

Article III
In Article 5 of the Convention, the following shall be added as paragraph 2 bis:
'2 bis. Each Contracting State shall likewise take such measures as may be necessary to establish its jurisdiction over the offences mentioned in Article 1, paragraph 1 bis, and in Article 1, paragraph 2, in so far as that paragraph relates to those offences, in the case where the

alleged offender is present in its territory and it does not extradite him pursuant to Article 8 to the State mentioned in paragraph 1(a) of this Article'.

Article IV
This Protocol shall be open for signature at Montreal on 24 February 1988 by States participating in the International Conference on Air Law held at Montreal from 9 to 24 February 1988. After 1 March 1988, the Protocol shall be open for signature to all States in London, Moscow, Washington and Montreal, until it enters into force in accordance with Article VI.

Article V
1. This Protocol shall be subject to ratification by the signatory States.
2. Any State which is not a Contracting State to the Convention may ratify this Protocol if at the same lime it ratifies or accedes to the Convention in accordance with Article 15 thereof.
3. Instruments of ratification shall be deposited with the Governments of the Union of Soviet Socialist Republics, the United Kingdom of Great Britain and Northern Ireland and the United States of America or with the International Civil Aviation Organization, which are hereby designated the Depositaries.

Article VI
1. As soon as ten of the signatory States have deposited their instruments of ratification of this Protocol, it shall enter into force between them on the thirtieth day after the date of the deposit of the tenth instrument of ratification. It shall enter into force for each State which deposits its instrument of ratification after that date on the thirtieth day after deposit of its instrument of ratification
2. As soon as this Protocol enters into force, it shall be registered by the Depositaries pursuant to Article 102 of the Charter of the United Nations and pursuant to Article 83 of the Convention on International Civil Aviation (Chicago, 1944).

Article VII
1. This Protocol shall, after it has entered into force, be open for accession by any nonsignatory State.
2. Any State which is not a Contracting State to the Convention may accede to this Protocol if at the same time it ratifies or accedes to the Convention in accordance with Article 15 thereof.
3. Instruments of accession shall be deposited with the Depositaries and accession shall take effect on the thirtieth day after the deposit.

Article VIII
1. Any Party to this Protocol may denounce it by written notification addressed to the Depositaries.
2. Denunciation shall take effect six months following the date on which notification is received by the Depositaries.
3. Denunciation of this Protocol shall not of itself have the effect of denunciation of the Convention.
4. Denunciation of the Convention by a Contracting State to the Convention as supplemented by this Protocol shall also have the effect of denunciation of this Protocol.

Article IX
1. The Depositaries shall promptly inform all signatory and acceding States to this Protocol and all signatory and acceding States to the Convention:

(a) of the date of each signature and the date of deposit of each instrument of ratification of, or accession to, this Protocol, and

(b) of the receipt of any notification of denunciation of this Protocol and the date thereof.

2. The Depositaries shall also notify the States referred to in paragraph 1 of the date on which this Protocol enters into force in accordance with Article VI.

IN WITNESS WHEREOF the undersigned Plenipotentiaries, being duly authorized thereto by their Governments, have signed this Protocol.

DONE at Montreal on the twenty-fourth day of February of the year One Thousand Nine Hundred and Eighty-eight, in four originals, each being drawn up in four authentic texts in the English, French, Russian and Spanish languages.

TC2F
Convention for the Supression of Unlawful Acts against the Safety of Maritime Navigation, done at Rome, 10 March 1988

The States Parties to this Convention,
Having in mind the purposes and principles of the Charter of the United Nations concerning the maintenance of international peace and security and the promotion of friendly relations and cooperation among States,
Recognizing in particular that everyone has the right to life, liberty and security of person, as set out in the Universal Declaration of Human Rights and the International Covenant on Civil and Political Rights,
Deeply concerned about the world-wide escalation of acts of terrorism in all its forms, which endanger or take innocent human lives, jeopardize fundamental freedoms and seriously impair the dignity of human beings,
Considering that unlawful acts against the safety of maritime navigation jeopardize the safety of persons and property, seriously affect the operation of maritime services, and undermine the confidence of the peoples of the world in the safety of maritime navigation,
Considering that the occurrence of such acts is a matter of grave concern to the international community as a whole,
Being convinced of the urgent need to develop international cooperation between States in devising and adopting effective and practical measures for the prevention of all unlawful acts against the safety of maritime navigation, and the prosecution and punishment of their perpetrators,
Recalling Resolution 40/61 of the General Assembly of the United Nations of 9 December 1985 which, inter alia, 'urges all States unilaterally and in cooperation with other States, as well as relevant United Nations organs, to contribute to the progressive elimination of causes underlying international terrorism and to pay special attention to all situations, including colonialism, racism and situations involving mass and flagrant violations of human rights and fundamental freedoms and those involving alien occupation, that may give rise to international terrorism and may endanger international peace and security',
Recalling further that Resolution 40/61 'unequivocally condemns, as criminal) all acts, methods and practices of terrorism wherever and by whomever committed, including those which jeopardize friendly relations among States and their security',
Recalling also that by Resolution 40/61, the International Maritime Organization was invited to 'study the problem of terrorism aboard or against ships with a view to making recommendations on appropriate measures',

Having in mind Resolution A.584(14) of 20 November 1985, of the Assembly of the International Maritime Organization, which called for development of measures to prevent unlawful acts which threaten the safety of ships and the security of their passengers and crews,

Noting that acts of the crew which are subject to normal shipboard discipline are outside the purview of this Convention,

Affirming the desirability of monitoring rules and standards relating to the prevention and control of unlawful acts against ships and persons on board ships, with a view to updating them as necessary, and, to this effect, taking note with satisfaction of the Measures to Prevent Unlawful Acts against Passengers and Crews on Board Ships, recommended by the Maritime Safety Committee of the International Maritime Organization,

Affirming further that matters not regulated by this Convention continue to be governed by the rules and principles of general international law,

Recognizing the need for all States, in combating unlawful acts against the safety of maritime navigation, strictly to comply with rules and principles of general international law,

Have agreed as follows:

Article 1

For the purposes of this Convention, 'ship' means a vessel of any type whatsoever not permanently attached to the sea-bed, including dynamically supported craft, submersibles, or any other floating craft.

Article 2

1. This Convention does not apply to:
   (a) a warship; or
   (b) a ship owned or operated by a State when being used as a naval auxiliary or for customs or police purposes; or
   (c) a ship which has been withdrawn from navigation or laid up.
2. Nothing in this Convention affects the immunities of warships and other government ships operated for non-commercial purposes.

Article 3

1. Any person commits an offence if that person unlawfully and intentionally:
   (a) seizes or exercises control over a ship by force or threat thereof or any other form of intimidation; or
   (b) performs an act of violence against a person on board a ship if that act is likely to endanger the safe navigation of that ship; or
   (c) destroys a ship or causes damage to a ship or to its cargo which is likely to endanger the safe navigation of that ship; or
   (d) places or causes to be placed on a ship, by any means whatsoever, a device or substance which is likely to destroy that ship, or cause damage to that ship or its cargo which endangers or is likely to endanger the safe navigation of that ship; or
   (e) destroys or seriously damages maritime navigational facilities or seriously interferes with their operation, if any such act is likely to endanger the safe navigation of a ship; or
   (f) communicates information which he knows to be false, thereby endangering the safe navigation of a ship; or
   (g) injures or kills any person, in connection with the commission or the attempted commission of any of the offences set forth in subparagraphs (a) to (f).
2. Any person also commits an offence if that person:
   (a) attempts to commit any of the offences set forth in paragraph 1; or

(b)   abets the commission of any of the offences set forth in paragraph 1 perpetrated by any person or is otherwise an accomplice of a person who commits such an offence; or

(c)   threatens, with or without a condition, as is provided for under national law, aimed at compelling a physical or juridical person to do or refrain from doing any act, to commit any of the of fences set forth in paragraph 1, subparagraphs (b), (c) and (e), if that threat is likely to endanger the safe navigation of the ship in question.

Article 4

1. This Convention applies if the ship is navigating of is scheduled to navigate into, through or from waters beyond the outer limit of the territorial sea of a single State, or the lateral limits of its territorial sea with adjacent States.

2. In cases where the Convention does not apply pursuant to paragraph 1, it nevertheless applies when the offender or the alleged offender is found in the territory of a State Party other than the State referred to in paragraph 1.

Article 5

Each State Party shall make the offences set forth in Article 3 punishable by appropriate penalties which take into account the grave nature of those offences.

Article 6

1. Each State Party shall take such measures as may be necessary to establish its jurisdiction over the offences set forth in Article 3 when the offence is committed:

(a)   against or on board a ship flying the flag of the State at the time the offence is committed; or

(b)   in the territory of that State, including its territorial sea; or

(c)   by a national of that State.

2. A State Party may also establish its jurisdiction over any such offence when:

(a)   it is committed by a stateless person whose habitual residence is in that State; or

(b)   during its commission a national of that State is seized, threatened, injured or killed; or

(c)   it is committed in an attempt to compel that State to do or abstain from doing any act.

3. Any State Party which has established jurisdiction mentioned in paragraph 2 shall notify the Secretary-General of the International Maritime Organization (hereinafter referred to as 'the Secretary-General'). If such State Party subsequently rescinds that jurisdiction, it shall notify the Secretary-General.

4. Each State Party shall take such measures as may be necessary to establish its jurisdiction over the offences set forth in Article 3 in cases where the alleged offender is present in its territory and it does not extradite him to any of the States Parties which have established their jurisdiction in accordance with paragraphs 1 and 2 of this article.

5. This Convention does not exclude any criminal jurisdiction exercised in accordance with national law.

Article 7

1. Upon being satisfied that the circumstances so warrant, any State Party in the territory of which the offender or the alleged offender is present shall, in accordance with its law, take him into custody or take other measures to ensure his presence for such time as is necessary to enable any criminal or extradition proceedings to be instituted.

2. Such State shall immediately make a preliminary inquiry into the facts, in accordance with its own legislation.

3. Any person regarding whom the measures referred to in paragraph 1 are being taken shall be entitled to:

   (a) communicate without delay with the nearest appropriate representative of the State of which he is a national or which is otherwise entitled to establish such communication or, if he is a stateless person, the State in the territory of which he has his habitual residence;

   (b) be visited by a representative of that State.

4. The rights referred to in paragraph 3 shall be exercised in conformity with the laws and regulations of the State in the territory of which the offender or the alleged offender is present, subject to the proviso that the said laws and regulations must enable full effect to be given to the purposes for which the rights accorded under paragraph 3 are intended.

5. When a State Party, pursuant to this article, has taken a person into custody, it shall immediately notify the States which have established jurisdiction in accordance with Article 6, paragraph 1 and, if it considers it advisable, any other interested States, of the fact that such person is in custody and of the circumstances which warrant his detention. The State which makes the preliminary inquiry contemplated in paragraph 2 of this article shall promptly report its findings to the said States and shall indicate whether it intends to exercise jurisdiction.

Article 8

1. The master of a ship of a State Party (the 'flag State') may deliver to the authorities of any other State Party (the 'receiving State') any person who he has reasonable grounds to believe has committed one of the offences set forth in Article 3.

2. The flag State shall ensure that the master of its ship is obliged, whenever practicable, and if possible before entering the territorial sea of the receiving State carrying on board any person whom the master intends to deliver in accordance with paragraph 1, to give notification to the authorities of the receiving State of his intention to deliver such person and the reasons therefor.

3. The receiving State shall accept the delivery, except where it has grounds to consider that the Convention is not applicable to the acts giving rise to the delivery, and shall proceed in accordance with the provisions of Article 1. Any refusal to accept a delivery shall be accompanied by a statement of the reasons for refusal.

4. The flag State shall ensure that the master of its ship is obliged to furnish the authorities of the receiving State with the evidence in the master's possession which pertains to the alleged offence.

5. A receiving State which has accepted the delivery of a person in accordance with paragraph 3 may, in turn, request the flag State to accept delivery of that person. The flag State shall consider any such request, and if it accedes to the request it shall proceed in accordance with Article 7. If the flag State declines a request, it shall furnish the receiving State with a statement of the reasons therefor.

Article 9

Nothing in this Convention shall affect in any way the rules of international law pertaining to the competence of States to exercise investigative or enforcement jurisdiction on board ships not flying their flag.

Article 10

1. The State Party in the territory of which the offender or the alleged offender is found shall, in cases to which Article 6 applies, if it does not extradite him, be obliged, without exception whatsoever and whether or not the offence was committed in its territory, to submit the case without delay to its competent authorities for the purpose of prosecution, through proceedings in accordance with the laws of that State. Those authorities shall take their decision in the same manner as in the case of any other offence of a grave nature under the law of that State.

2. Any person regarding whom proceedings are being carried out in connection with any of the offences set forth in Article 3 shall be guaranteed fair treatment at all stages of the proceedings, including enjoyment of all the rights and guarantees provided for such proceedings by the law of the State in the territory of which he is present.

Article 11

1. The offences set forth in Article 3 shall be deemed to be included as extraditable offences in any extradition treaty existing between any of the States Parties. States Parties undertake to include such offences as extraditable offences in every extradition treaty to be concluded between them.

2. If a State Party which makes extradition conditional on the existence of a treaty receives a request for extradition from another State Party with which it has no extradition treaty, the requested State Party may, at its option, consider this Convention as a legal basis for extradition in respect of the offences set forth in Article 3. Extradition shall be subject to the other conditions provided by the law of the requested State Party.

3. States Parties which do not make extradition conditional on the existence of a treaty shall recognize the offences set forth in Article 3 as extraditable offences between themselves, subject to the conditions provided by the law of the requested State.

4. If necessary, the offences set forth in Article 3 shall be treated, for the purposes of extradition between States Parties, as if they had been committed not only in the place in which they occurred but also in a place within the jurisdiction of the State Party requesting extradition.

5. A State Party which receives more than one request for extradition from States which have established jurisdiction in accordance with Article 7 and which decides not to prosecute shall, in selecting the State to which the offender or alleged offender is to be extradited, pay due regard to the interests and responsibilities of the State Party whose flag the ship was flying at the time of the commission of the offence.

6. In considering a request for the extradition of an alleged offender pursuant to this Convention, the requested State shall pay due regard to whether his rights as set forth in Article 7, paragraph 3, can be effected in the requesting State.

7. With respect to the offences as defined in this Convention, the provisions of all extradition treaties and arrangements applicable between States Parties are modified as between States Parties to the extent that they are incompatible with this Convention.

Article 12

1. State Parties shall afford one another the greatest measure of assistance in connection with criminal proceedings brought in respect of the offences set forth in Article 3, including assistance in obtaining evidence at their disposal necessary for the proceedings.

2. States Parties shall carry out their obligations under paragraph 1 in conformity with any treaties on mutual assistance that may exist between them. In the absence of such treaties, States Parties shall afford each other assistance in accordance with their national law.

Article 13

1. States Parties shall cooperate in the prevention of the offences set forth in Article 3, particularly by:

    (a) taking all practicable measures to prevent preparations in their respective territories for the commission of those offences within or outside their territories;

    (b) exchanging information in accordance with their national law, and coordinating administrative and other measures taken as appropriate to prevent the commission of offences set forth in Article 3.

2. When, due to the commission of an offence set forth in Article 3, the passage of a ship has been delayed or interrupted, any State Party in whose territory the ship or passengers or crew are present shall be bound to exercise all possible efforts to avoid a ship, its passengers, crew or cargo being unduly detained or delayed.

Article 14

Any State Party having reason to believe that an offence set forth in Article 3 will be committed shall, in accordance with its national law, furnish as promptly as possible any relevant information in its possession to those States which it believes would be the States having established jurisdiction in accordance with Article 6.

Article 15

1. Each State Party shall, in accordance with its national law) provide to the Secretary-General, as promptly as possible, any relevant information in its possession concerning:

    (a) the circumstances of the offence;

    (b) the action taken pursuant to Article 13, paragraph 2;

    (c) the measures taken in relation to the offender or the alleged offender and, in particular, the results of any extradition proceedings or other legal proceedings.

2. The State Party where the alleged offender is prosecuted shall, in accordance with its national law, communicate the final outcome of the proceedings to the Secretary-General.

3. The information transmitted in accordance with paragraphs 1 and 2 shall be communicated by the Secretary-General to all States Parties, to Members of the International Maritime Organization (hereinafter referred to as 'the Organization'), to the other States concerned, and to the appropriate international intergovernmental organizations.

Article 16

1. Any dispute between two or more States Parties concerning the interpretation or application of this Convention which cannot be settled through negotiation within a reasonable time shall, at the request of one of them, be submitted to arbitration. If, within six months from the date of the request for arbitration, the parties are unable to agree on the organization of the arbitration any one of those parties may refer the dispute to the International Court of Justice by request in conformity with the Statute of the Court.

2. Each State may at the time of signature or ratification, acceptance or approval of this Convention or accession thereto, declare that it does not consider itself bound by any or all of the provisions of paragraph 1. The other States Parties shall not be bound by those provisions with respect to any State Party which has made such a reservation.

3. Any State which has made a reservation in accordance with paragraph 2 may, at any time, withdraw that reservation by notification to the Secretary-General.

Article 17

1. This Convention shall be open for signature at Rome on 10 March 1988 by States participating in the International Conference on the Suppression of Unlawful Acts against the

Safety of Maritime Navigation and at the Headquarters of the Organization by all States from 14 March 1988 to 9 March 1989. It shall thereafter remain open for accession.

2. States may express their consent to be bound by this Convention by:
- (a) signature without reservation as to ratification, acceptance or approval; or
- (b) signature subject to ratification, acceptance or approval, followed by ratification, acceptance or approval; or
- (c) accession.

3. Ratification, acceptance, approval or accession shall be effected by the deposit of an instrument to that effect with the Secretary-General.

Article 18

1. This Convention shall enter into force ninety days following the date on which fifteen States have either signed it without reservation as to ratification, acceptance or approval, or have deposited an instrument of ratification, acceptance, approval or accession in respect thereof.

2. For a State which deposits an instrument of ratification, acceptance, approval or accession in respect of this Convention after the conditions for entry into force thereof have been met, the ratification, acceptance, approval or accession shall take effect ninety days after the date of such deposit.

Article 19

1. This Convention may be denounced by any State Party at any time after the expiry of one year from the date on which this Convention enters into force for that State.

2. Denunciation shall be effected by the deposit of an instrument of denunciation with the Secretary-General.

3. A denunciation shall take effect one year, or such longer period as may be specified in the instrument of denunciation, after the receipt of the instrument of denunciation by the Secretary-General.

Article 20

1. A conference for the purpose of revising or amending this Convention may be convened by the Organization.

2. The Secretary-General shall convene a conference of the States Parties to this Convention for revising or amending the Convention, at the request of one third of the States Parties, or ten States Parties, whichever is the higher figure.

3. Any instrument of ratification, acceptance, approval or accession deposited after the date of entry into force of an amendment to this Convention shall be deemed to apply to the Convention as amended.

Article 21

1. This Convention shall be deposited with the Secretary-General.

2. The Secretary-General shall:
- (a) inform all States which have signed this Convention or acceded thereto, and all Members of the Organization, of:
    - (i) each new signature or deposit of an instrument of ratification, acceptance, approval or accession together with the date thereof;
    - (ii) the date of the entry into force of this Convention;
    - (iii) the deposit of any instrument of denunciation of this Convention together with the date on which it is received and the date on which the denunciation takes effect;

(iv) the receipt of any declaration or notification made under this Convention;
(b) transmit certified true copies of this Convention to all States which have signed this Convention or acceded thereto.

3. As soon as this Convention enters into force, a certified true copy thereof shall be transmitted by the Depositary to the Secretary-General of the United Nations for registration and publication in accordance with Article 102 of the Charter of the United Nations.

Article 22

This Convention is established in a single original in the Arabic, Chinese, English, French, Russian and Spanish languages, each text being equally authentic.

IN WITNESS WHEREOF the undersigned being duly authorized by their respective Governments for that purpose have signed this Convention.

DONE AT ROME this tenth day of March one thousand nine hundred and eighty-eight.

TC2G
Protocol for the Supression of Unlawful Acts Against the Safety of Fixed Platforms Located on the Continental Shelf, done at Rome 10 March 1988

The States Parties to this Convention,
Being parties to the Convention for the Suppression of Unlawful Acts Against the Safety of Maritime Navigation,
Recognizing that the reasons for which the Convention was elaborated also apply to fixed platforms located on the continental shelf,
Taking account of the provisions of that Convention,
Affirming that matters not regulated by this Protocol continue to begoverned by the rules and principles of general International law,
Have agreed as follows:

Article 1

1. The provisions of Articles 5 and 7 and of Articles 10 to 16 of the Convention for the Suppression of unlawful Acts against the Safety of Maritime Navigation (hereafter referred to as 'the Convention') shall also apply mutatis mutandis to the offences set forth in Article 2 of this Protocol where such offences are committed on board or against fixed platforms located on the continental shelf.
2. In cases where this Protocol does not apply pursuant to paragraph 1, it nevertheless applies when the offender or the alleged offender is found in the territory of a State Party other than the State in whose international waters or territorial sea the fixed platform is located.
3. For the purposes of this Protocol, 'fixed platform' means an artificial island, installation or structure permanently attached to the sea-bed for the purpose of exploration or exploitation of resources or for other economic purposes.

Article 2

1. Any person commits an offence if that person unlawfully and intentionally:
(a) seizes or exercises control over a fixed platform by force or threat thereof or any other form of intimidation; or
(b) performs an act of violence against a person on board a fixed platform If that act is likely to endanger its safety; or

(c) destroys a fixed platform or causes damage to it which is likely to endanger its safety; or

(d) places or causes to be placed on a fixed platform, by any means whatsoever, a device or substance which is likely to destroy that fixed platform or likely to endanger its safety; or

(e) injures or kills any person in connection with the commission or the attempted commission of any of the offences set forth In subparagraphs (a) to (d).

2. Any person also commits an offence if that person:

(a) attempts to commit any of the offences set forth In paragraph 1; or

(b) abets the commission of any such offences perpetrated by any person or is otherwise an accomplice of a person who commits such an offence; or

(c) threatens, with or without a condition, as is provided for under national law, aimed at compelling a physical or juridical person to do or refrain from doing any act, to commit any of the offences set forth in paragraph 1, subparagraphs (b) and (c), If that threat is likely to endanger the safety of the fixed platform.

Article 3

1. Each State Party shall take such measures as may be necessary to establish its jurisdiction over the offences set forth in Article 2 when the offence is committed:

(a) against or on board a fixed platform while it is located on the continental shelf of that State; or

(b) by a national of that State.

2. A State Party may also establish its jurisdiction over any such offence when:

(a) it is committed by a stateless person whose habitual residence is in that State;

(b) during its commission a national of that State is seized, threatened, injured or killed; or

(c) it is committed in an attempt to compel that State to do or abstain from doing any act.

3. Any State Party which has established jurisdiction mentioned in paragraph 2 shall notify the Secretary-General of the International Maritime Organisation (hereinafter referred to as 'the Secretary-General'). If such State Party subsequently rescinds that Jurisdiction, it shall notify the Secretary-General.

4. Each State Party shall take such measures as may be necessary to establish its jurisdiction over the offences set forth in Article 2 in cases where the alleged offender is present in its territory and it does not extradite him to any of the States Parties which have established their jurisdiction in accordance with paragraphs 1 and 2 of this article.

5. This Protocol does not exclude any criminal jurisdiction exercised in accordance with national law

Article 4

Nothing in this Protocol shall affect in any way the rules of international law pertaining to fixed platforms located on the continental shelf

Article 5

1. This Protocol shall be open for signature at Rome on 10 March 1988 and at the Headquarters of the International Maritime Organization (hereinafter referred to as 'the Organization') from 14 March 1988 to 9 March 1989 by any State which has signed the Convention. It shall thereafter remain open for accession.

2. States may express their consent to be bound by this Protocol by:

(a) signature without reservation as to ratification, acceptance or approval; or

    (b) signature subject to ratification, acceptance or approval, followed by ratification, acceptance or approval; or

    (c) accession.

3. Ratification, acceptance, approval or accession shall be effected by the deposit of an instrument to that effect with the Secretary-General.

4. Only a State which has signed the Convention without reservation as to ratification, acceptance or approval, or has ratified, accepted, approved or acceded to the Convention may become a Party to this Protocol.

Article 6

1. This Protocol shall enter into force ninety days following the date on which three States have either signed it without reservation as to ratification, acceptance or approval, or have deposited an instrument of ratification, acceptance, approval or accession in respect thereof. However, this Protocol shall not enter into force before the Convention has entered into force.

2. For a State which deposits an instrument of ratification, acceptance, approval or accession in respect of this Protocol after the conditions for entry into force thereof have been met, the ratification, acceptance, approval or accession shall take effect ninety days after the date of such deposit.

Article 7

1. This Protocol may be denounced by any State Party at any time after the expiry of one year from the date on which this Protocol enters into force for that State.

2. Denunciation shall be effected by the deposit of an instrument of denunciation with the Secretary-General.

3. A denunciation shall take effect one year, or such longer period as may be specified in the instrument of denunciation, after the receipt of the instrument of denunciation by the Secretary-General.

4. A denunciation of the Convention by a State Party shall be deemed to be a denunciation of this Protocol by that Party.

Article 8

1. A conference for the purpose of revising or amending this Protocol may be convened by the Organization.

2. The Secretary-General shall convene a conference of the States Parties to this Protocol for revising or amending the Protocol, at the request of one third of the States Parties, or five States Parties, whichever is the higher figure.

3. Any instrument of ratification, acceptance, approval or accession deposited after the date of entry into force of an amendment to this Protocol shall be deemed to apply to the Protocol as amended.

Article 9

1. This Protocol shall be deposited with the Secretary-General.

2. The Secretary-General shall:

    (a) inform all States which have signed this Protocol or acceded thereto, and all Members of the Organization, of:

        (i)   each new signature or deposit of an instrument of ratification, acceptance, approval or accession, together with the date thereof;

        (ii) the date of entry into force of this Protocol;

(iii) the deposit of any instrument of denunciation of this Protocol together with the date on which it is received and the date on which the denunciation takes effect;

(iv) the receipt of any declaration or notification made under this Protocol or under the Convention, concerning this Protocol.

(b) transmit certified true copies of this Protocol to all States which have signed this Protocol or acceded thereto

3. As soon as this Protocol enters into force, a certified true copy thereof shall be transmitted by the Depositary to the Secretary-General of the United Nations for registration and publication in accordance with Article 102 of the Charter of the United Nations.

Article 10

This Protocol is established in a single original in the Arabic, Chinese, English, French, Russian and Spanish languages, each text being equally authentic.

IN WITNESS WHEREOF the undersigned, being duly authorised by their respective Governments for that purpose. have signed this Protocol.

DONE AT ROME this tenth day of March one thousand nine hundred and eighty-eight.

TC2H
Convention on the Marking of Plastic Explosives for the Purpose of Detection, signed at Montreal, on 1 March 1991
(MONTREAL CONVENTION 1991)

The States Parties to this Convention,

Conscious of the implications of acts of terrorism for international security;

Expressing deep concern regarding terrorist acts aimed at destruction of aircraft, other means of transportation and other targets;

Concerned that plastic explosives have been used for such terrorist acts;

Considering that the marking of such explosives for the purpose of detection would contribute significantly to the prevention of such unlawful acts;

Recognizing that for the purpose of deterring such unlawful acts there is an urgent need for an international instrument obliging States to adopt appropriate measures to ensure that plastic explosives are duly marked;

Considering United Nations Security Council Resolution 635 of 14 June 1989, and United Nations General Assembly Resolution 44/29 of 4 December 1989 urging the International Civil Aviation Organization to intensify its work on devising an international regime for the marking of plastic or sheet explosives for the purpose of detection;

Bearing in mind Resolution A27-8 adopted unanimously by the 27th Session of the Assembly of the International Civil Aviation Organization which endorsed with the highest and overriding priority the preparation of a new international instrument regarding the marking of plastic or sheet explosives for detection;

Noting with satisfaction the role played by the Council of the International Civil Aviation Organization in the preparation of the Convention as well as its willingness to assume functions related to its implementation;

Have agreed as follows:

Article 1

For the purposes of this Convention:

1. 'Explosives' mean explosive products, commonly known as 'plastic explosives', including explosives in flexible or elastic sheet form, as described in the *Technical Annex* to this Convention.

2. 'Detection agent' means a substance as described in the *Technical Annex* to this Convention which is introduced into an explosive to render it detectable.

3. 'Marking' means introducing into an explosive a detection agent in accordance with the *Technical Annex* to this Convention. 4. 'Manufacture' means any process, including reprocessing, that produces explosives.

4. 'Duly authorized military devices' include, but are not restricted to, shells, bombs, projectiles, mines, missiles, rockets, shaped charges, grenades and perforators manufactured exclusively for military or police purposes according to the laws and regulations of the State Party concerned. 6. 'Producer State' means any State in whose territory explosives are manufactured.

Article 2

Each State Party shall take the necessary and effective measures to prohibit and prevent the manufacture in its territory of unmarked explosives.

Article 3

1. Each State Party shall take the necessary and effective measures to prohibit and prevent the movement into or out of its territory of unmarked explosives.

2. The preceding paragraph shall not apply in respect of movements for purposes not inconsistent with the objectives of this Convention, by authorities of a State Party performing military or police functions, of unmarked explosives under the control of that State Party in accordance with paragraph 1 of Article 4.

Article 4

1. Each State Party shall take the necessary measures to exercise strict and effective control over the possession and transfer of possession of unmarked explosives which have been manufactured in or brought into its territory prior to the entry into force of this Convention in respect of that State, so as to prevent their diversion or use for purposes inconsistent with the objectives of this Convention.

2. Each State Party shall take the necessary measures to ensure that all stocks of those explosives referred to in paragraph 1 of this Article not held by its authorities performing military or police functions are destroyed or consumed for purposes not inconsistent with the objectives of this Convention, marked or rendered permanently ineffective, within a period of three years from the entry into force of this Convention in respect of that State.

3. Each State Party shall take the necessary measures to ensure that all stocks of those explosives referred to in paragraph 1 of this Article held by its authorities performing military or police functions and that are not incorporated as an integral part of duly authorized military devices are destroyed or consumed for purposes not inconsistent with the objectives of this Convention, marked or rendered permanently ineffective, within a period of fifteen years from the entry into force of this Convention in respect of that State.

4. Each State Party shall take the necessary measures to ensure the destruction, as soon as possible, in its territory of unmarked explosives which may be discovered therein and which are not referred to in the preceding paragraphs of this Article, other than stocks of unmarked explosives held by its authorities performing military or police functions and incorporated as

an integral part of duly authorized military devices at the date of the entry into force of this Convention in respect of that State.

5. Each State Party shall take the necessary measures to exercise strict and effective control over the possession and transfer of possession of the explosives referred to in paragraph 2 of Part 1 of the *Technical Annex* to this Convention so as to prevent their diversion or use for purposes inconsistent with the objectives of this Convention.

6. Each State Party shall take the necessary measures to ensure the destruction, as soon as possible, in its territory of unmarked explosives manufactured since the coming into force of this Convention in respect of that State that are not incorporated as specified in paragraph 2(d) of Part 1 of the *Technical Annex* to this Convention and of unmarked explosives which no longer fall within the scope of any other sub-paragraphs of the said paragraph 2.

Article 5

1. There is established by this Convention an International Explosives Technical Commission (hereinafter referred to as 'the Commission') consisting of not less than fifteen nor more than nineteen members appointed by the Council of the International Civil Aviation Organization (hereinafter referred to as 'the Council') from among persons nominated by States Parties to this Convention.

2. The members of the Commission shall be experts having direct and substantial experience in matters relating to the manufacture or detection of, or research in, explosives.

3. Members of the Commission shall serve for a period of three years and shall be eligible for re-appointment.

4. Sessions of the Commission shall be convened, at least once a year at the Headquarters of the International Civil Aviation Organization, or at such places and times as may be directed or approved by the Council.

5. The Commission shall adopt its rules of procedure, subject to the approval of the Council.

Article 6

1. The Commission shall evaluate technical developments relating to the manufacture, marking and detection of explosives.

2. The Commission, through the Council, shall report its findings to the States Parties and international organizations concerned.

3. Whenever necessary, the Commission shall make recommendations to the Council for amendments to the *Technical Annex* to this Convention. The Commission shall endeavour to take its decisions on such recommendations by consensus. In the absence of consensus the Commission shall take such decisions by a two-thirds majority vote of its members.

4. The Council may, on the recommendation of the Commission, propose to States Parties amendments to the *Technical Annex* to this Convention.

Article 7

1. Any State Party may, within ninety days from the date of notification of a proposed amendment to the *Technical Annex* to this Convention, transmit to the Council its comments. The Council shall communicate these comments to the Commission as soon as possible for its consideration. The Council shall invite any State Party which comments on or objects to the proposed amendment to consult the Commission.

2. The Commission shall consider the views of States Parties made pursuant to the preceding paragraph and report to the Council. The Council, after consideration of the Commission's report, and taking into account the nature of the amendment and the comments of States Parties, including producer States, may propose the amendment to all States Parties for adoption.

3. If a proposed amendment has not been objected to by five or more States Parties by means of written notification to the Council within ninety days from the date of notification of the amendment by the Council, it shall be deemed to have been adopted, and shall enter into force one hundred and eighty days thereafter or after such other period as specified in the proposed amendment for States Parties not having expressly objected thereto.

4. States Parties having expressly objected to the proposed amendment may, subsequently, by means of the deposit of an instrument of acceptance or approval, express their consent to be bound by the provisions of the amendment.

5. If five or more States Parties have objected to the proposed amendment, the Council shall refer it to the Commission for further consideration.

6. If the proposed amendment has not been adopted in accordance with paragraph 3 of this Article, the Council may also convene a conference of all States Parties.

Article 8

1. States Parties shall, if possible, transmit to the Council information that would assist the Commission in the discharge of its functions under paragraph 1 of Article 6.

2. States Parties shall keep the Council informed of measures they have taken to implement the provisions of this Convention. The Council shall communicate such information to all States Parties and international organizations concerned.

Article 9

The Council shall, in cooperation with States Parties and international organizations concerned, take appropriate measures to facilitate the implementation of this Convention, including the provision of technical assistance and measures for the exchange of information relating to technical developments in the marking and detection of explosives.

Article 10

The *Technical Annex* to this Convention shall form an integral part of this Convention.

Article 11

1. Any dispute between two or more States Parties concerning the interpretation or application of this Convention which cannot be settled through negotiation shall, at the request of one of them, be submitted to arbitration. If within six months from the date of the request for arbitration the Parties are unable to agree on the organization of the arbitration, any one of those Parties may refer the dispute to the International Court of Justice by request in conformity with the Statute of the Court.

2. Each State Party may, at the time of signature, ratification, acceptance or approval of this Convention or accession thereto, declare that it does not consider itself bound by the preceding paragraph. The other States Parties shall not be bound by the preceding paragraph with respect to any State Party having made such a reservation.

3. Any State Party having made a reservation in accordance with the preceding paragraph may at any time withdraw this reservation by notification to the Depositary.

Article 12

Except as provided in Article 11 no reservation may be made to this Convention.

Article 13

1. This Convention shall be open for signature in Montreal on 1 March 1991 by States participating in the International Conference on Air Law held at Montreal from 12 February to 1 March 1991. After 1 March 1991 the Convention shall be open to all States for signature at

the Headquarters of the International Civil Aviation Organization in Montreal until it enters into force in accordance with paragraph 3 of this Article. Any State which does not sign this Convention may accede to it at any time.

2. This Convention shall be subject to ratification, acceptance, approval or accession by States. Instruments of ratification, acceptance, approval or accession shall be deposited with the International Civil Aviation Organization, which is hereby designated the Depositary. When depositing its instrument of ratification, acceptance, approval or accession, each State shall declare whether or not it is a producer State.

3. This Convention shall enter into force on the sixtieth day following the date of deposit of the thirty-fifth instrument of ratification, acceptance, approval or accession with the Depositary, provided that no fewer than five such States have declared pursuant to paragraph 2 of this Article that they are producer States. Should thirty-five such instruments be deposited prior to the deposit of their instruments by five producer States, this Convention shall enter into force on the sixtieth day following the date of deposit of the instrument of ratification, acceptance, approval or accession of the fifth producer State.

4. For other States, this Convention shall enter into force sixty days following the date of deposit of their instruments of ratification, acceptance, approval or accession.

5. As soon as this Convention comes into force, it shall be registered by the Depositary pursuant to Article 102 of the Charter of the United Nations and pursuant to Article 83 of the Convention on International Civil Aviation (Chicago, 1944).

Article 14

The Depositary shall promptly notify all signatories and States Parties of:
1. each signature of this Convention and date thereof;
2. each deposit of an instrument of ratification, acceptance, approval or accession and date thereof, giving special reference to whether the State has identified itself as a producer State;
3. the date of entry into force of this Convention;
4. the date of entry into force of any amendment to this Convention or its *Technical Annex*;
5. any denunciation made under Article 15; and
6. any declaration made under paragraph 2 of Article 11.

Article 15

1. Any State Party may denounce this Convention by written notification to the Depositary.
2. Denunciation shall take effect one hundred and eighty days following the date on which notification is received by the Depositary.

IN WITNESS WHEREOF the undersigned Plenipotentiaries, being duly authorized thereto by their Governments, have signed this Convention.

DONE at Montreal, this first day of March, one thousand nine hundred and ninety-one, in one original, drawn up in five authentic texts in the English, French, Russian, Spanish and Arabic languages.

TECHNICAL ANNEX

PART 1: DESCRIPTION OF EXPLOSIVES

1. The explosives referred to in paragraph 1 of Article 1 of this Convention are those that:
   (a) are formulated with one or more high explosives which in their pure form have a vapour pressure less than 10-4 Pa at a temperature of 25°C;
   (b) are formulated with a binder material; and
   (c) are, as a mixture, malleable or flexible at normal room temperature.
2. The following explosives, even though meeting the description of explosive in paragraph 1 of this Part, shall not be considered to be explosives as long as they continue to be held or used for the purposes specified below or remain incorporated as there specified, namely those explosive that:
   (a) are manufactured, or held, in limited quantities solely for use in duly authorized research, development or testing of new or modified explosives;
   (b) are manufactured, or held, in limited quantities solely for use in duly authorized training in explosives detection and/or development or testing of explosives detection equipment;
   (c) are manufactured, or held, in limited quantities solely for duly authorized forensic science purposes; or
   (d) are destined to be and are incorporated as an integral part of duly authorized military devices in the territory of the producer State within three years after the coming into force of this Convention in respect of that State. Such devices produced in this period of three years shall be deemed to be duly authorized military devices within paragraph 4 of Article 4 of this Convention.
3.   In this Part:
'duly authorized' in paragraph 2(a), (b) and (c) means permitted according to the laws and regulations of the State Party concerned; and 'high explosives' include but are not restricted to cyclotetramethylenetetranitramine (HMX), pentaerythritol tetranitrate (PETN) and cyclotrimethylenetrinitramine (RDX)

PART 2: DETECTION AGENTS

A detection agent is any one of those substances set out in the following Table. Detection agents described in this Table are intended to be used to enhance the detectability of explosives by vapour detection means. In each case, the introduction of a detection agent into an explosive shall be done in such a manner as to achieve homogeneous distribution in the finished product. The minimum concentration of a detection agent in the finished product at the time of manufacture shall be as shown in the said Table.

Table:

Name of detection agent	Molecular formula	Molecular weight	Minimum concentration
Ethylene glycol dinitrate (EGDN)	C2H4(NO3)2	152	0.2% by mass
2,3-Dimethyl-2,3dinitro Butane (DMNB)	C6H12(NO2)2	176	0.1% by mass
para-Mononitrololuene (p-MNT)	C7H7NO2	137	0.5% by mass
ortho-Mononitrolotuene (o-MNT)	C7H7NO2	137	0.5% by mass

Any explosive which, as a result of its normal formulation contains any of the designated dectection agents at or above the required minimum concentration level shall be deemed to be marked.

5.3   TC3: REGIONAL INSTRUMENTS

TC3A
The Arab Convention on the Suppression of Terrorism, signed at a meeting held at the General Secretariat of the League of Arab States in Cairo on 22 April 1998[1]

Preamble

The Arab states signatory hereto,
Desiring to promote mutual cooperation in the suppression of terrorist offences, which pose a threat to the security and stability of the Arab Nation and endanger its vital interests,

Being committed to the highest moral and religious principles and, in particular, to the tenets of the Islamic Sharia, as well as to the humanitarian heritage of an Arab Nation that rejects all forms of violence and terrorism and advocates the protection of human rights, with which precepts the principles of international law conform, based as they are on cooperation among peoples in the promotion of peace,

Being further committed to the Pact of the League of Arab States, the Charter of the United Nations and all the other international convents and instruments to which the Contracting States to this Convention are parties,

Affirming the right of peoples to combat foreign occupation and aggression by whatever means, including armed struggle, in order to liberate their territories and secure their right to self-determination, and independence and to do so in such a manner as to preserve the territorial integrity of each Arab country, of the foregoing being in accordance with the purposes and principles of the Charter of the United Nations and with the Organization's resolutions.

Have agreed to conclude this convention and to invite any Arab State that did not participate in its conclusion to accede hereto.

Part One: Definitions and General Provisions

Article 1
Each of the following terms shall be understood in the light of the definition give;
1. Contracting State

---

[1] Translated from Arabic by the United Nations English translation service (Unofficial translation) 29 May 2000

Any member State of the League of Arab States that has ratified this Convention and that has deposited its instruments of ratification with the General Secretariat of the League.

2. Terrorism

Any act or threat of violence, whatever its motives or purposes, that occurs in the advancement of an individual or collective criminal agenda and seeking to sow panic among people, causing fear by harming them, or placing their lives, liberty or security in danger, or seeking to cause damage to the environment or to public or private installations or property or to occupying or seizing them, or seeking to jeopardize a national resources.

3. Terrorist offence

Any offence or attempted offence committed in furtherance of a terrorist objective in any of the Contracting States, or against their nationals, property or interests, that is punishable by their domestic law. The offences stipulated in the following conventions, except where conventions have not been ratified by Contracting States or where offences have been excluded by their legislation, shall also be regarded as terrorist offences:

    (a)   The Tokyo Convention on offences and Certain Other Acts Committed on Board Aircraft, of 14 September 1963;

    (b)   The Hague Convention for the Suppression of Unlawful Seizure of Aircraft, of 16 December 1970;

    (c)   The Montreal Convention for the Suppression of Unlawful Acts against the Safety of Civil Aviation, of 23 September 1971, and the Protocol thereto of 10 May 1984;

    (d)   The Convention on the Prevention and Punishment of Crimes against Internationally Protected Persons, including Diplomatic Agents, of 14 December 1973;

    (e)   The International Convention against the Taking of Hostages, of 17 December 1979;

    (f)   The provisions of the United Nations Convention on the Law of the Sea, of 1982, relating to piracy on the high seas.

Article 2

    (a)   All cases of struggle by whatever means, including armed struggle, against foreign occupation and aggression for liberation and self-determination, in accordance with the principles of international law, shall not be regarded as an offence. This provision shall not apply to any act prejudicing the territorial integrity of any Arab State.

    (b)   None of the terrorist offences indicated in the preceding article shall be regarded as a political offence. In the application of this Convention, none of the following offences shall be regarded as a political offence, even if committed for political motives:

    (c)   Attacks on the kings, Heads of State or rulers of the Contracting States or on their spouses and families;

    (d)   Attacks on crown princes, vice-presidents, prime ministers or ministers in any of the Contracting States;

    (e)   Attacks on persons enjoying diplomatic immunity, including ambassadors and diplomats serving in or accredited to the Contracting States;

    (f)   Premeditated murder or theft accompanied by the use of force directed against individuals, the authorities or means of transport and communications;

    (g)   Acts of sabotage and destruction of public property and property assigned to a public service, even if owned by another Contracting State;

    (h)   The manufacture, illicit trade in or possession of weapons, munitions or explosives, or other items that may be used to commit terrorist offences.

Part Two: Principles of Arab Cooperation for the Suppression of Terrorism
Chapter I: The Security Field
Section I: Measures for the prevention and suppression of terrorist offences:

Article 3
Contracting States undertake not to organize, finance or commit terrorist acts or to be accessories thereto in any manner whatsoever. In their commitment to the prevention and suppression of terrorist offence in accordance with their domestic laws and procedures, they shall endeavour:
I. Preventive measure:
    (1) To prevent the use of their territories as a base for planning, organizing, executing, attempting or taking part in terrorist crime in any manner whatsoever. This includes the prevention of terrorists; infiltration into, or residence in their territories either as individuals or groups, receiving or giving refuge to them, training, arming, financing, or providing any facilitation to them;
    (2) To cooperate and coordinate action among Contracting States, particularly neighbouring countries suffering from similar or common terrorist offences;
    (3) To develop and strengthen systems for the detection of the movement, importation, exportation, stockpilling and use of weapons, munitions and explosives and of other means of aggression, murder and destruction as well as procedures for monitoring their passage through customs and across borders in order to prevent their transfer from one Contracting State to another or to third-party States other than for lawful purposes;
    (4) To develop and strengthen systems concerned with surveillance procedures and the securing of borders and points of entry overland and by air in order to prevent illicit entry thereby;
    (5) To strengthen mechanisms for the security and protection of eminent persons, vital installations and means of public transportation,
    (6) To enhance the protection, security and safety of diplomatic and consular persons and missions and international and regional organizations accredited to Contracting Stages, in accordance with the relevant international agreements, which govern this subject;
    (7) To reinforce security-related information activities and to coordinate them with those of each State in accordance with its information policy, with a view to exposing the objectives of terrorist groups and organizations, thwarting their schemes and demonstrating the danger they pose to security and stability;
    (8) To establish, in each Contracting State, a database for the accumulation and analysis of information relating to terrorist elements, groups, movements and organizations and for the monitoring of developments with respect to the terrorist phenomenon and of successful experiences in counterterrorism, and to keep such information up to date and make it available to the competent authorities of Contracting States, within the limits established by the domestic laws and procedures of each State;
II. Measures of suppression
    (1) To arrest the perpetrators of terrorist offences and to prosecute them in accordance with national law or extradite them in accordance with the provision's of this Convention or of any bilateral treaty between the requesting State and the requested State;
    (2) To provide effective protection for those working in the criminal justice field;
    (3) To provide effective protection for sources of information concerning terrorist offences and for witnesses thereof;

(4) To extend necessary assistance to victims of terrorism;

(5) To establish effective cooperation between the relevant agencies and the public in countering terrorism by, inter alia, establishing appropriate guarantees and incentives to encourage the reporting of terrorist acts, the provision of information to assist in their investigation, and cooperation in the arrest of perpetrators.

Section II: Arab cooperation for the prevention and suppression of terrorist offences

Article 4

Contracting States shall cooperate for the prevention and suppressionof terrorist offences, in accordance with the domestic laws and regulations of each State, as set forth hereunder:

I. Exchanging of information

(1) Contracting States shall undertake to promote the exchange of information between and among them concerning:

(a) The activities and crimes of terrorist groups and of their leaders and members; their headquarters and training; the means and sources by which they are funded and armed; the types of weapons, munitions and explosives used by them; and other means of aggression, murder and destruction;

(b) The means of communication and propaganda used by terrorist groups, their modus operandi; the movements of their leaders and members; and the travel documents that they use.

(2) Each Contracting State shall undertake to notify any other Contracting State in an expeditious manner of the information it has concerning any terrorist offence that takes place in its territory and is intended to harm the interests of that State or of its nationals and to include in such notification statements concerning the circumstances surrounding the offence, those who committed it, its victims, the losses occasioned by it and the devices and methods used in its perpetration, to the extent compatible with the requirements of the investigation and inquiry.

(3) Contracting States shall undertake to cooperate with each other in the exchange of information for the suppression of terrorist offences and promptly to notify other Contracting States of all the information or data in their possession that may prevent the occurrence of terrorist offences in their territory, against their nationals or residents or against their interests.

(4) Each Contracting State shall undertake to furnish any other Contracting State with any information or data in its possession that may:

(a) Assist in the arrest of a person or persons accused of committing a terrorist offence against the interests of that State or of being implicated in such an offence whether by aiding and abetting, collusion or incitement;

(b) Lead to the seizure of any weapons, munitions or explosives or any devices or funds used or intended for use to commit a terrorist offence.

(5) Contracting States shall undertake to maintain the confidentiality of the information that they exchange among themselves and not to furnish it to any State that is not a Contracting State or any other party without the prior consent of the State that was the source of the information.

II. Investigations:

Contracting States shall undertake to promote cooperation among themselves and to provide assistance with respect to measures for the investigation and arrest of fugitives suspected or convicted of terrorist offences in accordance with the laws and regulations of each state.

III. Exchange of expertise:
- (1) Contracting States shall cooperate in the conduct and exchange of research studies for the suppression of terrorist offences and shall exchange expertise in the counterterrorism field.
- (2) Contracting States shall cooperate, within the limits of their resources, in providing all possible technical assistance for the formulation of programmes or the holding of joint training courses or training courses intended for one state or for a group of Contracting Sttes, as required for the benefit of those working in counterterrorism with the aim of developing their scientific and practical abilities and enhancing their performance.

Chapter II: The Judicial Field
Section I: Extradition of Offenders

Article 5
Contracting States shall undertake to extradite those indicated for or convicted of terrorist offences whose extradition is requested by any of these states in accordance with the rules and conditions stipulated in this convention.

Article 6
Extradition shall not be permissible in any of the following circumstances:
- (a) If the offence for which extradition is requested is regarded under the laws in force in the requested State as an offence of a political nature;
- (b) If the offence for which extradition is requested relates solely to a dereliction of military duties;
- (c) If the offence for which extradition is requested was committed in the territory of the requested Contracting State, except where the offence has harmed the interests of the requesting State and its laws provide for the prosecution and punishment for such offences and where the requested State has not initiated any investigation or prosecution;
- (d) If a final judgement having the force of res judicata has been rendered in respect of the offence in the requested Contracting State or in a third Contracting State;
- (e) If, on delivery of the request for extradition, proceedings have been terminated or punishment has, under the law of the requesting State, lapsed because of the passage of time;
- (f) If the offence was committed outside the territory of the requesting State by a person who is not a national of that State and the law of the requested State does not allow prosecution for the same category of offence when committed outside its territory by such a person;
- (g) If the requesting State has granted amnesty to perpetrators of offences that include the offence in question;
- (h) If the legal system of the requested State does not allow it to extradite its nationals. In this case, the requested State shall prosecute any such persons who commit in any of the other Contracting States a terrorist offence that is punishable in both States by deprivation of liberty for a period of at least one year or more. The nationality of the person whose extradition is sought shall be determined as at the date on which the offence in question was committed, and use shall be made in this regard of the investigation conducted by the requesting state.

Article 7
Should the person whose extradition is sought be under investigation, on trial or already convicted for another offence in the requested State, his concluded, the trial is completed or the sentence is imposed. The requested State may nevertheless extradite him on an interim basis for questioning or trial provided that he is returned to that State before serving the sentence imposed on him in the requesting State.

Article 8
For purposes of the extradition of offenders under this Convention, no account shall be taken of any difference there may be in the domestic legislation of Contracting States in the legal designation of the offence as a felony or a misdemeanour or in the penalty assigned to it, provided that it is punishable under the laws of both States by deprivation of liberty for a period of at least one year or more.

Section II: Judicial Delegation

Article 9
Each Contracting State may request any other Contracting State to undertake in its territory and on its behalf any judicial procedure relating to an action arising out of a terrorist offence and, in particular:
  (a) To hear the testimony of witnesses and take depositions as evidence;
  (b) To effect service of judicial documents;
  (c) To execute searches and seizures;
  (d) To examine and inspect evidence;
  (e) To obtain relevant documents and records or certified copies thereof.

Article 10
Each of the Contracting States shall undertake to implement judicial delegations relating to terrorist offences, but such assistance may be refused in either of the two following cases:
  (a) Where the request relates to an offence that is subject to investigation or prosecution in the requested State;
  (b) Where granting the request might be prejudicial to the sovereignty, security or public order of the requested State.

Article 11
The request for judicial delegation shall be granted promptly in accordance with the provisions of the domestic law of the requested State. The latter may postpone the execution of the request until such time as any ongoing investigation or prosecution involving the same matter are completed or any compelling reasons for postponement cease to exist, provided that the requesting State is notified of such postponement.

Article 12
  (a) A measure that is undertaken by means of a judicial delegation, in accordance with the provisions of this Conventions, shall have the same legal effect as if it had been taken by the competent authority of the requesting State
  (b) The result of implementing the judicial delegation may be used only for the purpose for which the delegation is issued.

Section III: Judicial cooperation

Article 13
Each contracting State shall provide the other States with all possible and necessary assistance for investigations or prosecutions relating to terrorist offences.

Article 14
(a) Where one of the Contracting States has jurisdiction to prosecute a person suspected of a terrorist offence, it may request the State in which the suspect is present to take proceedings against him for that offence, subject to the agreement of that State and provided that the offence is punishable in the prosecuting State by deprivation of liberty for a period of at least one your or more. The requesting state shall, in this event, provide the requested state with all the investigation documents and evidence relating to the offence.

(b) The investigation or prosecution shall be conducted on the basis of the charge or charges made by the requesting state against the suspect, in accordance with the provisions and procedures of the law of the prosecuting state.

Article 15
The submission by the requesting state of a request for prosecution in accordance with paragraph (a) of the preceding article shall entail the suspension of the measures taken by it to pursue, investigate and prosecute the suspect whose prosecution is being requested, with the exception of those required for the purposes of the judicial cooperation and assistance, or the judicial delegation, sought by the State requested to conduct the prosecution.

Article 16
(a) The measures taken in either the requesting State or that in which the prosecution takes place shall be subject to the law of the State in which they are taken and they shall have the force accorded to them by that law.

(b) The requesting State may try or retry a person whose prosecution it has requested only if the requested State declines to prosecute him.

(c) The State requested to take proceedings shall in all cases undertake to notify the requesting State of what action it has taken with regard to the request and of the outcome of the investigation or prosecution.

Article 17
The State requested to take proceedings may take all the measures and steps established by its law with respect to the accused both before the request to take proceedings reaches it and subsequently.

Article 18
The transfer of competence for prosecution shall not prejudice the rights of the victim of the offence, who reserves the right to approach the courts of the requesting State or the prosecuting State with a view to claiming his civil-law rights as a result of the offence.

Section IV: Seizure of assets and proceeds derived from the offence

Article 19
(a) If it is decided to extradite the requested person, any Contracting State shall undertake to seize and hand over to the requesting State the property used and proceeds

       derived from or relating to the terrorist offence, whether in the possession of the person whose extradition is sought or that of a third party.

(b) Once it has been established that they relate to the terrorist offence, the items indicated in the preceding paragraph shall be surrendered even if the person to be extradited is not handed over because he has absconded or died or for any other reason.

(c) The provisions of the two preceding paragraphs shall be without prejudice to the rights of any Contracting State or of bona fide third parties in the property or proceeds in question.

Article 20

The State requested to hand over property and proceeds may take all the precautionary measures necessary to discharge its obligation to hand them over. It may also retain such property or proceeds on a temporary basis if they are required for pending criminal proceedings or may, for the same reason, hand them over to the requesting State on condition that they are returned.

Section V: Exchange of evidence

Article 21

Contracting States shall undertake to have the evidence of any terrorist offence committed in their territory against another Contracting State examined by their competent agencies, and they may seek the assistance of any other Contracting State in doing so. They shall take the necessary measures to preserve such evidence and ensure its legal validity. They alone shall examination to the State against whose interests the offence was committed, and the Contracting State or States whose assistance is sought shall not pass this information to any third party.

Part Three: Mechanisms for Implementing Cooperation
Chapter I: Extradition Procedures

Article 22

Requests for extradition shall be made between the competent authorities in the Contracting States directly, through their ministries of justice or the equivalent or through the diplomatic channel.

Article 23

The request for extradition shall be made in writing and shall be accompanied by the following:

(a) The original or an authenticated copy of the indictment or detention order or any other documents having the same effect and issued in accordance with the procedure laid down in the law of the requesting State;

(b) A statement of the offences for which extradition is requested, showing the time and place of their commission, their legal designation and a reference to the legal provisions applicable thereto, together with a copy of the relevant provisions;

(c) As accurate a description as possible of the person whose extradition is sought, together with any other information that may serve to establish his identity and nationality.

Article 24

1. The judicial authorities in the requesting State may apply to the requested State by any of the means of written communication for the provisional detention of the person being sought pending the presentation of the request for extradition.

2. In this case, the State from which extradition is requested may detain the person being sought on a provisional basis. If the request for extraction is not presented together with the necessary documents specified in the preceding article, the person whose extradition is being sought may not be detained for more than 30 days from the date of his arrest.

Article 25

The requesting State shall submit a request accompanied by the documents specified in Article 23 of this Convention. If the requested State determines that the request is in order, its competent authorities shall grant the request in accordance with its own law and its decision shall be promptly communicated to the requesting State.

Article 26

1. In all of the cases stipulated in the two preceding articles, the period of provisional detention shall not exceed 60 days from the date of arrest.

2. During the period specified in the preceding paragraph, the possibility of provisional release is not excluded provided that the State from which extradition is requested takes any measures it considers necessary to prevent the escape of the person sought.

3. Such release shall not prevent the rearrest of the person concerned or his extradition if a request for extradition is received subsequently.

Article 27

Should the requested State consider that it requires supplementary information in order to ascertain whether the conditions stipulated in this Chapter has been met, it shall notify the requesting State accordingly and a date for the provision of such information shall be established.

Article 28

Should the requested State receive several requests for extradition from different States, either for the same offence or for different offences, it shall make its decision having regard to all the circumstances and, in particular, the possibility of subsequent extradition, the respective dates o when the requests were received, the relative seriousness of the offences and the place where the offences were committed.

Chapter II: Procedures for Judicial Delegation

Article 29

Request relating to judicial delegations shall contain the following information:
  (a) The authority presenting the request;
  (b) The subject of and reason for the request;
  (c) An exact statement, to the extent possible, of the identity and nationality of the person concerned;
  (d) A description of the offence in connection with which the request for a judicial delegation is being made, its legal designation, the penalty established for its commission, and as much information as possible on the circumstances so as to facilitate the proper functioning of the judicial delegation.

Article 30

1. The request for a judicial delegation shall be addressed by the Ministry of Justice of the requesting State to the Ministry of Justice of the requested State and shall be returned through the same channel.

2. In case of urgency, the request for a judicial delegation shall be addressed by the judicial authorities of the requesting State directly to the judicial authorities of the requested State, and a copy of the request shall be sent at the same time to the Ministry of Justice of the requested State. The request, accompanied by the documents relating to its implementation, shall be returned through the channel stipulated in the preceding paragraph.

3. The request for a judicial delegation may be sent by the judicial authorities directly to the competent authority in the requested State, and replies may be forwarded directly through this authority.

Article 31

Requests for judicial delegation and their accompanying documents must be signed and must bear the seal of the competent authority or be authenticated by it. Such documents shall be exempt from all formalities that may be required by the legislation of the requested State.

Article 32

Should an authority that receives a request for a judicial delegation not have the competence to deal with it, it shall automatically refer it to the competent authority in its State. In the event the request has been sent directly, it shall notify the requesting State in the same manner.

Article 33

Every refusal of a request for a judicial delegation must be accompanied by a statement of the grounds for such refusal.

Chapter III: Measures for the Protection of Witnesses and Experts

Article 34

If, in the estimation of a requesting State, the appearance of a witness or expert before its judicial authority is of particular importance, it shall indicate this fact in its request. The request or summons to appear shall indicate the approximate amount of the allowances and the travel and subsistence expenses and shall include an undertaking to pay them. The requested State shall invite the witness or expert to appear and shall inform the requesting State of the response.

Article 35

1. A witness or an expert who does not comply with a summons to appear shall not be subject to any penalty or coercive measure, not withstanding any contrary statement in the summons.

2. Where a witness or an expert travels to the territory of the requesting State of his own accord, he should be summoned to appear in accordance with the provisions of the domestic legislation of that State.

Article 36

1. A witness or an expert shall not be prosecuted, detained or subjected to any restrictions on his personal liberty in the territory of the requesting State in respect of any acts or convictions that preceded the person's departure from the requested State, regardless of his nation-

ality, as long as his appearance before the judicial authorities of that State is in response to a summons.

2. No witness or expert, regardless of his nationality, who appears before the judicial authorities of a requesting State in response to a summons may be prosecuted, detained or subjected to any restriction on his personal liberty in the territory of that State in respect of any acts or convictions not specified in the summons and that preceded the person's departure from the territory of the requested State.

3. The immunity stipulated in this article shall lapse if the witness or expert sought, being free to leave, remains in the territory of the requesting State for a period of 30 consecutive days after his presence is not longer required by the judicial authorities or, having left the territory of the requesting State, has voluntarily returned.

Article 37

1. The requesting State shall take all necessary measures to protect witnesses and experts from any publicity that might endanger them, their families or their property as a result of their provision of testimony or expertise and shall, in particular, guarantee confidentiality with respect to:

 (a) The date, place and means of their arrival in the requesting state;
 (b) Their place of residence, their movements and the places they frequent;
 (c) Their testimony and the information they provide before the competent judicial authorities.

2. The requesting State shall undertake to provide the necessary protection for the security of witnesses and experts and of members of their families that is required by their situation, the circumstances of the case in connection with which they are sought and the types of risks that can be anticipated.

Article 38

1. Where a witness or expert whose appearance, is sought by a requesting State is in custody in the requested State, he may be temporarily transferred to the location of the hearing where he is requested to provide his testimony under conditions and at times to be determined by the requested State. Such transfer may be refused if:

 (a) The witness or expert in custody objects;
 (b) His presence is required for criminal proceedings in the territory of the requested State;
 (c) His transfer would prolong the term of his detention;
 (d) There are considerations militating against his transfer.

2. The witness or expert thus transferred shall continue to be held in custody in the territory of the requesting State until such time as he is returned to the requested State unless the latter State requests that he be released.

Part Four: Final Provisions

Article 39

This Convention is subject to ratification, acceptance or approval by the signatory States, and instruments of ratification, acceptance or approval shall be deposited with the General Secretariat of the League of Arab States within 30 days of the date of such ratification, acceptance or approval. The General Secretariat shall notify Member States of the deposit of each such instrument and of its date.

Article 40

1. This convention shall enter into force on the thirtieth day after the date as of which instruments of ratification, acceptance or approval have been deposited by seven Arab States.

2. This Convention shall enter into force for any other Arab State only after the instrument of ratification, acceptance or approval has been deposited and 30 days have elapsed from the date of that deposit.

Article 41

No Contracting State may make any reservation that explicitly or implicitly violates the provisions of this Convention or is incompatible with its objectives.

Article 42

A Contracting State may denounce this Convention only by written request addressed to the Secretary-General of the League of Arab States.

Denunciation shall take effect six months from the date the request is addressed to the Secretary-General of the League of Arab States.
The provisions of this Convention shall remain in force in respect of requests submitted before this period expires.

Done at Cairo, this twenty-second day of April 1998, in a single copy, which shall be deposited with the General Secretariat of the League of Arab States. A certified copy shall be kept at the General Secretariat of the Council of Arab Ministers of the Interior, and certified copies shall be transmitted to each of the parties that are signatories to this Convention or that accede hereto.

IN WITNESS WHEREOF, the Arab Ministers of the Interior and Ministers of Justice have signed this Convention on behalf of their respective states.

TC3B
Convention of the Organisation of the Islamic Conference on Combating International Terrorism, adopted at Ouagadougou on 1 July 1999[2]

The Member States of the Organisation of the Islamic Conference,

Pursuant to the tenets of the tolerant Islamic Sharia which reject all forms of violence and terrorism, and in particular specially those based on extremism and call for protection of human rights, which provisions are parallelled by the principles and rules of international law founded on cooperation between peoples for the establishment of peace;

Abiding by the lofty, moral and religious principles particularly the provisions of the Islamic Sharia as well as the human heritage of the Islamic Ummah.

Adhering to the Charter of the Organisation of the Islamic Conference, its objectives and principles aimed at creating an appropriate atmosphere to strengthen cooperation and understanding among Islamic States as well as relevant OIC resolutions;

---

[2] Annex to Resolution No: 59/26-P.

Adhering to the principles of International Law and the United Nations Charter as well as all relevant UN resolutions on procedures aimed at eliminating international terrorism, and all other conventions and international instruments to which states acceding to this Convention are parties and which call, inter alia, for the observance of the sovereignty, stability, territorial integrity, political independence and security of states, and non-intervention in their international affairs;

Proceeding from the rules of the Code of Conduct of the Organization of Islamic Conference for Combating International Terrorism;

Desiring to promote cooperation among them for combating terrorist crimes that threaten the security and stability of the Islamic States and endanger their vital interests;

Being committed to combating all forms and manifestations of terrorism and eliminating its objectives and causes which target the lives and properties of people;

Confirming the legitimacy of the right of peoples to struggle against foreign occupation and colonialist and racist regimes by all means, including armed struggle to liberate their territories and attain their rights to self-determination and independence in compliance with the purposes and principles of the Charter and resolutions of the United Nations;

Believing that terrorism constitutes a gross violation of human rights, in particular the right to freedom and security, as well as an obstacle to the free functioning of institutions and socio-economic development, as it aims at destabilizing States;

Convinced that terrorism cannot be justified in any way, and that it should therefore be unambiguously condemned in all its forms and manifestations, and all its actions, means and practices, whatever its origin, causes or purposes, including direct or indirect actions of States;

Recognizing the growing links between terrorism and organized crime, including illicit trafficking in arms, narcotics, human beings and money laundering;

Have agreed to conclude this Convention, calling on all Member States of the Organization of the Islamic Conference to accede to it.

Part I: Definition and General Provisions

Article 1
For the purposes of this Convention:
1. 'Contracting State' or 'Contracting Party' means every Member State in the Organisation of the Islamic Conference that has ratified or adhered to this Convention and deposited its instruments of ratification or adherence with the General Secretariat of the Organisation.
2. 'Terrorism' means any act of violence or threat thereof notwithstanding its motives or intentions perpetrated to carry out an individual or collective criminal plan with the aim of terrorizing people or threatening to harm them or imperiling their lives, honour, freedoms, security or rights or exposing the environment or any facility or public or private property to hazards or occupying or seizing them, or endangering a national resource, or international facilities, or threatening the stability, territorial integrity, political unity or sovereignty of independent States.

3. 'Terrorist Crime' means any crime executed, started or participated in to realize a terrorist objective in any of the Contracting States or against its nationals, assets or interests or foreign facilities and nationals residing in its territory punishable by its internal law.

4. Crimes stipulated in the following conventions are also considered terrorist crimes with the exception of those excluded by the legislations of Contracting States or those who have not ratified them:

    (a) Convention on 'Offences and Other Acts Committed on Board of Aircrafts' (Tokyo, 14.9.1963).

    (b) Convention on 'Suppression of Unlawful Seizure of Aircraft' (The Hague, 16.12.1970).

    (c) Convention on 'Suppression of Unlawful Acts Against the Safety of Civil Aviation' signed at Montreal on 23.9.1971 and its Protocol (Montreal, 10.12.1984).

    (d) Convention on the 'Prevention and Punishment of Crimes Against Persons Enjoying International Immunity, Including Diplomatic Agents' (New York, 14.12.1973).

    (e) International Convention Against the Taking of Hostages (New York, 1979).

    (f) The United Nations Law of the Sea Convention of 1988 and its related provisions on piracy at sea.

    (g) Convention on the 'Physical Protection of Nuclear Material'(Vienna, 1979).

    (h) Protocol for the Suppression of Unlawful Acts of Violence at Airports Serving International Civil Aviation-Supplementary to the Convention for the Suppression of Unlawful Acts Against the Safety of Civil Aviation (Montreal, 1988).

    (i) Protocol for the Suppression of Unlawful Acts Against the Safety of Fixed Platforms on the Continental Shelf (Rome, 1988).

    (j) Convention for the Suppression of Unlawful Acts Against the Safety of Maritime Navigation (Rome, 1988).

    (k) International Convention for the Suppression of Terrorist Bombings (New York, 1997).

    (l) Convention on the Marking of Plastic Explosives for the purposes of Detection (Montreal, 1991)

Article 2

a. Peoples' struggle including armed struggle against foreign occupation, aggression, colonialism, and hegemony, aimed at liberation and self-determination in accordance with the principles of international law shall not be considered a terrorist crime.

b. None of the terrorist crimes mentioned in the previous article shall be considered political crimes.

c. In the implementation of the provisions of this Convention the following crimes shall not be considered political crimes even when politically motivated:

    (1) Aggression against kings and heads of state of Contracting States or against their spouses, their ascendants or descendants.

    (2) Aggression against crown princes or vice-presidents or deputy heads of government or ministers in any of the Contracting States.

    (3) Aggression against persons enjoying international immunity including Ambassadors and diplomats in Contracting States or in countries of accreditation.

    (4) Murder or robbery by force against individuals or authorities or means of transport and communications.

    (5) Acts of sabotage and destruction of public properties and properties geared for public services, even if belonging to another Contracting State.

    (6) Crimes of manufacturing, smuggling or possessing arms and ammunition or explosives or other materials prepared for committing terrorist crimes.

d. All forms of international crimes, including illegal trafficking in narcotics and human beings money laundering aimed at financing terrorist objectives shall be considered terrorist crimes.

Part II: Foundations of Islamic Cooperation for Combating Terrorism
Chapter I: In the Field of Security
Division I: Measures to Prevent and Combat Terrorist Crimes.

Article 3
I. The Contracting States are committed not to execute, initiate or participate in any form in organizing or financing or committing or instigating or supporting terrorist acts whether directly or indirectly.
II. Committed to prevent and combat terrorist crimes in conformity with the provisions of this Convention and their respective domestic rules and regulations the Contracting States shall see to:
  (a) Preventive Measures:
    (1) Barring their territories from being used as an arena for planning, organizing, executing terrorist crimes or initiating or participating in these crimes in any form; including preventing the infiltration of terrorist elements or their gaining refuge or residence therein individually or collectively, or receiving hosting, training, arming, financing or extending any facilities to them.
    (2) Cooperating and coordinating with the rest of the Contracting States, particularly neighbouring countries which suffer from similar or common terrorist crimes.
    (3) Developing and strengthening systems relating to detecting transportation, importing, exporting stockpiling, and using of weapons, ammunition and explosives as well as other means of aggression, killing and destruction in addition to strengthening trans-border and custom controls in order to intercept their transfer from one Contracting State to another or to other States unless they are intended for specific legitimate purposes.
    (4) Developing and strengthening systems related to surveillance procedures, securing borders, and land, sea and air passages in order to prevent infiltration through them.
    (5) Strengthening systems for ensuring the safety and protection of personalities, vital installations and means of public transport
    (6) Re-enforcing protection, security and safety of diplomatic and consular persons and missions; and regional and international organizations accredited in the Contracting State in accordance with the conventions and rules of international law which govern this subject.
    (7) Promoting security intelligence activities and coordinating them with the intelligence activities of each Contracting State pursuant to their respective intelligence policies, aimed at exposing the objectives of terrorist groups and organisations, thwarting their designs and revealing the extent of their danger to security and stability.
    (8) Establishing a data base by each Contracting State to collect and analyze data on terrorist elements, groups, movements and organizations and monitor developments of the phenomenon of terrorism and successful experiences in combating it. Moreover, the Contracting State shall update this information and exchange them with competent authorities in

(9) other Contracting States within the limits of the laws and regulations in every State.

(b) Combating Measures:

(1) Arresting perpetrators of terrorists crimes and prosecuting them according to the national law or extraditing them in accordance with the provisions of this Convention or existing Conventions between the requesting and requested States.

(2) Ensuring effective protection of persons working in the field of criminal justice as well as to witnesses and investigators.

(3) Ensuring effective protection of information sources and witnesses on terrorist crimes.

(4) Extending necessary assistance to victims of terrorism.

(5) Establishing effective cooperation between the concerned organs in the Contracting States and the citizens for combating terrorism including extending appropriate guarantees and appropriate incentives to encourage informing on terrorist acts and submitting information to help uncover them and cooperating in arresting the perpetrators.

Division II: Areas of Islamic cooperation for preventing and combating terrorist crimes.

Article 4

Contracting States shall cooperate among themselves to prevent and combat terrorist crimes in accordance with the respective laws and regulations of each State in the following areas:

First: Exchange of Information

1. Contracting States shall undertake to promote exchange of information among them as such regarding:

(a) Activities and crimes committed by terrorist groups, their leaders, their elements, their headquarters, training, means and sources that provide finance and weapons, types of arms, ammunition and explosives utilized as well as other ways and means to attack, kill and destroy.

(b) Means of communications and propaganda utilized by terrorist groups, how they act, movement of their leaders, their elements and their travel documents.

2. Contracting States shall expeditiously inform any other Contracting State regarding available information about any terrorist crime perpetrated in its territory aimed at undermining the interests of that State or its nationals and to state the facts surrounding the crime in terms of its circumstances, criminals involved, victims, losses, devices and methods utilized to carry out the crime, without prejudicing investigation and inquiry requisites.

3. Contracting States shall exchange information with the other Parties to combat terrorist crimes and to inform the Contracting State or other States of all available information or data that could prevent terrorist crimes within its territory or against its nationals or residents or interests.

4. The Contracting States shall provide any other Contracting State with available information or data that will

(a) Assist in arresting those accused of committing a terrorist crime against the interests of that country or being implicated in such acts either by assistance, collusion, instigation, or financing.

(b) Contribute to confiscating any arms, weapons, explosives, devices or funds spent or meant to be spent to commit a terrorist crime.

5. The Contracting States undertake to respect the confidentiality of information exchanged between them and shall refrain from passing it to any non-Contracting States or other parties without prior consent of the source country.

Second: Investigation
Each Contracting State pledges to promote cooperation with other Contracting States and to extend assistance in the field of investigation procedures in terms of arresting escaped suspects or those convicted for terrorist crimes in accordance with the laws and regulations of each country.

Third: Exchange of Expertise
1. Contracting States shall cooperate with each other to undertake and exchange studies and researches on combating terrorist crimes as well as exchange of expertise in this field.
2. Contracting States shall cooperate within the scope of their capabilities to provide available technical assistance for preparing programmes or holding joint training sessions with one or more Contracting State if the need arises for personnel required in the field of combating terrorism in order to improve their scientific and practical potential and upgrade their performance standards.

Fourth: Education and Information Field
The Contracting States shall cooperate in:
1. Promoting information activities and supporting the mass media in order to confront the vicious campaign against Islam, by projecting the true image of tolerance of Islam, and exposing the designs and danger of terrorist groups against the stability and security of Islamic States.
2. Including the noble human values, which proscribe the practice of terrorism in the educational curricula of Contracting States.
3. Supporting efforts aimed at keeping abreast of the age by introducing an advanced Islamic thought based on *ijtihad* by which Islam is distinguished.

Chapter II: In the Judicial Field
Section I: Extraditing Criminals.

Article 5
Contracting States shall undertake to extradite those indicted or convicted of terrorist crimes, requested for extradition by any of these countries in compliance with the rules and conditions stipulated in this Convention.

Article 6
Extradition shall not be permissible in the following cases:
1. If the Crime for which extradition is requested is deemed by the laws enforced in the requested Contracting State as one of a political nature and without prejudice to the provisions of Article 2, paragraphs 2 and 3 of this Convention for which extradition is requested.
2. If the Crime for which extradition is sought relates solely to a dereliction of military obligations.
3. If the Crime for which extradition is requested, was committed in the territory of the requested Contracting State, unless this crime has undermined the interests of the requesting Contracting State and its laws stipulate that the perpetrators of those crimes shall be prosecuted and punished providing that the requested country has not commenced investigation or trial.

4. If the Crime has been the subject of a final sentence which has the force of law in the requested Contracting State.

5. If the action at the time of the extradition request elapsed or the penalty prescribed in accordance with the law in the Contacting State requesting extradition.

6. Crimes committed outside the territory of the requesting Contracting State by a person who was not its national and the law of the requested Contracting State does not prosecute such a crime if perpetrated outside its territory by such a person.

7. If pardon was granted and included the perpetrators of these crimes in the requesting Contracting State.

8. If the legal system of the requested State does not permit extradition of its national, then it shall be obliged to prosecute whosoever commits a terrorist crime if the act is punishable in both States by a freedom restraining sentence for a minimum period of one year or more. The nationality of the person requested for extradition shall be determined according to the date of the crime taking into account the investigation undertaken in this respect by the requesting State.

Article 7
If the person requested for extradition is under investigation or trial for another crime in the requested State, his extradition shall be postponed until the investigation is disposed of or the trial is over and the punishment implemented. In this case, the requested State shall extradite him provisionally for investigation or trial on condition that he shall be returned to it before execution of the sentence issued in the requested State.

Article 8
For the purpose of extraditing crime perpetrators according to this Convention, the domestic legislations of Contracting States shall not have any bearing as to their differences with respect to the crime being classified as a felony or misdemeanor, nor as to the penalty prescribed for it.

Section II: Rogatory Commission.

Article 9
Each Contracting State shall request from any other Contracting State to undertake in its territory rogatory action with respect to any judicial procedures concerning an action involving a terrorist crime and in particular:
1. To hear witnesses and testimonies taken as evidence.
2. To communicate legal documents.
3. To implement inquiry and detention procedures.
4. To undertake on the scene inspection and analyse evidence.
5. To obtain necessary evidence or documents or records or their certified copies.

Article 10
Each Contracting State shall implement rogatory commissions related to terrorist crimes and may reject the request for implementation with respect to the following cases.
1. If the crime for which the request is made, is the subject of a charge, investigation or trial in the country requested to implement rogatory commission.
2. If the implementation of the request prejudices the sovereignty or the security or public order of the country charged with this mission.

Article 11

The request for rogatory mission shall be implemented promptly in accordance with the provisions of the domestic laws of the requested State and which may postpone its implementation until its investigation and prosecution procedures are completed on the same subject or until the compelling reasons that called for postponement are removed. In this case the requesting State shall be informed of this postponement.

Article 12

The request for a rogatory commission related to a terrorist crime shall not be refused on the grounds of the rule of transaction confidentiality for banks and financial institutions. And in the implementation of the request the rules of the enforcing State are to be followed.

Article 13

The procedure, undertaken through rogatory commission in accordance with the provisions of this Convention, shall have the same legal effect as if it was brought before the competent authority in the State requesting rogatory commission. The results of its implementation shall only be utilized within the scope of the rogatory commission.

Section 3: Judicial Cooperation.

Article 14

Each Contracting State shall extend to the other contracting parties every possible assistance as may be necessary for investigation or trial proceedings related to terrorist crimes.

Article 15

1. If judicial competence accrues to one of the Contracting States for the prosecution of a subject accused of a terrorist crime, this State may request the country which hosts the suspect to prosecute him for this crime subject to the host country's consent and providing the crime is punishable in that country by a freedom restraining sentence for at least one year or by a more severe sanction. In such a case the requesting State shall pass all investigation documents and evidence related to the crime to the requested State.
2. Investigation or trial shall be conducted on the grounds of the case or cases brought by the requesting State against the accused in accordance with the legal provisions and procedures of the country holding the trial.

Article 16

The request for trial on the basis of para (1) of the previous article, entails the suspension of procedures of prosecution, investigation and trial in the territory of the requesting State except those relating to the requisites of cooperation, assistance or rogatory commission sought by the State requested to hold the trial procedures.

Article 17

1. Procedures undertaken in either of the two States – the requesting State or the one where the trial is held – shall be subject to the law of the country where the procedure is executed and which shall have legal preeminence as may be stipulated in its legislation.
2. The requesting State shall not bring to trial or retrial the accused subject unless the requested State refuses to prosecute him.
3. In all cases the State requested to hold trial shall inform the requesting country of its action with respect to the request for trial and shall communicate to it the results of its investigations or trial proceedings.

Article 18

The State requested to hold trial may undertake all measures and procedures stipulated by its legislation regarding the accused both before and after the request for trial is received.

Section 4: Seized Assets and Proceeds of the Crime.

Article 19

If the extradition of a subject is decided, the Contracting State shall hand over to the requesting State the assets and proceeds seized, used or related to the terrorist crime, found in the possession of the wanted subject or with a third party.

Article 20

The State requested to hand over the assets and proceeds may undertake all necessary custodial measures and procedures for the implementation of its obligation. It may also retain them provisionally if required for penal action implemented therein or hand them to the requesting State on condition that they shall be returned for the same purpose.

Section 5: Exchange of Evidence.

Article 21

A Contracting State shall see to it that the evidence and effects of any terrorist crime committed on its territory against another Contracting State are examined by its competent organs and may seek assistance to that end from any other Contracting State. Moreover, it shall take every necessary step to safeguard the evidence and proof of their legal relevance. It may communicate, if requested, the result to the country whose interest were targeted by the crime. The State or States which have assisted in this case shall not pass this information to others.

PART III: Mechanism for Implementing Cooperation
Chapter I: Extradition Procedures

Article 22

The exchange of extradition requests between Contracting States shall be undertaken directly through diplomatic channels or through their Ministries of Justice or their substitute.

Article 23

A request for extradition shall be submitted in writing and shall include:
1. The original or an authenticated copy of the indictment, arrest order or any other instruments of identical weight issued in line with the conditions stipulated in the requesting State's legislation.
2. A statement of the acts for which extradition is sought specifying the dates and places, where these acts were committed and their legal implications along with reference to the legal articles under which they fall as well as a copy of these articles.
3. Description, in as much detail as possible, of the subject wanted for extradition and any other information such as to determine his identity and nationality.

Article 24

1. The judicial authorities in the requesting State may approach the requested State by any channel of written communication and seek the preventive arrest of the wanted subject pending the arrival of the extradition request.

2. In this case the requested State may effect the preventive arrest of the wanted subject. However, if the request for extradition is not submitted together with the necessary documents listed in the above article, the subject whose extradition is sought may not be detained for more than thirty days as of the day of his arrest.

Article 25
The requesting State shall send a request together with the documents listed in Article 24 of this Convention. If the requested State accepts the request as valid, its competent authorities shall implement it in accordance with its legislation and shall promptly notify the requesting State of the action undertaken.

Article 26
–   In all cases stipulated in the two articles above, preventive detention shall not exceed sixty days after the date of arrest.
–   Temporary release may be effected during the period stipulated in the previous article and the requested State shall take appropriate measures to ensure that the wanted subject does not escape.
–   Release shall not prevent the re-arrest of the subject and his extradition if it was requested after his release.

Article 27
If the requested State requires additional clarification to ascertain the conditions stipulated in this chapter, it shall notify the requesting State thereof and fix a date for provision of such clarifications.

Article 28
If the requested State received a number of extradition requests from various countries related to the same or diverse acts, this State shall decide upon these requests bearing in mind the circumstances and in particular the possibility of subsequent extradition, date of receiving the requests, degree of the danger of the crime and where it was committed.

Chapter II: Measures for Rogatory Commissions

Article 29
Rogatory Commission requests must specify the following:
1. The competent authority that issued the request.
2. Subject of the request and its reason.
3. The identity and nationality of the person being the subject of the rogatory commission (as may be possible).
4. Information on the crime requiring rogatory commission, its legal definition and penalty inflicted on its perpetrators along with maximum available information on its circumstances in order to ensure the efficient implementation of the rogatory commission.

Article 30
1. The request for rogatory commission shall be forwarded by the Ministry of Justice in the requesting State to the Ministry of Justice in the requested State and returned in the same way.
2. In case of expediency, the request for rogatory commission shall be directly forwarded by the judicial authorities in the requesting State to the judicial authorities in the requested State. A copy of this rogatory commission shall also be sent at the same time to the Ministry of

Justice in the requested State. The rogatory commission shall be returned together with the papers concerning its implementation in the way stipulated in the previous item.

3. The request for rogatory commission may be forwarded directly from the judicial authorities to the competent authority in the requested country. Answers may be sent directly through the said authority.

Article 31

Requests for rogatory commission and accompanying documents shall be signed or stamped with the seal of a competent authority or that authorized by it. These documents shall be exempted from all formal procedures that could be required by the legislation of the requested State.

Article 32

If the authority that received the request for rogatory commission was not competent enough to deal with it, it shall automatically transfer it to the competent authority in its country. If the request is forwarded directly the answer shall reach the requesting State in the same manner.

Article 33

Any refusal for rogatory commission shall be explained.

Chapter III: Measures for Protecting Witnesses and Experts

Article 34

If the requesting State deems that the appearance of the witness or expert before its judicial authorities is of special importance, reference thereto shall be made in its request. The request or summons shall include an approximate statement in terms of compensation, travel expenses, accommodation and commitment to make these payments. The requested State shall invite the witness or expert and inform the requesting State about his/her reply.

Article 35

1. No penalty nor coercive measure may be inflicted upon the witness or expert who does not comply with the summons even if the writ provides for such a penalty.

2. If the witness or expert arrives voluntarily to the territory of the requesting State, he shall be summoned according to the provisions of the internal legislation of this State.

Article 36

1. A witness or expert may not be subjected to trial, detained or have his freedom restricted in the territory of the requesting State, for acts or court rulings that preceded his departure for the requesting State, irrespective of his nationality, as long as his appearance before the judicial authorities of the said State is based on a summons.

2. No witness or expert, whatever his nationality, appearing before the judiciary of the State in question on the basis of a summons, may be prosecuted or detained or have his freedom restricted in any way on the requesting State's territory for other acts or court decisions not mentioned in the summons and predating his departure from the State from which he is requested.

3. The immunity privileges stated in this Article shall become invalid if a witness or expert remains on the requesting State's territories for over thirty consecutive days despite his ability to return once his presence was no longer requested by the judiciary, or if he returns to the requesting State's territories after his departure.

Article 37

1. The requesting State shall undertake all necessary measures to ensure the protection of a witness or expert from publicity that could endanger him, his family or his property as a result of his testimony and in particular:

    (a) To ensure confidentiality of the date and place of his arrival as well as the means involved.

    (b) To ensure confidentiality of his accommodation, movements and locations where he may be found.

    (c) To ensure confidentiality of the testimony and information given to the competent judicial authorities.

2. The requesting State shall provide necessary security required by the condition of the witness or expert and of his family, and circumstances of the case and types of expected risks.

Article 38

1. If the witness or expert who is summoned to the requesting State is imprisoned in the requested State, he shall be provisionally transferred to the location of the hearing at which he is to testify according to conditions and times determined by the requested State Transfer may be denied:

    (a) If the witness or expert refuses.

    (b) If his presence is necessary for undertaking criminal procedures in the territory of the requested State.

    (c) If his transfer would prolong his imprisonment.

    (d) If there are considerations militating against his transfer.

2. The transferred witness or expert shall remain in detention in the territory of the requesting State until he is repatriated to the requested Tate unless the latter requests his release.

PART IV: Final Provisions

Article 39

This Convention shall be ratified, or adhered to, by the Signatory States and the instruments of ratification or accession shall be deposited with the General Secretariat of the Organisation of the Islamic Conference not exceeding a period of thirty days as of the date of ratification or accession. The General Secretariat shall inform all Member States about any deposition and date of such instruments.

Article 40

1. This Convention shall enter into force thirty days after the deposit of the seventh instrument of ratification or accession at the OIC General Secretariat.

2. This Convention shall not be applicable to any other Islamic State until it deposits its instruments of ratification or accession with the General Secretariat of the Organisation of the Islamic Conference and after a period of thirty days of the date of deposition.

Article 41

It is not permissible for any Contracting State to make any reservation, explicitly or implicitly in conflict with the provisions of this Convention or deviating from its objectives.

Article 42

1. A Contracting State shall not withdraw from this Convention except by a written request to the Secretary General of the Organization of the Islamic Conference.

2. Withdrawal shall be affective six months after the date of sending the request to the Secretary General.

This Convention has been written in English, Arabic and French of equal authenticity, of one original deposited with the General Secretariat of the Organization of the Islamic Conference which shall have it registered at the United Nations Organization, in accordance with the provisions of Article 102 of its Charter. The General Secretariat shall communicate approved copies thereof to the Member States of the Organization of the Islamic Conference.

TC3C
European Convention on the Suppression of Terrorism, concluded at Strasbourg on 27 January 1977

The Member States of the Council of Europe, signatory hereto.

Considering that the aim ofthe Council of Europe is to achieve a greater unity between its Members:

Aware of the growing concerncaused by the increase in acts of terrorism;

Wishing to take effective measures to ensure that the perpetrators of such acts do not escape prosecution and punishment;

Convinced that extradition is a particularly effective measure for achieving this result.,

Have agreed as follows:

Article 1
For the purposes of extradition between Contracting States, none of the following offences shall be regarded as a political offence or as an offence connected with a political offence or as an offence inspired by political motives:
- an offence within the scope of the Convention of the Suppression of Unlawful Seizure of Aircraft, signed at The Hague on 16 December 1970:
- an office within the scope of the Convention for the Suppression of Unlawful Acts against the Safety of Civil Aviation, signed at Montreal on 23 September 1971:
- a serious offence involving an attack against the life, physical integrity or liberty of internationallyprotected persons, including diplomatic agents;
- an offence involving kidnapping, the taking of a hostage or serious unlawful detention;
- an offence involving the use of a bomb, grenade, rocket, automatic firearm or letter or parcel bomb if this use endangers persons;
- an attempt to commit any of the foregoing offences or participation as an accomplice of a person who commits orattempts to commit such an offence.

Article 2
1. For the purposes of extradition between Contracting States, a Contracting State may decide not to regard as a political offence or as an offence connected with a political offence or as an offence inspired by political motives a serious offence involving an act of violence, other than one covered by Article 1, against the life, physical integrity or liberty of a person.

2. The same shall apply to a serious offence involving an act against property, other than one covered by Article 1, if the act created a collective danger for persons.

3. The same shall apply to an attempt to commit any of the foregoing offences or participation as an accomplice of a person who commits or attempts to commit such an offence.

Article 3

The provisions of all extradition treaties and arrangements applicable between Contracting States, including the European Convention on Extradition, are modified as between Contracting States to the extent that they are incompatible with this Convention.

Article 4

For the purpose of this Convention and to the extent that any offence mentioned in Article 1 or 2 is not listed as an extraditable offence in any extradition convention or treaty existing between Contracting States, it shall be deemed to be included as such therein.

Article 5

Nothing in this Convention shall be interpreted as imposing an obligation to extradite if the requested State has substantial grounds for believing that the request for extradition for an offence mentioned in Article 1 or 2 has been made for the purpose of prosecuting or punishing a person on account of his race, religion, nationality or political opinion, or that that person's position may be prejudiced for any of these reasons.

Article 6

1. Each Contracting State shall take such measures as may be necessary to establish its jurisdiction over an offence mentioned in Article 1 in the ease where the suspected offender is present in its territory and it does not extradite him after receiving a request for extradition from a Contracting State whose jurisdiction is based on a rule of jurisdiction existing equally in the law of the requested State.

2. This Convention does not exclude anycriminal jurisdiction exercised in accordance with national law.

Article 7

A Contracting State in whose territory a person suspected to have committed an offence mentioned in Article 1 is found and which has received a request for extradition under the conditions mentioned in Article 6. Paragraph 1, shall, if it does not extradite that person, submit the case, without exception whatsoever and without undue delay, to its competent authorities for the purpose of prosecution. Those authorities shall take their decision in the same manner as in the case of any offence of a serious nature under the law of that State.

Article 8

1. Contracting States shall afford one another the widest measure of mutual assistance in criminal matters in connection with proceedings brought in respect of the offences mentioned in Article 1 or 2. The law of the requested State concerning mutual assistance in criminal matters shall apply in all cases. Nevertheless this assistance may not be refused on the sole ground that it concerns a political offence or an offence connected with a political offence or an offence inspired by political motives.

2. Nothing in this Convention shall be interpreted as imposing an abolition to afford mutual assistance if the requested State has substantial grounds for believing that the request for mutual assistance in respect of an offence mentioned in Article 1 or 2 has been made for the

purpose of prosecuting or punishing a person on account of his race, religion, nationality or political opinion or that person's position may be prejudiced for any of these reasons.

3. The provisions of all treaties and arrangements concerning mutual assistance in criminal matters applicable between Contracting States, including the European Convention on Mutual Assistance in Criminal Matters, are modified as between Contracting States to the extent that they are incompatible with this Convention.

Article 9

1. The European Committee on Crime Problems of the Council of Europe shall be kept informed regarding the application of this Convention.

2. It shall do whatever is needful to facilitate a friendly settlement of any difficulty which may arise out of its execution.

Article 10

1. Any dispute between Contracting States concerning the interpretation or application of this Convention, which has not been settled in the framework of Article 9, paragraph 2, shall, at the request of any Party to the dispute, be referred to arbitration. Each Party shall nominate an arbitrator and the two arbitrators shall nominate a referee. If any Party has not nominated its arbitrator within the three months following the request for arbitration, he shall be nominated at the request of the other Party by the President of the European Court of Human Rights. If the latter should be a national of one of Parties to dispute, this duty shall be carried out by the Vice-President of the Court or, if the Vice- President is a national of one of the Parties to the dispute, by the most senior judge of the Court not being a national of one of the Parties to the dispute. The same procedure shall be observed if the arbitrators cannot agree on the choice of referee.

2. The arbitration tribunal shall by down its own procedure. Its decisions shall be taken by majority vote. Its award shall be final.

Article 11

1. This Convention shall be open to signature by the Member States of the Council of Europe. It shall be subject to ratification, acceptance or approval. Instruments of ratification, acceptance or approval shall be deposited with the Secretary General of the Council of Europe.

2. The Convention shall enter into force three months after the date of the deposit of the third instrument of ratification, acceptance or approval.

3. In respect of a signatory State ratifying, accepting or approving subsequently, the Convention shall come into force three months after the date of the deposit of its instrument of ratification, acceptance or approval.

Article 12

1. Any State may, at the time of signature or when depositing its instrument of ratification, acceptance or approval, specify the territory or territories to which this Convention shall apply.

2. Any State may, when depositing its instrument of ratification, acceptance or approval or at any later date, by declaration addressed to the Secretary General of the Council of Europe, extend this Convention to any other territory or territories specified in the declaration and for whose international relations it is responsible or on whose behalf it is authorized to give undertakings.

3. Any declaration made in pursuance of the preceding may, in respect of any territory mentioned in such declaration, be withdrawn by means of a notification addressed to the Secre-

tary General of the Council of Europe. Such withdrawal shall take effect immediately or at such later date as may be specified in the notification.

Article 13

1. Any State may, at the time of signature or when depositing its instrument of ratification, acceptance or approval, declare that it reserves the right to refuse extradition in respect of any offence mentioned in Article 1 which it considers to be a political offence, an offence connected with a political offence or an offence inspired by political motives, provided that it undertakes to take into due consideration, when evaluating the character of the offence, any particularly serious aspects of the offence, including:
  – that it created a collective danger to the life, physical integrity or liberty of persons; or
  – that it affected persons foreign to the motives behind it; or
  – that cruel or vicious means have been used in the commission of the offence.

2. Any State may wholly or party withdraw a reservation it has made in accordance with the foregoing paragraph by means of a declaration addressed to the Secretary General of the Council of Europe which shall become effective as from the dated of its receipt.

3. A State which has made a reservation in accordance with paragraph 1 of this article may not claim the application of Article 1 by any other State; it may, however if its reservation is partial or conditional, claim the application of that article in so far as it has itself accepted it.

Article 14

Any Contracting State may denounce this Convention by means of a written notification addressed to the Secretary General of the Council of Europe. Any such denunciation shall take effect immediately or at such later date as may be specified in the notification.

Article 15

This Convention ceases to have effect in respect of any Contracting State which withdraws from or ceases to be a Member of the Council of Europe.

Article 16

The Secretary General of the Council of Europe shall notify the Member States of the Council of:
  – any signature;
  – any deposit of an instrument of ratification, acceptance or approval;
  – any date of entry into force of this Convention in accordance with Article 11 thereof;
  – any declaration or notification received in pursuance of the provisions of Article 12;
  – any reservation made in pursuance of the provisions of Article 13, paragraph 1;
  – the withdrawal of any reservation effected in pursuance of the provisions of Article 13, paragraph 2;
  – any notification received in pursuance of Article 14 and the date on which denunciation takes effect;
  – any cessation of the effects of the Convention pursuant to Article 15.

In witness whereof, the undersigned, being duly authorised thereto, have signed this Convention.

Done at Strasbourg, this 27th day of January 1977, in English and in French, both texts being equally authoritative, in a single copy which shall remain deposited in the archives of the

Council of Europe. The Secretary- General of the Council of Europe shall transmit certified copies to each of the signatory States.

En foi de quoi, les soussignês, dûment autorisês à cet effet, ont signê la prêsente Convention. Fait à Strasbourg, le 27 janvier 1977, en français et en anglais, les deux textes faisant êgalement foi, en un seul exemplaire qui sera dêposê dans les archives du Conseil de l'Europe. Le Secrêtaire Gênêral du Conseil de l'Europe en communiquera copie certifiêe conforme à chacun des Etats signataires.

TC3D

OAS Convention to Prevent and Punish Acts of Terrorism Taking the Form of Crimes against Persons and Related Extortion that are of International Significance, concluded at Washington, D.C. on 2 February 1971[3]

Whereas:

The defense of freedom and justice and respect for the fundamental rights of the individual that are recognized by the American Declaration of the Rights and Duties of Man and the Universal Declaration of Human Rights are primary duties of states;

The General Assembly of the Organization, in Resolution 4, of June 30, 1970, strongly condemned acts of terrorism, especially the kidnapping of persons and extortion in connection with that crime, which it declared to be serious common crimes;

Criminal acts against persons entitled to special protection under international law are occurring frequently, and those acts are of international significance because of the consequences that may flow from them for relations among states;

It is advisable to adopt general standards that will progressively develop international law as regards cooperation in the prevention and punishment of such acts; and

In the application of those standards the institution of asylum should be maintained and, likewise the principle of nonintervention should not be impaired,

The Member States of the Organization of American States

Have agreed upon the following articles:

Article 1
The Contracting States undertake to cooperate among themselves by taking all the measures that they may consider effective, under their own laws, and especially those established in this convention, to prevent and punish acts of terrorism, especially kidnapping, murder, and other assaults against the life or physical integrity of those persons to whom the state has the duty according to international law to give special protection, as well as extortion in connection with those crimes.

---

[3] Registered by the Organization of American States on 23 October 1986.

Article 2

For the purposes of this convention, kidnapping, murder, and other assaults against the life or personal integrity of those persons to whom the state has the duty to give special protection according to international law, as well as extortion in connection with those crimes, shall be considered common crimes of international significance, regardless of motive.

Article 3

Persons who have been charged or convicted for any of the crimes referred to in Article 2 of this convention shall be subject to extradition under the provisions of the extradition treaties in force between the parties or, in the case of states that do not make extradition dependent on the existence of a treaty, in accordance with their own laws.

Article 4

Any person deprived of his freedom through the application of this convention shall enjoy the legal guarantees of due process.

Article 5

When extradition requested for one of the crimes specified in Article 2 is not in order because the person sought is a national of the requested state, or because of some other legal or constitutional impediment, that state is obliged to submit the case to its competent authorities for prosecution, as if the act had been committed in its territory. The decision of these authorities shall be communicated to the state that requested extradition. In such proceedings, the obligation established in Article 4 shall be respected.

Article 6

None of the provisions of this convention shall be interpreted so as to impair the right of asylum.

Article 7

The Contracting States undertake to include the crimes referred to in Article 2 of this convention among the punishable acts giving rise to extradition in any treaty on the subject to which they agree among themselves in the future. The Contracting States that do not subject extradition to the existence of a treaty with the requesting state shall consider the crimes referred to in Article 2 of this convention as crimes giving rise to extradition, according to the conditions established by the laws of the requested state.

Article 8

To cooperate in preventing and punishing the crimes contemplated in Article 2 of this convention, the Contracting States accept the following obligations:

    (a) To take all measures within their power, and in conformity with their own laws, to prevent and impede the preparation in their respective territories of the crimes mentioned in Article 2 that are to be carried out in the territory of another Contracting State;

    (b) To exchange information and consider effective administrative measures for the purpose of protecting the persons to whom Article 2 of this convention refers;

    (c) To guarantee to every person deprived of his freedom through the application of this convention every right to defend himself;

    (d) To endeavor to have the criminal acts contemplated in this convention included in their penal laws, if not already so included;

    (e) To comply most expeditiously with the requests for extradition concerning the criminal acts contemplated in this convention.

Article 9
This convention shall remain open for signature by the Member States of the Organization of American States, as well as by any other state that is a member of the United Nations or any of its specialized agencies, or any state that is a party to the Statute of the International Court of Justice, or any other state that may be invited by the General Assembly of the Organization of American States to sign it.

Article 10
This convention shall be ratified by the signatory states in accordance with their respective constitutional procedures.

Article 11
The original instrument of this convention, the English, French, Portuguese, and Spanish texts of which are equally authentic, shall be deposited in the General Secretariat of the Organization of American States, which shall send certified copies to the signatory governments for purposes of ratification. The instruments of ratification shall be deposited in the General Secretariat of the Organization of the American States, which shall notify the signatory governments of such deposit.

Article 12
This convention shall enter into force among the states that ratify it when they deposit their respective instruments of ratification.

Article 13
This convention shall remain in force indefinitely, but any of the Contracting States may denounce it. The denunciation shall be transmitted to the General Secretariat of the Organization of American States, which shall notify the other Contracting States thereof. One year following the denunciation, the convention shall cease to be in force for the denouncing state, but shall continue to be in force for the other Contracting States.

In Witness Whereof, the undersigned plenipotentiaries, having presented their full powers, which have been found to be in due and proper form, sign this convention on behalf of their respective governments, at the city of Washington this second day of February of the year one thousand nine hundred seventy-one.

TC3E
OAU Convention on the Prevention and Combating of Terrorism, adopted at Algiers on 14 July 1999[4]

The Member States of the Organization of African Unity:

Considering the purposes and principles enshrined in the Charter of the Organization of African Unity, in particular its clauses relating to the security, stability, development of friendly relations and cooperation among its Member States;

---

[4] Entry into force in accordance with Article 20. Depositary: Secretary-General of the Organization of African Unity

Recalling the provisions of the Declaration on the Code of Conduct for Inter-African Relations, adopted by the Thirtieth Ordinary Session of the Assembly of Heads of State and Government of the Organization of African Unity, held in Tunis, Tunisia, from 13 to 15 June 1994;

Aware of the need to promote human and moral values based on tolerance and rejection of all forms of terrorism irrespective of their motivations;

Believing in the principles of international law, the provisions of the Charters of the Organization of African Unity and of the United Nations and the latter's relevant resolutions on measures aimed at combating international terrorism and, in particular, Resolution 49/60 of the General Assembly of 9 December 1994, together with the annexed Declaration on Measures to Eliminate International Terrorism as well as Resolution 51/210 of the General Assembly of 17 December 1996 and the Declaration to Supplement the 1994 Declaration on Measures to Eliminate International Terrorism, annexed thereto;

Deeply concerned over the scope and seriousness of the phenomenon of terrorism and the dangers it poses to the stability and security of States;

Desirous of strengthening cooperation among Member States in order to forestall and combat terrorism;

Reaffirming the legitimate right of peoples for self-determination and independence pursuant to the principles of international law and the provisions of the Charters of the Organization of African Unity and the United Nations as well as the African Charter on Human and Peoples's Rights;

Concerned that the lives of innocent women and children are most adversely affected by terrorism;

Convinced that terrorism constitutes a serious violation of human rights and, in particular, the rights to physical integrity, life, freedom and security, and impedes socio-economic development through destabilization of States;

Convinced further that terrorism cannot be justified under any circumstances and, consequently, should be combated in all its forms and manifestations, including those in which States are involved directly or indirectly, without regard to its origin, causes and objectives;

Aware of the growing links between terrorism and organized crime, including the illicit traffic of arms, drugs and money laundering;

Determined to eliminate terrorism in all its forms and manifestations;

Have agreed as follows:

PART I
SCOPE OF APPLICATION

Article 1
For the purposes of this Convention:
1. '*Convention*' means the OAU Convention on the Prevention and Combating of Terrorism.
2. '*State Party*' means any Member State of the Organization of African Unity which has ratified or acceded to this Convention and has deposited its instrument of ratification or accession with the Secretary General of the Organization of African Unity.
3. '*Terrorist act*' means:
    (a) any act which is a violation of the criminal law of a State Party and which may endanger the life, physical integrity or freedom of, or cause serious injury or death to, any person, any number or group of persons or causes or may cause damage to public or private property, natural resources, environmental or cultural heritage and is calculated or intended to:

    (i)   intimidate, put in fear, force, coerce or induce any government, body, institution, the general public or any segment thereof, to do or abstain from doing any act, or to adopt or abandon a particular standpoint, or to act I according to certain principles; or

    (ii) (ii) disrupt any public service, the delivery of any essential service to the public or to create a public emergency; or

    (iii) create general insurrection in a State;

  (b) any promotion, sponsoring, contribution to, command, aid, incitement, encouragement, attempt, threat, conspiracy, organizing, or procurement of any person, with the intent to commit any act referred to in paragraph (a) (i) to (iii).

Article 2

States Parties undertake to:

  (a) review their national laws and establish criminal offences for terrorist acts as defined in this Convention and make such acts punishable by appropriate penalties that take into account the grave nature of such offences;

  (b) consider, as a matter of priority, the signing or ratification of, or accession to, the international instruments listed in the Annexure, which they have not yet signed, ratified or acceded to; and

  (c) implement the actions, including enactment of legislation and the establishment as criminal offences of certain acts as required in terms of the international instruments referred to in paragraph (b) and that States have ratified and acceded to and make such acts punishable by appropriate penalties which take into account the grave nature of those offences;

  (d) notify the Secretary General of the OAU of all the legislative measures it has taken and the penalties imposed on terrorist acts within one year of its ratification of, or accession to, the Convention.

Article 3

1. Notwithstanding the provisions of Article 1, the struggle waged by peoples in accordance with the principles of international law for their liberation or self-determination, including armed struggle against colonialism, occupation, aggression and domination by foreign forces shall not be considered as terrorist acts.

2. Political, philosophical, ideological, racial, ethnic, religious or other motives shall not be a justifiable defence against a terrorist act.

PART II
AREAS OF COOPERATION

Article 4

1. States Parties undertake to refrain from any acts aimed at organizing, supporting, financing, committing or inciting to commit terrorist acts, or providing havens for terrorists, directly or indirectly, including the provision of weapons and their stockpiling in their countries and the issuing of visas and travel documents.

2. States Parties shall adopt any legitimate measures aimed at preventing and combating terrorist acts in accordance with the provisions of this Convention and their respective national legislation, in particular, they shall do the following:

  (a) prevent their territories from being used as a base for the planning, organization or execution of terrorist acts or for the participation or collaboration in these acts in any form whatsoever;

(b)   develop and strengthen methods of monitoring and detecting plans or activities aimed at the illegal cross-border transportation, importation, export, stockpiling and use of arms, ammunition and explosives and other materials and means of committing terrorist acts;

(c)   develop and strengthen methods of controlling and monitoring land, sea and air borders and customs and immigration check- points in order to pre-empt any infiltration by individuals or groups involved in the planning, organization and execution of terrorist acts;

(d)   strengthen the protection and security of persons, diplomatic and consular missions, premises of regional and international organizations accredited to a State Party, in accordance with the relevant conventions and rules of international law;

(e)   promote the exchange of information and expertise on terrorist acts and establish data bases for the collection and analysis of information and data on terrorist elements, groups, movements and organizations;

(f)   take all necessary measures to prevent the establishment of terrorist support networks in any form whatsoever;

(g)   ascertain, when granting asylum, that the asylum seeker is not involved in any terrorist act;

(h)   arrest the perpetrators of terrorist acts and try them in accordance with national legislation, or extradite them in accordance with the provisions of this Convention or extradition treaties concluded between the requesting State and the requested State and, in the absence of a treaty, consider facilitating the extradition of persons suspected of having committed terrorist acts; and

(i)   establish effective cooperation between relevant domestic security officials and services and the citizens of the States Parties in a bid to enhance public awareness of the scourge of terrorist acts and the need to combat such acts, by providing guarantees and incentives that will encourage the population to give information on terrorist acts or other acts which may help to uncover such acts and arrest their perpetrators.

Article 5

States Parties shall cooperate among themselves in preventing and combating terrorist acts in conformity with national legislation and procedures of each State in the following areas:

1. States Parties undertake to strengthen the exchange of information among them regarding:

(a)   acts and crimes committed by terrorist groups, their leaders and elements, their headquarters and training camps, their means and sources of funding and acquisition of arms, the types of arms, ammunition and explosives used, and other means in their

(b)   possession;

(c)   the communication and propaganda methods and techniques used by the terrorists groups, the behaviour of these groups, the movement of their leaders and elements, as well as their travel documents.

2. States Parties undertake to exchange any information that leads to:

(a)   the arrest of any person charged with a terrorist act against the interests of a State Party or against its nationals, or attempted tocommit such an act or participated in it as an accomplice or an instigator;

(b)   the seizure and confiscation of any type of arms, ammunition, explosives, devices or funds or other instrumentalities of crime used to commit a terrorist act or intended for that purpose.

3. States Parties undertake to respect the confidentiality of the information exchanged among them and not to provide such information to another State that is not party to this Convention, or to a third State Party, without the prior consent of the State from where such information originated.

4. States Parties undertake to promote cooperation among themselves and to help each other with regard to procedures relating to the investigation and arrest of persons suspected of, charged with or convicted of terrorist acts, in conformity with the national law of each State.

5. States Parties shall cooperate among themselves in conducting and exchanging studies and researches on how to combat terrorist acts and to exchange expertise relating to control of terrorist acts.

6. States Parties shall cooperate among themselves, where possible, in providing any available technical assistance in drawing up programmes or organizing, where necessary and for the benefit of their personnel, joint training courses involving one or several States Parties in the area of control of terrorist acts, in order to improve their scientific, technical and operational capacities to prevent and combat such acts.

PART III
STATE JURISDICTION

Article 6

1. Each State Party has jurisdiction over terrorist acts as defined in Article 1 when:
   (a) the act is committed in the territory of that State and the perpetrator of the act is arrested in its territory or outside it if this is punishable by its national law;
   (b) the act is committed on board a vessel or a ship flying the flag of that State or an aircraft which is registered under the laws of that State at the time the offence is committed; or
   (c) the act is committed by a national or a group of nationals of that State.

2. A State Party may also establish its jurisdiction over any such offence when:
   (a) the act is committed against a national of that State; or
   (b) the act is committed against a State or government facility of that State abroad, including an embassy or other diplomatic or consular premises, and any other property, of that State; or
   (c) the act is committed by a stateless person who has his or her habitual residence in the territory of that State; or
   (d) the act is committed on board an aircraft which is operated by any carrier of that State; and
   (e) the act is committed against the security of the State Party.

3. Upon ratifying or acceding to this Convention, each State Party shall notify the Secretary General of the Organization of African Unity of the jurisdiction it has established in accordance with paragraph 2 under its national law. Should any change take place, the State Party concerned shall immediately notify the Secretary General.

4. Each State Party shall likewise take such measures as may be necessary to establish its jurisdiction over the acts set forth in Article 1 in cases where the alleged offender is present in its territory and it does not extradite that person to any of the States Parties which have established their jurisdiction in accordance with paragraphs 1 or 2.

Article 7

1. Upon receiving information that a person who has committed or who is alleged to have committed any terrorist act as defined in Article 1 may be present in its territory, the State

Party concerned shall take such measures as may be necessary under its national law to investigate the facts contained in the information.

2. Upon being satisfied that the circumstances so warrant, the State Party in whose territory the offender or alleged offender is present shall take the appropriate measures under its national law so as to ensure that person's presence for the purpose of prosecution.

3. Any person against whom the measures referred to in paragraph 2 are being taken shall be entitled to:

    (a) communicate without delay with die nearest appropriate representative of the State of which that person is a national or which is otherwise entitled to protect that person's rights or, if that person is a stateless person, the State in whose territory that person habitually resides;

    (b) be visited by a representative of that State;

    (c) be assisted by a lawyer of his or her choice;

    (d) be informed of his or her rights under sub-paragraphs (a), (b) and (c).

4. The rights referred to in paragraph 3 shall be exercised in conformity with the national law of the State in whose territory the offender or alleged offender is present, subject to the provision that the said laws must enable full effect to be given to the purposes for which the rights accorded under paragraph 3 are intended.

PART IV
EXTRADITION

Article 8

1. Subject to the provisions of paragraphs 2 and 3 of this Article, the States Parties shall undertake to extradite any person charged with or convicted of any terrorist act carried out on the territory of another State Party and whose extradition is requested by one of the States Parties in conformity with the rules and conditions provided for in this Convention or under extradition agreements between the States Parties and within the limits of their national laws.

2. Any State Party may, at the time of the deposit of its instrument of ratification or accession, transmit to the Secretary General of the OAU the grounds on which extradition may not be granted and shall at the same time indicate the legal basis in its national legislation or international conventions to which it is a party which excludes such extradition. The Secretary General shall forward these grounds to the States Parties.

3. Extradition shall not be granted if final judgement has been passed by a competent authority of the requested State upon the person in respect of the terrorist act or acts for which extradition is requested. Extradition may also be refused if the competent authority of the requested State has decided either not to institute or terminate proceedings in respect of the same act or acts.

4. A State Party in whose territory an alleged offender is present shall be obliged, whether or not the offence was committed in its territory, to submit the case without undue delay to its competent authorities for the purpose of prosecution if it does not extradite that person.

Article 9

Each State Party undertakes to include as an extraditable offence any terrorist act as defined in Article 1, in any extradition treaty existing between any of the States Parties before or after the entry into force of this Convention.

Article 10
Exchange of extradition requests between the States Parties to this Convention shall be effected directly either through diplomatic channels or other appropriate organs in the concerned States.

Article 11
Extradition requests shall be in writing, and shall be accompanied in particular by the following:

(a)   an original or authenticated copy of the sentence, warrant of arrest or any order or other judicial decision made, in accordance with the procedures laid down in the laws of the requesting State;

(b)   a statement describing the offences for which extradition is being requested, indicating the date and place of its commission, the offence committed, any convictions made and a copy of the provisions of the applicable law; and

(c)   as comprehensive a description as possible of the wanted person together with any other information which may assist in establishing the person's identity and nationality.

Article 12
In urgent cases, the competent authority of the State making the extradition may, in writing, request that the State seized of the extradition request arrest the person in question provisionally. Such provisional arrest shall be for a reasonable period in accordance with the national law of the requested State.

Article 13
1. Where a State Party receives several extradition requests from different States Parties in respect of the same suspect and for the same or different terrorist acts, it shall decide on these requests having regard to all the prevailing circumstances, particularly the possibility of subsequent extradition, the respective dates of receipt of the requests, and the degree of seriousness of the crime.

2. Upon agreeing to extradite, States Parties shall seize and transmit all funds and related materials purportedly used in the commission of the terrorist act to the requesting State as well as relevant incriminating evidence.

3. Such funds, incriminating evidence and related materials, upon confirmation of their use in the terrorist act by the requested State, shall be transmitted to the requesting State even if, for reasons of death or escape of the accused, the extradition in question cannot take place.

4. The provisions in paragraphs 1,2 and 3 of this Article shall not affect the rights of any of the States Parties or bona fide third parties regarding the materials or revenues mentioned above.

PART V
EXTRA-TERRITORIAL INVESTIGATIONS (COMMISSION ROGATOIRE) AND
MUTUAL LEGAL ASSISTANCE

Article 14
1. Any State Party may, while recognizing the sovereign rights of States Parties in matters of criminal investigation, request any other State Party to carry out, with its assistance and cooperation, on the latter's territory, criminal investigations related to any judicial proceedings concerning alleged terrorist acts and, in particular:

(a)   the examination of witnesses and transcripts of statements made as evidence;

   (b) the opening of judicial information;

   (c) the initiation of investigation processes;

   (d) the collection of documents and recordings or, in their absence, authenticated copies thereof;

   (e) conducting inspections and tracing of assets for evidentiary purposes;

   (f) executing searches and seizures; and

   (g) service of judicial documents.

Article 15

A commission rogatoire may be refused:

   (a) where each of the States Parties has to execute a commission rogatoire relating to the same terrorist acts;

   (b) if that request may affect efforts to expose crimes, impede investigations or the indictment of the accused in the country requesting the commission rogatoire; or

   (c) if the execution of the request would affect the sovereignty of the requested State, its security or public order.

Article 16

The extra-territorial investigation (commission rogatoire) shall be executed in compliance with the provisions of national laws of the requested State. The request for an extra-territorial investigation (commission rogatoire) relating to a terrorist act shall not be rejected on the grounds of the principle of confidentiality of bank operations or financial institutions, where applicable.

Article 17

The States Parties shall extend to each other the best possible mutual police and judicial assistance for any investigation, criminal prosecution or extradition proceedings relating to the terrorist acts as set forth in this Convention.

Article 18

The States Parties undertake to develop, if necessary, especially by concluding bilateral and multilateral agreements and arrangements, mutual legal assistance procedures aimed at facilitating and speeding up investigations and collecting evidence, as well as cooperation between law enforcement agencies in order to detect and prevent terrorist acts.

PART VI
FINAL PROVISIONS

Article 19

1. This Convention shall be open to signature, ratification or accession by the Member States of the Organization of African Unity.

2. The instruments of ratification or accession to the present Convention shall be deposited with the Secretary General of the Organization of African Unity.

3. The Secretary General of the Organization of African Unity shall inform Member States of the Organization of the deposit of each instrument of ratification or accession.

4. No State Party may enter a reservation which is incompatible with the object and purposes of this Convention.

5. No State Party may withdraw from this Convention except on the basis of a written request addressed to the Secretary General of the Organization of African Unity. The withdrawal

shall take effect six months after the date of receipt of the written request by the Secretary General of the Organization of African Unity.

Article 20

1. This Convention shall enter into force thirty days after the deposit of the fifteenth instrument of ratification with the Secretary General of the Organization of African Unity.

2. For each of the States that shall ratify or accede to this Convention shall enter into force thirty days after the date of the deposit by that State Party of its instrument of ratification or accession.

Article 21

1. Special protocols or agreements may, if necessary, supplement the provisions of this Convention.

2. This Convention may be amended if a State Party makes a written request to that effect to the Secretary General of the Organization of African Unity. The Assembly of Heads of State and Government may only consider the proposed amendment after all the States Parties have been duly informed of it at least three months in advance.

3. The amendment shall be approved by a simple majority of the States Parties. It shall come into force for each State which has accepted it in accordance with its constitutional procedures three months after the Secretary General has received notice of the acceptance.

Article 22

1. Nothing in this Convention shall be interpreted as derogating from the general principles of international law, in particular the principles of international humanitarian law, as well as the African Charter on Human and Peoples' Rights.

2. Any dispute that may arise between the States Parties regarding the interpretation or application of this Convention shall be amicably settled by direct agreement between them. Failing such settlement, anyone of the States Parties may refer the dispute to the International Court of Justice in conformity with the Statute of the Court or by arbitration by other States Parties to this Convention.

Article 23

The original of this Convention, of which the Arabic, English, French and Portuguese texts are equally authentic, shall be deposited with the Secretary General of the Organization of African Unity.

ANNEX LIST OF INTERNATIONAL INSTRUMENTS

(a) Tokyo Convention on Offences and Certain Other Acts Committed on Board Aircraft of 1963;

(b) Montreal Convention for the Suppression of Unlawful Acts against the Safety of Civil Aviation of 1971 and the Protocol thereto of 1984;

(c) New York Convention on the Prevention and Punishment of Crimes against Internationally Protected Persons, including Diplomatic Agents of 1973; :

(d) International Convention against the Taking of Hostages of 1979;

(e) Convention on the Physical Protection of Nuclear Material of 1979;

(f) United Nations Convention on the Law of the Sea 1982;

(g) Protocol for the Suppression of Unlawful Acts of Violence at Airports Serving International Civil Aviation, supplementary to the Convention for the Suppression of Unlawful Acts against the Safety of Civil Aviation of 1988;

(h) Protocol for the Suppression of Unlawful Acts against the Safety of Fixed Platforms lo-
     cated on the Continental Shelf of 1988;
(i) Convention for the Suppression of Unlawful Acts against I Maritime Navigation of
     1988;
(j) Convention on the Marking of Plastic Explosives of 1991;
(k) International Convention for the Suppression of Terrorist Explosive Bombs of 1997;
(l) Convention on the Prohibition of the Use, Stockpiling, Production and Transfer of Anti-
     Personnel Mines and on their Destruction of 1997.

TC3F
SAARC Regional Convention on Suppression of Terrorism, signed at Kathmandu on 4 No-
vember 1987

The Member States of ohe South Asian Association Ffr Regional Cooperation (SAARC)

Mindful of the principles of cooperation enshrined in the SAARC Charter;
Recalling that at the Dhaka Summit on December 7-8, 1985, the Heads of State or Government of the Member States of the SAARC recognised the seriousness of the problem of terrorism as it affects the security and stability of the region;
Also Recalling the Bangalore Summit Declaration of 17 November 1986, in which the Heads
of State or Government of SAARC agreed that cooperation among SAARC States was vital
if terrorism was to be prevented and eliminated from the region; unequivocally condemned
all acts, methods and practices of terrorism as criminal and deplored their impact on life and
property, socio-economic development, political stability, regional and international peace
and cooperation; and recognised the importance of the principles laid down in UN Resolution
2625 (XXV) which among others required that each state should refrain from organising instigating, assisting or participating in acts of civil strife or terrorist acts in another state or
acquiesing in organised activities within its territory directed towards the commission of such
acts;
Aware of the danger posed by the spread of terrorism and its harmful effect on peace, cooperation, friendship and good neighbourly relations and which could also jeopardise the sovereignty and territorial integrity of states;
Have Resolved to take effective measures to ensure that perpetrators of terroristic acts do not
escape prosecution and punishment by providing for their extradition or prosecution, and to
this end,
Have Agreed as follows:

Article I
Subject to the overall requirements of the law of extradition, conduct constituting any of the
following offences, according to the law of the Contracting State, shall be regarded as terroristic and for the purpose of extradition shall not be regarded as a political offence or as an
offence connected with a political offence or as an offence inspired by political motives:
    (a) An offence within the scope of the Convention for the Suppression of Unlawful
         Seizure of Aircraft, signed at the Hague on December 16, 1970;
    (b) An offence within the scope of the Convention for the Suppression of Unlawful
         Acts against the Safety of Civil Aviation, signed at Montreal on September 23,
         1971;

(c) An offence within the scope of the Convention on the Prevention and Punishment of Crimes against Internationally Protected Persons, including Diplomatic Agents, signed at New York on December 14, 1973;

(d) An offence within the scope of any Convention to which the SAARC Member States concerned are parties and which obliges the parties to prosecute or grant extradition;

(e) Murder, manslaughter, assault causing bodily harm, kidnapping, hostage-taking and offences relating to firearms, weapons, explosives and dangerous substances when used as a means to perpetrate indiscriminate violence involving death or serious bodily injury to persons or serious damage to property;

(f) An attempt or conspiracy to commit an offence described in sub-paragraphs (a) to (e), aiding, abetting or counselling the commission of such an offence or participating as an accomplice in the offences so described.

Article II

For the purpose of extradition between SAARC Member States, any two or more Contracting States may, by agreement, decide to include any other serious offence involving violence, which shall not be regarded as a political offence or an offence connected with a political offence or an offence inspired by political motives.

Article III

1. The provisions of all extradition treaties and arrangements applicable between Contracting States are hereby amended as between Contracting States to the extent that they are incompatible with the Convention.

2. For the purpose of this Convention and to the extent that any offence referred to in Article I or agreed to in terms of Article II is not listed as an extraditable offence in any extradition treaty existing between Contracting States, it shall be deemed to be included as such therein.

3. Contracting States undertake to include these offences as extraditable offences in any future extradition treaty to be concluded between them.

4. If a Contracting State which makes extradition conditional on the existence of a treaty receives a request for extradition from another Contracting State with which it has no extradition treaty, the requested State may, at its option, consider this Convention as the basis for extradition in respect of the offences set forth in Article I or agreed to in terms of Article II. Extradition shall be subject to the law of the requested State.

5. Contracting States which do not make extradition conditional on the existence of a treaty, shall recognise the offences set forth in Article I or agreed to in terms of Article II as extraditable offences between themselves, subject to the law of the requested State.

Article IV

A Contracting State in whose territory a person suspected of having committed an offence referred to in Article I or agreed to in terms of Article II is found and which has received a request for extradition from another Contracting State, shall, if it does not extradite that person, submit the case without exception and without delay, to its competent authorities, so that prosecution may be considered. These authorities shall take their decisions in the same manner as in the case of any offence of a serious under the law of that State.

Article V

For the purpose of Article IV, each Contracting State may take such measures as it deems appropriate, consistent with its national laws, subject to reciprocity, to exercise its jurisdiction in the case of an offence under Article I or agreed to in terms of Article II.

Article VI

A Contracting State in whose territory an alleged offender is found, shall upon receiving a request for extradition from another Contracting State, take appropriate measures, subject to its national laws, so as to ensure his presence for purposes of extradition or prosecution. Such measures shall immediately be notified to the requesting State.

Article VII

Contracting States shall not be obliged to extradite, if it appears to the requested State that by reason of the trivial nature of the case or by reason of the request for the surrender or return of a fugitive offender not being made in good faith or in the interests of justice or for any other reason it is unjust or inexpedient to surrender or return the fugitive offender.

Article VIII

1. Contracting States shall, subject to their national laws, afford one another the greatest measure of mutual assistance in connection with proceedings brought in respect of the offences referred to in Article I or agreed to in terms of Article II, including the supply of all evidence at their disposal necessary for the proceedings.

2. Contracting States shall cooperate among themselves, to the extent permitted by their national laws, through consultations between appropriate agencies, exchange of information, intelligence and expertise and such other cooperative measures as may be appropriate, with a view to preventing terroristic activities through precautionary measures.

Article IX

1. The Convention shall be open for signature by the Member States of SAARC at the SAARC Secretariat in Kathmandu.

2. It shall be subject to ratification. Instruments of Ratification shall be deposited with the Secretary-General of SAARC.

Article X

The Convention shall enter into force on the fifteenth day following the date of the deposit of the seventh Instrument of Ratification with the Secretary-General of SAARC.

Article XI

The Secretary-General of SAARC shall be depository of this Convention and shall notify Member States of signatures to this Convention and all deposits of Instruments of Ratification. The Secretary-General shall transit certified copies of such Instruments to each Member State. The Secretary-General shall also inform Member States of the date on which this Convention will have entered into force in accordance with Article X.

In witness whereof the undersigned, being duly authorised thereto by their respective Governments, have signed this Convention.

(...)

TC3G
Treaty on Cooperation among the States Members of the Commonwealth of Independent States in Combating Terrorism, done at Minsk on 4 June 1999[5]

The States Parties to this Treaty, in the person of their Governments, hereinafter referred to as Parties,
Aware of the danger posed by acts of terrorism,
Bearing in mind the instruments adopted within the United Nations and the Commonwealth of the Independent States, as well as other international instruments, relating to combating the various manifestations of terrorism,
Wishing to render one another the broadest possible assistance in increasing the effectiveness of cooperation in this field,
Have agreed as follows:

Article 1
For purposes of this Treaty, the terms used in it mean:
'Terrorism' – an illegal act punishable under criminal law committed for the purpose of undermining public safety, influencing decision making by the authorities or terrorizing the population, and taking the form of:
- Violence or threat of violence against natural or juridical persons;
- Destroying (damaging) or threatening to destroy (damage) property and other material objects so as to endanger people's lives;
- Causing substantial harm to property or the occurrence of other consequences dangerous to society;
- Threatening the life of a statesman or public figure for the purpose of putting an end to his State or other public activity or in revenge for such activity;
- Attacking a representative of a foreign State or an internationally protected staff member of an international organization, as well as the business premises or vehicles of internationally protected persons;
- Other acts classified as terrorist under the national legislation of the Parties or under universally recognized international legal instruments aimed at combating terrorism;

'Technological terrorism' – the use or threat of the use of nuclear, radiological, chemical or bacteriological (biological) weapons or their components, pathogenic micro-organisms, radioactive substances or other substances harmful to human health, including the seizure, putting out of operation or destruction of nuclear, chemical or other facilities posing an increased technological and environmental danger and the utility systems of towns and other inhabited localities, if these acts are committed for the purpose of undermining public safety, terrorizing the population or influencing the decisions of the authorities in order to achieve political, mercenary or any other ends, as well as attempts to commit one of the crimes listed above for the same purposes and leading, financing or acting as the instigator, accessory or accomplice of a person who commits or attempts to commit such a crime;
'Facilities posing an increased technological and environmental danger' – enterprises, installations, plant and other facilities whose inoperability may lead to loss of human life, the impairment of human health, pollution of the environment or destabilization of the situation in a given region or a given State as a whole;
'Special anti-terrorist units' – groups of specialists formed by the Parties in accordance with their national legislation to combat acts of terrorism;

---

[5] Entry into force in accordance with Article 22

'Special items and supplies' – materials, machinery and vehicles, personal equipment for members of special anti-terrorist units including weapons and ammunition, and special items and equipment.

Article 2
The parties shall cooperate in preventing, uncovering, halting and investigating acts of terrorism in accordance with this Treaty, their national legislation and their international obligations.

Article 3
1. Each of the Parties shall, on signing this Treaty or carrying out the domestic procedures required for its entry into force, indicate its competent authorities responsible for implementing the provisions of this Treaty.
The Parties shall immediately notify the depositary of any changes with regard to their competent authority.
2. In implementing the provisions of this Treaty, the competent authorities of the Parties shall maintain direct relations with one another.

Article 4
1. In cooperating in combating acts of terrorism, including in relation to the extradition of persons committing them, the Parties shall not regard the acts involved other than criminal.
2. The nationality of a person accused of an act of terrorism shall be deemed to be his nationality at the time of commission of the act.

Article 5
1. The competent authorities of the Party shall, in accordance with this Treaty, other international agreements and national legislation, cooperate and assist one another by:
   (a) Exchanging information;
   (b) Responding to enquiries regarding the conduct of investigations;
   (c) Developing and adopting agreed measures for preventing, uncovering, halting or investigating acts of terrorism, and informing one another about such measures;
   (d) Adopting measures to prevent and halt preparations in their territory for the commission of acts of terrorism in the territory of another Party;
   (e) Assisting in assessing the condition of the system for physical protection of facilities posing an increased technological and environmental danger, and developing and implementing measures to improve that system;
   (f) Exchanging legislative texts and materials on the practice with respect to their application;
   (g) Sending, by agreement between interested Parties, special anti-terrorist units to render practical assistance in halting acts of terrorism and combating their consequences;
   (h) Exchanging experience on the prevention and combating of terrorist acts, including the holding of training courses, seminars, consultations and workshops;
   (i) Training and further specialized training of personnel;
   (j) Joint financing, by agreement between Parties, and conduct of research and development work on systems for and means of physically protecting facilities posing an increased technological and environmental danger;
   (k) Implementation on a contractual basis of deliveries of special items, technology and equipment for anti-terrorist activity.

2. The procedure for sending and executing requests for extradition, for the provision of legal aid in criminal cases and for the institution of criminal proceedings shall be determined by the international agreements to which the Parties concerned are parties.

Article 6

The Parties shall, through consultations, jointly draw up recommendations for achieving concerted approaches to the legal regulation of issues relating to the prevention and combating of terrorist acts.

Article 7

1. Cooperation under this Treaty shall be conducted on the basis of requests by an interested Party for assistance to be rendered, or on the initiative of a Party which believes such assistance to be of interest to another Party.

2. The request for the rendering of assistance shall be made in writing. In urgent cases requests may be transmitted orally, but must be confirmed in writing not later than 72 hours thereafter, including through the use of technical text transmission facilities.

If doubt arises as to the genuineness or content of a request, additional confirmation may be requested.

Requests shall contain:

  (a) The name of the competent authority requesting assistance and of the authority requested; a statement of the substance of the matter; the purpose of and justification for the request; and a description of the nature of the assistance requested;

  (b) Any other information that may be useful for the proper fulfilment of the request.

3. A request for the rendering of assistance transmitted or confirmed in writing shall be signed by the head of the requesting competent authority or his deputy and shall be certified by the seal of the competent authority.

Article 8

1. The requested Party shall take all necessary measures to ensure the prompt and fullest possible fulfilment of the request.

The requesting Party shall be immediately notified of circumstances that prevent or will substantially delay the fulfilment of the request.

2. If the fulfilment of the request does not fall within the competence of the requested competent authority, it shall transmit the request to an authority of its State which is competent to fulfil it, and shall imediately so inform the requesting competent authority.

3. The requested Party shall be entitled to request additional information that is in its view needed for the proper fullfilment of the request.

4. In fulfilling a request, the legislation of the requested Party shall be applied; however, at the request of the requesting Party, its legislation may be applied if that does not contradict fundamental principles of the legislation of the requested Party or its international obligations.

5. If the requested Party considers that immediate fulfilment of the request may impede a criminal prosecution or other proceedings taking place on its territory, it may postpone fulfilment of the request or tie its fulfilment to compliance with conditions determined to be necessary following consultations with the requesting Party. If the requesting Party agrees that assistance shall be rendered to it on the proposed terms, it shall comply with those terms.

6. The requested Party shall, at the request of the requesting Party, take the necessary measures to ensure confidentiality of the fact that the request has been received, the content of the request and accompanying documents, and the rendering of assistance.

If it is impossible to fulfil the request without maintaining confidentiality, the requested Party shall so inform the requesting Party, which shall decide whether the request should be fulfilled under those conditions.

7. The requested Party shall inform the requesting Party as soon as possible about the results of the fulfilment of the request.

Article 9

1. The rendering of assistance under this Treaty shall be denied in whole part or in part if the requested Party believes that fulfillment of the request may impair its sovereignity, security, social order or other vital interests or it is in contravention of its legislation or international obligations.

2. The rendering of assistance may be defined if the act in relation to which the request was made is not a crime under the legislation of the requested Party.

3. The requesting Party shall be notified in writing of a refusal to fulfil a request in whole or in part, with an indication of the reasons for refusal listed in paragraph 1 of this Article.

Article 10

1. Each Party shall ensure confidentiality of information and documents received from another Party if they are classified as restricted or the transmitting Party considers it undesirable that they should be made public. The level of security classification of such information and documents shall be determined by the transmitting Party.

2. Results of the fulfillment of a request obtained on the basis of this Treaty may not, without the consent of the Party providing them, be used for purposes other than those for which they were requested and provided.

3. Transmission to a third party of information obtained by one Party on the basis of this Treaty shall require the prior consent of the Party providing information.

Article 11

The competent authorities of the Parties shall exchange information on issues of mutual interest, including:

(a) Materials distributed in the territory of their States containing information on terrorist threats, terrorist acts in the course of preparation or committed and the identified intentions of given persons, groups of persons or organizations to commit acts of terrorism;

(b) Acts of terrorism in the course of preparation that are directed against the heads of State, internationally protected persons, staff of diplomatic missions, consular institutions and international organizations of the Parties and participants in State visits and international and national political, sporting and other activities;

(c) Instances of illegal circulation of nuclear materials, chemical, bacteriological (biological) weapons or their components, highly toxic chemicals and pathogenic micro-organisms;

(d) Terrorist organizations, groups and individuals that present a threat to the State security of the Parties and the establishment of contacts between terrorist organizations, groups or individuals;

(e) Illegal armed formations employing methods of terrorist activity, their structure, members, aims and objectives;

(f) Ways, means and methods of terrorist action they have identified;

(g) Supplies and equipment that may be provided by the Parties to one another to the extent of their ability;

(h) Practice with respect to the legal and other regulatory settlement of issues related to
     the extent of their ability;
(i) Identified and presumed channels for the financing and illegal delivery to the terri-
     tory of their States of weapons and other means of committing terrorist acts;
(j) Terrorist encroachments aimed at violating the sovereignity and territorial integrity
     of Parties;

Other issues of interest to the Parties.

Article 12

1. The Parties may, at the request or with the consent of the Party concerned, send representatives of their competent authorities, including special anti-terrorist units, to provide procedural, advisory or practical aid in accordance with this Treaty.

In such cases, the receiving Party shall notify the other Party in writing of die place and time
of and procedure for crossing its State border and the nature of the problems to be dealt with,
and shall promote and facilitate the necessary conditions for their effective solution, including unimpeded carriage of persons and special items and supplies and cost-free accommodation, food and use of the transport infrastructure of the receiving Party.

Any movement of a special anti-terrorist unit or of individual manbers of such a unit within
the territory of the receiving Party shall be possible only with special permission from and
under the control of the head of the competent authority of the receiving Party.

2. The procedure for the use of air, road, rail, river and maritime transport to provide aid shall
be determined by the competent authorities of the Parties in agreement with the relevant ministries and departments of the receiving Party.

Article 13

1. For purposes of the effective and timely provision of aid, the Parties shall, when special
anti-terrorist units cross the State border, ensure accelerated conduct of the formalities established by national legislation.

2. At the border crossing point, the commanding officer of a special anti-terrorist unit shall
present the nominal role of members of the group and list of special items and supplies certified by the competent authorities of the sending Party, together with an indication of the purposes of the Unit's arrival in the territory of the receiving Party, while all members of the
group shall present their national passports and I documents confirming that they belong to
competent authorities for combating terrorism.

3. Special items and supplies shall be exempt from customs duties and payments and must be
either used during the operation for the provision of aid or removed from the territory of the
receiving Party upon its conclusion.

If special circumstances make it impossible to remove the special items and supplies, the
competent authorities of the sending Party shall hand them over to the competent authorities
of the receiving Party.

Article 14

The decision on the procedure for conducting special measures under this Treaty shall be
taken by the competent authority of the receiving Party, taking into account the views of the
commanding officer of the incoming anti-terrorist unit of the other Party. If these views are
not taken into account, the commanding officer shall be entitled to refuse to participate in the
conduct of the special measure.

Article 15

1. The receiving Party shall refrain from any claims against a Party providing aid, including with regard to compensation for damages arising out of death, bodily injury or any other harm caused to the lives, health and property of natural persons located in the territory of the receiving Party, and also to juridical persons and the receiving Party itself, if such harm was inflicted during the performance of activities associated with the implementation of this Treaty.

2. If a participant in the special anti-terrorist unit of the sending Party inflicts harm on some person or organization while performing activities associated with the implementation of this Treaty in the territory of the receiving Party, the receiving Party shall make compensation for the harm in accordance with the provisions of national legislation which would be applied in the case of harm being inflicted by members of anti-terrorist units of the receiving Party in similar circumstances.

3. The procedure for repayment of expenses incurred by the sending Party, including expenses associated with the loss or complete or partial destruction of imported special items and supplies, shall be established by agreement between the Parties concerned.

4. If one of the Parties considers the damage caused by the actions of the special anti-terrorist unit to be disproportionate to the purposes of the operation, the differences of opinion that arise shall be settled at the bilateral level by the Parties concerned.

Article 16

For purposes of the implementation of this Treaty, the competent authorities of the Parties may where necessary hold consultations and working meetings.

Article 17

The Parties may, by mutual agreement and on the basis of separate agreements, conduct joint exercises of special anti-terrorist units and, on a reciprocal basis, organize training for representatives of another Party in their national anti-terrorist detachments.

Article 18

1. Materials, special items, technology and equipment received by the competent authorities of the Parties pursuant to this Agreement may be transferred to a third party only with the consent of and on the terms specified by the competent authority which provided such materials, special items, technology and equipment.

2. Information on the investigation methods of special anti- terrorist units and on the characteristics of special forces and of items and supplies used in providing aid under this Agreement may not be disclosed.

Article 19

The Parties concerned shall where necessary agree on the financial, organizational and technical and other conditions for the provision of assistance under this Agreement.

Article 20

1. This Treaty shall not limit the right of the Parties to conclude bilateral international agreements on issues which are the subject of this Treaty, and shall not affect the rights and obligations of Parties arising out of other international agreements to which they are parties.

2. The competent authorities of the Parties may conclude with one another agreements that regulate in more detail the procedure for implementation of this Treaty.

Article 21

Disputes arising out of the interpretation or application of this Treaty shall be resolved through consultations and negotiations between the Parties.

Article 22

This Treaty shall enter into force on the date of its signature, and for Parties whose legislation requires the completion of domestic procedures for its entry into force on the date of submission to the depositary of the relevant notification. The Parties shall notify the depositary within three months from the signature of this Treaty of the need to complete such procedures.

Article 23

This Treaty shall remain in force for five years from the date of its entry into force, and shall be automatically extended for further five-year periods unless the Parties adopt another procedure.

Each of the Parties may withdraw from this Treaty by sending written notification thereof to the depositary not less than six months prior to its withdrawal and after settling financial and other obligations that arose during the period for which this Treaty was in force.

The provisions of Article 18 of this Treaty shall continue to be applicable for a Party which withdraws from the Treaty for a further 10 years, and those of Article 10 indefinitely.

Article 24

Following the entry into force of this Treaty, it may with the consent of the Parties be acceded to by other States, including States which are not members of the Commonwealth of Independent States, by means of the transmission to the depositary of instruments of accession. Accession shall be deemed to take effect upon the expiry of 30 days from the date of receipt by the depositary of the latest notification by the Parties of consent to such accession.

Article 25

The depositary shall immediately notify the Parties of an accession to this Treaty or of the completion of domestic procedures required for its entry into force, of the date of entry into force of the Treaty and of the receipt by it of other notifications and documents.

DONE at Minsk on 4 June 1999 in one original in the Russian language. The original shall be kept in the Executive Committee of the Commonwealth of Independent States, which shall send to each State signing this Treaty a true copy thereof.

CHAPTER 6
EUROPE

6.1   INTRODUCTION

Following the September 2001 events, Europe appeared to have been waken up out of its sleep, also because some of the alleged culprits had been actively preparing their heinous crimes from a safe basis in Europe.

The European Commission reacted on September the 19th with two proposals to improve harmonization and cooperation in the fight against terrorism. These proposals should be seen in the context of a wider debate on judicial cooperation. In fact, efforts were already underway to simplify extradition procedures and the mutual recognition of arrest warrants. Indeed, the principle of mutual recognition of judgments had only been established a few years earlier (Tampere, 1999).[1] Against this background, the September 2001 events added momentum to the efforts to ensure greater cooperation in the Union. Yet, whilst studying the following Commission proposals, it should be underlined that under the 2001 EU/EC[2] structure, the Commission proposes, whereas the Council disposes.

> The European Commission is calling for greater harmonisation and closer cooperation in combating terrorism and crime. With the adoption today of two proposals for framework decisions on the fight against terrorism and the European arrest warrant, the Commission is getting down to the business of setting up genuine European cooperation in criminal matters on the basis of automatic mutual recognition between the Member States' judicial authorities.
>
> 'Terrorist acts are committed by international gangs with bases in several countries, exploiting loopholes in the law created by the geographical limits on investigators and often enjoying substantial financial and logistical resources', said António Vitorino, the Commissioner responsible for Justice and Home Affairs. 'Terrorists take advantage of differences in legal treatment between States, in particular where the offence is not treated as such by national law, and that is where we have to begin', he added.
>
> The current situation differs widely from one Member State to another. In most of them,

---

[1] 'Tampere' should be seen in the light of the Treaty of Amsterdam (1997, in force since 1 May 1999) by which major subjects were moved from the TEU to the TEC, from the so-called Third Pillar to the First Pillar, or, in other words from the 'capitals' to 'Brussels', from the Council to the Commission. Justice and Home Affairs was one of the subjects thus moved. A transition period of five years will come to an end on 1 May 2004. The Tampere October 1999 Council Meeting elaborated on the transition.

[2] It should be stressed that there are two treaties, two systems: the TEC, the Treaty of the European Communities, under which the Commission ('Brussels') enjoys significant powers, and the TEU, the Treaty of the European Union, which extends less far, and which leaves the main power with the respective capitals.

there are no specific rules on terrorism and terrorist acts are punished as offences under the ordinary law. Six Member States (Germany, Italy, France, Spain, Portugal and the United Kingdom) have specific legislation on terrorism, in which the words 'terrorism' or 'terrorist' are used explicitly.

Two proposals were adopted at the Commission meeting of the 19th of September:

First, a common definition of acts of terrorism and penalties on a commensurate scale. There is a list of offences treated as acts of terrorism where they are committed intentionally by individuals or groups against one or more countries or their institutions or population in order to threaten them and seriously undermine or even destroy their political, economic or social structures. It is proposed that such acts incur prison sentences ranging from a minimum of 2 years for the less serious offences to a minimum of 20 years for the most serious offences provided for by the proposal.

Second, a proposal to replace the traditional extradition procedures by a system of surrendering persons sought between judicial authorities on the basis of a European arrest warrant. This proposal proceeds from the principle of mutual recognition of judgments established by the Tampere European Council as the cornerstone of judicial cooperation. The underlying idea is that where the judicial authority in one Member State asks for the surrender of a person sought for an offence incurring at least four months' imprisonment, either having been convicted or still being prosecuted, the decision must be recognised and executed throughout the EU. To simplify and accelerate procedures as far as can be, a time-limit of three months is proposed. The principle of double criminal liability and the exception in favour of nationals are abolished. The proposal seeks to facilitate, wherever possible, the execution of the sentence in the country of arrest where that is where the person is most likely to be reintegrated into society.[3]

Two days later, on 21 September 2001, the Council declared at an extraordinary meeting that terrorism is a real challenge to the world and to Europe and that the fight against terrorism will be a priority objective for the European Union.

Remarkably, or so it appeared with hindsight, the European Parliament (the EU Parliament, that is) had adopted during the week preceding the September events a resolution (in fact: a recommendation) on the role of the Union in combating terrorism. Some paragraphs of this document are worth being quoted in full:

(...) E. whereas, over the past few years, the European Union has experienced an increase in terrorist activities within its borders, and there is hardly a country in Europe which has not recently been affected, directly or indirectly, by such acts of violence,

F. whereas these acts show that there has been a profound change in the nature of terrorism in the European Union and highlight the inadequacy of traditional forms of judicial and police cooperation in combating terrorism,

G. whereas this new form of terrorism stems from the activities of networks operating at international level, which are based in several countries and exploit legal loopholes arising from the geographical limits of investigations, sometimes enjoying extensive logistical and financial support,

---

[3] Above, in Chapter 3 on *aut dedere aut judicare* a description has been given of the subsequent developments in this domain.

H. whereas the increase in the number of terrorist acts committed in recent years in the European Union now makes it necessary to step up action to combat terrorism, while respecting the rights and freedoms enshrined in the European Convention on Human Rights and the European Union Charter of Fundamental Rights, (…)

and the EP hence made the following recommendations to the Council:

(1) Calls on the Council to adopt a framework decision with a view to approximating legislative provisions establishing minimum rules at European level relating to the constituent elements of criminal acts and to penalties in the field of terrorism.

(2) Calls on the Council to adopt a framework decision aimed at legislative harmonisation and the establishment of a European common area of freedom, security and justice, abolishing formal extradition procedures and adopting the principle of mutual recognition of decisions on criminal matters, including pre-judgment decisions, relating to terrorist offences, among the Member States of the European Union.

(3) Calls on the Council to adopt a framework decision establishing measures governing and guaranteeing the implementation of a 'European search and arrest warrant' with a view to combating terrorism in the context of action against crime, whether organised or not, trafficking in human beings and crimes against children, illegal trafficking in drugs and arms, and corruption and fraud, taking due account, in the event of more than one offence having been committed, of the gravity of each offence.

(4) Calls on the Council to adopt the appropriate legal instruments for the approximation of national legislation concerning the compensation of victims of terrorist crimes.

It is herewith underlined that these recommendations were very timely indeed.

As we have seen above, the Commission adopted two proposals on the 19th of September, one of which – included in full hereinunder – is the important proposal for a Council framework decision on combating terrorism.[4] On 10 December 2001, the Council of the European Union reached an agreement on a Common Position which provides for the application of specific measures in order to combat terrorism,[5] and in March 2002 the Commission submitted a proposal for a Council regulation on the same issue.

Moreover, as indicated in a Union report to the (SC) Counter-Terrorism Committee, the following activities took place:[6]

–   The Special Recommendations on terrorist financing adopted at the Extraordinary Plenary Meeting of the Financial Action Task Force on Money Laundering on 29-30 October 2001 relate to a number of the issues covered in Operative

---

[4] COM (2001) 521 final; 2001/0217 (CNS).

[5] Such a common position is of course not a binding instrument; it was the basis for many of the measures which are foreseen as the European Union's response to the provisions of UN SC Resolution 1373 (2001).

[6] The activities as listed in this Volume are based on, and more often than not reproduced from document UN S./2001/1297, containing a 27 December 2001 letter from the CTC chair to the chair of the SC, under cover of which was this report, which was sent by Belgium's Permanent Mission on 24 December 2001.

Paragraphs 1 and 2 of 1373. It is intended that these recommendations be at least partly implemented by measures taken within the framework of the Treaty on European Union (EU) and the Treaty establishing the European Community (EC).

– As to freezing accounts and assets at banks and financial institutions, it can be noticed that in the framework of restrictive measures against third States established under Articles 301 and 60 of the Treaty establishing the EC, the Council adopted a Regulation on 6 March 2001 (Council Regulation (EC) 467/2001) providing for the freezing of all funds and other financial resources belonging to any natural or legal person, entity or body designated by the 'Afghanistan Sanctions Committee' (established under SC Resolution 1267 (2001)) and listed in one of the annexes to the Regulation. As provided for under the terms of the Regulation, the European Commission has on four occasions amended the list annexed to the Regulation on the basis of decisions made either by the UN Security Council or the Sanctions Committee, adding new persons and entities to the list. The last three amendments target Osama bin Laden and the Al Qaida network.[7]

– the Council of the European Union, at its meeting on 10 December, reached agreement on a common position and a Regulation which together constitute a legal requirement to freeze and withhold the availability of funds, other financial assets and economic resources, to any previously identified natural or legal person, group or entity figuring in lists annexed to the legislation. It is expected that this legislation will enter into force early in 2002.

– Existing legislation (in the form of a Council Directive (91/308/EEC, adopted in 1991) aims to prevent the use of the financial system for money laundering. Its provisions include an obligation on financial institutions to maintain appropriate records and to establish money-laundering programmes. It also provides for the suspension of banking secrecy when necessary and an obligation to report suspicious transactions to reporting authorities. The 1991 Directive was amended on 19 November 2001. The new directive extends the prohibition of money laundering to most organised and serious crime. It also extends the coverage of the earlier directive to include a number of non-financial activities and professions which are vulnerable to misuse by money launderers. The EU Member States have agreed that all offences linked to the financing of terrorism constitute a serious crime under the directive.

– Measures aimed at prohibiting the supply of weapons to terrorists are covered by a Council Directive (91/477/EEC) of 1991 on the control of the acquisition

---

[7] In March 2002, the Commission submitted a proposal for a Council Regulation on this latter issue: COM (2002) 117 final; 2002/0059 (CNS). This regulation should be read in conjunction with Regulation 2580/2001.

and possession of weapons. This imposes a number of obligations on EU Member States, including the requirement to ensure that those acquiring or possessing firearms are not likely to be a danger to public order or safety. The directive also prohibits the acquisition and possession of certain types of firearms. On 16 October 2001, the Council adopted a decision authorising the signature of the UN Protocol on the illicit manufacturing of and trafficking in firearms, their parts, components and ammunition (annexed to the Convention against transnational organised crime) on behalf of the European Community. This paves the way for implementation of those aspects of the Protocol which are subject to Community competence.

–   The EU Code of Conduct on the exports of military equipment is an important tool in minimising the risk of European armaments being diverted to terrorist organisations. Further security is provided through the Council Regulation (EC) No 1334/2000 of 22 June 2000 governing dual use goods. The European Union has more generally been reconsidering its relations with third countries in the light of the stand taken by those countries in combating terrorism. On 17 October 2001, the Council adopted an objective set of indicators in order to help the EU to evaluate systematically its relations with third countries. The EU is undertaking a review of its relations with third countries in the light of this evaluation.

–   At its meeting on 20 September 2001, the Council agreed on a number of measures to intensify information exchange between EU Member States. These include regular meetings of the heads of Member States' anti-terrorist units, as well as of their intelligence agencies. Cooperation between EU Member States and Europol has also been stepped up, and includes the detachment of anti-terrorist specialists from Member States to work within Europol. The Council decision on 6 December 2001 to make Eurojust fully operational will also facilitate the exchange of operational information.

–   Article 23(1) of the Convention implementing the Schengen Agreement, which forms part of EC law, provides that aliens who do not fulfil or who no longer fulfil the conditions applicable within the territory of a Member State bound by the Schengen Agreement shall normally be required to leave the Schengen Territory immediately. When departure is not voluntary, or if the immediate departure of the alien is necessary for reasons of national security or public order, removal is to be carried out in accordance with the national law of the Member State in which the person was apprehended.

–   Harmonisation of legislation in this area should take place in the context of the Council Directive (2001/40/EC) of 28 May 2001 on the mutual recognition of decisions on the expulsion of third-country nationals, the aim of which is to ensure more effective enforcement of these measures and better cooperation between EU Member States.

– The Schengen Information (computer) System (SIS) offers several possibilities for preventing terrorists from using the territories of the EU Member States. Efforts are being made to improve the use of the SIS. For example: the authorities will encourage the introduction of warnings by default, and national warnings fulfilling the criteria for introduction into the SIS will be introduced as automatically as possible and should not require any additional operation from the initiating authority. In addition, the consultations foreseen about warnings on persons for the purposes of discreet surveillance will be simplified. At Europol, a task force composed of twenty specialists on anti-terrorism was created at short notice after 11 September and is now fully operational. In addition, existing EC legislation regulating data protection provides for flexibility in the exchange of information where this contributes to the fight against terrorism.

– On 6 December 2001, the Council reached political agreement on a Framework Decision on combating terrorism. This legislation includes a common definition of various types of terrorist offences and serious criminal sanctions. The legal text will be adopted shortly, and EU Member States have until the end of 2002 to implement the measures in their own criminal law. Political agreement has also been reached on a framework decision for a European arrest warrant. This is designed to supplant the current procedures of extradition between EU Member States and enable wanted persons to be surrendered to judicial authorities in other EU Member States without verification of the double criminality of the act for a wide range of offences, subject to agreed swift judicial review procedures.

– On 6 December 2001, the Council also reached political agreement on a text setting up the judicial cooperation unit Eurojust. Its objective is to improve and encourage cooperation between the competent national authorities, in particular by facilitating mutual legal assistance and the implementation of extradition requests.

– An Early Warning System was established by Council Resolution of 11 May 1999 for the transmission of information on illegal immigration and facilitator networks. This system is available to both EU Member States and candidate countries, and has been used increasingly since 11 September 2001. A uniform format for visas issued by EU Member States is required by a Council Regulation (EC) No 1683/95 of 29 May 1995. It provides for procedures and specifications to prevent the production and use of counterfeit or false visas.

– The European Union is intensifying its cooperation specifically with the United States in these areas. Following the events of 11 September 2001, the United States submitted to the EU Strategic Committee on Immigration, Frontiers and Asylum, at a joint meeting on 26 October 2001, proposals for cooperation in border control and migration management. These proposals are currently under examination.

–   The Council has taken a number of steps to enhance EU cooperation with third
    countries. High-level contacts have led in particular to a stepping up of law en-
    forcement and judicial cooperation between the EU and US. On 6 December
    2001 an agreement was signed which provides for cooperation and the exchange
    of non-personal information between Europol and the US, and negotiations have
    begun on an agreement on the exchange of personal data. Specific emphasis has
    been given to using the provisions in existing bilateral agreements to step up
    cooperation on counter-terrorism. More generally, the European Commission is
    examining the European Community's external aid programmes, budget lines
    and country strategies to establish what further assistance might be provided
    within the framework of the EC's existing assistance programmes. The EC is
    already providing assistance to a number of third countries in areas such as gov-
    ernance and the reinforcement of judicial and legal systems.

–   All EU Member States have now signed the Convention on the Suppression of
    terrorism financing. The EU has been promoting actively the signature and rati-
    fication by all States of all the UN conventions on terrorism (in particular the
    Convention on the Suppression of terrorism financing), as well as the comple-
    tion of the negotiations on the draft Comprehensive Convention on international
    terrorism. It has in particular taken advantage of all its political dialogue meet-
    ings with third countries, where terrorism now regularly features on the agenda,
    so as to address with those countries the specific issue of the terrorism conven-
    tions.

–   In March 2002, the Secretariat submitted to the EU Member States a draft list of
    concrete measures with regard to the implementation of the terrorist threat on
    the non-proliferation, disarmament and arms control of the EU.[8]

The above instruments also contain references to cross-border activities, illegal migration and such like, as well as the need to deny a safe haven to (would be) terrorists and their supporters. This aspect has been dealt with in the chapter on
Cross-Border Aspects, Chapter 7.

6.2   EUROPEAN PARLIAMENT 5 SEPTEMBER 2001

Sub-chapter 6.3 contains a draft Framework Decision on Combating Terrorism (6.3)
which was agreed upon by the European Commission in late September 2001 and
which was officially presented on 15 October 2001. The draft has been preceded by
an explanatory memorandum with a lengthy introduction and a commentary on each
of the Articles.

    This sub-chapter (6.2) contains the text of a 'resolution' adopted by the European
Parliament on 5 September 2001, which has been included in this Volume to underline the point that the legal pattern and the line of thought was well in place before

---

[8] Council Document 7115/02.

the 11th of September events. The latter events merely emphasized the need not to delay any action. It also shows that the EP recommendations appear to be in line with the Commission proposals. The framework Decision was about to be adopted by mid-2002. It is obviously not possible to include all EU/EC instruments on terrorism in this Volume, as much more has been agreed upon than the eye can see.[9]

---

[9] EU anti-terrorism plans are mostly based on JHA (justice and home affairs) proposals. A fairly complete list is contained in this footnote. Statewatch observatory has probably the most informative and up to date site and is herewith highly recommended. The list below is based on information found on that site and contains all the major justice and home affairs legislative proposals in the EU's action plan on terrorism.

Eurojust

Draft Council Decision setting up Eurojust, 12727/1/01, 19 October 2001

Decision 2000/799/JHA setting up a provisional Judicial Cooperation Unit (Eurojust), 14 December 2000

Legislature text of Decision setting up Eurojust (18 February 2002

Background report on above with Statements to be attached to the Decision (15 February 2002)

European arrest warrant

Proposed Framework Decision on a European Arrest Warrant from the Commission, COM (2001) 522, 19 September 2001

– Council of the EU (the Member States) response to the Commission proposal, 12646/01, 10 October 2001

– Council of the European Union final adopted text (including some corrections)

– Draft text of actual "European arrest warrant", 5327/02

Definition of terrorism

– Proposed Framework Decision on terrorism from the Commission, COM (2001) 521, 19 September 2001 (included in this Volume)

– Council of the EU (the Member States) response to the Commission proposal, 12647/01, 10 October 2001

Rapid information exchange on terrorist attacks [defines 'terrorist incidents'], 10524/5/01, 17 September 2001

Council of the EU draft position on definition of terrorism (14845/01) and later agreed Council position (14845/1/01)

Freezing of assets and evidence

– French, Swedish and Belgian proposal on the execution of orders assets and evidence 5126/01, 2 February 2001

Article 36 Committee report on the proposal on the execution of orders assets and evidence 12636/01, 10 October 2001

Commission proposal for a Council Regulation on specific restrictive measures directed against certain persons and entities with a view to combating international terrorism, COM (2001) 569, 2 October 2001

– Council Regulation (EC) No 467/2001 of 6 March 2001 prohibiting the export of certain goods and services to Afghanistan, strengthening the flight ban and extending the freeze of funds and other financial resources in respect of the Taliban of Afghanistan

– Commission Regulation (EC) No 1996/2001 of 11 October 2001 amending Council Regulation (EC) No 467/2001

Commission Regulation (EC) No 2062/2001 of 19 October 2001 amending Council Regulation (EC) No 467/2001

EU Extradition Conventions

– Convention on simplified ['consented'] extradition procedure between the Member States of the European Union, 10 March 1995 (still to be ratified by Belgium, France, Ireland, Italy & UK)

Convention relating to ['disputed'] extradition between the Member States of the European Union, 27 September 1996 (still to be ratified by France, Ireland, Italy & UK)

EU Mutual Legal Assistance Convention

Convention on Mutual Assistance in Criminal Matters between the Member States of the European

Union, 29 May 2000 (still to be ratified by all EU Member States)

Protocol to EU Mutual Legal Assistance Convention

– Protocol to the Convention on Mutual Assistance in Criminal Matters between the Member States of the European Union, 12234/01, 9 October 2001 (latest draft available to the public; Protocol signed on 16 October 2001)

Immigration and asylum (see also below, the chapter on cross border aspects)

– Immigration and asylum legislation is to be examined by the Commission with reference to 'safeguarding internal security', COM (2001) 743 final, 5 December 2001 (included in the annex to Chapter 7)

Commission communication on common EU policy on illegal immigration, COM (2001) 672 final, 15 November 2001

Joint investigation teams

– Initiative of the Kingdom of Belgium, the French Republic, the Kingdom of Spain and the United Kingdom for the adoption by the Council of a draft Framework Decision on joint investigation teams, 11990/01, 19 September 2001

Belgian, French, Spanish & UK proposed Framework Decision on joint investigation teams, 12442/01, 9 October 2001

Addendum to proposal extending its scope, 11990/01 ADD 1, 16 November 2001

Hacking & computer crime

Commission communication on 'cybercrime', COM (2000) 890, 26 January 2001

Commission proposal for a Framework Decision on 'attacks against information systems', Provisional text, 5. October 2001 (From 'Cryptome')

Background

Council of the European Union

Four Acts adopted by the Council of the European Union by written procedure, 27 December 2001: 1) Common Position on combating terrorism; 2) Common position on the application of specific measures to combat terrorism; 3) Regulation on specific restrictive measures directed against certain persons and entities; 4) Implementing Decision establishing the list provided for in Article 2(3) of the Council Regulation and the UN Security Council: Resolution 1373(2001), dated 28 December 2001

EU Justice and Home Affairs Council

– Conclusions of the Justice & Home Affairs special Council on terrorism, 3926/6/01, 20 September 2001

– 'Anti-terrorism road map' [1] - Justice and Home Affairs Aspects, 4019/01, 26 September 2001

– 'Anti-terrorism road map' [2] - Justice and Home Affairs Aspects, 4019/1/01, 2 October 2001

EU General Affairs Council

– Coordination of the implementation of the plan of action to combat terrorism [1, 12800/01], 16 October 2001

– Coordination of the implementation of the plan of action to combat terrorism [2, 12800/1/01], 17 October 2001

– Coordination of the implementation of the plan of action to combat terrorism [3, 13155/1/01], 24 October 2001

– Coordination of the implementation of the plan of action to combat terrorism [4, 13381/01], 31 October 2001

– Coordination of the implementation of the plan of action to combat terrorism [5, 13880/01], 15 November 2001

– Coordination of the implementation of the plan of action to combat terrorism [6, 14925/01], 7 December 2001

– Coordination of the implementation of the plan of action to combat terrorism [7, 14919/1/01], 13 December 2001

– Coordination of the implementation of the plan of action to combat terrorism [8, 5600/1/2002], 15 February 2002

– Coordination of the implementation of the plan of action to combat terrorism [9, 6811/02], 5 March 2002

European Commission

– Overview of EU action in response to the events of 11 September and assessment of their likely economic impact, COM (2001) 611, 17 October 2001.

However, apart form the framework decision, the Common Position of December 2001 (6.3.3) and the draft regulation of March 2002 (6.3.4) have also been included

European Parliament recommendation on the role of the European Union in combating terrorism[10]

The European Parliament,
– having regard to Article 29 of the Treaty on European Union, which specifically refers to terrorism as one of the serious forms of crime to be prevented and combated at European Union level by developing common action in the fields of police and judicial cooperation in criminal matters and approximating, where necessary, rules on criminal matters in the Member States,
– having regard to Article 31(e) of the Treaty on European Union, which empowers the European Union progressively to adopt measures establishing minimum rules relating to the constituent elements of criminal acts and to penalties in the fields of organised crime, terrorism and illicit drug trafficking,
– having regard to Article 39(3) of the Treaty on European Union, under which the European Parliament may make recommendations to the Council,
– having regard to the Universal Declaration of Human Rights, signed on 10 December 1948, and in particular Articles 1, 2, 3, 5, 7, 12, 13 and 19 thereof,
– having regard to the European Convention on the Protection of Human Rights and Fundamental Freedoms, signed in Rome on 4 November 1950, as amended by Protocol No 11, and in particular Articles 3, 5, 6, 8, 9 and 10 thereof,
– having regard to the European Union Charter of Fundamental Rights, officially proclaimed in Nice on 7 December 2000, and in particular Articles 1, 2, 4, 6, 7, 10, 11 and 19 thereof,
– having regard to the Convention on the prevention and punishment of the crime of genocide, approved by the United Nations General Assembly Resolution 260A of 9 December 1948,
– having regard to the European Convention on extradition, signed in Paris on 13 December 1957,
– having regard to the European Convention on mutual assistance in criminal matters, signed in Strasbourg on 20 April 1959,
– having regard to the European Convention on the international validity of criminal judgments, signed in the Hague on 28 May 1970,
– having regard to the European Convention on the transfer of proceedings in criminal matters, signed in Strasbourg on 15 May 1972,
– having regard to the Principles of international cooperation in the detection, arrest, extradition and punishment of persons guilty of war crimes and crimes against humanity, approved by General Assembly Resolution 3074 of 3 December 1973 (XXVIII), 28 UN GAOR supp. (30A) at 78, UN Doc. A/9030/Add. 1 (1973),

---

[10] 2001/2016(INI), TEXTS ADOPTED (1.) The European Union's role in combating terrorism (A5-0273/2001); the text has been slightly edited; the footnotes have been deleted.

- having regard to the Convention on the prevention and punishment of crimes against internationally protected persons, including diplomatic agents, approved on 14 December 1973,
- having regard to the European Convention on the suppression of terrorism, signed in Strasbourg on 27 January 1977,
- having regard to the International Convention against the taking of hostages, approved by General Assembly Resolution 34/146 of the United Nations on 17 December 1979,
- having regard to the European Convention on the transfer of sentenced persons, signed in Strasbourg on 21 March 1983,
- having regard to Recommendation 982 (1984), approved by the Parliamentary Assembly of the Council of Europe, on the defence of democracy against terrorism in Europe,
- having regard to its resolution of 18 April 1985 on measures to combat terrorism,
- having regard to its resolution of 11 July 1985 on air traffic safety and international terrorism,
- having regard to its resolution of 11 September 1986 on terrorism,
- having regard to its resolution of 10 March 1988 on terrorist acts on civil aviation,
- having regard to its resolution of 26 May 1989 on problems relating to combating terrorism,
- having regard to its resolution of 13 June 1991 on murders committed by terrorists in the Community,
- having regard to the Convention between the Member States of the European Communities on the enforcement of foreign criminal sentences, signed in Brussels on 13 November 1991,
- having regard to Recommendation 1170 (1991) adopted by the Standing Committee, acting on behalf of the Parliamentary Assembly of the Council of Europe, on 25 November 1991, about the European Convention on the suppression of terrorism,
- having regard to its resolution of 10 March 1994 on terrorism and its impact on security in Europe,
- having regard to the measures to eliminate international terrorism, approved by United Nations General Assembly Resolution 49/60 at the 84 th plenary meeting on 9 December 1994,
- having regard to the Council Act of 10 March 1995, drawing up the Convention on simplified extradition procedure between the Member States of the European Union,
- having regard to the Declaration on terrorism issued by the Ministers of the Interior and of Justice at the Informal Council Meeting of 14 October 1995 (La Gomera Declaration),
- having regard to Article 2(1) and (2) of the Convention on the establishment of a European Police Office (Europol Convention),
- having regard to the conclusions of the Madrid European Council meeting of 15/16 December 1995 with regard to measures to combat terrorism, and especially Annex 3 thereof,

– having regard to the public hearing on action to combat terrorism, held on 21 February 1996 by the Committee on Civil Liberties and Internal Affairs,

– having regard to its resolution of 4 July 1996 on the communication from the Commission to the Council and the European Parliament on the illicit traffic in radioactive substances and nuclear materials,

– having regard to the 25 measures to fight terrorism advocated by the seven leading industrialised countries (G7) and Russia on 30 July 1996 in Paris,

– having regard to the Council Act of 27 September 1996 drawing up the Convention relating to extradition between the Member States of the European Union,

– having regard to the Joint Action of 15 October 1996 adopted by the Council on the basis of Article K.3 of the Treaty on European Union concerning the creation and maintenance of a Directory of specialised counter-terrorist competences, skills and expertise to facilitate counter-terrorist cooperation between the Member States of the European Union,

– having regard to its resolution of 30 January 1997 on combating terrorism in the European Union,

– having regard to its resolution of 18 September 1997 on the Convention drawn up on the basis of Article K.3 of the Treaty on European Union, relating to extradition between the Member States of the European Union,

– having regard to the text of the Convention relating to extradition between the Member States of the European Union, approved by the Council on 26 May 1997,

– having regard to the International Convention for the suppression of terrorist bombings, approved by United Nations General Assembly Resolution 52/563 on 15 December 1997,

– having regard to the conclusions of the Cardiff European Council meeting of 15 and 16 June 1998, in particular with regard to mutual recognition of decisions on criminal matters,

– having regard to the Joint Action of 29 June 1998 adopted by the Council on the basis of Article K.3 of the Treaty on European Union on good practice in mutual legal assistance in criminal matters,

– having regard to the Council decision of 3 December 1998 instructing Europol to deal with crimes committed or likely to be committed in the course of terrorist activities against life, limb, personal freedom or property,

– having regard to the Action Plan of the Council and the Commission on how best to implement the provisions of the Treaty of Amsterdam on an area of freedom, security and justice, and in particular paragraphs 46, 47, 49 and 50 thereof, adopted by the Justice and Home Affairs Council of 3 December 1998,

– having regard to the Joint Action of 21 December 1998 adopted by the Council on the basis of Article K.3 of the Treaty on European Union on making it a criminal offence to participate in a criminal organisation in the Member States of the European Union,

– having regard to the conclusions of the Tampere European Council meeting of 15/16 October 1999,

– having regard to the Council recommendation of 9 December 1999 on cooperation in combating the financing of terrorist groups,

–   having regard to the conclusions of the Santa Maria da Feira European Council meeting of 19/20 June 2000, and in particular conclusion 51 thereof with regard to terrorism,
–   having regard to the programme of measures to implement the principle of mutual recognition of judicial decisions in criminal matters,
–   having regard to its resolution of 17 May 2001 on the mutual recognition of final decisions in criminal matters,
–   having regard to Articles 107 and 163 of its Rules of Procedure,
–   having regard to the report of the Committee on Citizens, Freedoms and Rights, Justice and Home Affairs (A5-0273/2001),

A. whereas the Union is founded on the indivisible and universal values of human dignity, freedom, equality and solidarity, respect for human rights and fundamental freedoms; whereas it is based on the principles of democracy and the rule of law, which are common to the Member States,

B. whereas the European Union respects fundamental rights, as guaranteed by the European Convention on the Protection of Human Rights and Fundamental Freedoms, signed in Rome on 4 November 1950, and as they result from the constitutional traditions common to the Member States as general principles of Community law,

C. whereas the European Union Charter of Fundamental Rights reaffirms the rights which result, in particular, from the constitutional traditions and international commitments common to the Member States, the Treaty on European Union and Community Treaties, the European Convention on the Protection of Human Rights and Fundamental Freedoms, the social charters adopted by the Community and the Council of Europe, and the decisions of the Court of Justice of the European Communities and the European Court of Human Rights,

D. whereas the European Union places the human person at the heart of its action by its decision to establish Union citizenship and create an area of freedom, security and justice,

E. whereas, over the past few years, the European Union has experienced an increase in terrorist activities within its borders, and there is hardly a country in Europe which has not recently been affected, directly or indirectly, by such acts of violence,

F. whereas these acts show that there has been a profound change in the nature of terrorism in the European Union and highlight the inadequacy of traditional forms of judicial and police cooperation in combating terrorism,

G. whereas this new form of terrorism stems from the activities of networks operating at international level, which are based in several countries and exploit legal loopholes arising from the geographical limits of investigations, sometimes enjoying extensive logistical and financial support,

H. whereas the increase in the number of terrorist acts committed in recent years in the European Union now makes it necessary to step up action to combat terrorism, while respecting the rights and freedoms enshrined in the European Convention on Human Rights and the European Union Charter of Fundamental Rights,

I. whereas procedural law, especially rules covering pre-trial orders, differs considerably from one Member State to another,

J. rejecting and condemning all acts of terrorism, which often subject the victims and their relatives and friends to unspeakable suffering, by causing them physical injury, disablement, psychological trauma and death and by ruining their lives,

K. expressing its sincere condolences to the families of victims of acts of terrorism and its deepest sympathy to those affected by terrorist attacks, and their families,

L. stressing that the victims of acts of terrorism and their families must be provided with effective material assistance and psychological support,

M. whereas, for the purposes of this recommendation, a terrorist act means any act committed by individuals or groups resorting to violence or threatening to use violence against a country, its institutions, its population in general or specific individuals which, for reasons of separatist aspirations, extremist ideological beliefs, religious fanaticism or desire for profit, is intended to create a climate of terror among official authorities, specific individuals or groups in society or the general public,

N. whereas all ideologies are legitimate provided they are expressed through dialogue and respect for democratic values, and hence terrorism is an expression of intolerance,

O. whereas democratic dialogue based on mutual respect and non-violence, aimed at upholding democracy, is the best means of resolving political, social and environmental conflicts and preventing conflicts from being used as a pretext for committing terrorist acts,

P. pointing out that in our democratic society any political, social or environmental conflict can and must be settled through the channels provided in a democratic and constitutional State, which means that there can be no justification for the use of terrorist violence,

Q. recommending that, as part of their action to prevent terrorism, Member States should pursue educational, social and other policies to combat social, economic and cultural exclusion and to build among young people a commitment to renounce all forms of violence and an understanding of how to use democracy to overcome conflict,

R. calling on the Member States to adopt effective measures to prevent a 'support framework' for terrorists being created and maintained, by prohibiting any form of participation in terrorist acts and preventing logistic, material and financial assistance to terrorist acts,

S. calling on the Member States to adopt effective measures to prevent the formation of, demonstrations by or collaboration between, violent groups in Europe which exploit legitimate social aspirations for their own ends,

T. whereas terrorist acts in the European Union should be considered as criminal acts whose aim is to alter political, economic, social and environmental structures in States governed by the rule of law by actually threatening to use violence or resorting to violence, as distinct from acts of resistance in third countries against state structures which themselves employ terrorist methods,

U. whereas, for the purposes of this recommendation, a terrorist association or organisation means any group composed of two or more people acting in collusion with a view to committing terrorist acts,

V. reiterating its unqualified rejection of terrorist organisations and terrorism in the European Union, which represent a denial of democratic values and the most fundamental of human rights, the right to life and which, as such, must be condemned in all circumstances,

W. whereas new forms of terrorist activity are constantly appearing, such as 'computer terrorism', which consists in destroying or damaging computer systems, including civilian or military databases and telecommunications systems, with a view to destabilising a State or putting pressure on public authorities, or 'environmental terrorism', with similar aims,

X. regretting the European Union's slowness in responding to the terrorist threat and the fact that there is as yet no coherent and legally binding set of coordinated measures, adopted by common accord, and whereas cooperation at all levels between central and regional government is necessary to fight terrorism,

Y. whereas, in view of the growing number of terrorist acts carried out using new methods such as chemical, biological and toxic substances, the Member States should take additional security measures in line with modern technological developments in order to ensure public safety,

Z. deeply concerned at the link which exists between terrorism and arms and drug trafficking,

AA. convinced that, in view of the democratic and constitutional structure of decision-making processes in the Member States, no ideological or other grounds can justify terrorist acts committed within the European Union and that, however political the reasons cited may be, such acts can only be considered as crimes, and even as crimes against humanity, which must be prosecuted, with due respect for the European Convention on Human Rights and the European Union Charter of Fundamental Rights,

BB. emphasising, consequently, that measures taken to combat terrorism must not, under any circumstances, be based on exceptional laws or procedures,

CC. whereas certain terrorist acts are orchestrated and carried out by groups organised at international level, which are explicitly or implicitly tolerated by certain States,

DD. whereas the European Union should provide for diplomatic, political and economic sanctions and deterrents to be used against third states which openly or secretly support acts of terrorism and terrorist groups,

EE. whereas the Treaty of Amsterdam opened up new opportunities for European Union action against certain criminal acts, and whereas, as a result of its entry into force, the European Union is responsible for adopting a catalogue of coherent measures, and not merely ad hoc proposals, to introduce coordinated action against terrorism within its borders,

FF. considering the possibilities based on Article 30 TEU of cooperation between Member States in the preservation of law and order and the maintenance of peace,

GG. whereas conclusion 33 of the Tampere European Council meeting of 15/16 October 1999 approved the principle of mutual recognition of judicial decisions, which should become the cornerstone of judicial cooperation in both civil and criminal matters within the Union, and stipulated that the principle should apply both to judgments and to other decisions of judicial authorities,

HH. whereas conclusion 35 of the Tampere European Council meeting of 15/16 October 1999 stated that it considered that the formal extradition procedure should be abolished among the Member States for persons fleeing from justice after having been finally sentenced, and replaced by a simple transfer of such persons, in compliance with Article 6 of the Treaty on European Union,

II. reiterating its confidence in the structures and operation of the Member States' legal systems and their capacity to guarantee a fair trial,

JJ. calling on Europol to publish annual reports on the terrorist threat in the Union and to inform the European Parliament on a regular basis about its activities and progress made in combating terrorism and to inform it promptly in the event of important developments,

KK. reminding the Council and Commission of the Treaty Articles which allow the Union to take an active interest in the problems of terrorism in Member States,

1. Makes the following recommendations to the Council:

(Recommendation 1)
– Calls on the Council to adopt a framework decision with a view to approximating legislative provisions establishing minimum rules at European level relating to the constituent elements of criminal acts and to penalties in the field of terrorism.

(Recommendation 2)
– Calls on the Council to adopt a framework decision aimed at legislative harmonisation and the establishment of a European common area of freedom, security and justice, abolishing formal extradition procedures and adopting the principle of mutual recognition of decisions on criminal matters, including pre-judgment decisions, relating to terrorist offences, among the Member States of the European Union.

(Recommendation 3)
– Calls on the Council to adopt a framework decision establishing measures governing and guaranteeing the implementation of a European search and arrest warrant with a view to combating terrorism in the context of action against crime, whether organised or not, trafficking in human beings and crimes against children, illegal trafficking in drugs and arms, and corruption and fraud, taking due account, in the event of more than one offence having been committed, of the gravity of each offence.

(Recommendation 4)
– Calls on the Council to adopt the appropriate legal instruments for the approximation of national legislation concerning the compensation of victims of terrorist crimes.

2. Instructs its President to forward this recommendation to the Council and, for information, to the Commission, as well as to the governments and parliaments of the Member States.

6.3   THE COMMISSION

In the context of this Volume no attention can be paid to the relationship between Council and Commission, not to the transition Justice and Home Affairs does find itself in, from the Third Pillar to the First Pillar, from the Union to the Community, from the TEU to the TEC, all per the 1997 Amsterdam Treaty. It is sufficient to underline the utmost relevance of framework decisions, common positions and Council regulations. All these instruments enjoy a tremendous impact and are more often than not binding.

6.3.1   **Proposal for a Council framework Decision on combating terrorism**[11]
(presented by the Commission late September; 'delivered' on 15 October 2001)

EXPLANATORY MEMORANDUM

1. INTRODUCTION

Terrorism constitutes one of the most serious threats to democracy, to the free exercise of human rights and to economic and social development. Terrorism can never be justified, whatever the target and the place where the offence is prepared or committed.

This has never been clearer than in the terrible aftermath of the unprecedented, tragic and murderous terrorist attacks against the people of the United States of America on 11 September 2001. These cowardly attacks highlight the need for an effective response to terrorism at the level of the European Union.

The European Union has set itself an objective in the Treaty on European Union to provide citizens with a high level of safety within an Area of Freedom, Security and Justice. This proposal, combined with the proposal to replace extradition within the European Union with a European Arrest Warrant, is a key element of the Commission's contribution to achieving this objective in the context of the fight against terrorism. It is vitally important that Member States of the European Union have effective criminal laws in place to tackle terrorism, and that measures are taken to enhance international cooperation against terrorism.

This proposal does not relate only to acts of terrorism directed at Member States. It also applies to conduct on the territory of the European Union which can contribute to acts of terrorism in third countries. This reflects the Commission's commitment to tackle terrorism at a global as well as European Union level. Indeed, the

---

[11] 501PC0521.

Commission is working closely with Member States and third countries to combat international terrorism within the framework of international organisations and existing international cooperation mechanisms, particularly the United Nations and the G8, with a view to ensuring the full implementation of all relevant international instruments.

The European Union and its Member States are founded on respect for human rights, fundamental freedoms, the guarantee of the dignity of the human being, and the protection of the these rights, both as regards individuals and institutions. Furthermore, the right to life, the right to physical integrity, the right to liberty and security and the right to freedom of thought, of expression and information are included in Articles 2, 3, 6, 10 and 11 of the Charter of Fundamentals Right of the European Union[12] (Nice, 7 December 2000).

Terrorism threatens these fundamental rights. There is hardly a country in Europe which has not been affected, either directly or indirectly, by terrorism. Terrorist actions are liable to undermine the rule of law and the fundamental principles on which the constitutional traditions and legislation of Member States' democracies are based. They are committed against one or more countries, their institutions or people with the aim of intimidating them and seriously altering or destroying the political, economic or social structures of those countries.

Terrorism takes different forms, ranging from murder, through bodily harm and threats to people's lives and kidnappings and on to destruction of property and damage to public or private facilities. Terrorism causes suffering to the victims and those around them. It destroys their personal hopes and expectations and the material basis of their livelihood, injuring them, inflicting psychological torture and causing death.

Terrorism has a long history behind it, but what makes modern-day terrorism particularly dangerous is that, unlike terrorist acts in the past, the actual or potential impact of armed attacks is increasingly devastating and lethal. This can result from the growing sophistication and ruthless ambition of the terrorists themselves, as demonstrated most recently by the horrific events in the United States on 11 September. Alternatively, it can result from technological developments (and easy access to information about these developments), whether in the traditional arms and explosives areas or in the even more terrifying fields of chemical, biological and nuclear weapons. In addition, new forms of terrorism are emerging. There have been several recent occasions where tensions in international relations have led to a spate of attacks against information systems. More serious attacks could lead not only to serious damage but even, in some cases, to loss of life.

The profound changes in the nature of terrorist offences highlight the inadequacy of traditional forms of judicial and police cooperation in combating it. Increasingly, terrorism stems from the activities of networks operating at international level, which are based in several countries and exploit legal loopholes arising from the geographical limits of investigations, sometimes enjoying extensive logistical and financial support. Given that there are no borders within the European Union and that

---

[12] OJ C 364, 18.12.2000, p. 1. The text as contained in this Volume has been slightly edited: most footnotes have been deleted.

the right of free movements of people is guaranteed, new measures in the fight against terrorism must be taken.

Terrorists might otherwise take advantage of any differences in legal treatment in the different Member States. Today, more than ever, steps are needed to combat terrorism by drawing up legislative proposals aimed at punishing such acts and strengthening police and judicial cooperation.

The objective of this Communication is to reinforce criminal law measures to combat terrorism. For that purpose, a proposal for a Framework Decision is submitted. Its objective is the approximation of the laws of the Member States regarding terrorist offences in accordance with Article 34(2)(b) of the Treaty on European Union (TEU).

2. INTERNATIONAL AND EU LEGAL INSTRUMENTS

The first steps in the fight against terrorism were made under the auspices of the United Nations, which promoted the Convention on offences and certain other acts committed on board aircraft (Tokyo, 14-9-1963). After this Convention some other conventions and protocols relating to terrorist acts were promulgated. The following are worth mentioning (...)

- UN Convention for the Suppression of Terrorist Bombings (New York, 15-12-1997);
- UN Convention for the Suppression of Financing Terrorism (New York, 9-12-1999).

These two last Conventions are particularly important. Article 2 of the Convention for the Suppression of Terrorist Bombings provides that any person commits an offence if that person unlawfully and intentionally delivers, places, discharges or detonates an explosive or other lethal device in, into or against a place of public use, a State or government facility, a public transportation system or an infrastructure facility with the intent to cause death or serious bodily injuries; or with the intent to cause extensive destruction of such a place, facility or system, where such destruction results in or is likely to result in major economic loss. The Convention for the Suppression of Financing Terrorism states that is an offence to provide or collect funds, directly or indirectly, unlawfully and intentionally, with the intent to use them or knowing that they will be used to commit any act included within the scope of the previously mentioned Conventions (apart from the Convention on offences and certain other offences committed on board aircraft, which is not included). This means that, even though in most of those conventions the words 'terrorism' or 'terrorist acts' are not mentioned, they are related to terrorist offences.

However, with regard to existing international Conventions, the most significant effort in the fight against terrorism, has been the European Convention on the Suppression of Terrorism (Strasbourg, 27-1-1977) under the mandate of the Council of Europe. This is the first Convention in which terrorism is treated generically, at least in the sense that it gives a list of terrorist acts. This convention does not consider this kind of offence as political offences, or as offences connected with a political offence, or as offences inspired by political motives. This is important for the purpose of the application of the conventions on extradition.

Articles 1 and 2 contain a list of offences considered to be terrorist acts. Article 1 refers to offences within the scope of the Convention for the Suppression of Unlawful Seizure of Aircraft (The Hague, 1970) and the Convention for the Suppression of Unlawful Acts against the Safety of Civil Aviation (Montreal, 1971), which refer to certain terrorist acts. Furthermore, offences involving an attack against the life, physical integrity or liberty of internationally protected persons (including diplomatic agents), offences involving kidnapping, taking of a hostage, serious unlawful detention, use of a bomb, grenade, rocket, automatic firearm or letter or parcel bomb, if this use endangers persons appear in the same list. Article 2 extends the concept of terrorist act to other offences such as those which involve an act of violence, other than one covered by Article 1, against the life, physical integrity or liberty of a person (paragraph 1); and against property if the act created a collective danger for persons (paragraph 2).

Most of these conventions have been signed and ratified by the majority of Member States, which means that they have to apply them. This proposal will facilitate the implementation of those conventions as far as they concern penal law since they refer to the same issue: terrorist offences.

At European Union level, Article 29 of the Treaty on European Union specifically refers to terrorism as one of the serious forms of crime to be prevented and combated by developing common action in three different ways: closer cooperation between police forces, customs authorities and other competent authorities, including Europol; closer cooperation between judicial and other competent authorities of the Member States; approximation, where necessary, of rules on criminal matters.

Regarding police cooperation (Article 30 of the TEU), it is worth mentioning Article 2(1) of the Convention on the establishment of a European Police Office, in which terrorism is included within its field of competence, and the Council Decision of 3 December 1998 instructing Europol to deal with crimes committed or likely to be committed in the course of terrorist activities against life, limb, personal freedom or property, which implements Article 2(2) of that Convention. Furthermore, the Council Joint Action of 15 October 1996 decided the creation and maintenance of a Directory of specialised counter-terrorism competences, skills and expertise to facilitate counter-terrorism cooperation between the MS of the EU.

Concerning judicial cooperation Article 31 of the TUE states that common action on judicial cooperation is to include facilitating and accelerating cooperation between competent ministries and judicial or equivalent authorities of the Member States in relation to proceedings and the enforcement of decisions (Paragraph A) and facilitating extradition between Member States (Paragraph B). In this field there are two important legal instruments: the Convention on simplified extradition procedure between the Member States of the EU (10 March 1995) and the Convention relating to extradition between Member States of the EU (27 September 1996), where Article 1 establishes that one of the purposes of that Convention is to facilitate the application between the Member States of the EU of the European Convention on the Suppression of Terrorism. Furthermore, the Joint Action of 21 December 1998 on making it a criminal offence to participate in a criminal organisation in the Member States of the EU refers to terrorist offences in Article 2(2).

However, it seemed necessary to improve these legal instruments in order to fight against terrorism in a more effective and efficient way. The conclusions of the Tampere European Council meeting of 15 and 16 October 1999 therefore established that formal extradition procedures should be abolished among the Member States as regards persons who are fleeing from justice after having been finally sentenced, and replaced by a simple transfer of such persons (Conclusion 35).

The European Parliament adopted (5 September 2001) a resolution concerning the role of the EU in combating terrorism, calling on the Council to adopt a framework decision to abolish formal extradition procedures, to adopt the principle of mutual recognition of decisions on criminal matters including pre-judgement decisions in criminal matters relating to terrorist offences and the implementation of the 'European search and arrest warrant', and to approximate legislative provisions establishing minimum rules at European level relating to the constituent elements and penalties in the field of terrorism.

Finally, regarding approximation of rules on criminal matters in the Member States, Article 31(e)[13] of the TEU calls for the adoption of measures establishing minimum rules relating to the constituent elements of criminal acts and to penalties in the field of terrorism, which is also mentioned in Paragraph 46 of the Action Plan of the Council and the Commission on how best to implement the provisions of the Treaty of Amsterdam on an area of freedom, security and justice (3 December 1998). This is the aim of this Framework Decision: implementing Article 31(e) of the TEU by approximating Member States' legislation concerning terrorist offences.

Additionally to Title IV of the TEU establishing the appropriate instruments for the fighting of terrorism at the Union's level and to coordinate action on an international level, the Union's commitment to contribute towards the emergence of a strong, sustained and global action against terrorism may require a political dialogue with or an action in relation to a non-Member State as well as coordination of Member States in international organisations and on international conferences. Without prejudice to the measures undertaken in the field of police and judicial cooperation, the addressing of all security aspects may call for complementary actions under, for example, the Common Foreign and Security Policy in order to enhance impact and ensure consistency of the Union's external relations.

3. MEMBER STATES LEGISLATION CONCERNING TERRORISM

In the European Union there are different situations in Member States in relation to legislation related to terrorism. Some have no specific regulations on terrorism. In

---

[13] In this Article organised crime and illicit drug trafficking are also mentioned and the Union is dealing with both of them. Concerning organised crime we should take into account the Joint Action 21 December 1998 on making it a criminal offences to participate in a criminal organisation in the MS of the EU. Regarding illicit drug trafficking the Commission presented a proposal for a Council Framework Decision laying down minimum provisions on the constituent elements of criminal acts and penalties in the field of illicit drug trafficking (COM (2001) 259 final, 23 May 2001).

these states, terrorist actions are punished as common offences. In other member States there are specific laws or legal instruments concerning terrorism where the words 'terrorism' or 'terrorist' are expressly mentioned and where some terrorist offences are expressly typified. This is the case in France, Germany, Italy, Portugal, Spain and the United Kingdom.

Most terrorist acts are basically ordinary offences which become terrorist offences because of the motivations of the offender. If the motivation is to alter seriously or to destroy the fundamental principles and pillars of the state, intimidating people, there is a terrorist offence. This point of view has been incorporated in Member States legislation concerning terrorism. Although the wording is different, they are essentially synonymous with each other.

The Criminal Code and the Code of Criminal Procedure in Greece have been substantially reshaped following the recent adoption of law no. 2928 of 27 June 2001. The French Criminal Code refers to terrorist acts as those that can alter seriously public order through threat or terror. The Portuguese Criminal Code mentions prejudice to national interests, to alter or to disturb State's institutions, to force public authorities to do or not to do something, and to threaten individuals or groups. The Spanish Criminal Code, as in France and Portugal, alludes to the aim of subverting the constitutional order and altering seriously public peace. A similar statement, to subvert the democratic order, is also mentioned in the Italian Criminal Code.

The UK legislation, Terrorism Act 2000, is the largest piece of terrorist legislation in the EU Member States. Terrorism is defined as meaning the use or threat of action where 'the use or threat is designed to influence the government or to intimidate the public or a section of the public' and 'the use or threat is made for the purpose of advancing a political, religious or ideological cause'; and that the action includes, among others, 'serious violence against a person', 'serious damage to property' or 'creating a serious risk to the health or safety of the public or a section of the public'.

4. A PROPOSAL FOR A FRAMEWORK DECISION

In view of Article 31(e) of the TEU, the legal background previously mentioned, and the fact that only six Member States have legal instruments covering terrorism, the present proposal for a Framework Decision for the approximation of the substantive laws of the Member States is clearly necessary. It concerns constituent elements and penalties in the field of terrorism, ensuring that terrorist offences will be punished by effective, proportionate and dissuasive criminal penalties. As a direct result, it will also facilitate police and judicial cooperation, since common definitions of offences should overcome the obstacles of double criminality requirement as long as it is a prerequisite for certain forms of judicial assistance. Furthermore, the existence of a common framework in the fight against terrorism in the EU will facilitate closer cooperation with third countries.

The key concept on which this proposal is based is the concept of a terrorist offence. Terrorist offences can be defined as offences intentionally committed by an individual or a group against one or more countries, their institutions or people, with the aim of intimidating them and seriously altering or destroying the political, economic, or social structures of a country. The implication is that legal rights affected by this kind of offence are not the same as legal rights affected by common offences. The reasoning here is that the motivation of the offender is different, even though terrorist offences can usually be equated in terms of their practical effect with ordinary criminal offences and, consequently, other legal rights are also affected. In fact, terrorist acts usually damage the physical or psychological integrity of individuals or groups, their property or their freedom, in the same way that ordinary offences do, but terrorist offences go further in undermining the structures previously mentioned. For this reason, terrorist offences and ordinary offences are different and affect different legal rights. Therefore it seems appropriate to have different and specific constituent elements and penalties for such particularly serious offences.

On the other hand, directing, creating, supporting or participating to a terrorist group must be considered independent criminal acts and must be dealt with as terrorist offences. In order to define the concept of a terrorist group we have to take into account the Joint Action of 21.12.1998 making it a criminal offence to participate in a criminal organisation in the Member States of the European Union, where terrorism is expressly mentioned.[14] Article 1 defines the criminal organisation as a structured association, established over a period of time, of more than two persons, acting in concert with a view to committing certain types of offence, which are subject to the penalties specified in the mentioned Article. Consequently, and following that definition, we can say that a terrorist group is a structured organisation, established over a period of time, of more than two persons acting in concert to commit terrorist acts.

This Framework Decision covers all terrorist offences prepared or committed within the borders of the European Union, whatever their target, including terrorist acts against interests of non EU Member States located in the EU.

Common definitions of offences and penalties are proposed. The proposal also contains provisions on liability and penalties for legal persons, jurisdiction, victims and exchange of information between Member States.

5. LEGAL BASIS

Article 29 of the TEU establishes that the Union's objective shall be to provide citizens with a level of safety within an area of freedom, security and justice by developing common action among the Member States in the fields of police and judicial cooperation, and by preventing and combating terrorism. The same Article provides for approximation, where necessary, of rules on criminal matters in the Member States, in accordance with Article 31(e). This Article states that common action on judicial cooperation in criminal matters shall include progressively adopting measures establishing minimum rules relating to the constituent elements of criminal acts and to penalties in the field, among other offences, of terrorism.

---

[14] OJ L 351, 29.12.1998, p. 1: 'Whereas the Council considers that the seriousness and development of certain forms of organised crime require strengthening of cooperation between the MS of the EU, particularly as regards the following offences: drug trafficking, trafficking in human beings, terrorism...'

Article 34(2)(b) of the TEU refers to framework decisions as the instruments to be used for the purpose of approximation of the laws and regulations of the Member States. Framework decisions are binding on the Member States as to the result to be achieved but leave to the national authorities the choice of the form and methods. This proposal will not entail financial implications for the budget of the European Community. (…)

6.3.2 Proposal for a COUNCIL FRAMEWORK DECISION on combating terrorism 2001/0217 (CNS) (Text)[15]

THE COUNCIL OF THE EUROPEAN UNION,

Having regard to the Treaty establishing the European Union, and in particular Article 29, Article 31(e) and Article 34(2)(b) thereof,
Having regard to the proposal from the Commission,
Having regard to the opinion of the European Parliament,

Whereas:
(1) Terrorism constitutes one of the most serious violations of the principles of human dignity, liberty, democracy, respect for human rights and fundamental freedoms and the rule of law, principles on which the European Union is founded and which are common to the Member States.
(2) All or some Member States are party to a number of conventions relating to terrorism. The European Convention on the Suppression of Terrorism of 27 January 1977 establishes that terrorist offences cannot be regarded as a political offences or as offences connected with political offences or as offences inspired by political motives. That Convention was the subject of Recommendation 1170 (1991) adopted by the Standing Committee, acting on behalf of the Parliamentary Assembly of the Council of Europe, on 25 November 1991. The United Nations has adopted the Convention for the suppression of terrorist bombings of 15 December 1997 and the Convention for the suppression of financing terrorism of 9 December 1999.
(3) At Union level, on 3 December 1998 the Council adopted the Action Plan of the Council and the Commission on how to best implement the provisions of the Treaty of Amsterdam on an area of freedom, security and justice. Terrorism was referred to in the conclusions of the Tampere European Council of 15 and 16 October 1999, and of the Santa María da Feira European Council if 19 and 20 June 2000. It was also mentioned in the Commission's Communication to the Council and the European Parliament on the biannual update of the scoreboard to review progress on the creation of an area of 'freedom, security and justice' in the European Union (second half of 2000). The La Gomera Declaration adopted at the Informal Council Meeting of 14 October 1995 affirmed that terrorism constitutes a threat to democracy, to the free exercise of human rights and to economic and social development.
(4) On 30 July 1996 twenty five measures to fight against terrorism were advocated by the leading industrialised countries (G7) and Russia meeting in Paris.
(5) The Convention based on Article K.3 of the Treaty on European Union, on the establishment of a European Police Office (Europol convention) refers in particular in Article 2

---

[15] Ed.: most footnotes have been deleted.

to improving the effectiveness and cooperation of the competent authorities in the Member States in preventing and combating terrorism.

(6) Other measures having an impact on terrorism adopted by the European Union are as follows: the Council Decision of 3 December 1998 instructing Europol to deal with crimes committed or likely to be committed in the course of terrorist activities against the life, limb, personal freedom or property; Joint Action 96/610/JHA of 15 October 1996 adopted by the Council on the basis of Article K.3 of the Treaty on European Union concerning the creation and maintenance of a Directory of specialised counter-terrorist competences, skills and expertise to facilitate counter-terrorism-cooperation between the Member States of the European Union; Joint Action 98/428/JHA of 29 June 1998 adopted by the Council on the basis of Article K.3 of the Treaty on European Union on the creation of a European Judicial Network,[16] with responsibilities in terrorist offences, in particular Article 2; Joint Action 98/733/JHA of 21 December 1998 adopted by the Council on the basis of Article K.3 of the Treaty on European Union on making it a criminal offence to participate in a criminal organisation in the Member States of the European Union,[17] and the Council Recommendation of 9 December 1999 on cooperation in combating the financing of terrorism.[18]

(7) The important work performed by international organisations, in particular the UN and the Council of Europe, must be complemented with a view to closer approximation within the European Union. The profound change in the nature of terrorism, the inadequacy of traditional forms of judicial and police cooperation in combating it and the existing legal loopholes must be combated with new measures, namely, establishing minimum rules relating to the constituent elements and penalties in the field of terrorism.

(8) Since these objectives of the proposed action cannot be sufficiently achieved by the Member States unilaterally, and can therefore, because of the need for reciprocity, be better achieved at the level of the Union, the Union may adopt measures, in accordance with the principle of subsidiarity as referred to in Article 2 of the EU Treaty and as set out in Article 5 of the EC Treaty. In accordance with the principle of proportionality, as set out in the latter Article, this Framework Decision does not go beyond what is necessary in order to achieve those objectives.

(9) Measures should be adopted applying not only to terrorist acts committed within the Member States but also to those which otherwise affect Member States. While police and judicial cooperation measures are the appropriate way to combat terrorism in the Union and on an international level, complementary actions may be adopted in order to enhance the impact in the fight against terrorist acts and ensure consistency of the Union's external relations.

(10) It is necessary that the definition of the constituent elements of terrorism be common in all Member States, including those offences referred to terrorist groups. On the other hand, penalties and sanctions are provided for natural and legal persons having committed or being liable for such offences, which reflect the seriousness of such offences.

(11) The circumstances should be considered aggravated where the offence is committed with particular ruthlessness, affects a large number of persons or is of a particular serious and persistent nature; or committed against persons whose representative position, including internationally protected person, as members of an executive or legislature or their work, dealing with terrorists, makes them terrorist targets.

---

[16] OJ L 191, 7.7.1998, p. 4.
[17] OJ L 351, 29.12.1998, p. 1.
[18] OJ C 373, 23.12.1999, p. 1.

(12) The circumstances must be mitigating if terrorists, renouncing their terrorist activity, provide the administrative or judicial authorities with some relevant information helping them to fight against terrorism.

(13) Jurisdictional rules must be established to ensure that the offence may be prosecuted.

(14) The European Convention on Extradition of 13 December 1957 is taken into account in order to facilitate prosecution when the offence is committed in a Member State which does not extradite its own nationals.

(15) In order to improve cooperation and in compliance with data protection rules, and in particular the Council of Europe Convention of 28 January 1981 for the Protection of Individuals with regard to Automatic Processing of Personal Data, Member States should afford each other the widest judicial mutual assistance. Operational contact points should be established for the exchange of information or adequate use should be made of existing cooperation mechanism for that purpose.

(16) Victims of certain kind of terrorist offences, such as threats, extortion, can be rather vulnerable. Each Member State should accordingly ensure that investigation or prosecution not be dependent on the report or accusation made by a person subject to the offence.

(17) This Framework Decision respects the fundamental rights and observes the principles recognised in particular by the Charter of Fundamental Rights of the European Union, and notably Chapter VI thereof.

HAS DECIDED AS FOLLOWS :

Article 1 – Subject matter
The purpose of this Framework Decision is to establish minimum rules relating to the constituent elements of criminal acts and to penalties for natural and legal persons who have committed or are liable for terrorist offences which reflect the seriousness of such offences.

Article 2 – Scope
This Framework Decision shall apply to terrorist offences:
    (a)   committed or prepared in whole or in part within a Member State; or
    (b)   committed by a national of a Member State; or
    (c)   committed for the benefit of a legal person established in a Member State; or
    (d)   committed against the institutions or people of a Member State.

Article 3 – Terrorist Offences
1. Each Member State shall take the necessary measures to ensure that the following offences, defined according to its national law, which are intentionally committed by an individual or a group against one or more countries, their institutions or people with the aim of intimidating them and seriously altering or destroying the political, economic, or social structures of a country, will be punishable as terrorist offences:
    (a)   Murder;
    (b)   Bodily injuries;
    (c)   Kidnapping or hostage taking;
    (d)   Extortion;
    (e)   Theft or robbery;
    (f)   Unlawful seizure of or damage to state or government facilities, means of public transport, infrastructure facilities, places of public use, and property;
    (g)   Fabrication, possession, acquisition, transport or supply of weapons or explosives;
    (h)   Releasing contaminating substances, or causing fires, explosions or floods, endangering people, property, animals or the environment;

   (i) Interfering with or disrupting the supply of water, power, or other fundamental resource;

   (j) Attacks through interference with an information system;

   (k) Threatening to commit any of the offences listed above;

   (l) Directing a terrorist group;

   (m) Promoting of, supporting of or participating in a terrorist group.

2. For the purpose of this Framework Decision, terrorist group shall mean a structured organisation established over a period of time, of more than two persons, acting in concert to commit terrorist offences referred to in paragraph (1)(a) to (1)(k).

Article 4 – Instigating, aiding, abetting and attempting

Member States shall ensure that instigating, aiding, abetting or attempting to commit a terrorist offence is punishable.

Article 5 – Penalties and sanctions

1. Member States shall ensure that terrorist offences and conducts referred to in Articles 3 and 4 are punishable by effective, proportionate and dissuasive penalties.

2. Member States shall ensure that terrorist offences referred to in Article 3 are punishable by terms of deprivation of liberty with a maximum penalty that is no less than the following:

   (a) the offence referred to in Article 3(1)(a): Twenty years;

   (b) the offence referred to in Article 3(1)(l): Fifteen years;

   (c) the offences referred to in Article 3(1)(c), (g), (h) and (i): Ten years;

   (d) the offence referred to in Article 3(1)(m): Seven years;

   (e) the offences referred to in Article 3(1) (f)and (j): Five years;

   (f) the offence referred to in Article 3(1)(b): Four years;

   (g) the offences referred to in Article 3(1)(d), (e), and (k) : Two years.

3. Member States shall ensure that ancillary or alternative sanctions such as community service, limitation of certain civil or political rights or publication of all or part of a sentence may be imposed for terrorist offences and conduct referred to in Articles 3 and 4.

4. Member States shall ensure that fines can also be imposed for terrorist offences and conduct referred to in Articles 3 and 4.

Article 6 – Aggravating circumstances

Without prejudice to any other aggravating circumstances defined in their national legislation, Member States shall ensure that the penalties and sanctions referred to in Article 5 may be increased if the terrorist offence:

   (a) is committed with particular ruthlessness; or

   (b) affects a large number of persons or is of a particular serious and persistent nature; or

   (c) is committed against Heads of State, Government Ministers, any other internationally protected person, elected members of parliamentary chambers, members of regional or local governments, judges, magistrates, judicial or prison civil servants and police forces.

Article 7 – Mitigating Circumstances

Member States shall ensure that the penalties and sanctions referred to in Article 5 may be reduced if the offender:

   (a) renounces terrorist activity, and

   (b) provides the administrative or judicial authorities with information helping them to:

      (i)   prevent or mitigate the effects of the offence,

(ii)   (ii) identify or bring to justice the other offenders,
(iii)   find evidence, or
(iv)   prevent further terrorist offences.

Article 8 – Liability of legal persons

1. Member States shall ensure that legal persons can be held liable for terrorist offences or conduct referred to in Articles 3 and 4 committed for their benefit by any person, acting either individually or as part of an organ of the legal person, who has a leading position within the legal person, based on:
(a) a power of representation of the legal person, or
(b) an authority to take decisions on behalf of the legal person, or
(c) an authority to exercise control within the legal person.

2. Apart from the cases provided for in paragraph 1, Member States shall ensure that a legal person can be held liable where the lack of supervision or control by a person referred to in paragraph 1 has made possible the commission of terrorist offences or conduct referred to in Articles 3 and 4 for the benefit of that legal person by a person under its authority.

3. Liability of a legal person under paragraphs 1 and 2 shall not exclude criminal proceedings against natural persons who committerrorist offences or engage in the conducts referred to in Articles 3 and 4.

Article 9 – Sanctions for legal person

1. Member States shall ensure that a legal person held liable pursuant to Article 8(1) is punishable by effective, proportionate and dissuasive sanctions, which shall include criminal or non-criminal fines and may include other sanctions such as:
(a) exclusion from entitlement to public benefits or aid,
(b) temporary or permanent disqualification from the practice of commercial activities,
(c) placing under judicial supervision,
(d) a judicial winding-up order,
(e) temporary or permanent closure of establishment which have been used for committing the offence.

2. Member States shall ensure that a legal person held liable pursuant to Article 8(2) is punishable by effective, proportionate and dissuasive sanctions or measures.

Article 10 – Jurisdiction

1. Member States shall establish its jurisdiction with regard to terrorist offences or conduct referred to in Articles 3 and 4 where the offence or conduct has been committed:
(a) in whole or in part within its territory; or
(b) by one of its nationals, provided that the law of that Member State may require the conduct to be punishable also in the country where it occurred; or
(c) for the benefit of a legal person that has its head office in the territory of that Member State; or
(d) against its institutions or people.

2. A Member State may decide that it will not apply, or that it will apply only in specific cases or circumstances, a jurisdiction rule set out in paragraph 1(b), (c) or (d).

3. Member States shall inform the General Secretariat of the Council and the Commission accordingly, where appropriate with an indication of the specific cases or circumstances in which the decision applies.

Article 11 – Extradition and prosecution

1. A Member State which, under its law, does not extradite its own nationals shall establish its jurisdiction over terrorist offences or conduct referred to in Articles 3 and 4 when committed by its own nationals on the territory of another Member State or against another Member State's institutions or people.

2. A Member State shall, when one of its nationals is alleged to have committed, in another Member State, an terrorist offence or conduct referred to in Articles 3 and 4, and it does not extradite that person to that other Member State solely on the ground of his nationality, submit the case to its competent authorities for the purpose of prosecution if appropriate.

In order to enable prosecution to take place, the Member State in which the offence or conduct was committed shall forward to the competent authorities of the other State all the relevant files, information and exhibits in accordance with the procedures laid down in Article 6(2) of the European Convention on Extradition of 13 December 1957. The requesting Member State shall be informed of the initiation and outcome of any prosecution.

3. For the purpose of this Article, a 'national' of a Member State shall be construed in accordance with any declaration made by that State under Article 6(1)(b) and (c) of the European Convention on Extradition.

Article 12 – Cooperation between Member States

1. In accordance with the applicable conventions, multilateral or bilateral agreements or arrangements, Member States shall afford each other the widest measure of mutual assistance in respect of proceedings relating to terrorist offences or conduct referred to in Articles 3 and 4.

2. Where several Member States have jurisdiction in respect of such offences, they shall consult one another with a view to coordinating their action in order to prosecute effectively. They shall make full use of judicial cooperation and other mechanisms.

Article 13 – Exchange of information

1. Each Member State shall designate operational contact points, which may be an existing operational structures or one newly established for this purpose, for the exchange of information and for other contacts between Member States for the purposes of applying this Framework Decision.

2. Each Member State shall inform the General Secretariat of the Council and the Commission of its operational contact point as referred to in paragraph 1. The General Secretariat shall notify that information to the other Member States.

3. Where a Member State has information relating to the future commission of a terrorist offence affecting another Member State, it shall provide that information to the other Member State. For that purpose operational contact points referred to in paragraph 1 may be used.

Article 14 – Protection and assistance to victims

Each Member State shall provide that investigations into or prosecution of terrorist offences over which it has jurisdiction shall not be dependent on the report or accusation made by a victim of the offence, at least in cases where Article 8(1)(a) applies.

Article 15 – Implementation and reports

Member States shall take the necessary measures to comply with this Framework Decision by 31 December 2002.

They shall communicate to the General Secretariat of the Council and to the Commission the text of any provisions they adopt and information on any other measures they take to comply with this Framework Decision.

On that basis the Commission shall, by 31 December 2003, submit a report to the European Parliament and to the Council on the operation of this Framework Decision, accompanied where necessary by legislative proposals.

The Council shall assess the extent to which the Member States have complied with this Framework Decision.

Article 16 – Entry into force

This Framework Decision shall enter into force on the third day following that of its publication in the Official Journal of the European Communities.

6.3.3   Council Common Position of 27 December 2001 on combating terrorism[19]

THE COUNCIL OF THE EUROPEAN UNION,

Having regard to the Treaty on European Union, and in particular Articles 15 and 34 thereof,

Whereas:

(1)   At its extraordinary meeting on 21 September 2001,the European Council declared that terrorism is a real challenge to the world and to Europe and that the fight against terrorism will be a priority objective of the European Union.

(2)   On 28 September 2001, the United Nations Security Council adopted Resolution 1373 (2001), reaffirming that terrorist acts constitute a threat to peace and security and setting out measures aimed at combating terrorism and in particular the fight against the financing of terrorism and the provision of safe havens for terrorists.

(3)   On 8 October 2001, the Council reaffirmed the determination of the EU and its Member States to play their full part, in a coordinated manner, in the global coalition against terrorism, under the aegis of the United Nations. The Council also reiterated the Union's determination to attack the sources which fund terrorism, in close cooperation with the United States.

(4)   On 19 October 2001, the European Council declared that it is determined to combat terrorism in every form throughout the world and that it will continue its efforts to strengthen the coalition of the international community to combat terrorism in every shape and form, for example by the increased cooperation between the operational services responsible for combating terrorism: Europol, Eurojust, the intelligence services, police forces and judicial authorities.

(5)   Action has already been taken to implement some of the measures listed below.

(6)   Under these extraordinary circumstances, action by the Community is needed in order to implement some of the measures listed below,

HAS ADOPTED THIS COMMON POSITION:

Article 1

The wilful provision or collection, by any means, directly or indirectly, of funds by citizens or within the territory of each of the Member States of the European Union with the intention that the funds should be used, or in the knowledge that they are to be used, in order to carry out terrorist acts shall be criminalized.

---

[19] 2001/930/CFSP; Official Journal L 344/90.

Article 2
Funds and other financial assets or economic resources of:
–   persons who commit, or attempt to commit, terrorist acts or participate in or facilitate the commission of terrorist acts;
–   entities owned or controlled, directly or indirectly, by such persons; and
–   persons and entities acting on behalf of or under the direction of such persons and entities, including funds derived or generated from property owned or controlled directly or indirectly by such persons and associated persons and entities, shall be frozen.

Article 3
Funds, financial assets or economic resources or financial or other related services shall not be made available, directly or indirectly, for the benefit of:
–   persons who commit or attempt to commit or facilitate or participate in the commission of terrorist acts;
–   entities owned or controlled, directly or indirectly, by such persons; and
–   persons and entities acting on behalf of or under the direction of such persons.

Article 4
Measures shall be taken to suppress any form of support, active or passive, to entities or persons involved in terrorist acts, including measures aimed at suppressing the recruitment of members of terrorist groups and eliminating the supply of weapons to terrorists.

Article 5
Steps shall be taken to prevent the commission of terrorist acts, including by the provision of early warning among Member States or between Member States and third States by exchange of information.

Article 6
Safe haven shall be denied to those who finance, plan, support, or commit terrorist acts, or provide safe havens.

Article 7
Persons who finance, plan, facilitate or commit terrorist acts shall be prevented from using the territories of the Member States of the European Union for those purposes against Member States or third States or their citizens.

Article 8
Persons who participate in the financing, planning, preparation or perpetration of terrorist acts or in supporting terrorist acts shall be brought to justice; such terrorist acts shall be established as serious criminal offences in laws and regulations of Member States and the punishment shall duly reflect the seriousness of such terrorist acts.

Article 9
Member States shall afford one another, as well as third States, the greatest measure of assistance in connection with criminal investigations or criminal proceedings relating to the financing or support of terrorist acts in accordance with international and domestic law, including assistance in obtaining evidence in the possession of a Member State or a third State which is necessary for the proceedings.

Article 10

The movement of terrorists or terrorist groups shall be prevented by effective border controls and controls on the issuing of identity papers and travel documents, and through measures for preventing counterfeiting, forgery or fraudulent use of identity papers and travel documents. The Council notes the Commission's intention to put forward proposals in this area, where appropriate.

Article 11

Steps shall be taken to intensify and accelerate the exchange of operational information, especially regarding actions or movements of terrorist persons or networks; forged or falsified travel documents; traffic in arms, explosives or sensitive materials; use of communication technologies by terrorist groups; and the threat posed by the possession of weapons of mass destruction by terrorist groups.

Article 12

Information shall be exchanged among Member States or between Member States and third States in accordance with international and national law, and cooperation shall be enhanced among Member States or between Member States and third States on administrative and judicial matters to prevent the commission of terrorist acts.

Article 13

Cooperation among Member States or between Member States and third States, particularly through bilateral and multilateral arrangements and agreements, to prevent and suppress terrorist attacks and take action against perpetrators of terrorist acts shall be enhanced.

Article 14

Member States shall become parties as soon as possible to the relevant international conventions and protocols relating to terrorism listed in the Annex.[20]

Article 15

Member States shall increase cooperation and fully implement the relevant international conventions and protocols relating to terrorism and United Nations Security Council Resolutions 1269(1999) and 1368(2001).

Article 16

Appropriate measures shall be taken in accordance with the relevant provisions of national and international law, including international standards of human rights, before granting refugee status, for the purpose of ensuring that the asylum-seeker has not planned, facilitated or participated in the commission of terrorist acts. The Council notes the Commission's intention to put forward proposals in this area, where appropriate.

Article 17

Steps shall be taken in accordance with international law to ensure that refugee status is not abused by the perpetrators, organisers or facilitators of terrorist acts and that claims of political motivation are not recognised as grounds for refusing requests for the extradition of alleged terrorists.

---

[20] Ed.: Not included; the list contains the usual international instruments, see Chapter 5.1 and 5.2.

The Council notes the Commission's intention to put forward proposals in this area, where appropriate.

Article 18
This Common Position shall take effect on the date of its adoption.

Article 19
This Common Position shall be published in the Official Journal.

Done at Brussels, 27 December 2001. For the Council, the President, L. Michel.

6.3.4 Proposal for a Council Regulation,[21] March 2002

(...)

EXPLANATORY MEMORANDUM

(1) Further to Resolutions 1267(1999) and 1333(2000) of the Security Council of the United Nations, the Council decided to impose a number of sanctions in relation to Afghanistan by means of Council Regulation (EC) No 467/2001, including in particular a ban on flights to Afghanistan, a ban on certain exports to that country and a freezing of funds.

(2) By means of Resolution 1390(2002) of 16 January 2002 the Security Council determined that the scope of both the financial measures and the prohibition to render services related to military activities, should be adjusted and that the remainder of these sanctions should be repealed. The adjusted financial measures and prohibition to render certain services target Usama bin Laden, the Al-Qaida network and the Taliban and a list of the persons, groups and entities concerned will be decided on by a UN Sanctions Committee. Taking into account that these measures are imposed in view of their role in international terrorism, without there being a link between the persons and groups concerned, and the new Government of Afghanistan, it is considered appropriate to adopt a new Regulation imposing such measures and to repeal the sanctions in relation to Afghanistan.

(3) In view of the explicit mention of terrorism in the texts, this new Regulation has been aligned as much as possible with Council Regulation (EC) No 2580/2001, which provides the framework for specific restrictive measures with a view to combating terrorism, directed against persons, groups and entities that have not been the subject of a specific determination by the Security Council or a UN Sanctions Committee.

Proposal for a COUNCIL REGULATION imposing certain specific restrictive measures directed against certain persons and entities associated with Usama bin Laden, the Al-Qaida network and the Taliban, and repealing Council Regulation (EC) No 467/2001 prohibiting the export of certain goods and services to Afghanistan, strengthening the flight ban and extending the freeze of funds and other financial resources in respect of the Taliban of Afghanistan

---

[21] COM (2002) 117 final; 2002/0059 (CNS).

THE COUNCIL OF THE EUROPEAN UNION,

Having regard to the Treaty establishing the European Community, and in particular Articles 60, 301 and 308 thereof,

Having regard to Common Position 2002/.../CFSP concerning restrictive measures against Usama bin Laden, members of the Al-Qaida organisation and the Taliban and other individuals, groups, undertakings and entities associated with them and repealing Common Positions 96/746/CFSP, 1999/727/CFSP, 2001/154/CFSP and 2001/771/CFSP,

Having regard to the proposal from the Commission,

Having regard to the opinion of the European Parliament,

Whereas:

(1) On 16 January 2002, the Security Council of the United Nations adopted Resolution 1390(2002) determining that the Taliban have failed to respond to its demands made in a number of previous resolutions and condemning the Taliban for allowing Afghanistan to be used as a base for terrorist training and activities. The Security Council also condemned the Al-Qaida network and other associated terrorist groups, for their terrorist acts and destruction of property.

(2) In this regard, the Security Council recalled the obligation to implement in full its Resolution 1373(2001) with regard to any member of the Taliban and the Al-Qaida organisation, but also with regard to those who are associated with them and have participated in the financing, planning, facilitation, preparation or perpetration of terrorist acts. By means of that Resolution the Security Council decided that a freezing of funds and other financial assets or economic resources should be implemented as against persons who commit, or attempt to commit, terrorist acts or who participate in or facilitate the commission of such acts, and that measures should be taken to prohibit funds and other financial assets or economic resources from being made available for the benefit of such persons, and to prohibit financial or other related services from being rendered for the benefit of such persons.

(3) The Security Council decided, inter alia, that the flight ban and export restrictions imposed on Afghanistan further to its Resolutions 1267(1999) and 1333(2000) should be repealed and that the scope of the freezing of funds and the prohibition on funds being made available, which were imposed further to these Resolutions, should be adjusted. It also decided that a prohibition on providing, to the Taliban and the Al-Qaida organisation, certain services related to military activities should be applied.

(4) These measures fall under the scope of the Treaty and, therefore, notably with a view to avoiding distortion of competition, Community legislation is necessary to implement the relevant decisions of the Security Council as far as the territory of the Community is concerned. For the purpose of this Regulation, the territory of the Community is deemed to encompass the territories of the Member States to which the Treaty is applicable, under the conditions laid down in that Treaty.

(5) In order to create maximum legal certainty within the Community, the names and other relevant data with regard to persons, entities and bodies whose funds should be frozen further to a designation by the UN authorities, should be made publicly known and a procedure should be established within the Community to amend these lists.

(6) The competent authorities of the Member States should, where necessary, be empowered to ensure compliance with the provisions of this Regulation.

(7) UN Security Council Resolution 1267 (1999) provides that the relevant UN Sanctions Committee may grant exemptions to the freezing of funds on grounds of humanitarian

need. Therefore, provision needs to be made to render such exemptions applicable throughout the Community.

(8) For reasons of expediency, the Commission should be empowered to amend the Annexes to this Regulation on the basis of pertinent notification or information by the UN Security Council, the relevant UN Sanctions Committee and the Member States, as appropriate.

(9) The Commission and the Member States should inform each other of the measures taken under this Regulation and of other relevant information at their disposal in connection with this Regulation, and cooperate with the relevant UN Sanctions Committee, in particular by supplying information to it.

(10) Member States should lay down rules on sanctions applicable to infringements of the provisions of this Regulation and ensure that the they are implemented. Those sanctions must be effective, proportionate and dissuasive.

(11) Taking into account that the freezing of funds is to be adjusted, it is necessary to ensure that sanctions for breaches of this Regulation can be imposed as of the date of entry into force of this Regulation.

(12) The measures referred to above were imposed by means of Council Regulation (EC) No 467/2001. In view of the need to adjust the freezing of funds and to repeal the remaining measures laid down therein, it is considered appropriate to repeal that Regulation and to adopt a new Regulation on the freezing of funds,

HAS ADOPTED THIS REGULATION:

Article 1
For the purpose of this Regulation, the following definitions shall apply:
1. 'Funds, other financial assets and economic resources' means assets of every kind, whether tangible or intangible, movable or immovable, however acquired, and legal documents or instruments in any form, including electronic or digital, evidencing title to, or interest in, such assets, including, but not limited to, bank credits, travellers' cheques, bank cheques, money orders, shares, securities, bonds, drafts and letters of credit.
2. 'Freezing of funds, other financial assets and economic resources' means the prevention of any move, transfer, alteration, use of or dealing with funds, other financial assets or economic resources, in any way that would result in any change in their volume, amount, location, ownership, possession, character, destination or other change that would enable the funds, other financial assets or economic resources to be used, including portfolio management.
3. 'Taliban' means: the Afghan faction which also calls itself the Islamic Emirate of Afghanistan.
4. 'Sanctions Committee' means: the Committee established by United Nations Security Council Resolution 1267(1999).

Article 2
1. All funds, other financial assets or economic resources belonging to, or owned or held by, a natural or legal person, group or entity designated by the Sanctions Committee and listed in Annex I shall be frozen.
2. No funds, other financial assets or economic resources shall be made available, directly or indirectly, to, or for the benefit of, persons, groups or entities designated by the Sanctions Committee and listed in Annex I.

3. Paragraphs 1 and 2 shall not apply to funds, other financial assets and economic resources for which the Sanctions Committee has granted an exemption. Exemptions granted by the Sanctions Committee shall apply throughout the Community.

Article 3

Without prejudice to the powers of Member States in the exercise of their public authority, it shall be prohibited to grant, sell, supply or transfer, directly or indirectly, technical advice, assistance or training related to military activities, including in particular training and assistance related to the manufacture, maintenance and use of arms and related matériel of all types, to any natural or legal person, group or entity listed in Annex I.

Article 4

1. The participation, knowingly and intentionally, in activities, the object or effect of which is, directly or indirectly, to circumvent Article 2 or to promote the transactions referred to in Article 3 shall be prohibited.
2. Any information that the provisions of this Regulation are being, or have been, circumvented shall be notified to the Commission.

Article 5

1. Notwithstanding the applicable rules concerning reporting, confidentiality and professional secrecy, natural and legal persons, groups and entities shall:
   (a) provide immediately to the Commission any information which would facilitate compliance with this Regulation, such as accounts and amounts frozen in accordance with Article 2. In particular information in respect of funds owned or controlled by persons listed in Annex I during the period of 6 months before the entry into force of this Regulation shall be provided.
   (b) cooperate with competent authorities in any verification of this information.
   (c) inform immediately the Commission on any transaction or activity where there is reasonable doubt about its compatibility with the provisions of this Regulation.
2. Any information provided or received in accordance with this Article shall be used only for the purposes for which it was provided or received.
3. Any information directly received by the Commission shall be made available to the competent authorities of the Member States concerned, as listed in Annex II.

Article 6

The freezing of funds, other financial assets and economic resources, in good faith and in accordance with this Regulation, shall not involve the natural or legal person, group or entity implementing it, or its directors or employees, in liability of any kind.

Article 7

1. The Commission shall be empowered to amend or supplement Annex I on the basis of determinations made by either the United Nations Security Council or the Sanctions Committee.
2. Without prejudice to the rights and obligations of the Member States under the Charter of the United Nations, the Commission shall maintain all necessary contacts with the Sanctions Committee for the purpose of the effective implementation of this Regulation.

Article 8

The Commission and the Member States shall immediately inform each other of the measures taken under this Regulation and shall supply each other with relevant information at their disposal in connection with this Regulation, in particular information received in accordance with Article 5 and in respect of violation and enforcement problems and judgements handed down by national courts.

Article 9
This Regulation shall apply notwithstanding any rights conferred or obligations imposed by any international agreement signed or any contract entered into or any licence or permit granted before the entry into force of this Regulation.

Article 10
1. Each Member State shall determine the sanctions to be imposed where the provisions of this Regulation are infringed. Such sanctions shall be effective, proportionate and dissuasive.
2. Pending the adoption, where necessary, of any legislation to this end, the sanctions to be imposed where the provisions of this Regulation are infringed, shall be those determined by the Member States in accordance with Article 13 of Regulation (EC) No 467/2001.
3. Each Member State shall bring proceedings against any natural or legal person, group or entity under its jurisdiction, in cases of violation of any of the prohibitions laid down in this Regulation by any such person, group or entity.

Article 11
This Regulation shall apply
– 	within the territory of the Community, including its airspace,
– 	on board any aircraft or any vessel under the jurisdiction of a Member State,
– 	to any person elsewhere who is a national of a Member State, and
– 	to any legal person, group or entity which is incorporated or constituted under the law of a Member State, and
– 	to any legal person, group or entity doing business within the Community.

Article 12
Regulation (EC) No 467/2001 is hereby repealed and, as regards the measures laid down in its Article 2, replaced by this Regulation.

Article 13
This Regulation shall enter into force on the day following that of its publication in the Official Journal of the European Communities. This Regulation shall be binding in its entirety and directly applicable in all Member States.

Annex I

List of persons, groups and entities referred to in Article 2
Legal persons, groups and entities [ed.: what follows are a great many names, institutions, banks etc, often together with detailed addresses, like:
– 	Aaran Money Wire Service, Inc., 1806, Riverside Avenue, Second Floor, Minneapolis, Minnesota, USA.
– 	Abu Sayyaf Group (aka Al Harakat Al Islamiyya)
– 	Afghan Support Committee (ASC), aka Lajnat Ul Masa Eidatul Afghania, Jamiat Ayat-Ur-Rhas Al Islamia, Jamiat Ihya Ul Turath Al Islamia, and Ahya Ul Turas; office locations: Headquarters - G. T. Road (Probably Grand Trunk Road), near Pushtoon Garhi Pabbi, Peshawar, Pakistan; Cheprahar Hadda, Mia Omar Sabaqah School, Jalabad, Afghanistan.

–   Al Baraka Exchange L.L.C., PO Box 3313, Deira, Dubai, UAE; PO Box 20066, Dubai, UAE.
–   Al Qaida/Islamic Army (aka "The Base", Al Qaeda, Islamic Salvation Foundation, The Group for the Preservation of the Holy Sites, The Islamic Army for the Liberation of Holy Places, The World Islamic Front for Jihad Against Jews and Crusaders, Usama Bin Laden Network, Usama Bin Laden Organisation)
–   Al Rashid Trust (aka Al-Rasheed Trust (…); - Also operations in Kosovo, Chechnya
–   Al Taqwa Trade, Property and Industry Company Limited (f.k.a. Al Taqwa Trade, Property and Industry) (f.k.a. Al Taqwa Trade, Property and Industry Establishment) (f.k.a. Himmat Establishment), c/o Asat Trust Reg., Altenbach 8, FL-9490 Vaduz, Liechtenstein.
–   Al-Barakaat Bank, Mogadishu, Somalia…. etc. etc]

Annex II

List of competent authorities referred to in Article 5
(to be completed by the Member States)

CHAPTER 7
CROSS-BORDER ASPECTS

Modern terrorism has proved to be successful thanks to fluid borders, relatively free movement, decreasing social cohesion and hence social control, increased interdependency, globalization and the need to ensure steady flows of goods, capital, services and people as well as major efforts relating to issues like data protection and the like. In the context of this Volume only three subjects have been touched upon: JUDICIAL COOPERATION (dealt with above in Chapter 3) and, covered by this Chapter 7.1 ARMS CONTROL as well as 7.2 MIGRATORY MOVEMENTS. The parts 7.3, 7.4 and 7.5 contain relevant material as produced by IOM, UNHCR and the EU respectively.

7.1   ARMS CONTROL

The arms trade and the proliferation of weapons are part and parcel of the terrorism issue. Of course, regard should also be had to either providing access or obtaining access to the information, knowledge and technology needed to produce arms in general, nuclear arms as well as biological and chemical weaponry in particular.

Universal adherence to instruments relating to weapons of mass destruction as well as the effective implementation of these instruments are important aspects of this line of thought. A list drawn up by the EU Council Secretariat would appear to be quite comprehensive:[1]

A. Accession
- Promote, at a political level, universal adherence to instruments relating to weapons of mass destruction (BWC, CWC, Geneva Protocol, NPT, CTBT, Safeguards Agreements and Additional Protocols with the IAEA, CPPNM);
- Lobby for the withdrawal of all relevant reservations on the Geneva Protocol;
- Act at a political level in view of reaching a wider adherence and effective implementation of other relevant instruments in the field of conventional weapons.

B. Implementation
- Compliance with obligations and commitments under the international instruments as agreed by the States Parties, including – where the international instru-

---

[1] Based on/quoting DG E VII, 7115/01, annex, dated 12 March 2002.

ments provide for – the destruction of prohibited weapons, the prevention of their diversion and illegal use, as well as the prevention of diversion of their technologies;

- Enactment and strict application of national implementation legislation as required by the international instruments;
- Full implementation of the Non-Proliferation Treaty and of the Final Documents of the 2000 and 1995 Review Conferences to the Non-Proliferation Treaty;
- Enactment of the provisions of the Convention of the Physical Protection of Nuclear Material (CPPNM) and encourage those concerned states to take into consideration relevant IAEA recommendations and to request, when appropriate, an IPPAS mission;
- Timely, consistent and full implementation of reporting obligations imposed either by the international instruments or by the final reports of review conferences (Chemical Weapons Convention declarations, BWC-CBMs, reports on the Amended II Protocol to the CCW, Article 7 reports regarding the Ottawa Convention) and the creation of necessary conditions for processing the resulting information (e.g. translate and process information coming from BWC-CBMs in usable databases);
- Implementation of confidence building measures like, inter alia, submission of national reports to the UN register on conventional weapons and expansion of the register;
- Implementation of the United Nations' programme of action on the fight against the illicit trade in small arms and light weapons and of the OSCE document on SALW.

C. Supervision and monitoring
- Reviewing the financial resources required by the international organisations like OPCW, CTBTO and IAEA in order to provide sufficient funding to enable them to discharge their monitoring activities, including those undertaken in the light of the new threats post September 2001, and ensuring that the funds provided are used in the most effective way;
- Sustaining and expanding the OPCW capabilities to conduct effective inspections especially challenge inspections and investigations into alleged use; more realistic and frequent training exercises, especially practice inspections, provide an ideal mechanism to maintain and enhance such capabilities;
- Supporting the statutory activities of the IAEA and strengthening its work to assist Member States to deal with the following:
  - physical protection of nuclear material and installations;
  - safe and secure management of radioactive sources including the implementation of the code of conduct on the safety and security of radioactive sources;
  - illicit trafficking in nuclear and radioactive material.

It is obvious that borders no longer exist to the extent that goods or services could be prevented from moving freely. This includes handbooks on making weapons, training in terrorist attacks, nuclear material and in particular items or goods which could have a perfectly legal objective but which could also be used in manufacturing the arms of mass destruction. One way or another, export control mechanisms need to be improved.

D. Export Controls

The Europeans submitted that attention should be paid to the following aspects:

- The assessment of appropriate ways of improving the existing export control mechanisms: Nuclear Suppliers' Group, Zanger Committee, Missile Technology Control Regime, Australia Group and the Wassenaar Arrangement, as a contribution in the fight against terrorism, in order to prevent the diversion by terrorists of any weapons or 'dual use' items or technologies.
- The establishment or further development of EU coordinating mechanisms with the aim to improve information exchange practices in different export control regimes and arrangements, in order to provide accurate and up to date information on risks of proliferation involving non-state actors and states that support them.
- The promotion, within the regimes and arrangements, common understanding and strict adherence to their guidelines, principles and practices.
- The promotion of the inclusion of 'prevention of terrorism' in the objectives of all existing export control regimes and arrangements.
- The promotion, where applicable, in the framework of intensified out-reach activities, of adherence to effective export control criteria by countries outside the existing export control regimes and arrangements.
- The examination of measures, in close cooperation with the Commission, to improve the enforcement of the common control system based on Council Regulation (EC) No. 1334/2000 on dual use items and technology and to consider whether there are further regulatory measures that could be adopted to render the control system more effective regarding non-proliferation by, among others, the following measures:
  - more regular exchanges of information between Member States (e.g. in the coordination group);
  - examine implementation by Member States of controls on transhipment, transit and post-clearance, according to the provisions of the Community customs code.
- An invitation to the relevant EU institutions to consider initiating a review of the denial notice system to ensure that it is operating efficiently after more than three years since its inception.

7.2   MIGRATORY MOVEMENTS

7.2.1   The UN

From the mid-1990s onwards, the status of migrants, asylum seekers and refugees became exposed to erosion. The criteria were somewhat sharpened, procedures were screened and the 'economy of procedures' became part of the equation, and increased knowledge and cooperation resulted on the one hand and decreased compassionate attitudes on the other had an impact on admission, recognition and return policies.

Part of this overall review was the increasing awareness that many of the asylum seekers were not necessarily fleeing from injustice but rather from justice as they might have committed acts which should be considered criminal and unjustifiable.

In the 1997 GA Declaration (51/210) to supplement the 1994 Declaration (49/60) it can be read:

> 3. The States Members of the United Nations reaffirm that States should take appropriate measures in conformity with the relevant provisions of national and international law, including international standards of human rights, before granting refugee status, for the purpose of ensuring that the asylum-seeker has not participated in terrorist acts, considering in this regard relevant information as to whether the asylum-seeker is subject to investigation for or is charged with or has been convicted of offences connected with terrorism and, after granting refugee status, for the purpose of ensuring that that status is not used for the purpose of preparing or organizing terrorist acts intended to be committed against other States or their citizens;
>
> 4. The States Members of the United Nations emphasize that asylum-seekers who are awaiting the processing of their asylum applications may not thereby avoid prosecution for terrorist acts.

This approach was to some extent copied in SC Resolution 1269 (1999). The line of thought developed in these instruments was continued in an even more straightforward manner in SC Res 1373 (2001), in which it was decided:[2]

(a)   to deny safe haven to those who finance, plan, support, or commit terrorist acts, or provide safe havens;

(b)   to prevent those who finance, plan, facilitate or commit terrorist acts from using their respective territories for those purposes against other States or their citizens;

(c)   to prevent the movement of terrorists or terrorist groups by effective border controls and controls on issuance of identity papers and travel documents, and through measures for preventing counterfeiting, forgery or fraudulent use of identity papers and travel documents;

(d)   to take appropriate measures in conformity with the relevant provisions of national and international law, including international standards of human rights, before granting refugee status, for the purpose of ensuring that the asylum seeker has not planned, facilitated or participated in the commission of terrorist acts; and

(e)   to ensure, in conformity with international law, that refugee status is not abused by the perpetrators, organizers or facilitators of terrorist acts, and that claims of political motivation are not recognized as grounds for refusing requests for the extradition of alleged terrorists.[3]

---

[2] Both GA Resolutions (Declarations) and SC Resolutions have been included in full in the annexes to respectively sub-chapter 4.1 and 4.2.

[3] The relevant 2002 Resolution of the (UN) Commission on Human Rights (April 2002) contains a paragraph to this same effect:

In the context of this chapter, the aspects under (a), (d) and (e) are of specific relevance and should be seen in the light of migration as such and refugee law in particular.

7.2.2 **IOM**

IOM stand for the International Organization for Migration, an intergovernmental organization which does not belong to the UN family.[4] As IOM claims that migration benefits migrants and society at large alike, it is obvious that IOM is somewhat worried by the negative impact of the September 2001 events on migratory movements in general. Yet, IOM is pragmatic enough to realize that some action needs to be taken and its February 2002 paper (included in the annex to this chapter) reflects a realistic approach, aimed at providing tools, rather than complaining about the adverse effects

7.2.3 **Refugee Law**

7.2.3.1 *The Refugee Convention*

Refugee law has long suffered under a misunderstanding as to the proper use of Art. 1F of the 1951 Refugee Convention. This article contains an exclusion clause and enumerates who shall not enjoy the benefits of the 1951 Convention. This article does not stand alone, but should be seen in the context of relevant clauses of the 1948 Universal Declaration of Human Rights and Art. 33.2 of the 1951 Convention. Most observers now agree that Art. 1F is indeed a most important clause which shall be applied vigorously.

A traditional argument relating to this proviso concerned the question whether Art. 1F should only be applied upon declaring Art. 1A2 applicable. In other words, it was promoted that the exclusion clause should only be used upon a decision on inclusion. Others were, obviously, of the opinion that such an order did not make sense and that the 1F exclusion question could be posed as a preliminary question, right at the start of the procedure. UNHCR now appears to agree with that line of thought.

'7. Calls upon States to take appropriate measures in conformity with the relevant provisions of national and international law, including international human rights standards, before granting refugee status, with the purpose of ensuring that the asylum-seeker has not planned, facilitated or participated in the commission of terrorist acts, and to ensure, in conformity with international law, that refugee status is not abused by the perpetrators, organizers or facilitators of terrorist acts and that claims of political motivation are not recognized as grounds for refusing requests for the extradition of alleged terrorists'.

[4] In its mission statement it can be read that IOM is committed to the principle that humane and orderly migration benefits migrants and society. As the leading international organization for migration, IOM acts with its partners in the international community to: (a) Assist in meeting the growing operational challenges of migration management; (b) Advance understanding of migration issues; (c) Encourage social and economic development through migration, and (d) Uphold the human dignity and well-being of migrants.

What remains is that the UNHCR appears to submit that a decision to declare Art. 1F applicable should be taken in proportion to the level of persecution the alleged offender could expect upon his/her return. This approach denies the absolute character of Art. 1F and would suggest that some terrorists should after all deserve some level of safe haven, only because the persecution upon return would be so serious. This, in the opinion of the present author, violates both the spirit and the text of Art. 1F as well as of the relevant Security Council resolutions, 1269 and 1373 in particular. In this respect it is also quite remarkable to note that the December 5th, 2001 UNHCR Note (included below, 7.4) concludes that the SC resolutions concerned are in line with international human rights law. There is no need to underline that SC resolutions, by definition, overrule whatever has been agreed upon in other fields of international law: human rights law does not dictate the actions and resolutions of the SC, but the SC 'dictates' in which direction human rights law might go. To all intents and purposes, however, major parts of this December 2001 UNHCR document concerned have been included in this Volume.

7.2.3.2 Article 1F [5]

Article 1F of the 1951 Refugee Convention raises many issues which, of course, are not limited to terrorist acts alone. Traditional war crimes these days probably represent the great majority of cases being considered under this proviso, but in view of the various developments, and also with regard to the agreement to declare terrorist acts as contrary to the purposes and principles of the UN, it is obvious that this particular group will, finally, receive the attention it has already deserved for so many years.

Art. 1F should be seen in the light of Art. 14.2 of the 1948 Universal Declaration of Human Rights and Art. 33.2 of the 1951 Refugee Convention.

Art. 14.2 denies the right to seek and enjoy asylum from persecution 'in the case of prosecutions genuinely arising from non-political crimes or from acts contrary to the purposes and principles of the United Nations'. It is obvious that this would *prima facie* exclude a fairly limited group of persons, particularly as it refers to actual prosecutions. Indeed, Article 1F covers a much wider group of people as it refers to the acts, not to prosecution *per se*. This is of particular importance as, in general, many persons 'participate in acts ... etc.', and only very few are put on trial.

Article 33.2 of the 1951 Refugee Convention indicates that some refugees do not enjoy protection against return to the country of origin, even if their life or freedom would be threatened for reasons of race, religion, nationality, membership of a particular social group or political opinion. It relates to refugees concerning whom there are reasonable grounds for considering them to be a danger to the security of the country in which they are in, or who, having been convicted by a final judgement of a particularly serious crime, constitute a danger to the community of that

---

[5] Based on my introduction to *Refugee Law in Context, The Exclusion Clause*, The Hague, Asser/Kluwer, 1999.

country. It is noteworthy that 'reasonable grounds' would appear to suffice, and that (would be) terrorists could indeed be regarded as a danger to the security of the country of asylum.

The third, and central element of this 'triptych' is Article 1F:

> The provisions of this Convention shall not apply to any person with respect to whom there are serious reasons for considering that:
> (a) he has committed a crime against peace, a war crime, or a crime against humanity, as defined in the international instruments drawn up to make provision in respect of such crimes;
> (b) he has committed a serious non-political crime outside the country of refuge prior to his admission to that country as a refugee;
> (c) he has been guilty of acts contrary to the purposes and principles of the United Nations.

It is quite obvious that terrorists and the complete group of accomplices, would, given the texts of the various terrorism instruments, fall under this Art. 1F, paragraph (b) in particular.

As we have seen elsewhere (e.g. the ICC sub-chapter 3.6) there is no need to declare an alleged offender a terrorist if the international humanitarian law (warfare) instruments could be applied (Art. 1F(a)). It is also noteworthy that all terrorism instruments have declared terrorist acts as 'non-political' by indicating that no justification whatsoever – be it of a political, religious, philosophical or other character – would be acceptable. Article 1F(b) is hence the most appropriate proviso to be applied.

Yet, recent developments, in particular the ones relating to the purposes and principles of the United Nations should also be considered to be of the utmost importance. Indeed, by declaring terrorist acts as contrary to the UN purposes and principles, the (would be) terrorist could also be considered to fall under Art. 1F(c). Forthcoming jurisdiction will prove whether, apart from 1F(b), regard shall also be had to 1F(c).

Of the utmost importance is the phrase 'serious reasons for considering' which is the basis for applying Art. 1F. This, indeed, falls far short of any 'trial', 'prove' or otherwise: an Administration could submit that it has 'serious reasons for considering' and it is then up to the person concerned[6] to prove that he/she does not belong to that category.

Finally, it should be emphasized that Art. 1F does not leave any room for proportionality. Art. 1F is absolute in character and is not subject to any form of trading, balancing or otherwise: it is either/or and not just 'a little bit.'[7]

---

[6] I do not use the term 'asylum seeker' as Art. 1F may also be applied retroactively, e.g. in the case of someone who has received refugee status, but who is subsequently (either through his acts, deeds or words, or thanks to new information) considered to fall under the terms of 1F.

[7] Likewise, a woman can not be 'a little bit pregnant.'

The above having been said, it is remarkable to note that even if Art. 1F would or should be considered applicable, and even if Art. 33.2 would come to the fore, (would be) terrorists would in some cases still find protection under regional instruments (e.g. the European Human Rights Convention, Art. 3), or the Convention against Torture (CAT, 1984, likewise Art. 3). In those cases efforts should be undertaken to see whether prosecution (*judicare*) would be possible, it having been agreed that if it concerns a terrorist, the alleged offender should either be put on trial or be extradited. In a great many cases, however, the prosecutor of the country of 'asylum' will find it difficult to successfully start a case. Emphasis should hence be put on the alternative of extradition. In the absence of any extradition agreements, time and energy need to be invested in ensuring that the alleged offender, or at least the 1F-client can be sent back, or handed over, without the person in question running the risk of being tortured, maltreated or subjected to other forms of inhuman treatment. More needs to be done to negotiate with the authorities of the countries of origin to ensure the due process of law.[8] This is considered to be part and parcel of both refugee law and terrorism law.

7.2.3.3 UNHCR

As indicated elsewhere in this Volume, terrorism can be dealt with under an increasing number of international instruments. Likewise, acts which may or may not amount to terrorism could be dealt with under at least one of the Art. 1F provisos. There is often no need to prove that it concerns terrorism to ensure that the assumed culprit does not deserve a safe haven.[9] For easy reference, the UNHCR document

---

[8] During his 'Nordic' years, the present author dealt with a number of hijackings from the USSR to Finland and Sweden. Whereas Sweden put the hijackers on trial in Sweden, Finland had successfully negotiated a return to the USSR and public, accessible trials during which the hijackers could make use of the services of Finnish defence lawyers.

[9] As an illustration/example (from AWR Bulletin 2000, issue 3-4, p. 194) we could consider could be had to e.g. the PKK (or: LTTE for that matter). Where it concerns the 'right to self-determination', UN GA Resolutions (2625[XXV], 50/6) clearly indicate that territorial integrity is to be upheld. Moreover, any conflict should be settled peacefully (pacific settlement of conflicts), which would indeed indicate that the use of force is not in conformity with international law including human rights. This argument is based on the presumption that the PKK bases its fight on the human right to self-determination. By linking up with human rights, Art. 29.3 UDHR automatically comes to the fore, and the individual responsibility towards the goals and principles of the UN is a realistic one. Hence the relevance of Art. 1Fc. As to Art. 1Fb it could be submitted that the PKK has been involved in a great many terrorist acts, which – irrespective of the 'political' character – fall within the realm of the article dealing with serious non-political crimes. Moreover, in many of the military encounters, the PKK (probably not unlike the Turkish army) has committed acts which should be considered contrary to the law of warfare. Art. 1Fa is applicable in many cases. As to the individual responsibility regard should of course be had to the Statute of Rome (July 1998) in which this aspect has been duly dealt with, and which clearly indicates that the group of persons falling under the Statute (and hence the competence of the future International Criminal Court) is far larger than hitherto thought, meaning that Art. 1F covers an even wider group, as the concept 'serious reasons for considering' is in itself wider than the ICC competence. It is, finally, of some interest to note that the PKK was declared by the EU a terrorist organization in early May, 2002.

containing a reaction to the September 2001 events has to a great extent been included in the Annex to this chapter.

7.2.3.4 *The EU*

As far as the EU is concerned, it indicated to the CTC chair (December 2001) on the issue of mechanisms that are in place for ensuring that asylum seekers have not been involved in terrorist activity before granting refugee status that the EU Council focused its work on the proposal for a Council Directive on minimum standards on procedures in Member States for granting and withdrawing refugee status. At its meeting on 6 and 7 December 2001, the Council adopted conclusions on this matter and took note of the Commission's intention to present a modified proposal. The Council also pursued its work concerning the proposal for a Council Directive laying down minimum standards for the reception of applicants for asylum in EU Member States and the proposal for a Council Regulation establishing the criteria and mechanisms for determining the EU Member State responsible for examining an asylum application lodged in one of the Member States by a third-country national. This Regulation will replace the 1990 Dublin Convention between EU Member States. Existing EC instruments in the field of asylum all contain standard provisions to allow persons thought to be terrorists or to pose a terrorist threat to be excluded from the right to international protection and residency or denied access to certain benefits.

On the 5th of December 2001 a document on exactly the relationship between protection and security saw the day of light. Major parts of this report have been included below (7.5.2), and is herewith submitted that that document contains a most useful survey which in some form or another will find its way into the implementation of European mainstream asylum and migration policy. Virtually all the relevant aspects have been duly dealt with, and represent a useful, pragmatic shift in perception, conception and pragmatism.

7.3   ANNEX IOM
INTERNATIONAL TERRORISM – A MIGRATION ISSUE?[10]

INTRODUCTION

International terrorism is, because of its cross-border dimensions, a migration issue. It touches on a range of matters directly affecting migration policy, in particular: immigration fraud (entry, residence and/or citizenship with illicit intent), national security, integration, ethnic/multicultural affairs and citizenship. But immigration policy, particularly on border control, is just one area where national and international enforcement measures can be taken against terrorism.

---

[10] Neil Clowes/Migration Management Services Department, IOM Geneva, January 2002, and published as an official IOM paper on 19 February 2002. This paper has been slightly edited for this Volume.

International terrorism is a test *in extremis* of the degree to which national immigration policies can continue to be relevant in an increasingly border-less world. Just as trade, capital and services are moving quickly and freely around the world, in ever complex globalised networks, so terrorist activities have a supra-national dynamic beyond the reach of many national law enforcement agencies.

The events of September 11 2001 have shown that terrorists frequently operate outside the purview of immigration enforcement, often with regular residence status, even citizenship (e.g. the Tunisian-born Belgian connected to criminal organizations related to Al Qaeda and the assassination of the Afghan leader of the Northern Alliance).

This scenario clearly calls for tighter control within existing immigration policies, but *remains principally a law enforcement matter*. The focus of most actions taken by governments since September 11 has been better intelligence and intelligence sharing within and among affected states. One option for some states is a clearer regulatory basis for rescinding status, including citizenship, and extraditing persons found to be associated with terrorism, when prosecuted.

IOM agrees with some observers[11] that, while immigration policy may not be central to counter terrorism, it can be an important vehicle for better application of law enforcement and intelligence. Immigration authorities can contribute to national/international intelligence through direct encounters with illegal immigrants and through partner networks with other law enforcement and immigration agencies.

Appropriate systems and mechanisms for information sharing among authorities and states need to be in place. But there also needs to be great care in policy, legislation and practice to protect the right of persons to be internationally mobile, and to protect the integrity of regular migration regimes.

IMMIGRATION POLICY ACTIONS AGAINST TERRORISM

IOM agrees with other commentators[12] that immigration policy reforms cannot prevent terrorism, but are key to any effort to combat it. Enhancement and upgrading of proven operational procedures within existing policies are even more crucial. In the wake of the September 11 events, most states have taken some action to tighten their immigration systems.[13] The focus is primarily on control through better information and identification systems, information sharing and inter-agency/inter-state cooperation. But there is also an increasing need to address the integration needs of migrants who may be vulnerable to recruitment for terrorist activities because of their experiences of alienation and exclusion in host societies.

IMPROVED INFORMATION AND IDENTIFICATION SYSTEMS

Measures are being adopted widely to enhance the integrity of security features and develop new ways of recording and verifying traveler and migrant identities. States which have large-scale passenger movements through their airports, and which rely on tourist and business visitors as wealth creators, must balance the need for security against the need to make the entry of bona fide persons as effortless as possible.

---

[11] Immigration and National security, Migration Policy Institute, Washington DC, September 28, 2001.

[12] Immigration and Terrorism: Policy reform Challenges, Phillip Martin and Susan Martin, 2001.

[13] The original paper contains an annex with a summary of the different national measures having been taken.

On the domestic front, a number of countries are planning to introduce replacement residence cards and other means of identification, which will incorporate special electronically-readable codes and be more resistant to forgery. This will provide greater certainty that the cardholder is the person originally issued the card.
New strategies being tested or considered include:

– *Biometrics*
One of the most commonly debated issues in international migration is how biometrics can aid the overlapping areas of migration, identity, tracking and data comparison. There are numerous trials underway across the world involving iris scans, facial geometry, hand geometry and finger print scans. All have their pros and cons and they seem to have been contradictory valuations. For example, facial geometry has been introduced at Fresno airport yet the police department in Tampa, Florida rejected facial recognition after a six week period dominated by false positives. Iris scans offer quick non-intrusive accurate matches but are more expensive than finger prints scanning devices. The sheer volume of passenger traffic makes visualizing a global integrated database difficult. The way forward for the travel industry will be by way of trusted passenger schemes where frequent travellers volunteer to undergo background checks prior to issue of a smart card. Such systems should be used with other systems to avoid the risk of over reliance and confidence on a single methodology. Whilst this is hardly likely to identify those posing security risks it takes out people from the system thereby enabling better targeted control mechanisms at points of entry and general intelligence work. (…)

– *Finger Printing*
The EURODAC system, established in 2000, and linked to the 'Dublin' Convention, is intended to establish a centralized European Union database on asylum seekers and other non-EU nationals apprehended while illegally crossing borders in the EU territory. It will include fingerprinting (to be erased if refugee status or citizenship is granted). (…)

INCREASED DATA EXCHANGE

All of the major immigrant-receiving states are looking at ways of increasing data exchange among authorities, with carriers and with other states. Germany is also pressing for an EU-wide TCN data base, centralized population register and common or standardized biometric measures throughout the EU. The EC echoes this with its proposal for discussion on a common European visa format with a shared database, including digitalized photographs. Within the EU, there is increasing use of CIREFI as a platform for increased routine exchange of immigration-related information. The CIREFI working group's original focus was the exchange of statistics on irregular migration, but it is now used more for sharing routine operational immigration information.

INCREASED BORDER CONTROL

Not surprisingly, the USA has taken steps to strengthen its border control. However, the recruitment and training of border guards takes time, as does the procurement of surveillance and other equipment, and it is likely to take 12-18 months before all objectives are reached. In the meantime, immediate needs are being met through the use of National Guards to boost border patrol strength from some 300 to 600-900; while regular recruitment takes place, and use is made of Department of Defense surveillance equipment and intelligence personnel. These actions are being taken in the context of the recently signed USA/Canadian agreement on tighter border security. This bilateral approach heralds a new intensity of cooperation in the joint management of a very porous North American border. In the South, the USA has committed to a substantial increase of border guards along the Mexico border, and will increase general cooperation on migration management with the Mexican authorities.

Those EU countries with Eastern borders to Central Europe are also increasing their guard patrols along the green borders. The move by the EC to establish a common border guard force, while not driven by the events of September 11, will clearly be influenced by them in terms of a suggested operational mandate.

TIGHTER ENTRY CONTROL

With limited resources, countries have recognised the value of flexible resource deployment towards problem areas. In busy airports, it is important to have the mechanisms to recognise emerging trends of bogus identities or false papers from particular points of departure. A number of countries in Western Europe and North America are thus investing considerably in intelligence and analysis. A great deal of entry control efficiency is dependent on advance information and trend analysis, often only possible where immigrant processing abroad is closely linked with border and in-country processing facilities.

– Shifting the Borders

Traditional border control regimes have increasingly shifted the locus of control abroad or further away from their immediate physical borders. There are obvious financial and political advantages to minimizing the arrival of irregular migrants on one's borders by doing so, the policy being one of 'prevention is better than cure'. There are limitations to what can be achieved. A number of countries have been criticized by humanitarian organisations for potentially interfering with the individual right to freedom of movement under international law. There are a number of typical 'offshore' control strategies employed by Governments, among them:

Passenger Pre–clearance – where immigration services work with carriers and intelligence/law enforcement agency operations in the country of origin or transit to clear passengers for entry at their final destination. This is crucial where criminal activity is aiding immigration fraud; and its cross-border nature calls for cross-border cooperation. The Immigration services of a number of countries post officers close to the centers of criminal activity.

Immigration Liaison Officers (ILOs) – are immigration enforcement officers posted close to the centres of criminal activity, or in source countries of irregular migrants to work with local law enforcement agencies and international agencies such as Europol to prevent irregular migration and help close down related illegal and criminal operations.

Airline Liaison Officers (ALOs) – these are immigration enforcement officers posted abroad to work with, and train, airline staff in the prevention of travel of persons with fraudulent documents or IDs. They often work in tandem with ILOs. The UK, for example, has steadily expanded its network of ALOs to over 20 around the world, and is now complementing this network with the posting of ILOs. The USA and Canada have agreed to expand the number of immigration officers working overseas to prevent and interdict, and to share intelligence as part of their combined response to terrorism.

Advanced Passenger Information (API) – by agreement between countries, and airlines and Governments, this permits passenger manifests to be sent ahead of the flight to the Immigration authorities of the country of destination, for pre-checking before arrival.

CARRIER SANCTIONS

Carrier liability legislation aims at making carriers accountable for embarking and delivering undocumented migrants or persons with forged papers. The sanctions underpin all other pre-embarkation activities abroad. Increasingly, governments are offsetting the sanctions with incentives for airlines to prevent embarkation of illegal or irregular migrants. This carrot-and-stick regime, underpinned by training of airline staff by ALOs, provides an extra cordon of defense against terrorism.

That cordon is further strengthened where pre-clearance and pre-embarkation processing is supported by solid and integrated migrant information systems of the kind used by Australia and New Zealand, which link visa issuance abroad with entry clearance at the port of entry and departure monitoring at the port of exit. These enable the authorities to match incoming with outgoing movements; eventually also to share this with other states' information systems – such as between Australia and New Zealand.

Carrier networks and initiatives have proven their usefulness to varying degrees. But there is also a danger of overkill, which could lead to a breakdown of cooperation among countries of origin, transit and destination if they are not managed in a cooperative way. It clearly becomes untenable for the host country if each country of destination seeks to post its own ALO at the same airports. Pre-clearance is less of an issue because this can be handled at consular or similar premises, where such exist.

The need for, and value of, external border control varies from state to state. Countries like Australia, with their blue borders and distance from others, are able to capitalize more on offshore clearance processes than many landlocked European countries with their porous green borders. Countries with a high reliance on external, as opposed to internal, control measures will wish to retain sole responsibility for ALO functions where the workload justifies it. They will not wish to delegate these functions, although sharing costs might be a possibility by undertaking work for others where volume of work is not an issue but strategic presence is. For other countries, including those with limited resources overseas, inter-state cooperation is the only way to continue/expand this activity – for example by doing each other's work, sharing resources/premises or sharing information.

The EU has brokered such cooperative arrangements through CIREFI, and some joint ALO initiatives have been launched. Similar forms of cooperation exist in other regions, e.g. under the Puebla Process, to override individual, national, political, ideological interests and set inter-governmental guidelines.

In the longer term, international organizations could play a role in setting such guidelines and standards.

TIGHTER INTERNAL MIGRATION CONTROLS

– Language Controls:
As an aid to determining nationality, more Western European countries have been looking into the concept of language analysis, based on Swiss and Swedish experiences in this area. For example, Germany is planning to legislate to provide for language analysis to be a nationality determinant. This will be particularly helpful in the area of undocumented and unco-operative cases.

In another context, in the USA for example, affidavits are no longer acceptable in one state as evidence of the ability to read English – which is a key requirement for a driver's licence; and in another state, non US citizens must go to regional drivers' licence processing centres, while nationals can use local centres.

– Tighter sanctions against Suspects:
The UK's new Anti-Terrorism, Crime and Security Act, which took effect on Friday 21 December 2001, enables authorities to jail suspected foreign nationals considered a threat to national security, who would normally not be subject to prosecution because of insufficient evidence, and who cannot be deported because they could be killed or tortured at home (subject to Review by Immigration Tribunal after 6 months).

– Control of ethnic/religious associations
In Germany, Interior Minister Schily banned a Cologne-based Union of Islamic Associations and Communities; and the Government is considering removing the current exemption for religious groups from the restrictions imposed by its law of association. In the USA there have been a considerable number of registered charities who have had their assets frozen.

– In-country identification
As already mentioned, a number of states are planning to improve their means of identifying asylum seekers and residents through new, electronically secure cards. To take the UK proposals as an example, asylum seekers are required to register in order to access social benefits. They are photographed and fingerprinted, and this data with other case-related information, is encoded in a chip located in a plastic-encased card. The chip is machine-readable both at the source of benefit payment and by mobile fingerprint readers carried by immigration officers. Verification of identity is also supplemented by enforcement/control information so that, for example, a missed interview will be flagged in the system – and as a result, no benefit will be paid out.

REGIONAL/INTER-COUNTRY COOPERATION

There are many examples of regional groupings and processes addressing the terrorism/migration issue. For example, within the European context the Schengen countries exercise a common visa policy under which a visa is valid for any Schengen country, and may be issued by one country for travel to another. There are obvious implications for integrity of standards, and these are aired at regular meetings. As there is no internal border control, there is more reliance on the external border controls of the country of entry. As a logical extension to these arrangements, the EC is advocating the idea of a common European border guard force. The French Government has also called for joint control of Europe's external borders and ALO networks in countries of origin.

– Schengen Information System (SIS) – provides vital support for the operation of the border-free system among the Schengen states. It acts as an 'alert list' of those who have committed offences. If a visa applicant's name appears in SIS, the visa is denied. Member States feed the system with information through national networks (N-SIS) which are connected to a central system and supplemented by the SIRENE network made up of representatives from the national and local police, customs and the judiciary.[14]

– EURODAC is an example of 'regional' cooperation compliance underpinned by legislation. The collection of fingerprints of asylum seekers to prevent repeat applications in each of the Member States of the EU has the potential to reduce uncertainty about who has been where.

---

[14] Migration Policy Institute, Background Paper, Immigration and National Security, September 28, 2001.

– *EUROPOL* – established under the Maastricht Treaty of 1992 – is a region-wide law enforcement support mechanism relying on intelligence from Member States on drugs, organized crime, terrorism and trafficking. It is developing a database to be operational in 2002. But EU cooperation on data exchange is only as good as the information available and shared by the Members, and permitted by member and EU data protection regimes. The fact that a data subject must give his/her consent to use of the information can hinder serious and quick information exchange. And data protection also limits the EU capacity to share information with non EU states.

USA/Canadian Agreement on border cooperation (November 2001) – As mentioned above, this agreement includes a mutual strengthening of border operations, among others to help end 'asylum shopping', (40% of Canadian asylum claimants arrive from the USA).
Other regions are engaged in dialogues which, *inter alia*, grapple with issues generated by concern over the movement of terrorists. A conference shortly to be held in Bali on irregular migration, to which Asian countries, IOM and UNHCR have been invited, is one such example.

Is Immigration Control the Solution?

IOM agrees with MPI's assessment that for large immigrant-receiving states, such as the USA with its ca. 500 million entries and exits per annum, *immigration controls can only be a 'needle in the haystack' measure to counter terrorism.*[15] While tightening the asylum process has, in countries like the USA, led to a reduction in the number of unfounded claims, there may be no linkage here with the deterrence of terrorism. Only the information/data collected is of obvious value if this can be cross-matched with other relevant data bases.

> In addition, terrorists do not need to be – indeed are unlikely to be – newcomers to a host country. With well-established support communities in the host country, the well-laid plans and global networking of terrorist organizations do not need to rely on traditional immigration to achieve their ends. As in the world of globalized commerce, the critical elements of terrorism can be mobilized and deployed without cross-border people movements. Accessing services for e.g. electronic bank transactions is possible through the Internet; and engagement of local sub-contractors can replace immigration.

Western governments tend to invest heavily in policing the permanent gateways to their countries and their asylum systems, both of which can, in the context of regional entities such as the EU, give access to other countries. They can also lay the foundations for high volume secondary temporary flows, e.g. visitors and temporary residents, who only need to demonstrate some real connection of a business or family nature, in order to enter for brief stays, but which can sometimes be converted into longer stay or permanent residence status. In many states, thus, it is the visitor and other temporary entry programs that potentially create the biggest open door for persons with illicit intentions. In general, large-scale movements, whether permanent or temporary, are difficult to check individually, also in post-emergency or conflict situations. But doing nothing is not an option. The best approaches appear to be those that combine intelligence-driven, flexible controls and fast response real time IT management systems (from passenger manifest analysis to biometric data comparisons). More robust identification and subsequent verification processes are available, and are beginning to

---

[15] Ibidem.

be used in resettlement programs run by the USA. It seems likely that more advanced and quicker processes will be deployed at overseas locations to provide more certainty and security, also on temporary travelers through verification on arrival. But these programs will only be as good as the calibre of the people and organizations responsible for their operation. The well-trained professional will continue to play a vital role.

UNINTENDED CONSEQUENCES OF INCREASED CONTROL MEASURES

Many believe, that the events of 11 September mean that discussions of migrant, refugee and asylum policies will now take place in a context where antiterrorist efforts take priority. Few doubt that conservative voices have been given more strength in arguing against liberal immigration and refugee policies. Anti-immigrant feelings in some European countries have encouraged right-wing parties to push door-closing agendas. There is also clearly a danger that too heavy an emphasis on admission control can skew or militate against a balanced migration policy. The stricter the regime and the more difficult it is to secure visas, the greater the potential for deterring bona fide visitors and businessmen. This can impact both on a nation's wealth, particularly where it is a trading nation, and on how it is perceived from the outside as a welcoming nation. The financial and political costs of too strict an immigration control regime can be high.

Domestically, the ever present tension between the rights of the individual and the security of the state can be thrown into sharp relief by such strict immigration regimes. Civil liberty groups will be watching new requirements brought in on the back of anti-terrorism legislation closely, and challenges on constitutional and proportionality grounds will be forthcoming. There may be fundamental differences of approach between the judiciary and the legislature, with the result that much time is spent in the courts.

The issue of identity cards, either for everyone or specific groups, will continue to be politically sensitive, particularly for countries which have no tradition of carrying identity cards such as the USA, UK and Australia.

CREATING THE RIGHT CLIMATE DOMESTICALLY

Ethnic/Multicultural Affairs Policies

How to cope with the 'ethnic affairs' side of the problem is often swept under the carpet by migration policy makers and commentators. Giving this subject increased prominence could well be one important way of addressing international terrorism; as post September 11 events have shown. There are two important reasons why governments urgently need to ensure effective integration strategies:

–   protection of migrants against a growing community backlash following September 11;
–   protection of migrants (and the general community) from being susceptible to recruitment to terrorism, e.g. through disaffection or alienation within their host community.

Integration policies have existed in states with long experience of immigration, and in the main have proven to be successful in ensuring a degree of social stability. Many immigrant-receiving states have legislation on equal opportunities designed to promote cultural and racial harmony; and positive discrimination is used to secure equal representation in certain professions. A range of other measures are in place to improve access to mainstream services and community activities. The most significant players in these initiatives are the NGOs, and community and ethnic support groups.

The EU is working towards a common European approach to social integration of third-country nationals, based on equal rights, free movement and some measures to enhance immigrants' economic and socio-cultural position against xenophobia and racial discrimination. A number of EC initiatives and programmes are already in place to support actions in this field.

All these initiatives are critical to a balanced approach to migration, and to ensuring that the minority phenomena of criminality or terrorism in the migration context do not compromise the integrity of regular migration or the right of persons to be mobile. They may need to be updated in the wake of September 11.

Employment Sector
The security of a state is inevitably undermined when there is a knowledge gap about who is in the country doing what. There is no doubt that pull factors play as important a role as push factors in the flow of irregular migration. No government can reduce these flows without co-operation from its own constituency.

Thus, if the employment sector does not cooperate with a government in the eradication of illegal working, the flow of irregular migrants seeking work will continue despite governments' best intentions and legislative prohibition.

Governments are increasingly taking action to provide legitimate outlets for economically-driven migration, including at the unskilled labour end of the market, in parallel with their evolving policies to eliminate illegal working.

SOME RECOMMENDATIONS TO GOVERNMENTS

The phenomenon, and the solutions, will be different for each state. For the large, immigrant-receiving states, the appropriate combination of the measures referred to earlier will need to be tested. They will need to draw the line between what is achievable and what is desirable.

For transit/destination countries with smaller, more manageable cross-border movements, border controls may well be more effective in identifying, apprehending and preventing terrorists and their affiliates than for large immigrant-receiving states.

Larger immigrant-receiving states may rather need to complement their offshore pre-emptive actions with tighter internal migration management; and work more closely with countries of origin and transit less able to cope with their illegal migration and security problems.But this would require strong cooperation and co-funding/investment by the better-endowed states.

The following general strategies are recommended for governments and international agencies:

- Put legislation in place that makes anti-terrorism a priority for all law enforcement and immigration authorities.
- Raise the interest/commitment of partner states to the same level.
- Improve globalised intelligence gathering and exchange.
- Strengthen targeted, rather than generalised, surveillance/law enforcement (through better information).
- Strengthen the capacity of Immigration programmes/procedures to allow better application of intelligence measures, and productive inter-state cooperation, e.g. as in the recommendations by MPI to the US Government to strengthen border management partnerships with Canada and Mexico.
- Human Rights organizations should train intelligence officials – i.e. work at the 'top end' as well as at the 'bottom end'.
- Analyse the need for community-focused actions to support integration of migrants and their protection from xenophobia and discrimination. Establish the same in legislation and practice.

Schematic Overview:
SUMMARY OF RESPONSES TO THE EVENTS OF 11 SEPTEMBER 2001

Austria	Schengen border and visa controls have been strengthened. The existing list of 21 visa-required countries have increased to 26. The number of countries for whom automatic referral back to Austria is required before issuance of a visa has been increased. Discussions on visa issuing standards under Schengen are underway. Security and intelligence sharing partnerships with Candidate countries are being sought.
Belgium	Measures to increase the amount of information collected about refugees to enable better questioning are being put in place and a more robust use of the exclusion clause of the Convention is expected.
Canada	Approximately CN$49 million dollars is being earmarked to strengthen certain areas of immigration and citizenship. A new residence card will be introduced for new immigrants. This will have security features and replace the paper document currently in use. The use of detention for new arrivals will increase where compliance with entry conditions is thought to be in doubt. A new emphasis is to be placed on pre-entry screening procedures with in-depth interviews and risk profiling. There will be a great deal of work with the US on border issues to maintain the present status quo including joint border intelligence and joint training.
Denmark	Tougher regime for asylum seekers and biometrics being considered.
Finland	Increasing the number of countries where referral to the police takes place before issuance of a visa.
Germany	Three billion DM budget against terrorism has been announced and the Border Guard will receive a share. The focus of measures will be on prevention of entry, and the passport format is being reviewed with a view to enhanced security features. Biometric data will be collected from visa applicants falling into certain categories. Those who are suspected of terrorist activities will be refused. Provision is being made for the selective fingerprinting of visitors on their arrival. Central photo database of passport photos will be established to combat identification substitution. Greater application of the Convention exclusion clause will be made. Measures are being taken to reduce restrictions on exchanging data, particularly in the exchange between carriers and authorities on passenger bookings and disclosure of information rules.

	The current exemption for religious groups from the restrictions imposed by the law of association is being removed. Changes in the banking laws to permit greater disclosure of information in cases involving suspected terrorists. Biometric feature to be incorporated into passports, visas and other ID Legal basis to be established for language analysis to be recognized as a nationality determiner
Italy	Recent events will impact to amend the current draft Bill, but it is too early to do more than speculate what these amendments might be.The use of biometrics in identification seems likely.
Netherlands	Anti people-trafficking units are being established. The circumstances under which the police may demand identification from people within the territory will be increased. Airline gate checks will be intensified and visa controls enhanced by means of fingerprinting. Increase in funding for biometry. Examining role of other biometrics for ID in passport.
Spain	New legislation has been drafted to tackle smuggling and trafficking with $10K fine plus 10 years imprisonment for traffickers Tougher laws on illegal employment with increased penalties for employers
Switzerland	New laws on carriers sanction Provision to tackle bogus marriages Increased smuggling penalties API agreements with carriers Biometric application New permanent residence card Data exchange provision between agencies
United Kingdom	A complete overhaul of Immigration and Asylum Legislation will take place with new legislation in 2002 seeking to redress some of the deficiencies revealed in implementing the 1999 legislation. They include; Measures relating to the reception, induction, detention and removal of failed asylum seekers. Changes to the offences and penalties relating to smuggling and trafficking. Compliance with security measures such as biometric tests and exclusion from the asylum system of suspected terrorists. The issue of smart cards to applicants to help identification and tracking. Greater use of the exclusion provisions of the Convention is also likely to emerge. This will be in addition to the Anti-terrorsm, Crime and security Act which took effect on 21 December 2001.

	New provision for the exchange of information between government departments and government and the private sector, including bulk data exchanges, to more easily screen for risk-profiled passengers.
Sweden	Migration Board and the appellate authorities will more regularly look into and test the possibility of asylum seekers being terrorists. Migration Board will work more closely with the police and intelligence services on cases to make better-informed decisions.
USA	The USA has now published comprehensive proposals tackling internal and external measures against terrorism.
	Build up to tripling to tripling of current staffing of the northern border.Inadmissability provisions on grounds of suspected terrorist activity are to be introduced. Measures relating to easier data exchange are proposed, including the exchange of information between governments. Mandatory detention for those certified to be a threat to national security. Greater use of technology and improvements of such things as machine readable passports will be examined, as will procedures for the better screening of the entry of immigrants and other individuals applying for visas for entry to the US, particularly students and those entering under the US Refugee Programme. Increased funding for more INS personnel at borders and overseas Joint exercises with Canada (see above)
Central America	Central American governments are reacting at the regional level. Issues are being discussed in such fora as the Legal, Defense and Security Sub-Committee of the Central American Commission of Security and the Pueblo Process.
IATA	Special conference in Arizona to discuss legal and some security issues took place in February 2002. Working groups and airlines will focus on airline and airport security and the use of booking and ticketing information in the context of risk profiling.
European Commission	Harmonizing judicial cooperation, border control and expanding the field of exchange of information (a new working group is being set up to focus on exchanges relating to combating terrorism.)
IGC	A workshop held in October 2001 focused on immigration control measures designed to reduce terrorist risks. It provided information on who is doing what, and will no doubt lead to further discussion at the full round at end June 2002 in UK.

7.4   ANNEX UNHCR

Addressing security concerns without undermining refugee protection; UNHCR's perspective
November 2001.

A. Introduction

1. In the aftermath of the attacks of 11 September 2001, security considerations are permeating policy responses on a wide range of issues. UNHCR endorses all efforts, multilateral or national, directed at eliminating and effectively combating international terrorism. UNHCR shares the legitimate concern of States to ensure that there should be no avenue for those supporting or committing terrorists acts to secure access to territory, whether to find a safe haven, avoid prosecution, or to carry out further attacks. The Office recognizes that appropriate mechanisms need to be put in place in the field of asylum as in other areas. At the same time care should be taken to ensure a proper balance with the refugee protection principles at stake. The observations and suggestions that follow are offered against this background and in response to the request, contained in SCR 1377 of 12 November 2001, for the newly established Counter-Terrorism Committee to explore with international organizations the promotion of best practice in the areas covered by this resolution.

B. General

2. UNHCR's main concern is twofold: that bona fide asylum-seekers may be victimized as a result of public prejudice and unduly restrictive legislative or administrative measures, and that carefully built refugee protection standards may be eroded. Current anxieties about international terrorism risk fuelling a growing trend towards the criminalisation of asylum-seekers and refugees. Asylum-seekers increasingly have a difficult time in a number of States, either accessing procedures or overcoming presumptions about the validity of their claims, which stem from their ethnicity, or their mode of arrival. The fact that asylum-seekers have arrived illegally does not vitiate the basis of their claim. Because they have a certain ethnic or religious background, which may be shared by those who have committed grave crimes, does not mean they, themselves, are also to be excluded.

3. Any discussion on security safeguards should start from the assumption that refugees are themselves escaping persecution and violence, including terrorist acts, and are not the perpetrators of such acts. Another starting point is that the international refugee instruments do not provide a safe haven to terrorists and do not protect them from criminal prosecution. On the contrary, they render the identification of persons engaged in terrorist activities possible and necessary, foresee their exclusion from refugee status and do not shield them against either criminal prosecution or expulsion.

4. UNHCR's overall conclusion is that dealing with the terrorist threat in the context of asylum does not require amendment of the principles on which refugee protection is based, but should benefit from a review and tightening of procedural security measures where necessary.

C. Admission/Access to refugee status determination

5. UNHCR appreciates that States may wish to strengthen border controls as one way of identifying security threats at the point of entry. Enhanced cooperation between border guards, intelligence services and immigration and asylum authorities of the State concerned, as well as with such organizations as Interpol, Europol and Eurodac could assist in the early identification of terrorist suspects. Increased security checks, including through the use of fingerprints, are understandable measures but there may be a risk of over-burdening procedures. Profiling and screening solely on the basis of religious or racial characteristics would, in UNHCR's view, be discriminatory and inappropriate.

6. The summary rejection of asylum-seekers at borders or points of entry may amount to *refoulement*. All persons have the right to seek asylum and to undergo individual refugee status determination. Each claim, even where there is a suspicion of involvement in grave criminal acts, must be determined on its own merits, and not against negative and discriminatory presumptions deriving from the nationality, ethnic origin or religious faith of the claimant. The refugee definition, properly applied, should lead to the exclusion of those responsible for serious criminal, including terrorist, acts. Since issues of exclusion can be complicated, UNHCR continues to advocate that they should continue to be dealt with in the regular asylum procedure, which allows for a full factual and legal assessment in the individual case by qualified personnel. Non-admission at borders and barring access to the asylum procedure not only endangers bona fide asylum-seekers but could serve, ironically, as an incentive to terrorism by encouraging those involved to seek entry through illegal means, thereby removing the possibility of identification through the interview process accompanying asylum adjudications.

7. Where there is a reasonable possibility that exclusion issues may arise in the case of an individual pursuing an asylum claim, States have an evident interest in expedient decision making processes. In such cases UNHCR continues to support a proper factual and legal assessment, but believes this could be accomplished through prioritized and expedited consideration of the claim by a specialized 'exclusion unit' within the refugee status determination process. Such unit would have expertise in relevant areas of refugee law and criminal law, specialist knowledge of terrorist organizations, and clear communication links with intelligence services and criminal enforcement agencies. Specialist expertise and clearly focused resources would enable prompt and quality decision making. UNHCR promotes the redesign of the regular asylum procedure in States to accommodate the setting up and operating of such a unit.

8. If the asylum-seeker is wanted by national courts or for extradition purposes, the examination of the claim could be deferred pending the completion of criminal law enforcement procedures.

9. In the case of individuals with regard to whom there are serious reasons to believe that they are seeking entry to prepare or commit terrorist offences, evidently there would be no obligation on the State in question to admit the person. This being said, there is an obligation of States to bring terrorists to justice as asserted most recently in SCR 1373 of 28 September 2001, which should presumably also be a factor in deciding whether to admit the person and how to respond to an asylum claim. As regards any asylum request lodged, its expedited examination would still be warranted.

D. Restrictions on the movement of asylum-seekers

10. The 1951 Convention relating to the Status of Refugees and its 1967 Protocol, as well as human rights law do not preclude restrictions on the movement of asylum-seekers, including detention as the exception, not the rule, if necessary in circumstances prescribed by law and subject to due process safeguards. Detention would justifiably be deemed necessary, where there are solid reasons for suspecting links with terrorism in the individual case. Proposals to introduce automatic detention of all asylum-seekers entering illegally or coming from particular countries, as are being considered in a number of States in response to the resurgence of fears about terrorism, are not supported by UNHCR. They would, in UNHCR's view, contradict long established guidelines on detention agreed by States, and could be seen as an arbitrary, even discriminatory response which could then come into conflict with international legal norms.

E. Sharing of data on asylum-seekers

11. UNHCR recognizes that the sharing of data between States is crucial to combating terrorism. States should, though, also take into account the well-established principle that information on asylum-seekers should not be shared with the country of origin. This could endanger the safety of the bona fide asylum-seeker and/or family members remaining in the country of origin. Best State practice indeed incorporates a strict confidentiality policy. Should it exceptionally be deemed necessary to contact the authorities in the country of origin, in case there is suspicion of terrorist involvement and the required information may only be obtained from these authorities, there should be no disclosure of the fact that the individual has applied for asylum.

F. Exclusion from refugee status

12. Those responsible for serious crimes are legally excluded from refugee status by virtue of the terms of the international refugee instruments. UNHCR encourages States to use the exclusion clauses rigorously, albeit appropriately. It also encourages States, which have not already done so, to incorporate the exclusion clauses of the 1951 Refugee Convention into national legislation. This is consistent not only with the dictates of refugee law, but also with Security Council resolutions which call on States not to provide refuge to terrorists, in particular SCR 1373 (2001) which calls for appropriate measures with regard to asylum-seekers. This being said, according to the latter resolution, such measures need to conform to international law, including international standards of human rights.

13. The crimes to which article 1F(a) of the 1951 Refugee Convention refer – crimes against peace, war crimes or crimes against humanity – are those so defined in international instruments and are to be interpreted in the light of a number of rapidly evolving sources of international criminal law. UNHCR concurs with the view that the 11 September attacks constituted a crime against humanity.

14. Article 1F(c) concerns acts contrary to the purposes and principles of the United Nations. This provision has always been understood as applying to persons acting on behalf of States or quasi-States because the United Nations' purposes and principles are intended to be a guide for States in their relations with each other. It remains to be seen how the assertion in SCR 1377 (2001) that acts of international terrorism are contrary to the purposes and principles of the Charter of the United Nations, may promote the application of article 1F(c) to a

broader circle of persons, in the specific context of acts of international terrorism which may be qualified as serious threats to international peace and security.

15. A central exclusion clause, from the perspective of international terrorism and fugitives from justice, is article 1F(b). It refers to 'serious non-political crimes' (committed outside the country of refuge), but this would generally encompass acts of terrorism as defined in relevant international conventions, notwithstanding any political motives behind such acts. This follows logically from the fact that the extradition clauses of these conventions have abolished the political offence exemption. Moreover, especially violent acts of terrorism are likely to fail the predominance and proportionality tests used in many jurisdictions to define political offences.

16. In view of the seriousness of the issues and the consequences of an incorrect decision, the application of any exclusion clause should continue to be individually assessed, based on available evidence, and conform to basic standards of fairness and justice. As mentioned earlier, this assessment should be located within the refugee status determination process, albeit taking place in specially tailored procedures for exclusion.

17. The assessment should also, in UNHCR's view, be sensitive to certain additional considerations. Firstly, crimes may not be of the same level of gravity as terrorist violence sufficient to warrant exclusion, in which case one has to take into account the consequences upon return of the person to his or her country of origin. Secondly, even though exclusion proceedings do not equate with a full criminal trial, the standard of proof ('serious reasons') has to be a higher threshold than a mere 'reasonable suspicion'. In the case of an indictment by an international criminal tribunal, this standard would automatically be met and moreover no further individual assessment would be necessary. Thirdly, exclusion requires individual liability, that is, the personal and knowing involvement of the individual in acts of terrorism.

18. Where, however, there is sufficient proof that an asylum-seeker belongs to an extremist international terrorist group, such as those involved in the 11 September attacks, voluntary membership could be presumed to amount to personal and knowing participation, or at least acquiescence amounting to complicity in the crimes in question. In asylum procedures, a rebuttable presumption of individual liability could be introduced to handle such cases. Drawing up lists of international terrorist organizations at the international level would facilitate the application of this procedural device since such certification at the international level would carry considerable weight in contrast to lists established by one country alone. The position of the individual in the organization concerned, including the voluntariness of his or her membership, as well as the fragmentation of certain groups would, however, need to be taken into account.

19. UNHCR fully appreciates the wish of States to tackle the financing and other forms of support of terrorist groups. This would best be done through domestic legislation. As such legislation may influence the interpretation of the exclusion clauses, it would have to be carefully drafted to be explicit as to the ramifications of such activities. In UNHCR's view it would go too far if, for instance, individuals demonstrating or collecting private contributions for groups that are engaged in armed conflicts, as defined in international humanitarian law, were to be automatically excluded from refugee protection, solely for this reason.

G. Cancellation of refugee status

20. Generalized suspicions based solely on religious, ethnic or national origin or political af-filiation do not justify a general review process. Cancellation of refugee status normally only follows evidence of fraud or misrepresentation as regarding facts central to the refugee deci-sion. This does mean that refugee status may be cancelled, if it emerges that one of the exclu-sion clauses would have applied to the individual, had all the relevant facts been known. Terrorist activity after arrival would normally lead to prosecution locally and/or expulsion, rather than cancellation of status.

H. Expulsion, including to the country of origin

21. UNHCR is concerned that States may be inclined to expel groups or individuals based on religious, ethnic or national origin or political affiliation, on the mere assumption that they may be involved in terrorism. International law, in particular article 33(2) of the 1951 Refu-gee Convention, does not prohibit the expulsion of recognized refugees, provided however that it is established in the individual case that the person constitutes a danger to the security or the community of the country of refuge. As this danger should outweigh the danger of re-turn to persecution, UNHCR wishes to emphasize that such expulsion decisions must be reached in accordance with due process of law which substantiates the security threat and al-lows the individual to provide any evidence which might counter the allegations.

22. Expulsion and exclusion are two different processes. Exclusion from refugee status is motivated by the severity of crimes committed in the past. It prevents fugitives from escaping justice for such crimes, just as, simultaneously, it protects the institution of asylum from abuse. Persons excluded do not deserve international refugee protection. Expulsion aims to protect the country of refuge and hinges on the appreciation of a present or future threat. The threshold for returning refugees to their country of origin – as an exception to the *non-refoulement* principle – has to be particularly stringent.

I. Extradition

23. International refugee law does not preclude the extradition for prosecution purposes of recognized refugees, much less of asylum-seekers. Extradition should, however, be granted only after the corresponding legal proceedings have been completed, and where it has been shown that the extradition is not being requested solely or principally as a means to return a person to a country for purposes which in fact amount to persecution. Although extradition clauses in recent international conventions no longer contain the political offence exemption for terrorist offences, they retain the non-persecution safeguard. UNHCR would recommend that the retention of this safeguard be mandatory rather than optional.

24. In case of a pending asylum procedure, it is conceivable that further consideration of the asylum claim be deferred until the proceedings in the extradition process enable informed de-cision making on whether or not exclusion from refugee status is justified. If the asylum-seeker is found excludable following consideration of his or her fear of persecution, the extradition could be decided upon without re-assessing the persecution element. If the asy-lum-seeker is not excluded and it is assessed that extradition would indeed amount to return to persecution, prosecution in the country of asylum is, in UNHCR's view, the appropriate response, based on the principle *aut dedere aut iudicare*.

J. Increasing criminal law enforcement

25. UNHCR would welcome the development and the swift adoption of a comprehensive Convention on International Terrorism and of other international or regional instruments, to serve also as an agreed framework for national legislation. UNHCR has already provided comments on the draft Convention and several pieces of national legislation. The closure of jurisdictional loopholes and clarity about the definition of terrorist offences would seem to be essential for combating terrorism effectively.

26. UNHCR appeals to governments, however, to ensure that the terms of international instruments and of domestic legislation do not imply any unwarranted linkages between asylum-seekers/refugees and terrorists. In addition, definitions need to be quite precise. If definitions are too broad and vague, there is a risk that the 'terrorist' label could be abused by some for political ends, for example to criminalize activities of political opponents. This is a matter of concern to UNHCR. It could well lead to recriminations amounting to persecution. The definition of terrorist offences is moreover likely to influence the interpretation and application of the exclusion clauses of the 1951 Refugee Convention in the future.

K. The continuing importance of refugee resettlement

27. There are signs that several refugee resettlement countries are disinclined to maintain their programmes at the promised levels, particularly for certain ethnic groups. Resettlement remains imperative, and continued support for resettlement is of vital importance. UNHCR is maintaining its efforts to diversify the number of resettlement countries and to strengthen its programmes, from emergency processing through to more systematic and elaborate use of resettlement to address durable solutions needs of refugees. UNHCR has no difficulty with an intensification of security screening, including finger-printing, of candidates for resettlement.

L. Combating racism and xenophobia

28. Equating asylum with a safe haven for terrorists is not only legally wrong and thus far unsupported by facts, but it serves to vilify refugees in the public mind and promotes the singling out of persons of particular races or religions for discrimination and hate-based harassment.

29. Since 11 September, a number of immigrant and refugee communities have suffered attacks and harassment based on perceived ethnicity or religion, heightening social tensions. While there are some asylum-seekers and refugees who have been, or will be, associated with serious crime, this does not mean that the majority should be damned by association with the few. Rather, the full application of the 1951 Refugee Convention and indeed of immigration policies generally is a key aspect of measures to combat xenophobia and reduce prejudice, which could otherwise provide the very conditions in which anger and extremism can flourish. As the UN Secretary-General stated on 24 September 2001: 'no people, no region and no religion should be condemned because of the unspeakable acts of a few individuals'.

30. Resolute leadership is called for at this particularly difficult time to de-dramatise and de-politicise the essentially humanitarian challenge of protecting refugees and to provide better understanding of refugees and of their right to seek asylum.

7.5   ANNEX EU/EC

On December 5th, 2001, the Commission of the European Communities, the European Commission (EC), issued a Working Document on the relationship between safeguarding internal security and complying with international protection obligations and instruments (COM/2001, 743 final). It covers various issues relating to freedom of movement and the security (read: terrorism) aspects, and focuses on the Exclusion Clause of the 1951 Refugee Convention and elaborates on other, future aspects of the relationship between freedom of movement and security, which, should indeed be seen in the context of the Copenhagen (1993) principle to create an area of freedom, security and justice. Later that month the Council adopted a Common Position in which a number of references of relevance to this issue of concern to this chapter.

7.5.1   Common Position: European Council, 27 December 2001
(excerpts on 'migratory movements', the subject of this chapter:[16])

Article 6
Safe haven shall be denied to those who finance, plan, support, or commit terrorist acts, or provide safe havens.

Article 7
Persons who finance, plan, facilitate or commit terrorist acts shall be prevented from using the territories of the Member States of the European Union for those purposes against Member States or third States or their citizens.

Article 10
The movement of terrorists or terrorist groups shall be prevented by effective border controls and controls on the issuing of identity papers and travel documents, and through measures for preventing counterfeiting, forgery or fraudulent use of identity papers and travel documents. The Council notes the Commission's intention to put forward proposals in this area, where appropriate.

Article 11
Steps shall be taken to intensify and accelerate the exchange of operational information, especially regarding actions or movements of terrorist persons or networks; forged or falsified travel documents; traffic in arms, explosives or sensitive materials; use of communication technologies by terrorist groups; and the threat posed by the possession of weapons of mass destruction by terrorist groups.

Article 16
Appropriate measures shall be taken in accordance with the relevant provisions of national and international law, including international standards of human rights, before granting refugee status, for the purpose of ensuring that the asylum-seeker has not planned, facilitated or participated in the commission of terrorist acts. The Council notes the Commission's intention to put forward proposals in this area, where appropriate.

---

[16] This Common Position has been included in full in Chapter 6

Article 17
Steps shall be taken in accordance with international law to ensure that refugee status is not abused by the perpetrators, organisers or facilitators of terrorist acts and that claims of political motivation are not recognised as grounds for refusing requests for the extradition of alleged terrorists.
The Council notes the Commission's intention to put forward proposals in this area, where appropriate.

7.5.2 Commission Working Document, 5 December 2001:
the relationship between safeguarding internal security and complying with international protection obligations and instruments[17]

This Working Document is the Commission response to Conclusion 29 of the Extraordinary Justice and Home Affairs Council Meeting of 20 September 2001, in which the Council invited the Commission to examine urgently the relationship between safeguarding internal security and complying with international protection obligations and instruments.[18]

---

[17] Slightly edited; footnotes deleted.

[18] This document has been set up as follows:
Introduction
Chapter 1: Mechanisms for excluding those not deserving protection from Refugee Convention status and other forms of international protection
    1.1. Application of exclusion clauses
        1.1.1   Terrorism in relation to the grounds for exclusion from the Refugee Convention
        1.1.2   Definition of terrorism
        1.1.3   Membership of a terrorist group
    1.2 Cancellation of Refugee Convention status
        1.2.1   Re-examination of refugee status granted
    1.3. Crimes committed on the territory of the country of refuge
    1.4 Asylum procedure
        1.4.1   Access to the asylum procedure
        1.4.2   The processing of asylum requests in extradition cases
            1.4.2.1 Suspension of the examination of an asylum claim
            1.4.2.2 Inadmissible asylum claims
        1.4.3   Treatment within the asylum procedure
            1.4.3.1 Assessment of the asylum claim in a regular asylum procedure
            1.4.3.2 Assessment of the asylum claim in an accelerated asylum procedure
        1.4.4   Standard of proof
        1.4.5   Right to appeal against the exclusion decision
    1.5 Administrative treatment of potential article 1(F) cases
        1.5.1   Special units in the asylum system for dealing with exclusion clauses
        1.5.2   Guidelines on the use of the exclusion clauses
        1.5.3   Information exchange mechanisms
    1.6 Dealing with security risk cases
    1.7 Exclusion from other forms of international protection
Chapter 2: Legal follow up to the exclusion of persons from Refugee Convention status or other forms of international protection
    2.1 Prosecution or extradition

Introduction

At the Extraordinary Justice and Home Affairs Council Meeting of 20 September 2001, following on the tragic events of the 11th of September in the USA, Conclusion 29 invited *the Commission to examine urgently the relationship between safeguarding internal security and complying with international protection obligations and instruments.* This specific subject has been and will remain a permanent concern to the Commission, and may result in the mid to long term in Proposals for (amended) legislation. In answer to the above invitation this Working Paper aims to provide, however, both a rapid reaction as well as a comprehensive review of the issue.

The European Council has in the aftermath of and in response to the 11th September events decided to develop an '*Action Plan on the fight against terrorism*'. This Plan covers several policy areas, including external, economic/financial, transportation and Justice and Home Affairs policy. With regard to Justice and Home Affairs, a separate plan of action has been developed, covering more particularly the policy areas of: judicial cooperation, cooperation between police and intelligence services, financing of terrorism, measures at the border and other measures. In the '*measures at the border*' Chapter of the Conclusions of the extraordinary JAI Council of 20 September 2001, within which Conclusion 29 is framed, other specific Conclusions relate to border control, issuing of identity documents, residence permits and visas, and the functioning of the Schengen Information System (SIS).

These specific Conclusions are very relevant in the fight against terrorism, and more generally they provide tools for States to strengthen national security. In particular pre-entry screening, including strict visa policy and the possible use of biometric data, as well as measures to enhance cooperation between border guards, intelligence services, immigration and asylum authorities of the State concerned, could offer real possibilities for identifying those suspected of terrorist involvement at an early stage. The functioning of Europol, Eurodac and the SIS can also substantially assist in the identification of terrorist suspects. However, these specific Conclusions are the subject of separate actions and follow up to be taken at the European and Member State level, and therefore fall outside the scope of this Paper. With this Paper, the Commission focuses on the mandate formulated in Conclusion 29.

This Document adopts a fourfold approach. Firstly, the Paper will analyse the existing legal mechanisms for excluding those persons from international protection who do not deserve such protection, focusing in particular on those suspected of terrorist acts. Subsequently, the Paper will consider which legal steps can possibly be taken by governments who are confronted with a person who is excluded from international protection regimes. The Paper will then elaborate in more detail on what actions can be initiated and taken at the European level regarding the issue at stake, in the short as well as in the mid to long term. Finally, the Paper will assess the adequacy of the internal security-related provisions in EC legislation and (future) Commission Proposals for Directives in the asylum and immigration field

The two main premises on which this Document is built are, firstly, that bona fide refugees and asylum seekers should not become victims of the recent events, and secondly that there should be no avenue for those supporting or committing terrorist acts to secure access to the territory of the Member States of the European Union. It is therefore legitimate and fully understandable that Member States are now looking at reinforced security safeguards to prevent terrorists from gaining admission to their territory through different channels. These could include asylum channels, though in practice terrorists are not likely to use the asylum channel very often, as other, illegal, channels are more discreet and more suitable for their criminal practices. Any security safeguard therefore needs to strike a proper balance with the refugee protection principles at stake. In this context the Commission fully endorses the line taken and expressed by UNHCR that, rather than through major changes to the refugee protection regime, a scrupulous application of the exceptions to refugee protection available under current law, is the appropriate approach.

Chapter 1
Mechanisms for excluding those not deserving protection from the Refugee Convention status and others forms of international protection

1.1 Application of the exclusion clauses
After the 11th September events, UNHCR has publicly called on States to 'scrupulously and rigorously' apply the exclusion clauses, as contained in Article 1(F) of the Refugee Convention, as that Convention was never intended to be a 'safe haven' for criminals, nor was it designed to protect them from criminal prosecution, but quite the opposite: to protect the persecuted and not the persecutors.

Article 1(F) of the Refugee Convention states that refugee status can not be granted to any person with respect to whom

(a) 'there are serious reasons for considering that:

he has committed a crime against peace, a war crime, or a crime against humanity, as defined in the international instruments drawn up to make provision in respect of such crimes;

(b) he has committed a serious non-political crime outside the country of refuge prior to his admission to that country as a refugee;

(c) he has been guilty of acts contrary to the purposes and principles of the United Nations.'

This Paper is not the appropriate framework for analysing in full detail the application of the three grounds listed in Article 1(F) of the Refugee Convention. In addition to guidelines issued by Member States, UNHCR has issued special guidelines on the application of this particular article. The Commission also likes to refer to other relevant documents issued by UNHCR, including background papers and notes for the UNHCR Standing Committee and within the context of UNHCR's Global Consultations process.

1.1.1 Terrorism in relation to the three grounds for exclusion from the Refugee Convention
In line with several United Nations General Assembly and Security Council Resolutions, most recently Resolution 1373 of 28 September 2001, and following international refugee law jurisprudence, the exclusion of persons involved in terrorist acts from refugee status may be based on either of the three grounds listed in the exclusion clause under Article 1(F), depending on the circumstances of the case.

–   Art 1F (a): as it has been recognised that terrorist acts may constitute 'war crimes' if committed in a war context.

–   Art.1F (b): in so far as particular cruel actions, even if committed with an allegedly political objective, can be classified as serious non-political crimes, and fall within the realm of extraditable offences.

–   Art. 1F (c) following UN General Assembly Resolutions 'Relating to measures combating terrorism', which declare that

'acts, methods and practices of terrorism are contrary to the purposes and principles of the United Nations' and that 'knowingly financing, planning and inciting terrorist acts are also contrary to the purposes and principles of the United Nations'.

1.1.2 Definition of terrorism
Rather than attempting to adopt a general definition of what constitutes terrorism, States have, until now, preferred to declare certain specific acts as terrorist crimes. They have identified a number of crimes within this category, such as those related to hijacking, hostage-taking and bomb attacks. Though within the United Nations context work has been accelerated with regard to the preparations for an international instrument on terrorism, there is no internationally agreed definition of terrorism as yet.

In this particular context it is even more relevant that the European Commission has recently adopted the *Proposal for a Council Framework Decision on combating terrorism* (which includes the establishment of minimum rules relating to the constituent elements of criminal acts) and the *Proposal for a Council Framework Decision on the European arrest warrant and the surrender procedures between the Member State*s. In particular an EU common definition of what constitutes terrorists offences, if incorporated in EU extradition treaties, may be a basis for relying on Article 1(F)(b). EU standards will also be a helpful way of illuminating UN standards of, for example, 'terrorist acts', and hence serve as an interpretative aid to the application of Article 1(F)(a) or 1(F)(c).

1.1.3 Membership of a terrorist group

Mere, voluntary, membership of a terrorist group may, in some cases, amount to personal and knowing participation, or acquiescence amounting to complicity, in the crimes in question, and hence to exclusion from refugee status. In this assessment the purpose of the group, the status and level of the person involved, and factors such as duress and self-defence against superior orders, as well as the availability of a moral choice should be taken into consideration. If it has been determined that the person is still an actual, active, present and willing member, the fact of mere membership may be difficult to dissociate from the commission of terrorist crimes.

1.2 Cancellation of Refugee Convention status

Refugee Convention status can be withdrawn, for instance if it is discovered that the person had committed serious crimes, including terrorist acts, before having been recognised as a refugee. In such cases refugee status may be cancelled, following the UNHCR Handbook on Procedures and Criteria for Determining Refugee Status.

1.2.1 Re-examination of refugee statuses granted

An active re-examination of the 'closed files' of persons granted a refugee status could be considered by Member States. However, such a re-examination should only be undertaken if there is a clear inducement for doing so, for instance based upon intelligence services' information, identifying security risks. A review of cases based solely on the grounds of nationality, religion or political opinion is not considered appropriate. If this re-examination would lead to the conclusion that someone has indeed committed crimes falling under the scope of the exclusion clauses, his/her refugee status could be cancelled.

1.3. Crimes committed on the territory of the country of refuge

In cases where a refugee has committed a serious crime, including terrorist acts, on the territory of the country of refuge, protection against expulsion can be withdrawn, in conformity with Article 32, '*The Contracting States shall not expel a refugee lawfully in their territory save on grounds of national security or public order*', and Article 33 (2) (on the prohibition of expulsion or return – 'refoulement'): of the Refugee Convention. The purpose of this latter article is to safeguard the receiving country from persons who present a danger to the public safety or the security of that country, and states that:

> 'The benefit of the present provision may not, however, be claimed by a refugee whom there are reasonable grounds for regarding as a danger to the security of the country in which he is, or who, having been convicted by a final judgement of a particularly serious crime, constitutes a danger to the community of that country'.

Article 33(2) therefore provides an exception to the principle of *non-refoulement,* laid down in Article 33(1). This means in essence that refugees can exceptionally be returned when there is a threat to the national security of the host country, and in case their proven criminal nature and record constitute a danger to the community. The various elements of these extreme and exceptional circumstances need, however, to be interpreted restrictively and require a high standard of proof. However, any person falling *within* the terms of Art. 33(2) may lawfully be expelled, even if the only option is to return him or her to the country in which persecution is feared, without prejudice to other international legal obligations of States, in particular Article 3 of the European Convention on Human Rights.

1.4 Asylum Procedure

1.4.1 Access to the asylum procedure

In order to implement in good faith, and 'fully and inclusively', the 1951 Refugee Convention it is indispensable to determine who fulfils the requirements of the Convention. Therefore all persons requesting asylum in the Member State responsible for assessing the claim, should be granted access to a procedure, enabling such assessment. *Automatic bars* to accessing an asylum procedure, even of suspected criminals, for instance by rejection at the border, without providing such persons access to an asylum procedure, could result in 'refoulement'. In addition this would not be in conformity with Article 4 of the *Proposal for a Council Directive on minimum standards on procedures in Member States for granting and withdrawing refugee status*.

Channelling all asylum seekers through an asylum procedure with a view to granting or denying refugee status is also necessary from a practical security perspective. It effectively provides the opportunity to identify possible suspects of crimes. Asylum seekers will be known and identified, their background thoroughly investigated in one or more interviews, and checked against all available information on countries, groups and events. In addition they will be easily 'tracked' during the procedure, even if they are not detained.

1.4.2 The handling of asylum requests in extradition cases

1.4.2.1 Suspension of the examination of an asylum claim

After access to the asylum procedure has been granted, it may however be decided to allow for the immediate suspension, the 'freezing' of the actual examination of the asylum request in the following two situations. Firstly, in cases in which an international criminal tribunal has indicted the individual who has claimed asylum. In such cases, the appropriate response would be to hand over the individual concerned to that tribunal for prosecution. The second possible ground for suspensing the examination of the asylum request would be where an extradition request from a country other than the country of origin of the asylum seeker, relating to serious crimes, is pending. In both cases the criminal proceedings would take priority over the actual the asylum procedure.

Following the criminal prosecution of these cases, and following the serving of an eventual punishment, the old situation of the asylum request would be 'unfrozen'. This would effectively mean that the asylum seeker would be transferred back to the country where he had an asylum request pending. If this approach is opted for, the *Proposal for a Council Directive on minimum standards on procedures in Member States for granting and withdrawing refugee status* would need to be changed to allow for such an approach.

1.4.2.2 Inadmissible asylum claims

An alternative legislative approach for dealing with asylum claims in cases where an extradition request or an indictment by an International Criminal Court has been made, could consist of the dismissal of an asylum claim as being 'inadmissible'. In this option it would be necessary to add to article 18 of the *Proposal for a Council Directive on minimum standards on procedures in Member States for granting and withdrawing refugee status 5*, dealing with the inadmissibility of certain claims for asylum, two new grounds for inadmissibility: namely in cases where an extradition request has been made by a country, other than the country of origin of the asylum seeker, or in cases of an indictment by an International Criminal Court. In the case of an extradition request, and if following criminal prosecution the asylum seeker wants to reapply for asylum, the revised article 18 should include a rule to the effect that the merits of such a renewed asylum claim is to be assessed by the Member State to whom the person has been extradited.

The advantage of both such approaches would be that the possibilities for the criminal prosecution of alleged criminals would not be hindered by the mere fact of the filing of an asylum request. It would also be an appropriate response to the several UN General Assembly Resolutions on 'Measures to Eliminate International Terrorism' which provide that, before considering whether to grant refugee status, States should take appropriate measures to ensure that the asylum-seeker has not participated in terrorist acts, taking into due account any relevant information as to whether the asylum seeker is subject to investigation for, is charged with, or has been convicted of offences connected with terrorism.

1.4.3 Treatment within the asylum procedure

The procedure assessing the claim for refugee status, based on the Refugee Convention, also includes the examination of the applicability of the exclusion clauses, contained in article 1(F) of that Convention. The rationale underlying these exclusion provisions is that certain acts are so grave as to render their perpetrators undeserving of protection as refugees. However, because exclusion from refugee status may have potentially life-threatening consequences, such decisions should be made *within* the asylum procedure, by the authority with expertise and training in refugee law and status determination, in the context of a comprehensive consideration of the refugee claim.

1.4.3.1 Assessment of the asylum claim in a regular asylum procedure

The standard rule for assessing claims for asylum should be that this is being done in a comprehensive, holistic and integral manner. This means that there should be a comprehensive examination of all the relevant facts underlying a claim for asylum. However, the possible applicability of the exclusion clauses should not be explored in all cases, as a matter of routine. It should only be explored in cases where there are specific reasons to believe that the person may fall under one of these clauses. Indeed facts justifying an examination of the applicant's excludability will normally emerge in the course of the 'inclusion phase' of the refugee status determination process, checking the reasons for recognising someone as a refugee, and may then be referred to during the 'exclusion phase' of the case.

1.4.3.2 Assessment of the asylum claim in an accelerated asylum procedure

There may however be cases in which it has been *prima facie* established that someone falls under the scope of the exclusion clauses. In such situations States should be entitled to channel such claims through an accelerated procedure. In such an procedure States are entitled to start with and, *if found applicable*, limit themselves to the particular examination of the applicability of the exclusion clauses, as a preliminary matter at the commencement of a hearing, without having the need to examine the 'inclusion clauses' of the Refugee Convention. 'Translated' legally, such cases could be considered to allow for a dismissal of the asylum claim as being 'manifestly unfounded', as to be then provided for in a revision of the *Proposal for a Council Directive on minimum standards on procedures in Member States for granting and withdrawing refugee status*. If this option would be pursued, the issue of whether or not an appeal against a dismissal of such a claim as manifestly unfounded should automatically have suspensive effect, needs to be further examined.

1.4.4 Standard of proof

In determining the applicable standard of proof in exclusion procedures, it has to be acknowledged that exclusion proceedings do not amount to a full criminal trial. The term *'serious reasons for considering'*, used in the chapeau to article 1(F), should be interpreted as meaning that the rules on the admissibility of evidence and the high standard of proof required in criminal proceedings do not need to apply in this respect. There is therefore no need to prove that the person has committed the act, which may justify exclusion from refugee status. It is sufficient to establish that there are serious reasons for considering that the person has committed those acts. The basis for such a conclusion must be clearly established. Thus, an investigation should be undertaken, checking the claimant's potential links with or involvement in violent acts. In order to consider the possibility of excluding refugee status as a result of individual liability for terrorist acts, the measure of personal involvement required must be carefully assessed. A person whose actions contribute to the crime, through orders, incitement or significant assistance, may be excluded from refugee status.

1.4.5 Right to appeal against the exclusion decision

The application of any exclusion clause must be individually assessed. The grounds for exclusion should be based solely on the personal and knowing conduct of the person concerned as well as on available evidence, and should conform to legal standards of fairness and justice. The person concerned should be entitled to lodge a legal challenge in the Member State concerned, as also provided for and according to the standards laid down in the *Proposal for a Council Directive on minimum standards on procedures in Member States for granting and withdrawing refugee status*.

1.5 Administrative treatment of potential article 1(F) cases

1.5.1 Special units in the asylum system for dealing with exclusion cases

Without prejudice to paragraph 1.4.5, and the right to appeal against a denial of refugee status before an independent Court, Member States may have different logistical arrangements for dealing with claims of suspected war criminals or terrorists. In some Member States special Units have been set up to which all security risk cases and cases of suspected involvement in serious violent acts or violations of human rights are forwarded. Other Member States are considering introducing standard 'front-security checks', by which all claims for asylum would be checked as regards potential security risks, running the personal data through the available and relevant databases. Such logistical measures are completely compatible with the legal international obligations incumbent upon Member States and could potentially prove useful.

Given the complexities involved, Member States that have no specialised 'Exclusion/Security Unit' within their asylum system could consider introducing it. Referral to such a Unit could either be called for where there are immediate suspicions of involvement in war or other serious crimes, such as terrorist involvement (for instance, where an asylum seeker is alleged to be a member of an extremist group practising violence), or where these suspicions emerge during the course of assessment under the normal asylum procedure. Although it is likely that only a relatively small number of cases would be involved, the specialised 'Exclusion Unit' could pursue examination. In order to function properly and effectively such a Unit should possess expertise in both refugee as well as criminal law and have an in-depth knowledge of terrorist organisations. Equally important for such a Unit would be its access to all regularly available countries of origin, and if necessary, classified information, and efficient working links with intelligence and criminal prosecution and enforcement bodies.

A specialised Unit would be able to undertake priority, expedited processing of cases with a potential exclusion element. Its resources and expertise would enable it to undertake a more thorough assessment of any asylum claim made by someone suspected of involvement in terrorist acts. The Unit could subsequently refer such cases to the office of the public prosecutor for criminal prosecution as the appropriate avenue for bringing suspected terrorists to justice. Its increased specialist expertise and clearly focused resources would enable prompt and quality decision making.

1.5.2 Guidelines on the use of the exclusion clauses

Some Member States have issued special internal guidelines on the application of the exclusion clauses of the Refugee Convention. These could assist in the identification of cases with a potential exclusion element as early in the process as possible. It could be considered to establish such guidelines at a European level, making use of the best practices at the national level.

1.5.3 Information exchange mechanisms

It could also be considered to set up information exchange mechanisms to help those Member States which do not have sufficient resources to benefit from the already existing expertise on these issues in some other Member States, in order to obtain information and support once they have a potential case. Such information exchange mechanisms could involve the setting up of contact lists and explore the usefulness of creating Intranet sites.

It could also serve to inform each other of the presence of an exclusion case, in order to avoid the person trying to obtain protection in another Member State. Within this context the establishment of a European list of 'Refugee Convention-excluded persons' could also be considered. Within the framework of information sharing it needs to be stressed that the normal rules with regard to the confidentiality of personal data, in particular as regards possible communication between a Member State and the person's country of origin need to be respected.

1.6 Dealing with security risk cases

Member States have a range of measures at their disposal to ensure that asylum seekers on their territory do not abscond during the procedure. These include holding asylum-seekers in reception centres, reporting requirements, regulations on informing the authorities about any change of address, and detention. Which measures are appropriate will depend on individual circumstances, although where there is evidence to show that an individual asylum seeker has criminal affiliations likely to pose a risk to public order or national security, detention would be an appropriate tool. It must however be acknowledged that in most systems there are limits to the detention of asylum applicants; also the legality and necessity of detention is subject to judicial review.

1.7 Exclusion from other forms of international protection

The findings of this Chapter 1 should be considered equally relevant in cases where someone has requested, respectively has been granted another form of international protection, such as subsidiary protection.

Chapter 2
Legal follow up to the exclusion of persons from Refugee Convention status or other forms of international protection

2.1 Prosecution or extradition

Following a denial of an appeal against the decision to exclude a person from refugee or subsidiary protection status, and according to the international law principle known as *aut dedere aut judicare*, the State is obliged to either surrender or prosecute the person excluded from protection regimes. The above principle provides for a solution to the inherent contradiction between the State's need, and indeed the obligation, to combat criminal acts such as terrorism, and the individual's entitlement to protection against refoulement. This principle is formulated, inter alia, in Article 7 of the European Convention on the Suppression of Terrorism.

2.2 Prosecution

2.2.1 Universal jurisdiction

With regard to the implementation of the above principle, the situation differs from one Member State to the other. Some Member States attempt to actively try such a person, if they have specific criteria to have jurisdiction in the case, or if their national criminal law provides for an universal competence. In such a legal system the State can actively prosecute and punish persons suspected of crimes of universal jurisdiction, without having regard to the territoriality of the crime committed or the nationality of the person suspected. However, it has to be acknowledged that it is often, de facto, not possible to prosecute the person for a criminal offence, given the strict rules on the admissibility of evidence and the high standard of proof required in the criminal justice systems of the Member States of the European Union. These standards are much higher than for refugee exclusion and/or expulsion proceedings. In particularly the availability of (reliable) witnesses has proved in practice to be a very serious obstacle for Member States in pursuing the successful criminal prosecution of those persons excluded from the Refugee Convention.

2.2.2 Future International Criminal Court

The future International Criminal Court (ICC) could play an important role in the context of the prosecution of persons covered by the exclusion clauses of the Refugee Convention. However, the current mandate of the Court, laid down in its Statute, does not cover terrorism as such, except if it is associated with the other serious crimes (of concern to the international community) regarding which the Court does have jurisdiction. These crimes are also of direct relevance to the interpretation and application of Article 1(F) of the 1951 Convention. The future ICC could also help to address problems where national refugee status determination procedures may lack access to relevant intelligence information and/or resources and tools, such as are available to a judge or prosecutor investigating such crimes. It is also envisaged that cooperation between the ICC and UN agencies, such as UNHCR, will be established. It could therefore be useful to consider establishing formal and confidential cooperation agreements between Member States and the ICC in potential Article 1F cases.

2.3 Extradition

If there is no possibility to bring the person to trial in the country of refuge, nor to have the person indicted by the International Criminal Court, then in principle such a person needs to be extradited; that is if extradition is legally and practically possible to either the country of origin, another Member State or another third country. In connection with extradition requests made against persons accused of having committed terrorist crimes, both the 1977 European Convention on the Suppression of Terrorism and the International Convention for the Suppression of the Financing of Terrorism provide that States Parties are not obliged to accede to the extradition, if they have substantial grounds for believing that such request has been made for the purpose of prosecuting or punishing the person on account of his/her race, religion, nationality, ethnic origin or political opinion or that compliance with the request would cause prejudice to that person's position for any of these reasons.

2.3.1 Legal obstacles to extradition or removal

Extradition may however be impossible because of legal obstacles. The protection against 'refoulement' as a consequence of the prohibition of certain treatments or punishments, provided for in human rights instruments such as the United Nations Convention against Torture, the International Covenant on Civil and Political Rights and the European Convention on Human Rights (ECHR) is namely absolute in nature, that is to say, it admits no exceptions. The European Court of Human Rights has repeatedly affirmed that the European Convention on Human Rights, even in the most difficult circumstances, such as the fight against terrorism and organised crime, prohibits, in absolute terms, torture and inhuman or degrading treatment or punishment. The European Court of Human Rights has emphasised that, unlike most of the substantive clauses of that particular Convention, Article 3 makes no provision for exceptions and no derogation from it is permissible even in the event of a public emergency threatening the life of the nation. Following the 11th September events, the European Court of Human Rights may in the future again have to rule on questions relating to the interpretation of Article 3, in particular on the question in how far there can be a 'balancing act' between the protection needs of the individual, set against the security interests of a state.

2.3.2 Legal guarantees in extradition cases
Extradition must be considered legal when it is possible to obtain legal guarantees from the State that is going to try the person, addressing the concerns connected to the potential violations of the European Convention on Human Rights. Such 'guarantees' by third States could for instance relate to the non-application of capital punishment in that particular case, although the law of that State allows for such punishment.

2.4 The legal position of persons excluded from protection regimes but who are non-removable
The question that remains unresolved -and which falls outside the scope of refugee/international protection law – relates to the status that must be accorded to persons who are disqualified from refugee status or other forms of international protection, who cannot be successfully prosecuted, and yet who cannot be expelled because of the absolute nature of the prohibition of 'refoulement' as laid down in some international and regional human rights instruments. There are no international legal instruments which regulate the status and rights of persons who are excluded from any protection status but cannot be expelled because of legal obstacles. However, the UN Committee on Human Rights has elaborated upon the obligation of States parties to 'keep' some aliens with long links in the country, despite their criminal activities.

The current situation of Member States having limited policy options for adequately dealing with excludable but non-removable persons is a very unsatisfactory one. The issue is therefore urgently in need of further examination, and eventual resolution at the European level. In this context it again has to be stressed that, despite the serious obstacles referred to earlier on, criminal prosecution by the international community, both at the global level as well as the Member States level, of those persons having committed crimes against humanity, war crimes or terrorist attacks, and excluded from protection regimes, is an appropriate response. In addition to their possible criminal prosecution it may also be necessary to harmonise the basic rights granted to this category of excludable but non-removable persons, and to assess the different means for dealing with these persons if they pose a security risk.

2.4.1 Harmonisation of basic rights granted to persons excluded from protection regimes but who are non-removable
The 15 Member States of the European Union deal differently with the excludable but non-removable persons. Some Member States do not grant any rights whatsoever to these persons except for the right not to be refouled. In other Member States, persons do get access to basic human rights, such as urgent medical health care and education for children. In still other Member States these persons are entitled to even more social and economic rights and benefits. This difference in treatment may call for a harmonised approach at the European level in order to remove potential 'pull factors' for persons not deserving international protection.

2.4.2 Detention and alternatives to detention of persons excluded from protection regimes but who are non-removable

Persons, who are excluded from protection regimes, yet who can not be removed, do not necessarily and automatically pose a risk to national security. For instance many of the war criminals, rightly excluded from the protection regimes by Member States, are not automatically detained by these States. Indeed, so far an administrative unlimited detention system has not been made use of in the Member States, and it may also be useful to further explore alternatives to full detention measures, such as 'residence surveille'.

However, there may be cases in which there is a need for the public to be protected against persons rightly excluded from the protection regimes, such as terrorists, who do pose a risk to the security of the State. In this context it is relevant to note the legislation recently proposed at Member State level with regard to *the detention of foreign nationals whose presence is believed to constitute a risk to national security and who are being suspected of being international terrorist*s. This legislation has been proposed in anticipation of situations where Article 3 of the ECHR prevents removal or deportation to a place where there is a risk that the person in question will suffer treatment contrary to that Article. If no alternative destination is immediately available then removal may not, for the time being, be possible, even though the ultimate intention to remove remains, once satisfactory arrangements have been made. Notwithstanding this continuing intention to remove a person who is being detained, it is not possible to say that 'action is being taken with a view to deportation' within the meaning of Article 5(1)(f) ECHR, interpreted by the European Court of Human Rights. To the extent that the envisaged detention in the above cases may therefore be inconsistent with the obligations under Article 5(1) ECHR the right of derogation conferred by Article 15(1) of the ECHR could be invoked, provided that the strict conditions laid down in Article 15(1) are met, and the envisaged 'measures are not inconsistent with (States) other obligations under international law'.

Chapter 3
Approximation of relevant legislation, regulations and administrative practices against the background of the Common European Asylum System

3.1 General framework
Continuing the work on these issues at the EU level can be done following the method and means explained in the Commission's Communication

> 'Towards a common asylum procedure and a uniform status, valid throughout the Union for persons granted asylum'[19] and followed up by the recent 'Communication on the common asylum policy, introducing an open coordination method-First Report by the Commission on the application of Communication COM (2000) 755 final of 22 November 2000'[20].

The establishment of the Common European Asylum System will follow a two-step approach. The relationship between safeguarding internal security and complying with international protection obligations must be fed into both steps. Indeed it is necessary to work on more efficient, well-informed and common procedures, more convergent interpretation and application of exclusion possibilities and on enhancing prosecution and detention possibilities, including alternatives to detention. It is also necessary to ensure that terrorists, against the background of international protection, face comparable treatment in all Member States.

---

[19] Brussels, 22.11.2000 COM (2000) 755 final.
[20] Brussels, 28.11.2001 COM (2001) 710 final.

If a terrorist is not granted an international protection status in one Member State or if the status is withdrawn or cancelled, he/she should expect the same treatment of his/her case in all other Member States.

3.2 Legislative harmonisation, accompanying measures, administrative cooperation and the Open Coordination Method

Quick progress should be made on the negotiation of the different Commission Proposals for Directives which are on the Council's table, and appropriate attention should be given to the provisions dealing with examination and decision making, exclusion, cancellation of status and withdrawal of benefits. Appropriate and quick transposition of the EC legislative instruments at the national level will also be necessary. The Commission will prepare regular reports on the implementation of these instruments. The *Contact Committees* created for monitoring the implementation will facilitate consultation between Member States and the Commission with a view to reaching similar interpretations of the relevant provisions and comparing national rules and practices. In addition case law developed by national and European courts or review bodies will need to be further analysed. A meeting with representatives of determining authorities and review bodies could be organised in 2002 in order to study trends and case law and discuss common problems and solutions.

A continuing investment on enhancing common analysis tools is needed. In this context National points of contact could be nominated for developing cooperation and exchange of information. The new programme *ARGO, an Action programme for cooperation in the fields of external borders, visas, asylum and immigration,*[21] could be used in order to support such administrative cooperation. The Commission has recommended the use of the *open coordination method*. An illustration of such a method specially designed for asylum policy can be found in the *'Communication on the common asylum policy, introducing an open coordination method'.*[22] Attention is drawn to the Second European Guideline proposed on the development of an efficient asylum system, offering protection for those in need, based on the full and inclusive application of the Geneva Convention and in particular on points G *('by identifying principles and techniques for improving the identification of individuals, covered by the exclusion provisions, who do not deserve international protection.')* and J *('by evaluating ... the use of cessation and exclusion clauses ...').* In order to implement this Guideline, Member States have to identify in their national action plans means and objectives to meet the European goal and to analyse the implementation of national and EC instruments. This will also facilitate comparing and identifying good practices and analysing the real impact and results of choices made. Finally, appropriate consultation of and cooperation with the UNHCR, relevant international organisations and third countries will also be required to efficiently and comprehensively address the issue which is the subject of this Paper.

All the above instruments will greatly assist in the identification of the necessary improvements, leading to the adoption of additional rules within the framework of the second step of the harmonisation of asylum policies in the European Union.

---

[21] Brussels, 16.10.2001 COM (2001) 567 final.
[22] Id at 9.

Chapter 4
Analysis of 'internal security'– related provisions in EC legislation and (future) Commission
Proposals for EC legislation in the asylum and immigration field

4.1 General Analysis
The current EC legislation or Commission Proposals for such legislation in the field of asylum and immigration all contain, currently, sufficient standard provisions to allow for the exclusion of any third country national who may be perceived as a threat to national/public security from the right to international protection, residency or access to certain benefits. However, in the framework of current and future discussions and negotiations of the different Proposals, these relevant provisions will be revisited in the light of the new circumstances, without prejudice to the relevant international obligations underlying the Proposals. The relevant provisions in the different Proposals are briefly analysed below, and, where appropriate, possibilities for clarifying or enhancing these provisions have been identified.

4.2 EC legislation in the field of asylum
4.2.1 Temporary Protection
The formally adopted Council *Directive on minimum standards for giving temporary protection in the event of a mass influx of displaced persons and on measures promoting a balance of efforts between Member States in receiving such persons and bearing the consequences thereof*[23] allows Member States in its Article 28(1)(b) to exclude a person from temporary protection if, amongst other grounds, there are reasonable grounds for regarding him or her as a danger to the security of the host Member State or, having been convicted by a final judgement of a particularly serious crime, he or she is a danger to the community of the host Member State.

4.2.2 EURODAC
The formally adopted *Council Regulation concerning the establishment of 'Eurodac' for the comparison of fingerprints for the effective application of the Dublin Convention*[24] allows for the prompt taking of the fingerprints of all fingers of every applicant for asylum of at least 14 years of age.

For the purposes of applying the Dublin Convention, it is necessary to establish the identity of applicants for asylum and of persons apprehended in connection with the unlawful crossing of the external borders of the Community. However, this will simultaneously assist Member States in knowing who is entering their territory, and subsequently enhance their national security.

4.3 Proposals for EC legislation in the field of asylum
4.3.1 Asylum procedures
The *Proposal for a Council Directive on minimum standards on procedures in Member States for granting and withdrawing refugee status*[25] allows in Article 26 for 'Cancellation of refugee status' on the grounds that circumstances have come to light that indicate that this person should never have been recognised as a refugee in the first place. Article 33(2)(c) also allows Member States to derogate from the rule of suspensive effect for appeals in cases where there are grounds of national security or public order.

---

[23] Directive (2001/55/EC) 20.07.2001.
[24] Regulation (2725/2000/EC) 11.12.2000.
[25] Id at 3.

As also referred to in paragraph 1.4.2.1, within the context of the forthcoming revision of this particular Proposal it could be considered to include rules allowing for a suspension of the asylum procedure in situations where an extradition request, relating to a serious crime, for an asylum seeker has been made by a State, other than the country of origin, or in cases of an indictment by an International Criminal Court. Alternatively, as explained earlier in paragraph 1.4.2.2, Article 18 of the Proposal, on the inadmissibility of certain claims for asylum, could be amended to the effect that it would allow in the above cases for the dismissal of an asylum claim as being inadmissible.

As elaborated upon in paragraph 1.4.3.2, the Commission is also considering deleting article 28(2)(b) of the Proposal, which states that cases where there are serious reasons for considering that the grounds of article 1(F) of the Refugee Convention apply can not be considered to constitute grounds for the dismissal of applications for asylum as being manifestly unfounded. Following this possible deletion an additional ground would then need to be added to article 28(1) allowing for the dismissal of asylum claims as being manifestly unfounded in those cases where it has been prima facie established that the exclusion clauses of the Refugee Convention apply.

4.3.2 Reception conditions

Following Article 22(1)(d) of the *Proposal for a Council Directive laying down minimum standards on the reception of applicants for asylum in Member States*,[26] Member States may reduce or withdraw reception facilities if an applicant is regarded as a threat to national security or there are serious grounds for believing that the applicant has committed a war crime or a crime against humanity or if, during the examination of the asylum application, there are serious and manifest reasons for considering that the grounds of Article 1(F) of the Geneva Convention may apply with respect to the applicant.

It could be considered to add a new paragraph (4)(a) to Article 22, regarding the reduction or withdrawal of reception conditions, to the following extent:

'Should the applicant's involvement in terrorist activities be established, either by his having taken an active part therein or by his having aided and abetted or provided financial support to terrorist organisations as defined by the European Union, before or after the application for asylum has been lodged, Member States must withdraw the routine reception conditions in respect of the applicant and enforce the legal protection measures provided for in their respective legislation'.

It is also relevant to mention in the context of this Paper that the current text of Article 7 of the Proposal allows, where appropriate, for a limitation of the freedom of movement of asylum seekers to a specific area of the national territory of the Member States.

4.3.3 State determination

In the Proposal for a Council regulation establishing the criteria and mechanisms for determining the Member State responsible for examining an asylum application lodged in one of the Member States by a third-country national[27] there are no specific provisions relating to national security. However, such articles are not necessary given that the Proposal contains no provisions relating to the granting/refusing of rights or status.

---

[26] Brussels, 3.4.2001 COM (2001) 181 final.
[27] Brussels, 26 .7.2001 COM (2001) 447 final.

4.3.4 Qualification for international protection

In Article 14 of the recent *Proposal for a Council Directive on minimum standards for the qualification and status of third-country nationals and stateless persons as refugees or as persons who otherwise need international protection*[28] Member States have to ensure that an applicant who falls within the terms of the exclusion clauses of the Refugee Convention is excluded from refugee status.

In its Article 17 this Proposal equally obliges Member States to ensure that an applicant who falls within the terms of those exclusion clauses is also excluded from subsidiary protection status. In the framework of the future discussion on this particular Proposal an additional paragraph (2) to article 19, relating to 'Protection from refoulement and expulsion' could be considered. This additional paragraph, in accordance with article 33(2) of the Refugee Convention, holds that the benefit of that provision (the non-refoulement obligation),

> 'may not be claimed by a person enjoying international protection whom there are reasonable grounds for regarding as a danger to the security of the Member State in which he is, or who, having been convicted by a final judgement of a particularly serious crime, constitutes a danger to the community of that Member State'.

The provisions in the above mentioned articles 14, 17 and the possibly to be proposed new provision to Article 19, are all without prejudice to Member States' other international obligations, in particular those deriving from article 3 of the European Convention on Human Rights and Fundamental Freedoms.

4.4 Proposals for EC legislation in the field of immigration

In the field of legal immigration, all three Commission Proposals for Council Directives so far submitted on the right to family reunification, the status of third-country nationals who are long-term residents, and the conditions of entry and residence of third-country nationals for the purpose of paid employment and self-employed economic activities already contain 'public order' clauses. These clauses allow Member States to refuse admission to third-country nationals for reasons of public policy or domestic security. It appears that a scrupulous application of these clauses is a more appropriate way of enhancing security than to substantially change the different Proposals at stake. The invocation of these grounds must be based exclusively on the personal conduct of the third country national concerned. In practice this means that current or past membership of a certain – terrorist – association might be interpreted as being linked to the 'personal conduct' of a person and might therefore justify the use of this 'public order' clause. Within the scope of the Directives, any discrimination based on race, ethnic origin, religion or beliefs, political opinions or membership of a national minority is explicitly excluded. The mere ethnic origin or nationality of a person could never justify the use of the 'public order' clause, as this would also be contrary to the principle of non-discrimination enshrined in Article 21 of the Charter of Fundamental Rights of the European Union.

4.4.1 Economic migration

Following Article 27 of the *Proposal for a Council Directive on the conditions of entry and residence of third-country nationals for the purpose of paid employment and self-employed economic activities*:[29]

> 'Member States may refuse to grant or to renew or revoke permits in accordance with this Directive on grounds of public policy, public security or public health. The grounds of

---

[28] Brussels, 12.9.2001 COM (2001) 510 final.
[29] Brussels, 11.7.2001 COM (2001) 386 final.

public policy or public security must be based exclusively on the personal conduct of the third-country national concerned'.

This provision gives Member States a large degree of discretion. The current drafting of Article 27 of the Proposal can therefore be considered to be sufficient and it is not deemed necessary to envisage a modification.

4.4.2 Family reunification

The *Proposal for a Council directive on the right of family reunification*[30] contains in its article 8 a provision on public order allowing Member States to refuse:

'the entry and residence of family members on grounds of public policy, domestic security or public health. The grounds of public policy or domestic security must be based exclusively on the personal conduct of the family member concerned'.

The same logic as set out in 4.4.1 applies equally in the context of this particular Proposal, and an amendment of the text is therefore not considered necessary.

4.4.3 Long-term residency status

The *Proposal for a Council Directive concerning the status of third-country nationals who are long term residents*[31] contains several national security-related provisions. The Commission is considering amending these provisions in the following manner: Following Article 7 on *Public policy and domestic security* Member States may refuse to *grant long-term resident status where the personal conduct of the person concerned constitutes an actual threat to public order or domestic security*. It is being considered to delete the word *actual* in paragraph 1. It is also proposed to delete in paragraph 2 of Article 7 the reference to the fact that *'Criminal convictions shall not in themselves automatically warrant the refusal referred to in paragraph 1'*. The same applies to Article 19, regarding the right to settle in another Member State. *With regard to* Article 13 *Protection against expulsion* the Commission is considering deleting paragraph 7 in which emergency expulsion procedures are prohibited against long-term residents. This provision applies once the third-country national has obtained long-term resident status, and he/she should therefore benefit from a higher level of protection. Nevertheless, emergency expulsion procedures can be justified in the case of a terrorism threat.

Finally, in Article 25 on the Withdrawal of residence permit it is stated that:

'(1) During a five-year transitional period, the second Member State may take a decision to expel a long-term resident and/or family members: on grounds of public policy or domestic security as defined in Article 19;

(2) Expulsion decisions may not be accompanied by a permanent ban on residence'.

In such cases, the second Member State shall expel the long-term resident only to the Member State that has granted him/her that status. In cases of a serious threat, as defined in art. 13(1), the second Member State should expel the long-term resident directly to his/her country of origin or to another country outside the European Union. The Commission is considering adding an article 2 bis: *'In case of an actual and sufficiently serious threat the procedure of article 13 may apply'*.

4.5 Future Proposals for EC legislation in the field of immigration
4.5.1 Students and other third-country nationals

The objectives of the future Proposal for a Directive on the conditions of entry and residence of third-country nationals for the purpose of study and self-employed economic activities are

---

[30] Brussels, 10.10.2000 COM (2000) 624 final.
[31] Brussels, 13.3.2001 COM (2001) 127 final.

considered to be best achieved by guaranteeing simultaneously the possibility for Member States to cater for their domestic security concerns. The Proposal will therefore include a clause allowing Member States to refuse the admission of a third-country national, the renewal of a residence permit or to revoke such a permit on grounds of public policy, public security or public health based exclusively on the personal conduct of the third-country national concerned. This drafting seems sufficiently wide to give Member States the necessary margin of maneuver to refuse admission or put an end to the stay of a third-country national if this is objectively required. The same provisions will be included in the Proposal for a Directive on the conditions of entry and residence of third-country nationals for other purposes.

4.5.2 Victims of trafficking

The Commission's services are currently preparing a Proposal for a Directive on a short-term permit to stay for the victims of trafficking. There is no right to this permit to stay as such, its issuing is subject to a set of conditions being met. One of the conditions for the delivery of the permit is that *'no considerations regarding public order or national security oppose this delivery'*. The same applies to the renewal and consequently the withdrawal of the permit. This wording seems sufficiently wide to enable Member States to protect their public order and national security.[32]

---

[32] (Ed.: see Proposal for a COUNCIL DIRECTIVE on the short-term residence permit issued to victims of action to facilitate illegal immigration or trafficking in human beings who cooperate with the competent authorities COM/2002/0071 final of 11 February 2002, adopted Spring 2002).

CHAPTER 8
CONCLUSIONS

Promoting the relevance of e.g. SC Res. 1373 has been a connecting thread through-out this Volume. But such an exercise can sometimes become ever so slightly frus-trating. Many observers must during May 2002 have wondered why EU countries would be willing to provide hospitality to 13 Palestinians who had obviously vio-lated a variety of international laws and deserve to be put on trial rather than being given their freedom.

The Bethlehem Church of the Nativity has been the scene of a 39-day siege during April-May 2002. It could also be submitted that a number of armed Palestin-ians, in violation of international law, had sought refuge in a building, which, apart from mainstream Humanitarian Law, had also been designated under relevant UNESCO Conventions as a site which should never be used as a refuge for whatever purpose.[1] Palestinian gunmen and others had taken to the Church when Israeli forces entered Bethlehem on April 2 and might in the process have taken unarmed Palestin-ians and a number of clergy as hostages.[2] Although in violation of recognized legal principles, and although the Israeli forces would in principle be entitled to enter the church by force, to a great extent depending on the military necessity, the Palestin-ians correctly guessed that the Israeli troops would not dare to use military force, in the wake of an outcry by the West.

Upon lengthy negotiations the stand-off was resolved, with the Palestinians leav-ing the church on May 10th enabling the Israeli forces to leave town shortly thereaf-ter.[3] Part of the deal was that some of the Palestinians would be banned to the Gaza strip where they were supposed to face trial, whereas the 13 main terrorists/militia-men were flown to Cyprus, from where they would be divided among a number of EU Member States and Cyprus.[4]

---

[1] See e.g. Juliette van Krieken, on The Buddhas of Bamian and Beyond, *IIAS Newsletter*, nr. 23, autumn 2000, and nr. 27, spring 2002, in which she gives a fairly complete and up to date overview of the accomplishments in the 'blue shield' field and the issue of the protection of cultural heritage which indeed includes the military necessity issue in the case of the illegal use of, indeed, churches (IIAS stands for the Leiden-based International Institute for Asian Studies).

[2] At the time of writing, it was not known whether or not the armed Palestinians had kept unarmed Palestinians, not to mention the clergy present in the Church, as hostages, but the April events at least suggested that heavy pressure was put by the gunmen on the unarmed Palestinians not to leave the church.

[3] Shortly thereafter hundreds of worshippers and clergy gathered for Greek orthodox services in the Basilica and Catholic rites at the neighbouring Church of St. Catherine (IHT, May 13, 2002). Some of the clergy had been particularly upset that the Palestinians, all of them Moslem, had used ('abused') the Church as a mosque.

[4] As indicated, under International Humanitarian Law it has been forbidden for armed fighters to seek refuge in a church. Yet, quite remarkably, many of the reactions (see e.g. the ASIL web-site discus-sion) focused on the question whether the 'deportation' as such was lawful. This may be indicative for the misinterpretation by the human rights lobby of the basics of humanitarian law.

What puzzles the present author is that at a time during which the ICC became a reality and during which the vow to fight terrorism and other international crimes was still being upheld and promulgated, hospitality was offered to persons who, under the terms of the main international instruments and SC Res. 1373 in particular – depending, however, on whether they could be labeled terrorists – should never be allowed a safe haven.

The above example shows that the relationship between politics and law, between wishful thinking and the reality on the ground, between words and actions, as well as between conventions and deals is often blurred. The example also shows that whatever the legal experts propose, and whatever governments agree upon, reality more often than not escapes the eager hands of those specialists. The Bethlehem saga is a proper reminder that the law is a tool, and not a purpose in itself. Of course, justice is the final goal, and the sooner we reach that goal, the better. Yet, patience is needed every now and then, as for instance exemplified in the Nuremberg and Tokyo examples which were only repeated and codified almost 50 years on.

That does not mean that the politician or legal expert should relax, particularly as regards this extremely relevant and important issue. Terrorism, after all, affects us all, directly and indirectly, emotionally and rationally. Methods need to be found to counter terrorism, and a legal framework should be firmly in place enabling the policy-makers and those who are supposed to implement such policy to carry out their task.

On the basis of what has been included in this Volume, it is quite obvious that now that the Security Council has become intensively involved in this issue it is that very UN organ that will continue to set the tone. The 2001 resolutions in this regard leave no room for any misunderstanding. The resolutions are binding and the status of the Security Council (also in relation to the General Assembly and the (Sub-)Commission on Human Rights) should be underlined again and again. That also means that the UN, and by definition the various delegations to the various UN gatherings, should ensure that the UN speaks with one voice, leaving no reason for whatever misinterpretation. This concerns the acceptance of a 'chain-of-command' with the SC and its Counter-Terrorism Committee in charge of policy-making and codification. It also means that the mandate of the Special Rapporteur may have to be redefined, as the Rapporteur submits views which every now and then do not fully coincide with the SC line of thinking, also as they are not limited to the human rights issue alone.

Based on the SC resolutions, the principle of *aut dedere aut judicare* deserves to be reinforced, including the acceptance of universal jurisdiction in appropriate cases. Of course, States should be able to first rely on fully exploiting their 'domestic' jurisdiction and secondly on the expanded extradition instruments. Universal jurisdiction should only be used as a last resort but in this respect it probably comes as no surprise that it is hereby submitted that the Princeton Principles on this issue are somewhat disappointing.

The question whether the ICC could in the future play an active role should be firmly kept on the agenda. The US 2002 action to counteract Clinton's signature under the Rome Statute should not be considered as final: new ideas will emerge, new administrations will be voted into office. The 7-year span as foreseen under the Rome Statute before any amendment would be possible, should be fully used. The ICC could and should prove its worth and the climate in 2009 may be surprisingly different from the one in 2002. Moreover, it should be underlined that many a terrorist act falls well within the parameters of the more traditional humanitarian law and criminal law and the perpetrators could already be brought to justice under those headings.

It is also worth the effort to screen the various existing international instruments on domestic jurisdiction, extradition and universal jurisdiction and to ensure that gaps, if any, are filled. Hereto the binding instructions as laid down in e.g. SC Res. 1373 should be taken as an appropriate starting point. The idea that the instruments concerned have been *de jure* amended by that resolution would appear to be going too far.

Special attention should be paid to the position of the 'accomplice', also because '1373' has extended the target group to include all those who possibly support terrorist acts. It is not yet known how this 'support-element' should exactly be interpreted, but efforts to downplay this very aspect should be regretted. Terrorism is too serious an issue to allow any leniency or unnecessary flexibility.

On the European level it is of interest to note that the efforts to coordinate any action against terrorists have coincided with the general efforts to turn the EU into an area of justice, security and freedom (in that order) which might include the (automatic) surrender of suspects in general rather than extensive extradition efforts, over and above the round up of the usual suspects as per the Casablanca Principles.

It is quite interesting to note that within the European Union the September 2001 events have been fully exploited to accelerate a process the contours of which had been laid down in the October 1999 Tampere Milestones.[5] This concerns in particular the arrest warrant developments which enable the judiciary to overcome the sometimes lengthy extradition procedures by replacing them with a 'surrender-mechanism'. It is also noteworthy that the EU appears to be willing to implement the relevant SC resolutions: of some anecdotal interest might be that the main EU instruments were published on 27 December 2001, exactly within the three months as indicated in SC Res. 1373 which indeed had been adopted on the preceding 28 September. But the willingness is also reflected in virtually all the related EU documents and the constructive relationship between the European leadership and the Security Council should be duly noted.

International law is about cross-border activities, cross-border impact and cross-fertilization. This whole Volume hence falls within this category, and contains issues which relate to public international law, criminal law and human rights law and be-

---

[5] Presidency Conclusions of the Tampere European Council, October 1999.

yond. The primary nature of public international law has been maintained throughout as reflected in the use of terms like 'chain of command'. Whether or not the Security Council is entitled to act as a legislative body has been answered by referring to Article 24 of the UN Charter, which, in the opinion of this author, might indeed amount to (re-)interpretation of existing laws, if not *de-facto* law-making.[6]

The direct impact of terrorism and the various answers has also had a tremendous impact on individuals on all sides of the divide: the victims, the offenders and all others who now feel that they have to surrender part of their freedom in exchange for increased security. It has been submitted that the Security Council dictates international law and thus human rights law as well and not the other way around. Statements indicating that SC Res. 1373 is in accordance with human rights law are of no relevance: if need be, human rights law will – *de facto* or *de jure* – be amended by the SC. This conclusion is of some importance as it can be noted that the human rights lobby[7] appears to focus on the – indeed often negative – side-effects of counter-terrorism measures. Yet, one should get the priorities straight and agree that re-balancing the security-freedoms equation should not focus on freedoms alone. The fragile balance between freedom security and justice deserves to be revisited.

An interesting group, and rightly addressed in UN and EU documents alike, are the asylum seekers and other migrants. Within this realm the effects of counter-terrorism measures can be best felt, and the language of '1373' should not be denied, in particular where it concerns safe haven and refugee status (Art. 1F of the 1951 Refugee Convention).

Attention has also been paid to armaments and related worldwide smuggling efforts, whereas issues like trafficking has been somewhat neglected: the scope of this Volume is indeed fairly limited.

Creating a new international legal order might be counterproductive. The present legal order, international criminal law in particular, encompasses a great many aspects which make a fairly successful fight against terrorism quite possible. As long as most terrorist offenders can be effectively dealt with under the existing legal framework one should not despair that a comprehensive convention will not be agreed upon in the short term. However, everything should be done to increase the impact and effectiveness of the present legal instruments.

Yet, by reshuffling certain instruments and by placing existing material in a different limelight it is easy to see that a new international legal order focusing on terrorism has firmly emerged. This is a positive development which deserves to be strongly supported. Only by providing a robust legal framework can the war against terrorism be successful. Part of the job has already been done, but much more lies ahead. It is of paramount importance that the legal world provides the badly needed support to their counterparts in the world of action. Together they can deliver, or rather: should deliver.

---

[6] See on Art. 24: Simma, *The Charter of the United Nations, A Commentary*, Oxford 1995, pp. 397-407.

[7] See e.g. the 2002 yearbook of Amnesty International.